SAMUEL SEABURY
1729-1796
A Study in the
High Church Tradition

SAMUEL SEABURY
1729-1796

A Study in the High Church Tradition

Bruce E. Steiner

Ohio University Press

Library of Congress Catalog Number:
ISBN-0-8214-0098-3
Manufactured in the United States of America by
The Oberlin Printing Co., Oberlin, Ohio
Designed by Hal Stevens

For the Memory of My Mother

CATHERINE ZWICKEY STEINER

CONTENTS

ILLUSTRATIONS AND MAPS

ACKNOWLEDGMENTS

IN SEARCHING OUT MATERIALS RELATING TO THE LIFE OF Samuel Seabury, I have received the assistance of many persons. To Dr. Niels H. Sonne I am indebted for the opportunity to examine Bishop Seabury's papers under ideal conditions during a visit to the General Theological Seminary. Similar courtesies were extended at Trinity College by Dr. Kenneth W. Cameron, Archivist of the Protestant Episcopal Diocese of Connecticut. In Edinburgh I enjoyed the hospitality of Canon Kenneth J. Woollcombe, Principal of the Episcopal Theological College, and was guided through the college's collections by Canon W. D. Cooper. Also helpful were the staff in charge of books and manuscripts at the following institutions: the Public Record Office, London, and the William Salt Library, Stafford; the Library of Congress, the Connecticut State Library, the Pierpont Morgan Library, the New York Public Library, the William L. Clements Library, and the Massachusetts Diocesan Library; Yale University, Columbia University, and the University of Virginia; the New-York Historical Society, the Connecticut Historical Society, the Historical Society of Pennsylvania, the American Antiquarian Society, and the Peabody Institute.

Once more I am happy to make my acknowledgments to Professor Bernard Mayo of the University of Virginia. Professor Mayo first introduced me to Samuel Seabury in a seminar discussion of Revolutionary literature, and while I have emphasized the other aspects of "A. W. Farmer's" career, I hope my study will meet with his approval; his constant help and encouragement are gratefully remembered.

A NOTE ON TERMINOLOGY

IN ORDER TO PRESERVE THE FLAVOR OF THE PERIOD, THE DE-nominational nomenclature employed by eighteenth-century New Englanders who belonged to the Church of England has generally been adopted in this study. Such persons were referring to themselves as "Episcopalians" and to their church as "the Episcopal Church" long before the Revolution. These terms, accordingly, have been preferred to the designations customary in colonial histories: "Anglicans" and "the Anglican Church." "Churchmen" was a label applied to members of the Church of England by both Congregationalists and Episcopalians; although the cognate "Churchmanship" does not often appear until well after 1800, it has proved too useful a word to be relinquished. "Dissenter," despite its invidious overtones, has been retained, since it conveniently designates the collective body of non-Episcopalians. New England's eighteenth-century Churchmen often referred to their Congregationalist neighbors as "Presbyterians" (as did many of the Congregationalists themselves). But to avoid confusion, this usage has been confined to quotations.

The geographical expressions of the period have also been retained. "Eastern churches" refers to those Episcopal churches east of the Hudson: that is, the churches of New England. "Southern churches" is a somewhat amorphous term. Before 1775 it was applied, by some New Englanders, only to those Episcopal churches which would today be designated as "Southern." But in the post-Revolutionary period it generally meant the churches south of New England. For most Episcopalians after 1783, the "Southern churches" and the "Eastern churches," taken together, included all the Episcopal churches of the United States. In this sense the terms are employed in the post-Revolutionary chapters.

PROLOGUE

"THE SMOKE OF YALE-COLLEGE"

IN THE EIGHTEENTH CENTURY, THE YALE COMMENCEment was an event fondly anticipated by Connecticut's Congregational clergy. For country ministers, caught in the round of their obscure parishes, the annual exercises offered a chance for visiting with old friends, for discussing something besides crops, the weather, and Deacon Goddard's prize ram. Together with the election at Hartford in May, Commencement provided a rare opportunity to escape from the rural routine, and the opportunity was eagerly embraced.[1] Come September, sedate parties of black-garbed gentlemen might be seen moving down the west bank of the Connecticut to strike southwest at Wethersfield or Middletown for Wallingford and the New Haven road. Ministers from the colony's southern towns had an easier route: the post road from New York to Boston passed directly through the college town. Traveling from the west, through Fairfield, Stratford, and Milford, or from the east, along the winding roads which lay beyond Saybrook ferry, they skirted the north shore of the Sound and were soon in sight of Yale. A party of undergraduates firing guns and brandishing flasks excited little comment. For Latin disputations and drunken revels, lengthy sermons and demolished necessary houses, were alike ingredients of a week-long celebration signaling release from nearly eleven months of classes.[2] Easing themselves from their saddles, Connecticut's ministers ignored the distressing, but not unexpected, evidence of Man's Fallen State. They had come to enjoy themselves.

For such men, the Commencement of 1722, on many accounts, should have been a notably happy one. Disputes about its location, which but a few years before had nearly brought the school to ruin, had now subsided.[3] Timber-built "Yale College," dedicated these four years, was acquiring a patina—and institutional dignity. And Rector Timothy Cutler (Harvard, 1701), a brilliant scholar, a man of commanding presence and dignity, "made a grand Figure as the Head of a College."[4] Three years in office, he formerly had been minister of Stratford's church, having been chosen as pastor after the organization in that town in 1707 of Connecticut's first Episcopal congregation made necessary the calling of a particularly talented individual.[5]

Upon his arrival at Stratford, the Massachusetts-born Cutler had received an enthusiastic welcome from the Connecticut clergy, but now, in September of 1722, there was a stiffness in their greeting. Strange rumors and surmises, detrimental to the rector, his teaching assistant, Tutor Daniel Browne (Yale, 1714), and a group of neighboring ministers—Samuel Johnson (Yale, 1714) of West Haven, James Wetmore (Yale, 1714) of North Haven, Jared Eliot (Yale, 1706) of Killingworth, John Hart (Yale, 1703) of East Guilford, and Samuel Whittelsey (Yale, 1705) of Wallingford—had been circulating through the colony. Men talked of their frequent meetings, of their supposed affection for Arminian tenets. The country was excited, and it was expected that Commencement would bring matters to a head: "people came expecting strange things."[6]

"Strange things"—the phrase was totally inadequate for the happenings of that Commencement! In Boston the amazed and sorrowful Judge Samuel Sewall was quickly put in mind of Revelations 16:15 and wrote to Connecticut's governor "that in this extraordinary and unexpected Alarm, we have a Demonstration that the Drying up the Great River Euphrates is near at hand." The more practically minded Joseph Moss (Harvard, 1699) of Derby besought the aid of Cotton Mather (Harvard, 1678): "We must put on our armour and fight," he declared, "or else let the good old cause, for which our fathers came into this land, sink and be deserted."[7] That the cause was sinking no one doubted. "How is the gold become dim! and the silver become dross! and the wine mixt with water!" was the popular cry.[8]

The liturgical conclusion of the rector's Commencement prayer—"And let all the people say, amen"—had excited much talk,[9] but it was the events of the following day, September 13, which produced real consternation. Confident that the rumors must prove baseless, the Yale trustees had summoned rector, tutor, and five suspected pastors to appear before them in the library, hoping thus to satisfy the people and safeguard the college's reputation. When they had come together, the question was put. According to Samuel Johnson, writing nearly half a century after the event, the trustees

> desired them to declare truly how the case was from the youngest to the eldest; and some of them declared that they doubted, and others that they were more fully persuaded of the invalidity of presbyterian ordination. This was matter of very great consternation, and they expressed much grief and concern and desired their declaration in writing which they gave. Sometime after they sent them a paper, wherein they entreated them to consider things over more attentively; and if possible, to get over their scruples and those that could not to desist [from officiating as Congregational ministers]; and now the country was full of a bitter clamor![10]

Formerly minister of the church of New London and a man of broad religious sympathies,[11] Governor Gurdon Saltonstall was anxious to reclaim the erring shepherds, if that were possible, and sent word to them and to the trustees to meet him in conference at New Haven in October, at which time and place the General Assembly would convene. The conference met,[12] and although the argument waxed so bitter that the governor soon ended it abruptly, it was not, from his viewpoint, wholly unsuccessful. The trustees' arguments, or others, convinced Eliot, Whittelsey, and Hart that they had been mistaken in their views, and they continued in the Congregational ministry.[13]

But for Cutler, Johnson, and Browne (and, as the event showed, Wetmore) there was no turning back. The High Church conviction that episcopacy was necessary to the very being of a Christian church (and an uninterrupted apostolic succession necessary for a valid episcopate) had been ripening in their minds for many years. They were now certain that they lacked a proper ministerial commission. Never in complete sympathy with the Standing Order, these men (and the friends who parted from them) had fallen greedily upon the library of new books presented to Yale in 1714 by Jeremiah Dummer, Connecticut's London agent. Feasting upon the works of Boyle, Newton, and Locke—volumes regarded with some suspicion by their colony's pastors—[14] the young scholars also had read, first with curiosity, then with mounting uneasiness, the books of certain Church of England divines. Patrick and Whitby, Potter and Tillotson, Sharp, Scott and Sherlock had raised new questions, unsettled old convictions.[15] Opinions were altered; practical questions of conduct were posed. A true *crise de conscience* developed, and from its ultimate implications the New Englanders shrank.

> It was . . . very grievous to them to think of going into conclusions that they knew would be very distressing to their friends and very grievous to their country. They therefore honestly tried to satisfy themselves if possible to continue as they were; they resolved to examine things impartially and read the best things on both sides of the question.[16]

Further study only strengthened their views. Troubled in mind, they resorted to those uneasy compromises and temporary shifts which ever have marked the convert's halting and unsteady advance.[17] (It would have been "much more agreeable" to him to have taken Episcopal Orders, Johnson later recalled when writing of his ordination at West Haven in 1720, yet while he thought it "very eligible," he did not then see it "necessary in point of conscience to conform.")[18] But now in 1722, with Commencement and conference over, the clean break had been made. Action succeeded compromise.

On November 5, supplied with ship's stores by Boston Churchmen, the erstwhile Yale rector, together with Samuel Johnson and Daniel Browne, sailed for Great Britain and ordination as ministers of the Church of England.[19] James Wetmore joined them in July, 1723, and shared the last month of an extended visit, which had been passed in interviews with bishops and lesser clergymen, visits to Oxford and Cambridge, conversations with officials of the Society for the Propagation of the Gospel in Foreign Parts,[20] sermons and services, and a good amount of sightseeing. Fitted out with appointments as S.P.G. missionaries, Cutler, Johnson, and Wetmore left London for Gravesend, in order to embark for America, July 26, 1723.[21] Arriving at Piscataqua in late September, they immediately began work at their respective posts: Cutler at newly formed Christ Church, Boston; Johnson among the Episcopalians of Stratford; and Wetmore as catechist and assistant minister of Trinity Church, New York.[22]

These events of 1722-23 form an instructive prologue to a biography of Samuel Seabury. For it is from them that a New England Churchmanship with native roots, quite different from the established religion of the Southern colonies, took its rise. And it was this Churchmanship—High in its theology, evangelical in its preaching, shaped by a convert clergy and laity of Puritan background—which molded Seabury's outlook and thought from his earliest years.[23] Born in 1729, he witnessed its development under the fostering care of the S.P.G. He knew all its formulators and was intimately acquainted with, or an active participant in, their various schemes and projects. As the leading American exponent of doctrines developed by Nonjuring divines of England and Scotland, he enlarged and deepened its theological content. As Bishop of Connecticut, he organized and consolidated the churches of the area where New England Churchmanship had made its strongest impact. In the controversies of 1782-92, he championed its distinctive features and secured for the Protestant Episcopal Church an organization and liturgy within which this native High Church tradition might grow and develop. He perhaps would not have approved its subsequent metamorphoses: into the American Oxford Movement, so ably championed by his brilliant grandson, Samuel Seabury (1801-1872),[24] and the Anglo-Catholicism of the present day. But because of him and the New England Churchmen whom he headed, these later developments became possible. Through them he continues to exercise on the present-day theology of the Protestant Episcopal Church an influence far greater than that of any of his contemporaries in the episcopate.[25] Transmuted and transformed, the High Churchmanship of Bishop Seabury yet remains a vital force.

I

"MY HONOURED FATHER"

IN 1722, AT THE TIME OF THE "GREAT APOSTACY," SAMUEL Seabury of Groton, Connecticut, was a student at Yale College. Obviously that school, exposed as the breeding ground of Arminian and prelatical tenets, was a dangerous place for an impressionable Congregational youth. Pious John Seabury, deacon in Groton's church, summoned his son home. The following summer Samuel was sent up to Cambridge, along with Dudley Woodbridge, son of Groton's pastor, who had likewise been rescued from the contagious atmosphere of New Haven. An outlay of £1 10*s* 10*d* secured him a Harvard diploma with the class of 1724, £1 of this amount going for the Commencement dinner. In 1727, prepared to maintain the negative of the question "Is it to be expected that Christ will personally govern on earth prior to the Last Judgment?" he returned with his class and took his M.A. degree.[1]

Partly because of his late entrance, Samuel ranked only twenty-eighth in a class of forty graduates. But young Woodbridge, with the same disability, achieved ninth place.[2] Since the college authorities made family standing the main consideration when assigning students their rank, it is obvious that Harvard did not regard the Seaburys as persons of much prominence. Still, they were of respectable standing and related by marriage to men important in the settlement of New England.

The family's American progenitor, John "Seaberry," a seaman, established himself in Boston by 1639, purchasing in November of that year Walter Merrye's house "and half an Acre under it in the Mylne field, and so is allowed for an Inhabitant."[3] Seabury does not seem to have belonged to Boston's church, but his wife Grace was admitted a member. About 1645 he removed his family to the island of Barbados, where he soon died, leaving, among other children, a son Samuel, baptized May 22, 1642.

Although Samuel Seabury presumably accompanied his parents to Barbados, he returned to Massachusetts within a few years. Entered at Harvard with the class of 1659, he left without taking a degree,[4] but residence at the college seems to have given him a certain amount of prestige. At Plymouth, October 1, 1661, as a member of the twelve-man jury of the General Court, he was "Mr. Samuell Saberry," the only juryman given a title.[5] Previous to this date he had settled at Duxbury, where he practiced medicine until his death.[6]

Evidently his neighbors considered Samuel Seabury a man of judgment and sound sense, for they frequently entrusted him with local office. A Duxbury selectman 1669-75, 1677, 1680-81, he was also, at various times, constable, surveyor of highways, a member of innumerable New Plymouth Colony juries, inspector of ordinaries in Duxbury (he secured a wholesale liquor license in 1678), and a representative of that town in the General Court held 30 October-1 November, 1676.[7] The one unfortunate blot on his otherwise respectable career involved a quarrel with Duxbury's pastor, in the course of which he treated in cavalier fashion the leading officials of New Plymouth. Holding court at Plymouth, March 5, 1666, the governor and assistants considered the case:

> Mr. Samuell Saberry, being summoned to this Court, appeered to make answare for that by writing under his hand and otherwise hee hath busied himselfe to scandulise and defame the minnestry of Duxburry; but not takeing notice thereof to acknowlidgment, and not giveing satisfaction in that behalfe, but rather the contrary, hee was exhorted and admonished by the Court unto his duty in that behalfe, and likewise warned to desist from such disturbing practices, the which if the Court shall receive further information thereof, hee must expect to be againe questioned about it, and be reddy to give better cecurity for his better walking, and soe for the present was released.[8]

Despite his bravado, Samuel Seabury probably took to heart the court's warning, for nothing more is recorded of the matter. It is not likely that the incident was typical of his relations with the Puritan clergy. At some date, probably subsequent to this unpleasant broil, he became a deacon of the Duxbury church.[9] And among Seabury's family connections were several of New England's more prominent ministers. His first wife, Patience Kemp, was the granddaughter of Ralph Partridge (Cambridge, 1599-1600), Duxbury's original pastor, a man greatly respected.[10] At the time of their marriage in 1660, Patience's stepfather, Thomas Thacher, served as pastor of Weymouth. Noted for his medical skill (he published, in 1677, the first medical book to appear from an American press),[11] Thacher must have enjoyed professional chats with his Duxbury relation. He achieved the pinnacle of clerical success, being installed in 1670 as first minister of Boston's Third Church.[12] A son, Peter Thacher (Harvard, 1671), half brother to Patience (Kemp) Seabury, won a measure of fame with theological publications. Pastor of Milton from 1681 until his death in 1727, he was reportedly very

> Careful that Christ's sheep should never feed
> On Arian, Popish, or Arminian Weed.[13]

Securing ample clerical connections by his first marriage, Samuel Seabury, in choosing a second wife, established close relations with the Old Colony's inner political circle. Patience Kemp, after bearing him ten children, died October 29, 1676. Within six months Seabury was wed to Martha Pabodie, granddaughter of the famous Pilgrim couple John and Priscilla (Mullins) Alden. Then approaching his eightieth year, John Alden had completed in 1676 twenty-six successive years in office as one of Plymouth's seven assistants.[14] He lived at Duxbury and probably was a frequent visitor in the Seabury household, which soon included two of his great-grandchildren. No doubt there would have been other children, but in August, 1681, Samuel Seabury, aged only forty, died.

John Seabury, the second son of Patience Kemp, was about seven years old at the time of his father's death.[15] His half uncle, Rodolphus Thacher, brother to the minister of Milton, became his guardian in July, 1682,[16] and presumably saw to his upbringing. Late in 1697 he married Elizabeth Alden, a first cousin of his stepmother. The marriage was a most reputable one, for in addition to the Aldens, it connected John Seabury through his mother-in-law with the prominent Southworth family. Constant Southworth (d. 1679), grandfather of Elizabeth Alden, had been Treasurer of New Plymouth Colony for many years.[17] His political career required no elaborate explanation: he was the stepson of Governor William Bradford.

Soon after their marriage, John and Elizabeth Seabury removed from Duxbury, first to Stonington, Connecticut, and then to the adjacent town of Groton, where they purchased land in 1704. There John Seabury plied his cooper's trade and, presumably, farmed. By 1716 he was a deacon of the Groton church,[18] and two years later he represented that town in the General Assembly. He had by Elizabeth Alden eight children, of whom Samuel, born July 8, 1706, was the fourth.

Having graduated from Harvard in 1724, Samuel Seabury looked about for a place to settle. The place was, doubtless, the only matter still to be determined. It is hardly likely that a man of John Seabury's comfortable but not lavish means had sent his son off to college without a definite understanding as to his future career. A clergyman Samuel would be: godly, orthodox, respected, and possibly wealthy, qualities united in Great-Uncle Peter Thacher. And in 1725 it appeared possible that he might be settled in the ministry in his native town.

Groton's minister, Ephraim Woodbridge (Harvard, 1701), was dying. In his son Dudley, Samuel Seabury's Yale and Harvard classmate, he had an obvious candidate to succeed him, and it was Dudley that the Groton church engaged to preach, at twenty shillings a Sabbath, on November 18, 1725. The agreement ran until the following March, but the death of the Reverend Ephraim on December 1 seems to have so disconcerted his son that Samuel temporarily took his place. He probably occupied Groton's pulpit the following Sabbath, and on the next, December 12, he exchanged with the great Eliphalet Adams (Harvard, 1694), his neighbor at New London.[19]

This arrangement, if it continued, lasted only a few weeks, but the possibilities of a settlement in Groton were not yet exhausted. As the town's population increased, the farmers living in the northern part, away from the seashore, moved to erect a second and more conveniently situated meetinghouse. Organizing the North Society, they voted early in February, 1726, "That Mr Samuell Sebury (or Sum other Preacher of the Gospel in Case he Refeuse) Should be Called to Preach among us for the Space of ten weeks." For the same stipend that Woodbridge received, Seabury was invited to preach four Sabbaths at Captain John Morgan's house, four at William Morgan, Jr.'s, and two at Ralph Hodard, Sr.'s.[20]

Although it has been repeatedly stated that Seabury accepted this call,[21] there is no definite evidence to that effect. If he did preach at North Groton, he left after his ten-week engagement. For on May 9, 1726, the North Society moved to secure Simon Backus (Yale, 1724) as its preacher, also on a temporary basis.[22]

And about this time, or shortly afterwards, Samuel Seabury was preaching in the recently formed parish of New Salem in nearby Colchester.

The New Salem engagement probably lasted about a year: an undated order to the parish collector survives, directing him to pay Seabury £52 15*s* 6*d*.[23] By November, 1727, however, the young ministerial candidate had moved on again and was located at distant North Yarmouth on the Maine frontier.[24]

North Yarmouth offered definite prospects of a permanent settlement. Although the town had been incorporated in 1680, King William's War had devastated it, and it was not until the 1720's that a vigorous resettlement program began. Among the most active leaders in this enterprise was Samuel's uncle, Deacon Samuel Seabury (1666-1763) of Duxbury. The deacon, along with his son-in-law and nephew, Samuel's brother David Seabury (1698-1750), settled in North Yarmouth by the summer of 1727.[25] It was, therefore, quite understandable that the committee of town proprietors, in seeking out a minister for the settlement, should pitch upon Samuel Seabury. In August, 1727, they engaged him at a salary of one hundred pounds a year.[26]

The candidate apparently gave satisfaction, and matters proceeded smoothly toward his ordination and settlement. (One ordination requirement, full church membership, was fulfilled March 6, 1727/8, when Groton's First Church received Seabury into communion.)[27] Meeting at Boston, April 19, 1729, the North Yarmouth committee of proprietors gave their approval to the plan:

> Whereas the Sub-Committee & Proprietors at North Yarmouth have made Choice of Mr Samuel Seabury to be settled & ordained in the Work of the Ministry in that Town, & have voted that the sum of Two Hundred Pounds in Province Bills shall be granted & paid to Him toward his Settlement,—One Half thereof to be paid in Four Months & the other Half Twelve Months after his Ordination: and have further voted that the sum of One Hundred & Twenty Pounds

> Salary shall be paid Him, one Half thereof in April & the other Half in October Yearly, & every year that He shall continue in the work of the Ministry in the said Town: which the other Proprietors here have consented to: Wherefore It is agreed & voted that the said Vote & Terms are approved of & consented to by the Committee, upon Condition that if it shall so happen that Mr Samuel Seabury shall not continue in the work of the Ministry in said Town three Years after his Ordination there, then He shall repay back unto the Committee or Selectmen of the Town for the Time Being the Two Hundred Pounds granted Him for his Settlement, Extraordinary Providences only Excepted.[28]

The date of his ordination was not far distant when Samuel Seabury returned to Groton in November, 1729, having arranged for Ammi Ruhammah Cutter (Harvard, 1725) to supply his pulpit.[29] His wife, Abigail Mumford, who seems never to have lived at North Yarmouth, had given birth to her eldest son Caleb at Groton in February. Now she was expecting another child, a second son, born the last day of November. Two Sabbaths later, in the icy cold of the First Society's meetinghouse, John Owen (Harvard, 1723) baptized the boy, naming him Samuel for his father.[30]

Thus far the ministerial career of Samuel Seabury had followed the usual pattern: graduation at Harvard, experience as a supply preacher in various pulpits, and eventually a call to a permanent settlement. But now that career abruptly changed. When Seabury next appeared in the records, March 23, 1729/30, Timothy Cutler of Boston's Christ Church, describing his old pupil as "a person who, upon true & regular conviction, is come into the bosom of our excellent Church," was recommending him for an S.P.G. mission.[31]

The alteration in Seabury's sentiments (or, at any rate, his final resolution) had been a matter of a few months or even weeks: the Congregational baptism of Samuel, Jr., as late as December 14 clearly indicates a swift decision. As for the cause of his conversion, it is impossible, at this date, to go beyond Cutler's brief statement. "True & regular conviction" in the Cutler lexicon meant a belief that episcopacy formed an essential part of a Christian church, and Seabury's subsequent actions show that he adhered to such a view. It has, indeed, been suggested that money difficulties at North Yarmouth perhaps induced him to change his ecclesiastical affiliations. Seabury's North Yarmouth experiences, however, were the common lot of any minister in a newly settled town, and evidence does not support the statement that, as late as August, 1729, he had received no part of his salary.[32]

Naturally, the alteration in Seabury's views had not taken place in a vacuum. The building of an Episcopal church in nearby New London and his marriage into a family of Episcopal converts, the Mumfords of Groton, had brought him into close contact with many Churchmen. This milieu (and, perhaps, impressions lingering from the days of Cutler's rectorship at Yale) certainly softened any antipathy he may have had toward the Church of England and made him receptive to its arguments.

Seabury's father-in-law, Thomas Mumford (1687-*c.*1765), came of a family long settled in the Narragansett country, that lush agricultural region of Rhode Island bordering on Connecticut. In the spring of 1720 he removed to Groton, establishing himself on the "Great farm" of the New London Winthrops, the region's magnates.[33] Although he rented this property as late as 1758, Thomas Mumford was no poor tenant. Mingling with the Winthrops on terms of social equality, he could pay them £700 currency as an annual rent, and he acquired a farm of his own in North Groton as well as land and buildings at the New London-Groton ferry. This last probably consisted of stores or warehouses, for Mumford was a merchant as well as a farmer.[34]

James MacSparran (Glasgow, 1709), S.P.G. missionary in charge of St. Paul's Church, Narragansett, provided Thomas Mumford's initial contacts with the Episcopal Church. Soon after arriving at his post in 1721, this energetic, convert-seeking clergyman married Hannah Gardiner, niece of Mumford's wife Hannah Remington (*c.*1687-1781).[35] Given this relationship, it was natural that MacSparran should officiate in Thomas Mumford's house when he ventured west to Groton in the summer of 1723 to conduct a baptism.[36] And within a short time he managed to bring into the Episcopal fold almost the whole Mumford connection,[37] subsequently the strongest supporters both of St. Paul's and of the church which became St. James's, New London.[38]

On November 3, 1723, MacSparran baptized at St. Paul's Hannah Mumford and her children, Thomas, Jr., and thirteen-year-old Abigail, "all Upon their own personall profession of faith." The following January he traveled to Groton, baptizing on this occasion the younger Mumford children, John and Caleb. And in November of 1724, on the same day that Hannah was admitted to the Holy Communion, Thomas Mumford himself was received into the Episcopal Church.[39] MacSparran also recorded in his register the marriage of Thomas Mumford, Jr., December 7, 1727,[40] but he did not officiate at the wedding of Thomas' sister Abigail and Samuel Seabury, which probably took place several months later. In view of the groom's connection with the North Yarmouth congregation, an Episcopal ceremony would hardly have been appropriate.

Upon becoming an Episcopalian, Thomas Mumford took an active part in gathering a congregation in neighboring New London, a project which MacSparran was promoting by occasional visits.[41] Mumford was not one of the twelve men (four of them definitely identified as Englishmen)[42] who subscribed £216 toward the erection of a church, June 6, 1725. But he served on the standing committee formed in September to carry on that work and busied himself with its affairs, purchasing a piece of ground on which to set the church and keeping a record of donations and subscriptions. He himself gave twenty pounds.[43]

A plan to secure the old building which the congregation of Trinity Church, Newport, was replacing and transport it to New London by water having failed,[44] Mumford and his colleagues made a contract with a local carpenter, June 30, 1726. For £75 Connecticut currency, John Hough agreed to erect a frame fifty feet long "from Inside to Inside," thirty-two feet wide, and with a stud of twenty-four feet. Besides "a Cover on each side," the structure was to have double doors at the west end and five windows, "the Roof half Flatt and the other Archt on each side, all to be Done substantiall in good & seasoned Timber now in the Possession of Major Peter Buor."[45] With an allowance of five pounds for liquor, the raising of the frame in the fall of 1726 was undoubtedly a very jovial occasion. In the following months workmen enclosed the building, installed glass in the windows, laid a subfloor, and constructed a neat pulpit and reading desk.[46]

Having made some progress toward completing their church—the third Episcopal edifice to be erected in Connecticut—the Churchmen of New London and Groton began efforts to secure a pastor. MacSparran had reported the formation of their congregation to the S.P.G. Secretary in the spring of 1726, adding that it was intended "speedily to apply to the Society for a Missionary." Without additional information, the S.P.G. declined to consider the case immediately,[47] and when, at their June, 1727, meeting, a formal address was received from New London, the members present agreed that no missionary could be dispatched "till the People have sent over an Account what they will certainly contribute yearly towards his Support."[48] Faced with this firm demand, Thomas Mumford and others got up an annual subscription of £40 15*s* currency.[49] The S.P.G., however, judged the amount too small, and the report of their decision reached Connecticut in the spring of 1730, just after Samuel Seabury had announced his adherence to the Church of England.[50]

When he decided to enter the Society's service, Seabury must have had strong hopes of being settled as missionary at New London. In April, 1730, before the secretary's letter arrived, MacSparran visited that congregation and helped draft an address which pleaded ("with all the importunity, the utmost necessity, and most earnest desire of a Gospel minister among us is able to inspire") that the young convert might be appointed New London's pastor. Informed of the S.P.G.'s decision, MacSparran wrote that Seabury would have not only the subscription but an additional twenty pounds: the law allowed Churchmen to pay their rates to their own pastor instead of the Congregational minister once a missionary had arrived.[51] With this additional information an appointment to New London might still be obtained, but the matter was anything but certain.

Sailing for England, probably in late May, Seabury carried good letters of recommendation from the New England clergy. Timothy Cutler wrote that his acquaintance with him was "earlier than my own Mission" (apparently a reference to his schooling at Yale) and added: "I have had further opportunity of informing myself of him from the Dissenters among whom he has preached, & find everything in favour of his sobriety & good conduct." MacSparran likewise reported that by the Congregationalists "he is well reported of for a virtuous conversation." James Honyman of Trinity Church, Newport, could not claim any long acquaintance, "but I have carefully enquired after his Character, and find it to be very good, and think him to be an ingenious Person." And Samuel Johnson (not as yet preeminent in S.P.G. councils, but an important friend to have) declared that the young man "has led a sober, virtuous and studious life, and now heartily embraces the principles of the Church of England."[52]

There does not appear to be any extant record of Seabury's ordering as deacon and priest. Bishop Edmund Gibson of London probably officiated at the ordinations, which must have been held sometime before August 21, 1730.[53] For on that date the Reverend Samuel Seabury, clergyman of the Church of England, appeared at the London monthly meeting of the S.P.G. "and offered his Service to be employed as the Societys Missionary in the Plantations."[54]

The interview, formidable though it must have seemed to the New Englander, was no doubt a quite informal affair, designed to put him at his ease. Besides Bishop Gibson, who held the chair, only nine members were present. This group ordered that Seabury should read Prayers and preach from I Thessalonians 5:17 and desired Dr. Baker, one of the persons in attendance, to report on his performance. Provided he acquitted himself satisfactorily, the Society would appoint him to New London with an annual stipend of fifty pounds sterling. The prospective missionary would also receive a library costing ten pounds, "five pounds worth of Small Tracts," and a dozen copies of Ostervald's catechism. To his unfinished church the Society was prepared to donate a folio Bible and Prayer Book, the Book of Homilies, a cushion for the pulpit, and a linen cloth for the Communion table.[55]

Samuel Seabury preached his probationary sermon in St. Michael's, Cornhill, on Sunday, August 30. Expounding his assigned text—"Pray without ceasing"—he proved himself "a preacher of great earnestness, directness of address, a devout spirit, and an excellent logician."[56] So a nineteenth-century critic judged the performance, and Dr. Baker presumably gave a similarly favorable account. The New London appointment—and the fifty pounds a year—followed as a matter of course. The Episcopalians of that town, treated most generously by the Society, were now to enjoy its bounty for a full half century. During that period, the S.P.G. expended more than £2000 sterling, paying the major portion of their minister's salary.[57]

After obtaining ordination and his appointment as missionary, Seabury prepared at once for the return voyage. Without any income for nearly a year, he could not afford a lengthy stay in England. He had little time for sight-seeing and no opportunity to make clerical friends and correspondents as Timothy Cutler and Samuel Johnson had done in 1722-23.[58] Mid-September found him far out upon the Atlantic, devising ways to pass the time of a most tedious thirteen-week voyage. At last, on December 9, 1730, the vessel entered the Thames and came to rest in New London's harbor.[59] The town's Episcopalians were waiting, "with such Expressions of Joy, as gave me good Satisfaction."[60] For the Mumfords, for Abigail Seabury, for Samuel himself, the day was, indeed, a happy one. But Deacon John and Elizabeth Seabury, sitting in their meetinghouse pew the next Sabbath morning, must have been visited with quite different emotions. The deacon's good friend, Joshua Hempstead of New London, revealed the Congregationalists' opinion of the newly arrived missionary in a diary entry of December 25:

> Cloudy & Windy . . . a Great Concourse of people at the Church to hear Mr Seabury preach a Christmas Sermon & to See fashions. it being New many went. he hath preacht but 2 Sabath days (Since he Received orders) here.[61]

On March 15, 1731, Seabury sent to the S.P.G. Secretary the first of those reports (written annually in the 1730's and afterwards at half-year intervals) which provide almost all our information as to his subsequent career. An S.P.G. report was pretty much what a missionary chose to make it. A man with the vision, energy, and ambition of Samuel Johnson would range over all of New England, suggesting plans, maneuvers, likely spots for new missions. Another type of minister (not often encountered in Connecticut) would complain incessantly of his people's neglect and of slights put on him by his brother clergymen. Samuel Seabury's reports resembled neither of these sorts. Optimistic in tone, they disclosed a story of quiet growth and consolidation which justified the assessment Samuel Johnson had expressed in the summer of 1731: "New London I think well provided for in Mr. Seabury," he informed the secretary, "and I hope the Church will flourish in that town."[62] Seldom did Seabury mention a brother missionary. Extraparochial matters and projects were mostly foreign to his little world, bounded as it was by Groton and New London, and varied by occasional services elsewhere. Johnson's first biographer, who knew Seabury well, took his measure accurately when he described him as an "excellent clergyman," a parish priest "worthy of all imitation."[63] And it is evident from his own S.P.G. reports that Samuel, Jr., did, in fact, mold his career as a missionary according to the pattern of "my honoured Father."[64]

Abigail (Mumford) Seabury had little, if any, influence upon her son, since she died when he was only eighteen months old, reportedly of "the pluritick fever." New London's chronicler of local happenings, Joshua Hempstead, recorded his attendance at her funeral, held toward nightfall in the rain, May 10, 1731.[65] "Mother" to young Samuel meant his father's second wife, Elizabeth Powell, married to the New London missionary by James MacSparran about a year after Abigail's death.[66] She was a daughter of the late Adam Powell, Newport merchant and active member of that town's Trinity Church. Her aged grandfather, the Huguenot Gabriel Bernon (1644-1736), both clergy and laity honored as the principal promoter of the Episcopal Church in Rhode Island.[67] It is evident from letters that Elizabeth (said to have been educated at Boston)[68] was brought up in a tradition of strict piety. She bore her husband at least six children[69] and proved a loving mother to Samuel, Jr.[70]

In New London the Seaburys lived, after about 1738, in a house which the missionary built on State Street near the Green.[71] For little Samuel the wharves and docks of the thriving port, which carried on an extensive West India trade and a coasting trade with New York, offered many attractions. There Grandfather Mumford had his stores and warehouses, filled with mysterious bales and hogsheads. Periodically, ships commanded by Uncles Thomas and John Mumford returned from distant ports, sometimes with wine from the island of Madeira. The New London-Groton Mumfords produced several other sea captains and transmitted the seafaring instinct to their Seabury kin: Samuel's elder brother Caleb would make many a voyage.[72]

Besides the harbor, there was much to interest a growing lad in the busy town of New London. When news of the marriage of Prince Frederick and Augusta of Saxe-Gotha arrived in July, 1736, the inhabitants held a parade, fired salutes, and drank healths for joy that the heir was wed to a good Protestant. Birthdays of the King and Queen they celebrated in a similar manner. A vast crowd could be brought together for such an event as the hanging of the Indian murderess Kate Jarrett, and Caleb and Samuel were doubtless there, wide-eyed as the rest. Colonel Gurdon Saltonstall presided at another important occasion, April 24, 1740, reading to the assembled townsmen the proclamation of war with Spain. By summer a tent had been set up on the militia training field where volunteers were drilling for the Cuban expedition.[73] What an exciting spot it must have been!

Possibly Abigail Mumford's elder son never showed any great liking for books and study. Such a trait would fit in well with his desire for the active life of a sea captain. At any rate, it was Samuel who was carefully educated, either in the town's grammar school, or, more likely, at home, and destined for Yale and the ministry.[74]

New London's Episcopal church (designated as St. James's about 1739)[75] gave Samuel's mind its bent and direction. The church during his father's thirteen-year pastorate was considerably altered from the barn-like structure raised by John Hough in 1726. At Easter, 1732, the standing committee relinquished its powers, and the congregation held its first annual election of a vestry, Thomas Mumford, Sr., being chosen one of the two churchwardens. Although the principal men who originally petitioned for a missionary soon died or removed, the congregation went ahead with their pastor's plan to finish the church. Repeated subscriptions, supplemented by the contributions of visitors passing through New London, secured the necessary funds to erect "An hansom & Commodious Communion pew," plaster the interior, and build a hundred-foot tower and spire.[76] (This last improvement and subsequent alterations eventually gave the edifice quite a Wren-like appearance.) Pews were a matter of individual enterprise. The vestry chalked off spaces on the floor and sold them, according to location, for ten to twenty pounds to parishioners willing to erect their own seats.[77]

A London merchant, traveling in 1739 from Boston to New York along the post road and stopping over the Sabbath at New London, would have judged his fellow Churchmen a rather uncouth lot had he stepped into St. James's for Morning or Evening Prayer. Shavings and boards and half-finished pews cluttered the floor, while rough benches and stools pieced out the completed seats.[78] No organ prelude embroidered the scene. Like any Congregational meetinghouse, St. James's had a man "to set the Psalms."[79] Kneeling as the service began, the merchant perhaps found himself the only person in that posture. Former Congregationalists held tenaciously to the habit of standing during prayer.[80] As for Mr. Seabury's sermon, it was long, extremely long, and utterly unlike those discourses of a Latitudinarian cast so fashionable in polite English circles. St. James's pastor did not believe in employing smooth, flowing periods and an overly genteel pulpit manner when souls stood in danger of damnation. Alternately threatening and pleading, he would cry out:

> Oh Daring hardned Sinner, thou must See the Ground on Which thou Standest Ready to give Way . . . Thou must See thy hopes all perish and burn up with the Dark Smoky fire of a Dispairing Conscience. then hell will Seem to Gape Wide to Receive you; And the week Uncertain thread of Life, will be all your Defense against its Devouring Jaws. . . .
>
> But Glory be to God thro Jesus Christ our Lord, there is While we Live mercy With God. if We Will Enter into his Mercy, And believe in his mercy, and flee to his mercy in Christ our Saviour & Love his Mercy. Delay not therefore Oh Sinner in time to Lift up thy Offending hands And Eyes, To a mercyful God, and with thy trembling heart and voice implore the mercy thou hast Long Despised. And implore that Grace thou hast often Resisted; implore the Assistance of Gods holy Spirit, which you have often treated with Scorn and as a thing of no value—[81]

Strange and uncomfortable though the Londoner must have found such a scene, ten-year-old Samuel saw nothing amiss in it. The service followed the same pattern at the North Groton church[82] and at St. Paul's, Narragansett, the only churches he is likely to have attended besides St. James's. Two-hour services, evangelical preaching, and High Church doctrine dispensed in a barely adequate liturgical setting: this he regarded as the Churchman's customary worship. When he served as St. James's rector half a century later, the pattern remained almost unchanged.[83]

From childhood Samuel also was thoroughly acquainted with the itinerant duty of an S.P.G. missionary. Besides officiating at New London twice on Sundays, his father had frequently to ride about the parish and to neighboring communities, preaching and baptizing in private homes.[84] It is likely that young Samuel sometimes accompanied him—to Hebron, for example, where he began work in 1736. In January of that year certain inhabitants of the town—about thirty miles from New London—asked Seabury to preach among them.[85] He complied with the request, he informed the S.P.G. Secretary, and found

> a numerous congregation, who attended the service of the Common Prayer with great seriousness; and when the service was concluded, there stayed of the company about thirty or forty persons, inquiring concerning the Church of England, and proposing the vulgar objections against it, besides many others which were raised entirely from falsehoods, and had no shadow of truth to support them; to all which I answered with truth, and the best reasons and arguments that my understanding and knowledge could suggest, and in this manner I conversed with them at least four hours, who, in fine, appeared very much surprised to find that they had always been prejudiced with so many false notions about the Church; wondering how men could leave its pious and holy communion, and, most of all, that any could have the conscience to load the established Church with so many odious and injurious slanders. They earnestly desired me to come again, and at their importunity I have visited them six times, twice of which hath been on Sundays. More than twenty families there and in some neigh-

> boring places do embrace the Church; and when I was last there, which was on the first day of this instant August [1736] I administered the Sacrament to fourteen communicants.[86]

Pleased with Seabury's report, the S.P.G. added Hebron to his cure (with an additional allowance of ten pounds per annum), and the New London missionary officiated there twice every quarter at the church which was soon erected. In 1738 thirty-two Hebron males, sixteen and upward, acknowledged him as their pastor.[87]

While New London was isolated both from Boston[88] and from the main center of Episcopal activity in Connecticut—the area about Stratford—Samuel Seabury, Jr., occasionally encountered his father's colleagues. James MacSparran, cousin by marriage, appears to have been a frequent associate of St. James's pastor.[89] S.P.G. missionaries traveling along the post road naturally put up at a brother's house. And in the spring of 1740, Elizabeth Seabury busied herself with preparations to entertain the greater part of New England's Episcopal clergy, for their annual Convention was to meet that year in New London.[90]

From east and west, along the post road, men rode in for the session on May 4: the ineffectual commissary of the Bishop of London, Boston's Roger Price (Oxford, 1718); Arthur Browne (Dublin, 1726) of distant Queen's Chapel, Portsmouth; from Rhode Island aging James Honyman of Newport, John Usher (Harvard, 1719) of St. Michael's, Bristol—a man much like his host, a model parish priest—and MacSparran; roughhewn Ebenezer Punderson (Yale, 1726) of North Groton; and, of course, that dominant personality, Samuel Johnson of Christ Church, Stratford, accompanied by his neighbors, Henry Caner (Yale, 1724) of Fairfield and John Beach (Yale, 1721) of Newtown.[91] The sole recorded business of the session was Commissary Price's pet project, the proposed mission at Hopkinton, Massachusetts. But it is unlikely that Samuel Johnson let the occasion pass without some reference to his ever-present concern, the procuring of a resident American bishop. He could not know that there would be any connection between this matter and the ten-year-old boy who had greeted the arriving clergymen. And of the assembled missionaries, only Henry Caner would live long enough to see Samuel Seabury's son a bishop.

When the Convention next met, at Newport in June, 1741, there is no doubt of the topic which occupied everyone's mind. With the landing of George Whitefield (Oxford, 1736) in that town, September 14, 1740, New England had begun to experience its Great Awakening.[92] Eastern Connecticut, where Seabury had but one S.P.G. colleague, was the principal area of revival activity in that colony,[93] and New London became the scene of wild disorders. Whitefield himself did not visit the town, and those who went to Norwich to hear him, October 24, 1740, were disappointed by his failure to appear. But at the end of April, 1741, Gilbert Tennent (Yale M.A., 1725) came to New London for a two-day bout of preaching.[94] The sparks he kindled soon blazed up, and by early summer the town was in the full throes of the revival. Under date of June 5, Joshua Hempstead wrote enthusiastically in his diary of "the wonderful work of God."[95] Samuel Seabury, in a letter penned the same day to the secretary, gave a rather different account of the matter. The Episcopalians, both at Hebron and New London, he assured the S.P.G., remained firmly attached to the Church. They were, however, much alarmed by the revivalists and their novel doctrines,

> The Effects of which are Really Surprizing: These people have meeting In New London almost every Night or Day And 'tis not uncommon (as I'm assured by persons of Good Sence & Integrity) To See ten or more Sceized at once with violent agitations, many Incapable of any Decency crying out of their Damned Estate, Some past Speaking at all, or So much as being able to stand, fall Down, as they pretend with the weight of their guilt, and the most of these continuing thus violently exercised (As they Say—with conviction) but a few hours, Do then Receive Comfort, the Spirit of God they Say witnesses with their Spirits that they are Converted & born again. Then follows

> Immediately Such raptures & transports of Joy as are more Surprizing than the Distresses; New London has for a week together been in such a Tumult that I was afraid the people would have been beside themselves; I have had my house full with people, Some under these Distresses and others Surprized at the Conduct of their Neighbours; tho I thank God I have never Seen any person in this way, but with cool reasoning, and by plain expositions of the Terms of Reconsciliation with God, they have been brought off from their amazing apprehensions, To a Just notion of the Doctrine of Repentance & the Remission of Sins; & beside my attendance at home for many Days together on people thus affrighted, I have been Invited to preach To a numerous Congregation at Lime [Lyme] about 7 or 8 miles from New London who Never heard the Liturgy many of them, and who Express'd great Satisfaction in my Explanation of those Doctrines about which New England Seems at present So much perplex'd.[96]

Looking on as his father moved among the crowd of terror-stricken persons, calming them with his "plain expositions of the Terms of Reconsciliation with God," young Samuel first acquired that hearty dislike of "Enthusiasm" which later marked his letters and sermons. Events in New London in the next three years reinforced this early bias. The town was visited by a constant stream of itinerant evangelists and kept in a continual uproar by the excitement of their meetings and sermons. Disorders multiplied, culminating in the famous public burning of "wicked books" (among them the writings of such Church of England luminaries as Tillotson, Beveridge, and Sherlock) by the half-mad James Davenport (Yale, 1738) and his followers on Sunday, March 6, 1743.[97] This "most extraordinary instance" of enthusiasm was reported to the S.P.G. by New London's missionary a few days after the event.[98] One can easily imagine the distaste and contempt with which his son viewed the wild proceedings near the town wharf. Such emotional excesses were easily criticized, and it is likely that young Samuel's mind dwelt exclusively on them. But in after years it was another aspect of the revivalistic technique which met his censure. Preaching to the people of

St. James's on the second Sunday after Epiphany, 1791, he scored the Pelagian attitude which, he believed, suffused the itinerants' discourses:

> The common mode of exhorting people to *come* to Christ, to *receive* Christ, to *embrace* Christ, to *close with* Christ, to *lean on* Christ, with others of the same import; without ever explaining what they mean by those expressions, or telling how Christ is to be found or embraced by us, may pervert the judgment & misguide the passions—it never can inform the understanding.
>
> If religion consists in our taking Christ, I fear I do not understand it. The Gospel, I apprehend, represents Christ as taking us, even as he took the little children in his arms. *Ye have not chosen me*, said Jesus to his disciples, *but I have chosen you*. Into his covenant God graciously takes us; if any one think we take God, let him shew how that can be done.[99]

Years before, in words almost identical to his grandson's opening sentence, Deacon John Seabury had dared to challenge Gilbert Tennent himself. As he listened to the preaching of the noted evangelist, Seabury's Old Light sentiments were outraged. Rising from his pew in the meetinghouse, he called out (according to the family tradition):

> Sir—You are continually crying—'Come to Christ,'—'Come to Christ,' 'Bring your sins to Christ;' But, sir, you do not tell us how to come or how to bring our sins to Christ. You speak as if they were to be put in a basket, and taken somehow to Him. Let us have instruction, as well as exhortation.[100]

Bad as he considered the New Light doctrines, Deacon Seabury continued to walk in the traditional New England Way. Let his pastor, John Owen, rave on like any illiterate itinerant and champion such men as Davenport![101] He and Elizabeth were old; they would not have to bear him much longer. Other members of the family judged differently, however, and as Samuel

Seabury surveyed his congregation on a Sunday morning in the 1740's, he saw the familiar faces of most of his brothers and sisters.

Several of the Seaburys had joined St. James's some years before the Great Awakening.[102] Joseph Latham, who married Samuel's eldest sister Patience in 1722, was in fact listed by his brother-in-law as one of the first petitioners for an S.P.G. missionary. This seems doubtful, but Latham had been an Episcopalian for several years by 1735.[103] John Seabury, Jr., (1704-1744) had his daughter Esther baptized by John Owen in 1734. But in 1738, at St. James's annual parish meeting, he and his younger brother Nathaniel (b. 1720) were voted pew No. 12. An innkeeper in New London, John Seabury became a vestryman the following year and served until his death.[104]

Neither of these Seabury brothers, nor Joseph Latham, left children who played any significant role in the affairs of St. James's. But about the time of the Great Awakening's beginning, the accession of Jonathan Starr (1705-1795) and his wife, Mary Seabury (1708-1807), added to that congregation a family who came, in time, to dominate all its proceedings. After the defection of certain of the Mumfords (as a result of Whig-Tory quarrels during the Revolution),[105] the Starrs and their numerous kin formed the backbone of St. James's. It was they who secured the rectorship—and a livelihood—for their impoverished cousin, Connecticut's bishop.[106]

Besides the Seabury connection, many other Congregationalist families of Groton and New London became Episcopal converts during Samuel Seabury's successful pastorate. Only four months in his mission, he noted in the spring of 1731 the accession of four households.[107] Such an achievement perhaps helped soften his disappointment that certain local Churchmen took their religious obligations rather lightly. Although Episcopalians constituted one sixth of the six hundred persons living in New London's thickly settled section—the port area—the average Sabbath crowd at St. James's numbered but fifty, and communicants were a mere handful: fourteen.[108] Yet the situation improved as the young rector brought the negligent to a sense of their duty and attracted additional converts. The church, he reported in 1733, was "plainly in a growing State."[109] A decade later the port, grown in size to about one thousand persons, had no less than two hundred thirty Churchmen. Fifty-six communicants provided a second index of the missionary's accomplishment. At Hebron's church, where he continued to officiate twice every quarter, forty persons attended at the administration of the Sacrament.[110]

Despite these accomplishments, the Reverend Mr. Seabury was not content to remain in New London. By 1742 he had a rapidly growing family. Samuel was to enter Yale in the fall of 1744; there were other sons to educate and daughters to provide for. His salary, he thought, was inadequate for these purposes. The congregation of St. James's had done their best. They regularly paid the £40 15*s* subscription promised him in 1730, giving it in the form of a contribution after Evening Prayer.[111] Indeed, they sometimes contributed a great deal more: in 1739 Seabury estimated his total annual "Perquisites" from the parish at £98 5*s* currency.[112] But Connecticut's paper was depreciating. The £98 5*s*, when converted into sterling, yielded only £18 12*s*, and this, joined with £60 sterling from the S.P.G., did not go far in an expensive place like New London.[113] The State Street family was in no danger of starvation (the minister seems to have had at least one Negro slave, and he had purchased, in September, 1741, a half interest in a New London ironworks).[114] Still, its income was too small to cover increasing needs. Earlier, in 1737, Seabury had asked the S.P.G. to transfer him to the Monmouth County, New Jersey, mission.[115] Nothing came of this request. But in 1742 he secured appointment as rector of Hempstead parish on western Long Island.

Seabury's hasty installation in this parish was closely associated with the smoldering feud between Churchmen and Dissenters which had existed in New York Province ever since the Ministry Act of 1693.[116] Under its provisions, the Church of England was able to secure a quasi-establishment in certain legally defined parishes, among them the parish of Hempstead, comprising the towns of Hempstead and Oyster Bay. All inhabitants, regardless of their denomination, paid taxes to provide the £60 in New York currency levied annually for Hempstead's Episcopal minister, and all freeholders might vote each January for the members of the parish vestry. Since the vestrymen need not be Churchmen, since a large majority of Hempstead's population were Dissenters,[117] and since no minister could receive the legal salary without being called by this vestry, possibilities for a first-class parish broil were ever present. Complicating the picture was the fact that within the parish there existed a second vestry made up exclusively of Churchmen and incorporated by royal charter[118] in 1735 to secure Episcopal control of the parish church, St. George's, recently built by voluntary contributors. Besides satisfying both these bodies, a prospective Hempstead rector also had to secure approval by the S.P.G., for the major part of his salary came from his missionary's stipend. Confusing though this situation was, it could exist in a form still more acute. As rector of Jamaica—the parish to the west of Hempstead—Samuel Seabury, Jr., would have to deal with no less than four separate vestries.

Late in 1742 Robert Jenney (Dublin, 1709), Hempstead's minister for many years, accepted a call to Christ Church, Philadelphia. On November 18, Samuel Seabury preached in St. George's. Since few of the parish vestry (the mixed Dissenter-Churchmen body) were present, he repeated his performance the following Sunday. He gave general satisfaction, and it was agreed that he should be given a call. Ordinarily, the S.P.G. would have been petitioned to approve his removal from New London, but Hempstead's Churchmen believed such a delay might be fatal. An answer could not be received from England before January, 1743, at which time the vestry election would be held. There were rumors that the Dissenters intended to combine and elect a purely Dissenting body, which should refuse to call any Episcopal minister. If Seabury were to become Hempstead's rector, the matter would have to be settled quickly.[119]

In order to pacify the S.P.G. (some of whose members were quite ruffled by his procedure), Seabury wrote to the secretary that he would accept the rectorship conditionally, holding himself subject to the final determination of the Society.[120] All arrangements having been completed, the two Hempstead vestries accepted Jenney's resignation. On December 5, the parish vestry issued its formal call to Seabury, presenting him to Lieutenant Governor Clarke for induction. Two days later, the candidate being in New York City, Clarke issued the requisite mandate, and on December 10, the rector of Jamaica officiating, Samuel Seabury was formally inducted into "the Real, personal and actual possession of the Parish Church of Hempstead aforesaid, of all the Rights, Glebes and Rectory thereunto belonging."[121]

Although he occasionally supplied Hempstead parish in the next few months, Seabury did not leave New London with his family until August, 1743.[122] Financially, he seems to have profited little by his removal. Hempstead's S.P.G. stipend—fifty pounds sterling—was smaller than that awarded New London-Hebron, while the legal salary, translated into sterling, was no great increase over New London's contributions. Seabury still had two churches to supply—St. George's and that at Oyster Bay—and there were many more Churchmen to care for at Hempstead.[123] The one concrete gain was a parsonage and glebe. The former the rector found in a wretched condition, but the parish promised to erect a new one and did so in the summer of 1745, Seabury describing it as "Verry Decent & Convenient."[124]

For St. James's, New London, the departure of its first minister was something of a disaster. The parish had hoped to appoint a New Englander as his successor and behaved so rudely toward the Irishman, Theophilus Morris (Dublin, 1729), whom the S.P.G. sent that he was forced to resign.[125] The case excited considerable interest and led to certain remarks, not very just in this instance, about clergymen who deserted poor New England missions for the livings of the New York Establishment.[126] If Samuel Seabury heard them, he probably gave them little attention. The S.P.G. knew his worth. Hard at work in his Hempstead mission, he could report to the secretary, just a year after his removal, that the Oyster Bay congregation was building a new church under his direction, and had "proceeded So far as to Raise a wood frame of 46 feet Long 34 wide & 20 feet to the Roof with a beautyfull Steeple 96 feet high, The Labourers being Daily at Work, I hope we Shall have It to performe Divine Service in this Winter."[127] A man who could produce results in the form of new churches, greatly increased congregations, and a healthy ratio of communicants to families did not have to fear the S.P.G.'s censure. And such achievements made up the quiet chronicle of Samuel Seabury's life. As the energetic parish priest, he made a favorable impression upon Hempstead's Churchmen:

> My father described him to me, as, seated on a strong sorrel horse, he made his way to Oyster Bay and Huntington, with his saddlebags strapped to his saddle. He was strongly built, but not tall, and he had a countenance which was intelligent and kindly, and showed decision and firmness. He wore a three-cornered hat, and small clothes and top boots. He rode well, but sometimes he could not make the journey in time to have service and return the same day.[128]

In the same month that Hempstead's rector proudly reported the erection of Oyster Bay's church, Samuel Seabury, Jr., left his father's parsonage and crossed to the other side of the Sound to enter Yale College. Working without family letters and reminiscences, or any autobiographical writings, it is a difficult matter to say much that is more than conjecture about his early years. One can sketch his Puritan ancestry and note the entrance of

Mumfords and Seaburys into that distinctive Episcopal communion which developed in New England after 1722. Something can be said of New London and of St. James's Church, of the Great Awakening, of the High Church missionary whose parental influence was so clearly decisive in molding his character. But of the boy himself nothing really is known except his physical appearance, derived from descriptions of him in later life. He was rather short, stocky, and powerfully built.[129] He had a full face, a high forehead, and dark green eyes.[130] In physical appearance, as well as in the cast of his mind, he was his father's son.

II

"A SOLID, SENSIBLE VIRTUOUS YOUTH"

IT WAS, PERHAPS, NOT WITHOUT A CERTAIN UNEASINESS THAT Samuel Seabury entered New Haven in the autumn of 1744 and made his way toward Yale College, still housed—as in the days of Rector Cutler—in a single wooden building and that now rather out of repair.[1] Sooner or later he must encounter Rector Thomas Clap (Harvard, 1722), and Clap's previous relations with his father had not been such that he could expect any warm welcome.

The clash between the two men had occurred in 1735. Clap at that time was pastor of the First Church in Windham, twenty-six miles north of New London. Exceedingly zealous for the strict maintenance of Congregational discipline, he had set up a committee of four deacons and three other laymen—the "Seven Pillars"—to make inquiries and report on members of his congregation suspected of committing notorious sin or giving scandal. Clap also conducted investigations on his own, and his pastorate (1726-40) was marked by an unusual number of public confessions.[2]

Most of the First Church was willing to submit to this stern regime, but Israel Folsom and his wife rebelled. Convicted by the pastor and "Seven Pillars" of "scandalous talk and reviling," they refused to confess before the congregation. Instead, they sent off an invitation to Samuel Seabury, desiring him to come and preach at Windham. He arrived in August, 1735, and found that the Folsoms had brought together a group of eighty, "of whom some stayed sundry hours with me after sermon was over, and were desirous to be informed concerning the Church of England; and upon my conversing with them they confessed that the Church had been sadly misrepresented, and that they should have a more favourable opinion of it for the future, and desired that I would come again."[3] Clap was enraged, and Congregational pressure soon put a stop to the Episcopal services. But the Folsoms, excommunicated from the First Church, left Windham for New London and were admitted to St. James's. This action (one of the few recorded which could be cited in support of the general Congregationalist explanation of Church of England conversions) further excited Pastor Clap. "It is a Disorderly and Scandalous thing," he complained to Benjamin Colman (Harvard, 1692), "for one Church or Community of Christians, to receive the Members of another Church while they are under Censure for Scandalous Immoralities in the Church where they belong."[4]

Probably Clap's anger had cooled by 1744. And Samuel Seabury would not have been at any disadvantage, in comparison with other Yale students, merely because he was an S.P.G. missionary's son. Before the erection of New Haven's Episcopal church in 1752, Clap's relations with Church students were fairly pleasant.[5] When he was chosen rector, Samuel Johnson described him to Bishop George Berkeley as "a solid, rational, good man, and much freer from bigotry than his predecessor." In a letter to his father, written in 1747, Johnson's son William Samuel spoke of Clap's "great friendship for you."[6] William Samuel had graduated with the class of 1744. Clap and the tutors allowed him to go home every third or fourth Sunday (he went to Stratford, if possible, for the monthly Communion), to attend the church at West Haven when the missionary officiated there, and to remain in his room, occasionally, at other times when Congregational services were held.[7]

It is likely that Yale similarly indulged other Episcopalians, including Samuel Seabury. The college rules, however, required all students to attend on the Sabbath, and on special days of feast or fast, at New Haven's First Church. Many a Sabbath Samuel had to sit in the meetinghouse pew while Pastor Joseph Noyes (Yale, 1709), reputedly the dullest preacher of his generation, delivered sermons and long extemporaneous prayers. Morning and evening prayers conducted by the rector, the college's Saturday religious exercises (in which the works of Ames and Wollebius and the Westminster Confession of Faith figured prominently), scholastic disputations and declamations:[8] all these familiar occurrences and, indeed, the general atmosphere of Yale gave Samuel Seabury an intimate acquaintance with the New England Way. When in his writings he discussed Congregational worship and doctrine, he spoke of matters he knew well.

No personal details of Seabury's college years have been preserved. He may have lived in the college hall or—more likely—lodged in New Haven. Cramped Yale College could accommodate less than half the student body in 1747, and Samuel, as a Churchman, had special reasons for preferring the greater freedom of the town. The curriculum he studied differed little from that his father had known. Essentially medieval, it concentrated on Latin, Greek, and Hebrew, on logic, rhetoric, geometry, geography, ethics and metaphysics. Clap, an ardent student of science, made significant additions in the fields of natural philosophy and mathematics. During his rectorship (1740-45) and presidency (1745-66) he put through a host of reforms, transforming Yale from a small, distinctly second-rate school into an institution which could challenge Harvard's position of leadership. Some of these reforms—the reorganization of the twenty-six-hundred-volume library and the addition of a third tutor—occurred before Seabury arrived at Yale. Others, notably the detailed code of college laws and the revolutionary charter of 1745, were adopted shortly after he entered.[9] What effect these institutional changes had upon his education, if any, is not known.

Seabury's Yale instructors were all competent men, but they do not seem to have made any deep impression on him. Chauncey Whittelsey (Yale, 1738), who had "a very happy talent at instruction and communicating the knowledge of the liberal arts and sciences," carried him through most of his freshman year.[10] In 1745-46 he was taught by Noah Welles (Yale, 1741), afterwards pastor of the Congregational church in Stamford and a noted anti-Episcopal polemicist. As a junior he had as his teacher John Whiting (Yale, 1740).[11] His final year, 1747-48, brought him a seasoned scholar in the place of recently graduated tutors: President Clap himself saw to the instruction of the seniors.

The class of 1748 included thirty-six students, an exceptionally large number. Seabury's rank in the class—fourth—gave evidence of his family's rise in the social scale.[12] Above him stood Richard Morris (of the New York manorial family), a representative of that important Connecticut clan the Fitches, and William Johnson, younger son of the Stratford missionary. Common backgrounds, as well as the fact that both were destined for the Episcopal ministry, provided a strong basis for friendship between Johnson and Seabury, and it is likely that they were often in one another's company. It was through his son that Samuel Johnson first became acquainted with Samuel Seabury. "He has lived 4 years much under my Eye," the leader of New England's Churchmen informed the S.P.G. in 1748, and "I can truly testifie of him that he is a solid, sensible Virtuous youth."[13]

There were other men, also important in Seabury's subsequent career, whose acquaintance he first made during his years at Yale. Isolated at New London, at New Haven he was only a few miles from such Church strongholds as Stratford and Fairfield, Newtown and Redding. Johnson and the clergy from nearby towns west of the Connecticut often visited New Haven, particularly at Commencement time. Letters to the S.P.G., written during the period of Seabury's residency at the college, reported many accessions from the student body.[14] The most important of these converts were two members of the class of 1745, Thomas Bradbury Chandler and Jeremiah Leaming, among Seabury's closest friends in after years.[15]

Chandler, who became a Churchman while a senior sophister,[16] was a man after Samuel Johnson's heart: witty, capable of immense labors, a true scholar, a convinced High Churchman, a planner of ecclesiastical campaigns. Seabury perhaps knew him intimately at Yale, for his father, when recommending Chandler to the S.P.G. in 1748, mentioned that he himself had "had a personal Acquaintance with him for nearly two years, & am well inform'd of his good Character at Yale Colledge."[17] Leaming, like Chandler a theological student of Samuel Johnson's, was cast in a rougher mold. Considerably older than his classmate (he was twenty-four when he entered the college), he lacked Chandler's urbanity and was later to display a certain eccentricity of character. There was always something of the rustic about Leaming, but deep piety, massive common sense, and an active though unwieldy pen made him a leader among Connecticut Churchmen. It is unlikely that Seabury formed a close friendship with him during their college years. The "Solid, sensible Virtuous youth" was shy. "I have always found a Backwardness in myself in contracting Intimacies," he once wrote. "My Friendships have therefore been but few, & those of a slow & gradual Groth."[18]

The Yale Commencement of 1748 attracted a large number of Episcopal clergy to New Haven. Samuel Johnson came, of course, to see young William graduate. Presumably Samuel Seabury, Sr., also attended, traveling from New York in company with Commissary Henry Barclay (Yale, 1734). In all, nine ministers assembled and "consulted the best things" for the Episcopal interest.

Among the candidates for degrees there were, Johnson noted, no less than ten—five bachelors and five masters—who acknowledged themselves Churchmen.[19]

Whether Samuel Seabury bore any distinguishing part in the exercises is not known: the bachelors' *theses* sheets of the period do not assign propositions to specific individuals. But Jeremiah Leaming (a few days returned from his ordination voyage and settled at Newport as assistant to James Honyman) must have annoyed many in the assembled crowd with his choice of a master's *quaestion.* The young apostate, they grumbled, had the hardihood to maintain the affirmative of "Whether an unbroken apostolic succession be necessary for a valid ordination?" Chandler, though equally zealous for episcopacy, preferred to be noncontroversial and thus submitted the conventional proposition that the Scriptures contained a complete philosophical, as well as theological, system. When he returned to take his M.A. in 1751, Samuel Seabury also proved discreet. "Was the Mosaic dispensation, with respect to religion, identical with that prefiguring dispensation revealed for the first time after the Fall?"[20] Yes, according to Mr. Seabury.

Like other members of his class who intended to take Episcopal Orders, Samuel Seabury, upon receiving his first degree, began to read Prayers and sermons to Churchmen who lacked the regular services of an ordained clergyman. No doubt he envied the situation of William Johnson. As a Berkeley Scholar, the Stratford missionary's son continued to reside at Yale, combining the intellectual pleasures of a college community with service to West Haven's Episcopalians.[21] Seabury's work in rural Long Island afforded no such delights. Yet it did allow him to profit from a constant professional association with his father.

More the Connecticut Puritan than he suspected, Samuel Seabury, Sr., had not been able to accustom himself to the free and easy ways of New York Province. The government, he complained, did nothing to encourage religion except continue the laws, made many years before, for the support of ministers in a few places. Personal religion counted not at all in the appointment of public officials—only considerations of party. "Profaneness meets with no frown from the Civil Majestrate, there being none to put any men to Shame for anything nor Doth the Civil Government seem To have any thing in View, but to Secure Interest & Property." (How shocking to the Puritan mind was the concept of a lay state!) The majority of his neighbors were persons the New Englander found quite uncongenial. "Indeed if a man will Laugh at Every Jest crack'd upon religion and Revelation, & Seem pleased with blasphemy which Infidels Call Wist, he will find himself caressed by many, but a grave Countenance and Serious Rebuke will not fail To get him Implacable Enemys."[22] In such a difficult mission the middle-aged minister needed the support of a like-minded colleague. The settlement of Samuel in the neighborhood would prove a great help and comfort, and while the lad finished his education at Yale, Hempstead's rector proceeded to create a congregation for him.

Stretching across Long Island from sea to Sound, Hempstead was a very large and populous parish. Within its boundaries were located two Dutch Reformed churches, two Quaker meetinghouses, a Baptist meetinghouse, and another occupied by a weak Presbyterian congregation. In order to care for the minority of Churchmen, Samuel Seabury frequently preached in private homes on weekdays, besides supplying the churches at Oyster Bay and Hempstead on Sundays. Such duty would have been enough for many missionaries, but in the spring of 1746 he began to venture outside his parish, preaching eighteen miles northeast of Hempstead at Huntington on the southern shore of the Sound.[23]

The situation at Huntington favored the establishment of an Episcopal congregation. There existed a small nucleus of Churchmen, the most prominent of the group being Henry Lloyd I (1685-1763), lord of the Manor of Queens Village, which covered the narrow peninsula between Cold Spring Harbor and Huntington Bay. Huntington's First Congregational Church was rent by divisions, a legacy of the Great Awakening.[24] Although its pastor, Ebenezer Prime (Yale, 1718), vigorously opposed Seabury's preaching, suggesting that he had no right to officiate at Huntington without consulting him, Hempstead's rector replied bluntly that he would work where he pleased: "My Great Design Is (as far as God Shall Enable me) To prosecute the Commission and command of our Lord in St. Luke 24:47 that Repentance and Remission of Sins Should be preached in his Name Among all Nations and this by Gods Grace I Shall do att huntington as I have Opportunity."[25]

Officiating at Huntington on weekdays, Seabury quickly made a number of converts. By the spring of 1747 people talked of building a church,[26] and in September subscriptions were opened. Twenty-nine persons agreed to pay various sums to Henry Lloyd, who himself contributed £143 7*s* in building materials, labor, and cash, an amount nearly equal to the total of the other subscriptions. In April, 1748, Lloyd ordered from Boston "5 thousand good merchantable boards for the Church in Huntington." The lumber soon arrived and work progressed rapidly, supervised by a four-man committee chosen by the subscribers. By the date of Yale's Commencement the church, it was reported, had been raised and "in a Little time will be Commodious for Publick use."[27]

Having created a congregation and built a church, Samuel Seabury made ready to approach the S.P.G. for aid. The Society was expected to provide a salary, first for a catechist (Samuel, Jr., was only eighteen and could not be ordained before November, 1753), and afterwards for a regular missionary. Hempstead's rector had devised an ingenious scheme for obtaining the necessary funds without putting his employers to any additional expense. Within his parish, the S.P.G. helped maintain two schools, paying Thomas Keble and Thomas Temple each ten pounds sterling per annum. By the spring of 1748 both men were unable to attend to their duties: Temple was old and very deaf and Keble hopelessly mad.[28] Seabury suggested, and the other New York missionaries agreed, that the Society might well withdraw their stipends, paying them instead to the support of the new church at Huntington. "Although it may Seem hard to turn a Superannuated Servant out of Bread," Commissary Barclay observed in a letter to the secretary, "It is more unreasonable that the Society Should be Burthen'd with them when Ample provision is made for the Poor by Law."[29]

Anticipating a favorable decision by the S.P.G., young Samuel prepared to take up his work at Huntington. Two weeks after his graduation, the Episcopalians of that town drafted a petition to the secretary, setting forth the rise and progress of their infant church and requesting that "Mr. Samuel Seabury the Son of Your Worthy Missionary, a young Gentleman (Lately Educated and Graduated at Yale College) of a Good Character, and Excellent hopes, may be Appointed the Society's Catechist in this Place, and Perform Divine Service Among us in a Lay Capacity." Included with the petition was a subscription totaling £17 3*s* currency, which the Huntington men agreed to pay annually to Samuel. On the same day, Hempstead's rector seconded this request in a personal letter to the secretary, in which he explained that Samuel intended to take Orders and would be guided by his father's advice in his post as catechist. Samuel Johnson sent a very favorable account of the candidate to the secretary. Commissary Henry Barclay, speaking for the Convention of New York's clergy, recommended that Seabury, "a Youth of an Amiable Character," be appointed according to Huntington's request. And Samuel himself, in his earliest extant letter, informed the S.P.G. that he heartily joined the Churchmen "in their Petition; and beg Leave to assure the Honourable Society that I shall do every Thing in my Power to advance true Religion, and the pious Designs of the Society amongst them."[30]

The secretary's reply to these communications, dated June 24, 1749, did not reach Hempstead until sometime in the autumn. Before the petition and accompanying letters arrived from Huntington, the Society had already decided to dismiss schoolmaster Keble, while still allowing the aged Thomas Temple his stipend. The ten pounds saved was, however, to be paid to Samuel as Huntington's catechist, the salary to be reckoned from Christmas, 1748. Alarmed by a report, forwarded by an immigrant English clergyman, that New England's candidates for Orders omitted certain prayers in reading service, the secretary warned Seabury that he should be particularly careful to teach his son "to read the Church Prayers, exactly without omitting any Part thereof, & [sic] Liberty which of late hath been taken by too many in their Service, and will be very highly resented by the Society."[31] Unfortunately for the Seaburys, the Hempstead rector had written to the Society prior to the receipt of this letter, informing them that Samuel, with the advice of Commissary Barclay and the other clergy, had officiated at Huntington on Sundays during the summer of 1749, "Reading part of our Lyturgie." When the secretary's letter came to hand (backed by others to the leading New England missionaries, which threatened dismissal from S.P.G. service for the "heinous misdemeanor" of designedly omitting or altering one word of the Prayer Book), this abridged service was instantly abandoned. In January, 1751, Samuel wrote the Society that he had constantly read Prayers at Huntington, "without deviating in any one Instance."[32]

For three years, from the summer of 1749 to the summer of 1752, Samuel officiated at Huntington, supported by his S.P.G. stipend of £10 sterling and the subscription of £17 3*s* currency got up by his congregation. On Sundays he read Morning and Evening Prayer and printed sermons "of Some of the most approved Divines of our Church." He also catechized the Huntington children. His duties must have left him more than sufficient time to study theology under his father's direction, for the

Episcopalians he served were not a large group. The usual congregation at Huntington's church (formally dedicated September 4, 1751, at which time it was "well nigh Compleated") numbered not more than sixty persons. An epidemic in the winter of 1749-50 carried off several of the principal members, men who had been particularly active, "by which means those that Remain Seem much Dispirited." The rector of Hempstead came three or four times a year to administer the Sacrament to the communicants.[33]

For a time Samuel kept the S.P.G. school at Oyster Bay, entering upon this work June 6, 1749, after the death of Thomas Keble. His father informed the Society that he had begun teaching at the request of the most influential persons in that town and asked that he be allowed the usual stipend of ten pounds. Noting that Oyster Bay was only six miles from Huntington, he wrote that the posts of schoolmaster and catechist might easily be combined.[34] The Society, however, does not seem to have granted Samuel any salary, and it is likely that he taught only a few months.

To supplement his income as Huntington's reader, Samuel earned some money from the practice of medicine.[35] It had always been intended that he should be a physician as well as a clergyman, two careers often combined in the eighteenth century. In order that he might have time to acquire a proper medical education, he eventually would interrupt his labors at Huntington, applying himself wholly to medicine until he reached the canonical age of twenty-four. Samuel Seabury outlined the plan to the secretary in his letter of September 30, 1748:

> My Son is now Studying Physic, and before he is of Age to present himself to the Society in person, I intend God willing that he Shall Spend one or two Years at Edenburgh in the Study of physic: I have been led into this manner of Educating him, from an hint taken from one of the honorable Societys Abstracts concerning their designed Oeconomy of their College [Codrington College] at Barbadoes. I Shall therefore Esteem it a great favour, if the Society will be pleased

> to approve this Method, and give him a place on their Books, and grant what may be recommended in his Favour by our Reverend Commissary with Regard to huntington.[36]

Samuel undoubtedly pursued his early medical studies, which began within a few days of his leaving Yale, under the direction of his father. Hempstead's rector is known to have practiced medicine from 1753 to 1759; he probably acted as a physician much earlier than that period. (Medicine, it has been noted, was a traditional occupation of the Seabury family, the first Samuel Seabury (1640-1681) and his son, Samuel, Jr. (1666-1763), both being practitioners.) When Samuel had acquired some knowledge, he began to doctor his neighbors, and during the last two years he officiated at Huntington, his medical business appears to have been considerable. No list of his fees survives, but they were probably the same as his father's. For a shilling, the Reverend Mr. Seabury would bleed a man or pull his tooth, or supply a patient with an emetic, a styptic, sudorific, cathartic, or blister plaster. House calls at night cost four shillings, twice the fee for those made during daylight hours. For three shillings, a dying patient could obtain both a visit from the physician and the draft of a will.[37]

Preacher, doctor, scrivener, the rector of Hempstead was also a teacher. By 1749 he had set up a Latin school in which he was preparing half a dozen young men for Yale. His reputation as an instructor brought him many pupils. Building a schoolhouse in the rear of the parsonage, he eventually secured an usher to assist him and in 1762 was able to charge thirty pounds currency per annum for each student, board, washing, and wood for the school fire being included.[38]

He needed all the money he could earn if Samuel's ordination voyage and Edinburgh studies were to be paid for. The young man appears to have had higher hopes than his father: the rector spoke only of Edinburgh, while Samuel wrote of studying "in one of the Universities of England or Scotland."[39] But Oxford and Cambridge were far too expensive. It would have to be Edinburgh, and there were funds enough for only a single year.

On January 5, 1751, Samuel asked permission of the S.P.G. "to come home as soon as I shall have compleated three Years in my present capacity." His request was considered at the Society's May meeting, and the members present agreed that the catechist might come to England whenever his father chose to send him. The secretary dispatched a pleasantly worded letter to Hempstead, informing the rector that the Society wished Samuel "a good Voyage, & all Success in his Studies, in England, or Scotland, as you shall determine for him. & when he is Qualified & of Age for Holy Orders, if it is desir'd, they will endeavour to provide a Mission for him."[40] Samuel replied that he would, indeed, seek a place in the Society's service after ordination and thanked the S.P.G. for its past favors. In July, 1752, he read Prayers at Huntington for the last time. His father wrote that the Church had gained ground in that town by his work and suggested that "under the Advantage of the Labours of a pious & Discrete minister," Huntington would soon become a flourishing congregation.[41] He did not have to say more; the secretary could read between the lines.

August found Samuel in New York, stowing his gear aboard a British-bound vessel. Probably the whole family had come to see him off, for Hempstead was only twenty miles from the Brooklyn ferry. The rector was not without his fears as he stood on the deck, repeating last-minute instructions and admonitions. By 1752, of twenty-nine men who had gone for Orders, Samuel Johnson reported no less than six as failing to return. (The chances of survival were, of course, rather high, but as Johnson once remarked, parents seemed unimpressed by the fact that only one youth in five perished!) Seabury could not but think of the fate of Jonathan Colton (Yale, 1745), intended for the church at Hebron which he himself had nurtured, who had died of smallpox on his homeward voyage in May of this very year.[42] But worrying would not benefit him or the boy! Bestowing his final blessing, the rector returned to the wharf. The vessel dropped down the East River, threaded its way among the islands in the bay, and crossed the bar at Sandy Hook. Samuel was on his way to Edinburgh.

As the young man whiled away the tedious hours of a month's or six weeks' voyage, he may still have yearned for Oxford or Cambridge. But since medicine was to be his second profession, Edinburgh was a much more suitable place. In the 1750's it had the best medical school in Europe. Even a single year passed there in the study of physic and anatomy, the specific studies mentioned to the secretary by his father,[43] would provide Samuel with a better medical education than the great majority of American physicians received.

The university's physical plant, a small collection of mean and motley buildings, would hardly impress a New Englander who had viewed the handsome brick pile of Connecticut Hall, dedicated by President Clap at the 1752 Commencement. Public-spirited citizens of Scotland's capital felt rather apologetic about the school's appearance. "A stranger, when conducted to view the University of Edinburgh," Principal William Robertson observed with some bitterness in 1768, "might, on seeing such courts and buildings, naturally enough imagine them to be alms-houses for the reception of the poor."[44] Few students lived on the premises, and Samuel probably took lodgings in the town.

Perhaps he roomed with a fellow American. Forty-six men from the colonies, at least fifteen of them Virginians, took medical degrees at Edinburgh in the period 1749-76.[45] Samuel must have known the wealthy New Yorker, James (later Sir James) Jay, brother of the Revolutionary statesman, who was graduated in 1753. (It is not likely, however, that Jay and Seabury became good friends; Samuel's Yale classmate, William Johnson, reported in 1756 that Dr. Jay had Latitudinarian tendencies: "His religion hangs somewhat loose upon him.")[46] No doubt there were other Americans attending classes at this time who, like Seabury, went unmentioned in the university records.[47] The medical degree required several years of study, and fewer than twenty students, on an average, were acquiring it each year in the 1750's.[48] The majority of the students at Edinburgh—the hundred and fifty, for example, who filled the anatomy theater of Alexander Monro, primus, for a typical lecture series in the 1740's—came for only a year or two.

Samuel's departure from New York in August probably was arranged so as to allow him plenty of time to arrive in Edinburgh before the start of Monro's course. The Professor of Anatomy lectured from October to May, teaching not only his subject, but also surgery and surgical treatment, and including some general lectures on physiology. Then nearing the end of his career (his son became joint professor with him in 1754), Monro originally had established Edinburgh's great reputation: the medical school dated from his appointment to the university faculty in 1720.

Edinburgh acquired a true medical faculty in 1726 with the addition of four professorships. Two of the first holders of these posts still taught in 1753, and one of them, John Rutherford, Professor of the Practice of Physic, must have been, after Monro, Samuel's principal instructor. Deliberate, meticulous, and not very exciting ("slow but absolutely sure" was the common university characterization), Rutherford carried his pupils through a course of lectures on Boerhaave's *Aphorisms*, supplementing this theoretical instruction with clinical lectures in the Royal Infirmary. This series, begun in the session of 1746-47, initiated that practical instruction in medicine for which Edinburgh became famous. Since all students of medicine could attend and the fee was very small, Samuel probably accompanied Rutherford on the hospital rounds.

Other members of the medical faculty of 1753 included Charles Alston, who delivered a course of lectures on materia medica;

Andrew Plummer, chiefly interested in chemical pharmacy; and the brilliant Robert Whytt, a disciple of Boerhaave, whose *Institutiones* served as the textbook in his course. Samuel perhaps attended some classes taught by these men. But since physic and anatomy were his principal concerns, he naturally would concentrate on Monro's and Rutherford's courses.

Few documents relating to Samuel Seabury's practice of medicine, after his return to America, are still extant. A single sheet, listing recipes for various "Decoctions and Infusions," survives in what was originally intended as a physician's notebook; many of the pages have been cut out, and others contain drafts of letters written after 1784. More medical preparations are described on the blank pages of a sermon booklet.[49] Although neither of these manuscripts can be dated with any precision, they seem to have been written prior to the Revolution. The decoctions and infusions are formal Latin prescriptions. Preparations of this type appear in the sermon-booklet collection, but homelier remedies are also included. For a scaly head, Dr. Seabury prescribed an ointment concocted of olive oil and tobacco ashes, rubbed over the head morning and night and covered with a cabbage leaf. The gravel should be cured by a teaspoonful of oven-dried leek fibers, powdered in a glass of white wine and taken twice daily. Herbal preparations were popular with the physician. Conserve of damask roses, the leaves of the English walnut (boiled with brown sugar), powder of roasted horsebeans, and broad plantain leaves sprinkled with wheat all had their uses.

The wording of his prescriptions shows that Seabury believed diseases resulted from an imbalance of the body's "humors," a natural opinion for one instructed by followers of Boerhaave. He seems, however, to have made some effort to keep up with current medical advances. When he was in England in 1784, he purchased two copies of William Cullen's *First Lines of the Practice of Medicine*, a new multivolume work, strong in its criticism of Boerhaave's system. The second copy Seabury undoubtedly presented to his son Samuel (1765-1795), who appears to have been studying medicine as early as 1782.[50]

Except during the Revolution, Seabury probably made little money from his medical practice. When he listed the sources of income he had enjoyed in 1775, in his claim for compensation as a Loyalist, he did not mention medicine.[51] His friend John Weatherhead, testifying under oath in support of this claim, declared that "He had some little practice of Physic, but believe he got little by it." As a refugee in New York City from 1776 to 1783, Seabury felt obliged to seek medical employment, since he was deprived of much of his former income. Appointed physician to the almshouse, he also engaged in private practice. Surviving tradesmen's bills list deductions for medical services he rendered their families. His reputation apparently was high. For attending the family of Colonel Frederick Philipse, he received fifty guineas on account and charged a larger fee. After the Revolution, he practiced only occasionally. Perhaps he always intended that his medical skill should be chiefly employed in connection with his pastoral duties, as a help rendered free of charge to parishioners and neighbors in low circumstances. Such a concept is suggested by the writer of a contemporary obituary, who declared that "the poor will miss his services as a physician and friend."[52]

Because of Seabury's consecration by bishops of Scotland's Episcopal Church in 1784, considerable interest has always attached to his relations with that body during his Edinburgh sojourn of 1752-53. Jacobites almost to a man, the Scottish Episcopalians were subject at that period to a crushing burden of penal laws, the most savage of which had been enacted after the unsuccessful rising in 1745.[53] Conforming to the numerous accounts of their secret worship is the well-known story (originally printed, it appears, in 1853)[54] of Seabury's first Sunday in Edinburgh. Asking his host where he might find an Episcopal service, the young man was directed to follow him through the streets, keeping far behind his guide, for "we are watched with jealousy by the Presbyterians." After many turns and windings, Seabury saw his host disappear into a large, dilapidated house on the side of a steep hill. Following the sound of his footsteps, he ascended to the fifth or sixth story and there, encountering the Episcopal congregation, "worshipped God according to the dictates of his conscience." One writer locates this conventicle in Carubber's Close and adds that Seabury, "in all probability," was confirmed by a Scottish bishop.[55]

The story is romantic, exciting—and almost certainly untrue. There seems to be no contemporary evidence to support it; those who have related it cite none. Seabury himself does not mention the tale. Neither is there any suggestion of an early acquaintance with the Episcopal Church in the many letters which he exchanged with the Scottish bishops after 1784. Furthermore, the statement that he attended the services of their proscribed body in 1752-53 is intrinsically improbable.

In order to worship according to the Book of Common Prayer, Seabury did not have to seek out a Jacobite congregation. Scotland had a number of Hanoverian Episcopal chapels, licensed according to law and supplied by clergymen ordained by English or Irish bishops. Such pastors were, in effect, without any episcopal supervision, and the Scottish bishops, into whose dioceses they had intruded, looked upon them bitterly as interlopers.[56] The concordat Seabury signed with his consecrators in 1784 severely censured these ecclesiastical free lances, but there is no reason to suppose the New Englander regarded them with any disfavor in 1752-53. At that early date there was at least one "licensed chapel" in Edinburgh, the forerunner of the commodious Cowgate Chapel, of which Seabury's friend, Myles Cooper (Oxford, 1756), was the senior minister from 1777 to 1785.[57] When Seabury's circumstances as a candidate for an S.P.G. mission are considered, there is every reason to suppose that he attended services at a government-approved establishment of this type.

Contemporaries did not regard the '45 as an exciting but hopeless venture. To them it seemed a very near thing, and when the revolt had been suppressed loyal addresses poured in upon George II. Meeting at Rye, the S.P.G. missionaries of New York (including, presumably, Samuel Seabury, Sr.) assured the monarch of "our detestation of the destructive and slavish Principles of Popery, and Jacobitism: Our utter Abhorrence of the traiterous and Unnatural Practices of the Rebels and their Accomplices."[58] In recommending candidates to the secretary, missionaries thought it necessary to mention political loyalty along with pastoral qualities. Given this atmosphere, it is most improbable that Samuel Seabury, "a Youth of good Genius, unblemish'd Morals, sound Principles in Religion and Government," preferred the worship of a hidden Jacobite congregation to that of Edinburgh's licensed chapel or chapels. Such a course would have been madness in one who intended to become an S.P.G. missionary.

The characterization of Seabury just quoted was penned by Commissary Henry Barclay in a typical letter of recommendation. Barclay, stimulated, no doubt, by Hempstead's rector, added that he had known Samuel ever since his graduation from Yale and thought him "one that had made as good a Proficiency in Literature, as the present State of Learning in America will admit of." James Wetmore of Rye, New York's senior missionary, also produced a favorable appraisal. Well acquainted with the Reverend Mr. Seabury's son, he knew him to be "firmly attached to our happy Constitution in Church and State, of an unblemish'd moral Character, and good Learning, and of so prudent Behaviour, that he will prove a worthy Missionary, if the Society shall please to receive him into their Service." Both Barclay and Wetmore suggested Samuel for the New Brunswick, New Jersey, mission. Hempstead's rector had earlier mentioned this appointment to the secretary, declaring that it would be a great satisfaction to have his son so near.[59]

Huntington would have been, of course, a better post in this respect. But the congregation remained small, too small to merit the full-time services of a minister. Moreover, since the missionaries of Hempstead and Brookhaven had charge of the adjacent territories, no congregation could conveniently be joined with it. New Brunswick was, therefore, the closest mission that Samuel could expect. And it was flattering to find that Commissary Barclay considered him suitable for the place. Barclay had written to the Society in October, 1752, explaining that the College of New Jersey probably would locate at New Brunswick. That town's Presbyterians wanted President Aaron Burr (Yale, 1735), an agreeable preacher and "a man of Sense," as their pastor, "Upon which Accountt It were to be wish'd, that some Gentleman could be found to Supply Mr Woods [the late missionary's] Place capable of Coping with him."[60]

Secretary Bearcroft thought Samuel equal to the task. "I wish your son all Success," he declared to Hempstead's rector. "If he presents himself to the Society this winter [1753-54] before New Brunswick is supplied, I will present him to the Board for it which I am sure [will] pay a particular Regard to him for your Sake." Samuel, he added, would receive the best available mission within a reasonable distance of Hempstead if someone else obtained New Brunswick before his arrival in London.[61]

Such a disaster, however, had not occurred when Seabury appeared before the S.P.G. at its October, 1753, monthly meeting. The proceedings resembled those his father had experienced in 1730. With Thomas Secker (then Bishop of Oxford and a leading advocate of an American episcopate) in the chair, the nine members present awarded him the New Jersey post. As for salary, Seabury would receive fifty pounds sterling per annum, the stipend to be paid from September 29, 1753.[62]

Shortly afterwards, Secretary Bearcroft gave Samuel a note of introduction to Thomas Sherlock, the elderly Bishop of London, informing that prelate that the bearer would be appointed to

New Brunswick should Sherlock find him worthy of ordination. (Courtesy alone required the conditional tense; no New England candidate ever failed the examination for Orders.) The secretary concluded with the statement that with Seabury "Mr William Smith [(Aberdeen, 1747)] recommended to your Lordship by the Clergy of New York & New England proposes to pay his Duty to your Lordship."[63]

Different in their talents and in almost every other respect, Seabury and Smith were frequently to clash in the councils of the Episcopal Church. It is interesting to find them linked in this manner at the very outset of their ecclesiastical careers. Samuel probably knew Smith before his departure from Huntington. The ambitious young man, two years older than Seabury, had emigrated to the colonies in 1751, coming over as tutor to the children of a Colonel Martin who lived on Long Island.[64] Now associated with the Philadelphia Academy, he was once again a Churchman (born into a family of Scottish Episcopalians, he had become a Presbyterian in order to secure a parish school)[65] and a candidate for Orders. Seabury, unacquainted at this date with Smith's religious metamorphosis, doubtless did not feel for him, in 1753, that deep-seated contempt which he later exhibited. As the two rode through the Kentish countryside toward Fulham Palace, residence of the bishops of London, the conversation, presumably, was pleasant.

The Hempstead rector had smoothed his son's way, writing to Bishop Sherlock in July, 1753. And on the very day that Bearcroft penned his introduction, he got off a second letter to the bishop—which he intended that Samuel should present—setting forth, in great detail, "what appears to me the great Obstacle to the Growth of the Church of England in the plantations." The difficulty, according to the middle-aged missionary, was the want of an American episcopate.[66]

The thought of the future Bishop Seabury handing such a document to Bishop Sherlock gives the letter a certain interest. But more significant than this coincidence of circumstances is the argument of Hempstead's rector, which reveals, once more, how deeply his Congregational background shaped the thinking of this convert High Churchman. Seabury did not even mention the practical consideration which Samuel Johnson always kept in the forefront: the hazards of the ordination voyage. It was the lack of discipline—discipline in the sense understood by Thomas Clap and Windham's "Seven Pillars"—which appalled the missionary and which, he hoped, "Some eminent Personage, Armed with the Apostolic Rod," might remedy. The only discipline the clergy could impose, Seabury lamented, was the suspension of notorious sinners from the Communion. "But where Controversies Subsist amongst our people of any Considerable note and on whose influence the Behaviour of others depends, as Such generally think themselves Superior to ordinary ministers, therefore our advice or Reproof with them has but little weight." Disputes often arose in the churches—"to the Great Scandal of Religion"—and there was none with authority to determine them. This "a truly apostolic Bishop" might do, as well as ordain, confirm, hold visitations, "give Countenance to the Diligent and faithful among the Clergie, & Reprove & Chastize the Insolent and Wicked." With such a person in America, the Church would become "the Joy of this part of the world." But while the authority of ordinary ministers was flouted and irreligious men preferred to posts of authority, while "Our Laws Against the open profonation of the Lord's Day, Either by Sports or Labour [are] Grown Obsolete; Our poor Church Can Scarcely hope to stand its ground against the present flood of Deism and profaneness." Nevertheless, if a bishop could not be obtained, Seabury hoped Sherlock would send over general instructions regarding the manner in which discipline might be imposed upon the laity, so that the clergy might act in concert and thus avoid censure and reproaches.

If Samuel had presented this letter to His Lordship of London (the reason why he did not do so is not known) that prelate, though touched by its earnestness, could hardly have failed to be amused by its picture of the venerated hierarch, restraining vice and punishing the evildoer. No one knew better than Thomas Sherlock that the disciplinary power the English bishops could wield was something less than the authority envisioned by a New England convert, relying on his abstract conceptions of episcopacy.

Samuel must have looked forward with great interest to his first interview with Sherlock. Although later Seaburys probably exaggerated his opinion of the bishop's theological attainments,[67] it is likely that his son Charles Seabury was correct when he judged that Sherlock's published sermons—famous in their day—served as models for his father's discourses.[68] The same characteristics—a concise, almost blunt, style, great plainness in exposition, and a distaste for the flowing period—mark the compositions of both men.

Sherlock perhaps exchanged more than the usual pleasantries with Seabury and Smith. When Samuel returned to America, he informed Thomas Bradbury Chandler (who quickly relayed the news to Samuel Johnson) that the bishop had declared to the King and Council his willingness to give ten thousand pounds for the support of an American bishop, provided such a person were sent out during his tenure of the see of London.[69] But it is more likely that Samuel picked up this news at some clerical tea table. He had plenty of time for visiting and sight-seeing. He could not be ordained before November 30 and was, in fact, ordained nearly a month after that date. Unfortunately for his biographers, he does not appear to have kept a diary of his London experiences, as did some other New England candidates. But a letter of Thomas Bradbury Chandler preserves one incident which impressed him greatly. Seeing the Archbishop of Canterbury's coach in the street, he peered inside and saw, not a brace of bishops riding with His Grace, but the Reverend Dr. Samuel

Chandler, a leading English Dissenter![70] Latitudinarianism was making great progress, great progress, indeed!

Samuel may have been confirmed during his stay in London. Some New Englanders made arrangements for the rite to be performed prior to ordination, while others, who perhaps could not fit it into their hectic round of play-going and sight-seeing, neglected the opportunity.[71] Samuel received deacon's Orders on December 21, 1753. A few days before that date, he had undergone the preparatory examination. The questions, probably, had not changed much by 1760, at which time Sherlock's examiner asked another American candidate to render a portion of the Greek Testament into Latin or English, translate a selection from Grotius' *De Veritate*, and, after putting the Thirty-Nine Articles into Latin, to explain—in Latin—their meaning.[72] William Smith was ordained on the same day as Samuel, the ceremony being performed at Fulham Palace. Sherlock, "in a very declining state of health," attended but could not officiate in person, and John Thomas, Bishop of Lincoln, acted in his stead.[73] Having subscribed the Articles, Smith and Seabury (and, probably, other candidates), entered the palace chapel, swore the usual oaths, and, after Morning Prayer, went through the requisite ceremony. Jacob Bailey (Harvard, 1755) an impressionable New England country boy, has left a vivid picture of the dinner which followed such an occasion:

> When we returned from the chapel, we were conducted into a vast hall, entirely composed of the finest marble. It was arched overhead, and was at least twenty feet high. All the walls, as well as the grand canopy, were covered with the most striking figures, so that this spacious apartment might truly be said to be fine without hangings, and beautiful without paint. In the middle stood a long table, covered with silver dishes. We sat down with his lordship of Rochester, the Bishop of London's lady, and several others, being, in all, twenty-one. We had ten servants to attend us, and were served with twenty-four different dishes, dressed in such an elegant manner, that many of us could scarcely eat a mouthful. The drinking vessels were either of glass or

> of solid gold. The Bishop was very sociable at table, but was seen to behave with a very important gravity. After paying eleven shillings a-piece for our [certificates of] orders, we drove into the city, and took a dish of tea together, and then parted in friendship.[74]

Two days later, also in the Fulham Palace chapel, Seabury and Smith were advanced to the priesthood, with Richard Osbaldeston of Carlisle as the officiating bishop. "Know Ye that at an Ordination holden by Us with the Aid and Assistance of Almighty God at the request and in the stead of the Right Reverend Father in God Thomas by divine permission Lord Bishop of London . . . We did admit and promote our beloved in Christ Samuel Seabury to the Holy Order of a Priest": so ran the formula of the certificate. Before Sherlock, Seabury declared that he would conform to the liturgy of the Church of England and received from him his license "to continue only during our Pleasure to perform the Office of a Priest in the Province of New Jersey in America in Reading the Common Prayers and performing other Ecclesiastical Dutys belonging to the said Office."[75] Probably he also secured an order from the bishop for the King's Bounty,[76] twenty pounds paid at the Exchequer to each clergyman going to the colonies.

In order to avoid the dangerous winter passage, or for some other reason, Seabury delayed his departure from England until March or April of 1754. He seems to have sailed with William Smith, who reached Philadelphia on May 22. Three days later Samuel arrived at New Brunswick, where he "received a most hearty Welcome from the People."[77] From New Brunswick he hurried to Hempstead for a joyous family reunion. His father was particularly happy with his appointment and wrote to the secretary: "My Son's safe arrival after 2 Years Absence so much improved & in the Society's Service upon a Mission not more than 50 Miles from me gives me such a sensible Satisfaction & joy that besides the Thanks due to Almighty God, it would be impossible for me to Suppress my Thanks to the Society for their great goodness to him."[78] Scotland and England had broadened the young man and given a certain polish to his manners. An admiring relative summed up the result in a few very eighteenth-century phrases: "Mr. Samuel Seabury has returned to America again; an excellent physician, a learned divine, an accomplished gentleman and a pious Christian."[79]

III

"MY SUCCESS HAS NOT BEEN EQUAL TO MY FIRST EXPECTATIONS"

ON JUNE 7, 1754, SAMUEL SEABURY SAID GOOD-BY TO THE family at Hempstead and set out for his New Jersey mission.[1] The journey, though short in the number of miles actually covered, required an elaborate combination of land and water transportation. Traveling west, through Jamaica and Flatbush, the missionary boarded a ferry at the tip of Long Island, crossed the two-mile expanse of the Narrows, then cut diagonally southwest across Staten Island. An eighteen-mile ride brought him to another ferry, which made the crossing between Staten Island and Perth Amboy. Twelve miles inland from that port, and on the opposite bank of the Raritan (fordable at this point, except during flood tide), lay the town of New Brunswick, "Small, but pretty well built."[2]

Proximity to Hempstead was the only thing that made New Brunswick attractive. There was neither glebe nor parsonage (though the parish, at the time it became an S.P.G. mission, had promised to provide both), and the church remained unfinished. Planned, "not in proportion to the present Congregation, but in proportion of their Expectation of increasing," the building was a handsome stone structure, designed to accommodate six hundred persons.[3] Its erection had come about as a direct result of the Great Awakening.

In 1739 the Dutch Reformed and Presbyterian churches of New Brunswick had as pastors Theodorus Jacobus Frelinghuysen and Gilbert Tennent, the leading evangelical preachers in their respective denominations. Both men had used revival methods long before Whitefield's first visit to New Brunswick in November of that year, but his successful preaching, on this and subsequent occasions, stimulated them to greater efforts. Those who disapproved attached themselves to William Skinner, S.P.G. missionary at Perth Amboy, who attended the nearby church at Piscataway, built on the north side of the Raritan. Enough persons became Churchmen that the original idea of building in wood was abandoned, and in 1743 the congregation laid the foundations of the stone church.[4]

Seabury was the second missionary to reside at New Brunswick, his predecessor, Thomas Wood, a graduate of New College, Oxford, having served from 1749 to 1752.[5] The newly ordained minister did not have to contend with Frelinghuysen, dead several years before his arrival, or with Tennent, who had removed to Philadelphia in 1744. Neither did President Aaron Burr, that "Man of Sense," prove a threat to Episcopal expansion, since the College of New Jersey, contrary to Commissary Barclay's expectations, had settled at Princeton. Indeed, at the time of Seabury's arrival, there was no minister of any sort in the town, and he had the satisfaction, as he informed the secretary in his first report, "of seeing several dissenters come to church, whom I hope will in time regularly conform."[6]

Seabury's pastorate at New Brunswick lasted less than three years. Great things could not be accomplished in such a short period, yet he did something to consolidate the infant church. From the S.P.G. the missionary secured a parochial library worth ten pounds (the sort his father had been given in 1730), as well as the customary folio Bible and Prayer Book.[7] He reported in the autumn of 1754 that his people intended to finish their church the next summer. The building was so far erected that Seabury conducted services in it throughout the period of his stay, but he was overly optimistic in supposing that it soon could be completed: the steeple did not rise until 1772.[8] His people, paying him forty pounds currency as a supplement to his S.P.G. stipend,[9] probably were hard put to it to find additional funds to expend on their ambitious edifice. They were not very numerous. In 1761 Ezra Stiles (Yale, 1746) noted that New Brunswick contained one hundred forty families, about sixty of them Presbyterians and a somewhat larger number members of the Dutch Reformed Church. Some thirty Episcopal families lived in the town and in adjacent Piscataway.[10]

The S.P.G. did not expect that its missionary would confine his labors strictly to New Brunswick. Wood's parish had stretched as far west as Trenton, and his successor did a considerable amount of itinerant work. During the summer of 1755, Seabury made several missionary journeys, preaching to large congregations, particularly at Cranbury, sixteen miles south of New Brunswick, and at Readington, twenty-five miles up the Raritan valley. The people, many of whom had never before heard an Episcopal minister, liked the young man and asked him to continue his visits. His success at Readington must have been considerable, for in October, 1756, he reported that he had baptized eighteen children there at different times during the past half year. He also baptized many children at a German Lutheran church, about twenty-one miles from New Brunswick, where he frequently preached at the request of the congregation.[11]

South of New Brunswick, at South River (or Spotswood), Seabury built up an organized congregation. In the summer of 1755 he was making regular visits to the town, settled mostly by Scots attracted to the province by the proprietors of East Jersey. Subscriptions for a church were set on foot and considerable amounts of money raised when, suddenly, the business came to "a full stop, the attention of the whole Province being engaged by the Motions of the French on their Frontiers." Because of the badness of the roads, Seabury could not travel to South River in the winter of 1755-56. But in the spring the subscriptions went forward, and he formally organized a parish. A wooden church, the frame of which had been raised by October, 1756, opened for services in 1759.[12] By that date Seabury, two years gone from New Brunswick, was settled at Jamaica on Long Island, the parish which adjoined his father's mission.

The possibility of Seabury's leaving had arisen within a few months of his arrival in New Brunswick. When Samuel Johnson, after more than thirty years at Christ Church, Stratford, left that congregation in 1754 to become the president of newly established King's College, New York, he considered Seabury as his successor (along with several other missionaries), only to decide that he would not "entertain the least thoughts of a remove." Johnson's statement may have been an accurate judgment of Seabury's state of mind at this time, but the situation altered radically in December, 1755, when Thomas Colgan (Dublin, 1722), rector of Jamaica, died of a quinsy. Within a week Johnson (who still thought that the New Brunswick missionary might be unwilling to leave his post) informed his son William that the Jamaica Churchmen "intend to try for Mr. Seabury, Junior."[13]

The situation at Jamaica approximated that which Seabury's father had encountered at Hempstead in 1742. The parish, made up of the three towns of Jamaica, Flushing, and Newtown, had a Dissenting majority: there were, in 1762, more than five hundred families belonging to Dutch Reformed, Presbyterian, Quaker, and other non-Episcopal congregations, while only about one hundred twenty families adhered to the Church of England.[14] But the Presbyterians of Jamaica village, descendants of New England Puritans, constituted a more formidable host than their fellows of Hempstead, whose ancestry was similar.[15] They had recovered both their parsonage and stone meetinghouse, seized by the Episcopalians early in the century under cover of the Ministry Act of 1693, and were strong enough to maintain a settled minister, something the Hempstead Presbyterians could not do. Until the coming of Colgan in 1734, repeated difficulties occurred concerning the stipend of sixty pounds currency, due under the 1693 statute to the Church of England rector.[16] Colgan enjoyed a quiet incumbency, but Churchmen feared that the parish vestry, dominated by Dissenters, would refuse to call an Episcopal minister now that he was dead. Events justified their apprehensions.

Commissary Henry Barclay outlined the situation to the secretary on January 9, 1756.[17] Should the Dissenters proceed with their plan and present one of their own ministers for induction, the governor, Sir Charles Hardy, would refuse to accept him, and the right of presentation thereupon would lapse into His Excellency's hands. In order that Hardy might then grant induction to the clergyman whom Jamaica's Churchmen might select, Barclay requested a general permission for any missionary to remove to Jamaica. This the S.P.G. willingly granted.

There was talk of presenting the minister of Jamaica's Dutch Reformed church to the Governor.[18] The parish vestry, however, chose instead Simon Horton (Yale, 1731), the rather ineffective pastor of the Presbyterian church of Newtown.[19] Hardy, according to prediction, refused to accept him and made ready to induct a suitable S.P.G. missionary. Some doubt existed in the summer of 1756 as to which clergyman would secure the post. Samuel Johnson had written to his son William, who had gone for Orders in 1755, suggesting that he might seek an appointment to Jamaica, and William gave the matter serious consideration. But to Johnson's great grief his son, after being ordained deacon and priest, contracted the smallpox, fatal to so many New England candidates, and died in London, June 20, 1756.[20] Jamaica's Churchmen were therefore able, without any hindrance, to invite Samuel Seabury as their pastor.

Sir Charles Hardy issued the requisite documents on January 12, 1757. The ceremony of induction took place the next day, with Commissary Barclay as the officiating minister. On January 23, a Sunday, Seabury completed the tedious formalities. In the parish church at Jamaica he read Morning and Evening Prayer, then "openly and publickly, before the Congregation," declared "his unfeigned Assent and Consent to the Use of all Things . . . contained and prescribed in the Book of Common Prayer." This was followed by a reading of the declarations of conformity to the liturgy of the Church of England which he had made before Bishop Sherlock and Governor Hardy. Afterwards Seabury delivered, for the benefit of the congregation, a third declaration of this type. Lastly, he read all Thirty-Nine Articles, declaring his assent to them and acknowledging "them and every one of them to be agreeable to the Word of God."[21] Those Jamaica Churchmen who had the patience to sit through this whole performance (known as "reading in") could, indeed, be certain that they had a canonical pastor!

The new rector suffered for want of a parsonage and glebe,[22] none having been provided for Jamaica's missionaries after the Presbyterians had recaptured their property. The lack of such conveniences was the more keenly felt because Seabury was no longer a bachelor. On October 12, 1756, in New York and probably at the house of the bride's uncle, Colonel William Ricketts, the young man had been married by his father to Miss Mary Hicks.[23]

Edward Hicks gave his son-in-law seventy-five pounds cash as a wedding present, a sum he could well afford. A Philadelphia businessman (he probably was still active in 1756, though he had retired to Staten Island by 1762), Hicks, according to Seabury, bore "the Character of an opulent Merchant, & lived in a fashionable & genteel Manner." A partial inventory of his property in 1763, listing much fine furniture and silver, supports this statement. Mary Seabury, motherless since childhood, obviously had been brought up in an environment much more luxurious than that her husband had known. A fortnight before his daughter's wedding, Edward Hicks presented her with the Negro slave who had been her personal attendant.[24]

Almost nothing is known of Samuel Seabury's wife. Her children, in their adult years, described her as "a lady of good sense, of cultivated taste, and of refined and generous feelings; . . . both as a wife and mother she was all that husband or children could desire."[25] Probably filial affection and fading memories painted a portrait somewhat more attractive than the sitter's features warranted. Mary Seabury did not live to see her husband a bishop. She died at New York in 1780, on the twenty-fourth anniversary of her marriage and in the forty-fourth year of her age, leaving six children, three sons and three daughters.[26]

Immediately after their marriage, Samuel Seabury and his wife appear to have established their home in a rented house at Newtown. By himself Seabury could have provided no better residence, but relying on his father-in-law's promise of a gift of four hundred pounds, he soon arranged to purchase a small farm half a mile east of Jamaica village. When he reminded Hicks of his pledge, the merchant told him he was out of cash, but declared that if the money could be borrowed, he would go surety for it and pay the interest. The unsuspecting son-in-law agreed to these conditions and secured his farm. The house, enlarged by Seabury, was filled with furniture, some of it old and some new (and cheap), which Hicks sent to Jamaica; much of it the young couple did not like, but thinking it a gift, they said nothing.[27] Seabury otherwise improved the property, consisting of twenty-eight acres of good tillable land, fourteen acres of woodland two miles distant, and eight acres of salt meadow "from which may be cut 20 loads of hay." A new barn was erected, and by 1762 the rector had purchased an ingenious screw press and cider mill capable of grinding fifty bushels of apples an hour, the fruit being supplied by the farm's fine orchard.[28]

Seabury's first years at Jamaica proved discouraging. He did not attempt to conceal his lack of tangible accomplishments from the secretary; on the contrary, he openly confessed, in a letter written in the fall of 1759, that he could not "give the honoured Society an account of my success in this Mission answerable to their pious care & expense."[29] Jamaica was a very difficult mission for one man to properly care for. There were three churches to be attended: Grace Church, the parish church, a wooden structure with thirty pews, opened in 1734 and now much out of repair; the equally shabby Newtown church, raised in 1735; and a small building at Flushing, little more than a wooden shell.[30] The three congregations bickered back and forth, more or less continually, concerning the schedule of services, each believing that it was being deprived of a fair share of the pastor's attention. In order to quell this discontent, Seabury, soon after his arrival, rearranged "the turns of Preaching" in a manner which increased his work but silenced—temporarily—the complainers.[31] The basic problem, however, remained unsolved. "Preaching once in three weeks at a place I find by experience will do little more than keep up the present languid sense of religion," the rector informed the secretary in October, 1759; "was it not for the steady tho' slow increase of the Congregation at Newtown I should be almost discouraged."[32]

The great obstacle to religion in Jamacia parish, according to Seabury, was the large number of persons tinctured with Quaker sentiments. His letters and those of his father show that Long Island had many families, descendants of members of the Society of Friends, who no longer kept up an active membership in the various meetings but retained the Quaker dislike of a "hireling clergy" and repudiated the concept (upon which the High Church clergy laid particular stress) of a sacrament-orientated religion. Jamaica's rector was particularly distressed that such families could be persuaded neither to present children for Baptism nor to receive the Holy Communion.[33] And their "corrupt Principles," he believed, had produced a noticeable effect on their neighbors' religious behavior. Declaring that they could spend Sunday as profitably at home as at meeting or church, most backsliding Quakers refused to take part in public worship, and many Episcopalians followed their example. Although Seabury made repeated efforts to enlarge the number, as late as 1764 he could persuade only twenty-seven persons out of the parish's one hundred twenty families of professed Churchmen to become communicants. This situation contrasted sharply with that existing at Hempstead, where his father, in the same year, and with a congregation of about the same size, had sixty-five communicants.[34] The Hempstead ratio of families to communicants might be considered unimpressive in Connecticut.[35] But it was excellent for New York, and Jamaica's rector grieved that he could not attain it.

Flushing—"in the last generation the grand Seat of Quakerism . . . in this the seat of Infidelity"[36]—was the town where Seabury's first efforts met with the least success. But when, about 1760, the religious condition of Jamaica began to improve (considered from the Churchmen's viewpoint), Flushing led the revival. Noting that affairs in his parish were "considerably mended," Seabury, writing to the secretary in October of that year, singled out the Quaker stronghold for particular comment. Many young people, children of Friends and Deists, had attended Episcopal services the past summer, worshipping "with great Decency." And Flushing was at last completing its barn-like church.[37]

The Episcopal revival received zealous support from three well-to-do New Yorkers—John Aspinwall, John Troup, and Thomas Grenfell—who had retired from business to end their days amidst the bucolic scenes of Jamaica parish. They seem to have been active in getting up petitions for royal charters, submitted to the provincial authorities in 1761. Charters were readily granted, incorporating Newtown's church under the name of St. James's, Flushing's church as St. George's, and Jamaica's under its long-established name of Grace Church. Establishing three ecclesiastical vestries in the parish, in addition to the Dissenter-dominated parish vestry, the charters also gave the Churchmen a much firmer control over the buildings they had erected by voluntary contributions, besides allowing them to hold other property as incorporated bodies.[38] Encouraged by the favorable response to their petition, the Episcopalians attending Grace Church got up a subscription for the thorough repair of that structure, John Troup making the handsome contribution of twenty pounds.[39]

At Flushing, Seabury noted much greater improvements. Although Thomas Grenfell gave some money, John Aspinwall, who had acquired his fortune through privateering,[40] was the Church's principal financial backer. When he settled at Flushing about 1759, only a dozen or so persons regularly attended the rector's services. Intent on a reformation, he soon invited Agur Treadwell (Yale, 1760), a Congregational convert, to set up a Latin school in Flushing and perform, with Seabury's approbation, the functions of a lay reader. This step having been taken, Aspinwall next laid out the money for finishing Flushing's church, on which he expended a total of £600 currency, making it "one of the neatest churches in America of its bigness." Acting with Treadwell, he drew off many converts from the Presbyterians and Quakers, building up a large Episcopal congregation.[41]

Newtown experienced a similar awakening. A local benefactor, one William Sackett, left by will a house and glebe (the annual value of which was variously estimated at between twenty and forty pounds sterling) to be appropriated to the use of such a clergyman as St. George's Church should think proper. Money was found for completing the church, a tower and steeple were added, and a fine bell secured.[42]

Thus, outwardly at least, Jamaica parish about 1762 appeared to be in a much more promising state than when Seabury had arrived from New Brunswick five years before. Lumber-and-plaster achievements, it was true, still were more in evidence than spiritual ones (the backwardness to receive the sacraments continued to trouble the rector), but a beginning had been made. And Seabury was quite willing to speed the revival by supporting Treadwell's application for Orders and settling him in the parish as his colleague.

President Johnson, Commissary Barclay, and Samuel Auchmuty, Barclay's assistant at New York's Trinity Church, joined Seabury and his father in explaining the proposed plan to the secretary in December, 1761.[43] Treadwell would take complete charge of Newtown and Flushing, the former giving him possession of its newly acquired glebe. In return for obtaining Seabury's exclusive services, the people of Grace Church, Jamaica, were expected to provide £25 currency annually in lieu of glebe and parsonage. Each town was then paying £20 of the salary assigned Jamaica's rector by the Ministry Act, and Seabury would continue to receive £40 from Flushing and Newtown. (This last provision may appear unusual, but it was not without precedent: the people of New Rochelle, included in Westchester parish as defined by the 1693 statute, paid their proportionate share of the rector's salary, although for many years they had an S.P.G. missionary as their pastor and received no help from Westchester.)[44] Finally, Treadwell should act as Seabury's subordinate; it was proposed to make him "joint & assistant Missionary." In order that the S.P.G. might not misinterpret the situation, President Johnson sent a private letter to the secretary, assuring him that the desire to settle Treadwell owed nothing "to any want of Fidelity & Assiduity in Mr. Seabury, who is a worthy Missionary." The desire to have a clergyman's services more frequently than once in three Sundays, and "Zeal for the Enlargement of the Church & promoting the Interests of true Christianity," alone actuated the petitioners.[45]

The three churches and Rector Seabury having given their approval to all arrangements, Treadwell sailed for England and ordination. Yet, when he appeared before the S.P.G. at its April, 1762, meeting, he received an appointment, not to Flushing and Newtown, but to the vacant mission of Trenton, New Jersey. At the same time, the Society sent Ebenezer Kneeland (Yale, 1761) to Flushing as catechist and lay reader.[46]

The reason for the appointments, according to President Johnson, was the obstinacy of Flushing's benefactor, John Aspinwall. Not content that Treadwell should be joint missionary with Seabury, Aspinwall insisted that he be given an independent appointment. But the Society proved unwilling to consent to a plan which might give occasion for the charge that it had attempted to divide a parish established by the civil authority.[47] So Flushing got nothing but a catechist, the S.P.G. providing the usual stipend of ten pounds.

This turn of events bitterly disappointed Aspinwall. Knowing that Seabury, as well as the S.P.G., was unwilling for Treadwell to have an independent position in the parish, he proceeded to vent his anger on the rector, abetted by less important figures in Flushing and Newtown. Poor Kneeland, unhappy in his situation, soon left the former church for Huntington, settling there as lay reader at the invitation of Hempstead's rector.[48] Aided by the resentful Treadwell (and, it must be confessed, by Seabury's imprudent conduct), Aspinwall succeeded in turning Jamaica parish into an ecclesiastical bear garden. By the end of 1764 these developments, coupled with unfortunate family difficulties, had all but destroyed Seabury's usefulness.

Soon after arriving at Trenton, Treadwell paid a visit to his old neighborhood. Had he acquainted Seabury with his coming, he would have been invited—"readily & gladly"—to preach in the three churches of the parish. Instead, he passed within a mile of the rector's house without calling on him, and on the next day, Sunday, February 13, 1763, occupied Flushing's pulpit after forcing the church doors, the key being in Seabury's possession. He repeated this performance the next Sunday, preached at Newtown on a weekday, and in a flagrant violation of the rector's pastoral rights, came to Jamaica and baptized a child almost on Seabury's doorstep. The injured clergyman complained loudly to the secretary, declaring that he could not account for Treadwell's conduct, "unless he acted under the Influence & direction of Mr John Aspinwall of Flushing, a man of low Birth & strong passions & violent in his resentments."[49] The Society demanded an explanation of Treadwell, who replied, in a somewhat lofty strain, that the custom of the country justified his preaching; he had scarcely thought "the Society would be troubled with a Complaint of this Nature." He conveniently omitted any mention of the Jamaica baptism, and the Society's committee, which seems to have been singularly obtuse in judging the forces at work in the parish, accepted his explanation, hinting that Seabury was a sender of frivolous complaints. Treadwell must have adopted a humbler tone in the personal explanation he made to Jamaica's rector. In the fall of 1764, Seabury informed the secretary, "with the greatest Pleasure," that "he hath given me all reasonable Satisfaction in the Case of which I complained to the Society."[50]

After Treadwell's intrusion, the situation in Jamaica parish steadily worsened. Not only were Flushing and Newtown aggrieved, but Grace Church, too, felt that it was being neglected. In an attempt to bring his quarreling congregations to "brotherly love and peace," Seabury met the Grace Church vestry at John Comes's inn on September 3, 1764, and proposed a new preaching schedule. On the Sundays he officiated at Flushing and Newtown, he would return home, both winter and summer, and hold an afternoon service at Grace Church; in this way Jamaica village would be supplied every Sunday. The vestry agreed to try the plan for a year and to continue it afterwards during pleasure. The schedule required much additional work on Seabury's part —more riding and no less than three services on summer Sundays—but if it brought peace, the harassed rector was willing to continue it "as long as my health & Strength of Body will permit."[51]

John Aspinwall, continually seeking to undermine Seabury's position, had been active in fomenting the discontent over the turns of preaching. Deeply affected by his whispering campaign, Seabury temporarily lost his balance. A few days after the meeting with Grace Church vestry, he took the extraordinary step of challenging his opponent in print. Readers of the *New-York Gazette*; *or*, *the Weekly Post-Boy* encountered this unusual advertisement on the third page of the September 13, 1764, edition:

> WHEREAS it hath been represented to me, that Mr. *John Aspinwall*, of Flushing, hath at various Times, and on various Occasions, traduced and aspersed my Character, especially in the City of New York, to my very great Detriment and Disadvantage; This is therefore to desire the Favour of that Gentleman, that if he hath any Thing to object against me, which he thinks deserves the Notice of Mankind, he would be honourable enough to do it in one of the public Papers, that I may have the *Opportunity at least* of vindicating myself. I must also desire he would insert all he has to say against me at one Time, and leave nothing for after Explanations; And if I was not affraid of laying too great a Burthen upon him, I would ask him to name the Proof he has to support his Allegations. Thus doing he will confer an Obligation that shall be always acknowledged by SAMUEL SEABURY
> *Jamaica, Sept. 11, 1764.*

Aspinwall was not long in replying. The next week's edition of the *Gazette* carried his own challenge, as well as a reprint of Seabury's advertisement. Addressing himself to the printer, the ex-privateer wrote as follows:

> Mr. HOLT,
> BY an Advertisement in your last Weeks Paper I find my self charged by Mr. Seabury, with having traduced his Character, much to his Disadvantage, and he desires me to insert my Objections against him in one of the Publick Papers, with my Proofs to support them, in answer to which I shall say nothing more at present than that if any Thing I have declared concerning him, has proved so detrimental to him as he pretends, he doubtless must have been informed what those Declarations were, and had he been desirous to wipe off the Aspersion, he might have done it without calling on me to repeat the Charges; or he

might have had his Remedy at Law, which lies open to him: Mr. Seabury may be assured that I shall be ready to answer him in Support of my Allegations, when ever he shall think proper to charge me with them in a Course of Law.
Flushing, September 19, 1764. JOHN ASPINWALL

The battle was now joined, and advertisements flew thick and fast.[52] Poor Seabury found himself at a distinct disadvantage. Aspinwall's challenge to the contrary, he really did not know the details of the charges brought against him. Writing to the secretary on October 6, he declared that his enemy had represented him in very unfavorable terms "but without descending to particulars, that I have been told of." Seabury added that Aspinwall was threatening to complain of him to the S.P.G., on what grounds he knew not, and expressed confidence that he would not suffer in the Society's estimation before he had had a chance to vindicate himself. His closing sentence revealed his lifelong inability to remain silent in the face of unjust criticism; always he must defend his reputation. He would act with moderation, he assured the secretary, but it would be such "Moderation, as I think consistent with what I owe to my own Character, upon which my Usefulness intirely depends."[53]

Admirable as was the sentiment, it seems extremely doubtful whether a newspaper controversy, extending over two months and coloring every issue but one during that period, was a prudent and profitable method of implementing it. Whatever the merits of the case, Seabury could hardly hope for a clear-cut victory. The casual reader, who knew nothing more of the matter than what appeared in the advertisements, must have decided that he had no victory at all. Seabury was never able to list the particular charges which Aspinwall had made, a point his opponent repeatedly hammered away at, suggesting that the rector was not unable, but rather afraid, to reveal them because they were true. His declaration that he did not seek a remedy at law because he disliked such a procedure, could not afford it, and that, anyway, the law did not provide a remedy in the case of certain injuries, must have sounded suspicious to many persons. It is obvious that Seabury failed of achieving his goals: the silencing of Aspinwall and the public vindication of his own character. And the controversy can only have weakened his position in turbulent Jamaica parish.

That position was not enhanced by another dispute in which the rector simultaneously engaged. Everyone who had access to the *New-York Gazette* could learn of his quarrel with John Aspinwall, but a few favored souls were reading an even better tale: the details of Seabury's unhappy relations with his father-in-law, Edward Hicks. Manuscript pamphlets, relating the story from the viewpoints of the two men, circulated on Long Island and Staten Island in the autumn of 1764.[54]

It has already been noted that Hicks promised his son-in-law four hundred pounds for a farm at the time of his marriage and that when Seabury reminded him of his promise, he pleaded he had no cash but would pay the interest and go surety for the sum if Seabury could borrow it. Under these conditions the rector obtained the money, but Hicks never paid the interest. After three years the lender, Nathaniel Marston, demanded the accumulated amount—eighty-four pounds when figured at seven per cent—and Seabury had to pay it. Without his father-in-law's help, the annual interest was an enormous burden, amounting to nearly half the legal salary paid by the parish. Furthermore, the rector's expenses were constantly increasing: his three daughters were born between 1758 and 1761. Seabury's situation would have greatly improved had he been able to collect a legacy of £350 due to his wife from the estate of her mother's parents. But this money, which Mary Seabury supposed was in the hands of her Uncle Ricketts, was instead in the possession of her father, and Edward Hicks would not pay it. It was no wonder, then, that Jamaica's rector, early in 1762, found it necessary to advertise his farm for sale. When he first settled in the parish, he had assumed—on the basis of assurances given by certain leading men—that a parsonage soon would be forthcoming. Disputes among the three congregations, however, had prevented anything from being done. If he was receiving a housing allowance in 1762, it was only a few pounds from the people of Jamaica village, not enough to make any dent in the ever-increasing debt which must somehow be paid to Marston. Unless Hicks paid what he owed, the farm would have to go.[55]

The evidence indicates that Seabury's difficulties were not so much with his father-in-law—an old man, somewhat reduced in circumstances, sick of the palsy, and totally dependent on his house slaves—as with his grasping brothers-in-law, William and Charles Hicks, who managed the family's affairs. William had a home on Staten Island, where Edward Hicks had come to live by 1762. Dissatisfied with his treatment, he sent repeated messages to Seabury to come and visit him. When the rector finally arrived (the precise date is not known, but it was sometime in 1762), Hicks told him he wished to move to Jamaica and make his home with his daughter. Seabury became quite blunt. He explained his own financial situation, reminded his father-in-law of the legacy, and told Hicks that he could not be received unless the money was paid and a reasonable compensation made for his support. To this the old man replied that William stood obliged to pay him an annuity of fifty pounds per annum. Seabury should have this for his room and board, four slaves in part payment of the legacy, and a mortgage on his furniture and plate until, a settlement having been made with William, he would be in a position to pay the rest. The rector agreed to these terms. Hicks could come, provided Mary Seabury consented, and of this he would be given word within a fortnight.

Before any message had been sent him, Hicks arrived at the Seabury house with one of his Negroes. He was, of course, taken in by his son-in-law, who subsequently managed to get his plate, furniture, and other slaves from William. Part of the legacy was now paid in the form of a bill of sale for the four slaves and in cash, raised by selling most of Hicks's household goods in New York, a modification of the Staten Island agreement which he himself proposed. The old man, however, refused to execute a mortgage of his plate, suggesting that Seabury was trying to take advantage of him. But he pressed his son-in-law to accept an outright conveyance of this property when he thought that creditors might attempt to seize it. Seabury roundly told him this suggestion was dishonest, Hicks grew angry, and a quarrel ensued. Soon afterwards, while the rector was from home, William Hicks came to Jamaica and received from his father, before two witnesses, a gift of one of the slaves already delivered to Seabury. To justify this singular procedure, Hicks declared to his son-in-law that the bill of sale given him had been a sham, devised to protect his debt-encumbered property. He quitted the Seabury home for his old quarters on Staten Island, and Seabury allowed two of the remaining three slaves (William Hicks had carried off his gift, a boy named Ben) to accompany him, since he could not get along without their services.

Jamaica's rector was now poorer than ever. He had lost three slaves valued at £220, as well as the amount due for Hicks's board and lodging, for which no payment had been made. And on November 20, 1763, probably some months after his departure from Jamaica, Hicks sent him a written order, demanding that he surrender the plate and those pieces of furniture which had not been sold.[56] Since money was owed him, Seabury refused. His father-in-law thereupon had him arrested.

Until this event the details of the dispute had probably been known to few outside the Hicks-Seabury connection. But the rector's arrest naturally gave rise to a good deal of gossip. Seabury drew up a written "State of the Case" between himself and his father-in-law. This document (surviving only in a fragmentary copy made by one of the Hickses) apparently was written for the guidance of a lawyer prosecuting Seabury's demands on his father-in-law, not as a justification intended to be read by the general public. Nevertheless, Edward Hicks, or more likely one of his sons, charged that Seabury handed the document about the neighborhood.

Accordingly, the Hickses got up a "Reply to the State of the Case" (Edward Hicks signed the paper but the whole seems to be in the hand of his son Charles), which painted the Jamaica rector as a villain of the deepest dye. Seabury, according to his father-in-law, was a liar, a hypocrite, a villainous sophist, a brute, and—it seems superfluous to have stated it explicitly—"a Disgrace to his Profession." Hicks had never promised him four hundred pounds for a farm, he had never agreed to give him a mortgage of his furniture and plate, he had never intended to convey his slaves to him as part payment of any legacy. Cunningly, artfully, Seabury had played his game, endeavoring to secure possession of all his father-in-law's property. That the Ricketts legacy had not been paid Hicks acknowledged, but he declared that he had certain charges to offer in reduction of it. What these charges were appears from a manuscript in Seabury's hand, presumably the draft of a rejoinder to the "Reply to the State of the Case." Hicks's ridiculous demands must have gone far toward discrediting that highly colored narrative in the eyes of most reasonable people. He wanted £250 for his daughter's board and clothing from the time of her mother's death until her marriage; £80 for the slave girl he had given her; the £75 cash wedding present; also the price of the cheap furniture he had sent the newlyweds. His spite was obvious, and Seabury made short work of the charges in his pamphlet. The available evidence does not record the details of the final adjustment of the Hicks-Seabury claims, but it appears that a settlement was reached in 1765.[57]

Weighed down with family troubles and financial difficulties and saddled with three quarreling congregations—in two of which he had powerful enemies—Samuel Seabury, by the fall of 1764, was in no position to minister effectively. There was little reason for him to remain at Jamaica. The principal circumstance which had held him there—"my own Desire of being near a most excellent Father, whom I dearly loved & whose Conversation I highly valued"[58]—no longer existed. Early in June Samuel Seabury, Sr., had returned from a short visit to New London a very sick man, and on the morning of June 15 he died, his illness—variously reported as a nervous disorder and an abscess of the side—having lasted twenty-one days.[59] "His disconsolate widow" (who had provided wine valued at £3 10*s* for a suitable funeral) raised a handsome stone over his grave in St. George's churchyard "In gratitude to the memory of the best of husbands."[60] To her brother-in-law she wrote: "My husband did not lay up treasures on earth; though I have reason to think he did in Heaven, where no rust doth corrupt; and my whole trust is in Him who hath said, 'He is the Father of the fatherless and the widow's God.' " The S.P.G. presented her with half a year's stipend, the usual allowance of a missionary's widow.[61]

As his wife's letter indicates, Samuel Seabury, Sr., left an inconsiderable estate.[62] He had intended to give their youngest son Nathaniel a liberal education, probably at King's College, and fit him, like his brother, for an S.P.G. mission. The family income, however, could not bear this expense after the Hempstead pastor's death, and Nathaniel temporarily became master of the school which the S.P.G. helped maintain at Westchester, on the northern shore of Long Island Sound.[63]

Samuel Seabury joined his brother as rector of Westchester late in 1766.[64] It may appear surprising that he waited so long before quitting an uncomfortable post, but he explained to the secretary that he had delayed his request for a transfer from Jamaica for two years, fearing the Society would think he "indulged a discontented rambling Disposition."[65] Opportunities to leave had been frequent enough. In the spring of 1761, when his difficulties with Edward Hicks were just beginning, Westchester's vestry first elected Seabury rector. However, the S.P.G., unaware of this action, appointed John Milner as its missionary.[66] Seabury gave way to him—he had not, perhaps, intended to accept the call anyway. The next year he was mentioned for New Haven's Trinity Church, which needed, according to Samuel Johnson, "some politer person" than Ebenezer Punderson as its pastor. Nothing came of this suggestion (Johnson declared that New Haven could not "make it worth his while"),[67] but when Punderson died in 1764, shortly after his removal to Rye, the people of that parish applied to Seabury. Although his several disputes were then raging in full force, Seabury so feared the Society's displeasure that he could not bring himself to ask for the Rye position. Putting the vestry off with a statement that he must have time to consider, he kept them waiting three months, then wrote that "as he could not settle his affairs at Jamaica, he was necessitated to continue there a year longer."[68]

Seabury's letters to the secretary held out hope that the situation at Jamaica was improving and that he could still do good there.[69] Unbiased observers disagreed. Writing to the secretary in the spring of 1765, Samuel Auchmuty expressed a wish that, "for the peace of the Church," he could be prevailed upon to settle in his father's mission, still unsupplied. "He is an ingenious deserving Man," the new rector of New York's Trinity Church added, yet "such unhappy Differences subsist between him, and the several principal people belonging to the Church in his Mission, that his removal would be highly prudent; especially, as the people at Hempstead are fond of Him, and wish his settlement among them."[70]

Seabury showed no interest in the Hempstead rectorship (the S.P.G. was about to cut its annual stipend from fifty to thirty pounds and there was little prospect the people would make good the loss).[71] But after Westchester had been some months vacant, he plucked up his courage and informed the secretary in December, 1765, of his willingness to accept the call which the vestry had given him on October 28. Financial necessity, he affirmed, was the reason he desired to remove. Since settling at Jamaica, he had expended near £300 currency more than he had received, "one half of all I can call my own." Repeatedly his hopes for a satisfactory housing arrangement had been dashed. Still, if the Society desired him to remain, he would do so, provided his superiors would oblige Jamaica to furnish him with a parsonage or house rent.[72]

When the secretary's answer arrived in September, Seabury was genuinely distressed at its sharp criticism of his congregations. "It would very much grieve me," he wrote, "should this Mission continue long unprovided with a Missionary, especially as I should think that Misfortune happened to it in some Measure through my Means, & as a great Part of it, is not to be charged with the same Unkindness to me."[73] He formally resigned Jamaica on December 1, 1766, two days before the governor, Sir Henry Moore, issued the papers for his settlement at Westchester. Myles Cooper performed the ceremony of his induction (which, for some reason, was delayed) on the first day of the following March.[74]

Seabury's call to this parish resulted from a clerical scandal, the details of which were eagerly retailed through New York and the neighboring colonies. According to Samuel Johnson, Westchester's religious life had greatly deteriorated by the 1750's. The minister, Thomas Standard, inducted in 1727, was so old and feeble that he could do little or nothing; influential "freethinkers" abounded; the public worship was treated with contempt.[75] Standard died early in 1760,[76] and, as has been noted, John Milner was appointed to succeed him. A recent graduate of the College of New Jersey, the new missionary (described by Johnson as "a hopeful Young Man")[77] sent off reports to the S.P.G. which recorded most encouraging progress. In fourteen months he baptized one hundred fourteen persons; the communicants, only a handful when he arrived, had increased to fifty-three by the summer of 1763. A royal charter was secured for St. Peter's,

Westchester, in 1762;[78] his people purchased a new glebe and in the spring of 1765 laid the foundations of a large stone church at Eastchester.[79] Reading Milner's enthusiastic letters must have been a pleasant exercise for a secretary who had also to examine the doleful communications forwarded from Jamaica by Samuel Seabury.

After four years of unbroken success, the Westchester rector's career came to an abrupt end. The report forwarded to the S.P.G. and believed by his parishioners declared that in a drunken stupor he had sexually assaulted a churchwarden's son. Milner refused to confess (and there was some reason, though not much, to doubt the truth of the story), but, in any event, he could no longer keep his post. About the beginning of June, 1765, he fled from New York to Virginia, where he became the rector of Newport parish in Isle of Wight County.[80] His success in securing a position did not heighten, one may suppose, the opinion which Seabury and his colleagues entertained of the Southern clergy.[81]

Whatever the Reverend Mr. Milner's morals may have been, he did confer on his successor one tangible benefit: the thirty-acre glebe, pleasantly situated near St. Peter's Church and furnished with a house, a new barn and outbuildings, the building and repairing of which had cost Milner nearly £200 currency. Seabury estimated that the parish (which was supposed to reimburse Milner) would have to spend an additional £100 on the parsonage, and he himself laid out £20 to put his fences in repair.[82] While it is unlikely that his personal agricultural labors exceeded such light tasks as directing the haymakers or reapers, the glebe gave Seabury some claim to be considered a true Westchester farmer. He raised hay, corn, buckwheat and flax, and had, in 1776, at least sixteen head of cattle and six swine.[83]

Seabury's cash salary was somewhat less than that he had received at Jamaica. Under the Ministry Act of 1693, Westchester paid its rector £50 currency, to which the S.P.G. added £40 sterling (before 1765 the stipend had been larger);[84] the comparable amounts in the Long Island parish were £60 and £50. But while he received less money, he did have the glebe, and his work was lighter. Although the legal parish defined by the 1693 statute included the towns of Westchester and Eastchester, the small Manor of Pelham, the more important manor held by the Morris family and called after them Morrisania, as well as the huge (and similarly named) Philipsburgh Manor, and the town of New Rochelle, Seabury steadily officiated in only a small part of this extensive territory. Colonel Frederick Philipse, the great magnate of the region, had erected a stone church on his estate, at Yonkers, in 1752-53, and after 1765 Philipsburgh Manor had its own S.P.G. missionary.[85] Its people, however, continued to pay their ministerial rates to Westchester's rector, as did those of New Rochelle, which, at the time of Seabury's arrival, was also a separate S.P.G. mission.[86] New Rochelle's Episcopal church, originally a French Huguenot foundation, had always been served by a French-speaking minister.[87] But when the incumbent died in 1766, the Society decided it no longer could supply a missionary. Until the Revolution, Seabury provided occasional services at New Rochelle. His attempt to secure an additional S.P.G. stipend for this work apparently was unsuccessful.[88]

The Westchester rector regularly served the churches of Westchester and Eastchester (New Rochelle was four miles beyond Eastchester, and its Episcopalians could easily attend that church).[89] Seabury probably never officiated in the ambitious stone structure, originally named St. John's, which Milner had begun shortly before his fall. Eastchester's Churchmen quickly expended £700 currency on the building, erecting the walls and covering them with a roof. At this point their resources failed, and as the governor refused Seabury's application for a brief allowing him to solicit contributions, the structure necessarily remained unfinished until after the Revolution.[90] The Eastchester church in which Seabury conducted services was a small, dilapidated building, raised about 1693. In form it resembled St. Peter's,

Westchester, a wooden structure twenty-eight feet square, covered with a pyramidal roof and topped by a bell cupola. Both churches looked like seventeenth-century New England meeting-houses and had, in fact, been designed as such, the towns of "East" and "West Chester" having been settled by Connecticut Puritans. Unlike Hempstead or Jamaica, however, the towns no longer had a significant body of Congregationalists-turned-Presbyterians, who might still have been resentful of the seizure of the meeting-houses, accomplished by Churchmen in 1702-03.[91] Within that part of the parish which Seabury served, there were not many Dissenters of any denomination: a few Presbyterians and Quakers at Eastchester, a larger group of Quakers at Westchester, and some "Presbyterian French" at New Rochelle. But the rector noted "many Families, especially among the lower Class, who do not even pretend to be of any Religion at all."[92]

After the interminable squabbling and backbiting of Jamaica, Seabury found his new parishioners a pleasant relief. Rather irregular in their attendance at service when he arrived, by 1769 they had grown "more constant & devout." "The Churches are generally well filled," he reported to the secretary, "& the Responses very decently made by a much greater Number than heretofore."[93] Officiating one Sabbath at Westchester and the next at Eastchester, the rector read Prayers and preached in the morning and catechized the children after Evening Prayer.[94]

The Churchmen he served did resemble those of Jamaica in one important particular: their reluctance to approach the Holy Communion. Milner's glowing reports to the contrary, Seabury could find only twenty-two communicants in 1767, and the number never increased to more than twenty-eight. Many of them received but once a year, the usual communicants at a single administration being ten or twelve.[95] (The frequency of Seabury's Communions is not known, but it is more likely that he followed the established Westchester practice of administering only at the three great festivals of Christmas, Easter, and Whitsunday than the New England custom of monthly Communion.)[96]

Not Quaker doctrine, but a fear of being unworthy, was the main cause of this backwardness. S.P.G. missionaries in Westchester County reported that their people were terrified by the exhortations in the 1662 Communion service (read by the minister during the actual administration and on the previous Sunday) which warned of the fate of those receiving without proper dispositions.[97] Although the missionaries considered these fears unreasonable and attempted to quiet them, they had no great success. The difficulties experienced by Seabury deeply impressed him, and their influence may be traced in the wording of the Communion service which he introduced into Connecticut in 1786 and in that subsequently adopted by the Protestant Episcopal Church.

Life at Westchester was uneventful. "With Regard to the Mission under my Care, I have no particular Information to give the Honoured Society"—so ran the usual opening sentence of the rector's letters to the secretary. Free of unpleasant relatives, Samuel and Mary Seabury enjoyed at Westchester a few years of comparative happiness. They had, by the time of their removal from Jamaica, four children—three daughters and a son. Violetta Ricketts and Abigail Mumford (named for the two grandmothers) had been born in 1758 and 1760, respectively. "Miss Maria," who was to become a lifelong spinster and the constant companion of her widowed father, followed in 1761. After four years the long-desired son and heir appeared, but Samuel died in early manhood, and, like his brother Edward, born at Westchester in 1767, he left no children. It was Seabury's youngest son, born May 29, 1770, and named, appropriately, Charles (the day marked the Feast of the Restoration of Charles II) who carried on the family name and perpetuated a unique clerical dynasty.[98]

Nathaniel Seabury, S.P.G. schoolmaster at Westchester, lived at his brother's parsonage during his brief stay in the parish. Besides the ten pounds sterling from the Society, paid him for teaching poor children gratis, he received one Spanish dollar per child each quarter from parents able to pay. The school, however, was small (it taught reading, writing, arithmetic, and the Church of England catechism) and rather ineffective as a charity. According to the rector, Westchester's poor either were unconcerned about the upbringing of their children, allowing them to remain idle, or else they kept them at home to work. Nathaniel had hoped to finance his education for the ministry with the proceeds from the school, but discouraged by the report that the Society might withdraw its support, he abandoned teaching, November 20, 1767. He afterwards became an innkeeper in Newark, New Jersey.[99]

Ultimately the Society decided to continue its stipend. Westchester's rector, exceedingly conscientious in his supervision of the school, selected as master his clerk, George Youngs, "who supports a very good Character, is a Communicant, & very well known, both to me & the People." Youngs gave satisfaction for several years, but in 1771 the disapproving Seabury reported to the Society that he had "become an Encourager of Conventicles, admitting stroling Independent and Methodist Teachers to hold forth at his House."[100]

In order to extricate himself from the debts he had contracted while at Jamaica,[101] Seabury eventually established his own school, designed "to prepare young Gentlemen for the College, the Compting-House, or any genteel Business for which Parents or Guardians may design them." Presumably modeled after that conducted by his father, it opened early in 1775 in the borough town of Westchester. To children who had learned their letters, the rector offered a better grade of instruction in the three R's than that provided by a half-educated S.P.G. schoolmaster. Older pupils could learn geometry and trigonometry and apply their knowledge to practical problems in classes on surveying and navigation. Youths "who are intended for a learned Education" obtained Latin and Greek. And all pupils were instructed in "the Principles of Morality, and the Christian Religion, by frequent short lectures, adapted to their Capacity."[102]

Within a few months the rector had attracted more than twenty pupils, including five from the island of Jamaica,[103] who boarded in Westchester, with "unexceptionable Families," at a cost of £20 currency per annum. Charging £6 currency for tuition, Seabury realized a very good profit. In 1775 the school produced nearly half of his total income. The whole Westchester's rector rated as the equivalent of £200 sterling. Judging himself to be "tho' not in wealthy, yet in easy Circumstances," he was capable of supporting a wife and six children "comfortably & Decently."[104]

In 1767-69 the clergy of New York and New Jersey attempted to persuade Seabury to exchange his agreeable living for a remote frontier mission. Sir William Johnson, noted Indian agent and land speculator, was at this time in close correspondence with Samuel Auchmuty, the New York rector, and with President Myles Cooper of King's College, both active in the S.P.G., of which Sir William had been admitted a member in 1766.[105] Relying upon Johnson's unrivaled knowledge of Indian affairs, the Society asked him to submit a general scheme for missions among the Six Nations. The baronet's reply suggested, in addition to missions properly in the Indian country, the possible establishment of one on his estate, Johnson Hall, located in the wilderness on the banks of the Mohawk River. He had settled, he explained, about one hundred thirty families, mostly Germans and members of the Lutheran and Reformed churches, on his lands and had erected for them a stone church and a parsonage in the village of Johnstown, which he was establishing about a mile from his residence. The people, he assured the secretary, too poor to maintain a German minister, would become Churchmen if a missionary lived among them. Such a man could also work with the Indians, hundreds of whom remained at Johnson Hall for at least six months in every year. A smaller number constantly resided there. To further the good work, Sir William would give possession of the parsonage, a glebe of twenty acres, and, if necessary, thirty pounds sterling to supplement the S.P.G. salary.[106]

The Society accepted the proposal, agreed to pay an annual stipend of forty pounds sterling, and began the hunt for a suitable missionary.[107] But the clergy of New York and New Jersey, meeting at Elizabethtown in October, 1767, decided to recommend a candidate, since it might be difficult to secure a man in England. Perhaps Thomas Bradbury Chandler recalled that Seabury (absent from the gathering) had once had some thoughts of undertaking a mission to the Senecas, a project dashed by the preliminaries of the French and Indian War.[108] At any rate, the clergy pitched upon the Westchester rector.

Cooper and Auchmuty hurried off glowing recommendations to Sir William. The baronet's prospective pastor, according to the King's College president, was "a Man of great good Sense, of a cheerful Disposition, and has a moderate Family. . . . Besides his being a good Divine and an agreeable preacher, his Skill in Medicine is also much esteemed." Trinity's rector gave a similar evaluation: "a man of Character, and of excellent parts, a good Divine, and an Able physician."[109] Greatly impressed (Seabury's medical skill seems to have been a strong point with him), Sir William turned a deaf ear to Provost William Smith, who was attempting to secure the Johnson Hall appointment for a protégé, Alexander Murray (Aberdeen, 1746).[110] Smith did not hesitate to speak disparagingly of Seabury to the baronet, and his whole move appears rather underhanded, considering that he probably was present at the meeting which had chosen the rector.[111]

Seabury showed interest in the proposal. But he was no longer young, he had a growing family, and he did not think the financial arrangements adequate. If he were to acquire any influence among the Indians, he would need a salary large enough to provide occasional entertainment for those visiting Johnson Hall. Furthermore, it was uncertain what provision there would be in the event of Sir William's death.[112] He therefore resisted the earnest prodding of Cooper and Auchmuty, who continued to mention his excellent qualifications in their letters to the baronet.

Auchmuty first wrote that Seabury ("undoubtedly . . . the fittest man I know to begin a mission, having sufficient Abilities, Constitution, Zeal and firmness for such an undertaking") would call at Johnson Hall in the spring of 1768, then promised a visit in the autumn, yet it was not until the following summer that the rector actually made the two-hundred-mile journey.[113] Unfortunately, he missed Sir William, departed for the Senecas' country a few hours before his arrival, but Johnson's son-in-law showed him around and explained the allowance and perquisites which a missionary would have. Seabury reported to the secretary that, though the country was attractive, the mission would not support a family man unless it were joined with that at the Mohawks' Castle, twelve miles from Johnson Hall. To this plan Sir William was unwilling to agree; he considered it absolutely necessary for the Mohawks' missionary to reside constantly among them. And since he did not believe he could offer a larger salary than that he had suggested, the plan fell through.[114]

Seabury, therefore, remained at Westchester for the remainder of his career as an S.P.G. missionary. The active years he spent in the Society's service were not nearly so successful as his father's had been. His stay at New Brunswick, though promising, had been too short, and his incumbency of Jamaica too hectic, for much to be accomplished. Even at Westchester he was disappointed by the results he achieved. In 1771 he wrote to the secretary:

> . . . though I think Appearances are something mended since I have been in this Mission, yet my Success has not been equal to my first Expectations. I find it very difficult to convince People that Religion is a Matter of any Importance. They seem to treat it as a Thing unworthy of their Attention, except on some particular Occasions, when they are otherwise disengaged. Many come frequently to Church & yet continue unbaptised. Others come constantly, & appear to behave devoutly, & yet cannot be prevailed upon to become Communicants: While many others pay not the least Regard to Religion of any Kind, nor on any Occasion. I shall however endeavour to do my Duty, & I

> hope, by God's Blessing, in due Time I shall see some good Fruit from my Labours.[115]

An eminently successful parish priest the Reverend Mr. Seabury was not. And yet he had qualities of mind and character which greatly impressed his clerical colleagues, as the correspondence concerning his proposed removal to Johnson Hall clearly shows. Because of his ability, in the period 1755-74 he moved gradually, and somewhat against his will, into the small group of Episcopal leaders. The often unhappy details of his pastorates are not the whole story of these years.

IV

"HIS WANT OF LEISURE & INCLINATION, & NOT HIS WANT OF ABILITIES"

SAMUEL SEABURY'S FIRST APPEARANCE ON THE LARGER STAGE of Episcopal affairs—that supra-parochial setting dominated by Samuel Johnson—took place within a few months of his return to America. Johnson and Johnson's pet project, King's College, New York (opened in July, 1754, a month after Seabury's settlement at New Brunswick), gave rise to a newspaper controversy in which the "Westchester Farmer" of later years first wielded his trenchant pen. Throughout much of 1755, in "Conjunction with a number of his Brethren and Friends," Seabury earnestly contended with the Presbyterian opponents of the newly founded institution.[1]

The struggle over New York's college had already been several years in progress. A majority of those who had promoted its establishment were Episcopalians, and Trinity Church offered the largest single gift for that purpose: land for a site, valued at £7,000 currency and granted on condition that the president should always be a member of the Church of England and that the college's morning and evening prayer should be the service of the Prayer Book or a compilation formed from it. Lutherans, as well as members of the French and Dutch Reformed churches, showed themselves willing to accept the terms of the Trinity benefaction, which was twice the value of the excise monies voted for the college by the Assembly and more than equal to the college fund, built up by a series of Assembly-authorized lotteries.[2] But "a notable set of young gentlemen of figure in New York,"[3] Presbyterians and graduates of Yale, opposed the plan, arguing that a purely nondenominational institution should be established instead. Led by William Livingston, the group strenuously attacked Trinity's terms in their periodical, *The Independent Reflector,* published in New York in 1752-53. The Churchmen, quite naturally, replied in kind. Young William Smith (then on the verge of his ordination voyage), Seabury's father, Johnson himself, and several other clerical writers issued rejoinders in the New York newspapers.[4]

This first paper war ended while Seabury was still in England. Events of 1754, however, prepared the way for a second, more prolonged contest. Johnson, notified in January of his election to the presidency of the college, established classes in the vestry room of Trinity Church. The Churchmen triumphed again on October 31, when, after many delays, Lieutenant Governor James DeLancey affixed the province seal to a college charter embodying the terms of the Trinity donation. Defeated by the executive, Livingston and his associates now concentrated on the Assembly, hoping to keep the excise monies and lottery funds out of the hands of King's College's newly appointed governors. On November 25, the day before the Assembly was to consider their bill for a nondenominational college, the Presbyterians issued the first of "The Watch-Tower" essays, printed in the *New-York Mercury.*[5]

A yearlong newspaper controversy followed. Regularly, on the front page of each weekly edition of the *Mercury,* "The Watch-Tower" (usually Livingston) gave out his opinions on public matters, sounding frequent warnings of Episcopal domination and pleading the merits of the nondenominational college bill. Defenders of the King's College charter, on the other hand, conducted an intermittent, guerilla-type warfare. The essays which they placed in the *Mercury* were short, few in number, and scattered. Uncomfortably situated, in that they were relying on the enemy's publisher to mount their counterattack, they could at first do no better: on January 6, 1755, the capital's other newspaper, the *New-York Gazette,* announced that it would take no part in the paper war, despite frequent requests to insert essays. But by spring the *Gazette's* printers, James Parker and William Weyman, had agreed to print a periodical for King's College partisans, a sort of Episcopal *Independent Reflector.* Entitled *John Englishman, In Defence of the English Constitution,* it limped along for ten numbers (and twenty-six consecutively numbered pages) and expired with the issue of July 5, 1755.[6]

According to his Loyalist memorial, written thirty years after these events, Seabury was responsible for a number of the anti-"Watch-Tower" essays and papers.[7] Since their writers, following the usual custom, adopted various pseudonyms ("Agricola," "Old England," "Philo-Patris," for example), it is impossible to identify with any certainty the contributions which the New Brunswick missionary made to the *Mercury* or *John Englishman.* Yet considering Seabury's medical background, it seems likely that he produced the final number of the latter publication, a witty and rather vulgar letter addressed to William Livingston as author of "The Watch-Tower," in which the writer (signing himself "Hermanus Paracelsus") offered a series of remedies for curing the Presbyterian champion of "a Disease, commonly called the *Scribendi Cocoethes*, or Itch of *Scribling.*" Livingston, however, refused to experiment with his opponent's prescriptions. "The Watch-Tower" survived *John Englishman* by four months, appearing for the last time in the *Mercury* of November 17, 1755.

Probably Seabury entered into this controversy (which resulted in King's College receiving the allotted excise monies and half the lottery funds) at the urging of his college acquaintance, Thomas Bradbury Chandler, settled since 1751 as S.P.G. missionary at St. John's Church, Elizabethtown, twenty-seven miles from New Brunswick by way of Woodbridge and Perth Amboy.[8] Chandler and Samuel Auchmuty (at this date only an assistant minister of Trinity Church) together penned a reply to the first number of "The Watch-Tower."[9] Several months later, writing to Samuel Johnson, Chandler noted that "Mr. Seabury the younger" (in "whom I expect to find an agreeable Neighbour") had lodged with him the previous night.[10] No doubt the King's College battle was the chief topic discussed by the two men. The cooperation between them, first recorded in this controversy, was to continue unbroken through a variety of Episcopal plans and projects until Chandler's death in 1790.

Besides Seabury, Chandler, and Auchmuty, the identifiable Episcopal participants in the 1754-55 literary war included Johnson's stepson, Benjamin Nicoll (Yale, 1734), and—probably—James Wetmore.[11] All these men were transplanted New Englanders (Auchmuty, born in Boston, had graduated from Harvard with the class of 1742),[12] and all were High Churchmen. It must have been gratifying, indeed, to President Johnson to observe that his type of Churchmanship had taken root outside the boundaries of Connecticut and Massachusetts. And yet the very fact of their High Churchmanship created difficulties for Seabury and his colleagues when they defended the King's College charter.

No formidable host by themselves, New York's Presbyterians could command a numerous force if they secured Dutch support.[13] The King's College men were acutely aware of this fact, and in both the *Mercury* and *John Englishman* their spokesmen dwelt fondly on the natural alliance which should subsist between Churchmen and adherents of the Dutch Reformed body, both being members of "Sister-Churches," the established denominations of England and Holland.[14] (Lest some person argue that the Presbyterian Church, established in Scotland, might also qualify as a "Sister-Church" in the province, one writer affirmed that New York's New Side Synod was, in fact, a body of Independents and had been expelled from the true Presbyterian synod.)[15] But there existed obvious limitations beyond which a High Churchman could not go in developing the concept of sister churches. The Dutch Reformed body had no bishops, no apostolic succession. Friendly offices and cordial relations were all a High Churchman could offer. New York Episcopal leaders carefully cultivated such contacts,[16] and their efforts had a certain success. A Low Church group of clergy, however, could have forged a warmer, more intimate alliance. And it is likely that Seabury, at least, even considered certain of the pro-Dutch statements made in 1755 to be more than he could assent to in conscience. When he next turned his attention to extraparochial affairs, he had only congenial High Churchmen to consider, and his sphere of action was not polyglot New York, but his native colony of Connecticut.

On the afternoon of October 19, 1757, Seabury delivered a sermon in St. John's Church, Stamford, under circumstances particularly unpleasant for one thoroughly acquainted with the growth of Connecticut's Episcopal Church. No S.P.G. missionary except Samuel Johnson had done more to promote that growth than John Beach of Newtown and Redding, and even Johnson himself could not exhibit such large, active congregations as Beach had built up in the previous quarter century.[17] John Beach was clearly the most successful parish priest produced by New England's Episcopal body, and yet it was he whom Seabury repeatedly censured in his "long and excellent Sermon," preached in a church crowded with Episcopalians and Congregationalists, where Beach himself sat within the young missionary's gaze.

The series of events precipitating this painful occasion had begun sometime in 1755 with the publication of another sermon, written by Newtown's missionary and entitled *A Modest Enquiry into the State of the Dead.*[18] Those persons who sympathized with Beach, while opposing the doctrine strenuously maintained in his lengthy pamphlet, declared him to be so afflicted by his wife's approaching death that he could not bear the thought that she must await the General Judgment before entering into eternal glory.[19] Be that as it may, Beach in his sermon presented an elaborate argument in support of the thesis that the resurrection spoken of in the New Testament takes place immediately at death: "our Souls are never in a naked state, or without a Body, but as soon as we pass out of this earthly Body, we enter into an heavenly Body, in which we live with Christ."[20] Christ's Coming, the Day of Judgment, the Last Day were to be interpreted as expressions of this event. A man's earthly body—no essential part of him, according to Beach—would never be reunited to his soul.[21]

Beach's peculiar eschatology disturbed his brother missionaries. The Newtown pastor was, however, a greatly respected figure, honored not only for his pastoral zeal but for his writings in defense of episcopacy. Colleagues, for this reason, failed to publicize their dissent, thereby giving the Congregational clergy an opportunity to move against a principal opponent. Appearing as the defender of orthodoxy, Fairfield County's Western District Association formally condemned the much discussed sermon and dispatched a report to the S.P.G. More than a year passed without any reply, but finally, in the spring of 1757, word arrived that steps had been taken to bring Beach to a correct opinion.[22]

The Society's action apparently consisted of instructions to James Wetmore of Rye, senior missionary in the neighborhood of Newtown and Redding, to convoke a meeting of his brethren, which should attempt to persuade Beach to recant his doctrine. Samuel Johnson, busy with college duties, was not directly involved, but he exercised his usual leadership: at Wetmore's request he prepared a long letter of advice for the meeting.[23] Someone—the secretary, Wetmore, or possibly Johnson—decided that, in addition to the private conference, a public sermon should be preached on the occasion, refuting the heretical theses Beach had maintained. And Wetmore chose Samuel Seabury to deliver it. "I thought it hard upon me," the preacher recalled in his old age, "and I told him that I was the youngest Clergyman in the Provinces." "I do not care for that," Wetmore replied, "you are better able to do it than anyone else, and I shall insist upon your doing it."[24]

The selection of Seabury, only twenty-seven years old, was a flattering tribute to his precocious abilities. Yet there were other reasons for Wetmore's choice. Naturally, none of Beach's Connecticut neighbors cared to undertake the task. Wetmore himself was an old friend; his neighbor, Standard of Westchester, superannuated. To summon President Johnson or Rector Barclay from New York would be to make more of the matter than Wetmore intended. Seabury, only a few months settled at Jamaica, had no intimate relations with Beach and probably would never serve in a Connecticut parish. Talented—and obscure—he suited Wetmore's purpose exactly.

Ebenezer Dibble (Yale, 1734) of Stamford served as host to the conference, which opened at his parsonage on the morning of October 18, 1757.[25] Besides Dibble and Beach, five Connecticut clergymen attended, also Wetmore, Seabury, and Seabury's father. Since the day marked the Feast of St. Luke, the company proceeded to church for Prayers, after which they returned to the parsonage and began discussing Beach's doctrine. By nine o'clock in the evening, the missionary had been brought to regard much of his teaching as erroneous.

Next morning discussion resumed, "with fresh endeavours to make further advances and with good success to our satisfaction." Seabury's sermon, preached in St. John's Church that afternoon, brought the conference to a close. The manuscript has not survived, but the general outline may be gathered from a report Wetmore sent to the secretary. According to Rye's rector, the preacher, "after proving the received Doctrine [of the Resurrection] according to the Creeds and Liturgy of our Church, answered all the objections as taken from Mr. Beach's Sermon." His arguments, the clergy hoped, would confirm Beach in the truth as well as convince the large assembly who likewise heard them.

The Stamford conference was a brief and ultimately unimportant incident with respect to Beach's fifty-year pastorate, yet it had significance in its effect on Seabury's subsequent career. The contacts linking him to Connecticut's Episcopalians in the forty years elapsing between his father's settlement at Hempstead and his own election as bishop were casual and few in number. Indeed, his choice as Bishop of Connecticut appears surprising when it is noted that his episcopal colleagues—White, Provoost, Madison, Claggett, and Smith—all had resided for many years in the states which became their dioceses. The considerations moving the ten clergymen who elected him in 1783 included, in all likelihood, his sermon in St. John's. That scene in the fall of 1757 was not one which Churchmen would forget. Nothing similar to the Beach case had previously occurred, or was to occur again, in the colonial history of New England's Episcopal Church. Seabury's youth, coupled with his first-rate performance (if Wetmore's account be trustworthy), must have impressed his clerical and lay audience.[26] And one of the Connecticut missionaries present—Christopher Newton (Yale, 1740)—was probably among the ten electors of 1783.[27]

For several years after the Stamford conference, Seabury seems to have confined his attention strictly to the affairs of his turbulent parish. His abilities and potential leadership were generally recognized. Writing to Archbishop Secker in 1759, President Johnson, discussing the clergy north of Pennsylvania, singled out Jamaica's rector and his friend, Thomas Bradbury Chandler, as coming young men.[28] (Chandler, however, got the warmer recommendation: his love of books and scholarly pursuits, as well as his enthusiasm for grand enterprises, gave him the edge in Johnson's affections; also, as has been noted, he had studied theology under Johnson's direction.) The King's College president, pondering the fact that he was growing old, that Beach was only a few years his junior, and that both of them must soon surrender the reins of leadership—a consideration underlined by the death, in 1760, of their old associate, James Wetmore—was anxiously searching for new clerical talent. Alarmed by the failure of Connecticut's missionaries to answer a clever and widely distributed anti-Episcopal pamphlet, he wrote off that colony's younger ministers as men of mediocre abilities. "We have good hands here, Chandler and young Seabury," he informed his son in a letter from New York of 1762, "but I can't get them to write, nor indeed do they know enough of some affairs for this business, but might be informed."[29]

The next six years witnessed the full development of the tendencies and hopes which Johnson had expressed in the letter just quoted. In 1768 Chandler, with some assistance from Seabury, was showering the printers with writings in support of the Episcopal cause. By this date, also, the leadership of the Church of England in the Northern colonies had clearly passed from the Connecticut missionaries to the clergy of the New York area. It is true that, until Johnson's death in 1772, this transfer of power was somewhat obscured. After his retirement to Stratford in 1763, New York Churchmen constantly consulted Johnson as an ecclesiastical elder statesman, and his influence on them was very considerable. Describing Connecticut as "a kind of ecclesiastical *Flanders,* where the Clergy are trained up to the Service, having seen many a dusty campaign," Chandler wrote him in 1766, declining a suggestion to publish in behalf of the Church on the ground that Beach and others needed no help "while they are under the direction of so able & experienced a General, as still continues on the Field."[30] As usual, however, Johnson had judged the situation correctly. He might advise but he could no longer command, and no one in Connecticut could take his place. Chandler, though affection led him to say otherwise, realized his friend had good reasons for his request. In a letter of 1767 he admitted that "New Jersey and New York seem sometimes to be the seat of ecclesiastical operations."[31] And so they were.

Although Seabury played a significant role in the ecclesiastical maneuverings of the 1760's, the supremely energetic and talented Chandler was a more important figure. Steeped in the same Episcopal tradition, the two thought alike on almost every question. But the High Church atmosphere of pre-Revolutionary New York was produced by other leaders besides these New Englanders. Associated with Chandler and Seabury, and of particular importance in the latter's career, were two immigrant clergymen, Charles Inglis and Myles Cooper.

Inglis, born in 1734, the son of a Church of Ireland clergyman, had emigrated to Pennsylvania as an indentured servant. Capable and ambitious, he succeeded despite his lack of formal education, becoming first S.P.G. missionary at Dover, Delaware, and then, in 1765, an assistant to Samuel Auchmuty at New York's Trinity Church. Marriages, first to the sister of Delaware's chief justice, then to a New York heiress, provided prestige and money which aided a brilliant career, capped in 1787 by his consecration as first Bishop of Nova Scotia. Very evangelical and a devoted High Churchman, Inglis fitted in well with the New Englanders, Samuel Johnson being particularly fond of him.[32]

Myles Cooper was a younger man, born in County Cumberland in 1737. Educated at Queen's College, Oxford, he had come to New York in the autumn of 1762 as Johnson's assistant, succeeding him as President of King's College the following year. A vigorous administrator, he increased that institution's enrollment, wealth, and prestige and produced a remarkable group of graduates. Jovial, fond of good living,[33] Cooper perhaps was deficient in that piety which may be traced in the writings and correspondence of Seabury, Chandler, and Inglis. But he became their intimate friend and, like Inglis, he enjoyed a close relationship with Johnson.[34]

These four men—Seabury and Chandler, Inglis and Cooper —counseled by the Stratford sage, were the active spirits, the planners, the writers who managed the affairs of their region's Episcopal Church, in other than purely parochial concerns, in the decade 1765-75. Their program, simple and unoriginal, was the establishment in America of that "primitive episcopate" which Johnson and the other Yale converts had come to consider as necessary to the being of a Christian church. A bishop or bishops derived from the apostolic succession who could ordain and govern the clergy and confirm the laity: this colonial High Churchmen sought from 1722 onward, finally reaching their goal in 1784 with the consecration of Samuel Seabury. For the other powers of English prelates—votes in Parliament, a certain control over education, probate jurisdiction, authority to cite persons before spiritual courts—they cared little or nothing. Such things Chandler and Seabury regarded as mere accretions, superadditions to the essential episcopal office.[35] Yet unfortunately for the swift achievement of the High Churchmen's plans, those who rejected their theology failed to distinguish between "primitive bishops," stripped to their purely spiritual powers, and lordly English hierarchs, endowed with vast revenues and political authority. To Virginia's Low Churchmen, New England's Congregationalists, or New York's Presbyterians, bishops were bishops![36]

In working toward their goal, Seabury and his associates made much use of clerical conventions. Several such organizations emerged in the late colonial period. Pastors in New Jersey, New York, and Connecticut set up conventions for their respective governments, while those serving churches in Boston's trade area —Maine and New Hampshire, eastern Massachusetts and Rhode Island—also formed themselves into a group. These bodies were offshoots of the defunct New England Convention, whose annual sessions—usually at Boston or Newport—had collected that section's scattered ministers in the period from 1725 to 1747.[37]

Connecticut's Convention, already a well-established institution when it first appears in the records in 1760, was perhaps the oldest. Assembling at towns throughout the colony, it met on the Wednesday in Trinity week (as had the parent organization in the 1740's) and by 1764 was scheduling a second, fall session, usually in connection with Yale's Commencement.[38] Such activity inspired other New England clergymen, brought together in August, 1765, for Timothy Cutler's funeral, to organize a yearly gathering at Boston.[39] Thus the region's northern Convention (for which Johnson's earliest protégé, Henry Caner, had long agitated)[40] came into being. It met from 1766 to 1774, originally in spring on the same day as the Connecticut body, but after 1767 in September.[41]

New Jersey's organization, largely the work of Thomas Bradbury Chandler, sat in various places. The earliest Convention of which records survive, it first assembled in November, 1758, and thereafter held at least one session each year before merging in 1767 with the Convention of New York.[42] This latter group had been formed the previous year, with Samuel Johnson, last survivor of the original Newport gathering of 1725 (then visiting New York for the King's College Commencement) serving as its first president.[43] By uniting, New York and New Jersey created an organization equal in size to the Connecticut and Boston bodies. Each of the three had approximately twenty members.

Formed to consider their members' common concerns, the conventions were perfect organs for drafting petitions to English authorities in favor of an American episcopate. Indeed, the New York Convention, as is clear from the preamble to its minutes, was organized specifically for the purpose of agitating for resident bishops.[44] Moreover, in order to coordinate their efforts, the New York, New Jersey, and Connecticut organizations (and, after 1767, the New York-New Jersey body) appointed delegates or proctors to attend each other's meetings.[45] This practice had the important effect of putting Seabury in contact with leading Connecticut figures. Generally that colony's clergymen selected as proctors Jeremiah Leaming, his college acquaintance and close associate of the post-Revolutionary period, and Abraham Jarvis (Yale, 1761), apparently the dominant figure in the Convention which elected him bishop. Seabury himself may well have enlarged his acquaintance among Connecticut's Churchmen by serving as a proctor. His name, however, does not appear on the few surviving lists.

Also important for the developments of the 1780's were certain differences of opinion and personal animosities which emerged from these colonial conventions. Mention has been made of the deep-rooted dislike which Seabury (and Chandler as well) felt for William Smith, Provost of the College of Philadelphia. While the extent of this feeling in the prewar years should not be exaggerated (Chandler, for instance, kept up a correspondence with Smith, 1769-74),[46] it definitely existed. Smith and his neighbor, the Reverend Richard Peters (Oxford D.D., 1770) of Christ Church and St. Peter's in Philadelphia, as well as Samuel Auchmuty, agreed that if an episcopate could not be obtained, commissaries should be appointed. An organizer par excellence, Smith had devised a scheme for American corresponding societies, associated with the S.P.G. and headed by the Society's appointed agents, the whole to be tied in with the commissarial system by securing the same men as commissaries and agents. Members of the S.P.G. and well supported by their handsome livings, he and his associates (and particularly Auchmuty, who perhaps thought himself eclipsed by Chandler) tended to look rather disdainfully on the missionaries as their employees.[47] Seabury and his colleagues, for their part, showed no enthusiasm for Smith's ambitious plan.

The provost, recently returned from England, outlined its provisions to the New Jersey Convention at Perth Amboy in September, 1764. Seabury, the Trinity rector, and other New York clergymen attended the meeting, and Seabury appears to have acted as its secretary—the extant minutes are in his hand.[48] Auchmuty joined Smith in pressing for the adoption of the proposal for agents in its original form, while Chandler and Seabury, and all the other missionaries present, successfully insisted on amendments strengthening their position as against the agents (who, presumably, would be Smith for the proposed Pennsylvania-New Jersey district and Auchmuty for that of Connecticut and New York).[49] The missionaries also opposed the Smith-Auchmuty proposal for commissaries, Chandler arguing—and Seabury agreeing—that the system had been tried and found wanting, and that if the English authorities believed the clergy's clamor for bishops could be quieted by appointing commissaries, they would trouble themselves no further about an American episcopate. Meeting at Shrewsbury in October, 1766, the New Jersey Convention appointed a committee to address the Bishop of London and the Society, expressing its opposition to commissaries and even to the modified plan for resident S.P.G. agents. Seabury was present, along with several other New York clergymen, and signed the address drafted by Chandler, as did Jarvis and Leaming, proctors from Connecticut.[50]

Smith, Peters, and Auchmuty were furious at these proceedings and wrote angrily of the missionaries' lack of subordination. "They take too much upon them," the imperious New York rector declared, "and will, unless they are soon convinced of their Error endeavor to Rule the Society & their Superiors."[51] The Chandler-Seabury forces had their own accusations. Elizabethtown's missionary implied in a letter to Samuel Johnson that Smith (sarcastically termed "the American Colossus") lacked "a due degree of affection either for the Church or her clergy, or right principles." Noting that New Jersey had as many as five missions vacant, he urged Johnson to procure proper men for them, adding that if Connecticut could not furnish a supply, "we shall have persons dropping in from the westward [the College of Philadelphia], and with such principles as that region has commonly produced."[52] Obviously the High Churchmen's dislike of Smith and suspicion of his Churchmanship, which exerted a noticeable influence in the struggle to organize a united Protestant Episcopal body, were sentiments of long standing, first revealed in the pre-Revolutionary campaign for an American episcopate.

Seabury helped launch the projectiles—petitions authorized by New Jersey's Convention in October, 1765—which signaled the start of this campaign. Although the timing of these applications (signed, perhaps, on the very day the Stamp Act went into effect) could hardly have been less opportune, Thomas Bradbury Chandler, the moving spirit in the affair, was convinced that a delay would achieve no good end. Warm, united applications were needed, he wrote Samuel Johnson: "what has the Church ever gained, and what have its enemies not gained by that thing which the courtesy of England calls prudence?"

His colleagues assigned Chandler the task of drafting their addresses to George III, the Archbishops of Canterbury and York, the Bishop of London, and the S.P.G. Secretary. Because of his Oxford connection, Myles Cooper, honored with the presidency of the Convention, was chosen to write the representations forwarded to the English universities. Possibly other New York clergymen took part in this meeting, held at Perth Amboy. At any rate, most of them, including Samuel Seabury, joined their New Jersey brethren a few weeks later at a convenient halfway point, the Staten Island parsonage of Richard Charlton (Dublin, 1726), for the signing of the seven petitions. Cooper immediately dispatched the original drafts to Stratford, so that the "Father of the Clergy" might be fully informed.[53]

A flood of private letters afterwards descended on the English authorities, reinforcing the Perth Amboy addresses. Samuel Johnson, who thoroughly approved them, wrote to his old friend Archbishop Secker, beseeching one or two bishops.[54] Inglis informed the secretary that he had talked with Dissenters of various denominations and found them not averse to an episcopate, so long as the bishops had no civil powers and they were not obliged to support them. "On a false Supposition that both these would take place," he declared, "all their Objections are founded."[55] Seabury in a letter to the same official reinforced his argument, as did Johnson, with a reference to the death, a few days before, of the last two candidates for Orders from the Northern colonies. After reporting briefly on the condition of Jamaica, he wrote:

> We have lately had a most affecting account of the loss of Messrs. Giles & Wilson the Society's Missionaries; the ship they were in being wrecked near the entrance of Delaware Bay & only 4 persons saved out of 28, their death is a great loss in the present want of Clergymen in these Colonies, & indeed I believe one great reason why so few from this Continent offer themselves for Holy orders, is because it is evident from experience that not more than 4 out of 5 who have gone from the Northern Colonies have returned; this is one unanswerable argument for the absolute necessity of Bishops in the Colonies. The poor Church of England in America is the only instance that ever happened of an Episcopal Church without a Bishop & in which no Orders could be obtained without crossing an Ocean of 3000 miles in extent, without Bishops the Church cannot flourish in America & unless the Church be well supported & prevail, this whole Continent will be overrun with Infidelity & deism, Methodism & New Light with every species & every degree of Scepticism & Enthusiasm, and without a Bishop upon the spot I fear it will be impossible to keep the Church herself pure & undefiled. And that it is of the last consequence to the State to support the Church here, the present times afford an alarming proof.[56]

A month after Jamaica's rector penned this appeal (news of the repeal of the Stamp Act had, in that interval, arrived in New York) the clergy of New York assembled at Samuel Auchmuty's house to further the campaign for American bishops. The proceedings of this first session of the New York Convention, as well as of the four held in the ensuing year, are known from the minutes kept by Seabury, who was elected secretary at this organizational meeting. All the leaders of the episcopate campaign put in an appearance: Johnson, now in his seventieth year, Dr. Thomas Bradbury Chandler (Johnson had recently procured him an Oxford D.D.),[57] Cooper and Inglis, and Abraham Jarvis from Connecticut.

The assembled clergy adopted conventional rules, one of which set up a standing committee to transact business between meetings, the direct ancestor of the present standing committees of the Protestant Episcopal Church's diocesan conventions. Seabury became a member of this five-man body on which Cooper and Auchmuty also served. The main item of the day was a decision to address the Society "to inform them of the death of Messrs. Wilson & Giles, & so inforce upon them the Representation made at the last Convention in New Jersey," that is, the Perth Amboy meeting of October, 1765. Seabury and his Yale classmate John Ogilvie (now, like Inglis, an assistant to Auchmuty at Trinity Church)[58] accordingly prepared a draft, which the meeting endorsed in an amended form.[59]

Despite discouraging reports, including one from Secker stating that the Perth Amboy petition to George III had not been presented because it arrived at the wrong time,[60] New Jersey's Convention continued to forward addresses across the Atlantic. The meeting at Shrewsbury in October, 1766, attended by Seabury, Cooper, and Inglis, has already been noticed in connection with its stand against commissaries and S.P.G. agents. But this session (which lasted at least two days, sat eight and nine hours at a time, and continued until two o'clock each morning) accomplished a good deal of other work. Descending somewhat in the hierarchical scale, the clergy agreed to petition the young Bishop of Oxford and the Master of the Temple to lend their aid. The Bishop of London's cool answer to his Perth Amboy address having been read, a reply was voted which, as afterwards drafted by Chandler, respectfully but insistently repeated the request for bishops.[61] Connecticut's Convention subsequently approved a similar letter to His Lordship (also in reply to an answer made by him to a petition for bishops) following the return of the colony's proctors—Leaming and Jarvis—from Shrewsbury.[62]

The most important result of the Shrewsbury meeting was the appearance, late the following year, of *An Appeal to the Public, in Behalf of the Church of England in America.* Hoping that a candid discussion of the scheme of "primitive bishops" would remove Dissenters' objections to an American episcopate, the Convention had appointed several men, including Seabury, to assist the overworked Chandler in preparing this exposition. Seabury and his fellows, however, did little or nothing, with the result that Chandler (often urged by Samuel Johnson to undertake such a production)[63] had ultimately to perform the task by himself.

Chandler showed an understandable annoyance at Seabury's lack of cooperation. He had begun work late in January, 1767, a day or two after encountering the new rector of Westchester at the New York Convention.[64] By the middle of April, when the Convention held another session, he had the whole pamphlet roughed out. Since Seabury could then give it only a cursory examination, Chandler promised it should be returned to him for criticism after Samuel Johnson had tried his hand at improvements.[65] Accordingly, the manuscript eventually came to Westchester, and there it stayed. Weeks went by without any word from Seabury, until at last the impatient Chandler sent Myles Cooper to pick up his production. Still Seabury sent no message, and the author, upon checking, found that his supposed assistant had made not a single correction or suggestion. "I think he ought to be punished for such misconduct," Chandler declared in a letter to Johnson, "& I shall move that by way of penance he shall perform some exercise for the service of the Church as I take him to be very capable, & that no friend be allowed him to consult with."[66] At least two such projects were proposed for Westchester's rector in the next few years, with what results will shortly be noted.

Had Seabury examined the *Appeal* with some care, he might possibly have saved Chandler from a serious error. As both the Archbishop of Canterbury and the Bishop of London afterwards observed, it was certainly a mistake to preface a pamphlet intended to quiet Dissenters' fears and dislikes with a High Church argument in favor of divine-right episcopacy.[67] Such material merely confused the practical issue of whether or not an American episcopate should be established and allowed the die-hard opponents of the proposal to range far afield in the newspaper battle which the *Appeal* occasioned—a battle in which Seabury wielded a pen in company with his friends.

The timing of the attack upon Chandler's pamphlet lent color to the Churchmen's assertion that the move was designed to enhance the fortunes of the Presbyterian-backed Livingston party.[68] Apparently published in November, 1767, the *Appeal* (printed in an edition of six hundred fifty copies)[69] excited little open opposition until shortly before the New York City election of March, 1768. At that time, according to its author, it became "the grand Engine" of the Livingstons, who labeled it proof of a plot to erect an Episcopal tyranny. "It is to no Purpose to deny the Charge," Chandler complained to Sir William Johnson, "and to refer to the *Appeal* for the Proof of it; since the Body of the Dissenters are determined not to read it, and to believe as best suits the Turn."[70]

Rejected by the capital's voters, the Livingstons turned to the newspapers. On March 14, William Livingston published in James Parker's *New-York Gazette; or, the Weekly Post-Boy* the first number of "The American Whig." With William Smith and John Morin Scott, old colleagues of *The Independent Reflector* and "The Watch Tower," as his principal assistants,[71] Livingston for the next sixteen months kept up a steady assault on the

Appeal, beseeching Dissenters to oppose the projected episcopate. For the first time the issue of American bishops, long discussed in pamphlets and private correspondence, came before the mass of the reading public.

Episcopal leaders could not ignore their opponents' assertions. Accordingly, late in March Chandler came over to New York and there closeted himself with his clerical associates. From this meeting emerged the decision to publish a weekly paper, "A Whip for the American Whig," in the *New-York Gazette, and Weekly Mercury,* edited by Hugh Gaine. Seabury, Cooper, and Inglis would be the principal managers of the series, for which Chandler—busy with a pamphlet defense of the *Appeal*—was to write an occasional essay. Ostensibly the production of "Timothy Tickle, Esquire," (who soon encountered an antagonist in "Sir Isaac Foot," producer of "A Kick for the Whipper") the "Whip" made its initial appearance in Gaine's paper of April 4, with Inglis supplying the number.[72]

A week before the launching of this series Seabury published a signed advertisement in the same journal, probably at the urging of his fellow "Whippers." "The American Whig" had charged that the Perth Amboy applications for bishops had slandered the Dissenters, picturing them as seditious plotters, disaffected to the King and his government. This accusation Westchester's rector now publicly denied. As Secretary to the United Convention of New York and New Jersey, Seabury had "particularly attended to, and carefully read, every petition that they have transmitted to England." The "Whig's" statement he found "absolutely, utterly and intirely false and groundless," and he demanded that its writer produce the evidence he relied upon.[73]

Livingston's group at once began a concerted effort to extract from Seabury certified copies of the addresses in question. Whether or not the Convention had made the reflections the "Whig" ascribed to it turned largely on the interpretation which a reader, motivated by his denominational bias, chose to make of their wording. For the "Whig," the mention in the petition to the S.P.G. Secretary of "those who are equally zealous in propagating the Principles of Independency both in Church and State"[74] would have been sufficient to justify his charges. Replying to Seabury's advertisement in one of his own, printed in Parker's *Gazette* of April 4, he airily declared that the burden of proof rested upon the Convention's secretary. The public would not be satisfied "with the bare *verbum sacerdotis*." They had a right to expect true copies of the petitions, "noting what was in the original drafts, and struck out by a few moderate members of the Convention, (for luckily for the colonies a few such there appeared to be, or no mortal can tell of what we should not have been accused) and that such publications be declared to be true copies, upon oath."[75]

Two weeks later the producer of "Whip" No. III—probably Seabury—ridiculed the "Whig's" assertions, whereupon that writer once more called for the evidence:

> As Mr. Seabury has again made his corporal appearance, tho' it was currently reported, that like Romulus, he was gone off in a thunder storm; and tho' not quite so pugnatious, seems as evasive as ever. The Author intends speedily to convince him (of what the public is already convinced) that the onus probandi always lies on the person possessed of the instrument concerning which the controversy is raised; and that the parties said to be calumniated in the petitions, cannot be satisfied with that strange departure in pleading, so apparent in his valedictory oration; but are justly entitled to a profert of the instruments, without any farther evasion or equivocation whatever.[76]

Seabury received a similar demand on May 8, in the form of a letter from the Reverend Dr. Ezra Stiles of Newport, principal promoter of the Convention of Presbyterians and Connecticut Congregationalists formed in 1766 to oppose an American episcopate.[77] Taking very lofty ground ("In this Age of *Truth & Liberty*, the Records of all ecclesiastical Bodies in the protestant World, we presume, lie open to public view & Examination;

and Extracts and Copies of the Proceedings thereof are freely permitted"), Stiles requested attested copies of the addresses, at least a copy of that prepared for George III. He had read Seabury's advertisement, he declared, and it would give him pleasure to see the secretary's statements confirmed by his own inspection of the much disputed papers.[78] Probably Stiles expected, even hoped to provoke, that refusal which could be interpreted to the Churchmen's disadvantage. He took care to work into his letter the statement that they sought a bishop supported by an American-raised revenue, not Chandler's inoffensive sort. Such a charge would infuriate Seabury; the secretary, in the last paragraph of his advertisement, had labeled it "a piece of effrontery and malice."

Stiles's letter lay unanswered for nearly a month. Having consulted with two or three of his brethren (probably Chandler, Inglis, and Cooper), Seabury finally on June 4 sat down to write a reply. He could not give out copies of the addresses on his own responsibility, he explained, because of a rule precluding such action without an order of the Convention. (The rule, dating from May 20, 1767, had been adopted as the result of certain difficulties with a ministerial candidate, not from any apprehension of the subsequent demands made on the secretary.)[79] And the clergy to whom he had shown the letter agreed with Seabury that willful misrepresentation by those opposed to an American episcopate made impossible, at the present time, the publication of any of the addresses. Several persons, consulted before the *Appeal* was published, had predicted such an assault on Chandler and his colleagues as "The American Whig" and his cohorts had made. But he himself, Seabury assured Stiles, had not shared their now substantiated fears:

> I was, I confess of a different opinion: I had such favourable sentiments of the Candour & friendly disposition of the Dissenters, that I imagined, they would have calmly & soberly pointed out the Disadvantages they apprehended, from the proposed plan, that they might

> have been removed. The Consequence here has been, that the plan is approved but the *thing* opposed. Now to oppose an American Episcopate upon any other Plan, than the one proposed, is fighting with a shadow, a meer non-entity; But to do this in such an illiberal abusive, scurrilous Manner, as has been done here, argues so bad a disposition, that I have no Inclination to give a Name to it.—The whole Body of the Clergy of the Church, have been represented, by the American *Whig* as *Tories*, that is, in the Estimation of that Faction, Traytors & Rebels to their King & Country. The Convention has been represented as a Number of false deceitful men, pretending to ask for one thing while they really are aiming at another.—When I denied publicly, that any accusation was made against the loyalty of dissenters; I was represented as a furious fellow, too much in a passion to know what he said—& that I really had affirmed a Matter of Fact, of which it was impossible I could be a competent judge.—Consider these things, Sir, & judge yourself, whether there is that probability of Candour & Moderation among the dissenters, which is sufficient to induce us to a compliance with your Demand.—Far be it from me to imagine that Dr. Stiles, is that void of Candour & Moderation—But then, it can not be thought that Dr. Stiles wants those Copies solely for his own inspection, & that no other person is to see them.

Although he had his doubts, the secretary declared, as to whether the proceedings of all ecclesiastical bodies were really as open as the Newport pastor asserted them to be, still, if that were the case, perhaps the Synod of New York and Philadelphia would care to join the United Convention of New York and New Jersey in publishing all their minutes and letters. Should this be done, the public would, indeed, have the necessary information to judge "whether the Church or Dissenters entertained sentiments the most favourable to universal liberty of Conscience." Seabury concluded the letter with a reaffirmation of his statement that the episcopate desired was that of the *Appeal*. If Stiles and his coreligionists apprehended "any inconveniences" from Chandler's plan, "when they are cooly & candidly pointed out, we will join our endeavours to yours to get them removed."[80]

So far as the secretary was concerned, the matter of the Perth

Amboy addresses was closed. Chandler printed those directed to the King and Archbishop of Canterbury in 1771.[81]

During the remaining months of 1768—and well into 1769 —Seabury continued to turn out essays for Gaine's *Gazette* according to the March agreement. "A Whip for the American Whig" appeared regularly in each week's issue, either in the form of a paper signed by "Timothy Tickle," or as a communication to that gentleman, supplemented on occasion by his admiring comments. It is impossible to determine how many times Seabury supplied the copy, though he certainly did so frequently. In 1783 he declared that in conjunction with Chandler and Inglis—Cooper was not mentioned—he had borne "the whole weight of the controversy with the American Whig."[82]

This statement reinforces the conclusion that Cooper, though assigned many publications by contemporaries, actually wrote very little.[83] Yet it cannot be accepted as completely accurate, since persons besides Seabury, Inglis, and Chandler contributed certain numbers to the "Whip" series.[84] Nevertheless, the anti-episcopate writers seem to have identified only Chandler and Seabury as their opponents as late as October, 1768.[85] The reading public accordingly considered Seabury to be a more active "Whipper" than he, in fact, was. This development led Westchester's rector into a comic-opera skirmish, irrelevant to the main struggle, but no more so than many another clash of the lengthy paper war. As a result, three of his contributions can be identified.

Gaine's *Gazette* of July 4, 1768, carried the fourteenth number of the "Whip," allegedly a letter from "An Independent" but probably the work of an Episcopalian.[86] The writer, among other matters, accused the Reverend Dr. Charles Chauncy (Harvard, 1721) of falsely stating in his *Appeal to the Public Answered* that the Society paid the expenses of candidates going to England for ordination. Actually this Boston foe of Chandler, in an attempt to show that the ordination voyage created no real hardship for American Churchmen, had quoted an old S.P.G.

publication, long obsolete, which promised such expenses would be paid. The discrepancy between Chauncy's statement and the "Whip's" paraphrase was pointed out with some warmth by a writer in Parker's *Gazette*, August 29, who acknowledged, in addition, that the S.P.G. did not at present reimburse candidates for their outlay, but asserted that this was because the churches expecting to enjoy their services, or private individuals, donated the necessary funds. Asserting that he himself had made such contributions, the writer described himself as a zealous Episcopalian, indeed a member of the S.P.G. Zeal for "decency, good manners, and a becoming treatment, especially of respectable characters," had impelled him to vindicate Chauncy from the aspersions of "An Independent," supposedly "Mr. S--b-r-y."[87]

Westchester's rector took great offense at "the *malevolent Strictures*, and *false Insinuations* contained in this Letter." As soon as possible, he availed himself of the invitation publicly extended by James Parker and called at his house to see the original, stated by the printer to be from "a gentleman of figure in *Boston*." But Parker, it developed, could not produce the usual sort of letter. His communication had for signature only the initials "B.W." (already known to Seabury, since they had appeared with the printed version); moreover, the date and address were in a hand different from the body. Roundly declaring that this was not the paper he had been led to expect, the rector demanded to know its author. After some shuffling and hesitation, Parker replied that it had been composed by Benning Wentworth, formerly Governor of New Hampshire, and affirmed that the paper he had shown Seabury was in Wentworth's autograph. Had Wentworth sent the paper to Parker? No, the printer answered, but Dr. Chauncy had sent it to a gentleman in New York, intending it for the *Gazette*. If Seabury doubted or denied that the paper was Wentworth's, Parker stood ready to prove his statement. His suspicions aroused by the variant handwritings, Parker's answers and evasive manner, the rector decided against continuing a conversation without witnesses. Telling Parker he had not lived up to his invitation, that he himself doubted Wentworth's authorship, and that the printer should hear from him again, Seabury left the house.

Prior to this conversation, Parker informed various other persons that the "B.W." letter had been written by Governor Wentworth. To test this declaration, "a Gentleman of Character"—no doubt Cooper or Inglis—contacted a friend in Portsmouth and inquired about the matter. The reply he received (probably from Arthur Browne of Queen's Chapel, Wentworth's pastor) enclosed a letter from the ex-governor himself, dated September 18, 1768. In it the indignant old gentleman declared "the Contents, and *every Clause*" of "B.W.'s" communication to be "a villainous Piece of Forgery." If the original letter could not be obtained, and it were thought advisable, Wentworth would pay the costs of a legal prosecution of Parker.

Armed with this formidable weapon and accompanied by a friend the Westchester rector paid a second call on the printer. He hoped to compare handwritings, but Parker (who complained that Seabury had not treated him like a gentleman during his last visit), after rummaging through some papers, declared he could not find his "B.W." letter. Still, he was certain—very certain—that Governor Wentworth had written it. Seabury then asked him to produce the proof he had spoken of in their previous encounter, whereupon Parker replied "that he was obliged immediately to attend a Corpse into the Country." However, if the rector would call upon Thomas Smith, a New York lawyer, he should find proof aplenty. He added that Chauncy had forwarded the letter to Smith.

With his companion in tow, Seabury next made his way to the lawyer's office and explained his business. Smith admitted that he had given the "B.W." letter to Parker but explained that it had come to him, not from Chauncy, but from the Reverend John Rodgers (Edinburgh D. D., 1768) of New York's Presbyterian church, who himself had received it from the doctor. He further declared Wentworth had given the letter to Chauncy, that it was not in his handwriting, since the governor was too old to write, yet drafted by his order and signed by him with his initials. Seabury observed that Wentworth did not live in Boston, to which Smith responded that he was visiting there at the time and that if Seabury wanted definite proof, an affidavit would arrive the following week establishing Wentworth's authorship.

Noticing that Smith did not actually use Wentworth's name, but spoke instead of "the Gentleman," Seabury questioned him closely and found that the lawyer had no real evidence the governor was "B.W." He merely thought Wentworth must be the man, because no other member of the S.P.G. had those particular initials (the list of members appeared annually in the Society's printed *Abstract*, copies of which were available in the colonies). Stepping to the door, Seabury announced that he had in his pocket such proof to the contrary as would surprise Smith and all concerned. After they had come into the street, he insisted the lawyer ought in justice to procure him an examination of Chauncy's covering letter to Rodgers, since he had busied himself in the publication of a paper in which the rector thought himself "very cruelly and unjustly treated." Smith answered that Seabury might do as he pleased. If he himself accidentally encountered Rodgers, he would mention the matter to him. As for saying that "B.W." was Wentworth, he had never made such a statement to Parker or any other person.

The intrepid rector now pursued his elusive quarry to the Reverend Mr. Rodgers' manse. Although the minister was absent from home, he was expected back from New Jersey that evening or the following morning. Seabury called at least twice the next day, only to find that Rodgers had not arrived. Soon afterwards he made a journey to Philadelphia. When he returned, Rodgers had departed for New England, so it was not until November that Seabury could arrange an interview. He found the Presbyterian pastor a man of "great Openness and Candour." Who "B.W." was Mr. Rodgers did not know. When he had recently been in Boston, Chauncy had mentioned the matter but without disclosing his identity. Seabury was welcome to view the doctor's letter, which described "B.W." as a Bostonian, a Churchman, and a member of the S.P.G. and declared that his paper had been written without Chauncy's solicitation and given to him to use as he saw fit. But Rodgers did not think himself at liberty to allow any extracts to be taken.

The story of his determined quest for "B.W."—related in even greater detail than the preceding narrative—made up the first of two signed articles published by Seabury in Gaine's *Gazette*, December 19, 26, 1768, as Nos. XXXVII and XXXVIII of the "Whip for the American Whig."[88] Having given this "just and faithful historical Account," he devoted his second "Whip" to reflections upon the now famous letter. The question of who paid the expenses of candidates' ordination voyages did not concern him. What interested the rector (the parallel with the Hicks-Seabury and Aspinwall-Seabury disputes was exact) was his good name and reputation. He would not remain silent while "B.W." accused him of "giving Dr. Chauncy the Lie," of making "rude and injurious Reflections on the Dr.," of being a "troublesome Person," of having "impertinently disturbed the Quiet of this Country for some time past." The public must know how badly he had been used, must read his vindication!

Declaring that "B.W." had penned his letter "With the most malevolent Party Rage, and with such Rancour and Ill-Nature as none but a Heart inflamed by Malice could dictate," Seabury indignantly repelled his aspersions. So far as the letter related to himself, it was completely false and groundless: "I positively declare, that I was so far from being the Author of the Paper to which he refers [the letter of "An Independent"] that I never saw it, heard of it, thought of it, or dreamed of it, 'til it made its public Appearance in Mr Gaine's Paper of July 4th." Seabury did not know who "B.W." was, and he did not care (an assertion which his search for that gentleman certainly contradicted!). As for giving Dr. Chauncy the lie—"a Form of Speech in which I do not allow myself to my menial Servants"—he had never troubled himself with anything the doctor might have included in his answer to Chandler's *Appeal*. The Westchester rector had read twelve pages of the Bostonian's performance, and he did not intend to read any more. "When an Author can calmly and seriously set himself to establish such wild Positions as that 'the Church of England does not teach the Divine Right of Episcopacy, and that her Reformers did not believe it,' I can spend my Time much more profitably than in giving him the Reading."

This lofty declaration was followed by satirical reflections on old men being tedious and positive in their writing and other barbed observations, the whole constituting a slashing attack upon Chauncy. Seabury might not know "B.W.'s" identity, but he had established the fact that the minister of Boston's First Church had forwarded his letter to New York for publication. The rector was in no gentle mood! In the middle of his assault, he paused to censure "B.W." for affixing those particular initials to his paper, noting—as Thomas Smith had observed—that they were those of Benning Wentworth and no other S.P.G. member. Upon examining the 1767 *Abstract*, he had found only four members—Governor Bernard, James Apthorp, Hugh Hall, and John Temple—who lived in Boston. Since he was not acquainted with any of them and could not think that they had occasion to treat him "in so injurious and cruel a Manner" as had "B.W.," he could not suppose that one of them had concocted the letter. "It remains then with Dr. Chauncy to produce his Author," Seabury declared, "or to take the Letter, with all its 'Fraud, Forgery, Villainy, Scandal, Falshood, and Baseness,' upon himself." He ended with an appeal to the doctor, calling upon him to make reparation for publishing a paper intended to wound the reputation of a man who had never done him any injury. "The Bread of myself and Family; nay more, my Usefulness as a Minister of Christ, depend upon that Character, which you have cruelly sported with, and most unjustly endeavoured to deprive me of."

Chauncy's reply to this onslaught eventually appeared in a Boston newspaper. His main point was that instead of apologizing to Seabury, he had a right to expect apologies himself, since he had been unfairly maligned. Asserting that he did not know Wentworth was an S.P.G. member, Chauncy explained that he had chosen the initials "B.W." to conceal the real author of the letter. The use of meaningless signatures, he supposed, was customary in newspaper controversies. As for exposing his defender, such a demand was sheer insolence. Chauncy would not allow Seabury to attack that individual as he himself had been attacked. To his letter the Boston pastor appended a shorter one from "B.W.," who declared he had no design to hurt Seabury's character. He had never heard anything particularly good or bad about him, "more than that he was generally thought to be the *American Whig Whipper*, or an Associate with him." However, the ranting style of the rector's anti-Chauncy polemic gave "B.W." but too much reason to think that he was, indeed, the writer who signed himself "An Independent." Signing his own letter "B.," he expressed the sarcastic hope that the initial would "not ingeniously be mistaken by Mr. S--b--y for my Lord Bute, or by the Spanish Ambassador for the Duke of Braganza."[89]

Seabury, sure—as always—of the rectitude of his conduct, must have raged as he read these retorts or examined the bitter criticism directed against him by "Sir Isaac Foot," Chauncy's ardent champion.[90] Needing similar support, he welcomed the appearance on his side of a certain Thomas Brown, "an Episcoparian [*sic*] by principle" and a member of Boston's Christ Church. Brown, after consulting two local Episcopal ministers, reprinted the rector's signed "Whips" in the *Boston-Gazette, and Country Journal*. Reporting his action, he offered to get others of Seabury's papers into the Boston journals and declared it his firm belief that Chauncy had produced the "B.W." letter.[91] That gentleman soon discovered his new antagonist. According to Brown, Chauncy inserted in the *Boston Weekly News-Letter* an anonymous letter to Seabury, to which was appended a postscript (written by two of his brethren) censuring Brown and his pastor, Mather Byles, Jr. (Harvard, 1751).[92] Seabury's helper responded with a newspaper article, "the substance of which," he explained, "may be to Strangers at a distance unintelligible but to people near home, cutting though just and unanswerable Reflections."[93] Boston's Congregationalists might have disputed the latter statement; no one could gainsay the former!

Seabury himself had again attacked Chauncy in "Whip" No. XLV, printed by Gaine, February 20, 1769.[94] A careful reading of his earlier productions, he declared, should convince Chauncy that he had not been charged with fraud and forgery. But if he refused to reveal "B.W.'s" identity, he must be held responsible for his villainy. Relying upon Brown's statement, the rector undoubtedly assumed that he had found "B.W.," and he repeatedly lashed out at Chauncy with sardonic thrusts and sallies. From Boston, Brown reported that the essay, as reprinted by the town's printers, had "met with an agreeable Reception by the good Sons of the Church; they think you have handled the Doctor admirably well, and that you are an excellent hand at Satire." Conversing with some of Chauncy's friends, Brown concluded that the whole affair had nettled the minister more than any other dispute in which he had ever engaged.[95]

This assessment may very well have been accurate. To Ezra Stiles, Chauncy described Seabury's latest "Whip" as a "low, school-boy, empty thing, I mean empty in regard of every thing but ill-nature, conceit, wrath and malice." If Rodgers had not imprudently mentioned his name, and if Parker had not affirmed that "B.W." was Governor Wentworth, when, in fact, he knew nothing of the matter, the whole controversy could have been avoided. As it was, the New York Episcopalians, clergy and laity, formed "the worst sett of men . . . upon the American continent," and Chauncy did not intend to dignify their spokesman's new address with any notice. There was, indeed, no need for him to do so, since "one of our top-writers" was preparing a rejoinder.[96] This writer turned out to be the well-known Samuel Adams, who published a letter to Seabury, signed "A Layman," in the *Boston-Gazette, and Country Journal* of March 27, 1769.[97] Condemning the rector for his attack upon an elderly gentleman "justly esteem'd for his great learning and piety," Adams handled severely Seabury's writing and supposed wit. "Your stile and manner," the Patriot leader asserted, "will never make you a model for elegance."

About this time, seven months after Parker had published the "B.W." letter, Seabury at last learned the true identity of his anonymous assailant. Starting from Chauncy's statement that "B.W." lived in Boston, he had written to each member of the S.P.G. residing in the town and requested him to state whether or not he was the author of the paper so signed. These letters Seabury dispatched about the middle of February, but already, under date of January 30, 1769, Governor Francis Bernard and the other members, with the single exception of John Temple, had signed a paper declaring they had not written, dictated, published, or delivered to be published the communication in question, neither had they known anything about it until it appeared in Parker's *Gazette*. Thomas Brown had been given the declaration to present to Temple, and great was his surprise when that gentleman refused to sign. This information (together with Brown's admission that he made a mistake in supposing Chauncy to be "B.W."), when added to the fact that Temple alone had failed to answer his personal inquiries, made Seabury extremely suspicious. On March 28 he sent Temple another letter; surely the Bostonian would agree he should use all lawful means "to discover the Author of that iniquitous Attack upon my Character." No reply seems to have been received. The conclusion was obvious: John Temple and "B.W." were the same person.[98]

This correspondence ended an exchange of charges and insults which, though it threw little or no light on the question of an American episcopate, did reveal Seabury's extraordinary sensitivity to public criticism. The battle of "Whig," "Whipper," and "Kicker" continued some months longer, "The American Whig" making his last appearance on July 24, 1769. Three weeks later Inglis reported his assessment of the outcome in a letter to the S.P.G. Secretary. "Our Paper war with the Dissenters is now over," he wrote. "They retired from the Field of Controversy with much Ignominy." Seabury concurred in his friend's opinion. All the "Whigs" had been answered, "and in the estimation of the public written down."[99]

Free of "The American Whig," the Westchester rector could turn his literary talents to that work in support of the Church of England which had been enjoined on him as penance for his failure to aid in the production of the *Appeal*. The ever-busy Chandler had outlined such a project even before the appearance of his own bulky pamphlet. In the summer of 1767, Chandler suggested to Samuel Johnson the production of a large-scale work refuting the assertion that the Church of England had originally championed Calvinism. The English reformers, he noted, had frequently been represented as supporters of the Genevan by Congregationalists and Presbyterians. Such persons insisted the Thirty-Nine Articles endorsed absolute predestination and reprobation and censured S.P.G. missionaries for preaching Arminian doctrine instead. New England's Episcopal clergy, over the years, had attacked this position in various pamphlets.[100] But Chandler had in mind a more scholarly refutation, an exhaustive work, "executed with delicacy."[101] And Seabury was the man to do it.

Chandler soon merged this proposal with another he had urged upon Seabury as early as 1765, a refutation of the "Connecticut Alcoran," no less a work than Jonathan Edwards' famous study of *Freedom of Will*, published in 1754. Seabury from the outset was somewhat less than enthusiastic. Much time elapsed before

Chandler could persuade him even to read the book, and then he refused to say whether or not he would undertake the task. "What I most fear," Chandler wrote Johnson, "is his Want of Leisure & Inclination, & not his Want of Abilities."[102] If he himself were to write the combined refutation he envisioned, it would mean four years of labor: a year of study, a year for a rough draft, another year of study, and a fourth year of revising for the press. The result, Chandler thought, would be a large octavo, divided into four books.[103]

Probably Seabury was unwilling to begin so ambitious a project. At any rate, he never published such a work. Not until the Congregationalist James Dana (Harvard, 1753) brought out his refutation of Edwards in 1770[104] did Chandler obtain a scholarly study covering part of the material he wanted discussed. Passing off Seabury's failure he wrote Samuel Johnson: "If the Dissenters will confute one another, it will save us the trouble."[105]

Baffled in his first attempt, Chandler came forward with a second proposal. One of the most popular polemical works against the Church of England, the collected tracts of Thomas De Laune entitled *A Plea for the Non-Conformists*, was reprinted at New York by the Presbyterians, apparently in 1769.[106] Intended for persons of low education, the *Plea* displayed little evidence of scholarship. Still, since it was supposed to have considerable effect, Chandler insisted it must be answered. In the autumn of 1769, he ordered various English refutations, intending to print an edition of the one he should judge the best. But on second thought Chandler decided an answer tailored to the local situation would best serve his purpose. "Mr. Seabury has undertaken it," he informed Johnson in April, 1770, "& has nearly compleated the Task." The Westchester rector, however, was not at all pleased with his work. Complaining of fatigue, he wrote Chandler: "I am tired & beat out. Had I suspected there was so much Nonsense, so much trifling, so much Falshood in the Way, I believe I never should have medled with him. It is the worst, the most disagreeable Task I ever undertook. Tis like suing a Beggar, or shearing a Hog, or fighting a Skunk." He added that he intended to dedicate the pamphlet to William Livingston and his crew.[107]

Chandler believed Seabury's publication would be "sensible & clever" but feared it might be too severe in its phraseology. Should this be the case, it would be necessary to make revisions before sending it to the press. Some attempt along this line was probably made, for nearly a year later the pamphlet remained unpublished. Writing to Johnson early in 1771, Inglis explained that the projected reprint of a biography of Archbishop Secker would have to be postponed, "as we shall speedily have three Publications on Hand; viz Chandler versus Chauncy—Leaming versus Wells, & Seabury versus Delaune."[108] Chandler's *Appeal Farther Defended* shortly appeared. Leaming's *Second Defence of the Episcopal Government of the Church* had already been printed. But Seabury's refutation of De Laune was never issued. Except for his "Whips," the Westchester rector published nothing between 1767 and 1774, while Chandler produced no less than eight books and pamphlets—nearly a thousand pages[109]—and Inglis, an important refutation of a William Livingston publication, as well as a scholarly defense of infant baptism.[110] Even the indolent Cooper managed to produce a textbook, *Ethics Compendium, in Usum Collegiorum Americanarum* (1774).

Unequal to his colleagues in the matter of publications, Seabury failed, in other ways, to participate fully in their intellectual activities. Unlike Chandler, Inglis, and Cooper, he never developed a real intimacy with Samuel Johnson. None of the interesting letters passing between New York and Stratford—letters concerned with new books, studies, ecclesiastical politics, English theological disputes—were intended for, or came from, the parsonage at Westchester. Both Inglis and Chandler enjoyed correspondences with leading English Churchmen, notably the Reverend Dr. Gloster Ridley (1702-1774),[111] but Seabury wrote no one except the S.P.G. Secretary.[112] Even in the colonies he had but a limited acquaintance, and he does not seem to have been anxious to enlarge his small circle of friends. In 1768 he declared that he had never been in Boston and had never written a letter to any person there.[113] When the Reverend Mather Byles, Jr., impressed by the rector's "Whips," sought a few months later to open a correspondence with him through the agency of Thomas Brown,[114] he appears to have repulsed the attempt.

Measured by the available indices, Samuel Seabury in January, 1774, was a less important figure in Episcopal circles than his three friends. That he had talents everyone admitted. But whether those talents could be employed, for any sustained period, in an enterprise of more than parochial scope was still uncertain. In his rise to an acknowledged position of leadership, 1774 was to prove an important year.

V

"PLAIN ENGLISH, FROM A PLAIN COUNTRYMAN"

THE CONTROVERSY WHICH ERUPTED BETWEEN GREAT Britain and the colonies in the decade following the peace of 1763 was viewed by Seabury and his associates, and by the Episcopal ministers of New England, from a long established and sharply defined perspective. Conscious of their numerical weakness and of the hostility engendered by their proselytizing activities, the clergy east of the Hudson had always looked to the British government for support and protection. That the Church of England, deprived of this buttress, could flourish or even survive in the colonies appeared to them almost inconceivable. Ebenezer Dibble voiced the general opinion in 1767. "God have mercy upon us," he wrote, "if the Provinces should throw off their connection, dependence and subjection to the Mother Country; for howmuchsoever they are divided in religious sentiment among themselves, yet they can unite heart and hand to oppose and check, if possible, the growth and progress of our holy Church."[1]

After 1765 the letters of S.P.G. missionaries in New York and New England contained many references to the developing contest.[2] Samuel Seabury, however, sent few letters of this kind. In a report of 1766 he briefly alluded to the Stamp Act.[3] In 1769 and again in 1770 he observed that "violent Party Heats" engrossed the people's attention, leaving "little or no Room for more serious & important Reflections." The disturbances, he thought, would eventually work to the Church's advantage, since "the more candid & responsible People" were acknowledging the advantages of her doctrines with regard to civil affairs, Churchmen being obliged to obey the government in all that was not sinful. These same individuals, he added, "seem heartily tired with the late Clamours for Liberty &c: As it appears evident that unbounded Licentiousness in Manner, & Insecurity to private Property must be the unavoidable Consequence of some late Measures, should they become prevalent."[4] Subsequent letters said nothing of the Revolutionary movement. Not until the spring of 1775 did he again touch upon the subject.

This casual attitude, amounting almost to apparent indifference, was certainly surprising in a man who was to produce the most famous of Loyalist publications. Yet it points up the fact that Seabury's activities as a Loyalist writer, so far as the evidence shows, began at a very late date, probably not before August, 1774. It is true that in 1783, when compiling a list of claims on the British government, he spoke of an early compact made with Chandler and Inglis, in which the three of them, taking into account the evident plots of the Dissenters against the English church and monarchy, agreed "to watch all publications either in News papers or Pamphlets and to obviate the evil influence of such as appeared to have a bad tendency by the speediest answers."[5] Yet this reference, it appears, was to no political compact, properly speaking, but rather to the decision of March, 1768, to counteract "The American Whig." Disposed to regard the struggle for an episcopate and that directed against the rebels as two campaigns of a single contest, Seabury—and Chandler, Inglis, and Cooper—saw no need to carefully distinguish them.

The former, however, long engrossed their attention. With a single exception,[6] none of their Loyalist writings, narrowly defined, was published prior to the meeting of the First Continental Congress.

It is natural to suppose that these clergymen, as early as the 1760's, were active members of the DeLancey faction, which produced the great majority of New York's Loyalists. But once again it has proved impossible to trace any political activity on their part prior to 1774. That the Westchester rector and his friends, like other Churchmen, supported the DeLanceys may be taken for granted. Moreover, Seabury was an intimate friend of at least two representatives of the clan: James DeLancey, grandson of Lieutenant Governor Cadwallader Colden, and Stephen James DeLancey, son of the late lieutenant governor, James DeLancey.[7] Still, it seems unlikely that he played any role in party councils. Lacking a freehold, he could not even vote.[8]

Without any identifiable background in political journalism or maneuvering, then, Seabury in 1774-75 wrote his superb Loyalist polemics ("Probably no pamphlets more readable, none more witty and brilliant, none argumentatively more effective, were called forth on either side of the question during the whole controversy"),[9] besides engaging in direct political action on a scale at least equal to that of any other Loyalist leader. Three of his productions—*Free Thoughts on the Proceedings of the Continental Congress*, *The Congress Canvassed*, and *A View of the Controversy Between Great-Britain and Her Colonies*—the rector cast in the form of addresses and signed with the pseudonym "A. W. Farmer." Probably Seabury intended that this signature should be understood by his associates and other initiates as meaning "A Westchester Farmer," the designation custom has awarded him. But "A. W. Farmer" or simply "A Farmer" (an abbreviated pseudonym appearing on the title page of *Free Thoughts*) was the signature mentioned by friend and foe alike in 1774-75 and during Seabury's lifetime. Employed in a manuscript as early as 1810,[10] "A Westchester Farmer" seems to have made his first appearance in print only in 1834.[11]

Before considering Seabury's pamphlets in detail, it may be well to mention the controversy which, at one time, revolved around the question of their authorship, particularly since the person to whom they were often assigned, Isaac Wilkins, was the Westchester rector's close friend and collaborator in various Loyalist activities.

Born on the island of Jamaica in 1741, Wilkins was brought to New York as a young boy. Educated by Seabury's father and, subsequently, by Samuel Johnson, he acquired important connections by his marriage to Isabella Morris of the Morrisania clan and served on the eve of the Revolution as the Assembly representative of the borough town of Westchester.[12] In 1785, then in exile, Wilkins explained his activities as a pro-British propagandist for the benefit of a commission investigating Loyalists' losses. Testifying under oath, he made a general claim to "some publications," specifying only "an Address to the Counties of New York."[13] He also declared (with a significant change in verbs) that he "was reputed" to be the author "of a Pamphlet under name of A. W. Farmer."[14] Wilkins' grandson, going beyond the second statement, insisted in 1858 that his ancestor had produced such a tract.[15] Basing this assertion, in part, on tradition, he seems also to have been influenced by historian Lorenzo Sabine, who in 1847 unhesitatingly assigned Wilkins two of the "A. W. Farmer" pamphlets.[16] Certain nineteenth-century scholars and library cataloguers, elaborating on Sabine, awarded the entire series to Westchester's representative or, following a writer of 1834,[17] declared the pamphlets the joint production of Seabury and Wilkins. Yet there is no evidence to indicate that the latter had any part in their manufacture.

Evidence in favor of Seabury's authorship, on the other hand, is overwhelming. In his Loyalist memorial of 1783, the rector explicitly declared himself to be the writer of the "A. W. Farmer" tracts.[18] Chandler, supporting the memorial with an affidavit, affirmed that Seabury had produced "all the pieces and pamphlets of which . . . he claims to have been the Author."[19] Myles Cooper, in a similar document, declared that his friend had published "several pamphlets under the signature of A. W. Farmer."[20] The Maryland Loyalist Jonathan Boucher (King's College A.M., 1771), one of Seabury's intimates in the post-Revolutionary era, discussed the late bishop's authorship at some length in a work published in 1797.[21] Additional evidence is to be found in the diary kept by Ambrose Serle, secretary to Admiral Richard, Earl Howe. Serle, on September 29, 1776, recorded that he had dined at Inglis' "Table with the Reverend Mr. Seabury of West Chester, author of those excellent Tracts, signed *A. W. Farmer*."[22] In the face of such testimonies, delivered by persons who were in the best position to obtain the facts, there can no longer be any doubt that Samuel Seabury, rector of Westchester, produced the "A. W. Farmer" pamphlets.

Shortly before embarking upon his career as a political writer, Seabury took more direct action in behalf of the Loyalist cause. Repeatedly he rode about Westchester County, voicing opposition to measures looking toward its inhabitants' appointment of delegates to the First Continental Congress.[23] Close to home, he had no success. Under the leadership of Wilkins' in-law, Colonel Lewis Morris, certain men of Westchester borough assembled August 20, 1774, and chose persons to attend a county-wide meeting where delegates were to be selected.[24] Elsewhere, however, Seabury's arguments (and those of other prominent Loyalists) seem to have had considerable impact, for besides Westchester borough, only Rye is known to have sent representatives. No doubt for this reason, the meeting—held at White Plains—abandoned the idea of a local Congressional deputation. Instead, the Patriots in attendance, following the precedent set by two of the county's towns,[25] authorized the delegates of New York City to act in their behalf at Philadelphia.[26] Such feeble action underlined the fact that in Westchester County, as in most of rural New York, ardent opponents of Britain's course as yet were few in number.[27]

The Congress began work on September 5, 1774. Until reports were obtained of its secret deliberations, Seabury and his friends could do little toward marking out the specific lines of a Loyalist critique. Chandler, however, was unwilling that the Patriots should escape criticism, even temporarily. Accordingly, writing under the signature "A North American," he published on September 8 *The American Querist, or Some [One Hundred] Questions Proposed Relative to the Present Disputes between Great Britain, and Her American Colonies*.[28] Printed by James Rivington, this thirty-one-page production is the earliest Loyalist pamphlet known to have been the work of one of the parties to the "Whip" compact of 1768. Readers speedily called for a second edition, satirically styled the tenth by the author. Its title page recorded the fate of one copy of the original issue: on the day of publication New York's Sons of Liberty, in full conclave, had committed the pamphlet to the flames, because "it contains some Queries they cannot, and others they will not answer." Such, at any rate, was Chandler's opinion.

Although Inglis followed up *The American Querist* with a series of newspaper essays (presumably those signed "A New York Freeholder," appearing in the *New-York Gazette, and Weekly Mercury*, September 12 to October 30),[29] Seabury wrote nothing—or, at least, nothing which has been identified. Away from the bustle of New York's mobs and coffeehouses, life in Westchester went on much as usual, the customary routine being broken only by an annual fair, beginning on the last Tuesday in October.[30] But the following Monday, nearly a week after the breakup of the Congress, New York received a detailed abstract of its proceedings.[31] *Rivington's New-York Gazetteer* published the documents on Thursday.[32] At last Seabury and his colleagues had texts of Congress' declarations and resolves, addresses and Association. The production of pamphlets could now begin in earnest!

That Loyalist criticism of the Philadelphia proceedings would meet with a ready reception seemed certain. Lieutenant Governor Cadwallader Colden reported to Lord Dartmouth that even in New York City—the all but spokeless hub of the colony's Revolutionary movement—people appeared "rather dissatisfied" with the Congress. "Merchants seem to disrelish the Non-Importation Association," he observed, "and if I am not much deceived, the Farmers will not bear the Non-Exportation."[33] To these two economic groups, then, Samuel Seabury addressed himself in an effort to frustrate the Congress' measures. Naturally he directed his first attempt at the farmers. A much larger group than the merchants, they were, for the most part, little affected by the Patriot movement. If the country people could be kept loyal, rebellious schemes might be stifled at the outset.

Chandler's quick publication of an anti-Congress pamphlet—*A Friendly Address to All Reasonable Americans*[34]—allowed Seabury to work leisurely without endangering the Loyalist cause. Not until November 16 did he finish or, at any rate, date his own production, issued a week later by Rivington.[35] "*Hear me, for I WILL Speak*!" was the motto blazoned on the first page, which bore a title reminiscent of the seventeenth century in its length. New Yorkers, after browsing through Rivington's wares, knew exactly what they were getting if they laid out their shillings for "A. W. Farmer's" *Free Thoughts on the Proceedings of the Continental Congress, Held at Philadelphia Sept. 5, 1774: Wherein Their Errors Are Exhibited, Their Reasons Confuted, and the Fatal Tendency of Their Non-Importation, Non-Exportation, and Non-Consumption Measures, Are Laid Open to the Plainest Understandings; and the Only Means Pointed Out for Preserving and Securing Our Present Happy Constitution: in a*

Letter to the Farmers, and Other Inhabitants of North America in General, and to Those of the Province of New-York in Particular.

Seabury built his argument upon two major premises. Having always lived in rural communities, he knew well the instinctive distrust which the countryman felt for the city dweller and particularly the city merchant. Settled among parishioners whose concerns seldom extended further than the possible yields of their flocks and fields, he judged that self-interest, measured in simple economic terms, was the crucial factor in determining the farmers' conduct. Consequently, he hammered away at the theme that the Congress' schemes for nonimportation, nonexportation, nonconsumption would ruin plain, honest tillers of the soil, while enriching grasping and unscrupulous townsmen. And he clothed his argument in the farmers' own language, utilizing homely expressions and figures of speech, the sort of talk he must have heard during many a pastoral visit and on Sunday mornings as he greeted his respectable but ill-educated flock.

The Congress, "A. W. Farmer" affirmed, had "either ignoantly misunderstood, carelessly neglected, or basely betrayed the interests of all the Colonies." Instead of a prudent plan for accommodating differences with the mother country, they had produced measures calculated to further "the ill-projected, ill-conducted, abominable scheme of some of the colonists, to form a republican government independent of Great-Britain." What would result from nonimportation agreements and similar economic restrictions? Riots, clamors, insurrections, rebellions in England, Ireland, and the West Indies, desired by the Congress in the hope of bending the British government to their will, but wholly unjust, since the English manufacturers, the Irish, the colonists in the Islands "have been no ways instrumental in bringing our distresses upon us." Such measures would alienate Great Britain, but they would not help America. "Can we think to threaten, and bully, and frighten the supreme government of the nation into a compliance with our demands? . . . . A single campaign, should she exert her force, would ruin us effectually."[36]

Keeping New York's products from foreign ports must inevitably work a similar result. Unable to get flaxseed from Manhattan, the Irish would secure it in Canada, the Baltic states, Holland. Simultaneously, the Floridas, the Mississippi region, Georgia (not represented in the First Congress), Canada, and Nova Scotia would obtain New York's West Indian traffic in horses and flour, lumber and fish. A shift in trade patterns, "A. W. Farmer" emphasized, was no temporary matter. When the Congress' restrictions were lifted, it would be next to impossible to regain old markets, as New York's fur merchants, victims of the last retaliatory scheme, could amply testify. Economic warfare, in short, must mean a severe financial loss for the province's rural inhabitants. And how insignificant were colonial grievances compared with that calamity!

> You know, my Friends, that the sale of your [flax] seed not only pays your taxes, but furnishes you with many of the little conveniences, and comforts of life; the loss of it for one year would be of more damage to you, than paying the three-penny duty on tea for twenty. Let us compare matters a little. It was inconvenient for me this year to sow more than one bushel of seed. I have threshed and cleaned up eleven bushels. The common price now is at least ten shillings; my seed then will fetch me five pounds, ten shillings. But I will throw in the ten shillings for expences. There remain five pounds: in five pounds are four hundred three-pences; four hundred three-pences currency, will pay the duty upon two hundred pounds of tea, even reckoning the exchange with London at 200 per cent. that is, reckoning 100£ sterling, to be equal to 200£ currency; whereas in fact it is only equal to 175 or 180£ at the most. I use in my family about six pounds of tea; few farmers in my neighbourhood use so much: but I hate to stint my wife and daughters; or my friendly neighbours when they come to see me. Besides, I like a dish of tea too, especially after a little more than ordinary fatigue in hot weather. Now 200 pounds of tea, at six pounds a year, will last just 33 years, and eight months. So that in order to pay this monstrous duty upon

> tea, which has raised all this confounded combustion in the country, I have only to sell the produce of a bushel of flax-seed once in THIRTY-THREE years. Ridiculous![37]

Shifting back to nonimportation, Seabury bore down heavily on the charge that such a scheme would fatten the purses of New York's merchants. These individuals, he observed, were certain to gain as the price of manufactured goods rose, owing to the lack of fresh stores. What would the farmers do when prices had advanced a quarter or a half? "To say that the prices of goods will not be raised, betrays your ignorance and folly. The price of any commodity always rises in proportion to the demand for it; and the demand always increases in proportion to its scarcity." It might be true that the merchants had declared that they would take only a reasonable profit, but who was to determine it? "Why, the merchants. Will they expose their invoices, and the secrets of their trade to you, that you may judge whether their profits are reasonable or not? Certainly they will not, and if they did, you cannot understand them; and, consequently, can form no judgment about them." The honor of the merchants must be the farmers' only reliance, and what a slender reed that was everyone knew.

> But no argument is like matter of fact. You have had one trial of a non-importation agreement some years ago. Pray how did you like it? Were the prices of goods raised on you then? You know they were. What remedy had you. A good Christian remedy indeed, but a hard one—patience—and patience only: The honour of the merchants gave you no relief—confound their honour—it obliged me—it obliged many of you, to take old moth-eaten cloths that had lain rotting in the shops for years, and to pay a monstrous price for them.[38]

"A. W. Farmer" buttressed such reasoning by shrewdly appealing to his rural audience's dislike of sophisticated urban dwellers. Merchants, he declared, indeed, the generality of citizens, treated country people with undeserved contempt. "They act as though they thought, that all wisdom, all knowledge, all understanding and sense, centered in themselves, and that we farmers were utterly ignorant of everything, but just to drive our oxen, and to follow the plough." Never did New Yorkers consult the countryman unless they could not do without him. "And then, all the plans are laid in the City before they are offered to us. Be the potion they prepare for us ever so nauseous, we must swallow it down, as well as we can."[39]

Page after page Seabury went on in this homely strain, feeding rural suspicions, attempting to deprive New York's city-based Patriot party of support it badly needed. Noting many farmers owed money, he vividly depicted the train of evils which would come upon country debtors when the nonexportation agreement took effect. Their crops, valueless because of the glutted market, would rot on their hands; interest could not be paid, principal could not be paid. Eventually the sheriff would appear, and farms must fall under his hammer, bought up for a few pence in the pound by creditors, rich merchants or usurers. "Glorious effect of Non-exportation! Think a little, and then tell me—when the Congress adopted this cursed scheme, did they in the least consider your interest? No, impossible! they ignorantly misunderstood, carelessly neglected, or basely betrayed you."[40]

Arguing against the assertion that encumbered farms need not be lost, since all legal processes except criminal cases would be stopped, Seabury introduced the story of farmer Dick Stubbs, whose tenant Peter Doubtful was corrupted by Tim Twistwell, "a Rascal from New-England" and a claimant to Stubbs's farm, "tho' he has no more right to it than the Pope of Rome." The moral of the tale was that farmers as well as moneylenders would suffer from the closing of courts, a practical consideration intended to illustrate "A. W. Farmer's" declaration that "The grand security of the property, the liberty, the lives of Englishmen, consists in the due administration of justice."[41]

Seabury employed the same sort of homespun dialectic in his

discussion of the Congress' nonconsumption agreement. Since the success of that agreement depended upon local committees of inspection, the rector labored mightily to prevent their being chosen. Outlining the committees' supposed workings and affirming that they would regulate every detail of a man's life, he called upon the farmers to reject them as instruments of tyranny. Summoning his loftiest strains of rural eloquence, "A. W. Farmer" attempted to shame his lethargic countrymen into a spirited defiance of the Congress:

> Will you be instrumental in bringing the most abject slavery on yourselves? Will you choose such Committees? Will you submit to them, should they be chosen by the weak, foolish, turbulent part of the country people?—Do as you please: but, by HIM that made me, I will not.—No, if I must be enslaved, let it be by a KING at least, and not by a parcel of upstart lawless Committee-men. If I must be devoured, let me be devoured by the jaws of a lion, and not *gnawed* to death by rats and vermin.
>
> Did you choose your supervisors for the purpose of enslaving you? What right have they to fix up advertisements to call you together, for a very different purpose from that for which they were elected? Are our supervisors our masters?—And should half a dozen foolish people meet together again, in consequence of their advertisements, and choose themselves to be a Committee, as they did in many districts, in the affair of choosing Delegates, are we obliged to submit to such a Committee?—You ought, my friends, to assert your own freedom. . . .
>
> But, however, as I said before, do as you please: if you like it better, choose your Committee, or suffer it to be chosen by half a dozen Fools in your neighborhood,—open your doors to them,—let them examine your tea-cannisters, and molasses-jugs, and your wives and daughters petty-coats,—bow, and cringe, and tremble, and quake, —fall down and worship our sovereign Lord the Mob.—But I repeat it, By H----n, I will not.—No, my house is my castle: as such I will consider it, as such I will defend it, while I have breath. No *King's* officer shall enter it without my permission, unless supported by a warrant from a magistrate.—And shall my house be entered, and my mode of living enquired into, by a domineering Committeeman? Before I submit, I will die: live *you*, and be slaves.[42]

"A. W. Farmer" closed his *Free Thoughts* with the plea that rural New Yorkers renounce all dependence upon congresses and committees. For a redress of grievances, they should rely upon their constitutional representatives. Probably these men would soon meet in General Assembly, and then the farmers must act:

> Present a petition to them, intreating them to take the matter into their own hands, and to labour earnestly to accomplish so blessed a purpose. But beware of giving them any directions *how* to proceed . . . . Only beseech them to heal this unnatural breach; to settle this destructive contention; that peace and quietness, and the firm protection of law, and good government, may again be our happy lot. Would the several counties, or towns in the province, conduct themselves in this manner, God, I am confident, would bless, and give a prosperous issue to so good a work.
>
> And whatever you may be taught by designing men, to think of the government at home, they, I am certain, would embrace us with the arms of friendship; they would press us to their bosoms, to their hearts, would we give them a fair opportunity. This opportunity our *Assembly* alone can give them. And this opportunity, I trust, they will give them, unless we prevent all possibility of accommodation, by our own perverseness, and ill conduct. And then, God only knows where our distresses may terminate.[43]

Having done what he could to steady the largest group of uncommitted New Yorkers in their loyalty, Seabury next addressed himself to the merchants. Nineteen miles from New York City by land (though only fifteen by water),[44] the rector seldom visited the capital. Most of his information concerning the activities of its traders he picked up from common report and from reading the newspapers.[45] Some additional facts, perhaps, were furnished by his half brother, David Seabury, proprietor of a mercantile establishment situated opposite the "Old Golden Key" in Hanover Square.[46] These sources enabled Seabury to turn out a serviceable twenty-seven-page pamphlet. Yet they were no substitute for those daily contacts which had familiarized him with the farmers' prejudices, moods, habits of thought. Accordingly, his address to the merchants, well written though it was, lacked the sure touch of *Free Thoughts*.

This second production, dated November 28 and listed by Rivington as "in the press" in his newspapers of December 8, 15, appeared sometime before December 22.[47] Its title was shorter and less bellicose than that chosen by "A. W. Farmer" for his original publication, simply *The Congress Canvassed: or, an Examination into the Conduct of the Delegates, at Their Grand Convention, Held in Philadelphia, Sept. 1, 1774. Addressed to the Merchants of New-York*. Nevertheless, the appended quotation from Cicero ("Do you look upon these Proceedings as the Counsels of Sobriety, or the Dreams of Inebriation? Do they seem to you the Deliberations of Wisdom, or the Ravings of Phrensy?")showed that the rector had not altered his views. In expounding them, he was, however, somewhat on the defensive. The merchants had not forgotten the stinging censures of *Free Thoughts*; he could not win the traders by flattery. "A. W. Farmer" therefore took the only course open to him. Assuring his chosen audience that he realized the importance of the mercantile interest to the community and knew "that the characters of many of you are truly respectable," he, nevertheless, claimed the honest farmer's right of uttering his views, let the chips fall where they might. "You must be content with plain English, from a plain countryman; I must have the privilege of calling a fig,—a Fig; an egg,—an Egg. If, upon examination, your conduct shall, in any instances, appear to be weak, you must bear to be told of it:—if wrong, to be censured: —if selfish, to be exposed:—if ridiculous, to be laughed at."[48]

Depicting all of New York's merchants as having taken part in sending the city's delegates to Philadelphia, "A. W. Farmer" invited them to view their representatives' dreadful handiwork. It was very difficult to account for the delegates' conduct, he declared, since they were acknowledged to be men of abilities and moderate views. To be sure, report had it that "some matters were *run* upon them"; they had agreed to be bound by the majority, and therefore they signed the Association. "Let these Gentlemen, however, remember, that though they might unfortunately, and imprudently have *tied up their hands*, yet their *feet* were at liberty." When the Congress proceeded to extremes, they might have walked out.[49]

Even though the delegates did assent to the Philadelphia measures, New York was not bound to carry them out. The merchants, "A. W. Farmer" roundly affirmed, had taken unfair advantage of the country people when they interpreted the refusal of many rural districts to choose delegates as an endorsement of those the city had selected. "Taking the whole province together, I am confident, your Delegates had not the voice of an hundredth part of the people in their favour."[50]

Nor was the situation greatly different in other colonies. Those who argued that, in certain instances, assemblies had appointed delegates did not impress Seabury. "Delegates, so appointed, are, at best, but delegates of delegates, but representatives of representatives." And, in this instance, they were not even that. The various components of an assembly—the two houses, the governor—had each to give an assent before any of its acts could be considered binding. But this had not happened in a single case. And if it had, and the assembly had possessed authority to send delegates to a congress, still "I am certain no provincial legislature can give them *such* powers as were lately exercised at Philadelphia."[51]

"But it is time to attend upon the Congress, and consider their proceedings." At this point "A. W. Farmer" traced out the sly steps by which Boston's Saints supposedly had moved toward their goal, securing the delegates' endorsement of the Suffolk Resolves, "this adopted brat of the congress." Everyone who wished for a reconciliation with Great Britain must condemn and abhor such wild declarations. As for himself, "A. W. Farmer" would not pass censures on any of the Congress' literary productions. A volume, not a pamphlet, would be needed for such a work; "nor would my patience hold out through so dirty a road, though I should find scarce anything to impede my progress; but positive assertions, without proof; declamations, without argument; and railing, without modesty."[52] He did intend, however, to expose the tyrannical principles upon which the Congress had proceeded and, for this reason, devoted many pages to showing that the delegates, without the slightest legal right, had assumed the powers of government, establishing regulations with the force of laws, providing penalties for those who violated them, and creating most arbitrary tribunals. Seabury's account of committees of inspection will serve to illustrate his argument:

> Here, gentlemen, is a court established upon the same principles with the *popish inquisition*. No proofs, no evidence are called for. The committee may judge from *appearances* if they please—for when it shall be made appear to a majority of any committee that the Association is violated, they may proceed to punishment, and *appearances*, you know, are easily *made*; nor is the offender's *presence* necessary. He may be condemned unseen, unheard—without even a possibility of making a defense. No jury is to be impannelled. No check is appointed upon this court;—no appeal from its determination.
>
> . . . . Poor, unhappy wretch, how I pity thee! Cast out from civil society! Nobody to have any dealings with thee! None to sell thee a loaf of bread, or a pot of tea-water, but such miserable outlaws as thyself! Perhaps thou hast drank a dish of *tea*, or a glass of *Madeira*, or hast used an English *pin*, or eaten Irish *potatoe*, imported out of due time;—and hast had the truth of thy unhappy case published, by the inquisition, in the Gazette: And is there no relief! Must thou expect no mitigation of thy punishment? None, my friend; thou hast committed the unpardonable sin against the Congress; and the utmost vengeance that they can inflict awaits thee!—Comfort thyself however in this—that thou art in no worse state than a few honest people, of whom I have read, in an old neglected book, who were not allowed to *buy* or *sell*, because they had not the *mark of the beast* in their *foreheads*.[53]

The New York merchants, "A. W. Farmer" affirmed, were no longer their own masters. They had chosen an extralegal body

—the Committee of Sixty, elected November 22, 1774—and subjected their business affairs, modes of living, and families' conduct to its supervision. Laws had given way to Congressional decrees. Magistrates found that the city's government was, in large part, taken out of their hands. True, the Committee of Sixty might consist of virtuous and honest men. "But is it then come to *this*? Your committee *will* not hurt you. Are you content to have your liberty and property dependent on the *Will* of the committee?"[54]

Seabury developed this last point in a lengthy discussion of the Congress' provisions for disposing of foreign goods arriving after the start of nonimportation. Merchants in such cases, he repeatedly emphasized, must surrender all control over their property. Nothing could excuse the cowardice which had led them to acquiesce in this state of affairs. "A. W. Farmer" saw no validity in the argument that men had consented to the appointment of delegates and agreed to abide by their decisions. Nor until "the legal and constitutional applications of our Assembly have failed," could he accept "necessity of the times" as justification for irregular measures. Seabury warned the capital's traders that their support of Congressional authority would, in all likelihood, assist the establishment of a "grand American Republic" in which New England would dominate New York. Calling for moderate proposals acceptable to Great Britain, he reinforced this appeal with somber prophecies as to the outcome of an armed test of strength. British arms would almost certainly prevail. "And then, after the most dreadful scenes of violence and slaughter.—CONFISCATIONS and EXECUTIONS must close the HORRID TRAGEDY."[55]

Irritating though *The Congress Canvassed* might be, the Committee of Sixty had little to fear from it. When the pamphlet first appeared, the nonimportation agreement had been in effect for about three weeks, and it continued to function smoothly.[56] But Seabury's *Free Thoughts* was quite a different matter. Patriot leaders showed alarm at the backwardness of the counties in adopting the Association. Most of rural New York had still to enlist under the Congress' banner,[57] and if calculating husbandmen should examine the rector's production, its appeal to their supposed self-interest, economically defined, might well carry the day. This consideration impressed "Z," correspondent of the *New-York Journal; or, the General Advertiser*. Writing from Kingston, December 21, 1774, he gave an account of the burning of a copy of *Free Thoughts* and commented:

> It is not my intention to enter into a minute examination of this pamphlet: To the sensible part of your readers, the specious, but false reasoning, (and in many instances the glaring falsehoods) which run through it, will be sufficiently obvious. Permit me only to observe, that it is calculated in a peculiar manner, above all other performances of the like nature, to impose on the ignorant and credulous—seldom extending their views beyond the narrow circle in which they move; and accustomed only to view things as they more immediately affect themselves, the minds of the illiterate and unthinking, rarely submit to those temporary hardships which are the means of procuring a much greater, tho' a more distant good.—It is for these reasons that the present performance is the more dangerous. The writer has adapted his style to the capacities of those to whom he has written. Is not the fate, then, it has met with in Kingston, worthy of imitation, wherever copies of it may be found?[58]

Several communities had already tried Kingston's approach to the problem posed by Seabury's homely style of argumentation. Others utilized it in the weeks which followed. On the evening of the day Rivington first offered the pamphlet for sale, two copies were burnt in separate gatherings in New York City, while additional ones provided fuel for a fire kindled at the printer's very door.[59] *Free Thoughts* (together with Chandler's *Friendly Address*) again fed the flames on December 1 as the fitting finale of a Patriot gathering at Elizabethtown, New Jersey.[60] Greater indignities awaited the pamphlet at Freehold in the same colony. Having been presented to the local committee, *Free Thoughts* was judged to be "calculated to deceive and mislead the unwary, the ignorant, and the credulous." Handed back to the people, it immediately received a covering of tar and turkey-buzzard feathers, "one of the persons concerned in the operation, justly observing, that although the feathers were pluckt from the most stinking fowl in the creation, he thought they fell far short of being a proper emblem of the author's odiousness to every advocate for true freedom." This same Patriot wished he might provide "A. W. Farmer" with a similar suit of clothing. Afterwards the pamphlet was nailed to the pillory post, "there to remain as a monument of the indignation of a free and loyal people."[61]

In the towns and precincts of Ulster County (possibly as a result of George Clinton's influence) the burning of *Free Thoughts* figured prominently in the meetings held to organize committees of inspection. Newspaper accounts of such events invariably contained some reference to the fear that Seabury's arguments might corrupt the ignorant countryman. The pattern emerged from a preliminary gathering of several towns, assembled at Hurley, January 6, 1775, which described *Free Thoughts* as being "artfully calculated to impose upon the illiterate and unthinking" and labeled its author an enemy of his country.[62] Setting up their committees, the men of Walkill and Shawangunk used precisely the same language, while those of New Windsor altered the Hurley phrase only slightly. Hanover's freeholders employed different words but expressed the identical sentiment.[63]

Patriots employed solutions other than the bonfire. As much as possible, they attempted to prevent the distribution of Rivington's newspaper and tracts. The printer insisted he opened his paper equally to Whig and Tory, and he did print pamphlets for both parties.[64] His paper's great circulation[65] and his enterprising selling techniques (he gave large discounts for pamphlets taken in dozen lots and solicited mail orders)[66] assured, however, a wide distribution for Loyalist propaganda. This situation the Patriots would not tolerate, particularly since Rivington's pro-British bias remained quite evident. Various groups, therefore, took action similar to that of the Hanover, New Jersey, committee of inspection. Meeting February 15, 1775, its members

> *Resolved unanimously*, That from several Pamphlets and Publications printed by James Rivington, of New-York, Printer, we esteem him as an incendiary employed by a wicked Ministry to disunite and divide us; and therefore we will not, for ourselves, have any connection or dealings with him, and do recommend the same conduct towards him to every person of this Township; and we will discountenance any Post-Rider, Stage-Driver, or Carrier, who shall bring his Pamphlets or Papers into this County.[67]

Such techniques of suppression (employed, perhaps, in many instances without any formal authorization) certainly curtailed the circulation of *Free Thoughts*. From Philadelphia, December 2, 1774, an unnamed correspondent informed Rivington of efforts in that city to prevent the pamphlet's being distributed. (Rivington, nevertheless, must send six dozen copies by the first stage; the writer and his friends were determined that *Free Thoughts* "shall be made known to that sort of people in our neighbourhood, for whose immediate purpose it was written.")[68] Sometime afterwards, a gentleman who tried to purchase copies in Annapolis learned that none had as yet been received.[69] Very possibly, watchful Patriots had "discountenanced" the carrier.

Despite efforts of this sort (and the New York orientation of its arguments), copies of *Free Thoughts* did travel considerable distances. The pamphlet's anti-Yankee passages severely limited whatever appeal it might have had to the eastward and, indeed, there is no clear evidence of attempts to send it into any of the New England colonies.[70] But, as the foregoing paragraphs have shown, it was to be found in New Jersey and, probably, in Pennsylvania. And its presence in Virginia is well documented: in March, 1775, Orange County's committee of inspection burned *Free Thoughts*—as well as copies of Seabury's subsequent pamphlets—which had been taken from a local parson. An account of the affair mentioned that these publications reportedly could be purchased in Williamsburg at the printing office of Alexander Purdie.[71]

Besides destroying *Free Thoughts* and seeking to suppress its distribution, Patriots took the obvious course of countering its possible effects with writings of their own. At least two newspaper refutations appeared, printed in Holt's *New-York Journal; or, the General Advertiser*. The first, signed "A Countryman" and dated from New Jersey, December 12, 1774, came out in three sections, in the issues of December 15 and December 29, 1774, and January 5, 1775. Angered by Seabury's obvious conviction that economic self-interest was the farmers' ruling passion, the writer indignantly rejected such a notion. "The value of three pence per pound duty, we are not contesting," he declared, "but the right of taxation." For "A. W. Farmer" to have noticed this would not, however, "have answered his end, as he supposed we ignorant farmers were not to be convinced by arguments of the head, but those of the pocket." On December 22, Holt published a much weaker production, allegedly the work of "A Weaver, in Harrison's Purchase, West Chester County." The "Weaver's" comparison of "A. W. Farmer" to Job's friends lacked point, but his appeal to the various economic classes to stand united in the struggle against Britain showed that he appreciated Seabury's strategy. "A Countryman" had issued a similar warning, declaring that "The designs of the *Farmer* are evident, viz. discord, anarchy, and destruction!"

More ambitious than these newspaper replies was the fat pamphlet entitled *A Full Vindication of the Measures of Congress*, written by Alexander Hamilton, then nineteen years old and a student of Cooper's at King's College. The work being in the press, Rivington on December 8 piously declared his hope that it would "meet with a gracious reception at the hands of every reader who has expressed disapprobation to the Free-thoughts of Farmer A. W."[72] Put on sale a week later,[73] the *Full*

Vindication compared unfavorably with Seabury's pamphlet in the matter of style. Yet it was an excellent production, given the writer's age, and its merits amply justified the confidence now placed in Hamilton by John Jay and James Duane. After reading his refutation of Seabury's arguments, these Patriot leaders took the youth in hand and started him on his public career.

Hamilton in his introductory paragraph attempted to minimize the influence of *Free Thoughts* and similar writings. "The impotence of such insidious efforts," he asserted, was "evident from the general indignation they are treated with; so that no material ill-consequences can be dreaded from them." Still, since the publications might have a tendency to mislead "a few," it was not an altogether useless task to bestow some attention upon them.[74] Hamilton divided his subsequent argument into two sections, a general address to all inhabitants and a specific appeal to the farmers of New York. Keeping close to Seabury's arguments, he sought to show that the technique of remonstrance and petition would produce no redress of grievances, that only a restriction of trade could have any effect, unless armed conflict might be considered a legitimate approach. Farmers, he warned, must repel any suggestion to enlist the aid of the General Assembly. Separating from the rest of the colonies and seeking "for redress alone, and unseconded, you will certainly fall a prey to your enemies, and repent your folly as long as you live."[75]

Seabury no doubt heard the rumors which assigned the *Full Vindication* to Hamilton. Probably he, like his friends, rejected the notion as preposterous. President Cooper declared a mere boy could not have produced such a tract and insisted it must be Jay's work.[76] Other persons perhaps ascribed it to William Livingston.[77] Whoever the author might be, Seabury was bent on challenging him. In a postscript appended to his *Congress Canvassed* (and dated December 16, the day following the publication of *A Full Vindication*) he mentioned that he had seen the pamphlet and was "neither frighted nor disconcerted by it." Since he preferred to vindicate his two productions at the same time, "A. W. Farmer" would wait ten days for his opponent's remarks on *The Congress Canvassed*.[78] Hamilton replied with "A Card" in Rivington's paper,[79] in which he declined to criticize Seabury's second pamphlet until the latter had issued any answer he might make to *A Full Vindication*. The young man also defended himself against the dreadful charge of having used improper grammar. This accusation (stemming from Hamilton's expression "his wit ridiculed") Cooper and Inglis repeated in their "Card in Reply," which appeared in the next issue of *Rivington's New-York Gazetteer*.[80]

Forced to confine his remarks to the *Full Vindication*, Seabury set to work upon *A View of the Controversy Between Great-Britain and Her Colonies: Including a Mode of Determining Their Present Disputes, Finally and Effectually; and of Preventing All Future Contentions*. The pamphlet, dated the day before Christmas, came from Rivington's press on January 5, 1775.[81] Shortly thereafter a copy received the honor of a public burning in a gathering of New York's Sons of Liberty.[82]

Seabury's third pamphlet failed to equal his earlier performances. The need to cut arguments according to Hamilton's pattern cramped his style considerably; he could not, as in *Free Thoughts* and *The Congress Canvassed*, strike out on his own. Nevertheless, "A. W. Farmer" managed to score good hits, notably in criticism of Hamilton's use of colonial charters and in an exposure of errors in the Patriot's account of taxes paid by English farmers.[83] And he still could write paragraphs of earthy, homespun rhetoric at least as lively as any in *Free Thoughts*. Consider, for instance, this amusing passage:

> Your next attempt is upon the imaginations of the farmers. You endeavour to fright them from obeying the parliament, by representing to them the danger of having taxes laid upon their tables, and chairs, and platters, and dishes, and knives and forks, and every thing else—and 'even every kiss their daughters receive from their sweet-

hearts,' and *that*, you say, would soon *ruin* them. No reflections, Sir, upon farmers daughters; they love kissing, 'tis true, and so did your mother, or you would scarce have made your appearance among us.

But I have a scheme worth all this table, and chair, and kiss taxing. I thought of it last night, and I have a violent inclination to write to Lord North about it, by the very next packet. It pleases me hugely, and I think, must please his Lordship, as it would infallibly enable him to pay the annual interest of the national debt, and I believe, to sink principal and all in fourteen years. It is no more than a moderate tax of four pence a hundred, upon all the fibs, falsehoods and misrepresentations of you and your party, in England and America.[84]

Besides rejoinders to Hamilton's arguments, *A View of the Controversy*, as its full title indicated, contained Seabury's plan for an accommodation of the dispute with Great Britain. The colonies, he readily admitted, were no longer infant plantations. Such indices as trade, population, extent of cultivated lands gave evidence of their maturity. "They want, and are entitled to, a fixed determinate constitution of their own." That constitution should unite them firmly to Great Britain and to each other and should mark clearly the line between British supremacy and colonial dependence. Without this, "A. W. Farmer" thought it idle to talk of a redress of grievances. "They naturally, they necessarily result from the relation which we at present stand in to Great-Britain."[85]

What form would a colonial constitution take? Seabury, avoiding thorny particulars, offered only a general outline based on the Patriot position of 1765. Assemblies would have exclusive rights of internal taxation, Parliament retaining authority to regulate trade by duties and bounties. The Lords and Commons also would possess power to enact "all general laws for the good of all the colonies." These arrangements, it was implied, were to be put into effect by Parliamentary statute. And a truly unified British Empire would result. "The dependence of the colonies on the mother country will be fixed on a firm foundation; the sovereign authority of Parliament, over all the dominions of the empire will be established, and the mother-country and all her colonies will be knit together, in ONE GRAND, FIRM, AND COMPACT BODY."[86]

Seabury offered several reasons in favor of such a plan. It must effectually safeguard American interests, since Britain could injure them only by an internal tax. "If they lay unnecessary, or oppressive duties on trade, they will immediately feel the effect; and as soon as the cause is pointed out, they will, for their own sakes, remove it." Moreover, the ideas underlying the proposed settlement seemed to comport with views expressed by the colonies' Parliamentary friends—Chatham, for instance—in the debates on the repeal of the Stamp Act. As for the settlement itself, it appeared so reasonable that "A. W. Farmer" believed "the justice of the nation will not refuse it, when applied for in a constitutional way." On the other hand, should the colonies raise their demands too high, they would lose everything. Parliament would never surrender the right to regulate their trade. Chatham's candid declarations illustrated this point. The choice, then, Seabury argued, lay between a scheme of the sort he was outlining—or civil war.[87]

There was certainly a good deal that could be said against "A. W. Farmer's" proposals. But Hamilton failed to make many really basic criticisms in *The Farmer Refuted*, the enormous pamphlet reply to *A View of the Controversy* (and *The Congress Canvassed*), which Rivington issued, after a long delay, on February 23.[88] By that date, the public had been reading, for more than a month, the fourth of Seabury's Loyalist pamphlets and the only one he published without the signature "A. W. Farmer." This was a short production (the text ran to only ten pages) entitled *An Alarm to the Legislature of the Province of New-York*.

It will be recalled that Seabury had urged farmers to seek a redress of grievances through their constitutional representatives. The Assembly was a body in which Loyalist sentiment might yet make itself felt in decisive fashion. True, its own loyalty was suspect; Lieutenant Governor Colden did not know just what steps it might take. But if he failed to summon it, an attempt probably would be made to convene a provincial congress.[89] Faced with this prospect, Colden issued his proclamation. Members responded but slowly, and it was not until January 13, 1775, that a sufficient number appeared to make a quorum.[90] Two questions stood in everyone's mind. Would the Assembly follow the precedent established by the other legislatures which had met since the Congress' dissolution and adopt its measures? And would it appoint delegates to the Second Congress, scheduled to assemble at Philadelphia in May?

Seabury did what he could to determine the answers. Apparently visiting New York just before the opening of the session, he held personal interviews with at least one third of the representatives.[91] His conversational arguments he reinforced with those of the anonymous *Alarm*, published on January 19,[92] before the Assembly had taken any important action.

The *Alarm* attempted to turn the Assembly against the Congress by appealing to its members' sense of *amour-propre*. It was the happiness of the British government and colonies, Seabury declared, that the people shared in the lawmaking process by electing one branch of the legislature. "But when they have chosen their representatives, that right, which was before diffused through the whole people, centers in their *Representatives alone*; and can legally be exercised by *none but them*." As the representatives were under the most solemn obligations to defend the liberties, rights, and properties of the people, so the people owed them honor and respect. If grievances existed, redress must be sought by way of the Assembly.

In the present dispute, however, the Assembly had been completely ignored. Its dignity had been trampled upon, its authority contravened. A committee of New York City, illegally chosen, had usurped authority over the whole province in arranging for the sending of delegates to Philadelphia. Meeting with other delegates, in a Congress which could claim no legal basis, they had devised mad schemes of commercial restriction and had returned to establish a most oppressive tyranny.[93] The Assembly, Seabury insisted, must first of all break that tyranny's chains:

> To YOU, Gentlemen, the good people of this province look for relief: on YOU they have fixed their *hopes*: from YOU they expect deliverance from *this intolerable state of slavery.* They have chosen YOU to be the *guardians* of their *rights,* and *liberties.* . . . If you *assert* your *own dignity*—If you maintain your own rights and privileges, we shall again be a *free* and *happy,* and, I trust, not an *ungrateful* people; but if you *prostitute the dignity of your House;*—if you betray the rights of your constituents, by confirming the decrees of the Congress;—*you* will thereby introduce a *foreign power* to *govern* and *tax* this province, and *we* shall be, of all men, the most wretched. —If laws made, and decrees passed, at *Philadelphia,* by the enthusiastic *republicans* of *New-England* and *Virginia,* are to bind the *people of this province, and extort money from them,* why, Gentlemen, do *you* meet? Is it barely to *register* their *edicts,* and to *rivet* the fetters of their tyranny on your *constituents?* Your constituents, in *that* case, would be better *without* you. You would be an useless burthen upon them: *worse* than useless; a snare and a trap to them. Your duty requires you to *interpose your authority,* and to break up this *horrid combination of seditious men,* which has already enslaved this province; and which was *intended* to draw the *faithful subjects of our most gracious Sovereign* into REBELLION and a CIVIL WAR.[94]

Moreover, Seabury—and Chandler, who published *What Think Ye of Congress Now?* on January 26[95]—wished the Assembly to forward addresses to the King, Lords, and Commons, soliciting the grant of a new American constitution. (Westchester's rector spelled out no details; representatives would find them in *A View of the Controversy.*) Congressional methods of proceeding, he affirmed, must call forth armed resistance on the part of Great Britain. In this case, "*Parliament* will probably *make a constitution for us,* without consulting *our* inclinations; and force us to accept it, at the mouths of their cannon." But by seizing the initiative, the Assembly might secure the colony's interests. And it could save from ruin the rest of America, even those colonies which had embraced the measures of Congress, by serving as "the mediatrix with Great-Britain."[96]

Seabury at a later date declined to speculate as to his influence over the Assembly.[97] He could, however, have noted that its Loyalist majority, led by Isaac Wilkins and by Colonel Frederick Philipse of Philipsburgh Manor, did pursue the course of action he suggested. A resolution to consider the work of the Congress was defeated by a comfortable margin. Another, looking toward a formal vote of thanks to the merchants for observing nonimportation, was likewise rejected. And the Assembly on February 23, 1775, negatived a third resolution, one declaring for a vote on the question of appointing delegates to the May Congress, by a vote of seventeen to nine. At the same time it approved addresses to the King and Parliament listing American grievances and pleading for a constitutional settlement.[98]

Generally speaking, these addresses embodied the ideas and, in several places, almost the phrases of Seabury's *View of the Controversy*.[99] Yet they were firmer in language and more forthright in demands. Because the remonstrance to the Commons and memorial to the Lords directly attacked the Declaratory Act of 1766—Parliament's affirmation of a right to make laws binding the colonies in all cases whatsoever—the two houses declined to receive them.[100] The strategy of New York's Loyalists therefore proved abortive in the face of British opposition. Seabury was bitterly disappointed. Referring to the addresses in an early draft of his Loyalist memorial, he maintained "that if they had been attended to, the rebellion could have proceeded no further."[101]

Active in the capital, Westchester's rector also continued to promote loyalty in his neighborhood. On March 3, by which date the Patriot party had decided to elect Congressional delegates through the machinery of a Provincial Convention, inhabitants of

Westchester borough assembled "in consequence of a summons" —whose, the records do not indicate. Rejecting any proposal to choose deputies to such a gathering, they endorsed the work of their representative, Isaac Wilkins (the Assembly was still sitting), and "peremptorily disowned all Congressional Conventions and Committees." Hilarity and good humor over tankards and bowls completed the proceedings of the day.[102]

Seabury, certainly a supporter, was probably the instigator of this assembly. And when the Patriots projected a general meeting of Westchester County at White Plains in order to sound freeholders on the question of electing delegates to the Provincial Convention, he joined with Isaac Wilkins to organize a second display of Loyalist strength.[103] Such a rebellious affair, they believed, could not be allowed to pass unnoticed, particularly since those who arranged it declared that persons failing to appear and vote would be presumed to have acquiesced in the proceedings.[104] Accordingly, a short address "to the Freeholders and Inhabitants of the County of Westchester" exhorted the King's supporters to gather at White Plains. Published in Rivington's paper[105] and signed "A White Oak," it was very much in the style of "A. W. Farmer."

On the morning of April 11, the two factions began to assemble, the Loyalists (shepherded by Seabury and Wilkins) putting up at Captain Hatfield's tavern and the Patriots at a similar establishment.[106] The hour appointed for the meeting—ten o'clock—passed without anything taking place, but about noon word came to Hatfield's that the opposing party were commencing business at the courthouse. With Wilkins and Colonel Frederick Philipse at their head, the Loyalists marched to the scene, where they found Colonel Lewis Morris acting as chairman. Wilkins stepped forward. The meeting, he declared, was an unlawful one and summoned for an unlawful purpose. To contest by a poll the expediency of appointing Convention delegates would be to acknowledge the authority of those who had convened it.

The friends of government, therefore, came only to protest against such proceedings and to show their detestation of all unlawful committees and congresses. They were resolved to continue steadfast in their allegiance to George III, to submit to lawful authority, and to abide by the measures for a redress of American grievances which the people's only true representatives, the General Assembly, had already taken. Joined by his followers, Wilkins emphasized this declaration with three huzzas. The company then returned to Hatfield's, singing as they went "the grand and animating song" of

> God save great George our King,
> Long live our noble King, &c.

Loyalist and Patriot accounts differ as to the strength of the parties present at the courthouse. Colonel Morris (whose partisans, after the departure of the Loyalists, unanimously agreed to elect delegates to the Provincial Convention and chose eight men, headed by Morris, for this purpose) gave no figures but affirmed that "a very numerous body of freeholders" had supported the Congressional measures. Wilkins and his followers he described as "an inconsiderable number." The anonymous Loyalist reporter, on the other hand, thought the total on each side about equal, both amounting to two hundred or, at most, two hundred fifty.

However large the force assembled by Wilkins and Seabury may originally have been, it greatly increased after the return to Hatfield's tavern. There a declaration embodying Wilkins' statements was exhibited for signatures. The mighty Colonel Philipse was the first to testify his loyalty. Wilkins followed him. Then came Seabury and next Luke Babcock (Yale, 1755), S.P.G. missionary at Philipsburgh Manor. In all, three hundred six men signed the protest, and six others, unable to attend at the Plains, subsequently asked that their names be added. These signatures when published in Rivington's paper formed an impressive bit of propaganda and one that Morris was not willing to let pass unchallenged. Having declared, in his original account, that the Loyalists at the courthouse included "many tenants, not entitled to vote," he now charged that of the three hundred twelve protesters, one hundred seventy had not the least claim to the franchise, many of them, in fact, being lads under age. Printing the names of the hundred and seventy, Morris headed his list with that of the landless Samuel Seabury.[107]

Morris' assertions may have been quite accurate. Yet the issue of whether or not the White Plains protesters could qualify as voters was less important than the fact that they had assembled and publicly challenged the Patriot claim of general popular support. The demonstration arranged by Seabury and Wilkins stands out as one of the few instances of joint action by a large group of New York Loyalists. Like Seabury's Assembly-based plan of accommodation, it reveals a grasp of the fact that mere passive resistance would never halt the Revolutionary tide.

Lexington and Concord made further demonstrations, indeed any manifestation of Loyalism, impossible. News of the affair arrived in New York City on Sunday afternoon, April 23,[108] about the time Seabury finished catechizing the children at Eastchester or Westchester church. The rector's rejoinder to Hamilton's *Farmer Refuted* (tentatively entitled *The Republican Dissected: or the Anatomy of an American Whig*) was then in Rivington's press.[109] But given the sudden change in circumstances, there could be no thought of issuing it. Instead, the Loyalist leaders sought shelter from the gathering storm.

Rivington published a halfhearted Patriot declaration.[110] This action did not save him; on the night of May 10, a disguised crowd prepared to seize the printer and President Cooper. Both escaped (Cooper fled through a back exit of the college, while his pupil, Hamilton, harangued the mob from the front stoop) and took refuge on a British man-of-war, the *King-Fisher*, lying in the North River.[111] Chandler, threatened by Sons of Liberty, fled from Elizabethtown a few days later. Arriving in New York, he found "every Thing in the utmost Confusion, and the Friends of Government under the severest Persecution." When he learned that the Patriots were making inquiries as to his whereabouts, he joined his friends on board the *King-Fisher*. Rivington remained there as late as June 7, but on May 20 Cooper and Chandler took passage on the *Exeter* for England.[112]

At Westchester Seabury and Wilkins had also experienced the Patriots' displeasure. As suspected Loyalist writers and prominent White Plains protesters, the rector and his friend became special objects of vengeance. Late in April word reached Seabury that New England troops, then at Rye, intended to seize him, together with Wilkins, that very night. Before these forces could travel the fifteen miles to Westchester, the two temporarily "retired."[113] Their wives took refuge at Morrisania with Mrs. Wilkins' mother, a Loyalist herself but protected from insult by the Patriotism of her son Gouverneur and her stepsons, Richard and Colonel Lewis Morris.[114] Wilkins subsequently embarked for England, after writing a farewell address to his countrymen, dated at New York, May 3, 1775.[115]

Samuel Seabury refused to flee. The situation, he informed the S.P.G. Secretary, was "very alarming"; still, he hoped he would be able to keep his station. The rebels had accused the clergy of conspiring with the Society and British Ministry to enslave America. Seabury did not think the retailers of the story believed a word of it, "But only intend it as an Engine to turn the popular fury upon the Church; which, should the violent schemes of some of our eastern neighbours succeed, will probably fall a sacrifice to the persecuting Spirit of Independency." Bleak though the future looked, the rector would hope for the best, trusting to the goodness of that God "who stilleth the raging of the Sea & the madness of the People."[116] With his S.P.G. report, he enclosed a short letter for Wilkins: little Isabella's rash was better; everything was peaceful at Westchester; the warship *Asia* had arrived;

the Provincial Convention had assumed the power of taxation; he had received Cooper's letter; few in the neighborhood had signed the Association.[117]

For the next six months nothing much happened. Seabury declined to open his church on the day appointed by Congress for a Continental Fast, and certain individuals reviled him for his refusal.[118] But on November 14 he wrote the secretary that "this mission is as quiet as I can reasonably expect." His two congregations, though not so numerous as formerly, were pretty regular in their attendance. From Christmas, 1774, until midsummer he had baptized twenty-seven white, and four Negro, infants. He had no new communicant.[119]

Wednesday, November 22, began like any weekday. The rector went to his school; at the parsonage his daughters, Violetta, Abigail, and Maria, dressed in caps and kerchiefs, sat down to work at the quilting frame. Suddenly, forty Connecticut horsemen surrounded the house, their commander, a Captain Lothrop, demanding to know where Seabury was. The troops were in no gentle mood. One of the girls had her clothes pierced by a bayonet, while the quilt was slashed to ribbons. Still, no one would tell the rector's whereabouts. Striking out on their own, the horsemen searched the neighborhood and soon found Seabury. They took him to the parsonage, then forced Mrs. Seabury to open his desk; hopefully, its contents might establish Seabury's identity with " A.W. Farmer." The rector, however, prudent man that he was, had preserved no working drafts or incriminating correspondence.[120]

By this time Seabury's horse had been located. Ordering him to mount up, the New Englanders set off for Kingsbridge, carrying not only the suspected pamphleteer but also Mayor Nathaniel Underhill of Westchester and Judge Jonathan Fowler of Eastchester, prominent signers of the White Plains protest. The company role but a short way before encountering their main body headed by Captain Isaac Sears, a leading New York Son of Liberty temporarily residing in New Haven. Sears placed Seabury and his fellows under a guard of about twenty men and ordered that they be sent to Horseneck. He himself, with seventy-four men, proceeded to New York, entered the town at noon with fixed bayonets, paraded down Broadway, and carried off the greater part of the types from Rivington's printing office. After spending several days disarming the Loyalists of Westchester County (apparently he had come from New Haven, at the request of the Westchester County committee, for this specific purpose),[121] the captain picked up his prisoners at Horseneck and on the same day, Monday, November 27, entered New Haven in triumph, escorted by a great number of Patriots on horseback and in carriages. Paraded through the streets, Seabury had to sit his horse in front of Sears's house while cannon fired salutes and the crowd huzzaed its hero. Afterwards he was sent, with an armed guard of four or five men, to the house of a Mrs. Lyman. New Haven's newspaper expressed the hope that he would there find "sufficient time and opportunity to compose sermons for the next Continental Fast."

Sears and his confederates showed little interest in Fowler and Underhill. The judge and mayor, anxious to escape confinement, signed statements offered by their jailors in which they expressed sorrow for having approved the White Plains protest and declared they would not, in the future, oppose the measures of Congress.[122] Within a day or two, they were on their way home. The Patriots, however, considered Seabury bigger game. About December 5 (but probably not in the evening of that day, for then all New Haven was greeting Mrs. Washington and Mrs. Gates on their way to Cambridge),[123] a guard brought the rector from the Lyman house to a tavern kept by Isaac Beers. There Captains Sears and Lothrop questioned him, as did several other persons. Seabury, according to his account, gave very explicit answers to the first queries. But seeing that a trap was being set, he soon refused to provide further information. Sears thereupon began to threaten. The Patriots, he declared, were not going to release Seabury unconditionally or make a compromise, as they had done in the case of Fowler and Underhill. Instead, the rector would remain a prisoner until the dispute with Great Britain should be settled.

Seabury now asked what charges had been made against him. His interrogators listed four: he had conspired with other persons to seize Captain Sears as he passed through Westchester County and spirit him aboard the *Asia* man-of-war; he had signed the White Plains protest; he had neglected to open his church on the day of the Continental Fast; and he had "written Pamphlets & newspapers against the Liberties of America." Whatever defense Seabury may have made was not considered adequate. Back he went to Mrs. Lyman's.

By the standards of twentieth-century warfare, Seabury's confinement was no very onerous one. But he himself became indignant at the restrictions his jailers imposed. They would not allow visits to friends even under guard. When the Reverend Bela Hubbard (Yale, 1758) invited him to read Prayers in Trinity Church, permission was refused. He could not use pen and ink except to write his family, and then the letters must be examined and licensed. He had also to bear the expense of his board and guard, which eventually amounted to not less than ten pounds sterling.

Seabury's first attempt to secure his freedom proved unsuccessful. When the judges of the Superior Court began their session at New Haven, he applied to them, apparently hoping to secure a writ of habeas corpus. The prudent jurists, however, decided it was "a Case not proper for them to interfere in." Shortly afterwards the meeting of the Connecticut legislature offered another opportunity. Captain Sears having been consulted, the rector was allowed to draft a memorial.

The resulting paper, dated December 20, came before the Assembly's lower house. Skillfully worded, it skirted the edges of equivocation with phrases implying friendship for the Patriot cause. Seabury first set down a detailed account of his imprisonment, then replied to the charges of his interrogators. He categorically denied involvement in any plot to seize Sears and affirmed, with exquisite casuistry, that he had written no pamphlets against the liberties of America. Indeed, he had acted to preserve those liberties, since by signing the White Plains protest he had registered support for the New York Assembly's attempt to secure a redress of colonial grievances! If this action constituted a crime, why had he been suffered to go so long unpunished, and why was he now singled out from more than three hundred signers to "endure the unexampled Punishment of Captivity and unlimited Confinement?" As for not opening his church on the day of the Continental Fast, the rector knew of the fast merely by rumor and had received no order from any congress or committee to observe it. Sears, he noted, had reported him to New York's Provincial Congress for his supposed neglect, only to have that body dismiss the complaint. Even if Seabury had been guilty as charged, he thought it unjust and cruel, arbitrary and tyrannical, that he should be removed from New York, to whose authorities he was solely amenable, and cited before a distant Connecticut tribunal. And since he had, in fact, committed no offense, justice demanded that the Assembly allow him to return home. A wife and six children depended "upon his daily Care for their daily Bread"; several families at Westchester required his services as a physician; his congregations were without a pastor; his pupils needed their teacher.

These arguments undoubtedly received a sympathetic scrutiny, for the chairman of the joint committee to which Seabury's memorial was referred was none other than William Samuel Johnson, son of the Stratford sage. High Church in his religious views, but a man widely respected by Congregationalists, Assistant (that is, Councillor) Johnson, as a passive Loyalist, was on the point of withdrawing temporarily from public life.[124] He might be expected to do what he could for Westchester's rector. And he had an excuse for doing a good deal: already his committee had under consideration a letter from the New York Congress demanding Seabury's release in polite, but unmistakable, language.[125]

The letter (and an accompanying resolution) represented a skillful balancing of divergent views within New York's Patriot party. City leaders resented Sears's bold-faced invasion of their metropolis. "Upon the whole the measure is condemned, by all the cautious and prudent among the whigs," Hamilton wrote to Continental Congressman John Jay.[126] Westchester men, on the other hand, were grateful for the fiery captain's assistance. Accordingly, the Provincial Congress, when drafting papers for transmission to Connecticut's governor, sought to achieve an acceptable blend of blame and praise. Dealing first in their letter with Sears's city venture, they then took up the abduction of Seabury and his neighbors, focusing on the rector's plight:

> Mr. Seabury, we are informed, is still detained. If such should be the case, we must entreat your friendly interposition for his immediate discharge; the more especially as considering his ecclesiastic character, which, perhaps, is venerated by many friends to liberty, the severity that has been used towards him may be subject to misconstructions prejudicial to the common cause. . . .

Succeeding sentences attempted to smooth feathers ruffled by this statement or by other critical remarks. The resolution formally thanking Sears for disarming Westchester Loyalists and authorizing similar help in the future should the county request it was directed toward this same end.[127]

After weighing the Congress' representations and those of the memorial, Johnson's committee sent in a report suggesting a hearing of Seabury's case before both houses of Assembly. This proposal accepted the rector's offer to appear either in person or by counsel; at the same time it called for testimony from "all parties Concern'd in said Transaction."[128] The hearing, Johnson obviously believed, would produce Seabury's immediate release. Continued confinement could not be justified, for Captain Sears was unable to prove his most serious charge, namely, that his prisoner had written the "A. W. Farmer" pamphlets. According to Seabury, he might easily have gained freedom by disowning these publications. But because he refused to accept or repudiate their authorship, he remained under guard while Sears contacted journeymen printers who had worked for Rivington at the time the pamphlets appeared. Since none of these men had the needed evidence, the captain failed to build a case.

The Assembly's lower house, however, had no desire to expose Sears. For this reason, it negatived the committee's report,[129] thus preserving his actions from an embarrassing public review. Yet the action, it seems, was premised upon an understanding that he would release the rector, as indeed he did on December 23. Seabury remained some time in New Haven, then returned to Westchester early in January. "How long I shall be able to continue here is very uncertain," he informed the secretary, adding: "I am determined to stay as long as I am permitted to discharge the Duties of my Mission, whatever personal Inconveniences it may subject me to."[130]

Until the evacuation of Boston on March 17, the Westchester neighborhood was relatively quiet. Thereafter small parties of American troops, traveling to New York to counter the expected British assault, began to make life miserable for Seabury and his family. Every day or two, and sometimes two or three times in a single day, they would come through Westchester, although the town lay a considerable distance from the main line of march. Knowing that the rector was suspected of being "A. W. Farmer," the soldiers always stopped at the parsonage to plague him. They would exclaim against the King, Lord North, the Parliament, the Church of England, its bishops, Episcopal clergymen and the S.P.G. But that vilest of all wretches, "A. W. Farmer," was their chief target. One man declared that he would give one hundred dollars to know his identity so that he might plunge a bayonet into his heart. Another was willing to crawl fifty miles in order to see him roasted. And while the troops raved on in this style, they were also demanding food, drink, and beds. So long as provisions held out, they remained in the parsonage, cursing and threatening their unwilling host. Often Seabury did not dare to go to bed. Locking the door of his room and arming himself as best he could, he spent the night walking the floor.[131]

After a month these invasions ceased. Again Seabury could carry out his parochial routine free, for the most part, from harassment. This state of affairs, however, proved only temporary, for when independence was declared, the situation once more became desperate. Sitting at White Plains, New York's Constitutional Convention passed a resolution, July 16, subjecting supporters of the King's cause to the penalty for treason—death.[132] About fifty armed men took up their station at Westchester, and Seabury, as he explained to the secretary, had to face a crucial dilemma:

> If I [publicly] prayed for the King, the least I could expect was to be sent into New England: Probably something worse, as no Clergyman on the Continent was so obnoxious to them. If I went to Church & omitted praying for the King, it would not only be a Breach of my Duty, but in some Degree countenancing their Rebellion, & supporting that Independency which they had declared. As the least culpable Course, I determined not to go to Church, & ordered the Sexton on Sunday Morning to tell any Person who should enquire, That till I could pray for the King, & do my Duty according to the Rubrick & Canons, there would be neither Prayers, nor Sermon. About half a dozen of my Parishioners, & a dozen rebel Soldiers came to the Church: The rest of the People, in a general Way declared, That they would not go to Church till their Minister was at Liberty to pray for the King.[133]

The imminent prospect of a battle between Washington's forces and those commanded by Sir William Howe induced the American commander to take stern measures against Loyalists who might offer assistance to the enemy. A large number of these people had left the Patriot-occupied capital for the more congenial atmosphere of Westchester. Such as could be located were now seized, and afterwards a roundup of local Loyalists began. To escape capture, Seabury kept out of sight most of the time, lodging away from home and visiting the parsonage for only an hour or two at a time. Persons upon whom he could depend, presumably Loyalist parishioners, brought him reports of local troop movements as well as other important news.[134]

Shortly before the British invasion of Long Island on August 22, two ships of war entered the Sound and took up a position within view of Seabury's house. Knowing he would be taken by the first Patriots sighting him (parties of armed men continually stopped at the parsonage under the pretext of buying something or seeking road directions and always asked for "the Gentleman of the house"), the rector's first thought was to go to them. But the beaches now were closely guarded. After the Long Island defeat of August 27, a body of American troops began to establish works near Kingsbridge while another took up a position within two miles of Seabury. Escape within the British lines became imperative, yet patrols still kept a close watch along the shore and Patriots had possession of every boat. Nevertheless, as luck would have it, on Sunday morning, September 1, soldiers from New Rochelle, ordered to replace a guard which had already left its station on a point of land a mile from the parsonage, mistook their route and marched to the wrong point. At once word came to the rector that the passage was open and a boat waiting. Hurrying to the beach, Seabury climbed aboard, traversed the Sound, and on the same day joined the army of Sir William Howe.[135]

Had he waited any longer, escape might have been impossible. The very next day American troops surrounded and searched the parsonage. A guard watched there for several nights, until Mrs. Seabury, now certain that her husband was safe within the lines, told them the rector had gone to Long Island. If they wanted him, they should visit the British camp where, no doubt, he would be very pleased to give them a meeting![136] The guard probably thought she was bluffing and continued to believe that Seabury had hidden himself nearby. New York's Committee of Safety maintained this theory. At a meeting held September 11 and attended by John Jay and James Duane, as well as five members from Westchester County, the Committee considered the fact that the rector "from his vicinity to the enemy, has opportunities of rendering them essential services." Accordingly, it resolved that Colonel Joseph Drake should seize and convey him to Fishkill. In that remote community, with a keeper, Colonel John Brinkerhoff, to watch his every move, he could do nothing to aid the British cause.[137]

Seabury, however, still with the King's army, was securely beyond the Patriots' reach. He accompanied the troops when they entered New York City and remained there several weeks, returning to Westchester County with General Howe in mid-October. Until the Battle of White Plains, October 28, the rector assisted Howe in every way he could, procuring guides, supplying information on the country about Westchester, and sketching from memory roads and rivers, hills and defiles—a type of service he had earlier performed on Long Island.[138]

Seabury found his farm and church a shambles. American troops had quartered at the parsonage, consumed or laid waste the glebe's hay and grain, pulled down fences, and transformed St. Peter's into a hospital, ruining the building in the process. Subsequently Howe's soldiers, after the landing at Throgs Neck, had made off with a horse, a yoke of oxen, cattle and swine. Despite the desolation, the rector hoped to stay on at Westchester. But he soon found that the British intended to quit the county, leaving it exposed to American incursions. Prudence dictated at least a temporary removal of his family to New York, and in November they abandoned the parsonage. A return was never possible. Until June, 1783, Samuel Seabury remained a refugee on Manhattan Island.[139]

After the happenings of 1774-76, life in New York was dull

and uneventful. Money proved to be the rector's principal problem. Although the S.P.G. continued its stipend, Seabury's other sources of income—the glebe, surplice fees, the legal salary, and the school—had all disappeared. Reduction from an annual income of £200 sterling to one of £40 would have been a personal disaster at any time, but wartime conditions made the blow particularly hard: as early as December, 1776, the price of foodstuffs in New York had more than doubled.[140]

Struggling to keep himself afloat, Seabury could do nothing for Loyalist parishioners he constantly encountered. Driven from their homes with a six-day supply of provisions, because they had refused to swear allegiance to the newly established state, many had taken refuge in New York, where they barely existed, lacking even common necessities. "To pity them & pray for them is all I can do," their pastor reported to the S.P.G. in the spring of 1777, adding that he had thus far "supported myself & Family with Decency."[141]

Chandler in London did what he could for his friend. "For my Part I have not been forgetful of You," he declared in a letter of April 8, 1776, conveying the welcome news that he had secured Seabury fifty pounds from an American clergy relief fund. "No man has, or ever had, more Love and Esteem for You than I; and it has been my constant Study how to do You every good Office in my Power."[142] But Chandler (probably responsible for the reprinting of Seabury's four pamphlets in London in 1775)[143] found his efforts clogged by difficulties, the more irksome because they were of the Westchester rector's making.

Chandler and Cooper, adept at advancing their interests, had early convinced British officials that their loyalty merited a reward. Even before they departed New York, the Treasury granted them annual pensions of two hundred pounds.[144] Seabury's lack of such assistance resulted largely, as Chandler plainly told him, from his own neglect. Surprised that the rector's "true Character" was not better known in England, he attributed this fact to Seabury's failure to write anyone but the secretary, to whom he had never sent any information except the necessary details of his mission. To overcome this difficulty, Chandler and Cooper, aided by some other persons, attempted to place Seabury's "Worth and Importance in a proper Light."[145] If the King's College president worked hard at this task, he perhaps did so in an effort to salve his conscience: the evidence indicates that this high-living cleric had obtained his two-hundred-pound pension, at least in part, by representing himself, or by allowing himself to be represented, as the author of the "A. W. Farmer" pamphlets.[146]

Seabury, prodded by Chandler's letters, made halting attempts to secure valuable English friendships. "If You had not heretofore been inattentive, to such Matters, it would have been much for your Interest," his old associate wrote, yet "it is better attending to them late, than not at all."[147] Recalling that the Reverend Dr. John Butler (who, as it developed, had just become Bishop of Oxford) had formerly taken some notice of him—presumably during his residence in Great Britain in 1752-54—Seabury asked Chandler to request permission for him to open a correspondence. A call was duly paid, but the bishop not being able to recall the acquaintance, Chandler—"for the present"—suppressed the proposal. A carefully worded letter, directed to Richard Terrick, Bishop of London, likewise produced no results: the bishop had died. The courtesy of his successor, Chandler thought, would probably occasion an answer, and "this will fairly prepare the Way for a Correspondence with his Lordship, which I hope You will cultivate."[148] If Seabury received such a letter, he failed to follow up his opening move. The secretary and Chandler (and possibly Cooper) remained his only English correspondents.

Chandler and Cooper did succeed in obtaining an Oxford D.D. for the rector (and also one for Inglis, who succeeded to the Trinity rectorship in March, 1777, following Auchmuty's death).

Chandler moved toward this goal with considerable care, lauding Seabury's achievements to the vice chancellor—"my particular Friend"—and securing the recommendations of the Archbishop of Canterbury and Bishop of London.[149] Although interested in his character, piety, and learning, Tory Oxford particularly valued Seabury's firm loyalty. Its diploma singled him out as one who "during the recent violent excesses of fanatical men, has stood with rare fidelity and unshaken fortitude in behalf of the *King* and the *Church* against the seditious contrivers of pious frauds."[150] Admission to the rights and privileges of the degree conferred no concrete benefits, but the degree itself gave the rector precedence, after Inglis, among the crowd of refugee clergy resident in New York.

Seabury's practice as a physician, his chief employment in the years 1776-83, has been mentioned in an earlier chapter. During that time, he also did duty as a minister whenever he had an opportunity. In the spring of 1777, he frequently assisted Inglis at St. Paul's and St. George's, survivors of the great New York fire of September, 1776, which had destroyed Trinity Church.[151] Officiating in these chapels, May 11, 1777, he preached on the relationship between reason and revelation, particularly in the study of Scripture. Criticism of his argument (by persons who apparently thought, though without much reason, that he approached a Latitudinarian position) produced a predictable response. Seabury published the sermon in order to vindicate his orthodoxy.[152] Shortly thereafter, he printed another, solicited by the Zion Lodge of Freemasons for their usual celebration of June 24.[153] His salutation on this occasion suggests membership in the fraternity. He had certainly become a member by 1782, in which year he addressed the newly formed Grand Lodge of New York Province.[154] Seabury's affiliation appears somewhat surprising, given the deistic tendencies of eighteenth-century American Freemasonry.[155] But the High Churchman continued a firm supporter of his brethren. As Bishop of Connecticut, he often officiated at Masonic celebrations.

Seabury obtained steady clerical employment in July, 1777, when Sir William Howe—grateful for the help he had rendered during the New York campaign—appointed him chaplain to the hospital established for the provincial, or Loyalist, troops.[156] Governor William Tryon commanded these forces, and it was at his request that Seabury preached, or, at any rate, printed a sermon delivered in their camp at Kingsbridge, September 28, 1777. Published as *St. Peter's Exhortation to Fear God and Honor the King, Explained and Inculcated*,[157] this typical Loyalist discourse expounded the doctrine that rulers must be obeyed in all things, except when they enjoined sinful acts. Seabury lauded the character of George III ("the *Vicegerent* of God, to whom He hath committed his Sword of Justice, and his Right and Power to govern the British Empire"), exposed the wickedness of the rebels, and passed severe censures on cowardly deserters. Tryon, no doubt, considered the performance a useful supplement to Inglis' *Christian Soldier's Duty Briefly Delineated*, also published at his request,[158] which had been heard at Kingsbridge three Sundays before.

Keeping the hospital chaplaincy, Seabury in January, 1778, added to it as an additional mark of Howe's favor the post of chaplain to the King's American Regiment of Foot, a Loyalist force headed by Colonel Edmund Fanning.[159] Later he secured a third chaplaincy, that of the *Renown* man-of-war.[160] These multiple appointments created no impossible work load, for the latter two were intended as sinecures, Seabury (like other refugee pastors who held similar positions) being repeatedly dispensed from attendance on his regiment and vessel. Their aggregate stipend was a most welcome assistance, one made doubly attractive by a chaplain's right to draw rations, which Westchester's former rector—by special favor—was allowed to do for each member of his family.[161]

Seabury supplemented his income as a physician and clergyman by writing for the New York newspapers. Although he is known to have been employed by Sir William Howe for this purpose,[162] the only detailed information on his operations dates from the period when Sir Henry Clinton succeeded Howe as Commander-in-Chief. In November, 1778, William Franklin, son of the statesman and, from the Loyalist point of view, Governor of New Jersey, conveyed to Clinton the suggestion that Seabury and Jonathan Odell (College of New Jersey, 1754) be hired to "keep the paper full of decent, well-meant essays" at a yearly salary of not more than fifty pounds apiece.[163] (Odell, a brilliant satirist in verse, had served at Burlington as an S.P.G. missionary and, like Seabury, had been employed by Howe.)[164] Clinton adopted the suggestion, and the two clergymen began to turn out articles, working under this arrangement at least as late as December, 1779.[165] Of their various pseudonyms, only "Britannicus" can be identified. Essays published under this signature, cast in the form of addresses to the rank-and-file supporters of the Congress, appeared at irregular intervals in six issues of Rivington's newspaper between December 19, 1778, and April 21, 1779.[166]

In his attempt to convince the mass of Patriots that they should abandon the power-mad political and military leaders who had deluded them, "Britannicus" treated such topics as depreciating Continental currency and the French alliance. Skillfully written, the essays, on the evidence of style, seem to be mainly the work of Seabury. Certain passages, notably in the second essay, bear a marked resemblance to the prose of *Free Thoughts*. Inglis, publishing about the same time, and likewise in Rivington's paper, the letters of "Papinian" (mostly addressed to Laurens and Jay),[167] probably cooperated closely with Seabury and Odell. Seabury later declared in his Loyalist memorial that the compact of 1768, earlier referred to, had been carefully observed until his departure from New York in 1783.[168] And since two of the four parties, Cooper and Chandler, were in Britain after 1775, he could not have made this statement unless he had coordinated propaganda efforts with Trinity's rector at certain times during the war years.

Like Inglis and Chandler, Seabury firmly believed Britain could subdue the Patriots. "I think the Rebellion is nearly at an End," he observed to the secretary in the spring of 1777, "Not that I imagine the Ringleaders are any Ways altered in their Sentiments or Designs: But Distress & Necessity must shortly produce an Effect which the most gracious offers have not been able to produce."[169] Holding firmly to his opinion, Seabury showed disgust at the dilatory tactics of the Howes and was positively furious with Lord North's peace overtures of 1778.[170] When the Carlisle mission failed to accomplish anything, he took heart that the war "would be conducted with more Vigour and Propriety than heretofore." Writing to Chandler, September 15, 1778, he even offered to forward his own plan for military operations if his correspondent (who had ready access to the Ministry) would convey it to Lord North. "Upon my Word, this is meer *Tantalization*," Chandler complained. "Why did You not send it to me, that I might have an Opportunity of presenting it to his Lordship? I promise *by these Presents*, that if You will send me your serious and best Thoughts upon this great Question, I will find some Way of introducing them to the Presence of Lord N[orth] or Lord G[eorge] G[ermain]."[171] Whatever the details of Seabury's plan may have been, the basic idea was certainly a massive assault on the American forces: in November, 1778, he asserted that the rebels could not withstand "the vigorous Efforts" of Great Britain for a single campaign, their resources being nearly exhausted.[172]

Yorktown failed to shake the confidence of Seabury's circle. "Our prospects in Europe & America are rather gloomy at present," Inglis admitted, "but they are not such as should make us despond, nor do I think our affairs irretrievable." The new Commander-in-Chief, Sir Guy Carleton, appeared willing to act "with Vigour"; this, plus a little judgment and common sense, would soon change everything.[173]

Loyalists officially maintained this posture as late as December, 1782. A week before Christmas Inglis and Seabury, along with sixty other persons, forwarded for Carleton's approval an address to George III. These signers characterized Patriot efforts to deprive the King of his colonies as "unwarrantable & nefarious," and pledged themselves to "contribute everything within our Power, to prevent their carrying this *most iniquitous Attempt* into Execution."[174] Iniquitous the design may have been, but it could hardly, at that date, be described as an "*Attempt*." And even the firmest Loyalists realized the hollowness of such words. Their hopes had, in fact, been dashed in August, when word reached New York of the King's decision that independence be proposed in the negotiations at Paris.[175]

Amid the "universal Consternation" which followed this news, Seabury came to a quick decision. Life in an American republic for the Loyalist Episcopal clergy generally, and for him in particular, would be almost impossible. Emigration was the only solution. To Nova Scotia, then, he would go, accompanied by his son-in-law, Colin Campbell, a Loyalist lawyer from Burlington, who had married Abigail Seabury in December, 1781.[176]

The next eight months proved exceedingly busy ones. Besides putting his own affairs in order, Seabury had also to arrange passage for thousands of other Loyalists. As he later explained to the Archbishop of York, when submitting a plan for uniting Nova Scotia firmly and permanently to the British Empire, he had served "as the principal agent in directing and superintending the emigration from New-York" until June, 1783.[177]

Seabury's activities probably began in August or early September, 1782. Loyalist refugees willing to emigrate and living, at that date, in the main section of Queens County, on Lloyd's Neck, and at Bergen (presumably Bergen Point, immediately north of Staten Island) chose agents to act for them. Seabury, selected by the Bergen group, became president of the fourteen-man board thus established, apparently by election of his fellow agents. The board having roughed out Nova Scotia proposals, he and Lieutenant Colonel Benjamin Thompson (afterwards, as Count Rumford, a leading minister of the Elector of Bavaria) approached the Commander-in-Chief. According to their plans, the Loyalists would receive from the British government ships and ship stores for the voyage and provisions or provision money sufficient to last a year. Warm clothing and medicine, millstones and window glass, weapons and nails, ploughs and other necessary tools and utensils should also be provided. Every family would obtain from three hundred to six hundred acres of useful land, and grants of two thousand and one thousand acres were to be set aside in each township for the support of a clergyman and a school, respectively. Carleton gave a general approval to the scheme, declaring that the terms finally agreed upon should be at least as generous.[178] At his suggestion, certain of the agents prepared to search out proper sites for settlement. Three hundred refugees—men, women, and children from every colony except Georgia—accompanied them to Annapolis, where they arrived October 19, 1782.[179]

Arrangements for this party, which departed New York in nine vessels, must have required many hours of work on Seabury's part. But with the autumn fleet gone, his task had just begun, for a large majority of the Loyalists had still to be transported. Throughout the winter Seabury perfected plans for a mass exodus. Ultimately, he managed to load nearly three thousand persons on board a first group of ships sailing from Sandy Hook, April 26, 1783. Most of the passengers came from Rhode Island, Connecticut, New Jersey or New York, and the number of Episcopalians was large: the hundred and sixty-four Loyalists of the *Union*, for example, were mostly members of Jeremiah Leaming's Norwalk congregation.[180] It is easy to picture Seabury at work upon the docks, checking details, settling quarrels about passage rights, discussing last-minute emergencies with his fellow agents. Perhaps it was there, on the crowded Manhattan waterfront, that Abraham Jarvis, Secretary of the Convention of Connecticut's clergy, first encountered him. Jarvis brought a message which soon altered Seabury's personal plans. At Woodbury on March 25, ten Episcopal ministers had met together in the house of the Reverend John Rutgers Marshall (King's College, 1770) and selected him, along with Jeremiah Leaming, as candidates for the Connecticut episcopate.

VI

"A FREE VALID AND PURELY ECCLESIASTICAL EPISCOPACY"

After writing his share of "whip" essays in 1768-69, Samuel Seabury, so far as the records show, took little or no part in further efforts to secure American bishops. Not so Inglis, Chandler, and Cooper. Until the Revolution, they planned and maneuvered, scribbled and pleaded, moving toward their goal by every available approach.

In 1770-71, encouraged by Cooper's report of episcopate activity among Maryland's ministers, Seabury's friends made a general effort to secure the support of the clergy in Virginia and the Carolinas. Premised upon the strategy of Samuel Johnson, who had often remarked that there was "no Hope of our obtaining an Episcopate untill the Southern Colonies where the Church is established joined us in petitioning for it,"[1] this letter-writing campaign produced an abortive movement in Virginia—and nothing else.[2] Undaunted, the United Convention of New York and New Jersey, in the autumn of 1771, got up petitions to George III, the two primates, five additional bishops, the S.P.G., the University of Oxford, and Lord Hillsborough, Secretary of State for the Colonies. Mostly written by Chandler, they were carried home by the King's College president, whose personal urgings, his friends hoped, would gain them a better hearing.[3] Again, nothing happened.

The Reverend Dr. George Berkeley occasioned the next approach. A son of Samuel Johnson's intimate friend, the famous philosopher, Berkeley toyed with the idea of temporarily leaving England and its corruptions for that bucolic High Church paradise: Connecticut. Johnson thereupon concocted a plan for drawing him into the episcopate campaign, intending that Berkeley should become the first American bishop.[4] Before the Stratford minister's death in January, 1772, the project of a visit had been given up. However, in August Berkeley again turned his attention to American affairs when a friend and former pupil, the pious Earl of Dartmouth,[5] succeeded Lord Hillsborough in his office. Writing to William Samuel Johnson, he declared he would rejoice to "devote my life to the service of the Episcopal interest" and suggested himself as a candidate for the colonial episcopate. Johnson forwarded this proposal (which envisioned an application for a resident bishop by one of the assemblies) to Myles Cooper, but received no very enthusiastic response.[6] Probably self-interest accounted for the president's coolness. In 1774 King's College professor John Vardill, then in England and in contact with Lord Dartmouth, was laying the groundwork for the appointment of both Cooper and Chandler as bishops, the colonies (including the West Indies) to be divided into a northern and a southern diocese.[7]

Chandler thought it certain that an episcopate would shortly be granted. Lord Dartmouth, he reported to William Samuel Johnson, was hearty in the cause and had made arrangements to discuss the matter with the Bishop of London. The Secretary of State was even considering bringing the matter immediately before Parliament. His Grace of Oxford, on the other hand, believing that Parliament had no concern with American bishops, thought it "best to wait for the event of the Boston Expedition."[8]

The first result of "the Boston Expedition"—the Battle of Lexington—was not, of course, very favorable to the appointment of American bishops. Entries in a memorandum book, however, show that Chandler, even after his flight to England in 1775, kept that long-sought object steadily in view.[9] And in the latter part of 1776 and the first months of 1777, when it appeared that another campaign would surely crush the rebellion, Chandler and his friends in New York confidently prepared plans for an American ecclesiastical settlement. At this point, Samuel Seabury once more became actively involved in the episcopate question.

Surely, the Episcopal clergy reasoned, the happenings of 1775-76 must have opened the Ministry's eyes, impressing upon them the fact that, in the colonies, Churchmen were the only true friends of Britain. (The Patriotism of most Episcopalians in the Chesapeake and more southerly colonies, of course, went far to undermine this conclusion, but, according to Seabury's argument, the planters' defection was not to be ascribed to their religion, but rather to their lack of attachment to it, to the introduction of "Deism, Republicanism & Presbyterianism," to the enormous load of British debts and that impatience of restraint which the command of "numerous herds of Slaves" produced, as well as to the prevalence of "Aristocratical Principles among the great Men.")[10] This being the case, it was needless to point out "that the Interest of the Church, & the Security of Government are inseparably connected." And accordingly, the clergy could not "doubt, but on the Restoration of Government here, the Church of England will be distinguished by particular Marks of Attention & Favor."[11]

Ambrose Serle, a gentleman fully as pious as his friend, Lord Dartmouth (whom he had served as an undersecretary), heartily endorsed such views.[12] Duties as secretary to Admiral Richard, Earl Howe, left Serle ample time for his favorite pastime: the working out of plans for a post-rebellion settlement. Inglis apparently met him, September 27, 1776, shortly after the British had taken possession of New York.[13] Two days later he introduced Serle to Seabury at Sunday dinner. "Much Conversation passed between us," Serle noted, "in which I found him to be, what his Writings indeed discover him, a very able and sensible Man, particularly intelligent in American Affairs, of great Wit in the Management of a Controversy, and (what very rarely happens to Men of Wit) of great Candor, Modesty, and good Nature." The topic canvassed at Inglis' table may be gathered from Serle's additional comment that "Till an Episcopate, founded only upon an ecclesiastical Bottom, is formed in America, 'tis to be feared, that the Church of England in them will dwindle to nothing."[14]

When Joseph Galloway arrived in New York in late December of 1776, Serle's taste for constitution-making found its full outlet. For months the two men were almost constantly in each other's company, comparing plans for a system "co-ordinate and conjunct (as far as possible) with the British Constitution, with a regular Symmetry in all its Parts or Provinces."[15] Initially they seem to have considered only political arrangements, but in the spring of 1777 Serle turned his attention to a religious settlement. He talked first to Inglis, with whom he found himself in complete agreement. The two of them, Serle wrote in his diary, were "to have a meeting with the Reverend Mr. Seabury & the [New York] Attorney General [John T. Kempe] to consider further of it." Prior to this meeting, Serle broached the matter to Galloway. Somewhat averse at first to a modified establishment of the Church of England, the Pennsylvanian came round when the secretary had fully outlined his views. Three days later, March 31, Galloway dined at Seabury's, together with Serle and Attorney General Kempe. Although Inglis was not present, this presumably was the meeting which he and Serle had projected. The secretary made no elaborate report of the conversation, merely observing that there had been "much pleasant & intelligent Discourse upon the Affairs & People of this Country."[16]

Plans for an American episcopate (and a general strengthening of the Episcopal position) were now proceeding apace on both sides of the Atlantic. Writing from London in May, 1777, in answer to a letter Seabury had sent him on March 27, Chandler expressed his eagerness to see the scheme "for the Settlement of the Church, which You have marked out," adding that he presumed it would correspond with his own ideas on the subject. For further information on developments in England, he referred Seabury to the letter which he was sending Inglis.[17] These developments, largely the work of Chandler, had come to a head that very day. After dampening the hopes of colonial petitioners for more than a decade, leading English prelates were taking active steps to obtain American bishops.

Chandler had begun his efforts in January. Attended by the Reverend Jonathan Boucher, he waited on John Moore, Bishop of Bangor, and requested him to propose the appointment of a special committee at the January meeting of the S.P.G. Such a body would prepare an account of the Society's early efforts to secure a colonial episcopate and the reasons for their failure, as well as a report on funds for an episcopate's support which had been donated to the Society. Its establishment Chandler regarded as a preparatory move toward "the grand Question."[18]

Apparently because the time before the meeting was too short, Bishop Moore was not able to complete his arrangements. Matters hung fire until April, when Moore called on Chandler and informed him that Bishop Robert Lowth of Oxford would be translated to the vacant see of London. Since Lowth had always taken an interest in the American churches and, moreover, was his good friend, Chandler was overjoyed.[19] In May the Society appointed a committee along the lines he had suggested. Probably Lowth instigated this action; in any case, the bishop was designated chairman. His colleagues included four other members of the bench, five lesser clergymen (Boucher among them), and three laymen. According to Chandler's account, the matter was introduced "by a Letter from Mr. Inglis, dated April 2d, to Dr.

Cooper, Mr. Vardill and myself, informing us, that the Clergy of New-York, &c., had authorized us to act in their Names in Behalf of the American Church."[20] From the date of this letter, it is obvious that it had been prepared as a result of those conversations which culminated in the conference held at Seabury's house on March 31.

Although the S.P.G. committee submitted a preliminary report at the Society's next meeting,[21] the indecisive campaign of 1777, culminating in the disaster of Saratoga, put a stop to further proceedings. This last attempt to secure a colonial episcopate (doubtless considered by its projectors the most promising ever made) is nevertheless of considerable interest, for it shows that Seabury and his friends, even in their hour of triumph over the Dissenters, intended, in the main, to adhere to that traditional New England concept of a purely spiritual episcopate expounded by Chandler a decade earlier in his *Appeal*. Proof of this is to be found in the draft of a plan for an American hierarchy, written in Seabury's hand, but probably prepared in cooperation with Inglis and Serle.[22]

Seabury prefaced his nine numbered proposals with an elaborate argument to convince the Ministry "that the easiest and most effectual Method of encouraging & promoting Loyalty in the Colonies, is to encourage & promote the Church of England." Specifically, he declared for the appointment of an undesignated number of bishops, whose only coercive authority over laymen would be the right to cite them as witnesses in cases involving delinquent clergymen. As regards civil government, the bishops, enlarging on the Virginia precedent of the Bishop of London's commissaries, were to be members of the councils of those colonies included in their dioceses. Assisting them in each colony would be one or two archdeacons, the number to depend upon the colony's size. These officials (whom Seabury expected to serve a regular parish cure) were to hold annual visitations in the several districts of their colonies. Twice a year they would convene courts to examine charges of clerical delinquency. Every clergyman in the district (or, as an alternative, those of a certain number of years' standing in the ministry) would be a member of this court and, unless accused or under censure, would act as a judge, decisions to be by a plurality of votes and the archdeacon to have only a casting vote in the case of a tie or, possibly, two votes. From this tribunal a convicted pastor could appeal to the bishop, whose judgment—given in his own court—was to be final. To guard against English-type abuses, no layman might be an officer in either ecclesiastical court. These proposals provided a minimum hierarchy designed for effective diocesan administration. They were moderate ones, adapted to the condition of the Church of England in the colonies.

Seabury intended that American bishops and archdeacons should enjoy fixed salaries. S.P.G. episcopate funds could provide some revenue. The probable plan for securing the remainder is suggested by entries in Serle's diary; the secretary noted that Inglis agreed with him on this point. Outlining for Galloway his proposed Episcopal establishment (which included the financing of parishes as well as dioceses), Serle declared it would not "create Expence to the Country, nor abridge in the least the Liberty of Conscience to all Sects." Glebes in the several provinces, he subsequently explained, would support the Church of England. Assigned by the Crown following the rebellion's suppression, they might conceivably be carved from the mass of forfeited lands.[23]

After 1777 the movement for American bishops collapsed, so far as available sources show, until the spring of 1783, when it was first revived by the Loyalist clergy who had taken refuge in New York. At Carleton's request, these men prepared a plan for a Nova Scotia episcopate. Arguments in favor of it, political and ecclesiastical, and the powers with which the bishop was to be entrusted were the familiar ones suggested in 1767 and 1777. Dated March 21, 1783, the proposals received the signatures of Inglis and Seabury and sixteen other clergymen, the incumbents and former incumbents of parishes from Boston to Prince George's County, Maryland. On March 26, the same individuals signified to Carleton their desire that Chandler, still in London, be appointed Bishop of Nova Scotia.[24] This action was taken the day after Connecticut's Convention had selected Seabury and Leaming, also a signer of the Nova Scotia proposals, as candidates for the Connecticut episcopate.

There were good reasons why the clergy of Connecticut should have been the first among those of the former colonies to attempt the securing of a resident bishop. Connecticut was removed from the main theaters of conflict, and its Episcopal organization had remained relatively intact. To be sure, four churches (out of some forty-eight) were burned by British raiders,[25] while of the twenty-two pastors of 1774, five left the state and three others—John Beach of Newtown and Redding being of this number—died during the war.[26] Still, almost every congregation, including those without ministers or buildings, was able to conduct services by virtue of the use of makeshift quarters, a heavy reliance on lay readers, and the willingness of the remaining clergy to provide vacant parishes with occasional help.[27] Beginning in 1780, the Convention resumed its Trinity week meeting, certainly an indication of comparatively stable conditions.[28] Indeed, according to John Rutgers Marshall of Woodbury, writing in April, 1782, "the Church in every part of the Colony is in very flourishing Circumstances Notwithstanding the troubles & Confusion of the present Day."[29]

Reports of frequent accessions substantiated this statement.[30] During the war Connecticut's Episcopal clergy continued to gather in converts. Inglis (no unbiased judge, of course) attributed this success to their firm Loyalism and avoidance of Revolutionary topics in sermons: Dissenting pulpits, he affirmed, "resounded with scarcely any Thing else than the furious politics of the Times, which occasioned Disgust in the more serious & thinking." He hazarded no numerical guess as to the increase, simply noting that it had been "surprizingly great" in some places.[31] Estimates of other persons varied considerably. Seabury afterwards gave thirty thousand as the number of Connecticut Churchmen in 1783, while Leaming put the figure at twenty thousand.[32] For 1774, a conservative estimate would be fifteen thousand.[33]

Whatever its precise strength, Connecticut's Episcopal Church in 1783 was obviously an active and growing body, served by a group of clergy who, with lay assistance, could provide for its basic needs and possessed of a pre-Revolutionary state-wide body, the Convention, which still functioned. The machinery for common action existed, and all agreed that action must be taken. To fill up vacant pulpits and to provide for the continued existence of the Church, means had to be adopted for securing a regular succession of clergymen. Old methods would not suffice. Candidates for the ministry who were citizens of the state of Connecticut could not take the political oaths required in the English ordination service, and the Bishop of London had no power to dispense from this statutory requirement. The only solution was the settlement of a resident bishop.[34]

A secondary consideration, but still an important one in spurring the Connecticut clergy to quick action, was the publication in Philadelphia early in August, 1782, of an anonymous pamphlet, *The Case of the Episcopal Churches in the United States Considered.* Written by William White (College of Philadelphia, 1765), rector of the Quaker capital's United Churches of Christ Church and St. Peter's, it was an epoch-making document, suggesting in broad outline the system of mixed clerical and lay conventions by which the Protestant Episcopal Church is still governed. The attention of the Connecticut clergy fastened, however, not so much on this proposal as on White's suggestion that the Episcopal churches, upon forming a national organization, should declare their intention to procure the historic episcopate as soon as possible but in the meantime should license unordained ministers to preach and administer the sacraments.[35] This plan, as White later explained, was the result of his conviction that Great Britain would cease military operations but refuse a formal recognition of American independence. In that event, it would be impossible to procure bishops from England; unless the Episcopal churches adopted a plan similar to his own, they must, in his opinion, inevitably collapse. Nearly all of them, he asserted (erroneously in the case of Connecticut) were closed for lack of ministers.[36]

Almost as soon as this pamphlet appeared, word arrived in Philadelphia of Great Britain's willingness to concede independence. White thereupon abandoned his plan for an irregular clergy. But believing that the other proposals he had made still had merit, he did not withdraw his production from circulation. *The Case of the Episcopal Churches* continued to be advertised in Philadelphia newspapers as late as November, 1782, and two new printings came out in 1783.[37] Since no addenda were included and no alterations made in the text, the Connecticut clergy, having no personal communication with White, naturally supposed that he still favored a temporary departure from episcopal ordinations.

Such a procedure, given the whole apologetic upon which New England's Episcopal Church had been erected since the events of 1722, could not but meet with the severest condemnation from Connecticut's ministers. Even a casual reading of White's pamphlet showed them that the author, though regarding episcopacy as a laudable, ancient, and apostolic institution, did not look upon it as essential to the very being of a church, as had Timothy Cutler and Samuel Johnson. Here at last in print, the High Churchmen must have reasoned, was positive proof of that lukewarmness, that lack of real attachment to Church principles of which they had always suspected the "Southern" clergy. Such conduct might have been expected from a man who had violated the most solemn obligations and rushed into rebellion against his lawful sovereign! The overthrow of White's scheme, the clergy concluded, was absolutely necessary for the preservation of the Episcopal Church, and the securing of a bishop from the historic succession would be the best method of accomplishing that end. Connecticut's own need to supply herself with duly ordained deacons and priests and the hope of preserving other Episcopal churches from what was regarded as a lamentable defection thus merged, in the eyes of the state's ministers, into a single project.

Careful to maintain their allegiance to George III until such time as he should formally release them, the clergy delayed taking any steps until news of the peace reached America early in 1783.[38] Winter snows must further have delayed the assembling of the Convention, which met at Woodbury in the parsonage of John Rutgers Marshall, on March 25, the Feast of the Annunciation.[39] Although no minutes are extant, the ten clergymen[40] present can be identified with some exactness by a process of elimination. Of Connecticut's fourteen Episcopal pastors (Gideon Bostwick of Great Barrington, Massachusetts, being included in this number), John Tyler (Yale, 1765) of Norwich and Daniel Fogg (Harvard, 1764) of Brooklyn, the only clergymen remaining in the region east of the Connecticut, are known, on the evidence of Tyler's statements, to have been absent from the Woodbury meeting.[41] A letter written by Ebenezer Dibble (Yale, 1734) of Stamford provides good evidence that he, too, did not attend.[42] The ministers who met at Woodbury, then, were in all likelihood, ten of the following eleven: John Rutgers Marshall (King's College, 1770), the host; Christopher Newton (Yale, 1740) of Ripton, who had been present when Seabury preached at the Stamford conference in 1757; Richard Mansfield (Yale, 1741) of Derby; Samuel Andrews (Yale, 1759) of Wallingford; Richard S. Clarke (Yale, 1762) of New Milford; Abraham Jarvis (Yale, 1761) of Middletown, Secretary to the Convention; Bela Hubbard (Yale, 1758) of New Haven; James Scovil (Yale, 1757) of

Waterbury; James Nichols (Yale, 1771) of Litchfield; Roger Viets (Yale, 1758) of Simsbury; and Gideon Bostwick (Yale, 1762) of Great Barrington. All of these men except Nichols, Jarvis, and Marshall were S.P.G. missionaries. At least one candidate for Orders, Ashbel Baldwin (Yale, 1776), also attended the Convention.[43]

Taking White's pamphlet into consideration, the clergy decided to send a formal protest to the author. They assured him that they, too, realized independence had broken the bond of union with the Church of England. New ecclesiastical arrangements would, of course, have to be made. But since bishops were the chief governors of the Church, Connecticut was unwilling to undertake important measures until it had secured a resident bishop, if that were possible. As for White's proposed departure from episcopal ordinations, such a plan was totally unacceptable. Connecticut agreed with what it took to be Chandler's opinion, that bishops are "as truly an ordinance of Christ, and as essential to his Church as the sacraments." White, on the other hand, the Convention plainly implied, favored episcopal government for reasons of mere expediency. Even if necessity could authorize a departure from it (and this Connecticut would not admit), no such necessity now existed. Not knowing White agreed with this last statement, the Convention argued in detail that the present time afforded the best opportunity ever for introducing an American episcopate. Its letter closed with an appeal for harmony:

> Nothing is further from the design of this letter than to begin a dispute with you; but in a frank and brotherly way to express our opinion of the mistaken and dangerous tendency of the pamphlet. We fear, should the scheme of it be carried into execution in the southern states [the states south of New England], it will create divisions in the Church at a time when its whole strength depends upon its unity for we know it is totally abhorrent from the principles of the Church in the northern [New England] states, and are fully convinced they will never submit to it. And indeed should we consent to a temporary departure from Episcopacy, there would be very little propriety in asking

> for it afterwards, and as little reason ever to expect it in America. Let us all then unite as one man to improve this favorable opportunity, to procure an object so desirable and so essential to the Church.[44]

Despite this concluding sentence, the Connecticut clergy had no plan for a united application for bishops by the churches of the several states. Their suspicions of Southern Latitudinarians and dislike of rebel pastors compelled them to pursue an independent course. From their letter White would never have known that they had chosen candidates for the episcopate at Woodbury. And until May, 1784, this fact was concealed from him, and, so far as the records show, from every other Patriot clergyman.[45]

In selecting a bishop, the Convention pitched upon the obvious man: Jeremiah Leaming. Author of two defenses of episcopacy, and the senior minister in date of ordination, Leaming was generally accorded the informal precedency earlier held successively by Samuel Johnson and John Beach. His withdrawal to New York at the time of the British raid on Norwalk and continued residence there did not make him an expatriate in his colleagues' eyes; they recognized this absence as a temporary one, necessitated by the fortunes of war.[46] After making its choice, the Convention roughed out—or, perhaps, authorized Secretary Jarvis to write later—an appeal to the Archbishops of Canterbury and York and the Bishop of London urging Leaming's consecration.[47] However, since the bishop-designate was both old (about sixty-six) and lame, it was thought well to have an alternate candidate in case he declined election when Jarvis should approach him. The nomination of Samuel Seabury followed.

Local pride probably had a good deal to do with this choice. The Connecticut-born refugee was, after all, an Oxford D.D. and, except for Inglis and the Reverend William Smith, the only one in the United States. With influential friends in Britain to help him—Chandler and Cooper—Seabury perhaps could obtain consecration more easily than any other candidate. He had helped his brethren in Connecticut in 1778-79, consulting the Bishop of

London (through the medium of Chandler) as to whether their churches—closed, for the most part, after independence—should be reopened and Prayers read, only omitting those for George III and the royal family.[48] If Leaming were unwilling to shoulder the burdens of the episcopate, the clergy would welcome such a man in his stead.[49]

Leaming was unwilling. The reasons he offered were those the Convention had envisioned: age and bodily infirmities.[50] Seabury was therefore applied to, and all the refugee clergy whom Jarvis consulted insisted he should accept. "I foresaw many & great difficulties in the way," he afterwards declared, "but yet none but what I hoped might be overcome; & I was sensible the attempt ought to be immediately made by somebody." Jarvis pointed out that he had no authority to make his proposals to anyone else and asserted that if Seabury refused, the whole affair, in his opinion, would drop. In the face of this pressure, the alternate candidate accepted the nomination.[51]

Suitable addresses and certificates were soon manufactured. Jarvis (or some other clergyman) shortened the appeal which he had brought to New York, removed certain tactless sentences,[52] and thoroughly reworked the whole, altering it to fit Seabury's instead of Leaming's situation. The candidate would present copies, dated April 21 and signed by Jarvis on behalf of the Connecticut Convention, to the archbishops and the Bishop of London.[53] Of the same date was a testimonial, endorsed by Inglis and his assistant, Benjamin Moore (King's College, 1768), by Jarvis, Leaming, and Jonathan Odell, and by the aged Isaac Browne (a Yale graduate who had been recommended for Orders in 1733 by Seabury's father,[54] and whose elder brother, Tutor Daniel Browne of Yale, had joined Cutler and Johnson in declaring for the Church of England in 1722). Affirming that they had been intimately acquainted with Seabury for many years, the signatories cited his learning and abilities, prudence and zeal, and declared they believed "him every way qualified for the sacred Office of a Bishop; the several Duties of which Office, we are firmly persuaded he will discharge with Honor, Dignity and Fidelity, and consequently with Advantage to the Church of God."[55] The testimonial alluded briefly to the White pamphlet in urging Seabury's candidacy; this matter had been dealt with in detail in the address, the Connecticut clergy doubtless considering it a good lever with which to pry a consecration out of the English prelates. Duplicates of another document, directed to the archbishops and the Bishop of London and signed by the same ministers (except for Jarvis, now returned to Middletown), and also by John Beardsley (King's College, 1761), refugee pastor from Poughkeepsie, were prepared on May 24.[56] They contributed the information that Seabury, if successful in his application, intended to settle at New London and there perform the work of an S.P.G. missionary in addition to his episcopal duties. Why, after all these papers, another testimonial should have been considered necessary is not clear, but on June 3 one was drafted and signed by Inglis, Moore, and Odell.[57]

How to finance his outward and return voyages, as well as his stay in England, was a problem which must have loomed large in Seabury's mind. The immediate difficulty was solved by his obtaining, temporarily, the chaplaincy of the warship *Chatham*, due to depart for home waters. This ensured free passage for himself and his son Samuel, a youth of seventeen.[58] Printer James Rivington—by now a close friend—provided necessary funds, both for the bishop-elect and the family he was leaving behind. On June 4, shortly before the *Chatham* sailed, Rivington loaned him £300 sterling. He afterwards advanced other sums to Miss Maria for the support of herself, Sister Violetta, and Brothers Edward and Charles.[59]

Seabury reached London on July 7,[60] where Chandler, no doubt, gave him a hearty welcome. This influential exile could be of particular service, for Robert Lowth and John Moore, the prelates with whom he had discussed the scheme of an American episcopate in 1777, were the men Seabury had first to win over. Lowth—old, feeble, and not very active—was still Bishop of London; Moore had exchanged Bangor for the primatial see of Canterbury in March, 1783. Presumably Chandler furnished Seabury with letters of introduction when the latter paid initial calls at Lambeth and Fulham. He took this action within a few days of his arrival, probably hoping that he could complete his business and return to Connecticut before the autumn storms.

At Fulham the reception was most cordial. Lowth gave full approval to the scheme, wished it success, and expressed willingness to join his brothers of Canterbury and York in granting the candidate episcopal Orders. From the conversation, however, Seabury gathered that the bishop did not intend to take the lead in pushing the affair. Lowth mentioned the state oaths in the consecration service, suggesting that they might prove an impediment to providing a bishop for a foreign state, yet he supposed the King's dispensation would remove the difficulty.[61] Seabury showed no alarm. He was well aware of this particular problem; the clergy had discussed it prior to his departure from New York and had proposed the same remedy.[62]

The interview at Lambeth did not go as well. His Grace of Canterbury, to be sure, was friendly and sympathetic and anxious that Seabury should succeed. But since a Parliamentary act had imposed the oaths in question, he feared a royal dispensation could not remove them. Such arguments as Seabury hastily devised failed to alter the primate's opinion. However, he did agree to submit it to the scrutiny of persons knowledgeable in these matters. And though he foresaw great difficulties in Seabury's way, he believed there was no reason to despair; hopefully, none would prove insurmountable.[63] Accepting his copy of the Connecticut appeal, Moore afterwards delivered it to Lord North, now Secretary of State for home and colonial affairs in his coalition with Charles James Fox.[64]

Seabury in reporting these conversations to the Connecticut

clergy emphasized that much time, patience, and hard work would be necessary to secure his consecration. The thought that English Dissenters might get wind of the plan and stir up Connecticut's authorities to lodge a formal protest against it troubled him a good deal. If anything of this sort were attempted, he believed it "best to avow your Design, & try what strength you can muster in the Assembly to support it." He would write again when he had returned from York, where he was going to consult the archbishop.[65]

This journey, begun about July 20, took Seabury as far north as Edinburgh, where he held a reunion with Myles Cooper, since 1777 senior minister of the Cowgate Chapel in the Scottish capital.[66] Samuel, Jr., accompanied his father and on July 29 took up quarters at the boarding house of Mrs. Christian Edwards. He remained in Edinburgh until the following spring, pursuing medical studies in the same manner as his father had done in 1752-53.[67]

By August 10 Seabury was back in London, convinced that his interview with Archbishop William Markham had accomplished little or nothing. He now believed success improbable, and his belief hardened almost to a certainty in the next few months. Like Lowth and Moore, the northern primate had been kindly and gracious. But the old difficulty of the state oaths remained, and new ones appeared. Both archbishops believed it improper to send a bishop where there was no established diocese and feared the candidate would become an object of contempt unless a competent and permanent fund existed for his support.[68] Much more important than these considerations, however, was the fact that Seabury's application lacked the sanction of the Connecticut government. Upon this immovable rock, hopes for an English consecration repeatedly shattered.

The difficulties posed by the lack of concurrence of the American civil powers apparently originated, not with the primates, but rather with Lord North. The North-Fox Ministry could not but be suspicious of Dr. Seabury's request. Episcopal appointments were subject to political control in England and in every Continental monarchy. Would not the governments of the newly independent states wish to exercise a similar authority? Moreover, since a decided opposition to the introduction of an American episcopate had developed before 1775, was it not reasonable to suppose it still continued? Britain had no wish to furnish a handle for the charge that she was interfering in delicate domestic concerns. In short, since Seabury could produce no Connecticut endorsement, it was most unlikely that the Ministry would allow a bill to pass through Parliament dispensing with the obligation of the state oaths. And without such a bill, the bishops believed they could not consecrate.[69]

Against such syllogisms argument was hopeless. "All that I could say had no Effect," the bishop-elect reported, "and I had a fair opportunity of saying all that I wished to say." His Grace of Canterbury was willing to consult the Crown Lawyer, as well as the bench of bishops when they came to London in November for the opening of Parliament. The final decision, Seabury supposed, would be made known to him about Christmas. As matters stood, it would almost certainly be a refusal. To accomplish anything further, Churchmen must consult the Connecticut government.[70]

On August 10 Seabury sent off a letter urging an application to the General Assembly. Should that body be willing to allow a bishop in the state but unwilling, because of his Loyalist activities, that he should be the bishop, the clergy were to elect a new candidate. "Let another be chosen, against whom they have no objections," he repeated in a later letter. "I will resign my pretensions most willingly, I will assist him most readily, & with all my power." The Episcopal laity, he believed, ought to join with the clergy in getting up the petition in order that it might carry more weight. As a form of insurance, application should also be made to the legislature of Vermont. For personal reasons, Seabury wanted the matter concluded as soon as possible. At present he was unprovided for; if he failed in his mission, he would have to find some position which would support his family. He could not remain in London beyond the next spring.[71]

From the date of his first letter, it is probable that Seabury expected his friends to approach the Assembly at its October session. Word of the result would reach him, therefore, in late November at the earliest and probably not before December. To fill up the time, he drafted, with Chandler's help, an address to be presented to the bench of bishops, in which he again sought (though certainly without much hope of success) to overcome the archbishops' objections to a consecration performed without the formal concurrence of the Connecticut authorities. An able document, the address argued that the state would put no obstacles in the way of a bishop. According to Seabury, Connecticut was divided politically along religious lines, with Old Light Congregationalists battling the New. Both groups were anxious to conciliate Churchmen, who by throwing their votes to one or the other could determine the outcome of elections.[72] Seabury also prepared, during this period of waiting, a long paper for the Archbishop of York urging an establishment for the Church of England in Nova Scotia.[73] And with the assistance of friends, he made the overtures which resulted a year later in his consecration by Scottish bishops.

Nowhere else in 1783 was there a body of Christians so closely resembling the Episcopal Church of Connecticut as in the region about Aberdeen, where the meager strength of Scotland's similarly named group was concentrated. These Episcopalians traced their succession of bishops to men consecrated in England in 1661 for the ancient northern sees; they regarded themselves as the faithful remnant of a national church, cruelly disestablished by the events of 1688-89. Modern scholarship, however, has convincingly demonstrated that the Church of Scotland of the Restoration period was, in no real sense, an Episcopal communion.

Before 1689 the substance of faith and worship was Presbyterian; bishops were merely grafts upon an existing structure.[74]

Scotland's Episcopal Church, as Seabury encountered it, really dated from 1725, when, about the time that Cutler and Johnson were beginning their work in New England, Bishop James Gadderar assumed the charge of the diocese of Aberdeen. Though a Scot, Gadderar had long been a resident of London and a close associate of English Nonjurors with advanced High Church views. His support of their position reinforced a doctrinal outlook which, though held by the Scottish bishops and at least some of their clergy, had as yet made little headway among the Episcopal laity. Gadderar's example of vigorous diocesan administration complemented the work of Bishop Thomas Rattray of Brechin, a theologian and liturgist of the first order. Aided by lesser figures, and in the face of the Scottish episcopate's bitter internal quarrels, the two men fashioned a distinctive Episcopal body.[75]

Active persecution of the Episcopal Church—at its height during Seabury's 1752-53 residence in Edinburgh—had ended well before 1783; once the hopelessness of the Stuart cause became evident, the reason for it disappeared. Nevertheless, the penal laws were still on the books, and fears that they might be revived exercised an inhibiting influence. Episcopalians remained a downtrodden minority. The laity numbered upward of ten thousand—a group no more than half the size of that found in Connecticut. The inferior clergy (always termed presbyters) had declined from about sixty in 1763 to perhaps forty-five men, ministering to congregations housed in lofts and barns, in private dwellings and in plain, shed-like chapels.[76] Most important church matters were transacted by the Episcopal College, headed by the Primus or presiding bishop. In 1783 the College consisted of five bishops, whose differing views represented the various forces at work within their communion.

William Falconar, consecrated as early as 1741 and since 1776

Bishop of Edinburgh, had recently resigned the post of Primus. Old and sickly, he was incapable of exercising any leadership. Three of his colleagues were almost equally decrepit: Charles Rose, Bishop of Dunblane and Dunkeld, a man fast verging on senility; Bishop Arthur Petrie of Moray, whose illnesses excited constant concern; and Robert Kilgour, Bishop of Aberdeen and Primus, the strongest of a feeble quartet. All of these elderly gentlemen were Jacobites, Bishop Rose having the strongest views on the subject, and all of them, through a combination of Nonjuring and Jacobite logic, regarded the English Church as schismatical. Incredible as it may seem, these men considered two tiny congregations at Newcastle and London and the household of Thomas Bowdler of Bath (father of the Shakespeare editor) as the true Church of England, these being the last remnants of that Nonjuring church whose bishops derived, in regular order, from Archbishop Sancroft and the other prelates ejected from their sees following the Revolution of 1688. After the death in 1779 of Robert Gordon, last bishop of this succession, his adherents, under agreements previously made, had placed themselves under the government of the Scottish episcopate.[77]

This arrangement was looked upon with considerable disfavor by the fifth member of the hierarchy, John Skinner, consecrated in 1782 as coadjutor to Bishop Kilgour. Although much younger than the other bishops at the time of his elevation, Skinner at once assumed the leadership of the Episcopal College. Counseled by his brilliant father, John Skinner of Linshart (country pastor, historian, poet, biblical critic and, according to Robert Burns, writer "of the best Scotch song ever Scotland saw"), Bishop Skinner attempted, gradually and tactfully, to loose the Episcopal Church from its impossible moorings.[78] The English Nonjurors, he thought, ought to be abandoned, and the Stuarts upon the death of "Charles III"—an event shortly expected—should be disavowed. Once his communion had recognized the Hanoverians and established friendly relations with the Church of England, repeal of the penal laws would follow, permitting Scotland's Episcopalians to operate elsewhere than in the shadows.[79] By 1804 Skinner's proposals, for the most part, had been successfully carried out. The first impetus toward their execution had come about as a result of the consecration of Samuel Seabury.

The suggestion that Seabury, if unsuccessful in England, should seek episcopal Orders from the Scottish bishops had been made even before he departed New York. In reporting his election to the Reverend Samuel Parker of Boston's Trinity Church, Daniel Fogg of Brooklyn (Parker's Harvard classmate) declared that the clergy had "even gone so far as to instruct" Seabury to take this action.[80] However, the wording of the addresses and testimonials argues against anything as definite as instructions. Seabury's correspondence with Scotland likewise makes no mention of any such direction. Since Fogg was not at the Woodbury Convention, he very likely misunderstood what was related to him. But in light of his statement, it is certain that an application to Scotland was at least suggested.

Seabury first approached the northern episcopate through the agency of two Scots living in London, the Reverend George Bisset (Aberdeen, 1759) and James Elphinston. Bisset, a Loyalist refugee and former rector of Trinity Church, Newport, appears to have been a native of Peterhead in Aberdeenshire, where Bishop Kilgour was living in 1783. Before his emigration to Rhode Island, he served as an assistant in a well-known school kept at Kensington by the eccentric Elphinston, a minor literary figure and a promoter of phonetic spelling. Elphinston's father was an Episcopal clergyman; his mother (cousin to the first rector of Trinity, Newport) was the niece of a Bishop of Orkney; he himself would shortly marry the niece of Bishop Falconar.[81]

Writing to the Reverend John Allan of Edinburgh in November, 1783, Elphinston asked him to secure from the Scottish bishops an answer to a question posed by Bisset (described simply as

"An American Clergyman, whom I have long known"). Bisset's "momentous enquiry," written on a separate slip of paper, was this: "Whether consecration can be obtained in Scotland, by an already dignified, and well-vouched American clergyman, now at London, for the purpose of perpetuating the Episcopal Reformed Church in America, particularly in *Connecticut*."[82] Allan forwarded both letter and inquiry to Bishop Kilgour, who thereupon sent out copies to his colleagues.

Months before the reception of these documents the Scots episcopate had canvassed the question of consecrating an American bishop. For this was not the first time the proposal had been made: in October, 1782, the Reverend Dr. George Berkeley, already mentioned in connection with pre-Revolutionary plans for a colonial episcopate, had come forward with a truly fantastic scheme. To Bishop Skinner, Berkeley (then a temporary resident of St. Andrews) suggested the consecration of an itinerant missionary bishop, who, like a latter-day Augustine or Boniface, would suddenly appear upon the American shore, there to "be reverently and gladly received by the poor Protestant Episcopalians, as Angels of God, nay even as Christ Jesus." Philadelphia, Berkeley thought, would be a likely spot ("The Quakers are a tolerating people"); for a candidate, he had in mind George Gleig, subsequently a Scottish bishop and Primus.[83] Skinner communicated this proposal to Bishops Kilgour and Petrie. It was, to be sure, totally unacceptable, but the depressed Episcopalians had no desire to offend by a curt refusal an important English ecclesiastic who seemed desirous of their friendship. Although Skinner gently put forward the obvious difficulties, the doctor's romantic enthusiasm would not down. Finally he quashed the scheme by neglecting to answer Berkeley's latest letter.[84] Their correspondence, however, had elicited Skinner's statement that should the Americans apply to Scotland for an episcopate, " 'tis not to be doubted but the Bishops of this Church, on a proper application, will think it their duty to extend the precious benefit to them."[85]

Bisset's inquiry, therefore, met with a generally good reception. Providing his colleagues agreed and the candidate (soon identified as "a Dr. Seabury . . . a man eminent for his piety and learning, but of distinguished courage and resolution")[86] could produce proper vouchers, Primus Kilgour was willing to consecrate. Bishop Petrie would do the same when assured that Seabury possessed the proper qualifications and Catholic principles. "The very prospect of the thing rejoices me greatly," he informed the Primus, "and, considering the sacred *depositum* committed to us, I do not see how we can account to our Great Lord and Master if we neglect such an opportunity of promoting His truth and enlarging the borders of His Church." Bishop Falconar's sentiments, however, were directly opposite; he would have nothing to do with the proposal. Still, the Bishop of Edinburgh prescribed to no one: "every gentleman," he declared, "may act as he thinks proper." The opinion of Bishop Rose gave Kilgour more uneasiness. "I have no objection to lay my hands upon this American doctor but one," the old Jacobite declared, "and that is, his having got his orders from the schismatical Church of England." A personal interview, he added, would probably clear up this difficulty. Informed of Rose's statement, Petrie tried to dispel the Primus' misgivings. If "tenderly handled," the point raised by their brother might be adjusted easily, since Dr. Seabury, "I am persuaded, is acting in diametrical opposition to Erastian principles."[87]

Bishop Skinner's attitude was characteristic. While as favorably disposed to the consecration as Kilgour or Petrie, he wondered why Seabury had failed in England. Were the reasons such as might expose the Scottish Episcopalians to danger if their bishops should act? George Berkeley, who had learned of Seabury's mission and was, as usual, insistent that the Scottish bishops consecrate immediately, had written Skinner shortly after the receipt of Elphinston's letter, declaring that the King, some Cabinet members, all the bishops except possibly His Grace of St. Asaph, "and all the learned and respectable clergy in our Church" would rejoice—"at least secretly"—if Scotland acceded to Seabury's request. If this were true, the bishop queried, why had that Church refused him? Berkeley's reply showed that the English bishops had not publicized Seabury's application. A close friend of Archbishop Moore, Berkeley supposed himself well-informed; so far as he knew, there had been no request "for the consecration of a Bishop in England to exercise his function *in partibus fanaticorum*." The Ministry, he insisted, would not resent action by Skinner and his colleagues. Dr. Cooper, "Preacher at the new English Chapel at Edinburgh," could vouch for Seabury's character. Let the Scottish bishops interpose, then, before English Dissenters and American sectaries should have had time to spin their schemes![88]

On December 13, Bishop Kilgour answered Bisset's "momentous enquiry" in the affirmative. Unaware of Berkeley's latest declaration, he took this decisive action never doubting Moore's rejection of Seabury. To the Reverend John Allan he wrote that all the bishops except Falconar ("whose declining state may well excuse him from taking any concern") had received with joy the proposal for "conveying Protestant Episcopacy to America, and enlarging the Borders of the Church of Christ." When satisfied as to Dr. Seabury's piety, learning, and principles, they would readily concur in his promotion. That this might be done, Kilgour hoped to see the doctor in Scotland as soon as should be convenient. In the meantime, he wanted to know whether Seabury's proposed consecration was merely his own idea or a scheme backed by other American clergymen. Also—and the positioning of the question showed its comparative unimportance in the Primus' eyes—what were the reasons for his lack of success in London?[89]

This letter (forwarded through Elphinston) must have reached Seabury about Christmas. But pleased though he was at the favorable outcome of his overtures, he would not act upon Kilgour's invitation until he learned the result of the Connecticut Churchmen's application to the Assembly. So long as the possibility of an English consecration remained, the candidate had no intention of setting out for Scotland. January of 1784 passed without any word. The February and March packets likewise produced no letters. Not until late April, by which time his patience was almost exhausted, did Seabury receive the necessary information.[90]

This long wait had resulted from the clergy's failure to learn of Seabury's difficulties. For some reason, the letters which he dispatched between August 10 and October 20 were delayed in transit. When they finally reached Connecticut, notifications went out, and shortly afterwards, on January 14, 1784, a thin Convention, attended by only six men, assembled at Wallingford in the parsonage of Samuel Andrews. This meeting chose Leaming, Jarvis, and Hubbard a committee to confer with leading members of the Assembly—then sitting at New Haven—on the question of the application Seabury desired.[91] Since the Assembly, which was engaged in a revision of the laws, had approved an act putting all Christian congregations on the same legal footing as those of the Standing Order and allowing them to tax their members for the clergy's support,[92] prospects appeared good. Hubbard and Leaming immediately went to work, sounding out deputies and assistants, the Secretary of the state, and even Governor Trumbull. The proposed episcopate was fully explained and Seabury acknowledged to be the candidate.

The cordiality which they encountered somewhat surprised the Convention's emissaries. That a bishop should be consecrated for Connecticut and that Seabury should be that bishop was perfectly agreeable to the legislators. But being canny politicians, they advised against any application for formal permission. The law placing all denominations on a level, they declared, comprehended Seabury's position. "Let a Bishop come; by that act, he will stand upon the same ground that the rest of the clergy do, or the church at large." An application of the type suggested, on the other hand, would arouse jealousies, giving room for the charge that Episcopalians were seeking a favored position. Opposition to a bishop might be excited. All in all, it was better to rest on the recently approved law. And this, when subjoined to their personal declarations, should satisfy the English authorities.[93]

Reporting these statements to the bishop-elect, Leaming, Jarvis, and Hubbard declared that they fully agreed with them. "Now if the opinion of the Governor & other members of the council explicitly given, in agreement with the most respectable Members among the representatives, who must be admitted to be competent Judges of their own civil polity, is reasonably sufficient to remove all scruples about the concurrence of the legislature, we cannot imagine that objection, will any longer have a place in the minds of the archbishops." A certified copy of the act in question would be forwarded by Leaming.[94]

Armed with this letter, Seabury, late in April, called upon the Archbishop of York. But before he could extract an opinion from Markham, the arrival of company abruptly concluded the interview. Advised by His Grace to show the communication at once to his brethren of Canterbury and London, the candidate set out for Lambeth and Fulham. On the way he paid a call on the Bishop of Oxford, a prelate who had shown him much attention and of whose abilities he had a very high opinion. Seabury emerged from this visit somewhat shaken: Bishop Butler, though full of compliments for the Connecticut clergy, did not believe their letter gave sufficient grounds on which to proceed. Fulham, however, restored his hopes. Old Bishop Lowth was approaching his dotage, and it took much effort on Seabury's part to make him understand the matter. Still, after he had grasped the new developments, Lowth declared that in his opinion every objection had now been met. An Act of Parliament removing the impediment of the state oaths, he supposed, could be easily obtained. And he hoped that His Grace of Canterbury would see the affair in the same light.[95]

After an unsuccessful attempt the following morning, Seabury obtained an interview with Archbishop Moore on May 1. The primate coolly observed that the permission spoken of in the committee's letter was only that of individuals, not of the Assembly in its corporate capacity, nor were the Episcopal laity joined in the application for consecration. Seabury found it difficult to be polite. The letter, he declared, spoke for itself. Had His Grace demanded the concurrence of the laity the previous autumn, it might easily have been obtained. If there were insuperable obstacles, he would drop the whole matter, but he hoped the archbishop would consult further with York and London. Moore replied he would do this when his health improved; just then he was very unwell. Seeing it no time to press the matter, Seabury took his leave, promising he would send back a copy of the committee's letter.[96]

The candidate felt discouraged. Yet he kept up his hopes, particularly since Moore, in discussing the Nova Scotia episcopate with Chandler on May 3, affirmed he would do everything in his power to obtain a bishop for Connecticut. "Upon the whole, you will perceive that your letter has done great service of itself," Seabury informed the Convention's committee, "& it has enabled me to open a new battery, which I will mount with the heaviest cannon & mortars I can muster, & will play them as vigorously as possible." He added that he was anxiously awaiting the Connecticut act supposedly being sent by Leaming, since the archbishop required it before he could take any further steps.[97]

By the end of May Seabury was frantic. In subsequent interviews, Moore had reaffirmed his stand that he must have the act before he could approach Parliament for a statute dispensing with the state oaths. But weeks went by and no word came from Leaming. If the act failed to arrive before Parliament rose, Seabury did not know what he would do. His difficulties seemed endless. "This is certainly the worst country in the world to do business in," he complained to Jarvis. "I wonder how they get along at any rate." Still, if only the Connecticut law would come, he could push matters to a crisis and decide the affair one way or the other.[98]

Finally, on June 17, the long-awaited act was received. Seabury considered it "liberal" and thought it would answer every purpose—if "fairly interpreted and abided by." Both archbishops believed the law removed the principal objections on the score of interference in American affairs. As for the much discussed Parliamentary act, although Moore thought it necessary, he admitted the majority of the bishops judged otherwise. Presumably these prelates were thinking in terms of a royal dispensation, not of the revolutionary solution Seabury had devised. To Jarvis he wrote: "I have declared my opinion, which is, that as there is no law relative to a Bishop who is to reside in a foreign state, the Archbishops are left to the general laws of the Christian Church, and have no need either of the King's leave or dispensation."[99] Bishop Petrie had not been mistaken when he observed that the American candidate was no supporter of Erastian principles!

Moore promised to consult the Attorney General and Solicitor General, both of whom seem to have agreed with him as to the need for Parliamentary approval. Whereupon the archbishop, in an hour-long meeting on July 21, gave Seabury encouragement that a clause permitting his consecration would find a place in the pending bill providing for the ordination of American deacons and priests, by the English bishops, without the taking of the usual oaths. Lord Chancellor Thurlow, the primate believed, had been persuaded to give his approval. In a few days Moore was to discuss the whole affair with Prime Minister Pitt. He also would explain it to those persons from whom he expected opposition. He confidently hoped that matters would end to Seabury's satisfaction, and when he had further information for him a note would be dispatched. "I am flattered with every prospect of success," the candidate noted in his letter of July 26, "but everything here is attended with uncertainty till it is actually done."[100]

Seabury's skepticism proved to be well-founded. Early in August the expected note from Lambeth arrived at his lodgings. Believing the matter had ended unsuccessfully—the communication was short and reserved in tone—he found that this was, indeed, the case. His Grace expressed great regret. He had done all he could, but the Cabinet would not allow the bill in question to sanction the consecration of an American bishop. Seabury inquired the reasons. Moore listed seven: the Cabinet could not take up such a proposal until the Nova Scotia episcopate was settled; they could not act unless the Congress requested a bishop or at least formally acquiesced in the sending of one; Connecticut was but a single state, and its consent had not been explicitly given; the application was only from the clergy, unsupported by any laymen; the Episcopal laity in the United States were averse to having resident bishops; the country was not divided into dioceses, nor was there any provision made for bishops; since a bishop had never been sent before 1775, it would look strange to dispatch one now and probably would create or augment anti-British feeling.[101] Could Dr. Seabury, the archbishop inquired, possibly surmount these objections?

Dr. Seabury stood in great danger of losing his temper. The interview continued for an hour and a half, and several times Moore demanded to know what the candidate meant by his expressions. Nova Scotia, Seabury declared, might be supplied with a bishop whenever the Cabinet chose. Since the Articles of Confederation prohibited Congress' interference in religious matters, any recourse to that body would infringe Connecticut's sovereignty. As for Connecticut's consent, the act he had shown the archbishop was equal to the most explicit declaration. The Connecticut clergy and not the laity being under the bishop's governance, they alone were the proper persons to make application. Connecticut's Churchmen desired an episcopate; the sentiments of "the Laity to the Southward" he was not concerned with. His diocese would consist of the Episcopal congregations of his state, who "in the knowledge of their religion & in attachment to it . . . were not exceeded by the people in any part of England, not even excepting the diocese of Canterbury." Salary arrangements concerned him, but they concerned no one else, and, as President of the S.P.G., Moore could himself remove this obstacle by appropriating to his support part of the legacies for American bishops. True, no bishop had been sent before the Revolution, but "having neglected a necessary duty for almost a Century was a very bad reason for continuing the neglect." The whole bill of objections, Seabury asserted, was founded in such ignorance and ill policy that it could only be intended as a flat refusal. Consequently, America's Churchmen would seek consecration elsewhere. As they parted, Moore requested him to use his influence to prevent such action. Seabury replied he could not do so without an absolute promise of succeeding in England. He would, however, call on the primate if he received any further information from America.[102]

"Unconnected, unsupported, unbefriended—nothing to rely on but the goodness of my cause & my own resolution, I have failed," the bishop-elect wrote Jarvis, "but I have no reason to blame myself." With the pre-Revolutionary battle for American bishops still fresh in his mind, Seabury had no difficulty piecing together an explanation. The influence of English Dissenters, particularly the Reverend Dr. Richard Price, who enjoyed close relations with Pitt, was, he believed, responsible for his rejection. Had North and Fox remained in office (their Ministry had fallen in December, 1783), he must have succeeded, since they allowed Moore full authority in managing ecclesiastical concerns.[103] To Churchmen the explanation appeared plausible; in fact, it had no validity. The events surrounding the subsequent consecration at Lambeth of William White and Samuel Provoost show that Pitt's decision of 1784 was based primarily on a desire to avoid giving any cause for offense to the newly independent nation. It is not too much to say that without the formal approval of Pennsylvania and New York—the states for whose churches they were consecrated—and the backing of officials of the Confederation government, notably John Adams, Minister to the Court of St. James, White and Provoost would have met with the same fate.[104]

Once hopes of an English consecration were at an end, Seabury again turned to Scotland. He had prepared for this eventuality in the winter and spring of 1784; writing to Leaming, he informed him of his negotiations with the northern episcopate and requested the clergy's opinion of a Scottish application.[105] As late as the end of August Seabury had received no reply to these letters. The reason, in all likelihood, was closely connected with the ministers' financial situation. Few if any of them had private resources, while only Hubbard, it was reported, had a congregation able and willing to furnish an adequate salary.[106] For this reason, pastors considered the continuation of S.P.G. stipends essential; the concern on this score as expressed in a petition of the Woodbury Convention[107] found an echo in many letters of the years 1783-85.[108] Now, should they direct Seabury to proceed to Scotland to receive consecration from a church of whose existence all but a few Englishmen were ignorant, and which was regarded, by most of those who knew of it, simply as a little knot of die-hard Jacobites,[109] could they expect the S.P.G. to continue them on its rolls? Better to rely on their candidate's well-known resolution. If consecration could be obtained in Scotland, Seabury would seek it. And having had no hand in the matter, how could they be blamed?

Seabury consulted various English and Loyalist clergymen and two lay members of the Society, all of whom approved his plans.[110] Accordingly, on the last day of August, he renewed his application to the northern bishops. In a letter to Myles Cooper, intended for their inspection, he excused himself for not having taken earlier advantage of their invitation, explained his failure in London, and sketched the situation of Connecticut's Episcopal Church. Should the Scottish episcopate now grant his request —"that a free valid and purely Ecclesiastical Episcopacy may, from them, pass into the western world"—thousands of Churchmen would bless them. Seabury believed he could conduct matters so that the chance of the Society's withdrawing the stipends of the Connecticut clergy might be next to nothing. As for himself, if his own stipend were in danger, he was ready to part with it. Since he wished to return to America before the winter storms, he hoped for a speedy answer.[111]

Cooper gave this letter to the Reverend John Allan, along with a short note attesting that "Dr. Seabury is recommended by several worthy Clergymen in Connecticut as a person worthy of Promotion, and to whom they are willing to Submit as a Bishop."[112] Allan forwarded these papers to the Primus and also sent copies to Bishop Petrie. The Scottish bishops had never understood that Seabury's original overtures were merely tentative, dependent upon the outcome of further developments in Connecticut and England; still, this renewed application was generally well received. "As Dr. Seabury had been so long silent, I reckoned the Affair had been dropped," Bishop Kilgour wrote to Petrie, "but as he accounts for his Conduct in so open & candid a Manner, I still think we should not deny his Request."[113] Presuming his three colleagues would agree with this position (Bishop Falconar had recently died), the Primus, without waiting for Bishop Rose's opinion, drafted a reply to Allan in Edinburgh. The Episcopal College, he declared, would be happy to grant Dr. Seabury bishop's Orders, although they were concerned he should have taken so long to apply to them and wished he had corresponded directly with one of their number in an affair of such moment. Because the Primus could not come to Edinburgh and Bishop Petrie's state of health did not permit a long journey, Aberdeen must be the place of consecration. The Primus hoped Dr. Seabury would send word at once of the date of his coming, so that all arrangements might be made. "May God grant us a happy meeting," the aged prelate concluded, "and direct all to the Honour and Glory of his Name and to the good of his Church."[114]

This letter, channeled through Myles Cooper, reached Seabury in London on October 11. Two days later he dispatched an answer directly to Kilgour, in which he thanked the Episcopal College "for the kind and Christian attention which they shew to the destitute and suffering Church in North America in general, and to that of Connecticut in particular," informing them, at the same time, that he would arrive at Aberdeen by November 10.[115] The bishop-elect was now fully determined on his Scottish venture and, either shortly before the sending of this letter or immediately thereafter, notified the Archbishop of Canterbury, doubtless in very tactful terms, that His Grace's last-minute effort to dissuade him had failed.

Moore made his move—and a very clumsy one it was—sometime in September, after Seabury had renewed his application to Scotland and before he had received any word as to its reception. From the S.P.G. Secretary the candidate learned that a mission in New Brunswick was available if he desired it. Directed to make this offer by the archbishop, the secretary pressed for an early answer. Seabury, uncertain as to whether the northern bishops would consecrate him, could not flatly refuse; if he failed of becoming Bishop of Connecticut, he must support his family in some fashion. For this reason, he accepted the proposition, telling the secretary at the same time that he considered a New Brunswick mission unequal to what he could rightfully expect from the Ministry and must, if possible, secure something better from them. (Commenting on this statement, he later remarked: "This I said in full confidence that my merit toward this government was at least equal to any man in my station: & from government I never had before nor have I since, been favoured with the least notice or attention.")[116]

Shortly afterwards, Seabury presented the Loyalist Commission with a claim for temporary support. While admitting his great services, its members did not believe the Treasury should pay him an annual allowance. But since his funds were so low that he could depart for New Brunswick only with much difficulty (which, he declared, he wished to do unless the Ministry provided for him in England), they recommended he be given a passage or twenty-five pounds for that purpose. However, as soon as Kilgour's letter arrived, Seabury laid aside all thoughts of an English living or a frontier mission. Moore received word that he had withdrawn his acceptance of the secretary's offer.[117]

Plans for the consecration at Aberdeen—set for Sunday, November 14—proceeded swiftly after the reception of Seabury's letter to the Primus. The only discordant note was introduced by Bishop Rose, who now stubbornly refused to take any part in the proceedings. Testy and suspicious (and not always quite coherent) the old Jacobite thought he detected plans for a sell-out to the Hanoverians. According to Bishop Skinner, the fact that the bishop-elect had communicated his request by means of Myles Cooper—the most prominent of those "licensed" Episcopal clergymen who did not acknowledge the authority of the Scottish episcopate[118]—particularly annoyed Rose. His feelings had been hurt, justifiably it would seem, by Kilgour's failure to wait for his opinion before replying. He also thought Seabury had treated the College shabbily and pointed out that "we have nothing but his *ipse Dixit* for all that he says, and the only recommendation he has [submitted] is Dr. Cooper and his own." Despite his colleagues' repeated urging, Rose could not be persuaded to come to Aberdeen, though he did agree that they might consecrate. Such recalcitrance visibly irritated the usually imperturbable Skinner. "If all the Bishops of the Church were to act agreeably to the Notions entertained by his Reverence of Dunblane & Dunkeld," he wrote Petrie, "the Apostolic Succession I fear would soon be at an End."[119]

Seabury knew nothing of this dissension when on Sunday, October 24,[120] he set out for Aberdeen. Frank and open as ever, he had no intention of sneaking out of London: the day before he left, he called upon both archbishops. Markham told him if he went through with his plans the S.P.G. would certainly discharge him. Moore, too, tried to dissuade the candidate, declaring that a Scottish consecration might create jealousies and schisms. The Moravian bishops in the United States, he apprehended, would thereby be induced to ordain Episcopal ministers, and the Philadelphia clergy would be encouraged to carry White's proposals into effect.[121] "I was told that I was *precipitate*," Seabury reported, "that I ought to wait, that things might mend. But *when*, or *how* they were to mend I was not told. Only general hopes & future expectations were held out to me."[122]

The primates' remonstrances Seabury easily discounted, since he believed they acted under pressure from the Cabinet and did not, in fact, speak their true sentiments.[123] This conviction must have been strengthened when he discovered Moore had privately assured the Scottish bishops that they ran no risk. Skinner, always more concerned about this point than his colleagues, had written George Berkeley and probably George Horne, Dean of Canterbury, requesting them, so it appears, to sound the archbishop. Berkeley thereupon informed Moore of the proposed consecration and begged him to send word at once if he thought the performance of it would endanger the bishops; if, however, His Grace believed no cause for alarm existed, a communication would be unnecessary. To Skinner, Berkeley reported that his letter produced no reply.[124]

Seabury traveled by way of Edinburgh, where he made the acquaintance of the Reverend John Allan and presumably spent some time with Myles Cooper.[125] At Edinburgh, too, he had the good fortune to receive a letter from Leaming, Jarvis, and Hubbard, still operating as a committee of the Connecticut Convention. Worried because he could produce no evidence that the clergy approved his applying to Scotland, he had determined to surmount this objection somehow should the Scottish episcopate introduce it.[126] But now—with the letter and an accompanying communication in hand—the possibility of such a difficulty vanished. Reluctantly, no doubt, because of fears of S.P.G. disapproval, and in general terms which protected the Connecticut missionaries as much as possible, the committee at a very late date had endorsed a Scottish consecration. Declaring that Seabury must come to America in episcopal Orders, they affirmed "their reliance on his zeal and fortitude to prosecute the affair in such way as he can." Secretary Jarvis in a separate letter wrote: "you may depend upon it you will be kindly treated in this State, let your ordination come from what quarter it will." In his packet he also included a second copy of Connecticut's law on the subject of religious equality.[127]

Filing these papers with earlier letters and testimonials, Seabury pushed on to Aberdeen. He arrived there Friday evening, November 5, and the next morning called upon Bishop Skinner, a resident of the town since 1775. Skinner took an instant liking to Seabury. "He seems to be truly Pious in his Sentiments," he informed Bishop Petrie, "fair, open & candid in his Disposition & without any of that Duplicity, which too often marks the Characters of those, who have much to do with this designing World."[128] Firm in his judgment, Skinner refused to alter it when, two days later, an excited letter arrived from the Primus, enclosing a protest against Seabury's advancement.[129]

The candidate and the bishop had earlier discussed Aberdeen's famous son, the Reverend Dr. William Smith, late of Philadelphia. Smith's ambitions lay behind the protest; it was the work of Alexander Murray,[130] the protégé he had attempted to slip into the Johnson Hall mission in 1767 after the clergy of New York and New Jersey recommended Seabury for the post.[131] Now a Loyalist refugee in London, Murray knew that Maryland's pastors had chosen Smith for their bishop in August, 1783.[132] Apparently he feared that if Seabury received episcopal Orders in Scotland and returned to America to consecrate other bishops by himself (a valid though extralegal procedure, the canons requiring three prelates for the rite),[133] his friend might never be raised to the episcopate. Murray was acquainted with the New York clergy's dislike of Smith, dating from the conventions of the 1760's; he perhaps knew, too, that Seabury felt the greatest contempt for the ex-provost, as a result of the now Loyalist, now Patriot stance which had eventually cost him his academic position.[134] At any rate, he believed Seabury was "Dr. Smith's avowed enemy."[135]

To stop Seabury's consecration, Murray, on October 28, sent a letter to an old schoolmate, the Reverend William Seller of Inverugie. He reported what was true and what Seabury readily acknowledged, namely, that both archbishops had earnestly advised against his going to Scotland. Murray, however, added certain embellishments; apparently they were of his own devising. The English primates, he affirmed, considered Seabury an unfit person for promotion, especially because of his active Loyalism. On this account (and for other reasons) Seabury would render the episcopal office suspect in America and would himself be entirely slighted. His whole course was precipitate: in the autumn, Dr. Smith was expected in England, "with recommendations from the States of America to be consecrated a Bishop." Implying that the Scots bishops would be in danger if they acted, Murray held out the possibility "of some immediate union, or better understanding, at least" with the English episcopate if they proceeded no further in the matter without corresponding with Archbishop Moore. He even went so far as to play upon the poverty of the northern prelates. If no correspondence with Canterbury could be opened, and if it were thought necessary to send someone from Scotland, instead of consecrating Seabury, the bishops should dispatch one of their own number, who would "find the candidates for Holy Orders abundantly liberal, making him donations from 10 to 20 guineas each at least, and in the course of the first year he would have no fewer than 200 to order for the 13 States."[136]

The Primus was inclined to discount this information (which Seller immediately had relayed), yet he could not shake off fears that there might be something to it. Skinner sought to convince him such apprehensions were groundless. When told of the contents of the protest, Seabury, he reported, had betrayed no alarm "and very little surprise, after he found that it proceeded from a partizan of Dr. Smith's." This behavior inspired Skinner's confidence, as did Seabury's candid account of his parting interviews with the archbishops. Kilgour, his coadjutor insisted, need fear nothing from that quarter: "tho' they dare not openly approve, . . . they have not the most distant thought of resenting the step he is now taking." As for the protest's personal reflections, the candidate's ample and enthusiastic testimonials made it impossible to give them any weight. Moreover, a short acquaintance with Seabury would convince the Primus that "they are ill founded and malicious, and serve only to place his character in a more amiable light, when contrasted with that of his unworthy rival (for his rival he seems to be) Dr. Smith, a man of no principle, honour, or integrity, and who, by all acounts, would be a disgrace to the Episcopal character."[137]

Steadied by this report, Kilgour decided to proceed, and on Friday afternoon, November 12, arrived at Skinner's house. Arthur Petrie, who had only a short distance to travel from Meiklefolla (like many of the Scottish bishops of the period, he resided outside his diocese), put in an appearance about the same time. After introductions, the three prelates and Seabury spent the rest of the day getting acquainted. Next morning they examined the documents he carried and completed plans for Sunday's rite, Kilgour having earlier expressed a wish that everything possible should be done "to add to the Solemnety of the important & sacred Action."[138]

The lack of any episcopal revenue compelled the bishops to seek their support by serving as ordinary pastors. To accommodate his congregation, Skinner had erected a large dwelling in

Long Acre Lane, using the upper two floors (or rather what appeared from the street to be such) as a place for worship.[139] Seabury's consecration took place in this chapel. Capable of holding between five hundred and six hundred people, it was crowded for the occasion with Episcopal laity and also a considerable number of presbyters, who, as one of them expressed it, found "myself possessed with a very strong desire to feast my eyes with the sight of the first orthodox Bishop of America."[140]

The service opened with Morning Prayer, the day being the twenty-second Sunday after Trinity. There followed a celebration of the Holy Eucharist, whether according to the English liturgy of 1662 or the Scots of 1764 is not known. After the recitation of the Nicene Creed, Bishop Skinner mounted the pulpit and preached on the apostolic commission from Matthew 28:18-20. A typical exposition of the High Church doctrine of episcopal succession, the sermon also contained a slashing attack on Erastian principles, sharpened, when it appeared in print, by the addition of various notes.[141] English friends of Scotland's Episcopal Church criticized the production as reflecting unfairly on their own episcopate,[142] and even a Scottish Episcopal clergyman censured it in *The Gentleman's Magazine* while defending Seabury's consecrators against an anonymous assailant.[143] The preacher, however, did not care. Not intending his discourse "for the Meridian of London," Skinner was at no pains, so he informed Jonathan Boucher, "to adapt it to the notions that are cherished under the warm Sunshine of civil Establishment."[144]

The sermon prefaced the actual consecration, performed after the manner of the English Ordinal. Kilgour, Petrie, and Skinner, dressed, it is believed, only in black gowns and bands, the vestments customarily worn by the Scots Episcopal clergy[145] (and resembling, for this reason, nothing so much as an ordaining council of New England Congregational ministers), stood in a semicircle with Seabury kneeling before them. The Reverend Alexander Jolly, confidant of Bishop Petrie, held the folio Prayer

Book from which the consecrators read.[146] When they had imposed their hands, the eucharistic liturgy continued. The proceedings ended with the bestowal of the episcopal blessing by the newly consecrated bishop.

That same Sunday Bishop Seabury preached at Evening Prayer in the Long Acre chapel. Scots Episcopalians, accustomed to a restrained delivery, were somewhat surprised by his earnest manner. The American bishop also used more gestures than was common in Scotland and emphasized his points by stabbing with a white handkerchief.[147] Unlike Skinner's sermon, this one was not printed, nor is it now to be located among the many manuscript discourses preserved in Seabury's papers.

Monday found the four bishops still together at Skinner's house, engaged in a work the Scots episcopate considered an essential part of the whole transaction. This was the approving of what was described, in the document itself, as a "CONCORDATE, or BOND OF UNION, between the Catholic remainder of the antient Church of Scotland, and the now rising Church in the State of Connecticut."[148] From the time of Seabury's first negotiations in 1783-84, Kilgour and his colleagues had envisioned such an agreement, which would establish intercommunion between the two bodies, allowing Scots in Connecticut and Yankees in Scotland (a rather small group of travelers, in either case) to participate fully in each other's worship.[149] The idea seems to have originated with the Primus, yet the instrument was mostly Skinner's work.[150] When preparing it, he examined some earlier agreements, in particular a concordat proposed by the Nonjuring bishops to the Patriarch of Constantinople in 1716. Two of its articles he incorporated into his draft.[151] The whole included seven articles, which, as he admitted, "might have been fewer in number, & comprised in a shorter Form, but I thought it well to branch them out, & enlarge them as I have Done, to give the Transaction the greater Appearance of suitable Gravity & Importance."[152]

Seabury seems to have given Skinner's production blanket approval; the articles as signed by the four bishops suggest no additions or deletions on his part. Their content reflected, not merely the desire for proper terms of union, but also Skinner's wish to secure Connecticut's support of measures and propositions directly applicable to the peculiar position of Scotland's Episcopal Church. The second article, for example, after declaring the Church to be Christ's Mystical Body and its chief governors the bishops, went on to affirm that lay deprivation could not affect the episcopate's spiritual authority—an obvious reference to 1689. This same sentiment can be traced in article III. To its declaration of full communion between Scotland and Connecticut was subjoined a lengthy condemnation of those "licensed" clergymen regarded by Skinner and his brethren as "schismatical Intruders . . . and uncommissioned Disturbers." Article IV of the concordat likewise revealed the predicament of the northern bishops. In order to establish a close conformity in the worship of the two churches and, at the same time, to obviate the difficulties arising from different forms of civil government, it called for a "prudent Generality in their public Prayers." How useful this declaration might become, should a repeal of the penal laws be sought while it was still necessary, because of the prejudices of old persons, to avoid praying for George III by name, Skinner could easily see; if the English authorities pressed him on this point, he would argue the sacredness of Connecticut obligations!

Despite such skill in drafting, the concordat was to prove of little benefit to Skinner and his colleagues. Not so the consecration which had produced it. This event triggered their Church's emergence from obscurity and isolation, for it created valuable contacts south of the Tweed. Scottish Episcopal theology subsequently excited the admiration, Scottish poverty and legal disabilities the indignation, of William Stevens, a leading London layman, and his cousin, Dean George Horne of Canterbury, after 1790 Bishop of Norwich. Equally sympathetic were Jonathan

Boucher, Sir James Allan Park, the Reverend George Gaskin, and the noted theologian William Jones of Nayland, the last of whom enjoyed a Scottish correspondence well before 1784. These individuals, High Churchmen all, aided the northern episcopate with money and advice (at the same time extending help to Seabury in Connecticut).[153] Their part in agitating the repeal of the penal laws—finally secured in 1792—was particularly important.[154]

Seabury remained with Bishop Skinner for several days after the signing of the concordat. Then, taking with him one of two duplicates engrossed on large vellum sheets, as well as his Latin certificate of consecration, two attested copies of the Scottish succession since 1688, and a letter exhorting the Connecticut clergy to receive him and comply with the concordat's terms,[155] he set out on his return journey to London. The bishop traveled by slow stages, stopping with presbyters along the way and enjoying what might have been termed a triumphal progress had the phrase not been so inapplicable to the reception Scottish Episcopalians could provide. By November 24 he was at Dundee, guest of John Strachan (Bishop of Brechin, 1787-1810) and Strachan's friends.[156] Three days later he reached Edinburgh, where he remained until December 7, visiting the Reverend John Allan and his brother, the Reverend Alexander Allan, William Abernethy Drummond (Bishop of Brechin, 1787, of Edinburgh, 1787-1805, of Glasgow, 1805-9), and other clergymen. Had Myles Cooper occupied his reading desk, the concordat's prohibition against attending services of "licensed" ministers might have caused Seabury some embarrassment. But Cooper was just then recovering from a nearly fatal illness.[157]

Everywhere the American bishop excited the most flattering comments. "From all that I could observe or judge of him," Bishop Petrie declared to Thomas Bowdler, leader of the tiny group of Scottish-governed English Nonjurors, he might "with becoming dignity fill an Archiepiscopal chair."[158] William Abernethy

Drummond, writing to Seabury after his departure from Edinburgh, spoke of "that *something* in you which drew the attention, & attracted the esteem of all who had the pleasure to approach you." He added: "In fact, I can assure you, upon my honour, that I have never seen, nor heard, of one single person, male or female, who had the happiness of seeing you either in publick or private, that did not entertain a very favourable opinion both of your head & heart." Bishop Rose, however, remained obdurate. "The Countenance," he informed his brother Petrie, "is a very false glass, to judge of one's Disposition."[159]

After the warm enthusiasm of Scotland, Seabury felt more keenly the chill in London's ecclesiastical atmosphere. Dean Horne congratulated him on his consecration, and the Bishop of Lincoln, brother to the Lord Chancellor, reportedly approved it. But both archbishops, according to all accounts, were much displeased.[160] Distressed and a bit angered by this situation ("Why should I be censured for obtaining that consecration in Scotland, which political motives, if not party prejudices, prevented me from obtaining here?"),[161] Seabury kept at a distance, "that the first Impressions might wear off, & cool Judgement resume its Authority." Only on the eve of his departure from London did he call upon the primates. He found them, in each case, in a friendly mood and willing, without any embarrassment, to discuss his Scottish journey. Markham and Moore believed both Seabury and the northern episcopate had acted from the best motives. They regretted he had proceeded as he had done but hoped none of the consequences they dreaded would occur. For Connecticut's Episcopal Church and its bishop they wished success and prosperity.[162]

These interviews must have strengthened Seabury's hopes for a continuation of S.P.G. stipends to the Connecticut clergy, himself included. While still at Edinburgh, he had written a long letter on the subject to Jonathan Boucher, expressing a wish to remain in the Society's service and affirming that his discharge as a missionary would produce a schism between the Church of England and that of Connecticut. "In truth, Sir," he observed with a certain pathos, "it is not the loss of 50£ per Annum that I dread, though that is an object of some importance to a man who has nothing, but the consequences that must ensue—the total alienation of regard and affections."[163] This letter, as well as subsequent ones,[164] emphasized that he had entered into no political agreements with the Scottish bishops and wished to form the Connecticut Church as near to the English model as was possible. That this desire might appear to conflict with the Scottish concordat, strangely enough, did not occur to Seabury; when the only person to whom he showed the document in London (probably Chandler) advised him to conceal it until the S.P.G. had come to some decision about the stipends, he could not see the need for any such precaution.[165]

The question of the stipends was still undetermined when Seabury sailed for America. He had expected the matter to be canvassed at the meeting of the Society held December 17, just after his arrival in London, but nothing was done then,[166] nor did any discussion take place at the January or February boards. On January 12, Seabury signed a receipt for half a year's stipend.[167] At the end of February, he wrote a long letter to the secretary, in which he summarized his actions since 1783 and declared his intention of remaining in communion with the Church of England (but also with the Episcopal Church of Scotland). Toward the close of the letter he referred to the question of the stipends:

> How far the venerable Society may think themselves justifiable in continuing me their Missionary, they only can determine. Should they do so, I shall esteem it a favour. Should they do otherwise, I can have no right to complain. Whatever may be their resolution, I beg them to believe that I shall ever retain a grateful sense of their favours to me, during thirty one years that I have been their Missionary: And that I shall remember, with the utmost respect, the kind attention which they have so long paid to the Church in that country for which I am now to imbark. Very happy would it make me could I be as-

sured they would continue their attention, if not in the same, yet in some degree—if not longer, yet during the lives of their present Missionaries, whose conduct in the late commotions has been irreproachable and has procured esteem to themselves and respect to that church to which they belong.[168]

Seabury originally intended to take a passage to New York, but by this date he had changed his mind, deciding instead to sail on board the *Chapman*, bound for Halifax, and then proceed to New London by coasters. Among other advantages, the arrangement would allow him to visit his son, Samuel, Jr., settled (although not permanently) in Nova Scotia or New Brunswick, and his married daughter, Abigail Campbell, now of St. John in the latter province.[169] The *Chapman* left Gravesend on March 13. An inbound brig having stopped it for some provisions, Seabury a week later dashed off final messages to friends, dating his notes "65 Leagues West from Lizard." He was well; there was a fine, fair gale; and he hoped for a short passage.[170]

The voyage, though very rough, did pass quickly enough. New London's *Connecticut Gazette* of May 13, 1785, reported: "Letters from Nova-Scotia, dated the 23[d] of April, mention the arrival at Halifax, of the Right Reverend Father in God, Doctor SAMUEL SEABURY, Bishop of the State of Connecticut; from whence he would in a very short time embark for this city, the place for his fixed residence." By April 29 Seabury had reached Annapolis Royal. On June 20 he landed in Newport, where he preached the following Sunday to crowded audiences at Trinity Church. Monday he went aboard yet another vessel and that same evening got to New London. Maria and Violetta, Edward and Charles had earlier removed there, while the bishop's Aunt and Uncle Starr, as well as other members of St. James's congregation, were also on hand to extend a hearty welcome.[171] A brief note to a London friend declared his reception had been "such as I could wish."[172]

Seabury's first concern was to arrange a meeting with the

clergy. He immediately wrote Abraham Jarvis, inviting him to come for a visit that they might fix the time and place.[173] Presumably the Convention's secretary accepted. In any case, a session was advertised for August 2, to be held in his own house at Middletown, that being the most central place.

As Seabury prepared for the Convention, he could not but wonder what sort of reception he would encounter. The clergy, of course, would be courteous, but would there be a certain coolness, some sign of hidden resentments? By June, if not before, the bishop must have known that the S.P.G. had resolved to cut off, after September 29, the salaries of all missionaries who chose to remain in the United States. Ostensibly it took this decision on the grounds its charter did not permit any expenditure in foreign dominions. But Loyalist Samuel Peters (Yale, 1757) reported from London, and Seabury himself believed, that the Aberdeen proceedings provided the real impetus. According to Peters (seldom a trustworthy source), stipends were continued until the autumn date because he asserted Seabury's going to Scotland was without the clergy's knowledge; the S.P.G., his argument ran, would do well to wait and see whether Connecticut accepted its would-be bishop.[174]

Official letters informing each missionary of the decision arrived in New York on July 11 with Chandler, who, after waiting two years for the settlement of the Nova Scotia episcopate, had decided to visit the family he had last seen in 1775.[175] That directed to Seabury—short, curt, and addressed, not to the Bishop of Connecticut, but merely to "The Revd. Dr. Seabury at New London"—could only confirm his opinion as to the reason for the Society's action. Seabury's letter of February 27 had been received, the secretary wrote. The S.P.G. approved his services as their missionary; his case was, of course, comprehended under the general decision they had adopted; any information he might wish to forward relating to the propagation of the gospel in foreign parts would be readily accepted.[176] That was all.

However serious Seabury's apprehensions became, Middletown at once obliterated them. The loss of S.P.G. stipends might be keenly felt, but the warmth of the clergy's reception showed it was not their governing concern.[177] Ten pastors assembled in Jarvis' parsonage on August 2 and chose Leaming (now rector of Christ Church, Stratford) as their president.[178] Seabury then waited formally upon the Convention, which requested his Aberdeen certificate and, after reading it, proclaimed him duly and canonically consecrated.

Next morning came the ceremony of installation. At eight o'clock the Convention assembled and reconsidered the address it would present. The document as originally drafted included a stinging criticism of Pitt and England's bishops;[179] this was now softened, but Connecticut's conviction that the episcopate had basely abandoned the Church's cause was still discernible in the final version.[180] Concluding its business, the Convention proceeded to the church and appointed four members to attend Seabury. This delegation thereupon returned to the parsonage, where Jarvis as spokesman gave notice that the clergy confirmed their former election and acknowledged their diocesan. Seabury accepting the post, they escorted him to the church. He entered the chancel and seated himself on an improvised cathedra, the clergy standing before him, just outside the altar railings. When Bela Hubbard had completed the address of welcome and recognition, he read a short reply. Like the Convention, Seabury had been tempted to strike out at Pitt, but on second thought, he, too, had revised his manuscript.[181] He thanked the clergy for their congratulations and for "assurances of supporting the Authority of your Bishop upon the true principles of the primitive Church, before it was controlled and corrupted by secular connections & worldly policy." After soliciting prayers, Seabury briefly alluded to his difficulties in England and closed with a tribute to the Scottish episcopate.[182] The clergy knelt for the apostolic blessing before returning to their pews.

Connecticut's Episcopal Church had accepted its bishop.

VII

"UPON TRUE EPISCOPAL PRINCIPLES"

CONNECTICUT PASTORS WERE NOT THE ONLY CLERGYmen to welcome Samuel Seabury at Middletown in August, 1785. Samuel Parker, rector of Trinity Church, Boston, also had come to the Convention; so had Benjamin Moore, an assistant minister of Trinity Church, New York. Their attendance was closely linked with efforts to form a united Protestant Episcopal Church in the newly independent states, the chief problem Bishop Seabury had to face in the period 1785-92. In order to understand his attitude toward a union and his attempts to achieve one, it is necessary, first of all, to sketch briefly the steps taken to organize a united Church prior to the Middletown Convention, the relation of the Connecticut clergy to them, and the assessment Seabury had made of this work.

The first suggestion for an interstate meeting of Episcopalians came from Abraham Beach (Yale, 1757), nephew of John Beach of Newtown and Redding and, since 1768, S.P.G. missionary at New Brunswick, New Jersey.[1] Wartime conditions had tended to isolate Beach from his colleagues to the eastward, this situation continuing as late as 1783. The result was that he failed, despite his Loyalism, to learn of Seabury's election. Writing William White of Philadelphia in January, 1784, Beach expressed concern that nothing was being done to consolidate the Church and provide it with bishops; as an initial move, he proposed a conference of ministers, to be held that spring in New Brunswick in connection with a meeting of the Corporation for the Relief of Widows and Children of Clergymen. White signifying his approval, Beach then contacted the clergy of Trinity Church, New York. Ultimately, it was agreed that the conference should assemble on Tuesday, May 11.[2]

Since Connecticut's clergy were not members of the corporation in question (chartered in 1769 by Pennsylvania, New Jersey, and New York), there was at first no thought of inviting them to New Brunswick. However, sometime in March, Benjamin Moore, who had signed Seabury's credentials, proposed their inclusion to Beach. "Though they have nothing to do with the 'Corporation for the Relief, &c' yet other matters," he observed, "may come before us in which it will be expedient to have their concurrence."[3] Acting on this suggestion, Beach wrote both Bela Hubbard and Abraham Jarvis, issuing a general invitation. Hubbard's answer is not extant, but early in May Jarvis sent word that none of the state's pastors would attend.

Basic to the decision was Connecticut's continuing fear of ideas advanced in William White's *Case of the Episcopal Churches*, this despite explanations furnished by that writer in response to the Woodbury Convention's protest.[4] That White would be at New Brunswick Jarvis probably knew from Beach's invitation; in any case, the whole tone of his reply revealed a suspicion that measures inconsistent with the doctrine of apostolic succession might still be attempted. It was, he wrote, perfectly true that the Church needed the assistance of "all her true sons." Yet these sons should exhibit a due degree of prudence, keeping in mind that they handled no "mere piece of secular manufacture, indifferently to be wrought into any shape or mould." To properly establish the Church "in the beginnings of this new Empire" would require the foundation of "a genuine Apostolical Episcopate," as well as "primitive and evangelical doctrine and discipline." Accordingly, Jarvis and his brethren, taking a first, necessary step, were attempting to secure a bishop. If they succeeded, they could then convene, "in the full powers of our [particular] Church," to deliberate on interstate matters. If they failed, they would welcome the exertions of all Episcopalians to achieve union and uniformity "by such measures as shall be regular and practicable." But until the result of Connecticut's application were known, her clergy, Jarvis believed, would take no action. Even if they had advice or counsel to offer, he was not at all certain it would carry any weight.[5]

From the actions taken at the New Brunswick conference, held, according to appointment, May 11, 12, 1784, it appears that Beach, at that time, had not yet received Jarvis' frigid communication. Ten clergymen attended—three from Philadelphia, three from New Jersey, and four from New York—besides several laymen, in town on other business.[6] The atmosphere of the gathering—the first since the peace to mingle Loyalist and Patriot Churchmen—though friendly, showed certain signs of strain. Benjamin Moore and the other New York ministers present shared, to some degree, Jarvis' apprehensions with respect to White and like-minded Patriots.[7] And they at once judged quite unacceptable White's suggestion that mixed conventions, laymen as well as pastors, should forthwith organize the Church in each state, this work to be then completed by an interstate General Convention of similar composition.[8] Somewhat diffident the New Yorkers did not reveal their attitude in formal session. But on the second morning, before discussion resumed, Moore took White aside, explaining that he and his friends hoped the conference would sanction no scheme of this sort, since they were already cooperating with Connecticut in an attempt to secure a bishop (again, as in the case of Jarvis' letter, Seabury's name went unmentioned). Pending the outcome of that attempt, they could not join in proceedings which might hazard its success.[9]

Moore's words had the desired effect: for the time being,

White's detailed proposals were put aside. Nevertheless, the New Brunswick meeting did move in a general—and consequently, from the standpoint of the New Yorkers, relatively unobjectionable—fashion toward organizing the Church at the national level. Calling for a second clerical and lay conference to discuss the matter (hopefully this would include men from every state), it set October 6 as the date and picked New York as the place. Surely, by that time, the result of the application for a bishop must be known. And if it had proved successful, the bishop obtained would be, of course, a welcome participant. To win Connecticut support for the plan of operations, Abraham Beach, Benjamin Moore, and Joshua Bloomer (King's College, 1758)—Seabury's successor as rector of Jamaica—agreed to explain and justify it to the state's clergy.[10]

This committee encountered no difficulties when it met the Connecticut Convention at New Milford on the Wednesday in Trinity week. Willingly the seven members present agreed to enter into a correspondence "for the settling a Uniformity in the Episcopal Church," at the same time appointing Leaming, Jarvis, and Richard Mansfield "to form a Plan, for such Settlement, and to report the same to the Convention that will be held at New Haven at the Time of the Commencement." Deputies to the New York conference would be selected at this September meeting.[11] The Convention, however, was averse to sending lay deputies, believing that the Connecticut laity did not expect or even wish to have any part in purely ecclesiastical concerns (which, as later developments showed, was indeed the case). "We informed them," Beach reported to White, "that it was thought necessary in some of the States, particularly in Pennsylvania, to associate some respectable Characters amongst the Laity, in Order to give *Weight & Importance* to the Church; but we meant not to prescribe to *other States*—provided the *End* was obtained, we would not differ with them as to the *Means*, if they were only *fair & honest*."[12] It was on this basis that a general union finally took shape in 1789; it might have been constructed years earlier had all parties acted according to Beach's moderate counsels.

The measures approved at New Milford, indicating a novel willingness on the part of Connecticut to take part in interstate consultations, are to be explained, no doubt, by the fact that the clergy, having notified Seabury in February of the Assembly's acquiescence in an episcopate, expected his appearance, in episcopal Orders, within a few weeks. When the Convention resumed deliberations at New Haven on September 8, it had received no word of Seabury's failure in England. Still, since he had not arrived, the assembled pastors reverted to their former position. Although designating John Rutgers Marshall a deputy to the New York conference, they decided he should carry with him a letter declaring Connecticut could take no steps toward a general union until the state should have a bishop, "which we have Reason to expect will be soon."[13] As drafted, this letter also registered the opinion that the framing of an ecclesiastical constitution and the revision of the liturgy, if done without the concurrence of "the principal Officer in our Church," would be "unprecedented, and unsanctioned by any authoritative Example." Consequently, it was hoped the conference would "agree to suspend the entering upon those general Points, until we can properly meet them upon an Affair of so great Moment, and joint Concern to them, to ourselves, and the whole American Church."[14]

The deputies who came together at New York on October 6 heard these sentiments, not only from Marshall, but also from Samuel Parker, representing Massachusetts and Rhode Island.[15] (Maryland, too, had but a single, clerical deputy; Pennsylvania and Delaware, New York and New Jersey—the other participants in the conference—sent laymen as well as pastors.) A strong High Churchman,[16] Parker, nevertheless, harbored no suspicions of William White. In fact, the two enjoyed a friendly correspondence on the general needs of the Church,[17] one result of which was Parker's recent revival of the pre-Revolutionary Boston Convention. Meeting September 8, the very day the Connecticut body held its session at New Haven, this Convention approved—for the most part—guidelines for a national union put forward in late May by Pennsylvania Churchmen and transmitted to Parker by White; it also authorized Parker's presence at New York.[18] But at the same time the clergy drew up a letter, markedly similar in its key passage to that entrusted to Marshall. Unanimously they declared

> that it is beginning at the wrong end to attempt to organize our Church before we have obtained a Head. Our Churches at present resemble the scattered Limbs of the body without any common Centre of Union, or Principle to animate the whole. We cannot conceive it probable or even possible to carry the Plan you [the Pennsylvanians] have pointed out into Execution before an Episcopate is obtained to direct our Motions, & by a delegated Authority to claim our Assent.[19]

From the minutes of the New York conference, it appears that this letter, together with the one formulated in New Haven, were read at the opening session, just after William Smith had been chosen president and Benjamin Moore, secretary.[20] Yet they had no effect, for most of the delegates wished to get on with the work of organizing the Church, leaving the securing of bishops to some later period. Because of the clear prohibition of the Connecticut Convention, John Rutgers Marshall could take no part in such proceedings. Samuel Parker, however, agreed to help draft the "fundamental Principles" of an ecclesiastical constitution.

Parker credited reports that Seabury's success was assured and, indeed, may have believed that his consecration had already taken place.[21] This being the situation, there was more than met the eye in the Boston rector's suggestion that in any General Convention the senior bishop present should preside. William Smith, keenly alive to anything which might interfere with his own ambitions, smoothly countered this move. To confine the presidency to the senior bishop, he observed, "might be sometimes inconvenient." Others agreeing, Parker's motion was amended to read: "That in every State where there shall be a Bishop duly consecrated and settled, he shall be considered as a Member of the [General] Convention, ex Officio." This declaration, and six others, formed the "fundamental Principles" which the conference recommended to the states represented (to those lacking deputies it "proposed" them) as the basis of a national union. Such a union, if all went well, would take shape in a General Convention, scheduled for Philadelphia in September of the following year.[22]

The "fundamental Principles" immediately appearing in print as a broadside, someone—probably Benjamin Moore—dispatched a copy to Seabury, who received it in London by December 27. Writing to Bishop Skinner on that date, he characterized the whole as "a very lame, if not a mischevous business." Smith's revision of Parker's proposal he thoroughly disliked, since he interpreted it as placing bishops on a level with other members in any General Convention session. Equally objectionable was the proposal that each state send lay as well as clerical members, the concurrence of both (deliberating in one body but voting separately) to be necessary for every measure. These arrangements, Seabury insisted, must bring bishops and pastors "into abject bondage." Doctrine, discipline, the liturgy would all be under lay control, thanks to "Dr. Smiths meddling, restless disposition, & the lax principles of the southern Clergy." Further information of the New York proceedings did not alter this initial judgment. Indeed, from a subsequent letter, it appears that Seabury misconstrued one account as reporting an attempt by the conference to institute the irregular ministry suggested by White in 1782![23]

Scottish associates did nothing to allay these exaggerated fears and suspicions. Skinner condemned the "fundamental Principles" as being "directly repugnant" to episcopacy's "Spirit and subversive of its original Design," while the Reverend Andrew Macfarlane insisted that the body producing them would—in a purer age—have been "esteemed Schismatical, or Rebellious, against the Catholic Church."[24] American observations, in certain instances, were fully as harsh and, in the case of James Rivington, much more pungently expressed. Wrote the editor: "As to the *Southern Bastards* I hope yourself, and every [one] of your Clergy will always keep aloof from them, You can never associate with absurdity & in consistance."[25]

Fortunately, other friends of Seabury took a more hopeful view of the situation. Jeremiah Leaming (who seems to have been acting on his own responsibility) decided to turn the welcoming Convention at Middletown in August, 1785, into a general gathering of Episcopal clergy from Pennsylvania northward. On July 14, he dispatched a very friendly letter to William White, inviting him and the other ministers of his state to come to Middletown for the purpose of discussing a union of all the churches. "We have no Views of Usurping any Authority over our Brothers and Neighbours," he declared, "but wish them to unite with us, in the same friendly manner, that we are ready and willing to do, with them."[26] A similar invitation to the New Jersey ministers was extended in a letter to Abraham Beach,[27] and another probably was forwarded to those of New York through the agency of Benjamin Moore. It is likely that Leaming sent yet a fourth invitation to Samuel Parker. At any rate, on July 28, Parker, meeting with the Reverend Edward Bass (Harvard, 1744) of Newburyport and the Reverend Nathaniel Fisher (Harvard, 1763) of Salem—the other members of a committee of correspondence appointed by the Boston Convention of September, 1784—received their authorization to attend at Middletown, "then & there to learn what measures they mean to adopt, in order to the maintaining uniformity of divine Worship in the episcopal Church, &c. &c. &c."[28]

Parker attended the Convention as directed. Moore also joined his Connecticut brethren, though only as an unofficial observer. But no other pastors—authorized persons or volunteers—appeared. A lack of time to complete necessary arrangements perhaps explains the absence of Beach and other Jersey men, for Leaming had acted at a very late date. In the case of the Philadelphia clergy, another factor operated, namely, suspicion as to Leaming's motives. Judging that he had made his move in an effort to forestall the General Convention set for September 27,[29] White politely declined his invitation and, at the same time, drafted a letter for Seabury, to which his fellow townsmen Samuel Magaw (College of Philadelphia, 1757), rector of St. Paul's, and the Reverend John Andrews (College of Philadelphia, 1765), head of the Episcopal Academy, also appended their signatures. This communication—the friendliest of overtures—warmly congratulated the bishop on his safe arrival. White continued:

> You will doubtless, Sir, be informed, that, in Consequence of Consultations held in the City of New-York, ecclesiastical Deputies from all the States in the Union are expected to assemble in this City, on the Tuesday before the Feast of St. Michael. Should the Bishop of Connecticut honor the Convention with his Presence, we shall not only share in the general Satisfaction & Advantage which will arise from it, but shall derive from our local Situation the Privilege of shewing him those personal Attentions which will be due to his Episcopal Rank & to his private Character; and, it is to assure him of our best Endeavours to render . . . a Visit agreeable to him, that we now trouble him with this Address.[30]

By sending such a letter, White did what he could to draw Seabury into the plan of organization emerging as a result of the New Brunswick and New York consultations. He had always intended that Connecticut's application for a bishop, if successful, should be used to the benefit of all the Episcopal churches,[31] and his old friend and teacher, the celebrated Loyalist Jacob

Duché (College of Philadelphia, 1757), repeatedly had urged him to this course. From London in December, 1784, Duché recommended "it warmly to you to give a proper, affectionate and, (I must say) Filial Reception to good Bishop Seabury . . . a *Scholar*, a *Gentleman*, and I am happy to be able to say (which I verily believe to be true) *a real Christian*." Some months later, after Duché had seen the "fundamental Principles" (of which he heartily disapproved), he again wrote White, listing Seabury's episcopal credentials and describing him as "just such a Bishop as you could have wished for." "Receive him therefore, I beseech you," he pleaded, "with Cordial Affection, and with that Christian Respect, which is due to his high & sacred Office—Suffer no Schism in the Church."[32] This advice, as his letter to Seabury showed, White was perfectly ready to follow. Yet he could not do so without the bishop's cooperation. And that he did not get.

If the Philadelphia rector was unwilling to come to Middletown, the Bishop of Connecticut, in August, 1785, was equally unwilling to visit Pennsylvania's capital. White's letter reached him at the Convention, and Samuel Parker (to whom White had written in June, expressing fears that the "fundamental Principle" regarding bishops was creating difficulties and wishing that it had stood as originally proposed)[33] used all possible arguments to persuade him to accept the invitation.[34] Seabury, however, refused to budge. White and the other Philadelphia clergy might be friendly and respectful, but he had no guarantee the deputies from other states shared their attitude. He could not bring himself to put the episcopal character in a position where it might be, in his view, snubbed and disregarded. What if he should attend the General Convention only to find himself seated among the mass of deputies while Dr. Smith occupied the president's chair? This specter would not down, and because of it the bishop remained at home.[35] "I want much to see you," he declared in a friendly reply to White and his brethren, "& yet I fear there are some impediments that will prevent my attending at your Convention." In a subsequent letter he explained to White that his duty as minister of St. James's, as well as financial circumstances ("I am utterly unprovided for so long a journey, not being, at present, master even of a horse"), must prevent his coming.[36] These excuses were genuine; if they failed to exhaust Seabury's reasons for declining White's invitation, they were the only ones he cared to give explicitly.

The bishop's more important reasons could be gathered from the long letter he sent to William Smith on August 15.[37] Like White, Smith had invited Seabury to the proposed General Convention when congratulating him upon his consecration. His letter, dated July 19, was a very cordial one—and with good reason, as Seabury discovered when he met with a paragraph in which Smith quoted a certain theologian as justifying consecrations performed by a single bishop acting in conjunction with two priests.[38] In his answer, Seabury took no notice of this overly obvious suggestion. But he criticized, frankly and at great length, the measures taken to organize the Episcopal Church in Maryland, of which he had been informed by a printed pamphlet Smith had forwarded.[39] Chandler, in two letters to William White written some weeks later, gave a similar critique of the proceedings of the Virginia Convention held in May, 1785.[40] Taken together, these communications provided an excellent summary of Connecticut's traditional concept of the Church and its government, and as the writers polished drafts in the parsonages at New London and Elizabethtown, the shades of Samuel Johnson and Timothy Cutler must have cheered their resolute paragraphs.

The so-called "federal plan" of church organization,[41] supported by Virginia and Maryland, called for state conventions, composed, according to proposals made at New Brunswick, of the pastor and an elected lay representation from each congregation; a General Convention, likewise suggested at New Brunswick and formally endorsed by the New York conference, would link the state bodies in a general union. White had first broached the broad outlines of this scheme in his *Case of the Episcopal Churches*, and in that pamphlet he labored to show that its basic principles derived from the existing pattern of English church government.[42] The High Churchmen, however, believing that the "federal plan" was of a piece with projects for American political union, opposed it with arguments based on their reading of the history of the apostolic and patristic periods. "The rights of the Christian Church," Seabury informed Dr. Smith, "arise not from nature or compact, but from the institution of Christ; & we ought not to alter them, but to receive & maintain them, as the holy Apostles left them." Chandler was equally explicit. "The Church is a Society founded by *Christ*," he declared in his first letter to White. "All ecclesiastical authority and jurisdiction must be derived from *him*, and not from any natural rights &c." So far as Connecticut Churchmen were concerned, John Locke's philosophy was irrelevant to the problem of an ecclesiastical union.

Working from this patristic position, Seabury and Chandler grouped their criticisms around two main features of the Maryland and Virginia proceedings: the rigid circumscribing of the bishop's authority and the admission of the laity to ecclesiastical synods. Especially obnoxious to them was the proposition, affirmed by both states, that the office of a bishop differed from that of a priest in nothing save the powers of ordination and confirmation and the right of precedency in ecclesiastical assemblies.[43] Government, Seabury believed, was as much an essential right of the episcopate as ordination; indeed ordination was only an aspect of government. "Whatever share of government Presbyters have in the Church," he declared, "they have from the Bishop, & must exercise it in conjunction with, or in subordination to him." As for the laity, though they might choose their minister, yet the bishop must approve their choice "because they are part of his charge; he has the care of their souls, & is accountable for them."

Such a concept of episcopal authority, Seabury asserted, did not imply a prelatical despotism. While the choice of a bishop properly belonged to the diocesan clergy, he was willing, under certain conditions, that this power should be shared with the laity (although "I do not apprehend that this was the practice of the primitive Church"). Summarizing that manner of exercising episcopal powers which Leaming had expounded in his sermon before the Middletown Convention,[44] and which he himself scrupulously observed, Seabury explained that the clergy were an episcopal council, to be consulted in every important measure. "The Presbyters have always a check upon their Bishop," he declared, "because they can, neither Bishop nor Presbyters, do any thing beyond the common course of duty without each other." This applied, however, only to diocesan matters, "for it does not appear that Presbyters had any seat in general Councils, but by particular indulgence."

When coupled with Seabury's refusal to accept lay representatives in church assemblies, this last statement amounted to a complete repudiation of any such body as the "federal plan's" General Convention. Chandler stated the High Churchmen's objection to lay deputies in a terse syllogism. Christ was the source of ecclesiastical authority; "this authority he was pleased to lodge in the hands of certain *officers* of his appointment, to be communicated to their successors;—those, therefore, who are *not officers* in the Church, i.e. *the Laity*, can have no share of ecclesiastical authority." (Chandler, nevertheless, did outline proposals for a consultative assembly of the laity, which, presumably, was only a temporary fixture, to be abolished after a general union of the Episcopal churches had been formed.) Seabury, accepting his friend's logic, pointed out that American laymen already enjoyed a large measure of control over the clergy's actions, since they provided their only financial support. If a pastor misbehaved, let his congregation appeal to the bishop, who, assisted by the clergy, would censure, suspend, or deprive, according to the facts of the case. If a bishop failed in his duty, the neighboring bishops were his proper judges. "Men that are not to be trusted with these powers," he bluntly declared, "are not fit to be Bishops or Presbyters at all."

This problem of delinquent clergymen colored Seabury's whole approach to the question of lay deputies, so much so that White came to believe he had almost a fixation on the subject.[45] As the plan for an episcopate which he drafted in 1777 showed, the bishop was particularly anxious that proper procedures be devised for removing unworthy ministers from their cures. But this discipline, he explained to Smith, could not be exercised by a mixed convention of laymen and ministers, because the former had no right to any such power. "That authority which confers power, can, for proper reasons, take it away: But where there is no authority to confer power, there can be none to disanul it." Discipline must, as a consequence, be left to the bishops.

Such views, Seabury feared, would not be welcomed by the General Convention. Yet they were identical, he believed, with the provisions of the Church's constitution "in its pure & simple state," and they were the views Connecticut had adopted, attempting to exhibit "to the world, in our government, discipline & order, a pure & perfect model of primitive simplicity." The bishop hoped the proposals finally sanctioned at Philadelphia also would bear the patristic stamp and that, to this end, the Convention deputies might be brought to reconsider the federal plan. Persistence in its objectionable features, his closing sentences plainly informed Smith, would render impossible a union with his flock:

> If any expression in this letter should seem too warm, I will be ready to correct the mode, but the sentiments I must retain till I find them wrong & then I will freely give them up. In this matter I am not interested. My ground is taken, & I wish not to extend my authority beyond its present limits. But I do most earnestly wish to have our Church in all the States so settled that it may be one Church, united in government, doctrine & discipline—that there may be no division

among us—no opposition of interests—no clashing of opinions. And permit me to hope that you will at your approaching Convention so far receed in the points I have mentioned, as to make this practicable. Your Convention will be large & much to be respected. Its determinations will influence many of the American States, and posterity will be materially affected by them. These considerations are so many arguments for calm & cool deliberation. Human passions & prejudices, &, if possible, infirmities should be laid aside. A wrong step will be attended with dreadful consequences. Patience & prudence must be exercised: And should there be some circumstances that press hard for a remedy, hasty decisions will not mend them. In doubtful cases they will probably have a bad effect.

May the Spirit of God be with you at Philadelphia; & as I persuade myself, the sole good of his Church is the sole aim of you all, I hope for the best effects from your meeting.

Chandler placed his remarks at White's disposal, to be publicized or suppressed as he saw fit. Seabury, on the other hand, explicitly requested Smith to lay his letter before the General Convention. The latter complying, hostile reactions to its arguments came from the delegations, who represented the states south of Connecticut, with the exceptions of North Carolina and Georgia. Indeed, so harsh was the language of certain laymen that some of the clergy, notably John Andrews of Philadelphia, felt it necessary to defend Seabury's action. Pointing to the fact that the Bishop of Connecticut had received the same invitation to the Convention as those who had attacked him, Andrews declared he had every right to express himself.[46]

Once critics had vented their dislike of his views, Seabury was completely ignored. The Convention did not give him the courtesy of a public reply, nor did his name appear in the published minutes of its proceedings. Choosing White (not Smith, as Seabury expected) for their president, the deputies, in a twelve-day session beginning September 27, proceeded to frame a general ecclesiastical constitution, largely on the basis of the "fundamental Principles" formulated at New York the previous October.[47] Thus by the middle of October, 1785, the Episcopal Church of

Connecticut, constituted, in its bishop's opinion, according to "the primitive pattern," stood in direct contrast to the Protestant Episcopal Church[48] of the Southern states, modeled according to a "federal plan" of a somewhat later date.

Political animosities, lingering from the Revolutionary period, played a part in determining this outcome: the General Convention was definitely a Patriot body.[49] Still, the disagreement was more fundamental than that. Differences between the aggressive High Churchmanship of New England, particularly Connecticut, and the traditional, nontheological Episcopalianism of the majority of Churchmen south and west of the Hudson were no longer, in 1785, matter for lament in the correspondence of Seabury and his fellows: they had become a topic of general discussion. Men for whom episcopacy and the concept of apostolic succession had been the rationale of membership in the Church of England were opposing men unaccustomed to giving their church's government much thought. When the crisis of the Revolution forced a consideration of such questions, this latter group had turned naturally to the principles of polity which they vigorously championed in the area of civil government. The deadlock ensuing in 1785 was, therefore, no casual phenomenon, but rather the result of deeply rooted contrasts. A person familiar with Connecticut's Churchmen and with their counterparts in, say, Virginia, could easily have predicted as early as 1760 that some such struggle would result from an attempt to unite the two groups organically.

To the antagonisms produced by varying forms of government were immediately added those created by separate attempts at liturgical revision. As late as July, 1785, Churchmen in all the states worshipped in much the same forms. Those who had been Loyalists—the New Englanders were the largest group—omitted the prayers for the King and royal family without substituting any in their place; Patriots, on the contrary, introduced some slight additions, as, for instance, a transformation of the prayer for Parliament, used during its sessions, into a prayer for Congress.[50] Essentially, however, the services of the Prayer Book of 1662 stood unaltered. This situation changed after the meetings at Middletown and Philadelphia, and by the autumn of 1786 the Episcopal churches presented a picture of liturgical chaos.

The making of alterations at Middletown was connected with Samuel Parker's efforts to extend Seabury's episcopal authority over Massachusetts-Maine, Rhode Island, and New Hampshire. From the time of his election, Parker had expected that he would exercise jurisdiction throughout this region,[51] and when the Boston rector came to Middletown, he sounded the Convocation[52] on the matter. According to its minutes, Connecticut's ministers "expressed their warmest Wishes" for the other New England clergy to be united with them under Seabury's direction. This happened on Thursday afternoon, August 4; the next morning the Convocation adjourned until Commencement week, after first appointing "Mr. Bowden, Mr. Parker & Mr. Jarvis as a Committee to consider of & make some Alterations in the Liturgy needful for the present Use of the Church."[53]

Meeting with Seabury on Friday and Saturday, the committee approved two separate liturgical revisions. The first, which was immediately put into effect in Connecticut by a formidable injunction issued as a printed broadside,[54] formally abrogated the observance of the state holy days[55] and accommodated Morning and Evening Prayer, the Litany, the Communion service, and the Catechism to the civil constitution of the American states. Most of these changes appear to have been worked out in London by Seabury and Chandler.[56] Without altering the services in any major way, they repaired the gaps created by simply omitting the royal prayers. No collect for Congress found a place in this revision—not, as Seabury wrote Governor Matthew Griswold, because of any "backwardness on that account," but because it was thought proper first to inquire whether the governor had any instructions to give.[57] Griswold's apparent failure to reply further delayed the matter,[58] much to the alarm of Congressman William Samuel Johnson. In December his pastor suggested that Seabury order the use of a suitable prayer by a newspaper notice,[59] but the bishop, true to his concept of the proper exercise of episcopal authority, declined such unilateral action. Not until the next session of the Convocation provided an opportunity for consulting the clergy did he authorize a collect, as well as a Litany supplication. Governor Samuel Huntington, furnished with copies, laid them before his Council and later reported: "We find nothing exceptional in the forms, & esteem them well adapted to the Occasion."[60]

Alterations of this sort were inevitable. Not so the more basic ones which formed the Middletown proposals, the second of the liturgical revisions. Although the impetus for them came from Samuel Parker, Seabury entered fully into the work. "Most if not all the proposed Alterations were such as we were under Obligation to you for or such as you readily agreed to," Parker declared in 1788.[61] No transcript of the proposals, as originally fashioned, is extant. They are known, however, in a generally identical edition (save for verbal differences), tentatively adopted by the Boston Convention after Parker's return from Middletown.[62] As one studies the proposals, it becomes obvious that Seabury was less attached to the Prayer Book of 1662 than has commonly been supposed.

Intent on producing more compact forms of worship, the bishop and his committee discarded repetitions in the English Prayer Book and cut out certain prayers and ejaculations. Thus they omitted the Lord's Prayer after the Apostles' Creed in Morning and Evening Prayer (it had been recited twice in these services), as well as in the Litany and at the opening of the Communion. Only the First Lesson was retained in Morning Prayer, while in the same service—and in the comparable one for the afternoon—the so-called "shorter Litany" disappeared completely. At the Communion, the minister might, if he chose, recite but once the rather lengthy formularies for the delivery of the bread and cup instead of repeating them to the individual communicants. Seabury's experiences at Westchester were responsible for the rewording of the Communion exhortations so as to remove the fears of damnation entertained by overly conscientious persons. Lastly, the four revisors made a beginning in altering the offices—they discarded the Gospel and Exhortation of the Baptismal service—but lack of time precluded more than the listing of other possible changes.[63]

In light of the controversy which later developed over the use of the creeds, the Middletown decisions with respect to these three confessions of faith are particularly significant. It was agreed that the Athanasian Creed, disliked by many Churchmen and regarded by Seabury as somewhat unsuitable for public worship (though perfectly orthodox!),[64] should no longer be recited. The Nicene Creed became optional, the minister, wardens, and vestry of each church being empowered to discontinue its use. The Apostles' Creed, the one with which the people were most familiar (they recited the Athanasian only on certain holy days and the Nicene only at the Communion) was to be read as formerly, but even here the revisors made an alteration, omitting the article of Christ's descent into hell.[65]

The Middletown proposals were precisely that. Unlike the changes set forth in the broadside of August 12, they were not to be adopted anywhere without further consideration. Seabury would submit them to his adjourned Convocation at New Haven in September, 1785, while Parker, at his express desire, agreed to offer them to the Boston Convention that same month.[66] The bishop was opposed to hasty measures. With his long letter to Smith of August 15, he enclosed a copy of his injunction, explaining also that further alterations had been suggested, and that, if "we come to any determination, the Brethren to the southward shall be informed of it." Several days later, when sending another broadside to White, he remarked that "Should more be done, it must be a work of time and great deliberation."[67]

The General Convention of 1785, besides forming an ecclesiastical constitution, produced its own revision of the Prayer Book. This "Proposed Book," as it has always been called, Seabury much disliked. High Churchmen of later generations censured it with equal severity. And yet, a comparison of the Philadelphia alterations with those of Middletown shows that the differences between them are, for the most part, unimportant. Historians and biographers have been quick to assume that the changes included in Seabury's injunction were the only ones devised in Connecticut. If this were true, the contrast with the Proposed Book would, indeed, be great. But, as has been pointed out, the bishop and his assistants had proceeded far beyond this point in their second revision.

The committee appointed by the General Convention to alter the liturgy was headed by William Smith. Smith had before him the broadside Seabury had dispatched; he had also another copy of the injunction and a copy of the Middletown proposals as adopted by the Boston Convention, which Parker had sent to White, hoping the General Convention would approve them.[68] Parker's strategy enjoyed a good measure of success. Anxious, as was White, to keep up friendly relations with the bishop, Smith sent Seabury a short note on October 2, the day before his committee submitted its report. "There will be no Alterations in the Liturgy proposed here," he declared, "but what will well agree with what are proposed by our Brethren in the Northern States."[69]

The Proposed Book generally conformed to this statement. In the area dealt with by the injunction, Smith's committee made much the same changes. As for the Middletown proposals, it adopted a few (for example, the wording of the First Communion Exhortation) exactly as they stood.[70] Others were incorporated in substance, among them many of the changes in the offices, suggested at Middletown and afterwards formally sanctioned at Boston. The Proposed Book displayed numerous verbal emendations; these were irritating to persons who revered the old forms but mostly inconsequential in themselves. And in some respects the nonpolitical part of the revision was more conservative than the comparable Connecticut production, for it retained both lessons in Morning Prayer and preserved the accustomed method of administering the eucharistic elements. Certain alterations Seabury definitely would have opposed (such as the complete disuse, not merely of the Athanasian, but also of the Nicene Creed, or the abridgment of the singing and reading Psalms), and a service of thanksgiving for the Fourth of July, introduced against White's protest,[71] he could never have approved. Still, when these differences between the Proposed Book and the Connecticut changes have been pointed out, the area of agreement remains large, a fact underlined by Parker, who commented to Seabury in January, 1786: "As far as I have yet examined, it strikes me as a matter of great Indifferency whether I should adopt ours or their Alterations, Provided I mean that theirs had been made by Episcopal Authority."[72]

Interesting as was this agreement, it was also, by January, 1786, quite irrelevant. While Parker might label the Middletown proposals "our alterations" (his reference was solely to them, for he had already adopted the changes of the injunction), Seabury no longer gave them his support. Months before, in fact, prior to the General Convention, the bishop had shifted course, gradually setting his face against any tampering with the 1662 text except that required by the political situation. This action pointed up the fact that New England Churchmen enjoyed less unity than the Middletown revisors had supposed.

The first step toward a regional adoption of the proposals, earlier statements have indicated, went off well enough. Parker laying both them and the injunction before the Boston Convention, September 7, 8, that body approved, with but two material exceptions (the omission of the Second Lesson in Morning Prayer and of the Gospel and Exhortation in the Baptismal Office),[73] all changes Seabury and his committee had fully discussed and likewise endorsed others—in the offices—which, for lack of time, they had simply listed. Besides Parker, three clergymen were present: Edward Bass of St. Paul's, Newburyport; William Willard Wheeler (Harvard, 1755), rector of the United Churches of Scituate, Marshfield, and Bridgewater; and Naththaniel Fisher of St. Peter's, Salem. Lay deputies appeared from all of these churches except Salem, as well as from Dedham and Stoughton, St. Michael's, Marblehead, Trinity Church and Christ Church, Boston, from Queen's Chapel, Portsmouth, and from St. Michael's, Bristol, and Trinity Church, Newport.[74] Such delegations had been invited mainly because the scattered churches of Massachusetts-Maine, New Hampshire, and Rhode Island (in number approximately half the Connecticut total) for the most part lacked pastors. Twenty-one clergymen served their area in 1775; a decade later, death and the fortunes of war had reduced that number to the four participating in the Convention. Clearly, common action was now impossible unless lay representatives were admitted.[75]

Practical considerations—among them the want of a bishop—likewise explained the Boston Convention's submission of its work to the individual congregations.[76] Each received a copy of Seabury's injunction, of which two or three words had been emended,[77] together with a recommendation that its changes be put into effect immediately. Congregations sanctioning the Middletown proposals were urged to delay their introduction until after the day to which the Convention stood adjourned. October 26 was tentatively selected as this date, by which time Parker hoped to have received word of favorable action by the Connecticut Convocation. Transcripts of the Convention's edition of the proposals he forwarded both to Bela Hubbard and to Seabury, with the request that the bishop send him "a copy of the alterations you shall agree to and enjoin upon your Clergy [at New Haven], that we may conform thereto."[78]

Had Seabury and his pastors, at this point, adopted the Middletown proposals—either the Boston edition or their own formulation—a uniform, revised liturgy might soon have come into use throughout the New England states. Such a development would have strengthened the bishop greatly vis-à-vis the Southern churches. But Seabury's concept of episcopal authority (and, perhaps, his disinclination to hurry the affair) prevented the taking of bold measures necessary to achieve this goal. Some of the Connecticut laity, still tinged with Loyalism, did not favor even the minor changes introduced by the Middletown injunction: statements about delaying alterations "till a little time shall have cooled down the tempers, and conciliated the affections of people to each other" can hardly be interpreted in any other sense.[79] Hearing that other changes, much more considerable ones, were in the making, congregations took alarm—in large part, it seems, from an emotional attachment to the 1662 book.[80] The body of the clergy, voicing this attitude at New Haven, apparently shared it, at least in some degree. In any case, they counseled caution, Bela Hubbard reporting to Parker that "As to the alteration proposed by your Convention in the good old book of Common Prayer, I can at present only say, that our Convocation are slow in taking up a matter of such consequence."[81] This reluctance determined Seabury against further alterations for the time being. Without the Convocation's approval, he could not, as he had explained to William Smith, perform any but the customary episcopal duties. And the Convocation was in no temper to endorse drastic moves.

Reports of the General Convention's transactions confirmed Seabury's judgment. As late as January, 1786, he had no first-hand information; although Smith had indicated he would forward a full account and a copy of the journal, in fact, he had not done so.[82] Suspicious at this failure—"They seem to be backward in letting their doings appear"[83]—the bishop believed the worst when rumor declared that the deputies had adopted a revolutionary liturgical revision, necessitating the new edition of the Prayer Book. (Seabury assumed the Philadelphia alterations had received final approval, whereas they had only been submitted to the state organizations.) News that the General Convention also had revised the Thirty-Nine Articles, reducing them to twenty, further intensified his fears. Everything, so it seemed, could be called into question and instantly settled, without the intervention of any bishop, and by persons whose scheme of government showed that they had no true grasp of the Church's structures.[84] Given this situation, Seabury grew more and more convinced that the Prayer Book of 1662, adapted to the country's civil state, should be clung to as the rock of stability and orthodoxy. Once he had fully embraced this view, even changes which he and his committee had made became objectionable when they appeared in the Proposed Book.

The failure of Connecticut's Convocation to sanction the Middletown proposals posed a dilemma for the other New England churches. Not until July, 1786, after repeated adjournments, did the Boston Convention again assemble. Only one congregation to whom they had been submitted had failed to approve the alterations sanctioned in September, 1785, yet by adopting them the session could align itself neither with the Connecticut clergy nor with the General Convention.[85] The deputies had before them the Proposed Book, which Smith hoped they would accept.[86] A disposition to do so existed, but as Parker explained to White, although the Boston edition of the Middletown proposals and the Philadelphia liturgy were

> in a great measure similar, yet, as there are some things wherein we disagree, it was thought best, all things considered, to leave it optional with the several Churches to adopt which they like best, or even to continue the use of the old Liturgy (the State prayers excepted) until we become complete in our officers and one common Liturgy is established by the first Order of the Clergy to whom alone we are of opinion, this matter appertains.[87]

Contributing to the Boston Convention's decision was the fact that the Proposed Book had met with much opposition in the

Southern states.[88] This failure to adopt it generally in the region represented at Philadelphia, together with the New England developments outlined in the preceding pages, soon led to a bewildering variety of services. By the autumn of 1786 certain churches, both in New England and to the southward, were worshipping according to the Proposed Book; others in New England had adopted the Boston version of the Middletown proposals; and at least one congregation, Trinity Church, Boston, was using a combination of the two![89] Throughout Connecticut, the only changes in the 1662 Prayer Book were those introduced by Seabury's injunction of August 12, 1785, plus the subsequently authorized prayers for the civil powers. Elsewhere in New England there were pastors who operated on this plan, while the Southern churches which disliked the Proposed Book retained the 1662 book with such alterations as they individually preferred.

Obviously this situation, unlike the deadlock with respect to church government, was not the consequence of deeply rooted principles, peculiar to the matter in hand and distinguishing New England (and more especially Connecticut) from the Southern states. It might well have been avoided—a Prayer Book acceptable to all groups could very likely have been formed in 1785-86—had not first the prospect of the deadlock, and then the thing itself, necessarily complicated the picture, preventing truly national negotiations, fostering mutual distrust and ill will. Producing the identical divisive effects and, at the same time, strengthening the deadlock was the animosity felt by many toward Seabury because of his Loyalist past.

Patriot Churchmen, whose opinions of episcopacy were influenced by their political views, had regarded "A. W. Farmer's" elevation with a disapproving eye. "I am very much dissatisfied with the appointment of this Bishop," Rufus King wrote to Elbridge Gerry on May 8, 1785. "I never liked the hierarchy of the Church—an equality in the teachers of Religion, and a dependence on the people, are Republican sentiments." Gerry replied that he was equally concerned about "the Connecticut Bishop"; the old Puritan colony, he feared, was running "into every Excess, religious moral & political."[90] Requested to furnish a candidate for Orders with a recommendation, George Washington grumpily noted in his diary that he had no "desire to open a Correspondence with the *new* ordained Bishop."[91] And Richard Henry Lee, writing from New York of "the mischievous high church principles that prevail with the nonjuring Episcopalians of these Northern regions," affirmed that with Seabury at their head, such men were "sufficient to disturb the Moderate Councils of any Whig assembly in the world."[92]

John Jay and James Duane, the leading Patriots among New York's Episcopalians, held strongly views of the sort just quoted, and in their family connection, Samuel Provoost (King's College, 1758), they found a most willing ally.[93] This clergyman of mediocre talents, long inactive in the ministry and with nothing to recommend him save his support of the Revolution, had gained the rectorship of Manhattan's Trinity Church in 1784, thanks to the intervention of the state government and against the wishes of a great majority of the parish, who desired Benjamin Moore as Inglis' successor.[94] Bishop of New York after 1787, Provoost found High Church theology as objectionable as Loyalist politics. His own opinions were Latitudinarian, so much so that an unsympathetic nineteenth-century critic could characterize him as "corrupt in doctrine, beyond what would now be sufferable in an intelligent lay-communicant."[95]

From the time he first learned of Seabury's consecration until the Bishop of Connecticut's death in 1796, Provoost exhibited for him an inveterate dislike, William White's well-meant disclaimers notwithstanding.[96] In letters to White, he vented his petty spite by labeling him "Dr. Cebra," although he knew perfectly well the correct spelling of his name. Had Provoost, Duane, and Jay had their way, Connecticut would never have been brought into a general ecclesiastical union. And in 1785-

86 Provoost did his best to ensure its exclusion by circulating a letter critical of Seabury's Scottish consecration.

This letter was the production of Granville Sharp, the noted English philanthropist. Romantic, eccentric, zealous for the introduction of bishops into the United States,[97] Sharp in his relations with supporters of the "federal plan" was a fit counterpart of the High Churchmen's Dr. Berkeley. Although he disclaimed any knowledge of Seabury or Scotland's Episcopal Church (and his statements, ludicrous in their errors, show that he spoke truly),[98] Sharp in February, 1785, dashed off a communication to James Manning (College of New Jersey, 1762), the Baptist President of the College of Rhode Island, in which he warned of Seabury's coming and counseled a careful scrutiny of his credentials on the grounds that the Scots succession might very well be defective.[99] Manning carried the letter to New York and, after showing it to various Congressmen, lent it to Provoost, who asked and received permission to copy the text. This transcript, Manning reported to Sharp, he intended to communicate to the neighboring clergy and later to members of the General Convention.[100]

Provoost carried out his plan. Upon arriving at New York on the way to Philadelphia, Convention deputy Henry Purcell (Oxford, 1763), rector of St. Michael's, Charleston, was introduced to Sharp's statements. Provoost, however, probably did not know that James Rivington counted Purcell an intimate friend. Informed of his action, the printer persuaded Purcell to talk with Benjamin Moore, who soon convinced him that Seabury's consecration was valid. The Carolinian, in fact, became the bishop's ardent champion, and in a letter dated September 15 begged him to send a refutation of Sharp which he might use at Philadelphia. Rivington, writing on the same sheet, seconded the request, urging Seabury to send a "justificatory epistle" which would show that he was "as perfectly episcopized as the Great Chrysostom himself."[101]

The bishop did not draft such a document, possibly for reasons of prudence, possibly because, about the time he received the plea, a pamphlet came from the New Haven press detailing his episcopal lineage from 1688.[102] Very likely this publicizing of the Scots succession—done at Seabury's instance—represented a direct response to Sharp's letter; almost certainly he knew of it before Purcell gave him notice.[103]

If Seabury sent copies of the pamphlet to Philadelphia, they probably arrived too late to be seen by the deputies. Provoost's circulation of his transcript among them did have, according to White, a certain effect.[104] Patriot Latitudinarians, noting Sharp's fears of the genuineness of the Scottish episcopate, likewise fastened upon his assertion that Scotland's Churchmen were a group of stalwart Jacobites. In their minds, dislike of unlimited submission, indefeasible hereditary right, and Loyalism easily merged, forming a second plausible objection to the acceptance of Connecticut's bishop. This is well-illustrated by Jay's statements to John Adams, then American Minister in London:

> The [General] convention are not inclined to acknowledge or have any thing to do with Mr. Seabury. His own high church principles, and the high church principles of those who ordained him, do not quadrate either with the political principles of our Episcopalians in general, or with those on which our revolution and constitutions are founded. . . . I confess I do not like the principles of the non-jurors; and, I think, the less patronage such opinions meet with among us, the better.[105]

Nothing would alter Jay's stand: the Secretary for Foreign Affairs was beyond persuasion. On the other hand, persons whose judgment was less influenced by political factors found that the New Haven pamphlet fully removed all difficulties. Stephen James DeLancey, pious old aristocrat and a friend from Westchester days, wrote Seabury in October, 1785, offering to devote his remaining years to that county's desolate churches. He would have applied for Orders earlier, DeLancey explained, but "the whig Clergy (sorry I am to use the term) said you were not

Lawfully Ordained & Desired me not to acknowledge you as A Bishop of our Church but by A pamphlet publish'd I trust by your permission there is no doubt of it."[106]

DeLancey added that the same clergy had predicted Seabury's formal rejection as a bishop by the General Convention. Provoost, however, lacked the strength to effect this. And he could not prevent candidates for Orders, resident in the states represented in the Convention, from procuring credentials and resorting to Connecticut's bishop. The Trinity rector was furious at these proceedings, since churches, by accepting the men as pastors, implicitly acknowledged Seabury's episcopal status. To White he complained: "If Private persons continue these recommendations to Dr Cebra the Validity of whose consecration as a Bishop has neither been acknowledged nor Discussed in Convention—I foresee that the Bands which united us together in Philadelphia will be converted into a Rope of Sand."[107]

It would be interesting to know White's reaction, since he was a guilty party, as were James Madison (William and Mary, 1771) and Thomas John Claggett (College of New Jersey, 1764), also future bishops, and William Smith. On the basis of their and other testimonials, Seabury in 1785-86 conferred deacon's and priest's Orders on some seventeen men who assumed posts outside Connecticut: six in Maryland, five in Virginia, two in New Jersey, one each in North Carolina, Pennsylvania, New York, and Rhode Island. In addition, he ordained three deacons (priested in subsequent years) to serve in New Hampshire and Vermont. Connecticut during this period was given six new pastors, bringing the number of the bishop's protégés to twenty-six.[108] A would-be poet found the mounting total impressive:

> From Harvards walls and Providence behold
> The sons of science flocking to thy fold,
> New York and Yale their learned offspring send,
> And Pennsylvania greets thee as her friend,
> While ruin'd temples rising from decay

Shall beam with Glory on thy Gospel day
Columbia's freemen shall united call
The[e] Father of our Church Episcopal.[109]

All of these men, whether intended for Connecticut or for other states, signed a subscription and received certificates of Orders reflecting Seabury's conviction that changes in the Prayer Book and Articles, made without episcopal approval, were quite unwarranted. At his first ordination, for example, the four candidates for the diaconate each declared they would use the Prayer Book of 1662 "as far as shall be consistent with the alteration to be made on account of the civil constitution of the state in which I shall live . . . & none other, unless in obedience to competent ecclesiastical authority."[110] What the bishop regarded as "competent ecclesiastical authority" is shown by the revision of this early form of subscription (used as late as November 27, 1785) which he was employing in 1788 and which he probably had devised after learning of the proceedings of the first General Convention. Ordained priest in Trinity Church, Boston, March 27, 1788, John Cosens Ogden (College of New Jersey, 1770) agreed to use the English Book as conformed to the American constitutions and to hold himself "subject to the Bishop of Connecticut to whose ecclesiastical authority I do promise all due obedience untill there shall be a Bishop regularly settled in the state [New Hampshire] where I shall reside."[111]

Seabury defended his subscriptions in an early letter to Bishop Skinner. "It seemed right to me," he explained, "to put those Gentlemen particularly, who were not under my immediate direction, under some restraint with regard to the mode of officiating; & as no other mode has yet been here agreed upon, the old one of course was adopted." This procedure had given offense to some of the Southern clergy, who discouraged candidates from applying, "telling them that I exacted an oath of obedience to myself without any limitations."[112] Such rumors reached Walker Maury (William and Mary, 1775), master of a grammar school in Williamsburg, Virginia. Before setting out for Connecticut, he inquired exactly what was demanded of candidates, "report having raised some difficulties, as well in regard to a subscription to doctrinal points, as to an oath of future dependence on your See."[113]

Seabury's reply proved satisfactory: Maury received Orders in Trinity Church, New Haven, in July, 1786.[114] However, complaints about the bishop's ordination practices continued, and much was said of them at the second General Convention, held in Philadelphia June 20 to June 26, 1786. There critics asserted that Seabury every day became more careless about proper titles and credentials. He had even made clergymen of "very illiterate persons, ignorant Methodists and others." (In this statement, there was at least some truth, for the bishop had indeed ordained several former Methodist preachers,[115] complying with a promise he had given Charles Wesley in London: "He told me he looked upon the Methodists in America, as sound members of the Church," Wesley reported to Chandler, "and was ready to Ordain any of their Preachers whom he should find duly qualified.")[116] Rumor also accused Seabury of taking large fees—"ten guineas and upwards"—or, at any rate, as much as candidates offered. He was further reported to have sent his episcopal charges to such of these men as served parishes outside Connecticut, enjoining them, in conformity to their subscription, not to use the Proposed Book.[117]

Except in the instance noted, no surviving evidence provides any support for these assertions. Nevertheless, they created considerable hostility to Seabury, and that hostility encouraged Provoost to act. With the help of his lay associates, he had secured from the New York Convention, June 13, a resolution "That the persons appointed to represent this church [in General Convention], be instructed not to consent to any act that may imply the validity of Dr. Seabury's ordinations."[118] Thus armed, Provoost (and Jay) launched an assault at Philadelphia, aided by Robert Smith (Cambridge, 1754), rector of St. Philip's, Charleston.

For Patriots, the reasons these men offered the deputies to support their claim that Seabury's consecration was schismatical—and his ordinations, in consequence, questionable—were singularly odd. You are accused, wrote William Smith, of "having broke off from the English Bishops, to whom, as being then an English subject, and resident in London, you owed obedience, &c.; and, deriving your consecration from Bishops whose consecration of English subjects is, by the laws of England, deemed invalid, &c."[119] This line of argument, quite different from that presented at the first General Convention, had been adopted because Seabury's critics, by this date, were unwilling to contest the validity of the Scots succession. Presumably, the publication of his episcopal lineage had convinced them that such an attempt must fail.

Robert Smith began the attack, moving on the second day of the Convention "That the Clergy present produce their Letters of Orders, or declare by whom they were ordained." His object was the unseating of Joseph Pilmore, a Seabury ordinee. However, some mistakenly interpreted the motion as impugning all ordinations by bishops of the Scottish line and as such an attack, not only upon Pilmore, but also upon one William Smith (Aberdeen, 1774), a young immigrant who, it is believed, had received Orders from Bishop Kilgour or Bishop Skinner.[120] Included in this number was Dr. William Smith. Immediately he came to his kinsman's[121] defense, calling for the previous question, in which action White seconded him. Their motion was lost, but the original one being put, the Convention determined it in the negative. This defeat compelled the anti-Seabury forces to become more specific. After some other business had been transacted, Provoost, seconded by Robert Smith, moved "That this Convention will resolve to do no act that shall imply the validity of ordinations made by Dr. Seabury." Again Dr. Smith moved the previous question, again White seconded, and again their efforts to suppress the motion failed. Yet the Charleston and New York rectors met with a swift rebuke. New Jersey, Pennsylvania, Maryland, Virginia, and Delaware voted against their motion; only their own delegations endorsed it.[122]

White, attempting to produce at least a surface harmony, next proposed that state conventions accept as pastors "no Clergymen professing canonical subjection to any Bishop, in any State or country, other than those Bishops who may be duly settled in the States represented in this Convention." He did not believe the men Seabury had ordained for posts outside Connecticut could be injured by such a ban—Pilmore explicitly denied their being put under "canonical subjection"—and if it would destroy apprehensions, let it be established! White's motion carried unanimously, as did a second, less innocent resolution, offered the following day by Robert Smith. It urged state conventions not to "admit any person as a Minister within their respective limits, who shall receive ordination from any Bishop residing in America, during the application now pending to the English Bishops for Episcopal consecration."[123]

Writing to White in September, Samuel Parker condemned the "coolness and Indifference" with which "some of the Gentlemen in your Convention speak of Bishop Seabury." This situation, the Bostonian feared, must produce a total rupture. Reaffirming his belief in the validity of Seabury's ordinations, he singled out Smith's ambiguously worded motion for particular criticism. If the deputies "meant to limit it, during the pending of your application to England, and were actuated herein from a principle of not doing anything that might give Umbrage to the English Bishops," it perhaps was a prudent step. But if they acted from other motives, Parker would interpret the motion as a declaration of war against the Bishop of Connecticut, foreboding "a settled and perpetual Enmity."[124]

Seabury's response to Smith's action is not recorded. Undoubtedly he must have resented it, even if it had produced no effects. And, in fact, the resolution did dissuade Southern candidates from seeking ordination.[125] Nevertheless, in the second half of 1786, Seabury had a more important matter to consider: the General Convention's application to England for bishops which had given Smith his opportunity. Ever since October, 1785, when the English episcopate had first been sounded on the subject, he had watched the application's progress with the greatest interest and had formulated, as a result of it, plans to secure a bishop for the remaining New England states.

Unlike Parker, who dreaded a schism should the Southern churches obtain any bishops except those of the Scottish line,[126] Seabury offered no objections to an episcopate derived from England. He heartily wished that all the states might secure bishops—provided they were bishops "upon true Episcopal principles." An episcopate formed according to the model of the General Convention's ecclesiastical constitution, "subject to the control of, & liable to be deposed by, a Consistory of Presbyters & Laymen," was to him intolerable. Such a system must be "Presbuterical in fact, though Episcopal in name"; its bishops, ordination mechanisms—nothing more! Before the English bishops took any decisive action, Seabury hoped they would carefully examine the Proposed Book, as well as the proceedings of the General Convention and those of the different states.[127]

Provoost believed the bishop was actively opposing the introduction of a Convention-style episcopate. "If we may judge from appearances Dr. Cebra and his friends are using every art to prevent the success of our Application to the English prelates," he reported to White at the end of 1785. "A close Correspondence is kept up between him Chandler &c. and a few days ago two large packets were seen at Rivingtons addressed to the Archbishop of Canterbury one of which it was imagined came from Dr. Chandler."[128]

Chandler certainly was guilty as charged. On the very day Provoost drafted his letter, he himself got off one to Seabury, criticizing the General Convention's proposed episcopate in the same manner as had his friend. To the Archbishop of Canterbury (who regularly received his reports), Chandler had given a full account of the Philadelphia proceedings. Although he could not believe the English bishops would "be accessory to such a degradation of their own Order," he nevertheless thought it necessary to put Moore on his guard.[129]

Seabury avoided such direct action: no letters passed between New London and Lambeth. But the bishop was not wholly idle. In late November, 1785, he went to Wallingford, where Jarvis and Hubbard and two other ministers gathered to assist him in an ordination. Hubbard, at the conclusion of this affair, wrote Samuel Peters in London, requesting the former Connecticut missionary "to employ your abilities in the service of a broken tattered Church." Specifically, Hubbard wanted Peters, "keeping us out of sight[,] to get published as occasion shall require, the following Squibs in the London Newspapers, you can improve upon them far & near."[130] These articles were compounded equally of Loyalism and staunch Churchmanship, and they formed a slashing attack upon the General Convention's work. Obviously Hubbard intended them for the eyes of the English bishops.

Whether Seabury penned all the Wallingford squibs is uncertain, but the one savagely assaulting Dr. Smith and his pretensions to the episcopate displays "A. W. Farmer's" unmistakable style. A satirical biography, it recounted Smith's shifts from the Scots Episcopal to the Presbyterian Church and then to the Church of England, as well as his Loyalist-Patriot maneuvers during the Revolution. In short, he was portrayed as an unprincipled changeling, also "ambitious, vain & intrieguing," dishonest in money matters, and a drunkard to boot! The bishop's trumpeting of these charges (long the subject of private comment)[131] is to be explained by his fear that plans were afoot to send Smith to London for consecration, he, upon his return, to consecrate White and Provoost.[132] Seabury's objections to the latter two men were not insuperable. Indeed, in London he and Chandler had agreed upon White as the logical choice for the Pennsylvania episcopate.[133] But Smith, if he could help it, should never be decked out in rochet and chimere! To Bishop Skinner, he declared that if the archbishops agreed to so censurable a consecration, they would have "great need to repeat daily the general Confession, 'We have left undone [those things which we ought to have done; And we have done those things which we ought not to have done].' "[134] His alarm, however, appears to have been groundless, for Inglis, constantly in Moore's company, reported the primate showed an equal determination that Smith should remain a simple clergyman.[135]

The General Convention's application to the English episcopate convinced Seabury that he must bolster his position with one or two congenial colleagues. Probably at no time had he fully embraced Parker's suggestion that he assume jurisdiction over all the churches of the New England states; a diocese that vast did not agree with his notions of strict episcopal supervision. In any case, the scheme was hanging fire. Acquainting Trinity Church, Newport, with the projected Boston Convention of September 7, 8, 1785, Parker had explained that its "grand object" would be to see if "we shall join with Connecticut and receive their Bishop; or, whether we shall choose a deputy or deputies to attend the general convention at Philadelphia in September, or adopt any other measures to continue as one communion."[136] By declining to appoint General Convention deputies and by endorsing the Middletown proposals, the Convention placed itself in a position to adopt the first alternative, but it took no definite step. And although Parker reported to Seabury that he expected the clergy "at their next meeting" to accept the bishop, paying him "the same submission and obedience the Clergy of Connecticut have done,"[137] the failure of the Boston Convention to reassemble as planned, on October 26, prevented early action.

Against the background of these developments, Seabury, November 28, 1785, addressed a letter to Parker from Wallingford. Consulting with certain pastors (presumably Jarvis and Hubbard, Samuel Andrews and James Scovil),[138] he had decided it would be best to secure a bishop "to the eastward," who, with representatives of his clergy, should meet with himself and similar proctors from Connecticut and establish a uniform liturgy. Seabury hoped Parker and his neighbors would take up this matter the following summer. Whether he intended to consecrate their candidate himself (should they select one) or—more likely—recommend him to Scotland, he did not say. He intended to be at New London "the last of this Week, & hope I shall not again be called out in the course of the winter, unless to give you a half-way meeting, in case you should think it advisable."[139]

Parker replied that such an interview was absolutely essential prior to the meeting of the Boston Convention, now adjourned until the week after Easter. But he rejected Seabury's proposal: "As to procuring another Bishop in the Eastern States, it cannot be accomplished at present, nor would it be at all necessary was there a person resident in them qualified for the Office, which is [not] now the Case." One bishop for the whole of New England was "fully sufficient."[140] This argument Seabury refused to accept, so with the goal of winning over Parker (as well as getting donations for a new St. James's, New London), he proposed a Boston visit instead of a halfway conference, "for I presume they will not be alarmed at the appearance of so harmless a Bishop as I am."[141] Accordingly, late March found him in the metropolis, pressing his views upon the Trinity rector.[142] Nothing came of their discussion, however, nor was the bishop, as Parker hoped, received by the clergy at the next Convention. The reasons why Parker's scheme failed do not appear in the extant correspondence, but unless Seabury proved adamantly opposed (which seems unlikely), they probably resulted from the division existing among the small number of Massachusetts pastors. Parker, the only one to correspond with Episcopal leaders in other states, had the support of Seabury's second cousin, Edward Bass, a man influenced by New England's traditional Churchmanship, although not in full agreement with all the bishop's views.[143] William Willard Wheeler and Nathaniel Fisher, whose rectorships did not antedate the Revolution, were, however, men of a very different sort. Reputed Socinians, or, at least, Socinian sympathizers, they showed no desire to subject themselves to any kind of episcopal supervision.[144]

Plans for a second bishop of the Scots succession having come to a temporary halt, Seabury concentrated his attention on the General Convention's application. Initially, it had produced a favorable reaction: the English prelates resolved to comply with its request provided no political difficulties intervened. None did, but reports (among them possibly the Wallingford squibs) reaching London that the Convention was departing from Church of England worship and doctrine, the prelates became more cautious, especially since the application said nothing about a revision of the Prayer Book and Articles.[145] A friendly but carefully worded letter was returned, indicating that Archbishop Moore and his colleagues must satisfy themselves as to the Convention's essential agreement with the English Church before they could provide an episcopate.[146] Jonathan Boucher, frequently consulted by Moore on American ecclesiastical affairs, sent Seabury a summary of this reply, which reached New London, May 24, 1786, just twelve days after the reply itself—signed by nineteen bishops—was delivered to Provoost at New York.[147] To Seabury the episcopate's statement was both a vindication of his own position and a warning that the Convention's application would be rejected, unless that body altered its plan of government. "I humbly beg pardon of the Bishops in England," he quipped. "They are not so low in principles as I feared they were."[148]

Seabury's assessment of the situation, it soon developed, was, from his point of view, overly optimistic. The bishops, upon examining the Proposed Book and newly modeled Articles, found, to their relief, that they did not favor Arian or Socinian tenets. Archbishop Moore disliked the liturgy, but if certain things in it were remedied, he was willing to consecrate.[149] In a second letter to the Convention he listed his terms: the article of the descent into hell should be restored to the Apostles' Creed and the Nicene Creed and Athanasian Creed reinserted in the Prayer Book, to the extent, at least, that their use might become discretional.[150] The letters of Chandler and Boucher's advice probably had some effect in formulating these requirements. Inglis' counsel certainly influenced Moore, and it was at his pleading that the archbishop, just before dispatching the letter (which was also signed by Archbishop Markham), inserted a sentence labeling the eighth article of the General Convention's constitution "a degradation of the Clerical, and still more of the Episcopal character."[151] Moore told the Convention rather plainly that this provision, relating to the state conventions' cognizance of offenses committed by bishops and ministers, ought to be revised. He also submitted forms for the testimonials the bishops-elect were to bring to England. Concerned with the individual candidate's learning, morals, and religious character, they were drafted in such strict and solemn terms that Smith, it was believed, would not be able to obtain them.[152] As for lay deputies, so strenuously opposed by Seabury, the archbishop said nothing at all.

Before the receipt of this letter, forwarded in June, 1786, the Convention, in its second meeting at Philadelphia, had already revised its constitution, providing that the presidency should be held by a bishop if one were present, and making rules for the trial and punishment of bishops and clergymen more in agreement with Seabury's notions.[153] These provisions, hopefully, would obviate Moore's objection to the eighth article. After the archbishop's communication arrived, an adjourned session, sitting at Wilmington, October 10, 11, made additional changes, restoring the article of the descent into hell and authorizing the discretional use of the Nicene, but not the Athanasian, Creed.[154] White did not think the wording of Moore's letter implied that the latter creed's reintroduction (or, indeed, any of his politely phrased requirements) was to be considered a *sine qua non* of consecration.[155] Both he and Provoost, chosen bishops by their state conventions, received testimonials at Wilmington, and without waiting to learn whether or not the several revisions had satisfied Moore, they sailed from New York in November. To Samuel Parker, Benjamin Moore observed: "It sometimes happens, in doubtful cases, that to act as if you were *sure* of success, is the most effectual way to obtain it. *Possunt quia posse videntur.*"[156] The maxim was applicable, for on Sunday, February 4, 1787, Archbishop Moore, assisted by Archbishop Markham and the Bishops of Bath and Wells and Peterborough, consecrated Provoost and White at Lambeth Palace.

Seabury had been kept well informed of the London measures leading to this event. Boucher sent him a report of the second letter to the General Convention, probably in the same packet in which it arrived, and Inglis, in September, 1786, forwarded a detailed account of the whole negotiation with the English prelates.[157] The expressions used by his friends may have given Seabury some hope that the Convention's constitution and liturgy would be judged objectionable, even with considerable revision. (At any rate, he regarded the departure of Provoost and White as hasty and premature.)[158] Yet, mulling over the reports, he must have focused upon the fact that the archbishop's criticism, compared to his own, was relatively mild. Such reticence produced first fear, then a growing conviction: Provoost and White would obtain the Orders they sought.

Sharing this view, Connecticut's clergy became anxious; in the event of the bishop's death, the "spirit of innovation" giving rise to the "Southern establishment" might wreak its havoc even in their state. To guard against such a development, they wished to choose a coadjutor and send him to Scotland for consecration.

Seabury agreed to the proposal.[159] At the same time, with support from his Convocation, he revived and coupled with it the idea of securing a bishop of the Scottish line for the other New England states. This latter scheme, however, had again no chance of being realized, since Parker remained opposed.[160]

The decision to supply Seabury with a coadjutor was taken at Wallingford in late February, 1787. Finding a willing candidate proved a problem for the Convocation. Leaming, the first choice, declined because of age and infirmities. Richard Mansfield, selected in his stead, felt that he could not bear the burdens of the episcopate. Why the clergy should have chosen these men is not clear. Both were older than Seabury, and although they were to outlive him, the contrary would naturally be assumed. A third attempt produced the logical candidate, Abraham Jarvis, the forty-seven-year-old secretary.[161] Jarvis declined giving an answer until the May session of the Convocation.[162] However, Seabury, presuming his acceptance, notified Bishop Skinner that he would embark on the first available vessel as soon as word was received that the plan "meets with the full approbation of my good and highly respected brethren in Scotland."[163]

Having sanctioned this strengthening of the High Church forces, Seabury next prepared to approach Provoost and White on the subject of a union. With Jarvis to back him, he could meet the Conventionists on better ground. The bishop's fears rose higher than his hopes,[164] but he had some reason for optimism. Lieutenant Colonel Edward Hicks, his brother-in-law, had written from London in January reporting a visit by White; Hicks gathered from their conversation that White had a good opinion of Seabury and desired "a perfect harmony & good understanding among his Brethren the other side of the Water."[165] Ultimately more encouraging (but of no use to Seabury at the time he made his decisions, since it arrived too late) was a second letter, from Inglis. He had conferred with Provoost, privately and in company with White, had sought to remove the doubts which they hinted as to Seabury's willingness to coalesce, and had come away firmly convinced that both men "wished to unite & hold a brotherly communication with You."[166] This line of conduct, Inglis added, had been strongly recommended by the Archbishop of Canterbury.

Seabury acted on May 1. Picking his words with care, he sent congratulatory messages to Provoost and White, expressing also his pleasure at Provoost's recovery from a serious illness. The second paragraph, the crucial one, was identical in both letters:

> You must be equally sensible with me of the present unsettled state of the Church of England in this country, & of the necessity of union & concord, among all its members in the United States of America, not only to give stability to it, but to fix it on its true & proper foundation. Possibly nothing will contribute more to this end than uniformity in worship & discipline among the Churches of the different States. It will be my happiness to be able to promote so good & necessary a work: And I take the liberty to propose, that before any decided steps be taken, there may be a meeting of yourself & Bishop White with me at such time & place as shall be most convenient; to try whether some plan cannot be adopted that shall in a quiet & effectual way, secure the great object which I trust we should all heartily rejoice to see accomplished. For my own part I cannot help thinking that the most likely method will be to retain the present Common Prayer Book, accommodating it to the Civil Constitution of the United States. The government of the Church, you know, is already settled: A body of Canons will however be wanted to give energy to the government, & to ascertain its operations.

Seabury warmly urged Provoost's attendance at the forthcoming session of the Convocation, to be held on the Thursday after Whitsunday. Originally scheduled for Norwalk,[167] it would now meet at Stamford, presumably in order that the Bishop of New York might have to travel no further than was absolutely necessary. White likewise was informed of the session, but Seabury regretted that time and distance probably would not permit his being present, the "more especially as I think it would greatly promote so essential an object as the union of all our Churches must be esteemed."[168]

Connecticut's bishop had employed a friendly tone; he had bestowed compliments freely. Yet it should be evident from the passage quoted that he had offered no real compromise. This fact was underlined by a letter to an English correspondent in which he reported his proposal of "an union of the Church of England through all the States, on the ground of the present Prayer Book only accommodating it to the Civil Constitution of this Country; And the government of the Church to continue unaltered."[169] If Provoost and White wished to unite with Seabury, they must accept the polity and liturgy of Connecticut's Church. Such an unconditional surrender they naturally refused.

Provoost, whose actions hardly accord with his declarations to Inglis, did not bother to reply and soon was reported to be considering the reordination of ministers who had received Orders in Connecticut.[170] White showed some signs of yielding on the question of the Prayer Book. With respect to the more basic matters at issue, he was, however, as firm as his correspondent. The Bishop of Pennsylvania's sentences, though polite, left no doubt as to his position:

> We have been informed (but perhaps it is a Mistake) that the Bishop & Clergy of Connecticut think our proposed Ecclesiastical Constitution essentially wrong in the leading Parts of it. As the general Principles on which it is founded were maturely considered & compared with the Maxims which prevail in the Ecclesiastical System of England; as they have received the Approbation of all the Conventions Southward of You & of one to the Northward; as they were not objected to by the Archbishops & Bishops of the English Church; & as they are generally thought among us essential to the giving of Effect to future Ecclesiastical Measures; I do not expect to find the Churches in many of the States willing to associate, on any Plan materially different from this. If our Brethren in Connecticut should be of Opinion, that the giving of any Share of the legislative Power of the Church to others than those of the Episcopal Order, is inconsistent with Episcopal Government; & that the requiring of the Consent

> of the Laity to Ecclesiastical Laws is an Invasion of Clerical Rights; in this case, I see no Prospect of my doing Good in any other way, than by contributing all in my Power to promote a Spirit of Love & Peace between us: although I shall continue to cultivate the Hope of our being brought at some future Day to an happy Agreement.[171]

By the summer of 1787, Seabury knew his efforts had failed. Connecticut held tightly to her traditional concepts of church government. The Southern churches, regarding that subject, were equally tenacious of their more recently formulated opinions. Prospects for a general ecclesiastical union seemed no more promising than they had been two years before. Indeed, the picture was darker; the deadlock, more complete.

VIII

"I HAVE DETERMINED TO GO TO PHILADELPHIA"

AFTER THE REJECTION OF SEABURY'S 1787 PROPOSALS, other spokesmen in the High Church camp sought to effect a loosely structured union of all Episcopalians, leaving disputed matters unreconciled. As early as 1786, Jeremiah Leaming had mentioned the idea to Abraham Beach: so long as there was agreement regarding articles of faith, churches might join hands although their liturgies and governments varied.[1] In letters to White, written shortly after the bishop's return from England, Leaming hinted at this approach, urging that Congressman William Samuel Johnson be sounded and that an early meeting be held by Seabury, White, and Provoost.[2] Simultaneously, Samuel Parker developed another plan for unity in diversity. "I cannot see why upon the Supposition of a different ecclesiastical form of Government, the Bishops of the several States may not agree in one common Liturgy & a uniformity of worship be preserved, if not of Discipline," he observed to White in July, 1787.[3]

Both Leaming and Parker linked the cause of union with the consecration of a fourth bishop by the three already in the United States. Scotland's episcopal succession and that of England might merge in the elevating of David Griffith, a New Yorker, a former

S.P.G. missionary in New Jersey, and now, in 1787, Bishop-Elect of Virginia.[4] That state's Convention, however, explicitly rejected the idea of joining Seabury with White and Provoost,[5] and while the Virginians might have reconsidered, Provoost's implacable dislike of Seabury must still have prevented its realization. Even White, though he desired a union and judged "that any Difficulties which have hitherty [sic] seemed in the Way might be removed by mutual Forbearance," scrupled to adopt such a course. To Parker he wrote, August 6, 1787:

> I will be very explicit with you on the Questions you put in regard to an Union with Bishop Seabury & the Consecration of Dr. Griffith. On the one hand, considering it was presumed a third was to go over to England, that the Institutions of the Church of that Country require three to join in the Consecration, & that the political Situation of the English Prelates prevents their official Knowledge of Dr Seabury as a Bishop, I am apprehensive it may seem a Breach of Faith towards them, if not an intend[ed] Deception in us, were we to consecrate without the usual Number, & those all under the English Succession; although it would not be inconsistent with this Idea, that another Gentleman under a different Succession should be joined with us.[6]

This letter and the similar one which Leaming presumably received[7] put an end to these particular efforts (although Leaming, as late as August, 1788, attempted to enlist William Samuel Johnson's aid in reviving the scheme of a joint consecration of Dr. Griffith).[8] Parker, who had never got the better of fears that the introduction of bishops of the English line would produce a schism, now judged the situation utterly hopeless. "I agree with you that White & Provoost will never form a Coalition with Bishop Seabury," he declared to Samuel Peters in September, 1787, "not that the former kissed Georges & the latter Jamess hand, but because Oil & Vinegar cannot unite, Whigs & Tories cannot act cordially together, one have a democratical Constitution to act by, the other a monarchical. Connecticut preserves the

Discipline of the primitive Church, New York & Philadelphia have fashioned theirs upon the principles of Republicanism."[9]

Whether Seabury knew of his friends' correspondence with White is uncertain. Still, he was not unaware of suggestions for union along the lines they had proposed. Bishop Skinner, spokesman for his colleagues, urged a similar plan in replying to Seabury's letter soliciting the consecration of a coadjutor. This request had created a dilemma for the Scottish episcopate, caught, as they were, between a desire to help the Bishop of Connecticut and a fear of antagonizing, by a second consecration, the English bishops, whose support they hoped to secure in negotiating repeal of the anti-Episcopal laws.[10] Understandably, they sought a way out: interpreting in the most optimistic light the information about Provoost and White which he had received from English friends (mainly, it would seem, from Boucher), Skinner urged Seabury to coalesce with the bishops of the English line on the basis of each side's retaining its own liturgy. Connecticut's coadjutor, in this way, could be consecrated in the United States. Nevertheless, should the "new Bishops either refuse Communion with your Church, or grant it only on terms, which you cannot in conscience comply with," Scotland would act. In that case, Skinner declared, "there would be no room left for us to hesitate in the Affair."[11]

Pleas for a coalition had earlier been voiced by Inglis,[12] and they were repeated by William Stevens, who wrote from London, July 4, 1787, two weeks after the date of Skinner's letter. "As you are distinct, independent churches, absolute conformity in all particulars is not necessary," the prominent layman asserted. "Agreement in essentials will be sufficient for giving each other the right hand of fellowship, and preserving the unity of the spirit in the bond of peace."[13] Boucher's opinion was identical. Seabury's friends, he observed, "seem to be anxious that, if it be practicable, You should coalesce with your Brethren now both North [Inglis had been consecrated Bishop of Nova Scotia,

August 12, 1787] and South of You. We see not, why this may not be done, without any Sacrifice either of Principles or Interests on either Side."[14]

Counsels of this sort, no matter how tactfully expressed, offended the Bishop of Connecticut. Although the evidence is not complete, it appears that sometime after the rejection of his proposals of May 1, 1787, Seabury had sent another letter to White, in which he suggested such a union as would formally authorize Connecticut's communicants and those of the Southern churches to receive the Sacrament in each other's congregations. In addition, clergymen ordained by the three American bishops might hold a parish charge in any of the states. (The much canvassed idea of a joint consecration perhaps formed yet another part of the bishop's proposal, for his Convocation agreed that "there might a Christian agreement take place so far as to establish the Church in America [that is, an agreement to consecrate bishops for the various states] if they could not agree on the particular mode of exercising the right of that Church.")[15] This letter never reached Philadelphia, and the resulting failure of White to send an answer Seabury interpreted as a calculated rebuff.[16] When, therefore, correspondents urged him to a coalition, he became indignant. Never one to bear in silence what he regarded as unjust criticism, he resented hints that *his* stiffness was the obstacle. To Parker he complained that "all the difficulty" lay with the Southern churches, "not with us in Connecticut," explaining:

> I have several times proposed & urged a union, it has been received & treated, I think, coldly. And yet I have received several letters urging such a union on me as tho' I was the only person who opposed it —this is not fair—I am ready to treat & settle the terms of Union on any proper notice. But Bishops White & Provoost must bear their part in it *actively* as well as myself. And we must come into the Union on even terms, [and not?] as underlings.[17]

Such was Seabury's state of mind when, in December, 1788, White broke his supposed silence. From a Connecticut ordinee recently settled near Philadelphia he had learned that a letter sent him by Seabury had drawn no reply; unaware of the bishop's later communication, he assumed the letter must be that of May 1, 1787, and that his answer, dated May 21, had miscarried. Conceivably, White might have done nothing more than repeat what he had then said. But the dangers of a continued impasse in negotiations increasingly impressed him, and, for this reason, he now showed an eagerness to compromise. Going beyond his stand of 1787, he offered concrete possibilities for an accommodation of the two principal matters at issue.

White's paragraph relating to the Proposed Book obviously was designed to persuade Seabury that a mutually acceptable liturgy might still be framed. Implying that the General Convention scheduled for July, 1789, probably would have views on this subject similar to those of his own clergy, he declared that the Pennsylvanians had never approved some parts of that production, "And, as to those we were for, I believe there are none we should not be disposed to give up, if they appear to give Offence in any considerable Extent." Lay deputies, White admitted, posed a thornier problem. Explaining why he thought the Southern churches would not give up this feature of their polity, he at the same time extended a second olive branch. "If any thing should be desired, for the Accommodation of the Church in any State where the Clergy will not admit & the Laity do not desire" lay representation, he would be "among the first to advocate some conciliatory Expedient for that purpose." To this end, and in order that all questions might be thoroughly treated, White hoped Seabury would appear at the forthcoming Convention session; should he not see his way clear to attend, perhaps some of his clergy might come instead.[18]

White's proposals were prophetic. A fresh start in the matter of Prayer Book alterations and a revised polity incorporating Connecticut's system into the "federal plan" would soon produce a united Episcopal Church. However, these ideas were as yet anathema to Bishop Provoost. Noting a suggestion of William

Smith that the General Convention's standing committee might extend a formal invitation to Connecticut, Provoost crisply registered his view. "An Invitation to the Church in that State to meet us . . . I conceive to be neither necessary nor proper," he wrote White in February, 1789, "not necessary, because I am Informed that they have already appointed two persons to attend the next general Convention without our Invitation—not proper; because it is publickly known that they have adopted a Form of Church government which renders them inadmissible as members of the Convention or Union."[19]

With this letter, Provoost enclosed a resolution calling upon New York's General Convention deputies to promote a union "by every prudent measure, consistent with the Constitution of the Church, and the Continuance of the Episcopal Succession in the English Line." As originally offered in his Trinity Church vestry, the resolution carried no qualifications, but Provoost, fearing concessions to Connecticut were afoot, had insisted that the deputies be bound strictly to the altered version before allowing it to pass unopposed in the state Convention.[20] New York's bishop maintained a position identical with that of Seabury in 1787: if the other side desired a union, it might have it only on the basis of complete surrender.

Seabury, of course, had no intention of accepting such terms. Neither, after he had thoroughly considered the matter, was he at all forward to develop the compromises White had suggested. Still smarting at the notion that he was standing in the way of a union and feeling that his Church, in some instances, had been treated by the General Convention "in a manner bordering on contempt," he saw a private conference with Provoost and White (the three of them to be attended by certain of their clergy) as the sole source from which an agreement might come. To hazard himself or his representatives in a mass of General Convention deputies—for so he ultimately interpreted White's invitation—was intolerable. "It must be a union of the Church in Connecticut with the Church of the Southern States upon just and reasonable

Samuel Seabury in his last years. Oil portrait by an unidentified artist.

Samuel Seabury 1706-1764. Oil portrait tentatively attributed to John Smibert.

The General Area of Samuel Seabury's Activities 1748-1783

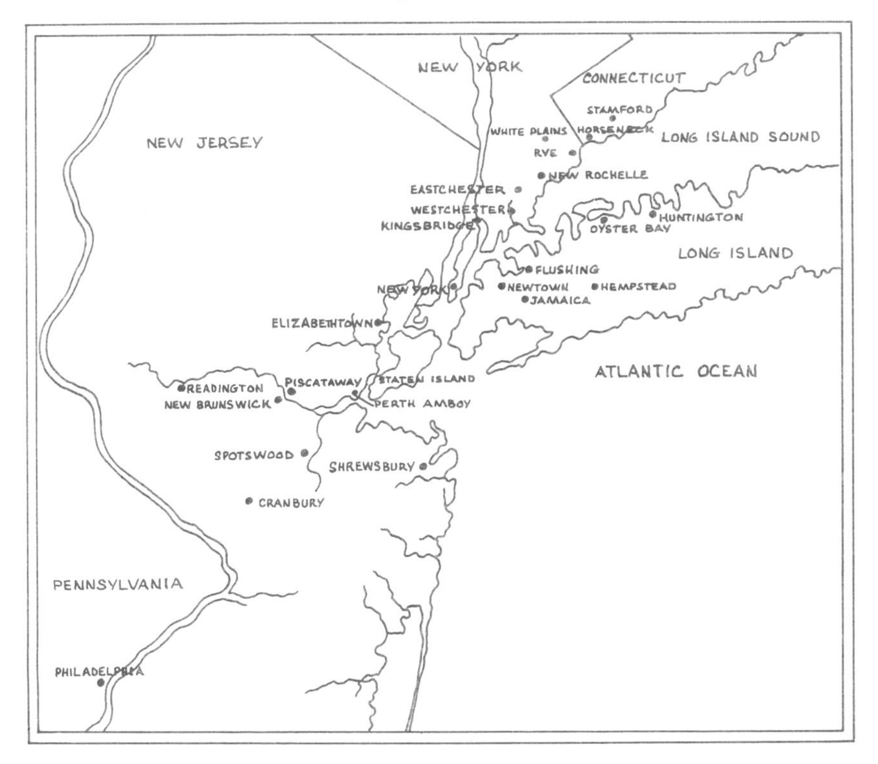

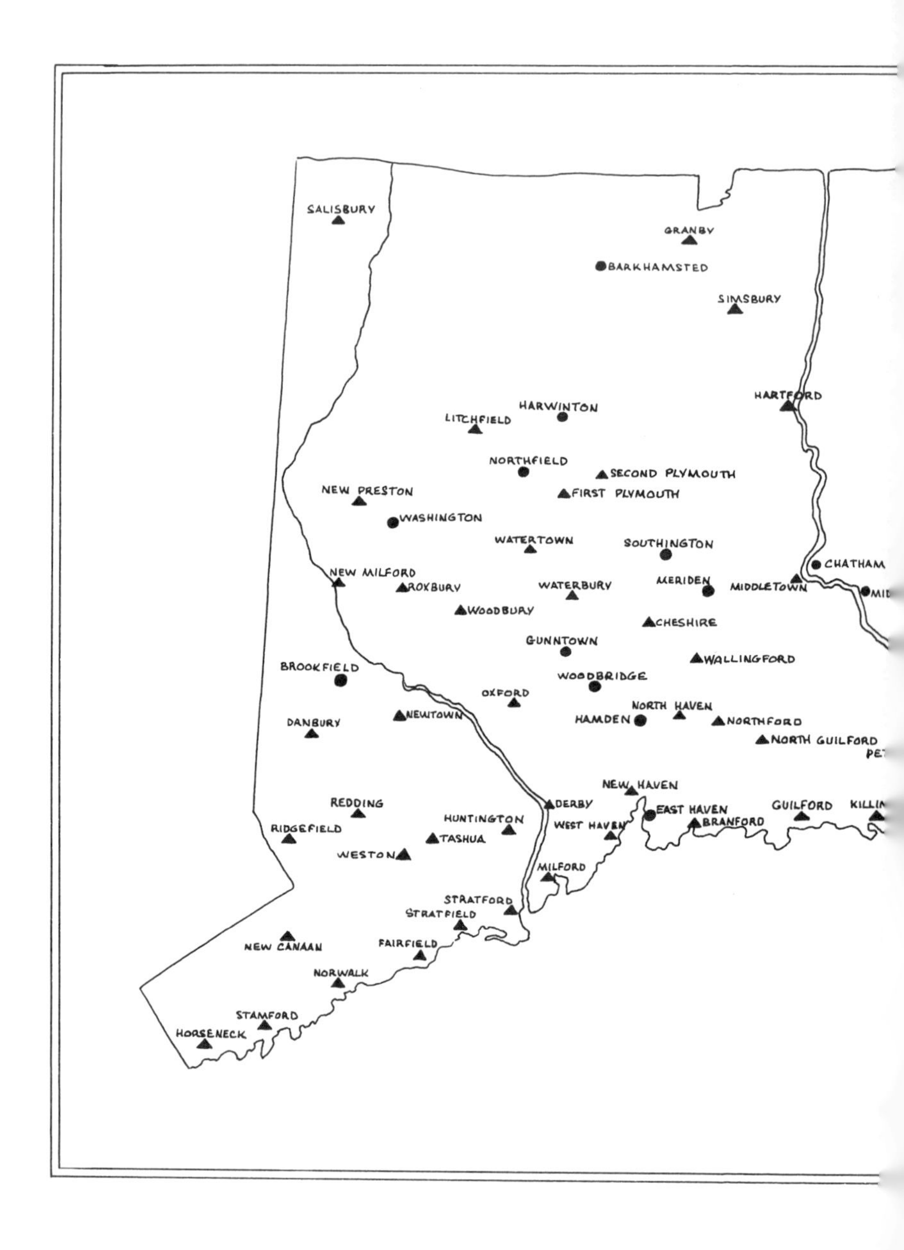
SALISBURY
GRANBY
BARKHAMSTED
SIMSBURY
HARTFORD
HARWINTON
LITCHFIELD
NORTHFIELD
SECOND PLYMOUTH
FIRST PLYMOUTH
NEW PRESTON
WASHINGTON
WATERTOWN
SOUTHINGTON
CHATHAM
NEW MILFORD
ROXBURY
WATERBURY
MERIDEN
MIDDLETOWN
WOODBURY
CHESHIRE
GUNNTOWN
WALLINGFORD
BROOKFIELD
WOODBRIDGE
OXFORD
NORTH HAVEN
HAMDEN
NORTHFORD
DANBURY
NEWTOWN
NORTH GUILFORD
NEW HAVEN
DERBY
REDDING
HUNTINGTON
EAST HAVEN
GUILFORD
RIDGEFIELD
WEST HAVEN
BRANFORD
TASHUA
WESTON
MILFORD
STRATFORD
STRATFIELD
NEW CANAAN
FAIRFIELD
NORWALK
STAMFORD
HORSENECK

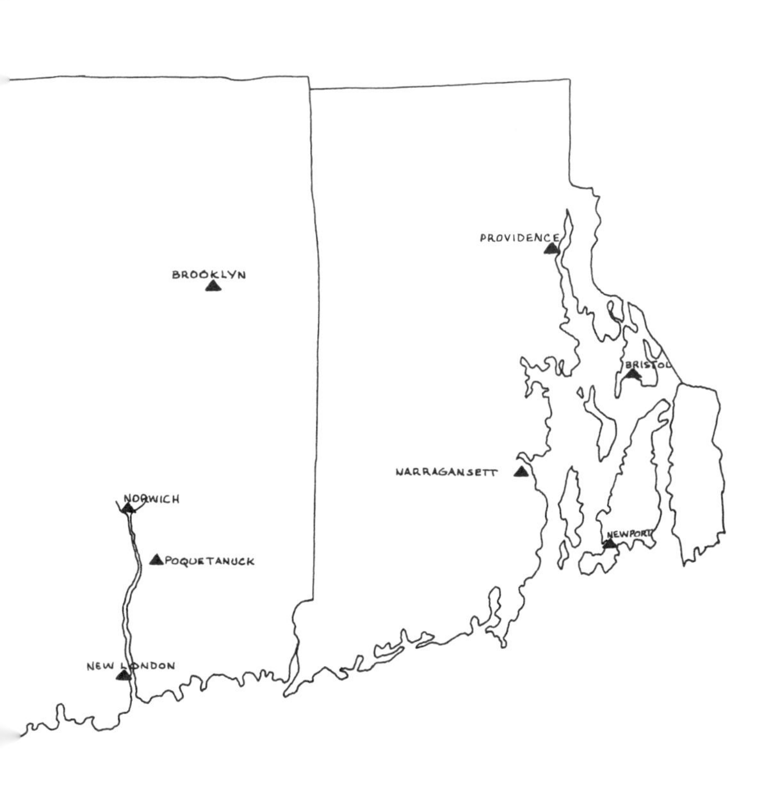

DIOCESES OF CONNECTICUT AND RHODE ISLAND
1796

▲ CONGREGATION FORMED BEFORE 1771

● CONGREGATION FORMED 1783-1794

3

FREE THOUGHTS,
ON
The PROCEEDINGS of
THE
CONTINENTAL CONGRESS,
Held at PHILADELPHIA Sept. 5, 1774:
WHEREIN
Their ERRORS are exhibited,
THEIR
REASONINGS CONFUTED,
AND
The fatal Tendency of their NON-IMPORTATION, NON-EXPORTATION, and NON-CONSUMPTION MEASURES, are laid open to the plainest UNDERSTANDINGS;
AND
The ONLY MEANS pointed out
For Preserving and Securing
Our present HAPPY CONSTITUTION:
IN
A LETTER
TO
THE FARMERS,
AND OTHER INHABITANTS OF
NORTH AMERICA
In General,
And to those of the Province of *New-York*
In Particular.

By a FARMER.

Hear me, for I WILL speak!

PRINTED IN THE YEAR M.DCC.LXXIV.

Title page of *Free Thoughts on the Proceedings of the Continental Congress*, one of Seabury's Loyalist pamphlets.

Samuel Seabury in the winter of 1784-1785. Oil portrait by Thomas S. Duché.

THE

Communion-Office,

OR ORDER

FOR THE ADMINISTRATION

OF THE

HOLY EUCHARIST

OR

SUPPER OF THE LORD.

WITH

PRIVATE DEVOTIONS.

Recommended to the Epiſcopal Congregations in *Connecticut*,

By the Right Reverend

BISHOP SEABURY.

NEW-LONDON:

Printed by T. GREEN, M,DCC,LXXXVI.

Title page of Seabury's version of the Scots Communion Office of 1764.

principles," he wrote Parker, "not a Subjection to them founded in a Majority of votes."[21]

Despite this stand, Seabury decided to sound his flock before replying to White. Pastors might give their opinions at the Convocation appointed for June 3, 1789, at Norwalk; prior to that date, a lay Convention, called to consider the Church's "external or temporal state," would provide a forum for rank-and-file Churchmen. The bishop expected the laity to express themselves freely, even to the point of commissioning General Convention deputies, should this be the wish. However, if the lay Convention took that step, he had no intention of permitting clergymen to accompany its representatives. A purely clerical delegation, on the other hand, was at least a possibility, for notwithstanding his own judgment, he was willing to leave the question to the Norwalk session.[22]

Seabury's apprehensions—if serious—were short-lived. Both pastors and people supported him, and on June 29 he reported their decisions to White. Since he intended his letter for the General Convention, he was careful to detail the precise reasons which would prevent members of Connecticut's Church from attending. He began with those of the laity:

> When the matter was proposed to the Lay Convention after some conversation, they declined every interference in Church government or in reformation of Liturgies. They supposed the government of the Church to be fixed, and that they had no right to alter it by introducing a new power into it. They hoped the old Liturgy would be retained, with little alteration; and these matters, they thought, belonged to the Bishops and Clergy, and not to them. They therefore could send no delegates, though they wished for unity among the Churches, and for uniformity of worship; but could not see why these great objects could not be better secured on the old ground than on the new ground that had been taken with you.

The sentiments of his clergy Seabury found equally gratifying:

> The Clergy supposed that, in your Constitution, any representation from them would be inadmissible without Lay delegates, nor

> could they submit to offer themselves to make a part of any meeting where the authority of their Bishop had been disputed by one Bishop, and probably by his influence, by a number of others who were to compose that meeting. They therefore, must consider themselves as excluded, till that point shall be settled to their satisfaction, which they hope will be done by your Convention.

Lastly, the bishop explained his own position; there had been enough skirting of the issue:

> For my own part, gladly would I contribute to the union and uniformity of all our Churches; but while Bishop Provoost disputes the validity of my consecration, I can take no steps towards the accomplishment of so great and desirable an object. This point, I take it, is now in such a state that it must be settled, either by your Convention, or by an appeal to the good sense of the Christian world. But as this is a subject in which I am personally concerned, I shall refrain from any remarks upon it, hoping that the candour and good sense of the Convention will render the further mention of it altogether unnecessary.

Seabury next proceeded to comment elaborately on the main topics of White's letter: lay deputies and liturgical revision. His remarks on the introduction of the laity into ecclesiastical councils were extremely sharp; two sentences, nevertheless, hinted at a possible agreement. Opening his discussion, the bishop explicitly affirmed what had appeared, somewhat less clearly, in his earlier correspondence: "The grand objection in Connecticut to the power of Lay delegates in your Constitution, is their making part of a judicial Consistory for the trial and deprivation of Clergymen." A postscript, however, showed that laymen might enjoy some power in the making of canons. "That the assent of the Laity should be given to the laws which affect them equally with the Clergy, I think is right, and I believe will be disputed no where," Seabury asserted, "and the rights of the Laity we have no disposition to invade."

Connecticut's objections to the Proposed Book the bishop

could not list without running his letter to an unreasonable length. "I will confine myself to a few, and even these I should not mention but from a hope they will be obviated by your Convention." To begin with, there was the matter of the Psalms. Abridging them constituted an "unwarrantable liberty"; never before had any church ventured to meddle with the sacred text. As for the creeds, while the Proposed Book's arrangements as modified in 1786 actually represented a more conservative approach than the Middletown proposals, Seabury seemed ignorant of the fact that the General Convention had revised its changes. In any case (and possibly as a result of the developments at Boston's King's Chapel), he now insisted that all three creeds should be retained exactly as they stood in the Prayer Book of 1662 lest the Church appear to countenance Arian or Socinian tenets or, on the other extreme, seem to deny the perfect humanity of Christ. Other objections to the Proposed Book were noted: the discarding of the word "Absolution" in the rubrics and of most of the references to "Regeneration" in the Baptismal Offices; a supposed discrepancy between the Offices of Baptism and Confirmation; the making of the Sign of the Cross discretional in Baptism (a change suggested at Middletown, but one which was now said to "exceedingly grieve" Connecticut because of "Our regard for primitive practice"); and the apparent rejection of the notion of an "intermediate state" in the Burial Office, "though, that this was a catholic, primitive and apostolical doctrine, will be denied by none who attend to this point." The Convention's Twenty Articles Connecticut regarded as no improvement on England's Thirty-Nine. A long paragraph discussed the deficiencies of the English Communion Office—repeated in the Office of the Proposed Book—and suggested improvements based on the Scots Office of 1764.

Seabury at this point advanced his old proposal for a private conference. Provoost and White, accompanied by clerical proctors, might meet with himself and similar delegates. "We should then be on equal ground, on which ground only, I presume, you would wish to stand, and I doubt not everything might be settled to mutual satisfaction, without the preposterous method of ascertaining doctrines, &c., &c., by a majority of votes." Hopefully, the General Convention would prepare the way for such an agreement; it could do so if it would remove "all obstructions."[23]

White did not immediately respond to this letter. But two weeks before the General Convention opened at Philadelphia, William Smith (recently restored to his college provostry) repeated White's informal invitation. Writing that he had seen Seabury's communication, he declined to enter into its arguments, declaring at the same time what was undoubtedly true, that an episcopal meeting of the sort Seabury had suggested would only widen the breach between Connecticut and the Southern churches. Smith begged the bishop to reconsider his stand; explicit provisions of the Conventionists' constitution to the contrary, he affirmed "there could be no reasonable Objection" to seating Seabury and several of his clergy in the General Convention as a "proper Representation" of Connecticut. "Although we should not perfectly agree respecting every proposed Alteration in the Liturgy, or even in some disputed Articles of Faith, or in Respect to the Share which Lay Members have in Points of Discipline & Government," yet in "Matters essential to General Uniformity & Concord we may & ought to be one Church."[24] Seabury must be got to Philadelphia! Then, Smith was certain, an agreement could be reached.

The Bishop of Connecticut, however, still held back. His reply to Smith of July 23, though very friendly, marked no advance over his letter to White. "The wish of my heart, & the wish of the Clergy, & of the Church people of this State, would certainly have carried me & some of the Clergy to your General Convention," he wrote, "had we conceived we could have done it with propriety." But while his consecration remained unrecognized and a Convention representation of both clergy and laity was required, no steps toward union could be taken. Philadelphia would have to provide the initiative:

> Before I wrote to Bishop White, I took the most deliberate pains to obtain the sentiments of both Clergy & Laity; & I should not now think myself at liberty to act contrary to their sentiments, even did not my own co-incide with theirs. I have however the strongest hope that all difficulties will be removed by your Convention—That the Connecticut Episcopacy will be explicitly acknowledged—& that Church enabled to join in union with you, without giving up her own Independency.

Seabury indicated the sort of coalition he had in mind, observing that he, too, realized there might be "a strong & efficacious union between Churches where the usages are different." He saw no reason why this should not be so in the present case, "as soon as you have removed those obstructions which, while they remain, must prevent all possibility of uniting."[25]

This declaration proved of great use to Smith when delegations from seven states assembled in Philadelphia's Christ Church, July 29, 1789. The third General Convention included many ardent well-wishers to the cause of union, among them a number of Seabury's friends. Benjamin Moore and Abraham Beach, though furnished with the instructions Provoost had insisted upon, formed the majority in the New York delegation, since five of the eight men chosen, including James Duane, failed to put in an appearance. Two ministers Seabury had ordained were present among the Maryland deputies, still headed by Smith, despite his removal to Philadelphia. Another of Seabury's ordinees, Joseph Pilmore, had been elected a deputy from Pennsylvania, as had the economist Tench Coxe, who strongly advocated an agreement with Seabury.[26] Even more important was the absence of Provoost, a victim of chronic migraine.[27] This latter situation allowed Smith to use his influence for conciliatory measures without exciting episcopal opposition. It gave the same freedom of action to Bishop White, Convention president *ex officio.*

A desire to settle matters with Connecticut, it soon appeared, was general. Smith, who received Seabury's letter of July 23 on the opening day of the Convention, probably showed it privately that evening to a number of persons. Next day an official reading of this communication and the longer one earlier forwarded to White placed the bishop's views before the entire gathering. At once the deputies unanimously resolved "That it is the opinion of this Convention, that the consecration of the Right Rev. Dr. Seabury to the Episcopal office is valid."[28] The General Convention now showed itself determined to accomplish a union, and the way to achieve or, at any rate, cement the necessary arrangements was marked out for it in an extraordinary document, the contents of which the deputies had learned just prior to the reading of Seabury's letters. Dated at Salem, June 4, 1789, it appeared in the minutes as "An act of the Clergy of Massachusetts and New Hampshire." The act bore the signatures of five ministers, and it called upon the Bishops of Connecticut, New York, and Pennsylvania to consecrate Seabury's cousin, Edward Bass of Newburyport, as their bishop.[29]

As might be expected, the Bass proposal was the result of Samuel Parker's management. White, it will be recalled, had explained to Parker his objections to a consecration of this sort when Parker first raised the subject in 1787. At the same time, he urged the procuring of a bishop from the English succession for Massachusetts. Such a move, he believed, would contribute to a union with Connecticut, presumably because, the canonical number of English prelates having been obtained, he and his colleagues might properly join Seabury in consecrating a fifth bishop.[30] White repeated this suggestion—and in more explicit terms—at the end of 1788, about the date he approached Seabury.[31] His letter (which strongly urged the sending of Massachusetts deputies to the General Convention) brought from

Parker the reply that an English bishop was an impossibility, but also this statement: "If there is any thing in the power of the Clergy here that could effect a Reconciliation between the Church of Connecticut & Philadelphia, it will, I am sure, be embraced with cheerfulness. Something I hope will be attempted in the Spring."[32] This "Something" was, of course, Bass's consecration, which evidently Parker thought White could be brought to support, his scruples notwithstanding.

The settlement of Seabury-ordained clergymen in Massachusetts and New Hampshire made it possible for Parker to break the local deadlock of 1785: Bass and himself countered by Fisher and Wheeler. Thomas Fitch Oliver (Harvard, 1775) in 1786 became rector of St. Michael's, Marblehead; John Cosens Ogden in 1788 began work at Queen's Chapel, Portsmouth; and in May, 1789, just before Parker took action, Tillotson Bronson (Yale, 1786) secured a post as supply minister for six months at Christ Church, Boston.[33] No canonist would have awarded Bronson a vote in the choice of a bishop, but Parker, intent on forming a general union of the churches, was not to be deterred by legalistic niceties. The rector of Christ Church, William Montague (Dartmouth, 1784), then making preparations for a voyage to Europe, agreed to support Parker's plan; he had received Orders from White.[34]

Before proceeding to the formal election of Bass, Parker consulted Seabury. The bishop approved the idea of a colleague "to the Eastward," and "from Mr Bass['s] Character & Standing in the Church," judged "he would worthily and Acceptably fill that Station." He himself stood ready to contribute "all in my power to accomplish an Event which I much wish." Still, he had doubts as to whether the other bishops would concur. White and Provost according to his information (derived from the former's letter of December 8, 1788) lay under obligation not to consecrate until a third bishop had been procured from England. "You can however make the experiment," he wrote, "or if you choose it, you can ascertain whether they would join in such a Consecration before Mr. Bass be elected."[35]

Parker decided to make the experiment. Without notifying Fisher and Wheeler, or giving any general notice to the Massachusetts and New Hampshire laity, he and his four confederates, together with their designated candidate, assembled in Salem, June 4, 1789, almost on Fisher's doorstep. There they drafted a formal instrument of election, the "act of the Clergy of Massachusetts and New Hampshire," copies of which were sent to the three bishops. The electors included in this document a candid statement of their motives: "that the people comitted to our respective charges may enjoy the benefit & advantage of those Offices, the administration of which belongs to the highest order of the Ministry, & to encourage & promote, as far as in us lies, a Union of the whole Episcopal Church in these States, & to perfect & compact this mystical body of Christ." To further promote the work of union, the Salem meeting appointed Parker the clergy's agent, giving him broad powers to attend any "Convocation to be holden in Pennsylvania or New York, & to treat upon any measures that may tend to promote an Union of the Episcopal Church throughout the United States of America, or that may prove advantageous to the Interests of said Church."[36]

Disappointed in his hopes of securing a supply for Trinity Church, Parker could not be present at the General Convention.[37] But White's copy of the "act," as earlier noted, was read to that body, July 30, 1789. Much of the next day the deputies spent in attending the Commencement of the University of Pennsylvania. However, on Saturday, August 1, and again on the Tuesday following, they deliberated the application for Bass's consecration, as well as points made in Seabury's letters, acting as a committee of the whole and with Provost Smith occupying the chair. Conciliatory decisions (shortly to be discussed) furnished basic materials for a union, yet as Smith afterwards explained to Seabury, "much Difficulty and Variety of Sentiment and Apprehension prevailed, respecting the *Means* [of constructing one]; in so far that there seemed more than a Probability of coming to no Decision." In this situation, Smith suggested an adjournment, promising that the next morning he would offer proposals acceptable to all.[38] The deputies adopted this suggestion, and the provost began to draft resolves, assisted by White, Benjamin Moore, and, of all people, Robert Smith of St. Philip's, Charleston, late Provoost's ally in anti-Seabury maneuvers.

White's position was most uncomfortable. Various speakers in the committee of the whole had taken it for granted that he and Provoost must concur in Bass's consecration should the Convention approve it. But the Bishop of Pennsylvania, still entertaining the scruples he had mentioned to Parker in 1787, had no intention of complying. Despite a good deal of pressure, he would not budge from his position that the negotiations with the English episcopate had been carried on in such a manner as to require three bishops of the English line before any consecration might be attempted. As a result, Smith had to include in his draft a recognition of this difficulty.[39] To make certain that Connecticut's leading lay Churchman did not interpret the statement in question as a slur on Seabury, Tench Coxe sent a lengthy explanation to William Samuel Johnson, now a United States senator.[40]

Smith finished his work on schedule, presenting the Convention with five resolves on Wednesday morning, August 5. "And I shall always account it among the happiest Incidents of my Life, and the best Service I have ever been able to render to the Church," he later wrote Seabury, that they "were Unanimously and almost instantly adopted, as reconciling every Sentiment, and removing every Difficulty which had before appeared to obstruct a General Union."[41] Following Parker's lead, the provost built his strategy around the consecration of Bass. His first resolve, listing the three prelates by name, declared "That a complete Order of Bishops, derived as well under the English as the Scots line of Episcopacy, doth now subsist within the United States of America." This order he next affirmed to be competent to every episcopal act, including consecration. After a third resolution, asserting it the duty of the churches represented in the Convention to respond to all reasonable petitions of sister churches in the United States, came the formal request that White and Provoost join Seabury in the proposed consecration. This fourth resolve was the significant one: prior to Bass's elevation, the New England churches were invited "to meet the Churches of these States, with the said three Bishops, in an adjourned Convention, to settle certain articles of union and discipline among all the churches." Lastly, Smith alluded to White's position. If any "difficulty or delicacy" prevented his or Provoost's compliance with the request, the Convention would address the English episcopate, hoping in this way to remove the impediment.[42]

The deputies to this Convention had come with full power to finally determine a general constitution. Seabury's letters to White and Smith made it clear that some changes would have to be made in existing arrangements. Moreover, from the bishop's insistence upon a private conference with White and Provoost to settle articles of union on some other basis than a majority of votes, it seemed obvious that he would not accept an invitation to the adjourned Convention unless such terms had first been worked out. A conference being impossible, the deputies did what they could by altering their proposed constitution in a manner which, they supposed, would meet Seabury's objections. Most of these basic changes were made prior to the Tuesday adjournment and the resulting formulation of Smith's facilitating resolves.

The revised constitution was a very different document from that tentatively adopted in 1785-86. Hitherto a unicameral body, the General Convention henceforth would consist of two houses, one made up of lay and clerical deputies, and the other of bishops endowed with a veto power which could be overriden only by a three-fifths vote. In the House of Clerical and Lay Deputies, provision was made for a reciprocal veto of the two groups represented: Connecticut's fears that laymen might outvote the clergy provided the inspiration for this amendment. Every state could send both lay and clerical deputies, but if its convention chose to appoint only one or the other, these persons sufficed for a due representation. When coupled with the constitution's silence as to the composition of the state conventions (the tentative constitution had required them to consist of lay and clerical deputies), this article amounted to an incorporation of the Connecticut system of government by bishop and Convocation into the "federal plan." The state conventions—in Connecticut, the Convocation—were to form rules for the trial of clergymen. In this way what Seabury had described to White as Connecticut's "grand objection" to lay deputies was lessened. Finally, after the adoption of Smith's resolves, the deputies decided to leave completely open the matter of liturgical revision. The eighth article of their amended constitution declared:

> A Book of Common Prayer, Administration of the Sacraments, and other Rites and Ceremonies of the Church, Articles of Religion, and a form and manner of making, ordaining, and consecrating Bishops, Priests, and Deacons, when established by this or a future General Convention, shall be used in the Protestant Episcopal Church in these States, which shall have adopted this Constitution.[43]

The abandonment of the Proposed Book, an acknowledgment of Connecticut's right to her local polity, and a radically remodeled General Convention: this Seabury could never have gained in any private conference of bishops and proctors. After appointing a committee of correspondence, the Convention broke up on Saturday, August 8, to meet again on September 29.[44]

Nearly three weeks passed without Seabury's receiving any official word from Philadelphia. However, Benjamin Moore wrote privately, informing him that the address authorized by Smith's resolve had been sent to the English primates, laying before them the problems raised by the Bass application. The bishop found this action repellent. "These steps, to me, look queer," he declared to Parker on August 26, "& shew a degree of thraldom both to the Convention & English Archbishops, that ought not to be." Moore had urged him to attend the adjourned Convention, and since "they have removed the objections I made, I should be much inclined to go, was it not for the promise I have made of visiting Portsmouth at that time." Having twice disappointed the good people of Queen's Chapel, Seabury did not know how he could form a third apology. "Let me have your opinion on that matter," he wrote, "& also whether I ought to go to Philadelphia without an official invitation, which yet I have not received."

Portsmouth! Parker's patience must almost have snapped at this point. But then came the last three sentences: "So far had I written when the Post brought me the proper official invitation, with the various Communications from the Convention. These I suppose you will also receive by this Post. I have determined to go to Philadelphia, & hope to see you there."[45] Parker could congratulate himself; his plan was working.

The letters to which Seabury referred were the product of the Convention's committee of correspondence—White, Smith, Samuel Magaw, Tench Coxe, and Francis Hopkinson—and of White and Smith acting individually. That from the committee, enclosing copies of the journal and of the address to the archbishops, pointed out what had been done to accommodate Connecticut in the matter of lay deputies and sought to quiet any fears remaining in Seabury's mind as to the Convention's attitude toward his consecration. The bishop's presence at the adjourned Convention was urged in the warmest terms.[46] Smith, spokesman for his colleagues, included in his own letter a long account of the resolves he had sponsored. Since he would not "entertain a Doubt but that you will attend," he invited Seabury to put up at his house. "The Reverend Dr. Benjamin Moore of New York" was to be his "other & only Guest, in a Chamber adjoining to & communicating with Yours; and he will accompany you either from New York, or Elizabeth Town to my House in Philadelphia, as you may agree to meet."[47] Smith was anxious lest Seabury put a wrong construction on White's refusal to join immediately in consecrating Bass, and the Bishop of Pennsylvania showed this same concern. White hoped his conduct would not be "misinterpreted by a Brother, for whom I entertain a sincere Esteem; & with whom I wish to be united in religious Labours." His obligations, he insisted, were not surmised with any desire to create difficulties, and he earnestly desired a release from them. As Seabury was to be the guest of Dr. Smith, White could not invite him to his own house "to which I had previously invited Bishop Provoost: & in which, I could not accommodate both, in a suitable Manner, & agreeably to my own Wishes."[48]

Or, it soon developed, agreeably to Provoost's wishes! The Bishop of New York would as soon have lodged in the Walnut Street prison as in a house containing Samuel Seabury. Still suffering from migraine, he could not attend the adjourned Convention, but in reproachful letters to White he registered his complete dissatisfaction, and that of Jay and Duane, with the constitutional changes the first session had made. Beach, Moore, and New York's lay deputy, he asserted, stating the case with complete accuracy, had "grossly deviated from their Instructions which were worded with their consent and at my particular request." The provisions of the tentative constitution declaring that each state should have a convention consisting of both lay and clerical deputies, and that both groups must be represented in the deputation sent to the General Convention, Provoost regarded as "fundamental Principles," to be "kept Inviolate." As for the address to the archbishops, the Bishop of New York, contrary to White's expectations,[49] would have no part in it. "What you stile an implied engagement to the English Bishops

I look upon . . . in regard to myself as a positive one—I entered into it Ex Animo, upon Principle; and do not wish to ask or to accept a releasement from it." So angry was Provoost that he considered withdrawing from the union or, at least, wished White to believe that he was weighing such action. "How far I shall be able in future to act in concert with the general Convention of the Protestant Episcopal Church will depend," he warned, "upon the proceedings at their next meeting."[50]

In Massachusetts the Convention's actions stirred up a veritable hornet's nest. Fisher and Wheeler, naturally angered that no one had consulted them in the choice of Bass, formally protested to Provoost in a letter of September 18. Although they had six churches under their care, yet they "were never informed of, nor made acquainted with, nor invited to, the Election of any Bishop, in any way or manner whatever, nor were we ever apprized of it, untill informed, by the public Newspapers; neither do we yet know where, when, and by whom such Bishop was elected." The two pastors utterly rejected Parker's scheme: if Bass received consecration, they would not acknowledge him. Moreover, they reported that their people, claiming a right to a voice in any election (and offended by the ignoring of Fisher and Wheeler), showed the same determination.[51]

In the bishop-elect's congregation, St. Paul's, Newburyport, a similar protest appeared. The vestry, meeting August 30, 1789, drafted a circular letter to all the churches of Massachusetts and New Hampshire, censuring the election on the grounds of secrecy and nonparticipation of the laity. The Seaburyites, it was hinted, proposed to erect an ecclesiastical tyranny: the vestry could not "divest ourselves entirely of an apprehension that a System of Ecclesiastical Government is contemplated in these States not perfectly consistent with that Freedom with which it hath pleased a merciful God in his Providence to bless us, and which has been so assiduously supported and Cultivated by our sister Churches in the Southern Government[s]." Inviting the churches to send lay delegates to a meeting at Salem on September 16, 1789, there to choose a lay deputation to attend at Philadelphia on September 29, the vestry urged those congregations who could not do so to designate as General Convention deputies Senator Tristram Dalton and Congressman Elbridge Gerry of Massachusetts and Congressman Samuel Livermore of New Hampshire. Presumably these men would be endorsed by the Salem gathering.[52]

This attempt to counter Parker's proceedings immediately collapsed for lack of support. The Trinity rector was in firm control of his congregation, the vestry of which, along with that of Christ Church, Boston, informed the men of Newburyport that they would willingly trust the concerns of the Church to the clerical deputy to the General Convention—Samuel Parker. St. Michael's, Marblehead, sent no reply, and Wheeler's congregations at Scituate, Marshfield, Braintree, Bridgewater, and Taunton, in spite of their reported anger at Bass's election, likewise made no response. Similarly, Fisher's congregation declined taking action. Queen's Chapel, Portsmouth, irritated by what it regarded as neglect on the part of the General Convention, would not agree to the sending of a lay deputy. Only the newly established church at Holderness, New Hampshire (of which Congressman Livermore was a member), gave any countenance to the plan.[53]

Rebuffed in this fashion, the Newburyport Churchmen resorted to unilateral action, appointing Dalton and Gerry as their General Convention deputies.[54] But these gentlemen never appeared at Philadelphia or, if they did so, were not allowed to take their seats. Parker charged that the whole agitation had resulted from conferences in New York between "a certain gentleman who has interested himself in Church matters in Massachusetts" (undoubtedly Senator Dalton of Newburyport), Provoost, Duane, and another New Yorker, probably Jay.[55] Whether or not this was true, it seems likely that the New Yorkers were in some way involved.[56]

Parker and his associates, undeterred by the momentary threat of a lay revolt, steadily pursued plans to assist Seabury at Philadelphia. In reply to their request for Bass's consecration, the Convention's committee of correspondence had forwarded to Boston a copy of the address to the English primates, as well as a letter "earnestly & affectionately" inviting the attendance of a Massachusetts-New Hampshire delegation.[57] When these arrived, Parker held a meeting at Newburyport, attended by Bass and Oliver, Ogden and Bronson. The clergy renewed his commission as their Convention deputy and got up instructions for him in line with Seabury's supposed objectives. Parker was to attempt to secure amendments to the constitution which would give the House of Bishops an absolute veto and ensure that bishops could be tried only by members of their own order. He should "endeavour that there be as little alteration as possible in the Liturgy." His principal task would be to "procure the junction of the Church of Connecticut upon just & honourable terms."[58]

The clergy likewise drafted an answer to the committee of correspondence, explaining that the amendments proposed with respect to the episcopate were needed to ease the minds of certain clergymen (apparently Rhode Island's two Episcopal pastors) "who cannot be persuaded to join with us without the concurrence of Connecticut & with a view to an universal Union of the Church." White, to whom they directed their letter, was further informed of their ardent wish for the removal of all difficulties impeding Bass's consecration, since if he did not receive episcopal Orders from the three bishops they had designated, "our intentions will be frustrated in a great measure."[59] Parker apparently carried this letter to Philadelphia. By September 27, he had got as far as New York, and there, at the home of Benjamin Moore, he held an interview with Seabury and with Connecticut's clerical deputies, Abraham Jarvis and Bela Hubbard.[60]

After receiving the Convention's formal invitation, Seabury

immediately had taken steps to assemble his clergy. He feared he could not get them together in time, though he assured White he would do what he could, "And I presume, on so sudden an Emergency, any little informality in the appointment of their Representatives will be overlooked."[61] The bishop himself did not attend the hastily summoned meeting, which took place at Stratfield (now Bridgeport) September 15, 16. With the Convention documents Seabury had provided spread before them, the ministers present decided—on the motion of John Bowden (King's College, 1772) of Norwalk—to send deputies to Philadelphia. Their extreme conservatism regarding the Prayer Book of 1662 was evidenced by the instructions given Jarvis and Hubbard. While the deputies received power "to confer with the General Convention on the subject of making alterations in the Book of Common Prayer," the "ratification of such alterations" was "expressly reserved to rest with the Bishop and Clergy of this Church."[62] The Convocation also retained the right to reject any other measures to which their proctors might assent.[63]

"Our imagination, nay every faculty of the devout Soul is ravished with the prospect of beholding Mount Zion raised as a City that is at *Unity* with herself," the rector of St. Paul's, Narragansett, declared to Provost Smith.[64] In New York, however, the representatives of the New England churches found the attitude somewhat different. The failure of Provoost to call upon Bishop Seabury (presumably a guest of Benjamin Moore) excited unfavorable comment.[65] Parker wrote to his brother-in-law that he had "some presentiments that nothing will be accomplished by the Convention." Provoost, Duane, and another person (probably Jay) were vehemently opposing a union with Seabury, and if the two New York laymen appeared at Philadelphia, "we shall bring nothing to pass."[66]

Neither of Provoost's associates did attend the Convention, but even as Parker wrote, a last-minute effort was being waged to prevent Seabury's taking a seat in that body. In all likelihood, it originated in Provoost's clique. To Tench Coxe and at least one other lay deputy the news was conveyed that Seabury was receiving half-pay as chaplain to the King's American Regiment. Coxe much desired a union with Connecticut, and this matter disturbed him. On September 25, he sent a letter to Senator Johnson, explaining that, in order to hold his commission, the bishop must have taken the oath of supremacy or allegiance, possibly both, and that "it is certainly a very serious question, whether a person professing and engaging *ecclesiastical submission* and *allegiance* to a foreign Church & Prince can set [*sic*] in our Convention."[67] Whether Coxe received Johnson's opinion, which he requested, does not appear, but White, in a dinner conversation on September 30, the day the Convention opened, satisfied his scruples, or those of the other deputy in question. Despite White's fears, no one pursued the matter further.[68]

Accompanied by Parker, Jarvis, and Hubbard, the Bishop of Connecticut, on the morning of that day, entered Christ Church "to confer with the Convention, agreeable to the invitation given him, in consequence of a resolve passed at their late session." Seabury produced his certificate of consecration and the three clergymen testimonials of their appointment, all of which were read. Little business was transacted until the following day, when the Convention (still a single house during these preliminary operations) transformed itself into a committee of the whole to consider a union with the New England churches. Although there was some opposition, a resolution then passed declaring "That for the better promotion of an union of this Church with the eastern Churches, the General Constitution established at the last session of this Convention is yet open to amendment and alterations, by virtue of the powers delegated to this Convention." Thereupon a committee was appointed to meet with Seabury and the Eastern deputies. Headed by William Smith, it included only known friends to union: Robert Smith of Charleston, Benjamin Moore, and, from the lay delegates, Richard Harison and Tench Coxe.

After the Convention adjourned for the day, this group met and easily agreed upon a report. Two amendments were proposed: the House of Bishops should have the right of originating measures (as the constitution then stood, it could only revise those proposed by the other House), and its veto should be absolute.[69]

The committee offering this report the next morning, the first amendment easily gained the Convention's approval. The second, too, had a good deal of support and, according to White, would probably have been adopted had not Robert Andrews, lay deputy from Virginia, voiced fears that his state would not accept an absolute episcopal veto. For this reason, the session referred the subject to the next Convention, the amendment being altered so as to require, in the meantime, a four-fifths vote (instead of the previous three-fifths) to override the bishops' negative.[70]

Seabury judged this compromise essentially defective. The prospect of any measure's passing without the episcopate's approval was, of course, extremely remote. But while the possibility remained, he and the other New Englanders, so White afterwards recalled, "thought that the frame of ecclesiastical government could hardly be called Episcopal."[71] Nevertheless, the bishop, and after him Jarvis, Hubbard, and Parker, reluctantly signaled their acceptance, signing the short declaration: "We do hereby agree to the Constitution of the Church as modified this Day in the Convention."[72] By this action of October 2, 1789, Connecticut, Massachusetts, and New Hampshire joined those states already represented in the General Convention: Pennsylvania, New Jersey, and New York, Maryland and Delaware, Virginia and South Carolina. After more than four years of largely fruitless negotiations, a united Protestant Episcopal Church had at last been formed.

Still, as an event of the next day showed, the union achieved was a tenuous one which might possibly be broken by disaffected elements. On October 3, the General Convention met for the last time as a unicameral body. White reported "that he had received certain letters from the Right Rev. Bishop Provost [*sic*], with a request that they may be communicated to the Convention; which were read accordingly."[73] The exact message of the letters is not known: they cannot definitely be identified with any now among White's papers, nor did White choose to mention them in his *Memoirs*. But since Provoost had asked him to lay before the session a copy of the New York deputies' instructions ("as I shall not think myself bound by any proceedings of said Delegates which run counter to the Tenor"),[74] the letters undoubtedly warned of consequences which might ensue if the Convention insisted on retaining its revised constitution. They failed, however, to produce any effect. Following their reading, White and Seabury retired. The persons remaining in the hall (the Convention was meeting in the State House and later removed to the College of Philadelphia) then resolved themselves into the House of Clerical and Lay Deputies and elected Provost Smith as their president.[75]

In the House of Bishops—rather a grandiloquent title for two men—Seabury and White transacted business according to simple forms White had devised. The most important of them provided that the senior bishop present should always preside, seniority to be reckoned from the date of consecration. As a result, Seabury became the first Presiding Bishop of the Protestant Episcopal Church. Attended by a secretary, the Reverend Joseph Clarkson (Pennsylvania, 1782), the bishops got through their work with great dispatch, largely because of the accommodating disposition each showed toward the other's views. Poles apart in their Churchmanship, White and Seabury could meet on the common ground created by personal integrity and a sincere desire for union, and, if they can hardly be said to have become intimates, they, nevertheless, came to regard one another with affection and respect. Looking back on this first meeting, the aged Bishop of Pennsylvania remembered it as wholly pleasant. "To this day," he wrote in his *Memoirs*, "there are recollected with satisfaction, the hours which were spent with Bishop Seabury on the important subjects which came before them; and especially the Christian temper which he manifested all along."[76]

Actions of the other House helped Seabury and White to draw together. Both men were of one mind when it came to protecting their conventional prerogatives, as the debate on liturgical revision soon showed. This establishment of a Book of Common Prayer was the session's chief work aside from the settling of the general constitution; it began with the deputies. Their House appointing committees to prepare the several things to be included, Parker offered the English Book as a working basis, asserting, at the same time, that no such status could be given the Proposed Book. (Among the deputies, Parker usually acted as New England's spokesman; Jarvis and Hubbard said very little, trusting him to make necessary points.) This move produced a controversy and, ultimately, the decision that the committees might operate without any basis, picking and choosing as they pleased. White and Seabury, who were present as spectators, seated on chairs to the right of the president, were much dissatisfied at this procedure. To White it seemed obvious that the deputies should accept the English Book as the Church's recognized liturgy and take the Proposed Book for what it was: a proposal. When this was not done, the bishops, if they chose to veto any particular change in the English liturgy, ran the risk of having no prayer or whatever else it was they rejected, instead of preserving the English text unaltered, as would have been the case had the Prayer Book of 1662 been acknowledged. The result, White believed, was an unfair curtailment of the episcopal negative. Joined by Seabury, he attempted to impress his view on several of the deputies, but without success. The House insisted, he later wrote, upon adopting "a mode of proceedings, in which they have acted differently from the conventions before and after them: who have recognized the contrary principles when any matter occurred to which it was applicable."[77]

Seabury probably interpreted the deputies' action as indicating a fondness for radical innovations. If so, he erred, for the Book of Common Prayer produced by the 1789 Convention (still, with some changes, the service book of the Protestant Episcopal Church) met most of the objections to the Proposed Book which he had outlined to White on June 29. The remodeling of the Communion liturgy, in line with the Scots service of 1764, was a personal triumph.[78] Elsewhere Seabury's success was less obvious, since he generally opposed all the departures from the English Book, even verbal ones, which went beyond his injunction of August 12, 1785.[79] He did perhaps favor the introduction of the Nicene Creed as an alternative to the Apostles' in Morning and Evening Prayer; this allowed a more fully developed Trinitarian formulary to be used in the customary Sunday worship. Again, while the substitution of a selection of reading Psalms in place of the abridgment offered by the Proposed Book lacked his endorsement (or White's, for that matter), he did not greatly concern himself, for the English arrangement of the Psalter might still be used at the minister's discretion.[80] The alternatives allowed in the reading of the Apostles' Creed were, on the contrary, a most serious matter. Seabury, very intent on keeping the creed in its ancient form, took alarm at the Convention's rescinding of its former decision to reinsert the article "He descended into Hell" so far as to permit the use of the form "He went into the place of departed spirits" or even the complete omission of the clause. And he became angry when the House of Clerical and Lay Deputies insisted on discarding the Athanasian Creed. White, though not sharing his fear that the total omission of the formulary would encourage Arian and Socinian views, nevertheless, agreed to its optional use. Even a conference of the two houses, however, could not bring the majority of deputies to support this measure.[81]

Seabury's objections to the Proposed Book's Catechism and Burial and Baptismal Offices produced no disputes, for the Convention adopted, except for a few changes, the old forms of 1662. The Sign of the Cross in Baptism did, it is true, remain optional, as in 1785. But the offices now sanctioned, unlike those of the earlier revision, explicitly declared the person baptized to be thereby "regenerated," a doctrinal statement which partly explains the anti-Seabury sentiments of nineteenth-century Episcopal Evangelicals. Churchmen of every party, on the other hand, were to approve this Convention's enlargement of the English Book's section of "Prayers and Thanksgivings," done mainly, it seems, at Seabury's urging. At least five of the nine additions—prayers "In Time of great Sickness and Mortality," "For a sick Person," "For a sick Child," "For a Person, or Persons, going to Sea," "For a Person under Affliction"—were his suggestions. Probably he himself had compiled them. In any case, he was using these prayers at St. James's, New London, as early as 1787.[82]

Having sanctioned a general constitution, canons, and a Prayer Book (and referred the question of adopting the Thirty-Nine Articles to a future session), the General Convention adjourned on Friday evening, October 16. Seabury remained in Philadelphia until Monday, then set out for New York by way of Elizabethtown, where he spent two days with Thomas Bradbury Chandler. Despite the cancer which hideously disfigured his face, and which, by now, had all but destroyed his sight, Chandler, as always, was cheerful and sprightly, delighting in the bishop's society, even though he felt a certain embarrassment because he could not always articulate sentences so as to make himself understood. "And in this way I understand he continued to the last, never uttering a complaint," Seabury declared when reporting his death the following year.[83] While the two men do not appear to have corresponded frequently after their return to America, Chandler's letters to Jonathan Boucher show that he thoroughly approved Seabury's conduct with respect to negotiations for a union.[84] Happy he must have been to hear of the successful outcome of the Philadelphia meeting.

Seabury's pleasure in talking with his old friend was soon marred, however, by the arrival of a hurried letter from White. Upon meeting with the committee for printing the new Prayer Book, White had discovered that the two houses had misunderstood one another as to the debated article in the Apostles' Creed. Seabury had mentioned some misgivings on this score before leaving Philadelphia, only to be assured by his colleague that they had no foundation. But now it definitely appeared that the deputies expected the clause "He descended into Hell" to be printed in italics and within brackets, an alteration the bishops had refused to accept.[85] Unimportant though the matter might seem, Seabury could not regard it as such. Knowing his people's extreme liturgical conservatism, he judged it would be a difficult enough matter to secure the acceptance of a Prayer Book which did not allow even a discretional use of the Athanasian Creed. And should the Apostles' appear with "such a mark of reproach as Crotchets & Italics will be," he could "not be answerable for consequences." From New York he begged the committee to publish the creed in its old form.[86] The members refusing, White, in order that the Prayer Book might go to press, finally put his signature to the Morning Prayer, stating, at the same time, that it did not imply the episcopate's assent to the disputed printing. Seabury approved White's action. "But it is to be remembered," he warned, "that that Article, printed in Italics & within crotchets, is not the Book to which I subscribed in Philadelphia." Accordingly, if he found it necessary, he had a perfect right to abandon the whole of the liturgical revision![87]

The irritable tone of Seabury's declaration should not obscure the fact that the fears giving rise to it had a certain foundation. Many in Connecticut did react most unfavorably to the new Prayer Book. Ebenezer Dibble, for example, writing Samuel Peters in November, 1789, lashed out at its "mutilations, omissions and alterations," which he saw as undermining orthodoxy. Dibble predicted the Convocation would reject the book. Not only that, it would break off all connection with the General Convention.[88]

While the Convocation took no such drastic action, neither was it in any hurry to approve the Philadelphia measures. Meeting at Litchfield in June, 1790, the clergy examined the constitution and canons, but deferred the question of adopting them until their next session.[89] At that time, it was hoped, each man would be able to obtain his own copy of the Prayer Book. "As I apprehended, so I still fear, there will be some difficulty in bringing our book into common use in this State," Seabury wrote White on September 1, qualifying his statement with the hope that "it will be done; If not at once, yet gradually in the course of a year or two."[90]

The Convocation reassembled in Newtown, September 30. Seabury, who was traveling with pastors from east of the Connecticut, did not arrive until the next afternoon. Prior to his coming, the constitution and canons were again considered, and there was an attempt to force through a vote, whether with the aim of defeating them is not known. In any case, the majority present rejected the motion. Once Seabury had taken his seat as president *ex officio*, the clergy took up the subject of the Prayer Book, reading out and discussing the Convention's changes in the 1662 text. Eighteen pastors thereupon voted to accept the revision, also the constitution and canons; one man dissented.[91] Bela Hubbard had earlier expressed the prevailing sentiment: "the terms are not altogether pleasing to us here but they are the best that could be obtained for the present[;] the door however is still open for amendments, & time & perseverance may produce something more favourable."[92]

The method to be taken in introducing the Prayer Book the Convocation left to the individual pastors. However, in order to offend congregational sensibilities as little as possible, it decided that all would "approach as near the *Old Liturgy* as a compliance with the Rubrics of the *New* will allow." For the same reason, the 1791 session resolved to use the Nicene Creed on Communion Sundays and the Apostles' at other times—the pattern imposed by the English Book.[93]

One cannot determine the date at which the revised liturgy came into use in Connecticut. It was certainly many months after that fixed for its adoption by the General Convention, October 1, 1790. Largely, this resulted from the slow distribution of the new books. Seabury's own congregation, for instance, could not readily purchase them before April, 1791, when the New London newspaper first advertised copies.[94] On the other hand, failure to use the revision at times represented complete disapproval of everything done at Philadelphia. A small minority in the diocese regarded the 1789 terms of union as requiring sacrifices which no true Churchman could make.

James Sayre (College of Philadelphia, 1765) was the spokesman of this group. Alone among the clergy attending the Newtown Convocation, Sayre refused to endorse the General Convention's proceedings. As soon as the Convocation voted approval, he entered a formal protest, recorded, at his desire, in the session minutes. He had several objections, all of them reducible to the fact that Seabury and the Connecticut proctors—and now the clergy as a whole—had consented to liturgical changes and the introduction of laymen into ecclesiastical synods. The distraught pastor (who had recently replaced the aged Leaming at Christ Church, Stratford) voiced his judgment of the latter development in the most unequivocal terms, declaring:

> That the said General Constitution of the Protestant Episcopal Church in the United States of America, does not import in it, that Form of the Government of the Church of Christ, which it's blessed & glorious Head impressed upon it; which is therefore, it's *proper, & only right* Government;—which was committed to the Apostles & their successors in office, since their day stiled Bishops; & which has therefore obtained the name of the Episcopal Government of the Church; but that the said general Constitution signed & approved as afore-

> said, is repugnant to the above-described *proper, only right,* & episcopal Government of the Church.[95]

The morning after he delivered this statement Sayre left the Convocation.[96] Within a short time, he succeeded in creating a schism which severed from the diocese its oldest congregation. The bishop's fears had been realized.

Seabury believed, as did Bishop White, who had known him since college, that Sayre was, to some extent, mentally deranged.[97] His violent denunciations of those disagreeing with him indicated as much. He owed a good deal to Seabury: in 1786 the bishop had obtained for him the rectorship of Trinity Church, Newport (which he resigned in 1788 because of opposition among some members of the congregation).[98] Gratitude, however, was not a virtue cultivated by the Reverend Mr. Sayre. From the pulpit of Stratford's church, after his departure from the Convocation, he railed against his benefactor in the most indecent language. The pastors of Connecticut, he affirmed, were a pack of Judases, nay, worse than Judas, for *he* got *something* for his treachery! Worst of all was their bishop: an enemy to truth and religion, totally unprincipled, a man who would adopt any religion just as it suited him and who was, in all likelihood, a concealed Roman Catholic![99]

Sayre rejected all connection with those he had labeled defectors, refusing to allow John Bowden, then living in retirement at Stratford, to assist in the administration of the Communion. When a letter from Seabury to Bowden, lost by the latter, was put into his hands, he read it to his congregation. Bowden countered by having a prominent member[100] read in a parish meeting, March 4, 1792, an address to the Stratford Churchmen, in which he pleaded with them to accept the measures of the General Convention. But Sayre (who also endeavored to spread his views in neighboring churches) had convinced his people that Seabury and the rest of the clergy had departed from the Church of their fathers: laymen were invading the sanctuary, the "good old Book of Common Prayer" had been mutilated! March 4, 1792, Christ Church voted to reject the Philadelphia measures.[101] By this action it soon placed itself in a state of schism, for the Convocation, meeting at East Haddam, February 16, had decided:

> That unless the Wardens & Vestrymen of Christ's Church in Stratford, shall transmit to the Right Reverend the Bishop of Connecticut, within 14 days after Easter-Monday next, a Notification, that the congregation of said Church, have adopted the constitution of the Protestant Episcopal Church, as settled by the general Convention at Philadelphia, in October 1789, they (the Congregation) will be considered as having totally separated themselves from the Church of Connecticut.[102]

Seabury took this step very reluctantly and then only as a last resort. Had Sayre, after the Newtown session, continued to use the English Book but without breaking the unity of the Church, he would have let it pass, trusting that time would remedy the situation. Wild charges, on the other hand, could not be ignored.[103] In April, 1791, he dispatched a sharp letter, censuring Sayre's conduct and urging him to "return to a better mind."[104] This producing no effect, Seabury addressed a second letter, to the Stratford congregation. A good illustration of his episcopal exhortations, it also provides a summary of his doctrine of church unity:

> The earnest desire of my heart, beloved Brethren, is that you may be kept in the way of truth which leadeth unto everlasting life. This way is in & through the Church of Christ, who is the way, the truth & the life. As there is only One God & Father of all, so there is only One Lord, One Faith, One baptism; & consequently One Church of Christ, which, though dispersed through the world, is united by the Unity & Communion of its Bishops: So that all the members of the Church keep up their unity with it by maintaining Communion with their Bishop through the medium of their Clergy. Judge, then, beloved, what must have been the feelings of my heart upon hearing

that there was great danger of your being led away from the unity of Christs Church by breaking off your Communion with your Bishop & Clergy. . . .

The ground of your conduct, I am told, is the Revised Prayer Book of the United States which has been adopted by the Bishop & Clergy of this State, & which Mr Sayre rejects with great warmth, & in his zeal interferes with the neighbouring Parishes, to the great disturbance both of the Clergy & People. At least this is what is reported of him. Consider, Brethren, that there is nothing in that Book which a pious Christian may not use with a good Conscience—nothing which contradicts the analogy of the Christian faith. The three Apostolic Orders of Bishops, Priests, & Deacons are fully retained, the Christian Priesthood duly supported, the Sacraments administered with solemnity—Consider also, that in the use of that book you will be in unity, & charity, & uniformity with your Brethren through the United States, Bishops, Clergy, & Laity, & of course in unity & charity with the Catholic Church; & that in any other way cannot be had. In the name of our Lord Jesus Christ, I beseech & exhort you Brethren, to weigh these things seriously & in the fear of God, & under a due sense of their great importance, & of the dreadful consequences of the want of them. . . .

I had resolved, by Gods assistance, to have visited your Church at my next visitation journey. But, Beloved Brethren, for such you will be to me as long as you shall permit our connection to subsist, How shall I be received? As your Bishop? How can that be?—If you disclaim Communion with the Clergy, you disclaim communion with him —And so you do if you hold communion with a Clergyman who refuses to communicate with them: For the different Congregations of Christs Church are not independent Societies: They are parts of a whole, & ought to consider and conduct themselves as such.

These things I have written with grief of heart, & with anxious forebodings of the fatal consequences of your present conduct, And duty to God & to you hath compelled me to this plainness of expression. Commending you, Beloved, to the grace & direction of the holy Trinity, Father, Son & Holy Ghost, I remain your affectionate friend & servant.[105]

This letter, like the earlier one to Sayre, went unheeded. Yet, despite the congregation's defiance of the Convocation's vote of February 15, 1792, Christ Church, by late August of that year, had moved to reconcile itself with the Bishop of Connecticut. Sometime before that date, Sayre abandoned his parish.[106] Staunch Churchman though he claimed to be, he now communicated with the Congregationalists. His continued efforts to arouse churches against the proceedings of 1789 led Seabury to excommunicate him, September 25, 1793. The bishop did not think Sayre would regard his authority, but he hoped, in this way, to put unwary parishes on their guard.[107] Issued with the approval of Convocation, the printed decree of excommunication was directed to be publicly read in all the churches of Connecticut and Rhode Island (since 1790 a part of Seabury's jurisdiction).[108] The other bishops also received copies. White, who had tried to reason with his old classmate during a visit that Sayre paid to Philadelphia, believed great allowances should be made because of his mental state. Still, he agreed Seabury had followed a proper course.[109]

Sayre was the only Connecticut pastor to steadfastly reject the revised liturgy. Of the others, Ebenezer Dibble showed the strongest distaste for the new Prayer Book. Perhaps for this reason, he had remained at home when the Convocation met at Newtown to consider it, and as late as the winter of 1791-92 he declined introducing it into his congregations: St. John's, Stamford, and Horseneck Chapel, Greenwich. For Dibble the bishop felt a good deal of affection. He was one of the dwindling number who could personally recall that day in October, 1757, when, in his own church, Seabury had first come to the notice of Connecticut's Churchmen with his sermon opposing the eschatology of John Beach. In the 1790's, with his son a Loyalist exile and his daughter still subject to fits of insanity first brought on by fear of the Revolution's mobs, Dibble was a broken man, unable to adjust to the postwar era.[110] The bishop gave him every indulgence he could, until the conduct of Sayre, who sought to influence congregations in Dibble's neighborhood, made it imperative that the Stratford rector be deprived of every vestige of support.

On February 22, 1792, a week after the Convocation had issued its ultimatum to Christ Church, Seabury approached Dibble, requesting him to "review in your own mind the ground & principles on which you have hitherto refrained from the use of the Prayer-book of the Church of the United States." In its tone of respectful affection and of regard for the services the old man had rendered in a ministry of more than forty years, his letter struck exactly the right note. No coercion would be attempted: "If you cannot use the book with a good conscience, I have not a word to say to prevail on you to do so." Seabury, nevertheless, hoped Dibble would adopt it in order to promote peace and unity. "Let me . . . *intreat you as a father, to review this matter*," he wrote, "& I have no doubt but that you will join with your brethren, & *walk by the same rule* in public ministrations."[111]

Dibble did not reply until after his church's Easter Monday meeting,[112] when he informed Seabury that the people had agreed to use the Prayer Book of 1789 as soon as a few copies could be procured. Sayre's "intemperate Zeal, & imprudent conduct," as well as the bishop's letter, convinced him that such action was necessary. "I confess I love the prayer book my Mother[113] gave me," he declared, "and think the Sacrifice great, but nevertheless wise & prudent, under the present State of the Church if a Coalition, with our brethren in the Southern States could no otherwise be effected."[114] As previously noted, this was the general opinion, and Sayre's departure from Christ Church, Stratford, several months later, marked the acceptance of the revised liturgy throughout the diocese. If there was little enthusiasm, there was, at least, acquiescence. Seabury's problems with respect to the union of 1789 had been solved, insofar as they originated within Connecticut.

The bishop's fears that those who disliked both him and the Connecticut Church might successfully rupture the union were laid to rest in September, 1792. In New York's newly rebuilt Trinity Church, during a General Convention, Seabury, White,

Provoost, and Bishop James Madison of Virginia consecrated a former Loyalist, Thomas John Claggett, as Bishop of Maryland. How apprehensive Seabury had been as to the permanency of the agreement of 1789 is shown by the fact that, even after the Convention assembled, he became convinced Provoost and Madison were plotting to exclude him from any part in this affair.

The proceedings of the adjourned Convention of 1789 had pleased Provoost no more than those of the summer session. To White he expressed his belief that when the laity found themselves reduced to "mere Cyphers," they either would raise disturbances to recover their rights or else would become lukewarm, allowing the Church to sink into insignificance. The bishop, nevertheless, had to admit that few New York Churchmen shared this judgment. His own vestry, approving the General Convention's work, refused to elect Jay as a deputy to the state Convention which would discuss it and bound the equally hostile Duane with instructions so unpalatable that he did not bother to attend. In other parishes, the Philadelphia measures enjoyed similar support, for the state Convention deputies unanimously declined to question them, much to the anger of Provoost, who, however, remained silent.[115]

Provoost's attitude, coupled with the long delay in printing the General Convention's journal, excited the suspicions of Benjamin Moore. "There is some secret Mischief lurking somewhere," he warned Parker, "which, on a proper Occasion, will come forth, & attempt to overturn all our Proceedings."[116] It seems unlikely that New York's bishop and his lay allies (who kept up a connection so close that Jay could be referred to as "the Guardian of Bishop Provoost")[117] seriously contemplated so revolutionary a move, although they do seem to have maintained contact with the anti-Parker elements in Massachusetts.[118] But if they could not expel Seabury from the union, neither would they display any inclination to treat him with friendliness—or even with common courtesy. Echoing his earlier letters to White, Provoost informed

James Madison, chosen Virginia's bishop in place of the deceased Dr. Griffith, that should the archbishops return a favorable reply to the General Convention's address, he still would join in no consecration until a third English bishop were present.[119] Before making this explicit declaration, he had attempted to force Madison to England by securing for him a testimonial specifically directed to the English prelates. Not only that, he framed the document in such a way that it could be certified by a bare majority of the standing committee appointed by the House of Clerical and Lay Deputies, and immediately dispatched it to the southward, without giving Parker and Hubbard, the New England members, any chance to protest.[120]

William Smith, chairman of the standing committee, censured this action as "very disrespectful" to the Eastern churches. With White's approval, Smith drafted another testimonial, so worded that Madison might use it either in England or America, and tried to ensure the New Englanders an opportunity to affix their signatures.[121] However, Provoost's stubborn stand made it necessary for Madison to go to London, whither he sailed in the summer of 1790.

If Seabury learned of the Bishop of New York's maneuverings in this affair, there is no mention of it in his correspondence. Writing to Boucher in October, 1790, he observed that White was "very friendly & apparently & I believe, sincerely rejoicing in the union of our Churches." Provoost, on the other hand, remained "reserved, haughty & sullen; & I believe chagrined—that any notice has been taken of me, or of the Church in Connecticut." No great harm could result from this, Seabury thought, except that "it keeps up a coldness where there ought to be none." Still, this was of little importance. When Madison returned from England, Provoost might become more friendly. If he did not, the bishops could then do without him. "And when Dr Bass, Bp Elect for Massachusetts, shall be consecrated, the succession in this country will be pretty secure."[122]

Seabury would have qualified his optimism had he known that the proposal to elevate Bass had been abandoned. The bishop-elect partially disqualified himself by marrying in November, 1789, within a few months of his first wife's death, a woman little more than half his age. Bass's clerical supporters disapproved,[123] and the continued opposition to his consecration on the part of Wheeler and Fisher, as well as of the Newburyport Churchmen, induced Parker to forego any thought of proceeding. Writing to his own congregation, Parker represented this decision as resulting from the fact that the clergy's application had achieved the union of the churches: "The end being effected, the means now cease." At the same time he admitted to a fear that dislike of the means might yet endanger the end. The Wheeler-Fisher-Newburyport forces had proposed a meeting of the Boston Convention at Salem, October 5, 1790. To Parker this suggested "a plan laid by some disaffected to the Church or actuated by private pique to break the Union & set aside the whole proceedings of the general Convention so far as respects this State."[124] No such plan developed. However, the Salem session did include in the diocesan constitution which it drafted a clause outlawing any surreptitious election of a bishop.[125]

Once he learned that Bass would not be consecrated, Seabury became more curious as to the character and views of Bishop Madison. He knew nothing about him personally, and the information he received from Boucher (who had employed Madison in his Caroline County, Virginia, school before the Revolution) was hardly encouraging. Boucher's first statements have not survived, but in a letter of August 1, 1791, referring to them, he expressed hope that Madison would turn out "a better Bishop than He was a Man, when long ago He lived with Me." Those persons who had met the Virginian in England, he observed, thought "Him sour, sullen, & supercilious: hence, I cannot but fear, He will attach himself to Bishop Provoost, rather than to White & You."[126]

An earlier report came from White immediately after Madison's return to America. White had met the newly consecrated President of William and Mary but once—about 1775—and though he had heard that Madison was "a Man of Science & irreproachable Morals," he did not appear to be wholly sure of him. "You will wish & pray with me," he wrote, "that he may be a Fellow-Labourer with us in building up our Church, on the true Gospel Plan."[127] Taken in conjunction with Boucher's statements this cryptic remark made Seabury very suspicious of Virginia's bishop. "In September next, our General Convention is to meet at New York," he informed his English correspondent in January, 1792; "then probably I shall know the part he will act—God grant it may be a proper one."[128]

Whatever Madison's attitude was by 1792, there had earlier been ample reason for distrust of this sort, as is shown by his account of Archbishop Moore's thoughts with respect to consecrations performed in the United States. Moore and his colleague, Archbishop Markham, had been very slow to respond to the General Convention's address of 1789 on this subject, presumably because their advising White and Provoost to join with Seabury in creating a fourth bishop would be tantamount to recognizing the validity of the Scots succession, whose powers of ordination Parliament did not acknowledge.[129] Although White in April, 1790, voiced surprise that their reply had not as yet reached America,[130] Madison, arriving in London several months later, found that the letter, while prepared, still remained to be sent. Seizing the opportunity to convey its contents informally, Moore read the text to him, then said he was sorry that he and Markham could not have expressed themselves more explicitly. "The Answer," Madison informed White, "rather evaded, than satisfied the principal Purport of the Address." As for Moore's private opinion:

> A few Days before I left London, the Archbishop requested a particular Interview with me. He said he wish'd to express his Hopes, &

> also to recommend it to our Church, that, in such Consecrations as might take Place in America, the Persons who had received their Powers from the Church of England would be alone concerned. He spoke with great Delicacy of Dr. Seabury, but thought it more advisable, that the Line of Bishops should be passed down from those who had received their Commission from the same source.[131]

The fact that Madison said not a word about disagreeing with this suggestion to isolate Seabury, White could only interpret as willingness to follow such a course, kindly protestations to the contrary in his *Memoirs* notwithstanding.[132] White's answer is not preserved. Nevertheless, there can be little doubt but that he flatly rejected Moore's advice, thus preventing further discussion.

On August 13, 1792, Seabury left New London to attend the General Convention. Traveling by way of Hempstead so as to visit his stepmother and other relatives and friends, he reached New York on September 4 and put up at the house of his friend, James Rivington.[133] The Convention did not begin its work until September 12. Sometime during the interval mutual friends, knowing that Seabury and Provoost had never taken any notice of each other during the former's visits to New York, and fearing their publicized coldness might affect the business of the session, proposed that Seabury make a courtesy call. William Smith suggested White as the man to arrange this meeting, to which both parties agreed. Accordingly, Seabury appeared at Provoost's house and accepted an invitation to dine there that evening, White and others being added to the party. "From that time," White wrote in his *Memoirs*, "nothing was [publicly] perceived in either of them, which seemed to show, that the former distance was the result of any thing else but difference in opinion."[134] If this is an accurate statement of the facts, it records no more than an effort to keep up the amenities. The Bishop of New York had not changed his judgment of Samuel Seabury.

When the House of Bishops assembled on September 12, Provoost and Madison expressed dislike of the rule which awarded its presidency to the senior bishop. Since Seabury and White opposed any change, dividing the House equally, the rule, if they had persisted in their view, must have remained unaltered. Seabury, however, in spite of White's urging, was not disposed to cling to his office if the arrangement proved disagreeable to others ("I had no inclination to contend who should be the greatest in the Kingdom of heaven").[135] At the same time, he was troubled, wondering if the opposition to him as Presiding Bishop indicated an extensive plot. The House took no decision, for the bishops shortly adjourned to Trinity Church, where Seabury preached to the assembled Convention. Those who knew of the misgivings with which he had come to New York saw a special significance in his discussion of love as "the grand cement and band of the Christian Church," the bond of perfectness, "which preserves the peace and unity of the Church under all possible circumstances."[136]

Next morning, before the Convention met, Seabury sent word to White that he wished to speak privately with him at the house of Benjamin Moore. Calling there, White found him much disturbed over the proposed consecration of Thomas John Claggett:

> He opened his mind to this effect—That from the course taken by the other two bishops on the preceding day, he was afraid they had in contemplation the debarring of him from any hand in the consecration, expected to take place during this convention—that he could not submit to this, without an implied renunciation of his consecration, and contempt cast on the source from which he had received it—and that the apprehended measure, if proposed and persevered in, must be followed by an entire breach with him, and, as he supposed, with the Church under his superintendence.

White believed Seabury was overwrought. He saw no evidence that Provoost and Madison were plotting; if they were, he would not support them. In the consecration of Claggett, he himself wished, and he supposed his absent colleagues did also, that all three bishops of the English line might take part along with the

Bishop of Connecticut. As for the presidency, he would not vote against the rule he had originated in 1789, but if Seabury temporarily absented himself from the House, Madison and Provoost might carry their suggestion that the office pass in turn from north to south. White solemnly pledged he would take no part in Claggett's elevation if the other bishops refused Seabury's assistance. "Hands were given in testimony of mutual consent in this design." Subsequently, the House altered its rule, Provoost becoming Presiding Bishop, and on September 17, all four of its members joined in consecrating the Bishop of Maryland.[137] Whether Seabury believed that White's behavior had convinced Provoost and Madison that they could not exclude him, or whether he decided that his suspicions had been groundless, does not appear.

The failure of the 1792 Convention to give the House of Bishops an absolute veto much displeased Seabury; deputies vigorously debated this question, only to refer it again to a later session.[138] Generally acceptable to him, on the other hand, was the chief work accomplished, the preparation of an Ordinal. He could approve all the changes made in the English texts, except one in the rite for the ordination of priests. This made optional the old form used in imposing hands: "Receive ye the Holy Ghost. . . . Whose sins thou dost forgive, they are forgiven, and whose sins thou dost retain, they are retained." Had Seabury not pleaded its merits, the form would simply have been discarded for the alternative now introduced, since White, Provoost, and Madison all objected to the second section.[139]

The proposal to adopt Articles (ultimately put aside for further consideration) resulted in a different alignment of the House. Seabury in 1789 had opposed giving a sanction to the Thirty-Nine Articles. Like his Scottish consecrators, he thought some of them too Calvinistic. He preferred the more Catholic expressions of the liturgy, which he considered an adequate exposition of doctrine. By 1792, however, the bishop had come to believe that articles were necessary, and that the Thirty-Nine would give more satisfaction than any others. White shared this opinion; so, it seems, did Claggett. But Madison resisted all articles on Latitudinarian grounds, in which position, White believed, he was supported by Provoost.[140]

A final question to come before the Convention involved an attempt to place the Church on the road toward possible reunion with the Methodists. The bishops sanctioned a resolution designed to achieve this, but the deputies would have nothing to do with it (in part, because its vague wording led to a misunderstanding of the intent).[141] The idea of a resolution was Madison's. He had first mentioned it to White as they traveled together to New York, and the latter, believing that reunion was impossible, had tried to dampen his enthusiasm with particulars of an exchange of letters and interviews between himself and the Reverend Dr. Thomas Coke (Oxford, 1768). Coke had written White in the spring of 1791, proposing such a union as would allow the Methodists to remain, for all time, a distinct society within the Episcopal Church. Some weeks later (White having held discussions with him in the interval), he addressed a second, and much longer, letter to Seabury. The main features of his plan, as therein explained, were the consecration of himself and Francis Asbury as Episcopal bishops, assurances that the Methodists would be given other bishops upon their deaths, and the reordination of the present Methodist clergy. Unlike White, Seabury seems to have made no response. His lack of courtesy might be criticized, but he can scarcely be accused of neglecting a genuine opportunity. Coke's overtures were merely private ones. He did not understand the American Methodists, and his efforts can most plausibly be interpreted as an attempt to strengthen his position as against Asbury, the real leader of the movement in the United States.[142]

Having completed their business, the bishops and deputies adjourned on the evening of September 19. Three days later, Seabury departed for Hempstead as a passenger in a farm wagon.[143] He never attended another General Convention.

IX

"SAMUEL, BY DIVINE PERMISSION BISHOP"

FROM 1785 UNTIL HIS DEATH, SAMUEL SEABURY, BESIDES performing the usual duties of a bishop, also officiated as rector of St. James's Church, New London. This combination of offices was natural, indeed inevitable, in a country where only the most meager episcopal revenue could be got from congregations often at difficulties to provide even for their parochial clergy. Seabury's contemporaries in the episcopate—White, Provoost, Madison, Claggett, and Robert Smith of South Carolina (consecrated in 1795)—all served in the dual capacity of rector and bishop, Madison and Smith discharging, in addition, the work of college presidents.

As rector of St. James's, Seabury enjoyed the use of a two-story, gambrel-roofed, clapboarded parsonage on New London's Main Street. Built in 1748 and considerably enlarged twenty years later,[1] it was managed for him by his spinster daughter, Miss Maria, who directed the work of a hired servant and a Negro slave named Nell.[2] The parsonage, with its cherry, mahogany, and walnut furniture, its china, queen's ware, and silver spoons, seems to have been an attractive, comfortable place. Trout rod and tobacco box gauged the bishop's modest measure of self-indulgence, while a library, grown to more than six hundred volumes by 1796, gave evidence of the manner in which he spent many of his hours.[3]

Most of Seabury's children established themselves in New London. By October, 1785, Samuel, Jr., combining the duties of apothecary and physician, had opened a shop "directly opposite the Parsonage-House," where drugs and medicines might be purchased by "Country Practitioners and others . . . at the New-York Prices."[4] In 1789 Dr. Seabury married a local girl, Miss Fanny Taber. He achieved no great position, for when he died in August, 1795, his estate was small and supposedly insolvent.[5] Very likely the bishop had to furnish him with cash on occasion, as well as to pay bills for his second son Edward, who, after unsuccessful attempts at a mercantile career, went off to England in 1795.[6] Equally inept at making money was a Seabury son-in-law, Charles Nicol Taylor. The Taylors seem to have joined the parsonage household about 1787; they had just established their own home when Taylor's death in September, 1792, forced his widow and children to return.[7]

All in all, the bishop's family must have been something of a disappointment to him. Even Charles, whom he ordained deacon in June, 1793, did not fulfill his hopes. Upright and conscientious, Charles also was awkward and ungainly, a young man of mediocre talents. "Simply a sensible and faithful minister of the Word," a kindly nineteenth-century writer noted, remarking at the same time that his chief difficulty always was the fact that people expected Seabury's son to be a good deal more.[8]

A list compiled by Ezra Stiles shows that Seabury's congregation in 1790 included at least fifty families.[9] This was a somewhat larger number than had attended St. James's in his father's time, yet he found parochial duty no impossible burden, particularly since he usually had a deacon as an assistant.[10] From July, 1792, through June, 1795, Seabury entered in a private register fifty baptisms performed by himself, also seven marriages and twenty-six burials, and, in addition, ten burials at which his son Charles had officiated.[11] Until 1787 his support as rector was a voluntary collection each Sunday; in that year the congregation tried a subscription, and in 1788, the new St. James's having been completed, owners of pews were taxed to provide an annual salary of eighty pounds. There were later attempts, all unsuccessful, to add to this meager amount.[12] The bishop paid his assistant out of his own pocket.

Among Seabury's parishioners were representatives of the Winthrops and the Saltonstalls, whose New London branches, during his boyhood, had been staunchly Congregationalist. Rosewell Saltonstall, grandson of the Governor Saltonstall who had presided over the conference held in 1722 between the Cutler-Johnson group and the Yale trustees, was chosen a churchwarden in 1786. He served in this post, along with Seabury's cousin, Jonathan Starr, Jr., throughout the bishop's rectorship.[13] John Still Winthrop and his brother, Basil Winthrop, great-grandsons of Governor John Winthrop (1606-1676), son of the Massachusetts governor and progenitor, first appear in the records of St. James's as vestrymen in 1752. The former's sons, William and Francis Bayard Winthrop, held the same office during the early part of Seabury's incumbency.[14]

To have such prominent men among them was a matter of pride to other members of St. James's. For Seabury, however, the presence of Saltonstalls and Winthrops could not compensate for the disappearance from the congregation of many of his Mumford relatives. In particular, he felt saddened by the loss to New London's First Church of Captain David Mumford, sometime vestryman and churchwarden.[15] Fiery in his opposition to George III, the captain had been a leader of St. James's Patriot faction.[16] Presumably he could not stomach the thought of Seabury as rector, although that prospect had induced most Patriot Churchmen to patch up matters with their Loyalist brethren, the two sides joining for "the reestablishment of their sacred dwelling," burned by Arnold's forces in 1781.[17]

Plans for rebuilding St. James's slowly advanced to the stage of construction, begun on July 4, 1785.[18] While the work went on, the First Church generously permitted Seabury to hold Sunday services in its meetinghouse.[19] Even with such help as he obtained from Boston's Episcopalians,[20] the problem of sufficient funds loomed large, and the building committee, one supposes, had no difficulty in heeding the congregation's direction "to lay out the money in the most frugal manner."[21] Fitted up with forty-one pews, ranging in price from twenty pounds (occupied by Francis Bayard Winthrop) to a group costing a third of that sum,[22] the church, placed on a site different from that of the original building, stood completed except for the steeple in the summer of 1787. A later incumbent, fond of the Gothic Revival's architectural concepts, passed it off as "a respectable structure, and not unchurchly, according to the ideas of the time."[23] But when erected it seemed "elegantly finished"; indeed, one observer thought it "the neatest building in the State."[24]

"Amazingly grand" was the consecration of St. James's, performed by the bishop on September 20, 1787, in connection with a session of the Convocation.[25] For such occasions, Seabury had adapted forms of prayer devised by the celebrated Bishop Thomas Wilson of Sodor and Man, no consecration service having been included in the Prayer Book of 1662.[26] Dressed in rochet and chimere and wearing the mitre which Inglis had got for him in London,[27] he entered the church accompanied by his clergy and moved down the aisle to the Communion table, reciting, during this procession, the Twenty-Fourth Psalm. Seating himself, he accepted from Warden Jonathan Starr, Jr., the congregation's deed of dedication, the reading of which preceded the actual consecration.[28] Morning Prayer, the Litany, and the Communion followed, and the whole proceeding must have occupied several hours, for Seabury's sermon (delivered from the text "The Lord loveth the gates of Sion, more than all the dwellings of Jacob") occupies no less than thirty-eight pages of closely written manuscript.[29]

St. James's was the second church consecrated by the bishop. In the summer of 1786, he had solemnly blessed St. Paul's, Norwalk, the former building of which had likewise been burned by British troops.[30] The other churches destroyed in this fashion—those at Ridgefield and Fairfield—were rebuilt about 1785 and in 1790, respectively, yet Seabury did not consecrate them, presumably because he received no request to do so.[31] The same reason—lack of an invitation on their part—must explain his failure to perform this office for a majority of the thirteen congregations which replaced outgrown or otherwise obsolete structures, and the ten which put up their first buildings, between 1784 and 1794. As for pre-Revolutionary churches, Seabury consecrated only two, both of them but recently completed.[32]

The casual attitude shown in this matter did not mean that congregations were also indifferent to the more ordinary work of the episcopate. All of them expected Seabury to visit their churches for the purpose of confirming. When preparing his first charge, delivered to the Middletown Convocation in August, 1785, the bishop took this rite as his chief topic. Anxious to dispel Latitudinarian notions that the laying on of hands was "a bare confirmation of the baptismal vow," he insisted that "it implies, and was originally understood to imply, the actual communication of the Holy Spirit." Since confirmation, in the absence of a bishop, had, of course, never been administered in Connecticut, Seabury thought it not unlikely that some Churchmen would neglect it, unless their pastors gave proper instruction. For this reason, he outlined for his clergy what he considered to be the scriptural grounds of the rite and listed the benefits resulting from it. Confirmation, the ministers were to explain to their congregations,

> . . . enters us into a new engagement to be the Lord's, and to lead a Holy and Christian life; it is a lasting admonition not to dishonor or desert our profession: it preserves the unity of the Church, by making men sensible of their obligations to maintain communion with those ecclesiastical superiors who are the successors of the holy Apostles; and it is a testimony of GOD's mercy and favor to them, if they receive it worthily; because his minister declares authoritatively that GOD accepts their proficiency, and, advancing them to the higher rank of the faithful, gives them a right to approach his Table and feast with their brethren on the sacrifice of the Holy Eucharist, the memorials of Christ's death; and by it also GOD condescends to communicate supernatural strength, even the gift of his blessed Spirit, to enable them to encounter and vanquish their spiritual enemies, and fulfill the terms of the Gospel.[33]

Daniel Fogg of Trinity Church, Brooklyn, was absent from the Middletown session. Although he subsequently informed Seabury—and in somewhat airy fashion—that he would not at present recommend confirmation to those already admitted to the Communion, the bishop's sharp reply seems to have brought him around.[34] Fogg probably stood alone in his opposition, for despite the loss of Seabury's visitation journal for 1785-90, it is evident that he confirmed great numbers early in that period. His first recorded administration of the rite was in the old Episcopal stronghold of Fairfield County, at St. John's, Stratfield, September 22, 1785.[35] The following summer found him again in the area; at Stratford he confirmed about four hundred and at Norwalk, an equally large group.[36] Immense crowds, Congregationalists as well as Churchmen, attended on such occasions, proving that New England's traditional aversion to bishops was more than equalled by the desire to see one in the flesh. Seabury—dignified, eloquent, a man of commanding presence—did not shame his adherents.[37] In the autumn of 1787, he came into Litchfield County. At St. Michael's, Litchfield, where he confirmed one hundred sixty-five, fifteen hundred people crowded into the church to hear his sermon. "His subject was the doctrine of the atonement, on which his observations were so striking that it was almost impossible to restrain the audience from loud shouts of approbation," the rector, Ashbel Baldwin, reported to a friend.[38] During this tour, the bishop entered Salisbury, the northwesternmost town in the state. It is likely that he ventured across the Massachusetts line into Berkshire County, confirming at Lanesboro and Great Barrington, for their minister, Gideon Bostwick, regarded himself as one of his clergy.[39]

Seabury usually conducted these visitations as he journeyed to and from sessions of the Convocation. They formed the major portion of his work as a diocesan; a Connecticut regulation of 1792,[40] and probably custom prior to that date, required him to repeat, once in every three years, his initial visit to each part of the state (or at least where there was a minister settled). In performing this duty, he used a horse, a borrowed chaise, sometimes the public stage, and, during his last years, usually a sulky.[41] Not until 1794 did the bishop fail to keep an appointment: because of rain, he was unable to reach Woodbridge on June 9. How determined he was to get through his schedule is shown by the fact that on the previous day, Whitsunday, he had preached morning and afternoon at New Haven's Trinity Church, confirmed thirty-five, and ordained Daniel Burhans priest—all this despite a slight stroke suffered while walking along one of the town's streets.[42] As early as July, 1792, he could report to Jonathan Boucher that he had "travelled more than 6,000 miles on Visitation & other Ecclesiastical duties, through exceeding rough roads, & with much fatigue of body, though with a willing & cheerful heart." He had confirmed, by that date, more than ten thousand persons.[43]

The Connecticut pastors Seabury directed fell naturally into two groups. The first consisted of those men, ordained in England and settled in the diocese at the time of his arrival, who continued at their posts.[44] Many of them contemplated a removal to Nova Scotia, New Brunswick, or some other place where they might secure an S.P.G. mission; Bela Hubbard considered settling in Nova Scotia as late as 1791.[45] Four of their colleagues—Clarke of New Milford, Scovil of Waterbury, Viets of Simsbury, and Andrews of Wallingford—finding it impossible to live without the Society's stipends, did emigrate to New Brunswick in 1786. This loss the bishop felt severely, for they were both able and hard-working.[46]

The second group—the clergy Seabury himself ordained—had never personally experienced the S.P.G.'s pounds sterling and so did not keenly feel the lack of them. Generally they had charge of two or more churches, few places being able to support a full-time pastor. Chauncy Prindle (Yale, 1776), for example, went to Christ Church, Watertown, and St. Peter's, Plymouth, in 1788; the latter congregation engaged him "for one half of the Time" and paid annually £37 10*s* lawful money "in produce Such as Beef Pork Butter Tallow Sheeps Wool Flax or any Sort of Grain with a Suitable proportion of Each Kind."[47] Salaries were lower than the abilities of the people warranted, Seabury believed, but he consoled himself with the thought that while the clergy's total dependence on their congregations had obvious drawbacks, still they were free of the Erastian pressures which came with an English Establishment.[48]

As a group, the bishop's protégés were perhaps inferior in talents, as they were almost certainly inferior in learning, to the earlier generations of Connecticut clergy.[49] A sizeable proportion lacked a college degree,[50] and those who did publish anything confined themselves, for the most part, to the occasional sermon. On the other hand, they seem, in general, to have been active, zealous pastors. Probably typical was Daniel Burhans; from distant Lanesboro he reported to Seabury in May, 1795, that although alone and "surrounded with the assaults of the enemies of the Cross of Christ," he hoped "to fight manfully," being "Blessed with the Prospect of the Prosperity of Zions kingdom Notwithstanding the insinuations of Schismatics, the malignant Shafts of Tom Pane & the Lukewarm zeal of Nothingarians."[51]

The Convocation, increasingly made up of these younger men, functioned throughout Seabury's episcopate as the principal diocesan governing body. True to his declaration of 1785, the bishop took no important action without its approval, but this he seldom had difficulty in securing. As an early biographer put it, "In his consultations with his brethren, he had a happy faculty of so drawing out their opinions upon points of difference, as to reconcile them with each other, and accommodate them to his own, until he impressed his own mind upon that of all his clergy."[52]

Beginning in 1792, members of the Convocation also were members of a newly created diocesan Convention, which likewise included deputies chosen by the laity. The appearance of this mixed body must have surprised many observers, given Seabury's often expressed dislike of lay participation in ecclesiastical assemblies. Those who investigated its operations soon discovered, however, that the Convention represented no invasion of the priesthood's rights. On the contrary, Seabury regarded it as a proper means for preserving the Church's essential unity.

Precedents for the mixed Convention could be found in three *ad hoc* lay conventions held in 1788-89. Before this time, the bishop had received no regular income from the diocese; that deficiency its laymen were now expected to remedy. In December, 1787, the Convocation scheduled the first of their meetings, appointing a committee to confer with representatives from all the state's churches at Waterbury on February 13, there to discover the "Grand Levy" or assessed property valuation of the membership of each and to judge whether an annual salary could be raised. Of the fifty or so churches in Connecticut, about two thirds sent deputies. Those who failed to do so probably were motivated by reasons which Ebenezer Dibble mentioned to Samuel Peters. "Many Churches are incapable of setling and supporting a minister," he wrote, "and others [are] taxed as high already to support those who officiate among them, as the Presbyterians are taxed for the support of their Religion."[53]

Despite the lack of a full representation, the Waterbury Convention unanimously voted Seabury one halfpenny in the pound, on the grand levy of the churches, to the amount of £250 annually, the grant to continue for two years. Parishes with deputies present were to confirm this vote; it was hoped that the others, notified by a newspaper advertisement, would give in their grand levy lists. At the same time the Convention requested all churches to send deputies to a second meeting at Wallingford, May 7, 1788, for the purpose of reviewing "the doings of the former Convention, and securing the Continuation of said Salary for the Support of the Right Reverend SAMUEL SEABURY, our Diocesan Bishop."[54]

How many churches responded to this appeal is not recorded. Nevertheless, the representation at Wallingford must have been more complete, for the session confirmed and made perpetual Seabury's salary and, in addition, selected persons to solicit subscriptions for an Episcopal Academy.[55] These same matters formed the agenda of a third lay Convention, assembled at Middletown on the second Wednesday in May, 1789.[56] Here Seabury obtained the declaration, relayed to White in his letter of June 29, that the laity had no right to interfere "in Church government or in reformation of Liturgies." An episcopal revenue and education were, however, quite different subjects. They came under the heading of the Church's "external or temporal state," and in the ordering of such matters, the laity, Seabury had explained to Bishop Skinner in 1788, might well have a share.[57]

The bishop intended to preserve this close restriction of lay activity when, in 1791, he decided upon the mixed Convention. As a result of James Sayre's actions at Stratford, he had become convinced that the unity of the Church might disappear unless congregations could be persuaded that they were parts of a larger whole. An annual meeting of their representatives to discuss common interests with himself and the body of the clergy, he judged, would create a sense of unity and dispel what had proved to be a very dangerous isolation. His motives were well summarized in a letter to an English friend, William Stevens:

> The state of the Church in this country is much the same as when I wrote last. The great difficulty is to get the several congregations to consider themselves as parts of one body, & to act in unison with each other. While they were Missions of the Society in England, their whole Ecclesiastical business was transacted with that Society, as distinct congregations; & they seldom had much intercourse with each other. A spirit of independency on each other hath, by that means, been introduced, which can only be overcome by time & patience.
>
> In order to remedy this inconvenience, which weakens the influence of the Church, I have prevailed with some of the principal & more understanding laity of the several congregations to meet annually on this subject; that by conversing on it, & on such subjects within their line as relate to the general good of the Church, they may become acquainted with each other, & with the general state of the several congregations. I have reason to hope this will promote union & intimate connection among them.[58]

At Watertown, October 5, 1791, the Convocation authorized the mixed body. Each clergyman, it was voted, should urge the choosing of at least one deputy by the people of his cure (which, as earlier noted, usually included two or more congregations). Assembling at New Haven the following year, these representatives would "be considered as a Committee of conference, to confer with the Convocation, at that time & place, on all matters that respect the temporal interest of the Church."[59] As a result of this decision, twenty ministers and twenty-four laymen came together in Trinity Church, New Haven, June 6, 7, 1792. The bishop presided *ex officio* and noted in his journal his complete satisfaction with their work.[60] Approving a diocesan constitution formally establishing the Convention, this organizational meeting designated the first Wednesday in June for its annual sessions. Upon Seabury's death, it would assemble within three months to name his successor; the right of election was to belong, first of all, to the clergy, but their choice must be ratified by a majority of the lay members. Among other provisions (the constitution had eight articles) was one establishing the procedure for electing lay deputies to the General Convention.[61] Such persons were immediately chosen, whose presence at New York in September, 1792, gave particular pleasure to Bishop White.[62]

Although a few congregations opposed some part or parts of the constitution when it came before them for ratification, the great majority signified their acceptance.[63] The Convention, accordingly, became a fixed feature of Connecticut's diocesan government. Its minutes resembled those of the Episcopal conventions of the other states, and a person who gave them a casual reading might well have supposed that the body had, together with the bishop, the full direction of extraparochial affairs. In fact the mixed Convention, like the lay conventions of 1788-89, confined itself almost exclusively to "temporal" matters: Seabury's support and the long-projected Episcopal Academy. When a session got through its agenda and adjourned, Seabury and the clergy, remaining behind, would resolve themselves into the Convocation, there to transact such business as they considered their exclusive province.[64] And each autumn, as before 1792, the Convocation held a second meeting.

Of the topics chiefly occupying the Convention during Seabury's episcopate, that of his salary received no satisfactory solution. In 1792 the lay members, noting that many parishes "through inattention have not altogether complied with" the provision made for its payment, urged churches to meet their current assessment. At the same time, in an effort to put the matter on a firmer basis, the Convention decided to seek a charter for a charitable corporation, donations to which would form the principal of a permanent episcopal fund.[65] Such a scheme could be expected to inflame old prejudices, and the Convention's committee, when approaching the Assembly in October, 1793, obviously kept that in mind. Episcopalians, they explained, "reprobate the Idea of supporting a Bishop in Luxury and Idliness [sic], yet they are strongly of Opinion, that the Labourer is worthy of his Hire."[66] This argument convinced the deputies but not the assistants; repeated efforts in 1794 and 1795 likewise failed to extract a charter.[67]

The other matter which concerned the Convention—the formation of an Episcopal Academy—was closely linked to Seabury's personal relations with the state's dominant religious group. Although the bishop counted individual members of the Congregational churches among his friends,[68] his encounters with the Congregational clergy, and particularly with their leader, Ezra Stiles (since 1778 President of Yale), were often unpleasant. Considering themselves to be as good scriptural *episcopi* as any Episcopal prelate, the ministers resented Seabury's assumption of the style "Bishop of Connecticut." Immediately upon his arrival in 1785, the General Association voted to recommend to their several associations that members adopt the title of "Bishop."[69] How long this form of address remained in use is uncertain; it continued for several years at least. As late as the summer of 1788, the New London *Connecticut Gazette* reported:

> At a Council of Bishops and Delegates convened at Hebron the 18th inst. the Rev. Samuel Kellogg was consecrated Bishop of the first Church in Hebron, late charge of the reverend and venerable Bishop Pomeroy. The clergy who officiated on the solemnity, were the Rev. Bishop Lockwood, Bishop Lathrop, (who preached a sermon well adapted to the occasion, from I Cor. iv. I.) Bishop Robbins, Bishop Brockway, Bishop M'Clure, Bishop Huntington, Bishop Par-

sons and Bishop Gurley. The whole was conducted with becoming solemnity and exemplary order.[70]

President Stiles was probably the moving spirit in organizing this comic-opera assault.[71] At the Yale Commencement of 1785 he gave further evidence of his dislike of prelatic pretensions. Seabury coming, though late, to the exercises (the Convocation was then meeting in New Haven), someone suggested to Stiles that he be given a place upon the stage. Replied the intrepid Puritan: "It would be invidious, among so *many bishops*, to discriminate Dr. Seabury."[72]

After this beginning, it was understandable that Seabury should refuse an invitation to dine with the assembled ministers, when Stiles, in May, 1787, came to New London for the ordination of Henry Channing (Yale, 1781) as pastor of the First Church.[73] The sermon preached by the president on this occasion,[74] utilizing the "Bishop" terminology and containing passages defending "presbyterian" ordination, stirred up a controversy in which John Bowden of Norwalk published a number of pamphlets setting forth the Episcopal position.[75] Seabury was not directly involved, but in 1791 he unwisely allowed himself to be persuaded to print an ordination sermon championing divine-right episcopacy, which some persons considered a continuation of the earlier exchange.[76]

The previous year, in an anonymous *Address to the Ministers and Congregations of the Presbyterian and Independent Persuasions*, the bishop had urged the union of these bodies with the Episcopal Church. Having corresponded on the subject with a prominent Congregationalist, Dr. Benjamin Gale of Killingworth,[77] he had—so he thought—grounds for believing his proposals might be well received, at least by the laity of these denominations. Seabury wrote in his opening paragraph:

My encouragement to this undertaking arises from observing, that candour and liberality of sentiment are increasing in the country, and that most of those objections against the Church of England which caused a separation from it, have in a great measure ceased to operate in the United States of America.—People of your persuasion can now look upon a gown or surplice without horror; and some of your own clergy make a respectable and dignified appearance when clothed in the former of those garments, or, at least, one very like it. They can be present at divine service in our churches, and use the Common-Prayer-Book with every appearance of sincere devotion. They can pay attention to Christmas and Good-Friday and seem to be sensible of the propriety of observing *those* days, at least, for the commemoration of the nativity and death of the blessed Redeemer: and your clergy, particularly in the eastern states, have generally adopted, and seem to be well pleased with, the stile and title of Bishop.

From these circumstances, I cannot but hope that the great difficulties in the way of an union between you and the Episcopal Church are at an end, and that all lesser matters may be obviated or removed by mutual explanations and concessions.[78]

The concessions, however, it soon became evident were to be made by the other side. A liturgy somewhat different from that of the Prayer Book might be allowed former Dissenters, but, in all other respects, the union would mean conformity to the Episcopal system. Seabury candidly explained his belief that the groups he was addressing lacked a true ministry ("You ask, 'Have we no authorized ministers? no valid sacraments?' To these questions, I shall return disagreeable answers"),[79] extolled liturgical worship as against extempore prayer, and pleaded the usefulness of the patristic writings in arriving at a correct interpretation of biblical passages. Within the limits imposed by eighteenth-century High Church theology, the *Address* was a competent production, conciliatory in tone and written with obvious desire for an agreement. Still, it was unthinkable that the Congregationalists or Presbyterians should choose to unite with the Episcopal Church on the basis of its terms.

Unpleasant incidents and hurt feelings continued to mar the bishop's relations with the Standing Order until his death. Episcopal clergymen might preach the annual election sermon in New Hampshire in 1790 and in Massachusetts in 1793,[80] but Seabury was never invited to perform the same office at Hartford, despite the fact that the Connecticut population included a much larger percentage of Churchmen. That the first societies of Fairfield and Norwalk should be granted five hundred pounds each by the Assembly to assist in replacing meetinghouses burned by the British, and the local Episcopalians left to finance their rebuilding themselves, the bishop considered unjustifiable partiality. The legislature readily authorized lotteries for constructing meetinghouses, he complained, while denying the Churchmen of Norwich the like privilege when their edifice was to be erected. Nor could the whole body of Episcopalians secure the desired charter for a corporation to manage the episcopal fund, "though a similar petition from Presbyterians would have been complied with, without hesitation."[81]

Fasts and thanksgivings caused a good deal of interdenominational bickering. In 1795, already under attack for a newspaper notice in which, styling himself "SAMUEL, by divine permission Bishop of Connecticut and Rhode-Island," he had ordered a collection in his churches for the relief of captives at Algiers,[82] Seabury was censured for his refusal to open St. James's Church on February 19, a day set aside for public thanksgiving by proclamation of President Washington. Since the date coincided with the second day of Lent, the bishop felt he could not comply.[83] For the same reason—a conflict with the Church's liturgical calendar—he declined to observe the annual Connecticut Fast, which, in spite of his efforts to work out some arrangement with Governor Huntington, had continued, so he charged, to "be appointed in Easter week, at least twice in three times."[84] The criticism of Seabury's failure to regard Washington's proclamation seems to have redirected the state authorities' attention to this related matter, for in 1795 the fast was appointed for Good Friday. This practice becoming fixed after 1797, the occasion for controversy disappeared.[85]

Possibly more irritating to Seabury than anything else was

the Assembly's "monstrous donation" of certain monies to Yale in 1792, estimated by some "at 10,000£ some even at 15,000£."[86] Such use of public funds was intolerable so long as President Stiles, supported by the school's exclusively Congregational trustees, denied Episcopal students permission to worship regularly in New Haven's Trinity Church[87] and, in general, kept up his zealous opposition to episcopacy. In Seabury's mind, the need to remove young Churchmen from his tutelage merged easily—and at an early date—with resentment of what the bishop regarded as Stiles's personal insults. Similar sentiments appearing among the clergy and laity,[88] he was able by 1788 to launch plans for a rival institution: the Episcopal Academy.

The academy's basic function, as Seabury saw it, would be to produce and train candidates for Orders. The proper theological education of such youths (and the improvement in learning of men already ordained) had been one of his first concerns. In England he had solicited books from acquaintances—though apparently without much success—in order to lay the basis for a clerical subscription library.[89] He returned to this project in 1788, hoping now to purchase "the Fathers of the Primitive Church in the originals, & their best Translations," to be supplemented, as funds allowed, with controversial works and "the Old Standard Authors of the Church of England."[90] Presumably the academy was to house this library. Its younger students would require another collection, of which books on the liberal arts would form but a part. The school, Seabury explained, was to be comprehensive in nature, "qualifying young Gentlemen for business in the different departments of life." With luck, this broad focus would produce a sizeable enrollment and, consequently, an adequate income.[91]

At Wallingford in May, 1788, the second *ad hoc* lay Convention chose a committee to frame the academy's constitution, to determine its location, and to solicit subscriptions. Headed by Seabury, it included, among others, Congressman William

Samuel Johnson, Jonathan Ingersoll of New Haven (Lieutenant Governor of Connecticut from 1816 to 1823), Jarvis, and Hubbard. These men with their associates met at New Haven on October 16,[92] and again on January 8, 1789, and got up a plan which they submitted to the public in the form of a printed subscription paper.

The religious regulations established by Seabury's committee were modeled on those in effect at King's College before the Revolution. All pupils might attend the church indicated by their parents, but they had also to be present at "Morning and Evening Prayers in the Academy—which Prayers shall be extracted from the Liturgy of the Church of England." Only an Episcopal clergyman could serve as the school's president, Seabury being designated as the first holder of that office. In managing the academy's affairs, he was to have the assistance of a board of fifteen governors, six Episcopal clergymen and nine laymen, four of whom must be Episcopal communicants. Initially, the governors would be chosen by those persons who subscribed at least ten dollars. As for a location, subscribers were to declare both the amount they would give absolutely and the amount they would furnish should the academy be placed in a specified town; if any town's subscription exceeded the others by two hundred pounds, it was to have preference.[93]

Seabury hoped that his school might open its doors in the summer of 1789. But it was soon evident that two thousand pounds in available subscriptions—the sum needed to begin operations—could not be raised. "Our Academy for the present lies still," Hubbard informed Samuel Peters, explaining that "Money in this part of the World is not very plenty."[94] This being the case, the bishop turned his attention elsewhere until 1792, when the Convocation decided that the clergy should make inquiries in their neighborhoods to discover what funds could now be got.[95] Again the response must have been unfavorable, for there is no record of further action.

Finally, in 1794, the Convention busied itself with the matter. A lay-clerical committee was appointed to frame another prospectus and subscription paper, and while the session's minutes were silent as to a location, Seabury wrote in his journal that the academy would be established in Stratford and that John Bowden—not he himself—was to have its direction.[96] However, when deputies and pastors came to examine the subscription papers the following year, it developed that Cheshire and Wallingford, as well as Stratford, would give generous financial aid in order to secure the school. The Convention accordingly chose persons to carry on discussions with the three towns and to meet at Major Bellamy's tavern in Hamden on July 1 to reach a final decision.[97] Cheshire, declaring its desire to "rescue from the expenses and the vices of Colleges and crowded cities, the means of useful improvement, and to implant them in the bosom of retirement and rural simplicity,"[98] won the contest. During the last months of Seabury's life, plans emerged for a large two-story brick building, crowned with a cupola and spire.[99] Construction began in the spring of 1796, the cornerstone being laid with Masonic rites on April 28.[100]

It appeared that Seabury's goal—a school where ministers might be "educated upon Church principles, that they might be able successfully to contend for Church principles"[101]—was about to be realized. The academy opened in June, 1796, with a constitution providing for instruction in the "English language, Philosophy, Mathematics, History, and every other science usually taught at Colleges."[102] Yet it never succeeded in gaining recognition as a school of higher learning. Repeatedly the Assembly rejected applications for a college charter. Not until Washington College at Hartford (subsequently renamed Trinity) opened in 1824 did Connecticut's Churchmen establish a real rival to Yale.

Besides superintending Connecticut, Seabury extended what help he could to the other Episcopal churches of New England.

Maine's few congregations had been desolated by the Revolution: "Our church is all going to pieces, the roof is coming down, the rafters and beams broke with heavy snows last winter. What application can we make to Dr. Seabury?" Major Samuel Goodwin of Pownalborough declared to his former pastor in 1785.[103] Pownalborough's church soon disappeared, but further up the Kennebec, St. Ann's, Gardinerstown (now Gardiner) was completed about 1793 with funds bequeathed by Seabury's cousin, Dr. Sylvester Gardiner. Joseph Warren (Harvard, 1790), ordained by the bishop, became its rector, the first Episcopal clergyman to settle in Maine since the Revolution.[104]

Seabury seems never to have ventured as far east as the Kennebec, but in 1791, after repeated invitations, he visited Portsmouth, New Hampshire. On June 26, the first Sunday after Trinity, he preached at the morning and evening services in St. John's Church (the former Queen's Chapel) and confirmed seventy-two persons. Three days later he added thirty-three to this number, at the same time raising to the priesthood Robert Fowle (Harvard, 1786), whom he had ordained deacon at New London in 1789 to serve the newly established church in Holderness, New Hampshire. Since Fowle's second ordination was the first such Episcopal ceremony to be performed within the state, hundreds crowded into St. John's, some of whom, Seabury complained, "little regarded the solemnity of the Office or the prosperity of the Church." Particularly objectionable to this group was the bishop's sermon, earlier mentioned, in which he strenuously defended divine-right episcopacy.[105]

Seabury, at some date prior to the Revolution, had acquired rights to land in the town of Bolton, later included in the state of Vermont. In 1787, before his parish and diocese had attempted to provide him with a fixed support, he planned an inspection of this property, thinking (not, it seems, very seriously) that he might settle in Bolton if he found it to his liking.

Illness in the family kept him at home, and it is doubtful that he ever visited Vermont:[106] the evidence of his journal shows that he certainly did not do so between 1791 and 1796. Still, he did his best to get missionaries for the state when the General Convention proposed sending them to the Western frontiers.[107] And he ordained a good number of ministers for the struggling Vermont churches: Tillotson Bronson for Strafford—and Hanover, New Hampshire—in 1786; Daniel Barber (Dartmouth A.M., 1801) for Pownal and Sandgate in the same year; Reuben Garlick for Manchester and Bethuel Chittenden for Tinmouth and Castleton in 1787; also Russell Catlin (Yale, 1784) for Arlington in 1792.[108] All of these churches were located in an area visited by Connecticut's S.P.G. missionaries just prior to the Revolution, and probably a large proportion of their members consisted of immigrants from that state. Despite the geographical difficulties involved, it is not surprising, then, to find that the first Vermont Convention, meeting at Sandgate, February 24, 1791, ordered a letter "to be addressed to the Right Rev. Samuel, Bishop of Connecticut, recommending the Church of this State to his pastoral regard, until a bishop is elected to preside over it."[109] Such a letter seems never to have been sent. At any rate, none reached New London, and although Seabury was privately informed of the Sandgate proceedings, the Vermont Convention proceeded no further. Later, it chose Bass of Newburyport bishop, and in 1794 the Loyalist refugee Samuel Peters. "Who they will elect next I know not," Seabury wrote the latter nominee, "but suspect all is not right."[110]

Seabury visited Boston in 1786 and 1788. He also stopped in the town in 1791 on his way to and from Portsmouth, preaching on both occasions in Trinity Church. Trinity was the scene of one of his earlier confirmations: March 24, 1786, he laid hands on about thirty of Samuel Parker's parishioners and afterwards performed the same office at Christ Church.[111] Local writers handled him roughly, charging that he took money from the candidates (probably because a collection was made to assist in rebuilding St. James's, New London) and ridiculing his interpretation of the rite.[112] In 1788 Seabury appeared in public at Boston only to preach,[113] but making a side excursion to Marblehead, where his partisan, Thomas Fitch Oliver, was rector of St. Michael's, he confirmed on Easter Sunday and Monday upward of one hundred twenty persons.[114] Returning from Portsmouth in 1791, he spent several days with another friend, Dr. Bass, at Newburyport. A crowd estimated at more than two thousand filled St. Paul's Church on Sunday afternoon, July 3, to hear his sermon, and since only fifty candidates could force their way through the aisles, he again confirmed the next morning.[115] "Your visit here & episcopal performances have given a respectability to our Church," Bass later reported. A Congregational pastor, who encountered Seabury at a tavern as he passed through Salem, likewise testified to the good impression the bishop had made. "He is a man of excellent person, good address, manly confidence," wrote William Bentley (Harvard, 1777), adding regretfully: "But he is rigorous in his discipline, & a true Churchman."[116]

Casual contacts with northern New England congregations formed a contrast to Seabury's close ties with the Episcopalians of Rhode Island. This was true even before 1790, the year he became the state's bishop. King's Church, Providence, where he first confirmed April 3, 1786, is a case in point. In September, 1789, Parker informing its members that the General Convention desired a representation from Rhode Island at the adjourned session, they authorized the bishop to act for them.[117] As for Trinity Church, Newport, it constantly consulted Seabury. In the spring of 1786, he received an invitation to become rector, the salary to be £100 sterling plus a house and garden.[118] The offer was tempting, given his uncertain support from St. James's, but Seabury rejected it. In his reply, July 17, 1786, he declared:

> I am much obliged to you, Gentlemen, and to the whole congregation of the Church at Newport, for the favorable opinion you entertain of me, manifested by your wishing to have me reside with you,

> and take charge of your Church. However agreeable such an event might be to me, the state of Connecticut does not seem to permit it. Since you turned your attention towards me, we have lost five clergymen, and I believe shall lose the sixth. This makes it a matter of more consequence that I stay with them, and endeavor to remedy the inconvenience that must arise on this occasion. And, indeed, should I accept your kind invitation, my necessary absence from you, would leave your Church unsupplied more frequently than it ought to be.

Trinity, the bishop suggested, would find a faithful pastor in James Sayre, then residing at Fairfield without a cure. "His character is irreproachable, and his piety and discretion may be depended on," he declared, lauding the clergyman in terms he scarcely would have used in the 1790's![119] The Newport congregation, duly impressed, engaged Sayre. An opposition to him soon developed, however, led by John Bours, formerly the church's lay reader. Both sides corresponded with Seabury, and in July, 1788, when he came to Newport to confirm, he talked with the two leaders. These efforts to heal the breach failing, Sayre resigned before the end of the year, although his party seems to have been the larger.[120]

Sayre's successor was William Smith, the young immigrant Scot earlier introduced.[121] After a brief career in Pennsylvania and Maryland, he had settled at St. Paul's, Narragansett, in July, 1787, Seabury getting this post for him.[122] Smith, an able liturgist and a man thoroughly imbued with the High Church views of the Scots Episcopalians, was probably the bishop's favorite clergyman. "I heartily wish to keep him in my neighbourhood," he wrote Bishop Skinner in November, 1788, "for he would be very useful to me in bringing our people to a better knowledge of the real principles of their Religion, & to more submission to Ecclesiastical discipline."[123] Members of Trinity Church who opposed Smith's settlement appealed to Seabury to persuade him to stay at Narragansett, but the bishop refused.[124] Once at Newport, he found himself surrounded by difficulties. Still, the storms he had to weather were smaller than the ones which had engulfed Sayre, with the result that he remained there until after Seabury's death.[125]

All the evidence points to Smith as the man responsible for Seabury's assuming the episcopal charge of Rhode Island. From the date of the initial proceedings, it seems evident that he was motivated by fear of what the Boston Convention—summoned by Massachusetts Churchmen opposed to Samuel Parker's measures—might do when it assembled at Salem, October 5, 1790.[126] Neither his own congregation, nor any of the other three in the state, was sending deputies to this meeting. On the other hand, given their traditional ties with the churches to the eastward, the possibility existed of their being pulled eventually into the Salem schemes. How was this danger to be avoided? The answer, presumably first formulated by Smith, was to place Rhode Island's Churchmen under Seabury's formal superintendence. Such a move would complete their polity, would give them their necessary head.

Smith acted after the Salem meeting had adjourned but before its decisions were published.[127] Notice being given, Trinity's parishioners came together on October 17 and voted to invite their sister congregations—St. Paul's, Narragansett, St. Michael's, Bristol, and King's Church, Providence—to join them in a union.[128] The latter two responded, sending representatives to the Rhode Island Convention, organized at Newport on November 18. This first session approved the measures of the 1789 General Convention, established a diocese,[129] and declared Seabury its bishop. (The Convention's minutes imply that he had earlier given his consent.)[130] At the direction of the lay delegates, Smith and Moses Badger (Harvard, 1761), the only Episcopal clergymen in Rhode Island, sent off an official notification:

> Confiding in your moderation and prudence, and beholding the decency and propriety with which you conduct your Episcopal admin-

istration in your diocese of Connecticut, as also esteeming you an able defender, as well as an avowed patron and propagator of Apostolic faith and practice, the aforesaid Convention has nominated and unanimously voted your Reverence, the Bishop and Ecclesiastical Superior of the Churches so represented; and of such others in this State as may in future accede to and become parts of the established Episcopacy of the United States; and in consideration of the many advantages which will naturally result from your superintendence, as well as to manifest our desire to promote and strengthen the unity of Christ's Apostolic Church, as far as in us lieth, the aforesaid Churches promise to pay to your Reverence all due and Christian respect and canonical obedence.[131]

Seabury's graceful reply was dated at New London, December 1, 1790:

Had I a high opinion of my own abilities, it is probable I should accept this instance of the good opinion your convention are pleased to entertain of me, with more confidence; next, however, to doing as well as we wish, is to do as well as we can.

Confiding then in the assistance and protection of Almighty God, and hoping, gentlemen, for your advice and support, and for the support of all good men, I do, in the fear of God, and under a sense of duty to the great Redeemer and Head of the Church, accept the charge your convention have thought proper to commit to me; and will exert my best efforts that their expectations from me may not be entirely disappointed.

By the divine permission I will visit your churches as soon as the spring season shall permit. . . .[132]

St. Paul's, Narragansett, it will be noted, sent no delegates to Newport. A majority of the congregation favored joining their brethren and acknowledging Seabury, but one Dr. Walter Gardiner, supported by some other members, held out. Before the Revolution, a certain John Case had bequeathed his estate, on the death of his widow (now, in 1790, a very aged woman), for the support of the bishop superintending St. Paul's Church. Until such a personage should appear, the property was to be utilized for the benefit of the church's poor. Hoping to control this estate, Gardiner and his friends got a charter from the Assembly incorporating themselves as the legal representatives of St. Paul's. The doctor, with an eye to the rectorship, tried to obtain Orders from Seabury while keeping the church independent of the bishop's authority. For obvious reasons, the standing committee of Rhode Island refused to recommend him. In 1793, therefore, Gardiner and his party joined themselves to the Boston (or Massachusetts) Convention. The Massachusetts standing committee supplying him with testimonials, he was ordained deacon by Bishop Provoost.[133]

Seabury, in light of their past relations, considered Provoost's action a deliberate affront, although Provoost assured Bishop White that he knew nothing of any division at Narragansett and that Seabury's close associates, Benjamin Moore and Jeremiah Leaming, had both assisted him in the ordination. Equally offended was the Rhode Island Convention. After investigating, it adopted a report declaring that "the Promotion of Dr. Gardner [*sic*] by Bishop Provost [*sic*] was directly contrary to the Constitution and Canons of the Protestant Episcopal Church." The affair ultimately came before the 1795 General Convention, the result being an additional canon designed to prevent any possibility of its repetition.[134] By this time Gardiner had quitted Narragansett, and its pro-Seabury faction was clearly in control. Immediately prior to the General Convention, the bishop had confirmed at St. Paul's, administering the rite in the same structure in which James MacSparran, some sixty years before, had received his mother and Mumford grandparents into the Episcopal Church.[135]

Seabury held visitations of his Rhode Island diocese in the summers of 1791, 1793, and 1795.[136] While these tours allowed him the company of "various good acquaintances"—among them certain Mumford connections—they also imposed fairly extensive work loads. Twice he took part in the Rhode Island

Convention, occupying the chair *ex officio* (which, in other years, was filled by a local pastor). The session he attended in 1793 largely concerned itself with the Gardiner case; that of 1795 tentatively approved a diocesan constitution and, among other considerations, appointed the state's first separate delegation to a General Convention.[137] At the parish level, the bishop preached, confirmed, and counseled. In addition, he held one ordination, that of John Usher (Harvard, 1743), lay reader at St. Michael's, Bristol, whom he ordered deacon and priest, July 28, 31, 1793. Rectors William Smith and Moses Badger, in requesting Usher's advancement, declared that there should "be a Person in holy Orders, to officiate upon the footing of Itinerancy within the limits of this State, when and wheresoever the CHURCH may more immediately require his services."[138] Seabury agreed and appointed Usher to do this work,[139] yet the missionary's great age ruled out the possibility of success.[140] In Rhode Island, growth and expansion would come only after 1800. The bishop could but strengthen the existing congregations.

X

"THE TRUE & REAL CHRISTIAN SACRIFICE"

THE IMPORTANT ALTERATIONS WHICH SAMUEL SEABURY made in the corpus of New England's High Church theology concerned the nature of the Holy Communion. Adopting the Nonjuring eucharistic views of his consecrators, he inculcated their teaching in several publications and in the Scottish catechism he issued for the use of the Connecticut and Rhode Island churches. Equally significant, from the standpoint of liturgical developments, was Seabury's adoption in 1786 of the liturgy enshrining this sacramental doctrine: the Scots Communion Office of 1764. Incorporated, in part, into the Communion service approved by the 1789 General Convention, the Scots Office created the principal difference between the liturgies of the Church of England and the Protestant Episcopal Church.

Eucharistic doctrine as taught by Seabury's New England predecessors had produced no Congregational critique. On the contrary, it served to point up the fact that the region's first High Churchmen, though discarding Calvinist predestination and reprobation, otherwise altered little their old faith as distinguished from their former polity. That this should be so, that convert pastors should often preach in the church what they had learned in the meetinghouse, was not unnatural. Puritan criticism of the English Establishment focused on matters other than dogma. The ministers of western Massachusetts declared in 1734 that they accepted the doctrinal portions of the Thirty-Nine Articles;[1] earlier spokesmen for the Standing Order had taken the same stand.[2] Thus both Congregationalist and Episcopalian could agree—and they did agree—on the meaning of the Holy Communion, at least so far as it was set forth in Article XXVIII, "Of the Lord's Supper."

Writings of Samuel Johnson provide good evidence of this sacramental consensus. In the *Short Catechism*, which he published in 1753, the answer to question 34—"What does that ordinance [the Communion] mean?"—might well have come from Increase or Cotton Mather. "It is a public, solemn, and religious eating bread, and drinking wine, in remembrance of the sacrifice of the death of Christ," Johnson affirmed, "wherein the bread represents his body, and the wine his blood."[3] Preaching at Queen's Chapel, Portsmouth, March 30, 1740, he had explained the Sacrament in a similar manner. The bread was "a memorial only, & representation of that thing [Christ's body] whose name it bears"; the wine, Christ's blood "no farther, than as it represents & commemorates that blood, & the Covenant ratified by the shedding of it." Those who received the elements worthily had "sealed" to them "all the advantages, which his death was intended to procure for mankind."[4] In the *Short Catechism* Johnson expressed the same idea, stating that reception of the Communion "implied," that is, signified, "The receiving of Christ and all the spiritual blessings he purchased by his death, namely pardon, grace and eternal life."[5]

This teaching, it is to be presumed, was familiar to Seabury from childhood. It appears, with some modification, in his earliest surviving sermon, delivered at New Brunswick in 1754. Taking as a text I Corinthians 11:23-26, the young minister affirmed that "The Sacrament of the Lord's Supper was instituted to be the Christian Sacrifice; and an emblem of the Sacrifice our blessed Redeemer made." In this "continual Sacrifice," the passion and death of Christ were repeatedly commemorated and the devout communicant was strengthened by those graces he particularly needed, "namely perserverance in well doing, and continual increase in the divine likeness; and sincere gratitude, and unfeigned joy and thankfulness to Almighty God, and our adorable Savior for the innumerable benefits which his precious Blood shedding hath obtained for us."[6]

The bishop's great-grandson, William Jones Seabury, quoted this sermon in an effort to show that the eucharistic views he expressed after 1784 "were not of any recent adoption, but had been woven into the texture of his faith and teaching throughout his whole priesthood."[7] Seabury's descendants had never taken kindly the statement of Bishop White in 1820 that his colleague's views had altered radically as a result of contact with the Scots Episcopalians.[8] Samuel Seabury (1801-1872), questioning his father, the Reverend Charles, on the subject, had been assured the contrary: Charles "had heard his father say that the opinions expressed on this subject in the first volume of his published Discourses [1793] were substantially those which he had always entertained, only that they were in his later years more clearly defined and matured."[9] This statement is partly accurate, for Seabury's views undoubtedly underwent a certain development, away from the traditional New England position, long before 1784. The New Brunswick sermon shows this: it is the product of a man familiar with seventeenth-century High Church glosses on the eucharistic Article.[10] Still, there are significant differences between its theology and that of the Nonjurors. If Charles Seabury recalled his father's words accurately, one must conclude that the bishop, like many a theologian, unconsciously minimized the extent to which he had adjusted his opinions in attempting to preserve an image of himself as being always intellectually consistent.

The eucharistic theology which Seabury took from Scotland was formulated early in the century by John Johnson of Cranbrook, inheritor of the High Church traditions of the Laudian school and Jeremy Taylor. Johnson lived and died a Church of England clergyman. On the other hand, the doctrines expounded in his two-volume work, *The Unbloody Sacrifice and Altar, Unvail'd and Supported* (1714, 1718), found their best reception among one faction of the English Nonjurors and that faction's close associates, the early leaders of Scotland's Nonjuring Episcopal Church. In preaching and writing, these men echoed Johnson's belief that the bread and wine offered by a minister who could accurately be described as a "priest" became a sacrifice in a very real sense—nothing less than the body and blood of Christ "in Power and Effect" (or, to use Seabury's phrase, "the life-giving body and blood of Christ in power and virtue").[11]

With the consecrated elements so defined, the Holy Communion, together with Baptism, came to occupy the central position in the individual's religious life. As Seabury put it: "when we worthily receive baptism, we obtain through Christ remission of all past sins, so when we worthily communicate at God's altar we obtain remission of all sins committed since baptism."[12] The Eucharist, in short, was the channel through which God's pardon and renewing grace reached the penitent Christian; it was not merely a matter, as in the case of Samuel Johnson's teaching, of a person signifying his acceptance of God's redemptive work or "sealing" his participation in the Redemption by partaking of the elements. Instead, the Communion constituted an essential means of salvation. Under ordinary circumstances, those who had an opportunity to participate in it and stubbornly refused had no grounds for believing God had accepted their profession of contrition. Johnson of Cranbrook wrote very explicitly on this point: "If Christ Jesus have instituted any Sacrifice, as necessary to be offer'd, in order to obtain this Pardon; we are never to presume, that we have gain'd the End, 'till we have us'd the Means."[13]

Such doctrines did not always go down easily. Particularly was this true if their expositor explicitly connected the apostolic commission "Whose soever sins ye remit, they are remitted unto them; and whose soever sins ye retain, they are retained" with the minister's granting or refusing either sacrament. William Smith of Newport did this before the Rhode Island Convention in 1793, Seabury pronouncing the sermon an excellent one.[14] Some of Smith's hearers, however, thought it popish, as is clear from the defensive preface he appended to the printed text. The Christian pastor, Smith affirmed, disclaimed any notion of "lording it over God's heritage," but in keeping with the sacred deposit committed to him, he must "lift up his voice like a trumpet, to declare to Judah his sin, and to Israel his transgression," and to promulgate—with accuracy—"the doctrine of repentance and remission of sin to all people, through Jesus Christ."[15]

More frequently, the cry of popery was focused, not on this aspect of Johnson's eucharistic theology (of which critics frequently knew little or nothing), but on sentences in the Scots Communion Office formulated in response to another of his conclusions. Study of the patristic liturgies had convinced Johnson that the Communion service of the 1662 Prayer Book contained fundamental defects. Like its model, the Roman Mass, it made the consecration of the elements to consist in the recital of Christ's words of Institution, whereas Johnson believed that the Institution must be followed by their Oblation, the whole to be completed with an Invocation for the descent of the Holy Ghost upon the bread and wine. The compilers of the Scots Office of 1764—William Falconar, Bishop of Moray and Primus, and Robert Forbes, Bishop of Brechin—took this teaching as a framework when they set about producing an elaborate Prayer of Consecration.[16] At the same time, they phrased the prayer, as well as other parts of the office, in such a manner as to bring censure upon themselves—and later Seabury. Specifically, the bishops included in their Invocation this petition: "And we most humbly beseech thee, O merciful Father, to hear us, and of thy almighty goodness vouchsafe to bless and sanctify, with thy word and holy Spirit, these thy gifts and creatures of bread and wine, that they may become the body and blood of thy most dearly beloved Son." In similar fashion, they provided that the celebrant upon delivering the cup to the communicant (a like form was given for the delivery of the bread) should declare: "The blood of our Lord Jesus Christ, which was shed for thee, preserve thy soul and body unto everlasting life."

Falconar and Forbes interpreted these sentences in the light of Johnson's teaching. When they prayed that the bread and wine might become Christ's body and blood, they meant body and blood "in Power and Effect." But their stark phraseology conveyed quite different notions to men unfamiliar with such beliefs. Provost William Smith is a case in point. Smith severed his connection with the Scottish Episcopalians more than a decade before Falconar and Forbes compiled their office, and he seems to have known nothing of Johnson's theology. After examining the Scots Prayer of Consecration in 1786, he wrote William White and Samuel Parker that it "favoured the doctrine of *Transubstantiation*."[17]

Given this situation—the ambiguity of certain wordings and the resulting probability of controversy—one might have expected Seabury to approach the Scots Office with a good deal of caution. Such was not the case. At Aberdeen he readily adopted, so it seems, the suggestion of the Scottish bishops that he propose its use to his clergy.[18] To be sure, he formally bound himself no further than to give the office careful consideration. This, however, is explained by the fact that the formal commitment was a part of the concordat of November 15, 1784, the text of which apparently was completed prior to Seabury's arrival and thus before the bishops could accurately gauge his willingness to accede to their wishes. The fifth and longest article dealt with the Communion Office. It modestly set forth the Scots position:

> As the Celebration of the holy Eucharist, or the Administration of the Sacrament of the Body and Blood of Christ, is the principal Bond of Union among Christians, as well as the most solemn Act of Worship in the Christian Church, the Bishops aforesaid [that is, Seabury and his consecrators: Kilgour, Petrie and Skinner] agree in desiring that there may be as little Variance here as possible. And tho' the Scottish Bishops are very far from prescribing to their Brethren in this matter, they cannot help ardently wishing that Bishop Seabury would endeavour all he can consistently with peace and prudence, to make the Celebration of this venerable Mystery conformable to the most primitive Doctrine and practice in that respect: Which is the pattern the Church of Scotland has copied after in her Communion Office, and which it has been the Wish of some of the most eminent Divines of the Church of England, that she also had more closely followed, than she seems to have done since she gave up her first reformed Liturgy used in the Reign of King Edward VI, between which and the form used in the Church of Scotland, there is no Difference in any point, which the primitive Church reckoned essential to the right Ministration of the holy Eucharist.—In this capital Article therefore of the Eucharistic Service, in which the Scottish Bishops so earnestly wish for as much Unity as possible Bishop Seabury also agrees to take a serious View of the Communion office recommended by them, and if found agreeable to the genuine Standards of Antiquity, to give his Sanction to it, and by gentle Methods of Argument and Persuasion, to endeavour, as they have done, to introduce it by degrees into practice without the Compulsion of Authority on the one side or the prejudice of former Custom on the other.[19]

When he made his commitments, formal and informal, Seabury was ignorant of the true background of the Scots Office. He obviously had misread the concordat, for he thought the office not merely similar to, but in fact identical with, that published in the First Prayer Book of Edward VI.[20] However, books and pamphlets obtained from Scotland shortly before he sailed for America enabled him to place the liturgy in its own distinctive context.[21]

Studying this extensive and, for an American clergyman, probably unique Nonjuring collection[22] as the *Chapman* cut her course across the Atlantic, Seabury gained the knowledge necessary to discuss the Scots Office intelligently with his clergy. Their possible criticisms of it he must answer, particularly any on the score of popery. Nevertheless, he saw no serious difficulties in the way of its introduction and, in fact, none developed. It is true that Ebenezer Dibble spoke in 1787 of opposition to the office; writing Samuel Peters, he noted that Seabury "hath made *an attempt* to alter the Communion Service," adding that "it was with *a noble Spirit rejected*, when palmed upon the Clergy by *dint of Episcopal Supremacy*."[23] Several factors, however, argue against the accuracy of Dibble's statement. Persuasion—and this over a period of time—not an episcopal injunction, was the plan envisioned by the concordat. Moreover, the revision of the English Office at Middletown in August, 1785, shows that the bishop was willing to keep that service in the Prayer Book as an alternative to the Scots. Finally, there is the rule that Seabury set for himself: to act only with the approval of the Convocation in all but routine duties. In every other instance, he faithfully observed it, and his own account of the steps leading to the introduction of the Falconar-Forbes liturgy fully accords with this concept of the exercise of episcopal authority.

The text of the Scots Office was available for inspection at Middletown, where Seabury's pastors presumably first made their acquaintance with it. A month later the New Haven session of the Convocation provided the opportunity for further examination, and in December the bishop informed Skinner that the office would certainly be accepted. He had heard of no objection; indeed, "most people are convinced of its superior excellency." On the other hand, since congregations knew nothing of the office (and had recently been frightened by the Middletown proposals), the clergy judged it best to wait a little, until sermons and conversation had prepared communicants for its reception. "I shall first introduce it here [St. James's, New London]," Seabury explained, "but I believe not till Easter Sunday [1786], as I should choose to have the aera marked by one of our great Festivals."[24]

Another reason for not using the office immediately was the issuance of the Proposed Book by the General Convention of 1785. Seabury found himself in a difficult position, trying to counteract the Southern attempt at a thoroughgoing liturgical revision, while, at the same time, he himself planned radical "improvements" as regarded the Communion. He was afraid, he wrote Skinner, that the Southerners "would plead our example" if Connecticut took up the Scots Office.[25] And, as the event showed, his apprehensions were well-based. In the report of the second General Convention which William Smith prepared for him in July, 1786, the matter received specific mention. Seabury, according to this account, stood charged with forbidding his ordinees to use the Proposed Book, "while at the same time you are said, of your own authority, to be making very great alterations from the English Liturgy, especially in the administration of the blessed Sacrament of the Lord's Supper, striving, as Archbishop Laud did, to introduce again some of those superstitions of which it had been cleared at the Reformation."[26]

Despite misgivings, Seabury went ahead. Working from an unidentified edition of the Scots Office, he produced *The Communion-Office, or Order for the Administration of the Holy Eucharist or Supper of the Lord, with Private Devotions, Recommended to the Episcopal Congregations in Connecticut, by the Right Reverend Bishop Seabury*.[27] Published at New London in 1786, this service differed from that of 1764 in only a few details, almost all of them slight verbal changes.[28] Several alterations, however, were of some importance. The Exhortation with which the office began (Seabury and other users of the office probably prefaced it with the Ante-Communion of the 1662 Prayer Book)[29] was remodeled for the reason the English Exhortation had been tentatively remodeled at Middletown: in order to quiet the apprehensions of scrupulous communicants. As for the rubrics, Seabury directed the celebrant to put a little pure water into the cup containing the wine, the practice, he believed, being justified by primitive example.[30] This might seem a small matter, yet it was not accounted so by eighteenth-century liturgists: disputes concerning the "mixed cup" and other "Usages" had fragmented the English Nonjuring body in the reign of George I. Even in the 1780's, there were those, like Granville Sharp, who condemned Scots Episcopalians for doing silently what the bishop publicly ordered to be done.[31]

Equally insignificant, to the uninitiated, was Seabury's revision of the opening sentence of the Prayer of Consecration. He replaced a phrase—"who (by his own oblation of himself once offered)"—with the equivalent one in the 1662 service: "who made there (by his one oblation of himself once offered)." The latter statement, in its context, affirmed that the Son's offering of himself to the Father was made upon the cross. Bishops Forbes and Falconar disagreed. Holding with Johnson of Cranbrook[32] that Christ began his oblation in the institution of the Eucharist and merely completed it on Calvary, they worded their sentence in general terms, leaving the place and time of the sacrifice undesignated. Seabury in 1793 defended this position.[33] The wording of his office shows that he had not as yet adopted it in 1786: his development as a supporter of Johnson's theology, in other words, was a gradual, not a sudden, process.

The bishop's discussion of the Eucharist in the charge he delivered to his Convocation at Derby in September, 1786, further underscores this point. He compressed his thoughts into a few paragraphs, and there is, to be sure, some danger of seeing a distinction where none exists if one compares them with more extensive treatments. Still, reading this charge in conjunction with publications he issued in 1789 and 1793, it is at once noticeable that the ideas of Johnson of Cranbrook appear with much greater clarity in the latter.[34]

Although Seabury may have introduced the modified Scots Office into St. James's at Easter, 1786 (as he had indicated he would do in his letter to Skinner), it was during the Derby session that it was authorized for general use throughout the diocese.[35] One authority writes that "Bishop Seabury's Communion-Office seems to have been almost, if not quite, universally adopted by the clergy of Connecticut."[36] This conclusion is very likely true, but there is little direct evidence to support it. The statement of Dibble, earlier quoted, is the only contemporary expression of opinion on the matter, by a Connecticut pastor, that the present writer has uncovered. Indeed, after the publication of the office and its endorsement, the whole subject dropped from view until the possibility of union brought it once again to the fore in the early summer of 1789.

Seabury, taking a realistic view of the situation, knew that it would be impossible to persuade the churches of the other states to relinquish the English Office (reproduced, with no significant changes, in the Proposed Book) for the liturgy he had introduced. Nor did his doctrinal views compel him to require this sacrifice. While he now thought the English Office seriously defective, it could be corrected with judicious Scottish transplants. In that way he would avoid its wholesale condemnation, no unimportant consideration when his general plan was to preserve the Prayer Book of 1662 substantially unaltered.

Such reasoning illuminates the remarks on the subject included by Seabury in the lengthy letter he sent White on June

29, 1789. Noting that "a number of very respectable" English theologians could be cited in his support, he set down as the English Office's

> grand fault . . . the deficiency of a more formal oblation of the elements, and of the invocation of the Holy Ghost to sanctify and bless them. The Consecration is made to consist merely in the Priest's laying his hands on the elements and pronouncing, "*This is my body*, &c., which words are not consecration at all, nor were they addressed by Christ to the Father, but were declarative to the Apostles. This is so exactly symbolizing with the Church of Rome in an error; an error, too, on which the absurdity of Transubstantiation is built, that nothing but having fallen into the same error themselves, could have prevented the enemies of the Church from casting it in her teeth. The efficacy of Baptism, of Confirmation, of Orders, is ascribed to the Holy Ghost, and His energy is implored for that purpose; and why He should not be invoked in the consecration of the Eucharist, especially as all the old Liturgies are full to the point, I cannot conceive. It is much easier to account for the alterations of the first Liturgy of Edward the VI, than to justify them; and as I have been told there is a vote on the minutes of your Convention *anno*. 1786, I believe, for the revision of this matter, I hope it will be taken up, and that God will raise up some able and worthy advocates for this primitive practice, and make you and the Convention the instruments of restoring it to His Church in America. It would do you more honour in the world, and contribute more to the union of the Churches than any other alterations you can make, and would restore the Holy Eucharist to its ancient dignity and efficacy.[37]

Seabury's basic objection to the English Office (formulated, as earlier noted, by Johnson of Cranbrook) likewise is seen in an anecdote related by White. On Sunday, October 11, 1789, during the adjourned session of the General Convention, White invited Seabury to consecrate the eucharistic elements at Philadelphia's Christ Church. The bishop declined. When the hour for worship arrived, White once more pressed him to officiate. Again he refused, commenting with a smile: "To confess the truth, I hardly consider the form to be used, as strictly amounting to a consecration."[38]

The implications of this position explain the degree of joy which Seabury experienced when the adjourned session fell in with his suggestions for revising the English Office. Although other changes were made, the essential alteration in 1789 was the substitution of the Scots liturgy's Prayer of Consecration, with its well-defined (and, according to the bishop, properly arranged) Institution, Oblation, and Invocation, for the equivalent prayer in the 1662 service. Seabury had White's support in bringing this about. White could see nothing wrong with the English Office. Nevertheless, as regarded the Scots compilation, "he always thought there was a beauty in those ancient forms, and can discover no superstition in them."[39]

In adopting the Scots Prayer, the General Convention made one significant change in its wording, which does not seem to have been fully agreeable to Seabury.[40] It will be recalled that the Invocation of the 1764 office pleaded that the eucharistic elements might "become the body and blood of thy most dearly beloved Son." The 1789 revision kept intact the clause immediately preceding these words: "And we most humbly beseech thee, O merciful Father, to hear us; and, of thy almighty goodness, vouchsafe to bless and sanctify, with thy word and Holy Spirit, these thy gifts and creatures of bread and wine." But it continued in this manner, taking its wording from the 1662 service: "that we, receiving them according to thy Son our Saviour Jesus Christ's holy Institution, in remembrance of his Death and Passion, may be partakers of his most blessed Body and Blood."

This mixed phraseology resulted indirectly from the activities of Seabury's Scottish friend, William Smith of Newport. Following his arrival in the United States in 1784, Smith used the Prayer of Consecration of the 1764 office first at churches near

Philadelphia and later in Stepney Parish, Somerset County, Maryland, where he settled in July, 1785. Subsequently, Provost William Smith, then the principal figure among the Maryland clergy, asked that he lay aside his innovation and return to the 1662 text. Smith refused (he could "not so far depart from the Apostolic practice, as to adopt the use of a prayer which manifestly is abridged & mutilated") and reported his action to Seabury.[41] In reply, the bishop explained "how that matter stands in the Concordate, & what is proposed to be done here; & . . . encouraged him to continue as he has begun—at least till he has a Bishop to direct him—if the peace of his parish & the Church will any ways permit it."[42] The affair received an adjustment in the spring of 1786, Maryland's Convention, in deference to the Stepney rector, working an expression from the Scots Invocation into the English Office so as to produce an acceptable wording, which was almost identical with that found in the Scots Prayer of Consecration as altered in 1789.[43] It was intended that this change should come before the General Convention for its possible adoption, and Seabury's letter to White of June 29, 1789, showed that he believed something of this sort was attempted. In fact, the wording was put aside until 1789, when the Convention resurrected it with the idea of reconciling all persons to the form taken from the 1764 office.

Most Episcopalians received the Communion Office of 1789 without any adverse comment. But the reaction of one indignant gentleman pointed the way to later theological clashes. The celebrated Dr. Benjamin Rush in 1788 formally connected himself with one of Bishop White's congregations, believing that the Episcopal Church, as a result of the revisions included in the Proposed Book, had abandoned many of its doctrinal and liturgical "absurdities." "By their restoration by Bishop Seabury, I was thrown out of its pale," he observed to ex-President Adams in 1808. Specifically, Rush objected to the Baptismal Offices of 1789, with their explicit declarations in support of infant regeneration, and the Scots Prayer of Consecration which, even in its modified form, he saw as "favouring transubstantiation."[44]

The introduction of the full Scots Office into Connecticut in 1786 and the later incorporation of its principal feature into a liturgy used throughout the United States[45] did not exhaust Seabury's advocacy of a eucharistic life based on Johnson of Cranbrook's teachings. In addition, the bishop tried to increase the number of communicants in his congregations and to enlarge their schedules of sacramental celebrations. These two goals were to him of major importance. If the Eucharist was the channel through which the benefits of Christ's sacrifice, including the forgiveness of sins, were conveyed to the individual Christian, then obviously it was necessary for all men to become communicants and for all communicants to appear often at the altar. "As the bread of this world, frequently taken, is necessary to keep the body in health and vigour," Seabury explained in 1793, "so is this bread of God, frequently received, necessary to preserve the soul in spiritual health, and keep the divine life of faith and holiness from becoming extinct in us."[46]

Probably Seabury exerted himself the more urgently because of a falling off in the absolute total of Connecticut's communicants or, at least, a lowering ratio of communicants to adult Churchmen. While the absence of records comparable to the S.P.G. reports makes impossible a detailed comparison with the pre-Revolutionary period, isolated instances of decline seem significant. At Newtown in 1774 John Beach had two hundred thirty communicants in about one hundred twenty families; by 1799 the number was down to one hundred sixty, although the families then totaled one hundred forty. Similarly, in Seabury's own congregation in 1787, fewer than thirty people could be found at any celebration, whereas, in 1743, his father counted fifty-six.[47] Possibly these were extreme cases: the overall pattern may have been somewhat better. Still, Seabury in the 1780's was worried about the small number receiving the Sacrament in many churches. And he was greatly concerned that few of those who did approach the altar were men. (This, too, was particularly noticeable at St. James's, for the record of admissions to the Communion which he kept during his rectorship lists the names of forty women as against seventeen men.)[48] Delinquent males were to be found even among Connecticut's First Family of Churchmen: in 1789 Senator William Samuel Johnson of Stratford had to remind his son, Samuel William (born 1761), "as I have your Brother, of your too long neglect of Joining in full Communion with the Church of Christ."[49]

Seabury touched upon these matters in his published charge of 1786.[50] Failing to achieve much of a response, he decided upon a truly radical step. Except for the clergy of London and Westminster, New England's Episcopal ministers were unique in the eighteenth-century Church of England with respect to their general practice of monthly celebrations.[51] But Communion once a month, though better than once a quarter, was, in the bishop's opinion, still insufficient. If the Sacrament were made available at no more frequent intervals, people could never be brought to understand the real need for its reception. Weekly Communion, accordingly, should in time become the Connecticut norm.

Seabury presented this idea in a short address to the New London congregation, apparently delivered on Christmas Day, 1788. What he was about to say, he declared in his first sentence, had "long lain rather heavily on my mind." Study of the Scriptures and patristic writings (the latter probably at second hand, in the works of Johnson of Cranbrook and similar writers) had convinced him that for the early Christians, the Eucharist and public worship were synonymous terms. Moreover, the compilers of the English Prayer Book, as was evident from its arrangement, had intended that the Holy Communion should be administered every Sunday and holy day. These considerations disturbed him:

> I cannot help thinking it would be a reproach to a Christian Bishop, that in a Church where he constantly attends, the bread of God should ever be wanting on his Table. For this is the true & real Christian sacrifice, & succeeds in the Christian Church in the room of the daily sacrifice in the Jewish.
>
> My wish & design therefore is that the Communion be, for the future, administred every Sunday—And, if it please God to bless my endeavours, that at Easter it be administered every day for seven days after; And on Whit-sunday & six days after, according to the direction of the Church.
>
> Now whether this matter succeed, depends on you, my friends. It cannot reasonably be expected that every Communicant should constantly attend on every Sunday. Sickness, accidents, the cares of life, perturbations of mind, may sometimes discompose the best people for so solemn a service. But I do hope & expect, that there will on every Sunday be a sufficient number for the decent Celebration of the Holy Mysteries.[52]

Most Connecticut Churchmen first encountered the bishop's proposal in a twenty-three-page pamphlet, published at New Haven in 1789 under the title *An Earnest Persuasive to Frequent Communion; Addressed to Those Professors of the Church of England, in Connecticut, Who Neglect That Holy Ordinance.*[53] Claiming that the situation demanded "plainness of speech, and freedom of admonition," Seabury pleaded with such persons to hear him out, as he sought "to stir you up to the practice of a duty which I suppose an indispensable one, and in the neglect of which you live in a constant state of sin against your God."[54] The great excuse offered him for not communicating was a feeling of unworthiness. Striving to counter it, to quiet fears of damnation (as he earlier had attempted to do by revising the Exhortation of the 1764 Communion Office), the bishop argued that no individual could really be "worthy," free from all shortcomings and human infirmities. "God accepteth of what a man hath," he counseled scrupulous souls, "and requireth not that which he is unable to give." Those who tried to do their duty must, then, come confidently to the altar: "to receive baptism is not a more express command of Christ than to receive the Holy communion; and why there should be more solicitude about the one than the other, I cannot conceive."[55]

In explaining the nature of the Eucharist and its benefits, Seabury combined the teaching of Johnson of Cranbrook with the terminology of Puritan New England. The Eucharist, he declared, was "a covenanting rite." By Baptism the Christian originally entered into covenant with God, only to find this agreement subsequently broken—and of no effect—as the result of sin. A merciful God allowed the covenant to be renewed "at his Holy table"; there we "repeat our vows of obedience, and regain our title to his heavenly promises."[56]

Closing paragraphs presented the bishop's case for weekly Communion. Its general introduction he saw as a gradual process, dependent not on episcopal commands, but on a deepening understanding of the Eucharist on the part of each congregation.[57] Actually, there is no evidence that any church, except St. James's, attempted this schedule. There weekly celebrations may have continued for some time, but ultimately they disappeared. So forgotten were Seabury's efforts that the more venturesome leaders of the American Oxford Movement, who adopted a weekly Eucharist in the 1840's, came to be regarded as the first promoters of the practice in the Episcopal churches.[58]

No doubt the bishop believed the rising generation of Churchmen might frequent the Sacrament if their religious education gave a greater emphasis to its importance. This was, in all likelihood, one of the reasons which induced him to reprint in 1791 the catechism of Bishop George Innes of Brechin (d. 1781), although the consideration mentioned in his prefatory advertisement was the fact that the Episcopal Church's authorized Catechism (the same as that of the Church of England) said nothing about the duties owed God's ministers or the transmission of clerical authority.[59] These deficiencies the Scottish catechism remedied with properly High Church questions and answers,[60] at the same time providing a detailed explanation of Johnson of Cranbrook's eucharistic theology.[61] In its pages the laity first traced out that theology's full implications. And from this edition, as from a storehouse, High Church catechetical compilers took—directly or indirectly—individual questions and answers, complete pages, even whole sections.

As this selective borrowing indicates, the transmission of Nonjuring theology was incomplete. Certain statements of the Innes production proved too "Primitive" for Seabury's congregations to absorb. Repeated reading failed to remove the initial suspicion that they harbored a popish taint;[62] consequently, the first American edition of the complete text was also the last. In Rhode Island, the Scottish catechism soon was superseded (to some extent at least) by the catechism produced in 1798 by a Seabury ordinee, Abraham Lynsen Clarke (Yale, 1785). About half of Clarke's material came directly from Innes.[63]

A much more influential publication was that which came to be known as the "Old New York Diocesan Catechism." It was first issued in 1802 by Benjamin Moore, Seabury's old friend and Provoost's successor as bishop.[64] Except for unimportant consolidations, page after page reproduced Innes' words almost exactly, although Moore did make significant excisions and incorporated some statements from John Lewis' conventional *Church Catechism Explained* (1700). The work achieved great popularity, as is shown by the fact that a leader of the American Oxford Movement, Bishop William R. Whittingham, used the eleventh edition (1824) when producing a reprint for the Maryland diocese.[65] From an earlier edition, James Morss (Harvard, 1800) of Newburyport got Innes material for his catechism of 1815. Bishop John Henry Hobart (College of New Jersey, 1793) likewise took Innes items from Moore's compilation when he prepared the often reprinted *Church Catechism Enlarged*, originally published in 1827.[66]

The important Nonjuring doctrines these writers preserved

included a stridently High Church explanation of the ministry (which fact partly accounts for Episcopal Evangelicals' intense dislike of the Hobart catechism).[67] Again, they set forth with considerable clarity Johnson of Cranbrook's teaching as to the meaning of the Eucharist. Yet, at the same time, the Eucharist's central position, so evident in Innes' catechism (and in Seabury's own writings) disappeared. This is particularly noticeable in the case of Hobart, the leading High Churchman of his generation.

Innes related the Sacrament to the daily-bread petition of the Lord's Prayer and affirmed that the duties of the Sabbath were "To offer and receive the Holy Eucharist, and to attend all the public Offices of the Church."[68] Hobart interpreted the petition exclusively in light of the Christian's physical needs. Sunday duties he listed as "going regularly to church, both morning and afternoon"; "reading good books"; "private and family worship"; "teaching those who may be under my care, or who have need of my instructions"; "visiting the sick and the afflicted."[69] So different was this emphasis that the source of the Hobart catechism's formal eucharistic teaching can easily be overlooked. The shift here fully developed, like the abortive plan for weekly Communion as a general norm, marks the limits of Seabury's success in grafting Johnson of Cranbrook's full theology onto the native High Church tradition.

Seabury's collected sermons provide his best-known exposition of that theology, as well as of his High Church opinions in general. With the help of Benjamin Moore, James Rivington brought out two volumes in 1793 as *Discourses on Several Subjects*,[70] and before his death the bishop prepared a third, published in 1798.[71] Comprising nine hundred pages, these sermons displayed the unpretentious style of the "A. W. Farmer" pamphlets. Seabury expounded some forty-three biblical texts, treating a variety of topics in a fashion his friends conceived to be truly excellent. From England, Boucher sent congratulations, March 3, 1794:

> I have not yet read more than half a dozen of them; & I say no more than I really think, when I declare that a Majority of them are Equal to any in our Language. I can perceive, indeed, that, as You say, they are not all of Equal Merit: but, upon the whole, it is an admirable Collection; & much would You have had to answer for, had You withheld so useful a Work from the World. I no where know a Man, who can in so unassuming & unaffected a Manner, communicate such deep & important Information. They are not the worse, even for these Latitudes & these Times, for their being so very Scriptural: & all the Alteration I could have thought of making, had I been consulted Years ago, would have been the throwing, if I could, a little more Animation, & perhaps a little more Terseness & Elegance into your generally plain, clear, proper & strong language.[72]

Boucher's statements found an echo in the judgment of a nineteenth-century Scots Episcopal writer:

> . . . the same characteristics mark them all, viz., a close adherence to primitive truth, an independent and systematic mode of presenting old truths in diction at once terse, solid, lucid, and dignified, a tight hold of his argument, and an honest delivery of the preacher's whole mind. Modern High Churchmen may think some truths to be understated, and Low Churchmen will certainly think the sacramental teaching exaggerated, but no one will ever accuse Seabury of looking to the right or left of his convictions. Equally striking is the infrequency with which he cites any other authority than that of Scripture for the propositions he maintains.[73]

As early as 1788, Seabury had projected his first two volumes. Pleased that former Congregationalists continued to declare themselves Episcopalians, he, nevertheless, suspected that some were not actuated by the best motives, and he noticed they retained many "Independent" notions.[74] With the *Discourses*, he might firmly ground such Churchmen (and any others with defective views) in High Church doctrines. At the same time, he could perfect the diocese's general religious outlook. His sermons, in short, would "get this Church into better order before I die, and . . . keep it so when I am gone."[75]

Although not as all-pervasive as the bishop hoped, the influence of the *Discourses* proved to be very great. Naturally, pastors and candidates for Orders bought and studied them. So did especially pious laymen. More important was their frequent use (either in the original editions or the 1815 reprint) by Connecticut's lay readers, who supplied every desk and pulpit at one time or another, besides serving, on a regular basis, those which were otherwise vacant a quarter, one half, or even three quarters of the time. Sunday upon Sunday, lay readers presented Seabury's sermons, drilling his ideas into their respective congregations.[76] Given this widespread distribution and the resulting impetus to High Church thinking, one must rank the *Discourses* with the Communion Office of 1789 and the Innes catechism when considering his impact on Episcopal worship and teaching.

High Churchmen in England appreciated the importance of Seabury's contribution. Particularly enthusiastic were four closely associated individuals: Jonathan Boucher, George Horne, William Jones of Nayland, and William Stevens, earlier mentioned collectively as benefactors of Scotland's Episcopal Church.[77] Since Thomas Bradbury Chandler was their friend,[78] it was inevitable that they should meet Seabury during his stay in London. Indeed, Boucher and Stevens were often in his company between 1783 and 1785.[79]

Viewing Connecticut as the very citadel of true Church principles, this group was much concerned when its bishop and clergy lost their S.P.G. stipends. Unable to supply comparable funds, they determined that Seabury at least should not suffer. Specifically, Boucher, Stevens, and Horne (Jones had no income to spare) formed a compact with seven like-minded English gentlemen to supply him with fifty pounds each year. This subscription, of which Seabury was informed in the spring of 1786, continued to be paid until his death.[80] It opened the way for many interesting correspondences, but the bishop, as usual, failed to take full advantage of such opportunities. He wrote with fair regularity to Boucher and Stevens, forwarding what he hoped would be interesting items of news.[81] He also presented them with copies of his publications and received from Stevens some useful works, notably a hundred copies of Jones's *Course of Lectures on the Figurative Language of the Holy Scriptures* and a second hundred of the same author's *Essay on the Church.*[82] Yet with Jones himself (who kept Seabury's likeness in his study),[83] the bishop exchanged no letters, nor does he seem to have corresponded with Horne. Since the religious revival which began at Oxford in 1833 had its origins in the Boucher-Horne-Jones-Stevens circle in the same way as the American Oxford Movement stemmed from Seabury,[84] it would be a pleasant task to detail the latter's relations with his English counterparts. The evidence of the Seabury papers, however, shows that, except in the case of Boucher, no very intimate connection existed.

EPILOGUE

"A WILLING HEART TO DO MY DUTY"

BY THE SUMMER OF 1795, SEVERAL YEARS OF ILL HEALTH had impressed upon Seabury the fact that, at sixty-five, he was an old man.[1] Writing to Bishop White of the forthcoming General Convention, scheduled for Philadelphia in September, he declared his full intention of attending, but added: "my strength [is] declining & langour succeeding so can promise myself nothing but the decays & infirmities of age." The journey was a long one; still, he would do what he could, "& hope by God's goodness to be with you."[2]

Kept at New London by the sudden death of Dr. Samuel Seabury in late August, the bishop received from the ever-courteous White a full report of the Convention's proceedings. Seabury's name had come before the session in connection with an anonymous pamphlet written by his old defender of 1785, Henry Purcell of St. Michael's, Charleston. The South Carolina rector's feelings for him, it now appeared, had completely altered. In his production, entitled *Strictures on the Love of Power in the Prelacy*, he vehemently assaulted Seabury while censuring, in wild and intemperate language, a defense of the full episcopal negative,[3] which he supposed him to have written. Only the intervention of the House he had insulted saved Purcell, a clerical deputy, from being included by name in his own House's condemnation of the *Strictures*. "The Share which you personally have in his reflections cannot escape your Notice," White observed when forwarding a copy; nevertheless, he thought it "too low & absurd to give you Pain."[4]

In the middle of October, Seabury began his last visitation, traveling to East Haddam, East Plymouth and Harwinton, to Litchfield and Wallingford, North Haven and Branford. As he passed through East Haven, his horse fell, throwing him out of the sulky; he escaped with a bruised knee and preached and confirmed later in the day. Back in New London by November 4, he transcribed rough notes into the visitation journal and concluded his account with a characteristic passage:

> In this journey I traveled 134 miles, preached 10 times, administered the Communion 5 times, & confirmed 198 persons.—And now, All glory to God for his innumerable benefits. Thou, O God, tookest me out of my mothers womb; Thou hast preserved me ever since; Thou hast provided me with the comforts and decencies of life; Thou hast vouchsafed me the means of grace, and the hope of glory; Thou hast raised me to an honourable station in thy Church; Thou hast given me a willing heart to do my duty in it—confirm that ready disposition; Let thy Holy Spirit ever direct it to thy glory & the good of thy Church; Continue thy blessings to me; Bless also thy Church; May thy goodness lead me to love Thee above all things, thro' Jesus Christ. Amen.[5]

Although friends noticed that Seabury's health was worsening,[6] the new year found him still able to continue his parochial duties. On Thursday evening, February 25, accompanied by his daughter, Miss Maria, he paid a call at the home of Rosewell Saltonstall. The family, exceedingly devout Episcopalians,[7] had often entertained the bishop, who doubtless took a certain pleasuse in contemplating their portraits of the Puritan leader Sir Richard Saltonstall and of one of the seventeenth-century Winthrops.[8] As regarded religion, New England had changed a good deal in a century and a half!

Perfectly well upon entering the house, Seabury was not there five minutes when a sharp pain stabbed through his chest. Saltonstall and a son led him into another room to lie down; reviving somewhat, he rejoined the company. Within a short time, he again had to withdraw. He collapsed, suffered an attack of apoplexy, and died almost immediately.[9]

John Tyler of Norwich preached the funeral sermon in St. James's Church the following Sunday. Afterwards, a vast crowd accompanied the coffin to what is now the Cedar Grove Cemetery.[10] There Seabury's body remained until 1849, when it was reinterred in a crypt beneath New London's third Episcopal edifice, built from Gothic Revival plans drawn by Richard Upjohn. Over this resting place, parish and diocese erected an elaborate and costly monument in the form of an altar-tomb: the sort of memorial the Oxford Movement considered proper for a bishop.[11] The Reverend Dr. Samuel Farmar Jarvis (Yale, 1805) supplied a Latin inscription, which duly recorded that the deceased had first "brought from Scotland, into the Anglo-American Republic of the New World, the Apostolic Succession."[12] More revealing of Seabury's character was a sentence the doctor's father had included in a letter to Samuel Peters, April 4, 1796. "Bishop Seabury," Abraham Jarvis declared, "was a man who thought and spoke for himself; what he spoke he thought."[13]

FOOTNOTES

PROLOGUE

"THE SMOKE OF YALE-COLLEGE"

1. The number of ministers attending Commencement naturally increased as Yale grew in size and dignity and came to count an increasing proportion of Connecticut's ministers among its alumni. About 1714, before the college had settled at New Haven, "perhaps a score of nearby coast and river-town ministers" were present at the exercises in Saybrook's meetinghouse. Edwin Oviatt, *The Beginnings of Yale (1701-1716)* (New Haven, 1916), p. 257. At the Commencement held September 12, 1792, eighty or ninety pastors put in their appearance. *The Literary Diary of Ezra Stiles, D.D., LL.D., President of Yale College*, edited by Franklin Bowditch Dexter (New York, 1901), III, 474.

2. Louis Leonard Tucker, *Puritan Protagonist: President Thomas Clap of Yale College* (Chapel Hill, 1962), pp. 242-43, 246; Oviatt, *Beginnings of Yale*, pp. 356-61.

3. *Ibid.*, pp. 304-43, 350, 361-77.

4. Stiles, *Literary Diary*, II, 339-40.

5. Clifford Kenyon Shipton, *Sibley's Harvard Graduates* (Cambridge, 1933-), V, 46.

6. Samuel Johnson, "Memoirs of the Life of the Rev. Dr. Johnson, and Several Things Relating to the State Both of Religion and Learning in His Times," *Samuel Johnson, President of King's College, His Career and Writings*, edited by Herbert and Carol Schneider (New York, 1929), I, 14. The title of this four-volume publication is misleading; except for the letters of Johnson's correspondents, it consists entirely of his own writings. Cited hereafter as Johnson, *Writings*.

7. Samuel Sewall to Gurdon Saltonstall, October 15, 1722, *Letter-Book of Samuel Sewall (Collections of the Massachusetts Historical Society, Sixth Series*, I, II, Boston, 1886-88), II, 144; Joseph Moss to Cotton Mather, October 2, 1722, *Documentary History of the Protestant Episcopal Church, in the United States of America, Containing Numerous Hitherto Unpublished Documents Concerning the Church in Connecticut*, edited by Francis Lister Hawks and William Stevens Perry (New York, 1863-64), I, 67.

8. John Davenport and Stephen Buckingham to Increase and Cotton Mather, September 25, 1722, *Ibid.*, I, 68.

9. *Ibid.*, p. 69.

10. Johnson, "Memoirs," *op. cit.*, p. 14.

11. The Church of England missionaries George Keith and John Talbot, stopping at New London, September 13, 1702, while on a tour from New Hampshire to Philadelphia, preached there that forenoon and afternoon, "we being desired so to do by the Minister, Mr. *Gurdon Saltonstall,* who civilly Entertained us at his House, and expressed his good affection to the Church of England." George Keith, *A Journal of Travels from New-Hampshire to Caratuck, on the Continent of North-America* (London, 1706), p. 43.

12. Account in Johnson, "Memoirs," *op. cit.*, pp. 14-15.

13. Wrote Johnson's friend and first biographer: "it has often been observed of them, to their honour, that, amidst all the controversies in which the [Episcopal] church was engaged during their lives, they were never known to act, or say, or insinuate, any things to her disadvantage." Thomas Bradbury Chandler, *The Life of Samuel Johnson, D.D., the First President of King's College, in New York* (London, 1824), p. 30.

14. Johnson, "Memoirs," *op. cit.*, p. 6.

15. *Ibid.*, pp. 7, 10-13. A more complete list of the books examined by the group may be reconstructed from Johnson's careful record of his reading 1719-22. "Catalogue of Books Read by Samuel Johnson from 1719 to 1756," Johnson, *Writings*, I, 497-500.

16. Johnson, "Memoirs," *op. cit.*, p. 13.

17. Contemporary Congregational critics, as well as certain historians, seizing upon the evidence of such actions, have pictured the Yale group as dissimulators and hypocrites. Modern writers generally level this charge only against Timothy Cutler. The wealth of documents now available in the case of Samuel Johnson clearly acquits him of any such accusation, while no direct evidence of the state of Browne's and Wetmore's minds, in the years immediately prior to 1722, appears to be extant. The case against Cutler has been summed up most recently by Clifford Kenyon Shipton, who writes: "Mere conversion might have been taken less seriously, but Rector Cutler's case seemed to include duplicity and treachery of the worst sort. A reasonable interpretation of his statement to the trustees was that he had deliberately given up a pastorate in which his conversion, honestly confessed, would have done little harm to the New England system, for a position from which he might corrupt the Congregational church at its source and make a breach in the very foundations. Over his own signature he gave Hollis, the benefactor of Harvard, the worst possible statement of his case: 'I was never in judgment heartily with the Dissenters, but bore it patiently until a favorable opportunity offered. This has opened at Boston [the establishment of Christ Church], and I now declare publicly what I before believed privately.'" Shipton, *Sibley's Harvard Graduates*, V, 51-52.

This interpretation appears to rest on very faulty foundations. What Shipton terms Cutler's "statement to the trustees" is, in fact, the *report* of that statement which two of them (bitter over the rector's defection) sent to the Boston Mathers. John Davenport and Stephen Buckingham to Cotton and Increase Mather, September 25, 1722, Hawks and Perry, *Documentary History*, I, 69-70. That Shipton's assessment of this report is a "reasonable interpretation," the present writer does not agree, nor does he believe anyone will find it so who does not share that marked anti-Episcopal bias which colors a number of Shipton's sketches. As for the other piece of evidence, the statement over Cutler's "own signature" is not, actually, such a document, but rather a passage from a letter written by Thomas Hollis to Benjamin Colman, giving his version of a conversation with Cutler (Hollis hoped to win him back to Congregationalism and proposed a conference between them) after the latter's arrival in England. Quoted in Josiah Quincy, *History of Harvard University* (Boston, 1860), I, 365.

In weighing the statements of Davenport, Buckingham, and Hollis, proper allowance must be made for their state of mind. Cutler and his associates ("degenerate offspring" in what appear to be the words of Cotton Mather) they considered as betrayers of New England's very reason for being. Accordingly, they were ill-equipped to judge the events of 1722 with any degree of dispassion. Even if their letters receive substantial credit, when these are considered in conjunction with the account in Johnson's "Memoirs," a fairly consistent picture emerges of sincere but troubled men, anxiously trying to elude the obvious implications of their newly formed convictions. The mental state of Cutler, Browne, and Johnson, prior to 1722, would seem to be that which Hart, Wetmore, and Whittelsey affirmed was theirs at the Commencement of that year: "they should go on to administer Sacraments, &c., as before, for awhile, waiting for further light; but if they could get no better light than now they had, thought that, in time, it would come to pass with them that they should proceed no further to minister at the altar, without a re-ordination by a Bishop." Joseph Moss to Cotton Mather, October 2, 1722, Hawks and Perry, *Documentary History*, I, 66. This, the present writer submits, is a much more reasonable interpretation of the evidence than is Shipton's.

18. Johnson, "Memoirs," *op. cit.*, p. 12. See also in this connection Johnson's "My Present Thoughts of Episcopacy with what I conceive may justify me in accepting Presbyterial Ordination. Written at West Haven, Dec. 20, Anno. Dom. 1719," Johnson, *Writings*, III, 3-8. This document is an extremely important illustration of the state of mind of the Yale group at this date.

19. Johnson included a brief account of his voyage to, and residence in, England in his "Memoirs," *op. cit.*, pp. 15-19. More details are provided by the many extracts from his diary, November 4, 1722—September 22, 1723, printed in Eben Edwards Beardsley, *Life and Correspondence of Samuel Johnson, D.D., Missionary of the Church of England in Connecticut, and First President of King's College, New York* (New York, 1874), pp. 23-54.

20. Hereafter referred to by the usual designations: the S.P.G. and the Society.

21. Daniel Browne died in London of smallpox shortly after his ordination. Beardsley, *Samuel Johnson*, pp. 40, 41, quoting Johnson's diary entries, April 13, 16, 1723.

22. Wetmore in 1726 became rector (and S.P.G. missionary) of Rye, New York, the Westchester County parish which bordered on Connecticut. Remaining there until his death in 1760, he always maintained close ties with Johnson and the other Episcopal ministers of Connecticut. Robert Bolton, *History of the Protestant Episcopal Church, in the County of Westchester, from Its Foundation, A. D. 1693, to A. D. 1853* (New York, 1855), pp. 236-40, 286-87.

23. For the distinctive features of New England Churchmanship, as they emerged in the pre-Revolutionary decades, see Bruce E. Steiner, Samuel Seabury

and the Forging of the High Church Tradition: a Study in the Evolution of New England Churchmanship, 1722-1796 (University of Virginia Doctoral Dissertation, 1962), I, 16-125.

24. Seabury's own Churchmanship was that of his grandfather, but he welcomed and defended the ideas of the Tractarians. Edward Rochie Hardy, "Samuel Seabury, 1801-1872," *Dictionary of American Biography*, edited by Allen Johnson and Dumas Malone (New York, 1928-37), XVI, 530-31. His son, William Jones Seabury (1837-1916), held to the family theology, and in his *Memoir of Bishop Seabury* (New York, 1908) attacked the Anglo-Catholicism of his day. See, for example, his comments on the Holy Eucharist, pp. 340-46.

25. It is, of course, generally agreed that the influence of Bishop William White of Pennsylvania on the *organizational structure* of the Protestant Episcopal Church is paramount.

CHAPTER I

"MY HONOURED FATHER"

1. Shipton, *Sibley's Harvard Graduates*, VII, 432-33, 448.

2. *Ibid.*, VII, 291.

3. Quoted in Arthur Adams, "The Seabury Family," *Historical Magazine of the Protestant Episcopal Church*, III (September, 1934), p. 122; cited hereafter as *HMPEC*. The extant information concerning the ancestors of Samuel Seabury (1706-1764) has been conveniently assembled, *Ibid.*, III, 122-26, from which, unless otherwise stated, the account here given is derived.

4. Shipton, *Sibley's Harvard Graduates*, VI, 339.

5. *Records of the Colony of New Plymouth in New England*, edited by Nathaniel B. Shurtleff (Boston, 1855-61), VII, 101.

6. *Peirce's Colonial Lists, Civil, Military and Professional Lists of Plymouth and Rhode Island Colonies . . . 1621-1700*, compiled by Ebenezer W. Peirce (Boston, 1881), p. 113. Peirce also lists as a physician Samuel Seabury, Jr. (1666-1763); if a further search of the records should establish that his brother, John Seabury (*c.* 1673-1759), likewise practiced medicine, an interesting medical dynasty would be revealed, since John Seabury's son, grandson, and great-grandson —Samuel Seabury (1706-1764), Bishop Samuel Seabury (1729-1796), and Samuel Seabury (1765-1795)—were all practitioners.

7. *Ibid.*, pp. 42-43, 54; Shurtleff, *Records of the Colony of New Plymouth*, IV, 12, 91, 180, V, 19, 35, 42, 56, 60, 91, 113, 123, 143, 164, 214, 230, 264, VI, 34, 59, VII, 101, 105, 119, 219.

8. *Ibid.*, IV, 140-41.

9. *Vital Records of Duxbury, Massachusetts, to the Year 1850* (Boston, 1911), pp. 149, 150.

10. Cotton Mather, *Magnalia Christi Americana*; *or, the Ecclesiastical History of New England*; *from Its First Planting, in the Year 1620, unto the Year of Our Lord 1698* (Hartford, 1855), I, 404-5.

11. Thomas Thacher, *A Brief Rule to Guide the Common People of New-*

England How to Order Themselves and Theirs in the Small Pocks, or Measles (Boston, 1677).

12. Mather, *Magnalia Christi Americana*, I, 488-97.

13. Edward H. Dewey, "Peter Thacher, 1651-1727," Johnson and Malone, *Dictionary of American Biography*, XVIII, 390, quoting the Reverend John Danforth (Harvard, 1677).

14. Peirce, *Colonial Lists*, p. 4. Alden was an assistant 1632, 1634-39, 1650-86, and treasurer 1656-59.

15. According to his gravestone in the cemetery of St. George's Church, Hempstead, Long Island, he was eighty-six years old when he died, December, 1759. "St. George Church and Cemetery Records—Hempstead, L.I.," *The Daughters of the American Revolution Magazine*, LXXXVII (May, 1953), p. 671.

16. Shurtleff, *Records of the Colony of New Plymouth*, VI, 91.

17. Peirce, *Colonial Lists*, p. 4. Southworth served as treasurer 1659-79 and was an assistant 1672-78.

18. Joshua Hempstead, *Diary . . . Covering a Period of Forty-Seven Years, from September, 1711, to November, 1758* (*Collections of the New London County Historical Society*, I, New London, 1901), p. 62.

19. *Ibid.*, p. 164; Shipton, *Sibley's Harvard Graduates*, V, 130-31, VII, 448.

20. Records of the Second or North Ecclesiastical Society, Groton, 1725-1826, I, 2-3, Connecticut State Library.

21. The assertion first appears in Frances Manwaring Caulkins, *History of New London, Connecticut, from the First Survey of the Coast in 1612 . . .* (Hartford, 1852), p. 419.

22. Records of the Second or North Ecclesiastical Society, Groton, I, 4.

23. Connecticut Archives, Ecclesiastical Affairs, First Series, III, document 140, Connecticut State Library.

24. The date of his arrival in North Yarmouth is fixed by the minutes of a meeting of that town's proprietors' committee, April 19, 1729, which stated that two years' salary would be due him in November of that year. Quoted in William M. Sargent, "The Old Church," *Old Times: a Magazine Devoted to . . . the Early History of North Yarmouth, Maine*, IV (January, 1880), p. 461.

25. Samuel Dorrance Seabury, "Seabury Family," *Old Times*, III (July, October, 1879), pp. 373-74, 376-77; Sargent, "The Old Church," *op. cit.*, p. 461; William Hutchinson Rowe, *Ancient North Yarmouth and Yarmouth, Maine, 1636-1936, a History* (Yarmouth, 1937), pp. 32-33.

26. In *Ibid.*, p. 118, Seabury's pay is erroneously put at £150; records of the proprietors' committee (Sargent, "The Old Church," *op. cit.*, p. 461) reveal the correct sum.

27. Admissions and Baptisms of the First Congregational Church, Groton, Connecticut, 1727-1811 (copy), p. 6, Connecticut State Library.

28. Quoted in Sargent, "The Old Church," *op. cit.*, pp. 461-62.

29. It has been generally assumed that Seabury publicly severed his con-

nection with North Yarmouth at this time, but there is no reason to suppose that its people did not expect his return or that Cutter was engaged in any other capacity than as supply minister while Seabury attended his wife during the birth of her child. Rowe, *Ancient North Yarmouth and Yarmouth*, pp. 118-19; Edward Russell, "History of North Yarmouth," *Old Times*, II (January, April, October, 1898), p. 265.

30. Groton Births, Marriages, Deaths 1704-1853 (copy), p. 128, Connecticut State Library; Admissions and Baptisms of the First Congregational Church, Groton, p. 25.

31. Timothy Cutler to the S.P.G. Secretary, March 23, 1729/30, *Historical Collections Relating to the American Colonial Church*, edited by William Stevens Perry ([Hartford], 1870-78), III, 256.

32. For which, see Shipton, *Sibley's Harvard Graduates*, V, 434. Proprietors' committee records (Sargent, "The Old Church," *op. cit.*, pp. 461-62) indicate some difficulty in collecting that part of Seabury's salary owed by nonresident proprietors. But it appears that those resident at North Yarmouth paid their share, and when, April 19, 1729, the proprietors' committee laid a rate to pay Seabury the total amount of two years' salary, it specifically ordered that the collector should "deduct out what Mr Samuel Seabury hath already received by Order of the Committee." Shipton's statement that Seabury "went back to Groton without his pay" rests on no documentary evidence whatever.

33. Wilkins Updike, *A History of the Episcopal Church in Narragansett, Rhode Island, Including a History of Other Episcopal Churches in the State*, edited by Daniel Goodwin (Boston, 1907), I, 478-79; Hempstead, *Diary*, pp. 97, 614, 703.

34. *Ibid.*, pp. 518, 567; Estate of Thomas Mumford, Town of Groton, 1766, No. 3784, Connecticut State Library; Caulkins, *History of New London*, p. 441.

35. "Records of St. Paul's Church, Narragansett," Updike, *History of the Episcopal Church in Narragansett*, II, 466.

36. *Ibid.*, p. 471.

37. The family's previous religious affiliations are unknown; they may, however, have been Quakers, as were the Gardiners. See James MacSparran to Edmund Gibson, August 11, 1730, Fulham Palace Transcripts, Library of Congress.

38. The pre-Revolutionary records of the Narragansett and New London churches list the services of the Mumfords—as wardens, vestrymen, members of committees, and heavy contributors—on almost every page. See Records of St. James's Protestant Episcopal Church, New London, 1725-1874, I, 7-70, Connecticut State Library; "Records of St. Paul's Church, Narragansett," *op. cit.*, *passim.*

39. *Ibid.*, pp. 471-72, 475.

40. *Ibid.*, p. 491.

41. *Ibid.*, pp. 471, 472, 482, 487, 488, 491, 493, 494; James MacSparran to the S.P.G. Secretary, April 12, 1726, abstracted in S.P.G. Manuscript Journals, V, 106 (this journal and all other S.P.G. manuscripts hereafter cited are copies in the Library of Congress); James MacSparran to Henry Cary, August 20, 1752, Updike, *History of the Episcopal Church in Narragansett*, III, 24-25.

42. Caulkins, *History of New London*, pp. 440-41.

43. Records of St. James's Protestant Episcopal Church, New London, I, 7-8, 10, 13, 18.

44. New London standing committee to James MacSparran, February 25, 1725/6, *Ibid.*, I, 10; James MacSparran to New London standing committee, March 21, 1725/6, *Ibid.*, I, 11-13.

45. Records of St. James's Protestant Episcopal Church, New London, I, 14.

46. *Ibid.*, I, 14, 19-23; Samuel Seabury, Sr. to the S.P.G. Secretary, May 3, 1742, Hawks and Perry, *Documentary History*, I, 180.

47. James MacSparran to the S.P.G. Secretary, April 12, 1726, abstracted in S.P.G. Manuscript Journals, V, 106.

48. *Ibid.*, V, 129.

49. S.P.G. Manuscript A 23, pp. 145-46. Seventeen men signed the subscription, dated December 5, 1727; Mumford put himself down for £5 a year.

50. S.P.G. Manuscript Journals, V, 223-24; James MacSparran to the S.P.G. Secretary, May 20, 1730, Hawks and Perry, *Documentary History*, I, 142.

51. Samuel Fairbanks and other inhabitants of New London, Groton, and places adjacent, to the S.P.G. Secretary, April 13, 1730, *Ibid.*, I, 140, supplemented by S.P.G. Manuscript A 23, p. 109; James MacSparran to the S.P.G. Secretary, May 20, 1730, Hawks and Perry, *Documentary History*, I, 142.

52. Samuel Johnson to the S.P.G. Secretary, May 5, 1730, *Ibid.*, I, 140-41; James MacSparran to the S.P.G. Secretary, May 20, 1730, *Ibid.*, I, 142; Timothy Cutler to the S.P.G. Secretary, March 23, 1729/30, Perry, *Historical Collections*, III, 256; James Honyman to the S.P.G. Secretary, May 6, 1730, S.P.G. Manuscript A 23, p. 113.

53. And in the case of Seabury's ordination to the priesthood, after July 8, 1730, the day he attained the canonical age of twenty-four.

54. S.P.G. Manuscript Journals, V, 259.

55. In order to partly reimburse Seabury for the expenses of his voyage, the Society ordered that his salary should begin from Lady Day (March 25, 1730). *Ibid.*

56. William H. Moore, *History of St. George's Church, Hempstead, Long Island* (New York, 1881), p. 90. At the time Moore wrote, the sermon was in the possession of a Seabury descendant.

57. Seabury, serving New London 1730-43, Theophilus Morris, pastor for a few months in 1743, and Matthew Graves, pastor 1748-80, all received the S.P.G. stipend of £50 a year. For Graves see Maud O'Neil, "Matthew Graves: Anglican Missionary to the Puritans," *British Humanitarianism, Essays Honoring Frank J. Klingberg*, edited by Samuel Clyde McCulloch (Philadelphia, 1950), pp. 124-44.

58. Samuel Seabury, Sr., to the S.P.G. Secretary, March 15, 1730/1, S.P.G. Manuscript A 23, p. 144.

59. Samuel Seabury, Sr., to the S.P.G. Secretary, May 3, 1742, Hawks and Perry, *Documentary History*, I, 180.

60. Samuel Seabury, Sr., to the S.P.G. Secretary, March 15, 1730/1, S.P.G. Manuscript A 23, p. 142.

61. Hempstead, *Diary*, p. 229.

62. Samuel Johnson to the S.P.G. Secretary, June 2, 1731, Hawks and Perry, *Documentary History*, I, 146.

63. Chandler, *Life of Samuel Johnson*, p. 62.

64. Samuel Seabury to the S.P.G. Secretary, January 5, 1750/1, S.P.G. Manuscript B 18, p. 294.

65. Hempstead, *Diary*, pp. 234-35.

66. "Records of St. Paul's Church, Narragansett," *op. cit.*, p. 511.

67. *Annals of Trinity Church, Newport, Rhode Island, 1698-1821*, edited by George Champlin Mason (Newport, 1890), pp. 11-12, 31; Updike, *History of the Episcopal Church in Narragansett*, I, 479-514.

68. *Ibid.*, I, 478.

69. Adam, David, Nathaniel, Jane, Elizabeth and Abigail. Some writers have added another child, Mary, the wife of Jonathan Starr of New London, but she was the sister, not the daughter, of Samuel Seabury, Sr. Elizabeth (Powell) Seabury to James Helme, July 15, 1764, *Ibid.*, I, 146-47; Benjamin F. Thompson, *The History of Long Island; from Its Discovery and Settlement, to the Present Time* (New York, 1843), II, 32; Shipton, *Sibley's Harvard Graduates*, VII, 440; *Abstracts of Wills on File in the Surrogate's Office, City of New York, [1665-1800]* . . . (*Collections of the New-York Historical Society, Third Series*, XXV-XXXVIII, New York, 1893-1905), VI, 347-48.

70. Elizabeth (Powell) Seabury to Samuel Seabury, July 15, 1787, February 28, 1790, Samuel Seabury Papers, General Theological Seminary.

71. Deeds, John Plumbe to Samuel Seabury, Sr., September 29, 1737, April 27, 1738, Samuel Seabury, Sr., to Edward Palmes, November 26, 1743, New London Land Records (copy), XII, 25-26, 104-5, XV, 42-43, Connecticut State Library; Robert A. Hallam, *Annals of St. James's Church, New London, for One Hundred and Fifty Years* (Hartford, 1873), p. 33; Caulkins, *History of New London*, p. 444.

72. *Ibid.*, p. 441; Hempstead, *Diary*, pp. 340, 367, 687, 690; James Gregory Mumford, *Mumford Memoirs, Being the Story of the New England Mumfords from the Year 1655 to the Present Time* (Boston, 1900), pp. 94, 96-97, 113, 190. Little is known of Bishop Seabury's only full brother, who lived at various times in Groton and New London. In 1754 he subscribed £10 toward repairing St. James's Church and, in 1758, 10*s* for the recasting of its bell. Records of St. James's Protestant Episcopal Church, New London, I, 39, 44. His wife Esther gave birth to a son John in 1763, in which year he purchased a house, barn, and shop in New London. New London Births, Marriages, Deaths 1646-1854 (copy), p. 269, Connecticut State Library; deed, Silas Church to Caleb Seabury, October 7, 1763, New London Land Records, XIX, 84. He had described himself as of Groton when he made his will, January 28, 1762 (being bound on a voyage to sea), and was styled Captain Caleb Seabury at the proving of the will in Groton, May 2, 1772. Estate of Caleb Seabury, Town of Groton, 1772, No. 2680, Connecticut State Library.

73. Hempstead, *Diary*, pp. 305, 330, 331, 334, 363, 366-67.

74. For New London's school, see Caulkins, *History of New London*, pp.

398-401. Shipton, citing Samuel Seabury, Sr., to the S.P.G. Secretary, July 6, 1743 (S.P.G. Manuscript B 11, p. 269), states that Seabury kept a school at New London, but the letter has no reference to it. Shipton, *Sibley's Harvard Graduates*, VII, 435.

75. Samuel Seabury, Sr.'s, *notitia parochialis*, November 12, 1739, S.P.G. Manuscript B 7, p. 63.

76. Samuel Seabury, Sr., to the S.P.G. Secretary, August 22, 1735, Hawks and Perry, *Documentary History*, I, 161-62; Samuel Seabury, Sr., to the S.P.G. Secretary, May 3, 1742, S.P.G. Manuscript B 10, pp. 117-18; Records of St. James's Protestant Episcopal Church, New London, I, 15.

77. Evidently these prices were too steep for some parishioners, for the congregational meeting held Easter Monday, 1741, voted that seats should be built "for the poor." *Ibid.*, I, 29.

78. The vestry, meeting September 21, 1739, noted that "Sundry persons had taken up Spaces in the Church for pews, and had long Neglected to build & pay for the same." *Ibid.*, I, 28.

79. The "Clerk to said parish to set the Psalms" first appears in the records in 1767. *Ibid.*, I, 55. It seems likely, however, that the office had existed since the beginning of the church.

80. Matthew Graves to the S.P.G. Secretary, September 7, 1748, S.P.G. Manuscript B 16, p. 58; Hallam, *Annals of St. James's Church, New London*, p. 90.

81. Samuel Seabury, Sr., Sermon from Psalm 24: 115, annotated as preached at Oyster Bay, May 23, 1762, General Theological Seminary.

82. Organized in 1733-34 by Ebenezer Punderson, Samuel Seabury's close associate at Yale and, like his friend, a convert to High Church principles. Samuel Seabury, Sr., to the S.P.G. Secretary, March 30, 1734, August 22, 1735, Hawks and Perry, *Documentary History*, I, 158-59, 160-62; Franklin Bowditch Dexter, *Biographical Sketches of the Graduates of Yale College with Annals of the College History* (New York, New Haven, 1885-1912), I, 336-37.

83. Hallam, *Annals of St. James's Church, New London*, pp. 89-91.

84. The colonial register of St. James's has disappeared, but the private record of baptisms, marriages, and burials kept by Bishop Seabury 1792-95, during the last years of his rectorship, shows that he constantly married and baptized in private homes. It reveals just that sort of clerical routine which the colonial register of St. Paul's, Narragansett, exhibits. Records of St. James's Protestant Episcopal Church, New London, II, 7-16; "Records of St. Paul's Church, Narragansett," *op. cit.*, pp. 459-605, *passim*. See also the agreement of Roger Price *et al.* to supply Westerly church, May 23, 1733, S.P.G. Manuscript A 24, pp. 354-55; Samuel Seabury, Sr., to the S.P.G. Secretary, June 23, 1734, June 5, 1741, May 3, 1742, *Ibid.*, p. 180, S.P.G. Manuscript B 9, p. 73, S.P.G. Manuscript B 10, p. 118; Samuel Seabury, Sr., to the S.P.G. Secretary, August 22, 1735, November 2, 1742, March 25, 1743, Hawks and Perry, *Documentary History*, I, 160-61, 184, 190.

85. The Hebron Episcopal congregation originated in a parish dispute which resulted in the dismissal, about 1734, of the Congregational pastor John

Bliss. Bliss and some of his former parishioners subsequently became Churchmen. Dexter, *Biographical Sketches of the Graduates of Yale*, I, 97-98.

86. Samuel Seabury, Sr., to the S.P.G. Secretary, August 11, 1736, Hawks and Perry, *Documentary History*, I, 162-63, corrected by S.P.G. Manuscript A 26, p. 247.

87. Samuel Seabury, Sr., to the S.P.G. Secretary, November 12, 1739, October 10, 1740, S.P.G. Manuscript B 7, pp. 61-62, S.P.G. Manuscript B 9, p. 119; Connecticut Archives, Ecclesiastical Affairs, First Series, X, document 327b. Some of these men lived in towns bordering on Hebron.

88. In 1769 New London's Episcopal minister noted: "Vessels go frequently hence to New York, seldom to Boston." Matthew Graves to the S.P.G. Secretary, January 15, 1769, Hawks and Perry, *Documentary History*, II, 121.

89. "Records of St. Paul's Church, Narragansett," *op. cit.*, p. 504; James MacSparran, *A Letter Book and Abstract of Out Services Written during the Years 1743-1751* . . . , edited by Daniel Goodwin (Boston, 1899), pp. xxxiv, 3, 83.

90. These early New England Conventions have been little studied. Although it is likely that they met annually, 1725-47, first on an informal basis and afterwards at the direction of the Bishop of London's commissary, evidence is lacking for certain years. Salem's S.P.G. missionary noted in 1744 that the stated date for the Convention's assembling was the Wednesday after Trinity Sunday. Charles Brockwell to the S.P.G. Secretary, July 28, 1744, Perry, *Historical Collections*, III, 384-86.

91. Arthur Browne *et al.* to the S.P.G. Secretary, May 4, 1740, Hawks and Perry, *Documentary History*, I, 170-71. Absent from this session were two Boston clergymen and the pastors of churches at Salem, Newbury, and Braintree—all in the Bay colony—and at Providence.

92. For an early account of Whitefield's preaching, see Timothy Cutler to the S.P.G. Secretary, December 5, 1740, Perry, *Historical Collections*, III, 346-47.

93. See the statistical analysis in *Extracts from the Itineraries and Other Miscellanies of Ezra Stiles, D.D., LL.D., 1755-1794, with a Selection from His Correspondence*, edited by Franklin Bowditch Dexter (New Haven, 1916), pp. 298-99.

94. Hempstead, *Diary*, pp. 368, 375.

95. *Ibid.*, p. 377.

96. Samuel Seabury, Sr., to the S.P.G. Secretary, June 5, 1741, S.P.G. Manuscript B 9, pp. 72-73.

97. Caulkins, *History of New London*, pp. 449-59; *Gentleman's Progress, the Itinerarium of Dr. Alexander Hamilton*, edited by Carl Bridenbaugh (Chapel Hill, 1948), p. 161.

98. Samuel Seabury, Sr., to the S.P.G. Secretary, March 25, 1743, Hawks and Perry, *Documentary History*, I, 189.

99. Samuel Seabury, "The duty of fulfilling all righteousness," Sermons, V, 97-98, Samuel Seabury Papers.

100. Moore, *History of St. George's Church, Hempstead*, p. 87, quoting "MSS. of Rev. Dr. Sam. Seabury, p. 6." Samuel Seabury (1801-1872) prepared

memoranda for a projected life of Bishop Seabury, which were utilized by his son, William Jones Seabury, as well as by Moore. Most of his information presumably came from his father, Charles Seabury (1770-1844).

101. Shipton, *Sibley's Harvard Graduates*, VII, 244-47.

102. The content and manner of Owen's preaching may have had something to do with this. He appeared very early as a champion of revivalistic methods; visiting Northampton in the spring of 1735, he endorsed the awakening produced there by the preaching of Jonathan Edwards. *Ibid.*, VII, 245.

103. Samuel Seabury, Sr., to the S.P.G. Secretary, August 22, 1735, Hawks and Perry, *Documentary History*, I, 161. Latham was not one of seventeen men who subscribed £14 15*s* for the support of a New London missionary in 1727; neither was he among the petitioners for a missionary in 1730. Subscription of John Shackmaple *et al.*, December 5, 1727, S.P.G. Manuscript A 23, pp. 145-46; Samuel Fairbanks and other inhabitants of New London, Groton, and places adjacent, to the S.P.G. Secretary, April 13, 1730, Hawks and Perry, *Documentary History*, I, 140, supplemented by S.P.G. Manuscript A 23, p. 109.

104. Admissions and Baptisms of the First Congregational Church, Groton, p. 28; Records of St. James's Protestant Episcopal Church, New London, I, 27-34; Hempstead, *Diary*, p. 436.

105. See *supra*, p. 316.

106. Records of St. James's Protestant Episcopal Church, New London, I, 38, 41, II, 42; Hallam, *Annals of St. James's Church, New London*, pp. 52-53, 119-20; Groton Births, Marriages, Deaths, pp. 141-42; Admissions and Baptisms of the First Congregational Church, Groton, pp. 6, 24, 28, 31. Groton's First Church admitted Jonathan and Mary Starr to full communion in 1729.

107. Samuel Seabury, Sr., to the S.P.G. Secretary, March 15, 1730/1, S.P.G. Manuscript A 23, pp. 142-43.

108. Samuel Seabury, Sr., to the S.P.G. Secretary, January 5, 1731/2, *Ibid.*, pp. 248-49; Samuel Seabury, Sr., to the S.P.G. Secretary, August 22, 1735, Hawks and Perry, *Documentary History*, I, 160.

109. Samuel Seabury, Sr., to the S.P.G. Secretary, May 5, 1733, S.P.G. Manuscript A 24, p. 321.

110. Samuel Seabury, Sr.'s, *notitia parochialis*, March 25, 1743, S.P.G. Manuscript B 11, p. 138.

111. Samuel Seabury, Sr., to the S.P.G. Secretary, August 22, 1735, Hawks and Perry, *Documentary History*, I, 161; Samuel Seabury, Sr., to the S.P.G. Secretary, January 3, 1736/7, S.P.G. Manuscript A 26, p. 266; Guy Palmes, Thomas Mumford *et al.* to the S.P.G. Secretary, May 10, 1751, S.P.G. Manuscript B 19, p. 137. MacSparran most likely was mistaken in supposing that the Churchmen ever intended to *add* their rates to the subscription. Seabury's letters to the S.P.G. Secretary contain no reference to a plan of this sort.

112. Commissary Roger Price's account of the incomes of New England's S.P.G. missionaries, 1739, S.P.G. Manuscript B 7, p. 17.

113. Samuel Seabury, Sr., to the S.P.G. Secretary, January 3, 1736/7, S.P.G. Manuscript A 26, p. 266. Fairfield's S.P.G. missionary reported a decade later

that the cost of living in his own town and in New London was higher than anywhere else in Connecticut. Henry Caner to the S.P.G. Secretary, February 12, 1746/7, Hawks and Perry, *Documentary History*, I, 231.

114. His will mentions his slave Newport, whose name would indicate that he had become Seabury's property at the time of his marriage with Elizabeth Powell. *Abstracts of Wills on File in the Surrogate's Office, City of New York*, VI, 347. For the ironworks, see the following deeds: Jonathan Rogers to Samuel Seabury, Sr., September 30, 1741, Samuel Seabury, Sr., to Samuel Latimore, August 5, 1743, to Benjamin Alford, August 1, 1743, September 11, 1746, New London Land Records, XIII, 117-18, 296, XV, 56, XIV, 134.

115. Samuel Seabury, Sr., to the S.P.G. Secretary, January 3, 1736/7, S.P.G. Manuscript A 26, p. 266.

116. Conveniently printed in Bolton, *Protestant Episcopal Church, in the County of Westchester*, pp. xv-xvi.

117. Samuel Seabury, Sr.'s, *notitia parochialis*, September 30, 1745, S.P.G. Manuscript B 13, p. 451.

118. Printed in Moore, *History of St. George's Church, Hempstead*, pp. 288-97.

119. John Darton *et al.* to William Vesey, November 18, 1742, S.P.G. Manuscript B 10, p. 190; William Vesey to the S.P.G. Secretary, December 8, 1742, December 9, 1743, *Ibid.*, pp. 147-48, S.P.G. Manuscript B 11, pp. 257-58.

120. Samuel Seabury, Sr., to the S.P.G. Secretary, December 7, 1742, S.P.G. Manuscript B 10, pp. 196-97; Philip Bearcroft to William Vesey, June 14, 1743, *Ibid.*, p. 430.

121. Jenney's certificate of resignation and Seabury's certificate of presentation, order for induction, and certificate of induction appear in Moore, *History of St. George's Church, Hempstead*, pp. 75, 80-83.

122. Thomas Keble to the S.P.G. Secretary, April 4, 1743, S.P.G. Manuscript B 11, p. 274; Samuel Seabury, Sr., to the S.P.G. Secretary, December 15, 1743, *Ibid.*, p. 271.

123. Some 750, according to Seabury's *notitia parochialis*, March 26, 1746, S.P.G. Manuscript B 14, p. 165.

124. Moore, *History of St. George's Church, Hempstead*, pp. 92-95; Samuel Seabury, Sr., to the S.P.G. Secretary, September 30, 1745, S.P.G. Manuscript B 13, p. 450.

125. S.P.G. Manuscript B 11 includes many letters relating to this affair.

126. Roger Price to the S.P.G. Secretary, November 20, 1745, Perry, *Historical Collections*, III, 395.

127. Samuel Seabury, Sr., to the S.P.G. Secretary, October 14, 1744, S.P.G. Manuscript B 13, p. 448.

128. Moore, *History of St. George's Church, Hempstead*, pp. 91-92, quoting John Bedel (1771-1863), senior churchwarden of St. George's.

129. Illustrated by the "only tale which appears to have survived in regard to the Bishop's boyhood . . . being once sent by his father to drive some cows out of the garden, he threw a stone which struck one of them with such force as al-

most to cause her death—an incident which served as a caution to him to use his uncommon strength with more moderation in future." Seabury, *Memoir of Bishop Seabury*, p. 3.

130. Hallam, *Annals of St. James's Church, New London*, pp. 74-75; Daniel Burhans to William B. Sprague, January 9, 1850, William B. Sprague, *Annals of the American Pulpit* (New York, 1857-69), V, 157. Burhans (1763-1853) received deacon's and priest's Orders from Seabury.

CHAPTER II

"A SOLID, SENSIBLE VIRTUOUS YOUTH"

1. Hamilton, *Gentleman's Progress*, p. 166; *Some Cursory Remarks Made by James Birket in His Voyage to North America 1750-1751* (New Haven, 1916), p. 36.

2. Tucker, *Puritan Protagonist*, pp. 40-42.

3. Samuel Seabury, Sr., to the S.P.G. Secretary, August 22, 1735, Hawks and Perry, *Documentary History*, I, 160-61.

4. Tucker, *Puritan Protagonist*, p. 43, quoting Thomas Clap to Benjamin Colman, December 8, 1735. Folsom's name appears on a list (compiled in 1738) of New London men who acknowledged Samuel Seabury as their pastor. Connecticut Archives, Ecclesiastical Affairs, First Series, X, document 327a.

5. For the subsequent controversy regarding the regular attendance of such scholars at Episcopal services, see Tucker, *Puritan Protagonist*, pp. 166-83.

6. Samuel Johnson to George Berkeley, October 3, 1741, Johnson, *Writings*, I, 102; William Samuel Johnson to Samuel Johnson, June 22, 1747, *Ibid.*, I, 123.

7. Samuel Johnson to the S.P.G. Secretary, January 10, 1743/4, Hawks and Perry, *Documentary History*, I, 204-5.

8. Tucker, *Puritan Protagonist*, pp. 78-79, 134-35, 171-74, 183-84, 187-89.

9. *Ibid.*, pp. 63-93, 263-70.

10. Quoted in Dexter, *Biographical Sketches of the Graduates of Yale*, I, 613, from the funeral sermon delivered by Ezra Stiles. For the Yale faculty, 1744-48, see Stiles, *Literary Diary*, III, 516.

11. Dexter, *Biographical Sketches of the Graduates of Yale*, I, 655-56, 693-95.

12. *Ibid.*, II, 143.

13. Samuel Johnson to the S.P.G. Secretary, September 29, 1748, S.P.G. Manuscript B 16, p. 65.

14. James Wetmore to the S.P.G. Secretary, October 3, 1745, Bolton, *Protestant Episcopal Church, in the County of Westchester*, p. 276; Samuel Johnson to the S.P.G. Secretary, October 1, 1746, Hawks and Perry, *Documentary History*, I, 223.

15. Bibliographies of their writings are included in the accounts in Dexter, *Biographical Sketches of the Graduates of Yale*, II, 23-28, 39-43.

16. Stiles, *Literary Diary*, III, 398.

17. Samuel Seabury, Sr., to the S.P.G. Secretary, March 25, 1748, S.P.G. Manuscript B 16, pp. 92-93.

18. Samuel Seabury to an unidentified woman; undated but written after 1775 (draft), Samuel Seabury Papers.

19. Samuel Johnson to the S.P.G. Secretary, September 29, 1748, S.P.G. Manuscript B 16, pp. 64-65.

20. *Quaestiones pro Modulo Discutiendae sub Reverendo D. Thoma Clap, Collegii-Yalensis, Quod est Divina Providentia, Novo-Portu Connecticutensium, Praeside. In Comitiis Publicis a Laureae Magistralis Candidatis, MDCCXLVIII* [New London, 1748], *Quaestiones Pro Modulo Discutiendae . . . In Comitiis Publicis a Laureae Magistralis Candidatis, MDCCLI* [New London, 1751] (broadsides). The *quaestiones* of Leaming, Chandler, and Seabury are printed in small type, which indicates that they—like the great majority of those listed for any given class—were not, in fact, used in the exercises.

21. Samuel Johnson to the S.P.G. Secretary, March 28, 1749, Hawks and Perry, *Documentary History*, I, 252; Dexter, *Biographical Sketches of the Graduates of Yale*, II, 166.

22. Samuel Seabury, Sr., to the S.P.G. Secretary, March 26, 1752, S.P.G. Manuscript B 20, pp. 156-57.

23. Benjamin F. Thompson and Charles J. Werner, *History of Long Island from Its Discovery and Settlement to the Present Time* (New York, 1918), III, 142, 150, 161; Robert Jenney to the S.P.G. Secretary, June 27, 1728, Moore, *History of St. George's Church, Hempstead*, pp. 56-58; Samuel Seabury, Sr., to the S.P.G. Secretary, December 15, 1743, March 25, October 14, 1744, March 26, 1747, S.P.G. Manuscript B 11, p. 271, S.P.G. Manuscript B 13, pp. 446, 448, S.P.G. Manuscript B 15, p. 139.

24. Address of certain inhabitants of Huntington and places adjacent, to the S.P.G., September 30, 1748, S.P.G. Manuscript B 16, p. 144.

25. Samuel Seabury, Sr., to [Ebenezer Prime], *c.* 1746 (draft), Samuel Seabury Papers.

26. Samuel Seabury, Sr., to the S.P.G. Secretary, March 26, 1747, S.P.G. Manuscript B 15, p. 139.

27. Subscription papers and building accounts, *Papers of the Lloyd Family of the Manor of Queens Village, Lloyd's Neck, Long Island, New York, 1654-1826*, [edited by Dorothy C. Barck] (*Collections of the New-York Historical Society, Third Series*, LIX-LX, New York, 1927), I, 395-97, 413, 417-20, 462; Henry Lloyd I to Henry Lloyd II, April 29, 1748, *Ibid.*, I, 403; address of certain inhabitants of Huntington and places adjacent, to the S.P.G., September 30, 1748, S.P.G. Manuscript B 16, pp. 144-45.

28. Thomas Temple to the S.P.G. Secretary, December 29, 1746, S.P.G. Manuscript B 14, pp. 166-67; Samuel Seabury, Sr., to the S.P.G. Secretary, March 25, 1748, S.P.G. Manuscript B 16, pp. 91-92.

29. Samuel Seabury, Sr., to the S.P.G. Secretary, September 30, 1748, *Ibid.*, pp. 123-24; Henry Barclay to the S.P.G. Secretary, November 7, 1748, *Ibid.*, pp. 138-39.

30. Address of certain inhabitants of Huntington and places adjacent, to the S.P.G., September 30, 1748, *Ibid.*, pp. 144-46; Samuel Seabury, Sr., to the S.P.G. Secretary, September 30, 1748, *Ibid.*, pp. 122-24; Samuel Johnson to the S.P.G. Secretary, September 29, 1748, *Ibid.*, p. 65; Henry Barclay to the S.P.G. Secretary, November 7, 1748, *Ibid.*, p. 138; Samuel Seabury to the S.P.G. Secretary, November 10, 1748, *Ibid.*, p. 142.

31. Philip Bearcroft, S.P.G. Secretary, to Matthew Graves, June 23, 1749, to Samuel Seabury, Sr., June 24, 1749, S.P.G. Manuscript B 17, pp. 416-17, 411-12; Thomas Temple to the S.P.G. Secretary, December 8, 1749, *Ibid.*, p. 218.

32. Samuel Seabury, Sr., to the S.P.G. Secretary, September 30, 1749, *Ibid.*, p. 209; Philip Bearcroft, S.P.G. Secretary, to James MacSparran, October 4, 1749, to Matthew Graves, October 5, 1749, *Ibid.*, pp. 433, 443; Samuel Seabury to the S.P.G. Secretary, January 5, 1750/1, S.P.G. Manuscript B 18, p. 294.

33. Samuel Seabury, Sr., to the S.P.G. Secretary, September 30, 1749, March 26, October 1, 1750, March 26, September 30, 1751, S.P.G. Manuscript B 17, p. 209, S.P.G. Manuscript B 18, pp. 287, 291, S.P.G. Manuscript B 19, pp. 184, 186; Samuel Seabury to the S.P.G. Secretary, January 5, 1750/1, January 6, 1752, S.P.G. Manuscript B 18, p. 294, S.P.G. Manuscript B 20, p. 162.

34. Samuel Seabury to the S.P.G. Secretary, September 30, 1749, S.P.G Manuscript B 17, pp. 208-9. Keble died before the news of his dismissal by the S.P.G. arrived from England.

35. Henry Onderdonk, *The Annals of Hempstead; 1643 to 1832; Also, the Rise and Growth of the Society of Friends on Long Island and in New York, 1657 to 1826* (Hempstead, 1878), p. 76. Onderdonk, who had access to Samuel Seabury, Sr.'s, account book, states—apparently on the basis of its entries—that Samuel, Jr., began the practice of medicine in January, 1750.

36. Samuel Seabury, Sr., to the S.P.G. Secretary, September 30, 1748, S.P.G. Manuscript B 16, p. 123.

37. Onderdonk, *Annals of Hempstead*, p. 76.

38. Hempstead, *Diary*, p. 530; Moore, *History of St. George's Church, Hempstead*, p. 103, quoting advertisement dated March 27, 1762, from the *New-York Mercury*.

39. Samuel Seabury to the S.P.G. Secretary, January 5, 1750/1, January 6, 1752, S.P.G. Manuscript B 18, p. 295, S.P.G. Manuscript B 20, p. 162.

40. Samuel Seabury to the S.P.G. Secretary, January 5, 1750/1, S.P.G. Manuscript B 18, p. 295; S.P.G. Manuscript Journals, XII, 27; Philip Bearcroft, S.P.G. Secretary, to Samuel Seabury, Sr., August 1, 1751, S.P.G. Manuscript B 19, p. 356.

41. Samuel Seabury to the S.P.G. Secretary, January 6, 1752, S.P.G. Manuscript B 20, pp. 162-63; Samuel Seabury, Sr., to the S.P.G. Secretary, October 13, 1752, *Ibid.*, p. 159.

42. Samuel Johnson to John Berriman, October 30, 1752, Johnson, *Writings*, I, 159; Samuel Johnson *et al.* to unnamed correspondent, July 13, 1753, *Ibid.*, III, 249; Dexter, *Biographical Sketches of the Graduates of Yale,* II, 35-36.

43. Samuel Seabury, Sr., to the S.P.G. Secretary, October 13, 1752, S.P.G. Manuscript B 20, p. 159.

44. Quoted in Alexander Grant, *The Story of the University of Edinburgh during Its First Three Hundred Years* (London, 1884), II, 193.

45. "List of the American Graduates in Medicine in the University of Edinburgh, from 1705 to 1866, with Their Theses," *New England Historical and Genealogical Register*, XLII (April, 1888), pp. 159-61.

46. William Johnson to Samuel Johnson, April 3, 1756, Johnson, *Writings*, I, 250.

47. Eben Edwards Beardsley, *Life and Correspondence of the Right Reverend Samuel Seabury, D.D., First Bishop of Connecticut, and of the Episcopal Church in the United States of America* (Boston, 1881), p. 6.

48. For the medical school of Seabury's day, see Grant, *Story of the University of Edinburgh*, I, 217-29, 299-300, 304-6, 313, 315, 317-18, 329, II, 386-87, 393, 401-2, 411, from which the following account is drawn.

49. Both these manuscripts are in the Samuel Seabury Papers.

50. Account with James Youle, July 17, 1782, receipt from John Rivington & Sons, Booksellers, for books purchased August 6, 1784, Samuel Seabury Papers.

51. Memorial of Samuel Seabury, October 20, 1783, American Loyalists: Transcript of the Manuscript Books and Papers of the Commission of Enquiry, XLI, 561 (this manuscript and the other Loyalist transcripts hereafter cited are in the New York Public Library).

52. Testimony of John Wetherhead, September 18, 1784, *Ibid.*, XLI, 573; John Wetherhead to the Loyalist Commissioners, [*c.* November 1, 1784], A.O. 13 (American Loyalists' Claims, Series II) / 105, ff. 46-47, Public Record Office; certificate dated May 17, 1781, and signed by Samuel Seabury as physician to the New York almshouse, Historical Manuscripts Commission, *Report on American Manuscripts in the Royal Institution of Great Britain* (London, 1904-1909), II, 280; Samuel Seabury to the S.P.G. Secretary, November 12, 1777, abstracted in S.P.G. Manuscript Journals, XXI, 267; accounts with Thomas Bartow, February 18, 1779, and with Robert Coupar, March 10, 1779, Edward Hicks to Samuel Seabury, January 4, 1787, Samuel Seabury Papers; New London *Connecticut Gazette*, March 3, 1796.

53. Summarized in the "Case of the Episcopal Clergy in Scotland, and of the Laity of their Communion," drawn up by James Allan Park in 1789 and printed in John Skinner, *Annals of Scottish Episcopacy, from the Year 1788 to the Year 1816, Inclusive* . . . (Edinburgh, 1818), pp. 101-8.

54. [Flavel S. Mines], *A Presbyterian Clergyman Looking for the Church* (New York, 1849-53), Part 2, pp. 321-22. See also Beardsley, *Samuel Seabury*, p. 7; Seabury, *Memoir of Bishop Seabury*, pp. 5-6.

55. *The Guardian's* American correspondent to the editor of that publication, September 14, 1904, in *The Guardian*, September 28, 1904.

56. John Skinner of Linshart, *An Ecclesiastical History of Scotland, from the First Appearance of Christianity in That Kingdom, to the Present Time* . . . (London, 1788), II, 671-72; George Grub, *An Ecclesiastical History of Scotland from the Introduction of Christianity to the Present Time* (Edinburgh, 1861), IV, 43-44; John Skinner to George Gaskin, April 29, 1790, Skinner, *Annals of Scottish Episcopacy*, pp. 172-75.

57. Deed of submission to the bishops of the Scottish Episcopal Church of the trustees and vestrymen of Cowgate Chapel, February 26, 1805, *Ibid.*, pp. 366-68; Clarence Hayden Vance, "Myles Cooper, M.A., D.C.L., LL.D., Second President of King's College, Now Columbia University, New York City," *Columbia University Quarterly*, XXII (September, 1930), pp. 281-82.

58. New York's S.P.G. missionaries to George II, September 18, 1746, S.P.G. Manuscript B 14, pp. 110-12. James Wetmore as senior missionary signed the address in the name of his brethren.

59. Henry Barclay to the S.P.G. Secretary, June 27, 1753, abstracted in S.P.G. Manuscript Journals, XII, 279; James Wetmore to the S.P.G. Secretary, July 2, 1753, abstracted in *Ibid.*, XII, 279-80; Samuel Seabury, Sr., to the S.P.G. Secretary, April 18, 1753, abstracted in *Ibid.*, XII, 268-69.

60. Henry Barclay to the S.P.G. Secretary, October 3, 1752, S.P.G. Manuscript B 20, pp. 131-32.

61. Philip Bearcroft, S.P.G. Secretary, to Samuel Seabury, Sr., August 1, 1753, *Ibid.*, p. 432.

62. S.P.G. Manuscript Journals, XII, 279-80.

63. Philip Bearcroft, S.P.G. Secretary, to Thomas Sherlock, October 23, 1753 (copy), Archives of the Protestant Episcopal Diocese of Connecticut, Trinity College.

64. Horace Wemyss Smith, *Life and Correspondence of the Rev. William Smith, D.D., . . . with Copious Extracts from His Writings* (Philadelphia, 1879-1880), I, 17-21.

65. Samuel Seabury to [Jonathan Boucher], December 14, 1785 (copy), Hawks Papers, Church Historical Society.

66. Samuel Seabury, Sr., to Thomas Sherlock, October 23, 1753, Samuel Seabury Papers. This letter refers to Seabury's earlier communication of July, 1753.

67. William Jones Seabury declared: "He was fond . . . of repeating a saying common among the younger Clergy of that day in reference to the two Sherlocks, William, Dean of St. Paul's, and his son, Thomas, Bishop of London, 'that the father was the soundest Divine in England except the Son.' " Seabury, *Memoir of Bishop Seabury*, p. 7. This seems doubtful, for Seabury scarcely ever mentions Sherlock in the notes appended to his published writings.

68. *Ibid.* Sherlock's collected sermons, originally published in four volumes, 1754-58, were often reprinted.

69. Thomas Bradbury Chandler to Samuel Johnson, February 26, 1755, Hawks Papers.

70. *Ibid.*

71. Seabury's Yale classmate William Johnson and Samuel Fayerweather (Harvard, 1743) were confirmed by Bishop Secker of Oxford at St. Paul's, London, a few days before their ordination as deacons in March, 1756. William Johnson to Samuel Johnson, March 12, 1756, Johnson, *Writings*, I, 244. However, Edward Winslow (Harvard, 1741) and John Tyler (Yale, 1765) make no mention of confirmation in the diaries of their ordination voyages. Diary of Edward Winslow, 1754-55 (copy), New York Public Library; *The Rev. John Tyler's Journal, May 4 to November 1, A.D. 1768* (San Francisco, [1894]).

72. William S. Bartlet, *The Frontier Missionary: a Memoir of the Life of the Rev. Jacob Bailey, A.M.* . . . (New York, 1853), pp. 61-62, quoting Bailey's diary entry, February 29, 1760.

73. Smith, *Life and Correspondence of the Reverend William Smith*, I, 39, quoting Smith's diary entry, December 21, 1753; certificate of Samuel Seabury's ordination as deacon, December 21, 1753, Samuel Seabury Papers.

74. Bartlet, *Frontier Missionary*, pp. 62-63, quoting Bailey's diary entry, March 2, 1760. For a similar description, see William Johnson to Samuel Johnson, March 19, 1760, Johnson, *Writings*, I, 245.

75. Seabury's certificate of ordination as priest, declaration of conformity, and license, all dated December 23, 1753, Samuel Seabury Papers.

76. Tyler, *Journal*, pp. 10, 12.

77. Smith, *Life and Correspondence of the Reverend William Smith*, I, 45, quoting Smith's diary entry, May 22, 1754; Samuel Seabury to the S.P.G. Secretary, October 10, 1754, abstracted in S.P.G. Manuscript Journals, XIII, 30.

78. Samuel Seabury, Sr., to the S.P.G. Secretary, October 11, 1754, abstracted in *Ibid.*, XIII, 29-30.

79. Seabury, *Memoir of Samuel Seabury*, p. 9, quoting the letter of an unnamed relative.

CHAPTER III

"MY SUCCESS HAS NOT BEEN EQUAL TO MY FIRST EXPECTATIONS"

1. Onderdonk, *Annals of Hempstead*, p. 76.

2. Birket, *Some Cursory Remarks*, pp. 49, 70. A somewhat longer route utilized the Brooklyn-Manhattan, Manhattan-Staten Island, and Staten Island-Elizabethtown Point ferries. *Ibid.*, p. 49.

3. Nelson R. Burr, *The Anglican Church in New Jersey* (Philadelphia, 1954), p. 545, quoting William Skinner to the S.P.G. Secretary, December 7, 1742; Samuel Seabury to the S.P.G. Secretary, October 10, 1754, abstracted in S.P.G. Manuscript Journals, XIII, 30.

4. Burr, *Anglican Church in New Jersey*, pp. 543-47, has an excellent account of the origins of the parish.

5. Biographical sketch in *Ibid.*, pp. 653-54.

6. Samuel Seabury to the S.P.G. Secretary, October 10, 1754, abstracted in S.P.G. Manuscript Journals, XIII, 30.

7. *Ibid.*, XIII, 30-31.

8. Burr, *Anglican Church in New Jersey*, p. 546.

9. *Ibid.*, p. 548.

10. Stiles, *Itineraries and Other Miscellanies*, p. 107.

11. Samuel Seabury to the S.P.G. Secretary, October 9, 1755, October 10, 1756, abstracted in S.P.G. Manuscript Journals, XIII, 100, 215; Samuel Seabury, Sr., *A Modest Reply to a Letter from a Gentleman to His Friend in Dutchess-County, Lately Published by an Anonymous Writer* (New York, 1759), p. 15.

12. Samuel Seabury to the S.P.G. Secretary, October 9, 1755, October 10, 1756, abstracted in S.P.G. Manuscript Journals, XIII, 100, 215; Burr, *Anglican Church in New Jersey*, pp. 551-52.

13. Samuel Johnson to William Samuel Johnson, January 20, December 16, 1755, Johnson, *Writings*, I, 209, 230.

14. Samuel Seabury's *notitia parochialis*, October 8, 1762, S.P.G. Manuscript B 2, p. 572.

15. In 1705 the Episcopal ministers of Hempstead and Jamaica declared: "The ancient settlers have transplanted themselves from New England & do still keep a close correspondence & are buoyed up by Schismatical Instructions from that Interest which occasion all the disturbance & opposition we meet with in both our parishes." William Urquhart and John Thomas to the S.P.G. Secretary, July 4, 1705, *The Documentary History of the State of New York*, edited by Edmund Bailey O'Callaghan (Albany, 1849-51), III, 209.

16. Henry Onderdonk, *Antiquities of the Parish Church, Jamaica, (Including Newtown and Flushing,)* . . . (Jamaica, 1880), pp. 11-49; Thompson and Werner, *History of Long Island*, III, 142, 150, 161, 240-46.

17. Henry Barclay to the S.P.G. Secretary, January 9, 1756, abstracted in S.P.G. Manuscript Journals, XIII, 136-37.

18. Samuel Johnson to William Johnson, January 10, 1756, Johnson, *Writings*, I, 231.

19. Biographical sketch in Richard Webster, *A History of the Presbyterian Church in America, from Its Origin until the Year 1760, with Biographical Sketches of Its Early Ministers* (Philadelphia, 1857), p. 433.

20. Samuel Johnson to William Samuel Johnson, December 12, 21, 1755, April 21, 1756, Johnson, *Writings*, IV, 37-39, I, 254; Samuel Johnson to William Johnson, December 16, 1755, January 10, 1756, *Ibid.*, I, 230, 231; William Johnson to Samuel Johnson, February 13, March 12, 19, 31, 1756, *Ibid.*, I, 239, 243-44, 246, 248-49; William Johnson to William Samuel Johnson, May 5, 1756, Beardsley, *Samuel Johnson*, p. 219; Dexter, *Biographical Sketches of the Graduates of Yale*, II, 166-67.

21. Letter of institution, January 12, and statement of conformity, January 23, 1757, Samuel Seabury Papers; order for induction, January 12, and certificate of induction, January 13, 1757, New-York Historical Society.

22. Samuel Seabury to the S.P.G. Secretary, January 26, 1757, abstracted in S.P.G. Manuscript Journals, XIII, 259.

23. Seabury, *Memoir of Bishop Seabury*, p. 25.

24. Edward Hicks's order for the delivery of personal property, November 20, 1763, also Samuel Seabury, Further Account of the Case between Edward Hicks and Samuel Seabury, *c.* November, 1764, Samuel Seabury Papers.

25. Seabury, *Memoir of Bishop Seabury*, pp. 25-26.

26. *A History of the Parish of Trinity Church in the City of New York*, edited by Morgan Dix (New York, 1898-1906), I, 435, quoting obituary in the New York *Royal Gazette*, October 14, 1780.

27. Samuel Seabury, State of the Case between Edward Hicks of Staten Island

and Samuel Seabury junior of Jamaica, Long Island, *c.* 1764, also Seabury, Further Account of the Case between Edward Hicks and Samuel Seabury, *c.* November, 1764, Samuel Seabury Papers.

28. Advertisement of the sale of Samuel Seabury's farm, *New-York Mercury* (Supplement), February 15, 1762.

29. Samuel Seabury to the S.P.G. Secretary, October 10, 1759, O'Callaghan, *Documentary History of the State of New York*, III, 194.

30. Samuel Seabury to the S.P.G. Secretary, October 6, 1760, March 26, 1762, S.P.G. Manuscript B 2, p. 556, S.P.G. Manuscript B 3, p. 464; George Harison to unnamed correspondent, January 2, 1762, Onderdonk, *Antiquities of the Parish Church, Jamaica*, p. 63.

31. Samuel Seabury to the S.P.G. Secretary, March 28, 1758, abstracted in S.P.G. Manuscript Journals, XIV, 104.

32. Samuel Seabury to the S.P.G. Secretary, October 10, 1759, O'Callaghan, *Documentary History of the State of New York*, III, 195, corrected by S.P.G. Manuscript B 2, p. 550.

33. Samuel Seabury to the S.P.G. Secretary, October 2, 1757, abstracted in S.P.G. Manuscript Journals, XIV, 78-79; Samuel Seabury to the S.P.G. Secretary, October 10, 1759, March 26, 1764, June 28, 1765, O'Callaghan, *Documentary History of the State of New York*, III, 195-96, 199, 200; Samuel Seabury to the S.P.G. Secretary, March 28, October 6, 1760, S.P.G. Manuscript B 2, pp. 552-53, 556; Samuel Seabury, Sr., to the S.P.G. Secretary, March 26, 1764, *Ibid.*, pp. 494-95. A similar situation existed in Providence County, Rhode Island. See Stiles, *Itineraries and Other Miscellanies*, p. 106.

34. *Notitiae parochiales* of Samuel Seabury, Sr., and Samuel Seabury, March 25, 1764, S.P.G. Manuscript B 2, pp. 497, 580.

35. October 20, 1763, Samuel Johnson wrote to Thomas Secker, Archbishop of Canterbury, with reference to certain Connecticut congregations: "I observe one thing happier in those parts than I doubt in most of the King's dominion, which is, that there are sometimes at least as many communicants as families and in some places many more; and as many men as women." Hawks and Perry, *Documentary History*, II, 55. See also Bela Hubbard to the S.P.G. Secretary, January 30, 1767, *Ibid.*, II, 107; Samuel Andrews to the S.P.G. Secretary, October 2, 1773, *Ibid.*, II, 191; John Beach to the S.P.G. Secretary, October 20, 1773, April 12, 1774, *Ibid.*, II, 192, 195.

36. Samuel Seabury to the S.P.G. Secretary, October 10, 1759, O'Callaghan, *Documentary History of the State of New York*, III, 195, corrected by S.P.G. Manuscript B 2, p. 550.

37. Samuel Seabury to the S.P.G. Secretary, October 6, 1760, S.P.G. Manuscript B 2, p. 556.

38. Samuel Seabury, Sr., to the S.P.G. Secretary, January 4, 1762, *Ibid.*, p. 479; petition of Samuel Seabury and others of the town of Jamaica to Cadwallader Colden, April 8, 1761, O'Callaghan, *Documentary History of the State of New York*, III, 324; Thompson and Werner, *History of Long Island*, III, 320-21, 349-50; Onderdonk, *Antiquities of the Parish Church, Jamaica*, pp. 50-60.

39. Subscription, May 1, 1761, *Ibid.*, pp. 61-62.

40. Samuel Seabury to the S.P.G. Secretary, March 26, 1763, O'Callaghan, *Documentary History of the State of New York*, III, 198.

41. George Harison to unnamed correspondent, January 2, 1762, Onderdonk, *Antiquities of the Parish Church, Jamaica*, pp. 62-63.

42. *Ibid.*; Samuel Seabury, Sr., to the S.P.G. Secretary, January 4, 1762, S.P.G. Manuscript B 2, p. 479.

43. Samuel Johnson *et al.* to the S.P.G. Secretary, December 5, 1761, abstracted in S.P.G. Manuscript Journals, XV, 205-6.

44. Daniel Bondet to the S.P.G. Secretary, November 12, 1717, Bolton, *Protestant Episcopal Church, in the County of Westchester*, pp. 427-28; John Bartow to the S.P.G. Secretary, November 15, 1722, *Ibid.*, p. 434; Pierre Stouppe to the S.P.G. Secretary, August 10, 1733, *Ibid.*, p. 445.

45. Samuel Johnson to the S.P.G. Secretary, January 10, 1762, S.P.G. Manuscript B 2, pp. 302-3.

46. S.P.G. Manuscript Journals, XV, 222.

47. Samuel Johnson to William Samuel Johnson, October 18, 1762, Johnson, *Writings*, I, 324.

48. Ebenezer Kneeland to the S.P.G. Secretary, April 10, 1763, abstracted in S.P.G. Manuscript Journals, XV, 408; Samuel Johnson to the S.P.G. Secretary, May 10, 1763, abstracted in *Ibid.*, XV, 393.

49. Samuel Seabury to the S.P.G. Secretary, March 26, 1763, O'Callaghan, *Documentary History of the State of New York*, III, 198, corrected by S.P.G. Manuscript B 2, p. 573.

50. S.P.G. Manuscript Journals, XV, 394; Agur Treadwell to the S.P.G. Secretary, April 9, 1764, abstracted in *Ibid.*, XVI, 160; Samuel Seabury to the S.P.G. Secretary, October 6, 1764, S.P.G. Manuscript B 1, p. 54.

51. Preaching schedule, September 3, 1764, Onderdonk, *Antiquities of the Parish Church, Jamaica*, p. 64; Samuel Seabury to the S.P.G. Secretary, October 6, 1764, S.P.G. Manuscript B 1, pp. 52-53.

52. *New-York Gazette; or, the Weekly Post-Boy*, September 13, 20, 27, October 4, 11, 18, 25, November 8, 1764. Some of the advertisements appeared in more than one issue.

53. Samuel Seabury to the S.P.G. Secretary, October 6, 1764, S.P.G. Manuscript B 1, pp. 52-54.

54. Seabury, State of the Case between Edward Hicks of Staten Island and Samuel Seabury junior of Jamaica, Long Island, *c.* 1764; Edward Hicks, Reply to the State of the Case between Edward Hicks of Staten Island and Samuel Seabury junior of Jamaica, Long Island, November 10, 1764; Seabury, Further Account of the Case between Edward Hicks and Samuel Seabury, *c.* November, 1764. Unless otherwise stated, all details of the Hicks-Seabury dispute are drawn from these pamphlets in the Samuel Seabury Papers.

55. Advertisement of the sale of Samuel Seabury's farm, *New-York Mercury* (Supplement), February 15, 1762; Samuel Seabury to the S.P.G. Secretary, December 17, 1765, S.P.G. Manuscript B 2, pp. 591-93.

56. Edward Hicks's order for the delivery of personal property, November 20, 1763, Samuel Seabury Papers.

57. Among the Samuel Seabury Papers is a conveyance of three Negroes from Seabury to Edward Hicks, November 1, 1765.

58. Samuel Seabury to the S.P.G. Secretary, December 17, 1765, S.P.G. Manuscript B 2, p. 591.

59. Hallam, *Annals of St. James's Church, New London*, p. 33; *New-York Mercury*, June 18, 1764; *New-York Gazette; or, the Weekly Post-Boy,* June 21, 1764. Shipton states that Seabury, Sr., sailed for England in June, 1763, and returned just a year later, citing as his source a letter from Elizabeth (Powell) Seabury to James Helme, June 15, 1764, printed (from an inaccurate transcript) in Updike, *History of the Episcopal Church in Narragansett*, I, 146. Shipton, *Sibley's Harvard Graduates*, VII, 439. But this is clearly impossible. The Hempstead rector sent letters, dated from that town, to the S.P.G. Secretary, Sepember 30, 1763, March 26, 1764, S.P.G. Manuscript B 2, pp. 492-95.

60. Onderdonk, *Annals of Hempstead*, p. 76, quoting Samuel Seabury, Sr.'s account book; gravestone inscription, quoted in Moore, *History of St. George's Church, Hempstead*, pp. 105-6.

61. Elizabeth (Powell) Seabury to James Helme, July 15, 1764, Updike, *History of the Episcopal Church in Narragansett*, I, 146-47; S.P.G. Manuscript Journals, XVI, 185; Samuel Seabury to the S.P.G. Secretary, April 8, 1765, S.P.G. Manuscript B 2, pp. 584-85.

62. For his will see *Abstracts of Wills on File in the Surrogate's Office, City of New York*, VI, 347-48.

63. John Milner to the S.P.G. Secretary, December 21, 1764, abstracted in S.P.G. Manuscript Journals, XVI, 299; Samuel Seabury to the S.P.G. Secretary, April 8, 1765, S.P.G. Manuscript B 2, p. 584.

64. Samuel Auchmuty to the S.P.G. Secretary, November 12, 1766, *Ibid.*, p. 88.

65. Samuel Seabury to the S.P.G. Secretary, October 7, 1766, *Ibid.*, p. 597.

66. Samuel Johnson to the S.P.G. Secretary, April 30, May 15, 1761, *Ibid.*, pp. 294-95, 297.

67. Samuel Johnson to Thomas Secker, July 13, 1760, Hawks and Perry, *Documentary History*, I, 311; William Samuel Johnson to Samuel Johnson, December 31, 1762, Johnson, *Writings*, I, 329; Samuel Johnson to William Samuel Johnson, January 3, 1763, *Ibid.*, IV, 90.

68. Churchwardens and vestrymen of Rye to the S.P.G. Secretary, February 21, May 27, 1765, S.P.G. Manuscript B 3, pp. 552-53, 556.

69. Samuel Seabury to the S.P.G. Secretary, April 8, October 1, 1765, S.P.G. Manuscript B 2, pp. 583-85, 588-90.

70. Samuel Auchmuty to the S.P.G. Secretary, May 3, 1765, *Ibid.*, pp. 35-36.

71. Samuel Seabury to the S.P.G. Secretary, April 8, 1765, *Ibid.*, p. 583; Leonard Cutting to the S.P.G. Secretary, April 9, 1767, *Ibid.*, pp. 508-9; Samuel Seabury to the S.P.G. Secretary, June 28, 1765, O'Callaghan, *Documentary History of the State of New York*, III, 200; Daniel Burton, S.P.G. Secretary, to William Smith, September 20, 1765, Hawks Papers; S.P.G. Manuscript Journals, XVI, 185.

72. Churchwardens and vestrymen of Westchester to the S.P.G. Secretary,

October 28, 1765, S.P.G. Manuscript B 3, pp. 739-40; Samuel Seabury to the S.P.G. Secretary, December 17, 1765, S.P.G. Manuscript B 2, pp. 591-93.

73. Samuel Seabury to the S.P.G. Secretary, October 7, 1766, *Ibid.*, pp. 597-99.

74. Samuel Seabury to the S.P.G. Secretary, June 25, 1767, *Ibid.*, p. 605; letters of admission and institution, December 3, 1766, Samuel Seabury Papers; order for induction, December 3, 1766, and certificate of induction, March 1, 1767, New-York Historical Society.

75. Samuel Johnson to the S.P.G. Secretary, October 27, 1755, December 21, 1757, Johnson, *Writings*, I, 225, IV, 42-43.

76. Churchwardens and vestrymen of Westchester to [Thomas Secker], August 1, 1760, S.P.G. Manuscript B 3, p. 714.

77. Samuel Johnson to the S.P.G. Secretary, October 20, 1759, S.P.G. Manuscript B 2, p. 288.

78. Printed in Bolton, *Protestant Episcopal Church, in the County of Westchester*, pp. 73-77.

79. John Milner to the S.P.G. Secretary, October 3, 1761, June 29, 1762, June 4, December 10, 1763, June 8, 1764, June 7, September 10, 1765, S.P.G. Manuscript B 3, pp. 719-36.

80. John Milner to the S.P.G. Secretary, September 10, 17, 1765, February 3, 1768, *Ibid.*, pp. 735-36, 737, 745; churchwardens and vestrymen of Westchester to the S.P.G. Secretary, October 28, 1765, *Ibid.*, p. 739; Myles Cooper to the S.P.G. Secretary, December 20, 1765, *Ibid.*, p. 850; Samuel Auchmuty to Samuel Johnson, September 2, 1765, Hawks Papers; Samuel Auchmuty to the S.P.G. Secretary, September 25, 1765, S.P.G. Manuscript B 2, pp. 47-51; Edward Lewis Goodwin, *The Colonial Church in Virginia . . .* (Milwaukee, 1927), p. 294.

81. Writing to Archbishop Thomas Secker, November 10, 1766, Samuel Johnson conceded that a few Southerners might be "faithful parish priests though not public spirited." The rest, however, were either "very negligent" or "very wicked." Johnson, *Writings*, I, 379. See also Thomas Bradbury Chandler to Samuel Johnson, June 9, 1767, *Ibid.*, I, 407-8.

82. John Milner to the S.P.G. Secretary, June 4, December 10, 1763, June 8, 1764, September 10, 1765, S.P.G. Manuscript B 3, pp. 722, 727, 730, 736; Samuel Seabury to the S.P.G. Secretary, June 25, 1767, S.P.G. Manuscript B 2, p. 604.

83. Samuel Seabury to the S.P.G. Secretary, December 29, 1776, *Ibid.*, p. 653; memorial of Samuel Seabury, October 20, 1783, and Seabury's supporting testimony, American Loyalists: Transcript of the Manuscript Books and Papers of the Commission of Enquiry, XLI, 568, 572.

84. S.P.G. Manuscript Journals, XVII, 35; Samuel Seabury to the S.P.G. Secretary, June 25, 1767, S.P.G. Manuscript B 2, pp. 604-5.

85. Bolton, *Protestant Episcopal Church, in the County of Westchester*, pp. 486-98.

86. Daniel Bondet to the S.P.G. Secretary, November 12, 1717, *Ibid.*, p. 428; Pierre Stouppe to the S.P.G. Secretary, August 10, 1733, *Ibid.*, p. 445; Frederick Philipse to the S.P.G. Secretary, September 30, 1765, S.P.G. Manuscript B 3,

pp. 635-36; Harry Munro to the S.P.G. Secretary, December 26, 1766, *Ibid.*, p. 655.

87. For the history of the church prior to 1766, see Bolton, *Protestant Episcopal Church, in the County of Westchester*, pp. 387-470.

88. Samuel Seabury to the S.P.G. Secretary, June 25, 1767, S.P.G. Manuscript B 2, pp. 601-2; Myles Cooper *et al.* to the S.P.G. Secretary, July 8, 1768, S.P.G. Manuscript B 3, pp. 915-16.

89. Samuel Auchmuty to the S.P.G. Secretary, October 24, 1766, S.P.G. Manuscript B 2, p. 80; Samuel Seabury to the S.P.G. Secretary, June 25, 1767, *Ibid.*, p. 602.

90. Samuel Seabury to the S.P.G. Secretary, June 25, 1767, April 8, 1771, *Ibid.*, pp. 600-601, 630; vestry of Eastchester to the rector, churchwardens, and vestrymen of Trinity Church, New York, 1801, Boston, *Protestant Episcopal Church, in the County of Westchester*, pp. 380-81.

91. *Ibid.*, pp. 2-3, 8-9, 357-62; Thomas Standard to the S.P.G. Secretary, November 5, 1729, *Ibid.*, p. 59; undated address of Eastchester Churchmen to the S.P.G., *Ibid.*, pp. 366-67.

92. Samuel Seabury to the S.P.G. Secretary, June 25, 1767, S.P.G. Manuscript B 2, p. 605.

93. Samuel Seabury to the S.P.G. Secretary, October 10, 1769, *Ibid.*, p. 616.

94. Samuel Seabury to the S.P.G. Secretary, June 25, 1767, October 1, 1768, *Ibid.*, pp. 602-3, 563.

95. Samuel Seabury to the S.P.G. Secretary, June 25, 1767, April 15, 1769, October 8, 1771, S.P.G. Manuscript B 2, pp. 600, 614, 632.

96. For the Westchester practice, see John Bartow to the S.P.G. Secretary, December 1, 1707, Bolton, *Protestant Episcopal Church, in the County of Westchester*, p. 18; John Bartow's account of Westchester parish, July 13, 1724, *Ibid.*, p. 48; John Milner to the S.P.G. Secretary, June 29, 1762, June 7, 1765, S.P.G. Manuscript B 3, pp. 719, 732. For data concerning New England administrations, see *infra*, p. 460.

97. John Milner to the S.P.G. Secretary, June 29, 1762, S.P.G. Manuscript B 3, p. 719; Harry Munro to the S.P.G. Secretary, December 26, 1766, *Ibid.*, p. 653; Ephraim Avery to the S.P.G. Secretary, March 25, 1766, Bolton, *Protestant Episcopal Church, in the County of Westchester*, p. 317; Samuel Seabury to the S.P.G. Secretary, October 8, 1771, S.P.G. Manuscript B 2, p. 632.

98. Seabury, *Memoir of Bishop Seabury*, pp. 403-4. Seabury seems to have had at least one other child, born in the spring of 1769, who, presumably, died in infancy. See Samuel Auchmuty to Sir William Johnson, April 6, 1769, Sir William Johnson Papers, Library of Congress.

99. Thompson, *History of Long Island*, II, 32; Nathaniel Seabury to the S.P.G. Secretary, October 7, 1765, December 26, 1766, October 3, 1768, July 22, 1769, S.P.G. Manuscript B 3, pp. 741-42, 743, 748, 750; Samuel Seabury to the S.P.G. Secretary, December 28, 1767, October 1, 1768, S.P.G. Manuscript B 2, pp. 607-8, 564-65.

100. Samuel Seabury to the S.P.G. Secretary, October 1, 1768, October 8, 1771, *Ibid.*, pp. 565, 632.

101. Samuel Seabury to the S.P.G. Secretary, December 29, 1776, *Ibid.*, p. 654.

102. Advertisement of Seabury's school, *Rivington's New-York Gazetteer,* February 23, 1775.

103. Memorial of Samuel Seabury to the General Assembly of Connecticut, December 19, 1775 (draft), Samuel Seabury Papers.

104. Advertisement of Seabury's school, *Rivington's New-York Gazetteer,* February 23, 1775; memorial of Samuel Seabury, October 20, 1783, and Seabury's supporting testimony, American Loyalists: Transcript of the Manuscript Books and Papers of the Commission of Enquiry, XLI, 561, 571-72.

105. Daniel Burton, S.P.G. Secretary, to Sir William Johnson, May 26, 1766, Sir William Johnson Papers.

106. Sir William Johnson to the S.P.G. Secretary, November 9, 1766 (draft), to Myles Cooper, December 1, 1767 (draft), Sir William Johnson Papers.

107. S.P.G. Manuscript Journals, XVII, 511.

108. Samuel Seabury to the S.P.G. Secretary, October 1, 1768, S.P.G. Manuscript B 2, p. 567.

109. Myles Cooper to Sir William Johnson, November 6, 1767, Samuel Auchmuty to Sir William Johnson, November 19, 1767, Sir William Johnson Papers.

110. William Smith and Thomas Barton to Sir William Johnson, November 25, 1767, Sir William Johnson to Myles Cooper, December 1, 1767 (draft), to Samuel Auchmuty, December 2, 1767 (draft), to William Smith, December 18, 1767 (draft), to the S.P.G. Secretary, December 23, 1767 (draft), Sir William Johnson Papers.

111. William Smith to Sir William Johnson, January 8, 1768, Sir William Johnson Papers; Burr, *Anglican Church in New Jersey,* pp. 294-95.

112. Samuel Auchmuty to Sir William Johnson, November 19, 1767, Sir William Johnson Papers; Samuel Seabury to the S.P.G. Secretary, October 1, 1768, S.P.G. Manuscript B 2, pp. 566-67.

113. Samuel Auchmuty to Sir William Johnson, January 13, November 14, 1768, Sir William Johnson Papers.

114. Samuel Auchmuty to Sir William Johnson, August 21, November 14, 1769, Sir William Johnson to Samuel Auchmuty, December 1, 1769 (draft), Sir William Johnson Papers; Samuel Auchmuty to the S.P.G. Secretary, August 10, 1769, S.P.G. Manuscript B 2, p. 142; Samuel Seabury to the S.P.G. Secretary, October 10, 1769, *Ibid.,* pp. 617-18; Sir William Johnson to the S.P.G. Secretary, December, 1769, *Ibid.,* pp. 347-48.

115. Samuel Seabury to the S.P.G. Secretary, January 3, 1771, *Ibid.,* p. 628.

CHAPTER IV

"HIS WANT OF LEISURE & INCLINATION, & NOT HIS WANT OF ABILITIES"

1. Memorial of Samuel Seabury, October 20, 1783, American Loyalists: Transcript of the Manuscript Books and Papers of the Commission of Enquiry, XLI, 559-60.

2. John Howard Van Amringe *et al., A History of Columbia University, 1754-1904* (New York, 1904), pp. 3-4, 9-12, 33; Beardsley, *Samuel Johnson,*

p. 189; Samuel Johnson to Thomas Herring, June 25, 1753, to William Samuel Johnson, May 27, 1754, to Thomas Sherlock, July 6, 1754, Johnson, *Writings*, IV, 3, 11, 20; Henry Barclay to Samuel Johnson, November 4, 1754, *Ibid.*, IV, 24-25; Henry Barclay *et al.* to the S.P.G. Secretary, November 3, 1755, *Ibid.*, IV, 39-40.

3. Samuel Johnson to Thomas Herring, June 25, 1753, *Ibid.*, IV, 3.

4. Carl Bridenbaugh, *Mitre and Sceptre: Transatlantic Faiths, Ideas, Personalities, and Politics 1689-1775* (New York, 1962), pp. 144-57, has an extended account of the controversy, which, however, is marred by the anti-Episcopal bias displayed throughout this study. See also Dorothy Rita Dillon, *The New York Triumvirate: a Study of the Legal and Political Careers of William Livingston, John Morin Scott, William Smith, Jr.* (New York, 1949), pp. 31-37; Thomas Jones, *History of New York during the Revolutionary War, and of the Leading Events in the Other Colonies at That Period*, edited by Edward Floyd DeLancey (New York, 1879), I, 3-7.

5. Van Amringe *et al.*, *History of Columbia University*, pp. 16-18; Dillon, *New York Triumvirate*, pp. 37-39; Bridenbaugh, *Mitre and Sceptre*, pp. 157-65.

6. This paragraph is based on an examination of the files of the *New-York Mercury* and *New-York Gazette* for 1754-55 and of the ten numbers of *John Englishman*. The New York Public Library has a complete run of this very rare periodical.

7. Memorial of Samuel Seabury, October 20, 1783, American Loyalists: Transcript of the Manuscript Books and Papers of the Commission of Enquiry, XLI, 559-60.

8. Van Amringe *et al.*, *History of Columbia University*, p. 10; Burr, *Anglican Church in New Jersey*, p. 593; Birket, *Some Cursory Remarks*, p. 47.

9. William Samuel Johnson to Samuel Johnson, December 6, 1754, Johnson, *Writings*, IV, 31; Samuel Johnson to William Samuel Johnson and William Johnson, December 8, 1754, *Ibid.*, IV, 33.

10. Thomas Bradbury Chandler to Samuel Johnson, February 26, 1755, Hawks Papers.

11. Samuel Johnson to William Samuel Johnson and William Johnson, December 8, 1754, Johnson, *Writings*, IV, 33.

12. Biographical sketch in Shipton, *Sibley's Harvard Graduates*, XI, 115-27.

13. Jones, *History of New York during the Revolutionary War*, I, 2; Samuel Johnson to William Samuel Johnson and William Johnson, June 10, 1754, to Thomas Sherlock, July 6, 1754, Johnson, *Writings*, IV, 16, 20-21.

14. See, for example, "John Englishman's true Notion of Sister-Churches," *John Englishman, In Defence of the English Constitution*, [April 9, 1755].

15. Letter from a "country Correspondent, a Lover of Peace, and a true Friend to the Dutch-Church," signed "J.V.D.," *New-York Mercury* (Supplement), April 14, 1755.

16. It often is forgotten that an abortive arrangement of 1754 would have transformed King's College into a joint Church of England-Dutch Reformed enterprise. Henry Barclay to Samuel Johnson, November 4, 1754, Johnson, *Writings*, IV, 25; Samuel Johnson to William Samuel Johnson and William

Johnson, November 25, 1754, *Ibid.*, IV, 26; Van Amringe *et al.*, *History of Columbia University*, pp. 10-11.

17. John Eliot, *A Biographical Dictionary, Containing a Brief Account of the First Settlers and Other Eminent Characters . . . in New-England* (Boston, 1809), pp. 51-52; Sprague, *Annals of the American Pulpit*, V, 82-85; Dexter, *Biographical Sketches of the Graduates of Yale*, I, 239-43; Stiles, *Itineraries and Other Miscellanies*, pp. 77, 218.

18. The full title of the work, published at New London, ran as follows: *A Modest Enquiry into the State of the Dead. By Which It Appears to the Enquirer, That There Is No Intermediate State; But the Resurrection Immediately Succeeds Death. Humbly Propos'd to the Consideration of Those Who Love Christ's Appearing.*

19. Seabury, *Memoir of Bishop Seabury*, p. 16. The anecdote as here reproduced represents Beach's wife as being recently dead when he composed his sermon, but she did not die until the summer of 1756. Dexter, *Biographical Sketches of the Graduates of Yale*, I, 241.

20. Beach, *A Modest Enquiry into the State of the Dead*, p. 10.

21. *Ibid.*, pp. 10-25.

22. Moses Mather and Noah Welles to the S.P.G. Secretary, December 24, 1755 (copy), Philip Bearcroft, S.P.G. Secretary, to Obadiah [sic] Mather and Noah Welles, February 28, 1757 (copy), Samuel Seabury Papers.

23. Beardsley, *Samuel Johnson*, pp. 236-37.

24. Seabury, *Memoir of Bishop Seabury*, p. 17.

25. The account which follows is based upon the minutes of the conference, forwarded by Wetmore to the S.P.G. Secretary with a letter dated November 2, 1759, S.P.G. Manuscript Journals, XIV, 258-60.

26. See Seabury, *Memoir of Bishop Seabury*, p. 17 for a relevant anecdote.

27. For a discussion of the identity of the electors, see *supra*, pp. 187-88.

28. Samuel Johnson to Thomas Secker, July 25, 1759, Johnson, *Writings*, I, 290.

29. Samuel Johnson to William Samuel Johnson, December, 1762, Beardsley, *Samuel Johnson*, p. 272. See also William Samuel Johnson to Samuel Johnson, December 31, 1762, Johnson, *Writings*, I, 329; Samuel Johnson to William Samuel Johnson, January 3, 1763, *Ibid.*, IV, 90.

30. Thomas Bradbury Chandler to Samuel Johnson, February 5, 1766, Transcripts of Early Letters by Samuel Johnson (Stratford), Thomas Bradbury Chandler, John Henry Hobart, 1754-1830, pp. 19-21, Archives of the Protestant Episcopal Diocese of Connecticut.

31. Thomas Bradbury Chandler to Samuel Johnson, March 31, 1767, Johnson, *Writings*, I, 395.

32. John Wolfe Lydekker, *The Life and Letters of Charles Inglis* (London, 1936), *passim.*

33. To his fellow college president, William Smith of Philadelphia, Cooper wrote, April 9, 1770: "Don't you want to see Your Friends in New York? I am sure You do. Well then, come at the Time of our Commencement and Convention

[of the New York and New Jersey clergy]—the third Tuesday of next Month. I have got some Segars—and Beer of a most *delicate Texture*: and Beef Steaks, I hope, You will find in plenty. As for mental food, at a Commencement—or in a Methodist-meetinghouse, I know you have too much Experience to expect it; and therefore you will not be disappointed." Hawks Papers.

34. Vance, "Myles Cooper," *op. cit.*, pp. 261-86, *passim.*

35. The classic statement of the High Churchmen's concept of an American episcopate is Thomas Bradbury Chandler's *An Appeal to the Public, in Behalf of the Church of England in America* (New York, 1767).

36. The view that the effort to secure colonial bishops actually was—in the main—an aspect of a general struggle to achieve Episcopal dominance (and its corollary, the primacy of political motives among the supporters of an American episcopate) is a central theme of Bridenbaugh, *Mitre and Sceptre.* The present writer does not believe that the evidence sustains this interpretation.

37. See *supra,* note 90, p. 376.

38. For the Connecticut Convention, see *Diocese of Connecticut: the Records of Convocation A.D. 1790-A.D. 1848*, edited by Joseph Hooper (New Haven, 1904), pp. 7-8, 30; John Beach to the S.P.G. Secretary, April 22, 1760, Hawks and Perry, *Documentary History*, I, 306; Ebenezer Dibble to the S.P.G. Secretary, October 1, 1767, October 8, 1770, *Ibid.*, II, 112, 159; Godfrey Malbone to the S.P.G. Secretary, May 17, 1772, *Ibid.*, II, 187-88; Jeremiah Leaming to the S.P.G. Secretary, September 26, 1773, *Ibid.*, II, 190-91; Stiles, *Itineraries and Other Miscellanies*, pp. 118-19, *Literary Diary*, I, 244; Samuel Johnson to Thomas Secker, July 12, 1760, Johnson, *Writings*, I, 294; Charles Inglis to William Samuel Johnson, June 17, 1772, *Ibid.*, I, 489-90; St. George Talbot to the S.P.G. Secretary, September 10, 1762, Bolton, *Protestant Episcopal Church, in the County of Westchester*, p. 539; Ebenezer Punderson to the S.P.G. Secretary, November 12, 1762, S.P.G. Manuscript B 3, p. 538; St. George Talbot to the S.P.G. Secretary, July 1, 1763, S.P.G. Manuscript B 2, p. 717; Samuel Auchmuty to the S.P.G. Secretary, October 24, 1766, *Ibid.*, pp. 81-82; Charles Inglis to the S.P.G. Secretary, October 17, 1767, *Ibid.*, p. 222; Samuel Johnson to Richard Terrick, September 14, 1764, *The Fulham Papers in the Lambeth Palace Library, American Colonial Section, Calendar and Indexes*, compiled by William Wilson Manross (Oxford, 1965), p. 16; Jeremiah Leaming to the S.P.G. Secretary, May 6, 1768, abstracted in S.P.G. Manuscript Journals, XVII, 520; Joseph Lamson *et al.* to the S.P.G. Secretary, May 25, 1769, abstracted in *Ibid.*, XVIII, pp. 217-18; Ezra Stiles to Francis Alison, October 4, 1768, Dexter, *Biographical Sketches of the Graduates of Yale*, III, 264; Ebenezer Dibble *et al.* to Sir William Johnson, September 14, 1769, O'Callaghan, *Documentary History of the State of New York*, IV, 378-79.

39. William McGilchrist to the S.P.G. Secretary, June 27, 1766, Perry, *Historical Collections*, III, 524.

40. Henry Caner to the S.P.G. Secretary, December 8, 1760, and enclosed proposals, *Ibid.*, III, 459-61; Henry Caner to Thomas Secker, January 7, 1763, *Ibid.*, III, 490. Caner in 1747 had exchanged his Connecticut mission for the rectorship of King's Chapel, Boston.

41. For the Boston Convention, see William McGilchrist to the S.P.G.

Secretary, June 27, 1766, *Ibid.*, III, 524; Henry Caner *et al.* to the S.P.G. Secretary, September 22, 1768, *Ibid.*, III, 541; Henry Caner to Jacob Bailey, May 17, 1766, Bartlet, *Frontier Missionary*, p. 83; *Letters and Diary of John Rowe, Boston Merchant, 1759-1762, 1764-1779*, edited by Anne Rowe Cunningham (Boston, 1903), pp. 136, 285; "Records of St. Paul's Church, Narragansett," *op. cit.*, pp. 575, 581, 583-84, 590, 598-99, 602; *Boston Post-Boy*, September 26, 1768, September 24, 1770, September 30, 1771, September 14, 1772, September 13, 1773, September 19, 1774; Boston *Massachusetts Gazette*, September 25, 1769; William Willard Wheeler to Jacob Bailey, December 22, 1774, Jacob Bailey Papers, Library of Congress.

42. Burr, *Anglican Church in New Jersey*, pp. 286-96; "The Seabury Minutes of the New York Clergy Conventions of 1766 and 1767," edited by Walter Herbert Stowe, *HMPEC*, X (June, 1941), p. 154. The formation of the United Convention, scheduling sessions each year both in New Jersey and New York, amounted to a regularization of the existing situation. By 1767 many men from New York were attending New Jersey's meetings, while Jersey pastors were frequenting those held at Manhattan. *Ibid.*, pp. 132-35; New Jersey clergy, "assisted by the Revd: Messrs: Charlton, Auchmuty, Seabury & Milner of New York, and Mr: Neill of Pensylvania," to the S.P.G. Secretary, September 30, 1764, abstracted in S.P.G. Manuscript Journals, XVI, 221-24.

43. "The Seabury Minutes of the New York Clergy Conventions of 1766 and 1767," *op. cit.*, pp. 132-36.

44. *Ibid.*, p. 132.

45. *Ibid.*, pp. 132, 135, 143, 155; Thomas Bradbury Chandler to Samuel Johnson, October 19, 1766, September 9, 1768, Johnson, *Writings*, I, 369, 446; Samuel Johnson to the S.P.G. Secretary, November 10, 1766, *Ibid.*, I, 377; Charles Inglis to William Samuel Johnson, June 17, 1772, *Ibid.*, I, 489-90; Thomas Bradbury Chandler to Samuel Johnson, September 3, 1767, Hawks Papers; Charles Inglis to the S.P.G. Secretary, October 17, 1767, S.P.G. Manuscript B 2, p. 222; Ezra Stiles to Francis Alison, October 4, 1768, Dexter, *Biographical Sketches of the Graduates of Yale*, III, 264; Ebenezer Dibble to the S.P.G. Secretary, October 8, 1770, Hawks and Perry, *Documentary History*, II, 159.

46. Thomas Bradbury Chandler to William Smith, November 25, 1769, May 2, 1770, June 14, November 30, December 15, 1773, January 11, February 12, April 13, 1774, Hawks Papers; Thomas Bradbury Chandler to William Smith, April 28, 1773, William Smith Papers, Church Historical Society.

47. Samuel Auchmuty to the S.P.G. Secretary, May 1, 1767, June 8, August 16, 1770, S.P.G. Manuscript B 2, pp. 100-101, 147-48, 153-54.

48. "Copy of a Plan for establishing corresponding Societies &C—," Samuel Seabury Papers.

49. William Smith to Richard Osbaldeston, April 17, 1764, Smith, *Life and Correspondence of the Reverend William Smith*, I, 348-49; New Jersey clergy, "assisted by the Revd: Messrs: Charlton, Auchmuty, Seabury & Milner of New York, and Mr: Neill of Pensylvania," to the S.P.G. Secretary, September 20, 1764, abstracted in S.P.G. Manuscript Journals, XVI, 221-24; Hugh Neill to the S.P.G. Secretary, October 18, 1764, Perry, *Historical Collections*, II, 364-66.

50. Summary of address of New Jersey Convention to Richard Terrick,

[October 10, 1766], Johnson, *Writings*, I, 389-91; Thomas Bradbury Chandler to Samuel Johnson, October 19, 1766, *Ibid.*, I, 369-70; Edgar Legare Pennington, "Colonial Clergy Conventions," *HMPEC*, VIII (September, 1939), pp. 201-3.

51. Samuel Auchmuty to the S.P.G. Secretary, December 20, 1766, S.P.G. Manuscript B 2, pp. 91-94. See also William Smith to Richard Terrick, November 13, 1766, Smith, *Life and Correspondence of the Reverend William Smith*, I, 401; Richard Peters to Richard Terrick, November 14, 1766, Manross, *Fulham Papers . . . American Colonial Section, Calendar and Indexes*, p. 115; Samuel Auchmuty to Samuel Johnson, January 3, February 14, 1767, Hawks Papers.

52. Thomas Bradbury Chandler to Samuel Johnson, October 19, 1766, Johnson, *Writings*, I, 370-71. See also Thomas Bradbury Chandler to Samuel Johnson, March 31, 1767, January 22, 1768, *Ibid.*, I, 395, 433; Thomas Bradbury Chandler to Samuel Johnson, December 5, 1767, Transcripts of Early Letters . . . 1754-1830, pp. 67-68.

53. Thomas Bradbury Chandler to Samuel Johnson, November 12, 1765, Johnson, *Writings*, I, 356-57; Pennington, "Colonial Clergy Conventions," *op. cit.*, pp. 200-201. Auchmuty designated Johnson "the Father of the Clergy" in a letter to him, dated March 27, 1771, Hawks Papers.

54. Samuel Johnson to Thomas Secker, May 2, 1766, Johnson, *Writings*, I, 361.

55. Charles Inglis to the S.P.G. Secretary, May 1, 1766, S.P.G. Manuscript B 2, pp. 209-10.

56. Samuel Seabury to the S.P.G. Secretary, April 17, 1766, O'Callaghan, *Documentary History of the State of New York*, III, 200-201.

57. Thomas Bradbury Chandler to Samuel Johnson, August 20, 1764, Johnson, *Writings*, I, 343; Samuel Auchmuty to Samuel Johnson, June 12, 1766, *Ibid.*, I, 362.

58. Dexter, *Biographical Sketches of the Graduates of Yale*, II, 175.

59. Samuel Johnson *et al.* to the S.P.G. Secretary, May 22, 1766, S.P.G. Manuscript B 3, pp. 892-95.

60. Thomas Secker to Samuel Johnson, July 31, 1766, Johnson, *Writings*, III, 286-88.

61. Summary of New Jersey Convention's address to Richard Terrick, [October 10, 1766], *Ibid.*, I, 389-91; Thomas Bradbury Chandler to Samuel Johnson, October 19, 1766, *Ibid.*, I, 369-70; Pennington, "Colonial Clergy Conventions," *op. cit.*, pp. 200-201.

62. Samuel Johnson *et al.* to Richard Terrick, October 8, 1766, Hawks and Perry, *Documentary History*, II, 100-102.

63. Thomas Bradbury Chandler to Samuel Johnson, September 5, October 19, 1766, January 9, 19, 1767, Johnson, *Writings*, I, 366, 370, 385-87, 387-88; Chandler, *Life of Samuel Johnson*, pp. 113-15. Chandler, in his letter of January 9, declared that not a sheet of the *Appeal* should be printed until Johnson had examined it, and his letters, hereafter cited, show that the Stratford rector was his constant critic and assistant.

64. Thomas Bradbury Chandler to Samuel Johnson, February 21, 1767, Samuel Johnson Correspondence, Columbia University; "The Seabury Minutes of the New York Clergy Conventions of 1766 and 1767," *op. cit.*, p. 143.

65. Thomas Bradbury Chandler to Samuel Johnson, March 31, 1767, Johnson, *Writings*, I, 396; Thomas Bradbury Chandler to Samuel Johnson, April 15, 1767, Samuel Johnson Correspondence; "The Seabury Minutes of the New York Clergy Conventions of 1766 and 1767," *op. cit.*, p. 150.

66. Thomas Bradbury Chandler to Samuel Johnson, July 14, 1767, Transcripts of Early Letters . . . 1754-1830, pp. 55-57.

67. Thomas Bradbury Chandler to Samuel Johnson, July 7, 1768, Johnson, *Writings*, I, 444-45.

68. Charles Inglis to Samuel Johnson, March 22, 1768, Hawks Papers; "A Whip for the American Whig," No. 4, *New-York Gazette, and Weekly Mercury*, May 2, 1768; Carl Lotus Becker, *The History of Political Parties in the Province of New York, 1760-1776* (Madison, 1909), pp. 59-60.

69. Thomas Bradbury Chandler to Samuel Johnson, August 20, 1767, Transcripts of Early Letters . . . 1754-1830, pp. 63-65; Thomas Bradbury Chandler to Samuel Johnson, [November, 1767], Samuel Johnson Correspondence.

70. Thomas Bradbury Chandler to Sir William Johnson, March 4, 1768, Sir William Johnson Papers.

71. Charles Inglis to Samuel Johnson, March 22, 1768, Hawks Papers; Thomas Bradbury Chandler to Samuel Johnson, April 7, 1768, Johnson, *Writings*, I, 436; Samuel Johnson to William Samuel Johnson, April 22, 1768, to Thomas Secker, May 10, 1768, *Ibid.*, I, 438-41.

72. Thomas Bradbury Chandler to Samuel Johnson, April 7, 1768, *Ibid.*, I, 436-37; Charles Inglis to Samuel Johnson, March 22, 1768, Hawks Papers.

73. *New-York Gazette, and Weekly Mercury*, March 28, 1768, *A Collection of Tracts from the Late News Papers, &C. Containing Particularly the American Whig, a Whip for the American Whig, with Some Other Pieces . . .* (New York, 1768-69), I, 12-13. Seabury's statement provides additional evidence of the virtual union of the New Jersey and New York clergy even before 1767. He may well have acted as secretary at Perth Amboy in 1765, as he seems to have done in 1764. See *supra*, pp. 103-4.

74. Burr, *Anglican Church in New Jersey*, p. 353, quoting New Jersey Convention's address to the S.P.G. Secretary, October 3, 1765.

75. *New-York Gazette; or, the Weekly Post-Boy*, April 4, 1768, *Collection of Tracts*, I, 35.

76. *New-York Gazette; or, the Weekly Post-Boy*, April 25, 1768, *Collection of Tracts*, I, 96-97.

77. Edmund S. Morgan, *The Gentle Puritan, a Life of Ezra Stiles, 1727-1795* (New Haven, 1962), pp. 203-4, 241-50.

78. Ezra Stiles to Samuel Seabury, March 8, 1768, Samuel Seabury Papers.

79. "The Seabury Minutes of the New York Clergy Conventions of 1766 and 1767," *op. cit.*, p. 158.

80. Samuel Seabury to Ezra Stiles, June 4, 1768 (draft), Samuel Seabury Papers.

81. Thomas Bradbury Chandler, *The Appeal Farther Defended; in Answer to the Farther Misrepresentations of Dr. Chauncey* (New York, 1771), pp. 21-27.

82. Memorial of Samuel Seabury, October 20, 1783, American Loyalists:

Transcript of the Manuscript Books and Papers of the Commission of Enquiry, XLI, 561.

83. Vance, "Myles Cooper," *op. cit.*, pp. 274-76.

84. The author of "Whip" No. 10, for example, described himself as a retired lawyer in his letter to "Timothy Tickle," dated from Dutchess County. *New-York Gazette, and Weekly Mercury*, May 30, 1768, *Collection of Tracts*, I, 171-72. Chandler once implied that a good number of persons wrote at least one "Whip." To Samuel Johnson he wrote, July 7, 1768: "The scene in New York of *whigging, whipping*, etc., is not pleasing to me; but yet I think that so long as there are Whigs, there ought to be Whips, however I wish some of them were applied with more judgment and discretion. But where so many people are in their turn to have a lick at the Whig, it is not to be expected that all will acquit themselves with equal prudence, dexterity and decency." Johnson, *Writings*, I, 444.

85. Inglis was first mentioned by name in "Whig" No. XXXIII, *New-York Gazette; or, the Weekly Post-Boy*, October 24, 1768, *Collection of Tracts*, II, 228.

86. *New-York Gazette, and Weekly Mercury*, July 4, 1768, *Collection of Tracts*, I, 276-81.

87. Dated Boston, August 5, 1768, the letter was reprinted by Seabury in "Whip" No. XXXVII, *New-York Gazette, and Weekly Mercury*, December 19, 1768, *Collection of Tracts*, II, 339-40. The account which follows is based upon this "Whip."

88. *New-York Gazette, and Weekly Mercury*, December 19, 26, 1768, *Collection of Tracts*, II, 338-44, 351-55.

89. *Boston-Gazette, and Country Journal*, January 30, 1769.

90. No. XXXIV of "A Kick for the Whipper," *New York Gazette; or, the Weekly Post-Boy*, January 23, 1769, *Collection of Tracts*, II, 404-6.

91. Thomas Brown to Samuel Seabury, January 30, 1769, Samuel Seabury Papers.

92. Reprinted in the *New-York Gazette; or, the Weekly Post-Boy*, February 20, 1769.

93. Thomas Brown to Samuel Seabury, March 20, 1769, Samuel Seabury Papers. The article, in the form of a communication signed "C.Y.," was published in the *Massachusetts Gazette*, February 16, 1769.

94. *New-York Gazette, and Weekly Mercury*, February 20, 1769.

95. Thomas Brown to Samuel Seabury, March 20, 1769, Samuel Seabury Papers.

96. Charles Chauncy to Ezra Stiles, March 20, 1769, Stiles, *Itineraries and Other Miscellanies*, pp. 447-48.

97. William V. Wells, *The Life and Public Services of Samuel Adams . . .* (Boston, 1865), I, 249-50. The letter is reprinted in *The Writings of Samuel Adams*, edited by Harry Alonzo Cushing (New York, 1904-8), I, 322-32.

98. Thomas Brown to Samuel Seabury, March 20, 1769, Samuel Seabury to John Temple, March 28, 1769 (draft), Samuel Seabury Papers.

99. Charles Inglis to the S.P.G. Secretary, August 12, 1769, S.P.G. Manu-

script B 2, p. 231; memorial of Samuel Seabury, October 20, 1783, American Loyalists: Transcript of the Manuscript Books and Papers of the Commission of Enquiry, XLI, 561.

100. For example, Samuel Johnson, *A Second Letter from a Minister of the Church of England to His Dissenting Parishioners* (Boston, 1734), in Johnson, *Writings*, III, 49-53; also, Ebenezer Punderson, *The Nature and Extent of the Redemption of Mankind by Jesus Christ, Stated and Explained* (New Haven, 1758), p. 16.

101. Thomas Bradbury Chandler to Samuel Johnson, July 14, 1767, Transcripts of Early Letters . . . 1754-1830, pp. 58-59; Thomas Bradbury Chandler to Samuel Johnson, August 20, 1767, Johnson, *Writings*, I, 416.

102. Thomas Bradbury Chandler to Samuel Johnson, September 3, 1767, Hawks Papers.

103. Thomas Bradbury Chandler to Samuel Johnson, January 22, 1768, Johnson, *Writings*, I, 433-34.

104. *An Examination of the Late Reverend President Edwards's 'Enquiry on Freedom of Will.'* A continuation appeared in 1773.

105. Thomas Bradbury Chandler to Samuel Johnson, March 14, 1771, Johnson, *Writings*, I, 476.

106. John Ogilvie and Samuel Seabury to the S.P.G. Secretary, May 19, 1769, S.P.G. Manuscript B 3, p. 919; Thomas Bradbury Chandler to Samuel Johnson, April 21, 1770, Hawks Papers; Webster, *History of the Presbyterian Church in America*, pp. 579-80. The New York Public Library has what appears to be a copy of this edition; the place of printing is not indicated.

107. Samuel Seabury to Thomas Bradbury Chandler, [*c.* April, 1770], quoted in Thomas Bradbury Chandler to Samuel Johnson, April 21, 1770, Hawks Papers.

108. Charles Inglis to Samuel Johnson, February 5, 1771, Hawks Papers.

109. *Appeal to the Public* (1767), *Appeal Defended* (1769), *Appeal Farther Defended* (1771), *Address from the Clergy of New-York and New-Jersey, to the Episcopalians in Virginia* (1771), *Sermon Preached . . . October 2d, 1771* (1771), *Candid Remarks on Dr. Witherspoon's Address to the Inhabitants of Jamaica and the Other West-India Islands* (1772), *Appendix to the American Edition of the Life of Archbishop Secker* (1774), *Free Examination of the Critical Commentary on Archbishop Secker's Letter to Mr. Walpole* (1774). Chandler during this same period also wrote his biography of Samuel Johnson (largely a reworking of Johnson's memoirs), but the work was first printed only in 1805.

110. *A Vindication of the Bishop of Landaff's Sermon* (1768), *An Essay on Infant Baptism* (1768).

111. Charles Inglis to Samuel Johnson, December 10, 1768, July 3, 1770, April 30, 1771, Hawks Papers; Thomas Bradbury Chandler to Samuel Johnson, September 5, 1770, Transcripts of Early Letters . . . 1754-1830, pp. 90-93.

112. Thomas Bradbury Chandler to Samuel Seabury, April 8, 1776, Samuel Seabury Papers.

113. "Whip" No. XXXVIII, *New-York Gazette, and Weekly Mercury*, December 26, 1768, *Collection of Tracts*, II, 351.

114. Thomas Brown to Samuel Seabury, March 20, 1769, Samuel Seabury Papers.

CHAPTER V

"PLAIN ENGLISH, FROM A PLAIN COUNTRYMAN"

1. Ebenezer Dibble to the S.P.G. Secretary, October 1, 1767, Hawks and Perry, *Documentary History*, II, 111.

2. For New England, see the letters printed in Hawks and Perry, *Documentary History*, II, 81-203; also Edward Winslow to the S.P.G. Secretary, January 8, July 1, 1766, June 30, September 29, 1768, January 2, July 4, 1769, January 1, July 1, 1771, January 1, 1772, January 1, July 1, 1774, Perry, *Historical Collections*, III, 521-22, 525, 540-41, 542, 543-44, 547, 556, 558, 563-64, 565-66, 572-73. Winslow, stationed at Braintree, Massachusetts, appears to have mentioned the subject more frequently than any other missionary.

3. Samuel Seabury to the S.P.G. Secretary, April 17, 1766, O'Callaghan, *Documentary History of the State of New York*, III, 201.

4. Samuel Seabury to the S.P.G. Secretary, December 27, 1769, March 29, 1770, S.P.G. Manuscript B 2, pp. 620, 624-25.

5. Memorial of Samuel Seabury, October 20, 1783, American Loyalists: Transcript of the Manuscript Books and Papers of the Commission of Enquiry, XLI, 560. Inglis, when submitting his claims, made a similar statement: "That your Memorialist observing a restless and seditious spirit to prevail in some parts of America long before the proceedings there occasioned any public Alarm, had formed a resolution in conjunction with some of his intimate friends particularly the Revd. Dr. Thomas Bradbury Chandler the Revd. Dr. Myles Cooper and Revd. Dr. Samuel Seabury to watch all publications that were disrespectful to Government or the parent State, or that tended to a breach between Great Britain and her Colonys and to give them an immediate answer and refutation, which resolution he and they punctually adhered to as often as an occasion was offered—" Memorial of Charles Inglis, February 10, 1784, *Ibid.*, XLII, 543. Like Inglis, Chandler listed Cooper as a party to this agreement (which information accords with contemporary references to the 1768 compact). In 1782 he declared that he and his friends had joined together for the purpose of "watching all that should be Published, whether in Pamphlets or News-Papers, and for suffering no thing to pass unanswered, that had a tendency to lessen the respect or affection that was due to the Mother Country." Vance, "Myles Cooper," *op. cit.*, p. 274, quoting from a manuscript in the Public Record Office, London, "The case of Thomas Bradbury Chandler, etc. 27 November, 1782."

6. A series of articles signed "Popliocola," the joint production of Cooper and Professor John Vardill of King's College; published in 1773, they advocated the reception and purchase of the East India Company's tea. Becker, *History of Political Parties in the Province of New York*, p. 103; Vance, "Myles Cooper," *op. cit.*, p. 27; memorial of John Vardill, November 16, 1783, and Vardill's supporting testimony, American Loyalists: Transcript of the Manuscript Books and Papers of the Commission of Enquiry, XLII, 37-38, 47.

7. Memorial of Samuel Seabury, October 20, 1783, *Ibid.*, XLI, 562-63; memorial of James DeLancey, February 20, 1784, *Ibid.*, XLI, 253-55; Samuel Seabury's testimony in support of James DeLancey's memorial, *Ibid.*, XLI, 267-68; Stephen James DeLancey to Samuel Seabury, October 26, 1785, Samuel Seabury Papers; Bolton, *Protestant Episcopal Church, in the County of Westchester*, pp. 548-50; Lorenzo Sabine, *Biographical Sketches of Loyalists in the American Revolution with an Historical Essay* (Boston, 1864), I, 363-70; Alice Mapelsden Keys, *Cadwallader Colden: a Representative Eighteenth Century Official* (New York, 1906), pp. 23, 131.

8. Lewis Morris "To the PUBLIC," May 7, *Rivington's New-York Gazetteer*, May 11, 18, 1775.

9. Moses Coit Tyler, *The Literary History of the American Revolution, 1763-1783* (New York, 1898), I, 349. Tyler's account includes large extracts from Seabury's pamphlets. See *Ibid.*, I, 334-55.

10. Robert Troup to John Mason, March 22, 1810, "Alexander Hamilton Viewed by His Friends: the Narratives of Robert Troup and Hercules Mulligan," edited by Nathan Schachner, *William and Mary Quarterly*, *Third Series*, IV (April, 1947), p. 214.

11. John C. Hamilton, *The Life of Alexander Hamilton* (New York, 1834), pp. 26-38.

12. Howard Swiggett, *The Extraordinary Mr. Morris* (Garden City, 1952), pp. 12-13, 24-25, 48; Onderdonk, *Annals of Hempstead*, p. 76; Sabine, *Biographical Sketches of Loyalists*, II, 431-34; Bolton, *Protestant Episcopal Church, in the County of Westchester*, pp. 111-19; memorial of Isaac Wilkins, undated, American Loyalists: Transcript of the Manuscript Books and Papers of the Commission of Enquiry, XVII, 43-49.

13. *Short Advice to the Counties of New-York*, the production of "a Country Gentleman"; first advertised in *Rivington's New-York Gazetteer*, December 8, 1774.

14. Testimony of Isaac Wilkins, December 13, 1785, in support of his memorial, American Loyalists: Transcript of the Manuscript Books and Papers of the Commission of Enquiry, XVII, 51.

15. Gouverneur Morris Wilkins to William B. Sprague, June 7, 1858, Sprague, *Annals of the American Pulpit*, V, 464.

16. Lorenzo Sabine, *The American Loyalists, or Biographical Sketches of Adherents to the British Crown in the Revolution . . .* (Boston, 1847), p. 702. Sabine repeated his statement—unchanged—in the enlarged, two-volume edition of this work.

17. Hamilton, *Life of Alexander Hamilton*, pp. 26-38.

18. Memorial of Samuel Seabury, October 20, 1783, American Loyalists: Transcript of the Manuscript Books and Papers of the Commission of Enquiry, XLI, 563-65. Preparing his memorial in England, probably without the help of copies of his pamphlets, Seabury made several mistakes. The pamphlet which he described as *The Congress Canvassed* was, in fact, *A View of the Controversy*; *The Congress Canvassed* he termed "an Address to the Merchants of New York."

19. Thomas Bradbury Chandler's affidavit, October 31, 1783 (copy), Samuel Seabury Papers.

20. Myles Cooper's affidavit, September 29, 1783 (copy), Samuel Seabury Papers.

21. Jonathan Boucher, *A View of the Causes and Consequences of the American Revolution; in Thirteen Discourses, Preached in North America between the Years 1763 and 1775: with an Historical Preface* (London, 1797), pp. 556-57.

22. *The American Journal of Ambrose Serle, Secretary to Lord Howe, 1776-1778*, edited by Edward H. Tatum (San Marino, 1940), p. 116.

23. Memorial of Samuel Seabury, October 20, 1783, American Loyalists: Transcript of the Manuscript Books and Papers of the Commission of Enquiry, XLI, 562.

24. *Rivington's New-York Gazetteer*, September 2, 1774.

25. Bedford and Mamaroneck.

26. Minutes of the Rye meeting, August 10, 1774, *American Archives: Consisting of a Collection of Authentick Records, State Papers, Debates, and Letters and Other Notices of Publick Affairs, Fourth Series*, compiled by Peter Force (Washington, 1837-46), I, 703; minutes of the New York City Committee of Correspondence, August 29, 1774, *Ibid.*, I, 325.

27. Only three of New York's thirteen counties were represented in the Congress by their own delegates. Becker, *History of Political Parties in the Province of New York*, pp. 139-41.

28. *Rivington's New-York Gazetteer*, September 8, 1774. On Chandler's authorship of this tract (and subsequent Loyalist productions), see Vance, "Myles Cooper," *op. cit.*, pp. 275-76.

29. Philip Davidson, *Propaganda and the American Revolution, 1763-1783* (Chapel Hill, 1941), p. 253.

30. Advertised in *Rivington's New-York Gazetteer*, October 13, 1774.

31. Cadwallader Colden to William Legge, Earl of Dartmouth, November 2, 1774, Force, *American Archives, Fourth Series*, I, 957.

32. *Rivington's New-York Gazetteer*, November 3, 1774.

33. Cadwallader Colden to William Legge, Earl of Dartmouth, November 2, 1774, Force, *American Archives, Fourth Series*, I, 957.

34. First listed for sale in *Rivington's New-York Gazetteer*, November 10, 1774. Chandler produced this pamphlet before the abstract of the Congress's proceedings arrived at New York but after it was known that the delegates had adopted the Suffolk Resolves and would adopt a policy of nonimportation.

35. Although *Free Thoughts* was advertised in *Ibid.*, November 24, 1774, as published that day, Rivington had previously sold a great many copies. "C. D----" to John Holt, undated, in *New-York Journal; or, the General Advertiser*, November 24, 1774.

36. [Samuel Seabury], *Free Thoughts on the Proceedings of the Continental Congress* . . . ([New York], 1774), pp. 3-6.

37. *Ibid.*, pp. 6-8.

38. *Ibid.*, pp. 9-10.

39. *Ibid.*, p. 11.

40. *Ibid.*, pp. 14-15.

41. *Ibid.*, pp. 15-17.

42. *Ibid.*, pp. 17-19.

43. *Ibid.*, pp. 22-23.

44. So he stated in the advertisement of his school, *Rivington's New-York Gazetteer*, February 23, 1775.

45. [Samuel Seabury], *The Congress Canvassed: Or, an Examination into the Conduct of the Delegates, at Their Grand Convention* . . . ([New York], 1774), p. 4.

46. David Seabury to Samuel Seabury, June 18, 1774, Samuel Seabury Papers; advertisement of David Seabury, merchant, *Rivington's New-York Gazetteer*, September 8, 1774; David Seabury's certificate, January 20, 1784, and his supporting testimony, American Loyalists: Transcript of the Manuscript Books and Papers of the Commission of Enquiry, XVII, 201-4; Thompson, *History of Long Island*, II, 32.

47. First advertised for sale in *Rivington's New-York Gazetteer* of that date.

48. [Seabury], *The Congress Canvassed: or, an Examination into the Conduct of the Delegates, at Their Grand Convention*, pp. 3-4.

49. *Ibid.*, pp. 4-6.

50. *Ibid.*, pp. 8-9.

51. *Ibid.*, pp. 9-11.

52. *Ibid.*, pp. 11-13.

53. *Ibid.*, pp. 14-16.

54. *Ibid.*, p. 16.

55. *Ibid.*, pp. 16-27.

56. Becker, *History of Political Parties in the Province of New York*, pp. 167-69.

57. *Ibid.*, pp. 169-73.

58. *New-York Journal; or, the General Advertiser*, January 12, 1775 (Supplement).

59. "C.D----" to John Holt, undated, *Ibid.*, November 24, 1774.

60. *New-York Gazette, and Weekly Mercury*, December 19, 1774.

61. *New-York Journal; or, the General Advertiser*, April 6, 1775 (Supplement).

62. *Ibid.*, February 2, 1775.

63. *Ibid.*, February 16, 23, 1775; Force, *American Archives, Fourth Series*, II, 132-33.

64. Travelers found Rivington's busy shop the ideal place to secure literature on the controversy. Under date of March 13, 1775, Robert Honyman of Hanover County, Virginia, then in New York on his way to Newport and Boston, wrote in his diary: "After Breakfast went to Rivington's shop; lookt over the Titles of a number of Pamphlets & intend when I return [from New England] to get a compleat set, & he is the only man to furnish me with both sides of the question."

Colonial Panorama 1775: *Dr. Robert Honyman's Journal for March and April*, edited by Philip Padelford (San Marino, 1939), pp. 31-32.

65. Davidson, *Propaganda and the American Revolution*, pp. 225-26.

66. For typical advertisements, see *Rivington's New-York Gazetteer*, December 29, 1774, February 9, 23, 1775.

67. Force, *American Archives, Fourth Series*, I, 1240-41.

68. *Rivington's New-York Gazetteer*, December 8, 1774.

69. "AGRICOLA" to James Rivington, December 19, 1774, *Ibid.*, January 5, 1775.

70. For lack of space, John Holt omitted from his *New-York Journal*; *or, the General Advertiser*, January 19, 1775, "A piece from Middletown, on the evil tendency of a pamphlet lately published, entitled Free Thoughts, &c." The Middletown referred to may have been either the Connecticut or the New Jersey community of that name.

71. Force, *American Archives, Fourth Series*, II, 234-35.

72. *Rivington's New-York Gazetteer*, December 8, 1774.

73. Advertised in *Ibid.*, December 15, 1774, as having been published that day.

74. [Alexander Hamilton], *A Full Vindication of the Measures of Congress* . . . , in *The Papers of Alexander Hamilton*, edited by Harold C. Syrett *et al.* (New York, 1961-   ), I, 46.

75. *Ibid.*, I, 78.

76. Robert Troup to John Mason, March 22, 1810, "Alexander Hamilton Viewed by His Friends," *op. cit.*, p. 214.

77. Hamilton's second pamphlet, *The Farmer Refuted*, was definitely ascribed to Livingston. Hercules Mulligan's reminiscences of Alexander Hamilton, *c.* 1810-15, *Ibid.*, p. 211.

78. [Seabury], *The Congress Canvassed*: *or, an Examination into the Conduct of the Delegates, at Their Grand Convention*, [p. 28].

79. *Rivington's New-York Gazetteer*, December 22, 1774.

80. *Ibid.*, December 29, 1774; Lydekker, *Life and Letters of Charles Inglis*, pp. 146-47.

81. *Rivington's New-York Gazetteer*, January 5, 1775.

82. *Ibid.*, January 12, 1775.

83. [Samuel Seabury], *A View of the Controversy between Great Britain and Her Colonies* . . .(New York, 1774), pp. 11-14, 34.

84. *Ibid.*, pp. 34-35.

85. *Ibid.*, p. 19.

86. *Ibid.*, p. 21.

87. *Ibid.*, pp. 21-22.

88. *Rivington's New-York Gazetteer*, February 23, 1775. As early as January 12, the *Gazetteer* carried an advertisement that the pamphlet was then printing and would be issued as soon as possible.

89. Cadwallader Colden to William Legge, Earl of Dartmouth, December 7, 1774, January 4, 1775, Force, *American Archives, Fourth Series*, I, 1030, 1092.

90. The Assembly's journal, January 10-April 3, 1775, is printed in *Ibid.*, I, 1281-1324.

91. Memorial of Samuel Seabury, October 20, 1783, American Loyalists: Transcript of the Manuscript Books and Papers of the Commission of Enquiry, XLI, 564.

92. *Rivington's New-York Gazetteer*, January 19, 1775.

93. [Samuel Seabury], *An Alarm to the Legislature of the Province of New-York, Occasioned by the Present Political Disturbances, in North America: Addressed to the Honourable Representatives in General Assembly Convened* (New York, 1775), pp. 4-7.

94. *Ibid.*, pp. 7-8.

95. *Rivington's New-York Gazetteer*, January 26, 1775. Joseph Galloway's plan of union was printed as an appendix to this pamphlet, Chandler's own suggestions to the Assembly having appeared on pp. 42-48.

96. [Seabury], *An Alarm to the Legislature of the Province of New-York*, pp. 8-13.

97. Memorial of Samuel Seabury, October 20, 1783, American Loyalists: Transcript of the Manuscript Books and Papers of the Commission of Enquiry, XLI, 564.

98. Becker, *History of Political Parties in the Province of New York*, pp. 175-77.

99. The addresses are printed in the Assembly's journal, Force, *American Archives, Fourth Series*, I, 1313-21.

100. Edmund Burke to the Committee of Correspondence of the New York General Assembly, June 7, 1775, Ross J.S. Hoffman, *Edmund Burke, New York Agent, with His Letters to the New York Assembly and Intimate Correspondence with Charles O'Hara, 1761-1776* (Philadelphia, 1956), pp. 267-71.

101. Memorial of Samuel Seabury, [October 20, 1783] (draft), Samuel Seabury Papers.

102. *Rivington's New-York Gazetteer*, April 6, 1775.

103. Memorial of Samuel Seabury, October 20, 1783, American Loyalists: Transcript of the Manuscript Books and Papers of the Commission of Enquiry, XLI, 562.

104. The Patriots' notification of the meeting—signed by Colonel Lewis Morris and eleven other persons and dated March 28—appeared in *Rivington's New-York Gazetteer*, April 20, 1775.

105. *Ibid.*, April 6, 1775.

106. The account which follows is based upon the Patriot report of the White Plains meeting, written by Colonel Lewis Morris, and an anonymous Loyalist report, both of which appeared in *Ibid.*, April 20, 1775. Except for the advertisements, they occupied the entire front page of the newspaper.

107. Lewis Morris "To the PUBLIC," May 7, *Rivington's New-York Gazetteer*, May 11, 18, 1775; the list of names appears in the latter paper.

108. Becker, *History of Political Parties in the Province of New York*, p. 193.

109. *Rivington's New-York Gazetteer*, March 9, April 13, 20, 1775.

110. *Ibid.*, May 4, 1775.

111. Frederick Jay to John Jay, May 11, 1775, John Jay Papers, Columbia University; Cadwallader Colden to William Legge, Earl of Dartmouth, June 7, 1775, *Documents Relative to the Colonial History of the State of New-York . . .*, edited by Edmund Bailey O'Callaghan and B. Fernow (Albany, 1853-87), VIII, 581; Hercules Mulligan's reminiscences of Alexander Hamilton, *c.* 1810-15, "Alexander Hamilton Viewed by His Friends," *op. cit.*, p. 211; Robert Troup's additional reminiscences of Alexander Hamilton, February 12, 1821, *Ibid.*, p. 219; Memorandums of Thomas Bradbury Chandler, 1775-86 (copy), p. 2, Archives of the Protestant Episcopal Diocese of Connecticut.

112. *Ibid.*, pp. 1-3; Cadwallader Colden to William Legge, Earl of Dartmouth, June 7, 1775, O'Callaghan and Fernow, *Documents Relative to the Colonial History of the State of New York*, VIII, 581.

113. Samuel Seabury to the S.P.G. Secretary, May 30, 1775, S.P.G. Manuscript B 2, pp. 641-42; memorial of Samuel Seabury, October 20, 1783, American Loyalists: Transcript of the Manuscript Books and Papers of the Commission of Enquiry, XLI, 565.

114. *Historical Memoirs of William Smith, Historian of the Province of New York, Member of the Governor's Council and Last Chief Justice of That Province under the Crown, Chief Justice of Quebec*, edited by William H. W. Sabine (New York, 1956-58), [I], 223.

115. Printed in *Rivington's New-York Gazetteer*, May 11, 1775.

116. Samuel Seabury to the S.P.G. Secretary, May 30, 1775, S.P.G. Manuscript B 2, pp. 641-42.

117. Samuel Seabury to Isaac Wilkins, May 30, 1775, Bolton, *Protestant Episcopal Church, in the County of Westchester*, pp. 87-88.

118. Memorial of Samuel Seabury, October 20, 1783, American Loyalists: Transcript of the Manuscript Books and Papers of the Commission of Enquiry, XLI, 565.

119. Samuel Seabury to the S.P.G. Secretary, November 14, 1775, S.P.G. Manuscript B 2, p. 644.

120. Unless otherwise stated, the details of Seabury's seizure and confinement are drawn from the following sources: Samuel Seabury to the S.P.G. Secretary, January 13, December 29, 1776, *Ibid.*, pp. 646, 648-49; memorial of Samuel Seabury to the General Assembly of Connecticut, December 20, 1775, Connecticut Archives, Revolutionary War, First Series, I, document 436; memorial of Samuel Seabury, October 20, 1783, American Loyalists: Transcript of the Manuscript Books and Papers of the Commission of Enquiry, XLI, 566-67. Jones, *History of New York during the Revolutionary War*, I, 65-68, has a near-contemporary account (written *c.* 1783-88), but it contains many inaccuracies.

121. See the New York Provincial Congress's vote of thanks to certain inhabitants of Connecticut, December 12, 1775, *Journals of the Provincial Congress, Provincial Convention, Committee of Safety and Council of Safety of the State of New York, 1775-1776-1777* (Albany, 1842), I, 214.

122. Published in the New Haven *Connecticut Journal*, December 6, 1775, and in the *New-York Journal*; *or, the General Advertiser*, December 7, 1775.

123. New Haven *Connecticut Journal*, December 6, 1775.

124. George Cuthbert Groce, *William Samuel Johnson: a Maker of the Constitution* (New York, 1937), pp. 99-111.

125. Appointment of a committee of the General Assembly to consider the letter of Nathaniel Woodhull, President of the New York Provincial Congress, to Jonathan Trumbull, December 12, 1775, Connecticut Archives, Revolutionary War, First Series, I, document 437.

126. Alexander Hamilton to John Jay, November "21," 1775, Alexander Hamilton Papers, New York Public Library.

127. *Journals of the Provincial Congress, Provincial Convention, Committee of Safety and Council of Safety of the State of New York*, I, 210; Nathaniel Woodhull, President of the New York Provincial Congress, to Jonathan Trumbull, December 12, 1775, *Ibid.*, I, 213-14; Alexander McDougall to John Jay, December 14, 18, 1775, John Jay Papers.

128. Report of a committee of the General Assembly to consider the letter of Nathaniel Woodhull, President of the New York Provincial Congress, to Jonathan Trumbull, December 12, 1775, Connecticut Archives, Revolutionary War, First Series, I, document 438.

129. *Ibid.*

130. Samuel Seabury to the S.P.G. Secretary, January 13, 1776, S.P.G. Manuscript B 2, p. 646.

131. Samuel Seabury to the S.P.G. Secretary, December 29, 1776, *Ibid.*, p. 649; memorial of Samuel Seabury, October 20, 1783, American Loyalists: Transcript of the Manuscript Books and Papers of the Commission of Enquiry, XLI, 566-67.

132. Alexander Clarence Flick, *Loyalism in New York during the American Revolution* (New York, 1901), pp. 118-19.

133. Samuel Seabury to the S.P.G. Secretary, December 29, 1776, S.P.G. Manuscript B 2, pp. 649-50.

134. *Ibid.*, pp. 650-51; Flick, *Loyalism in New York*, p. 119.

135. Samuel Seabury to the S.P.G. Secretary, December 29, 1776, S.P.G. Manuscript B 2, pp. 651-52.

136. *Ibid.*, pp. 652-53.

137. *Journals of the Provincial Congress, Provincial Convention, Committee of Safety and Council of Safety of the State of New York*, I, 621.

138. Memorial of Samuel Seabury, [October 20, 1783] (draft), Samuel Seabury Papers; John Wetherhead to the Loyalist Commissioners, [*c.* November 1, 1784], A.O. 13 (American Loyalists' Claims, Series II)/105, ff. 46-47.

139. Samuel Seabury to the S.P.G. Secretary, December 29, 1776, S.P.G. Manuscript B 2, pp. 652-56; memorial of Samuel Seabury, October 20, 1783, American Loyalists: Transcript of the Manuscript Books and Papers of the Commission of Enquiry, XLI, 567-68.

140. Samuel Seabury to the S.P.G. Secretary, December 29, 1776, S.P.G. Manuscript B 2, p. 653.

141. Samuel Seabury to the S.P.G. Secretary, March 29, 1777, *Ibid.*, pp. 663-64.

142. Thomas Bradbury Chandler to Samuel Seabury, April 8, 1776, Samuel Seabury Papers. Subsequently, Seabury received an additional £50 from this source. Samuel Seabury to the S.P.G. Secretary, November 12, 1777, abstracted in S.P.G. Manuscript Journals, XXI, 267.

143. Richardson and Urquhart published as separate items Seabury's three "A. W. Farmer" tracts, also Chandler's *Friendly Address*; they combined *An Alarm to the Legislature of the Province of New-York* and Chandler's *What Think Ye of Congress Now?* into a single pamphlet.

144. Vance, "Myles Cooper," *op. cit.*, p. 279; examination of Thomas Bradbury Chandler's claim for temporary support, 1782, American Loyalists: Transcript of the Manuscript Books and Papers of the Commission of Enquiry, XLI, 234-35.

145. Thomas Bradbury Chandler to Samuel Seabury, April 8, 1776, Samuel Seabury Papers.

146. Jonathan Boucher twice alluded to this matter. In a book published in 1797, he declared that Seabury's "A.W. Farmer" pamphlets had been "attributed to another Gentleman," to whom the British government "granted an handsome pension." Writing to Seabury in 1789, he spoke of this gentleman as "our late friend of Punnical Memory." Jeremiah Leaming, in a letter to Samuel Peters in 1787, after referring to three supposed friends who had used him basely, observed: "I am not the only man, that has been chosed [sic] by the triumvirate, Bishop Seabury had his share of it; for one of them received a pension of £200 per Annum for writing the peice *A. W. Farmer*: when they all three knew, Doctor Seabury was the author." Boucher, *View of the Causes and Consequences of the American Revolution*, p. 556; Jonathan Boucher to Samuel Seabury, July 30, 1789, Samuel Seabury Papers; Jeremiah Leaming to Samuel Peters, May 25, 1787, "Letters of the Reverend Doctor Jeremiah Leaming to the Reverend Doctor Samuel Peters, Loyalist Refugee in London, and One Time Bishop Elect of Vermont," [edited by E. Clowes Chorley], *HMPEC*, I (September, December, 1932), pp. 180-81.

Myles Cooper, who was considered a punster and enjoyed a £200 pension, and who died May 20, 1785 ("our late friend"), would seem to be the person Boucher had in mind. If so, he probably had a confederate in John Vardill, his colleague at King's College. Vardill (a rather unsavory character) came to England for ordination in 1774 and immediately established a connection with the Ministry. An intimate of Cooper and Chandler, he presumably secured their pensions for them. In the case of Chandler, he could argue for a grant on the grounds of his pamphlets: *The American Querist* and *A Friendly Address* (considering only those pamphlets which were published in 1774 and of which Vardill may be presumed to have had information). But it is difficult to see why Cooper should have been considered worthy of a pension—unless Vardill had represented him as the author of the "A. W. Farmer" pamphlets; his biographer was not able to discover a single Loyalist pamphlet which could with certainty be attributed to him. Against this hypothesis must be noted the fact that Samuel Peters, on the back of Leaming's letter, jotted down the names of Chandler, Auchmuty, and Vardill as members of the triumvirate and listed Cooper among those who had been "deceived" by them. This identification, however, appears to be mere guesswork. In the introduction to his edition of the "A. W. Farmer" pamphlets, Clarence H. Vance, accepting Cooper as the person to whom Boucher referred, declared that the latter "maliciously slandered" the King's College President; but Vance's attempt to prove that Cooper did not claim the pamphlets is not supported by the evidence he presents. It is true that, as noted in the text, Cooper in 1783 furnished Seabury with an affidavit stating that Seabury had written them. Under the circumstances, however, he could hardly have refused his associate's request for such a statement, and at that late date he probably thought there was little danger in complying with it. Examination of John Vardill's claim for temporary support, 1782, American Loyalists: Transcript of the Manuscript Books and Papers of the Commission of Enquiry, II, 122-25; memorial of John Vardill, November 16, 1783, and supporting testimony, *Ibid.*, XLII, 37-53; Vance, "Myles Cooper," *op. cit.*, pp. 274-77; Samuel Seabury, *Letters of a Westchester Farmer*, edited by Clarence H. Vance (White Plains, 1930), pp. 37-39.

147. Thomas Bradbury Chandler to Samuel Seabury, July 5, 1777, Samuel Seabury Papers.

148. *Ibid.*; Thomas Bradbury Chandler to Samuel Seabury, May 16, 1777, Samuel Seabury Papers.

149. Thomas Bradbury Chandler to Samuel Seabury, July 5, December 9, 1777, June 2, 1778, Samuel Seabury Papers.

150. Translation of Seabury's D.D. diploma, Samuel Seabury Papers; the Latin original, dated December 15, 1777, is also in this collection.

151. Serle, *American Journal*, pp. 170, 220, 225.

152. Samuel Seabury, *A Discourse on II Tim. III. 16. Delivered in St. Paul's and St. George's Chapels, in New-York, on Sunday the 11th of May, 1777* (New York, 1777). The author discussed the censures passed on this production in a prefatory "Advertisement."

153. Samuel Seabury, *A Discourse on Brotherly Love, Preached before the Honourable Fraternity of Free and Accepted Masons, of Zion Lodge, at St. Paul's Chapel, in New-York, on the Festival of St. John the Baptist, One Thousand Seven Hundred and Seventy-Seven* (New York, 1777).

154. Samuel Seabury, *A Sermon, Preached before the Grand Lodge, and the Other Lodges of Ancient Freemasons, in New-York, at St. Paul's Chapel, on the Anniversary of St. John the Evangelist, 1782* (New York, 1783). An extract from the minutes of the Grand Lodge, thanking "our Reverend Brother Doctor SEABURY" for his effort, appears on a preliminary leaf.

155. Herbert M. Morais, *Deism in Eighteenth Century America* (New York, 1934), pp. 148-51.

156. Memorial of Samuel Seabury, October 20, 1783, American Loyalists: Transcript of the Manuscript Books and Papers of the Commission of Enquiry, XLI, 568; Samuel Seabury to the S.P.G. Secretary, November 12, 1777, abstracted in S.P.G. Manuscript Journals, XXI, 266-68. Preferring S.P.G. duty, Seabury in the letter just cited requested permission to relinquish the nominal charge of Westchester for the Staten Island mission, provided a return to Westchester continued to be out of the question. The Society approved, but because of enemy raids he found it impossible to reside on the island. Other clergymen, less obnoxious to the Patriots, supplied the post with his consent. Samuel Seabury to the

S.P.G. Secretary, January 20, 1778, January 16, 1779, September 6, 1780, May 5, 1782, abstracted in *Ibid.*, XXI, 296, 473, XXII, 169-70, 291-92; Charles Inglis to the S.P.G. Secretary, August 10, 1780, abstracted in *Ibid.*, XXII, 172; William Walter to the S.P.G. Secretary, September 27, 1781, abstracted in *Ibid.*, XXII, 334; Samuel Seabury to the S.P.G. Secretary, November 22, 1778, June 24, 1782, S.P.G. Manuscript B 2, pp. 666, 670.

157. New York, [1777].

158. William Tryon to Charles Inglis, September 12, 1777, incorporated in the memorial of Charles Inglis, February 10, 1784, American Loyalists: Transcript of the Manuscript Books and Papers of the Commission of Enquiry, XLII, 554-57.

159. Memorial of Samuel Seabury, October 20, 1783, *Ibid.*, XLI, 568. The formal certificate of appointment, dated February 14, 1778, and signed by Sir Henry Clinton, is in the Samuel Seabury Papers.

160. John Wetherhead to the Loyalist Commissioners, [*c.* November 1, 1784], A.O. 13 (American Loyalists' Claims, Series II)/105, ff. 46-47.

161. *Ibid.*; King's American Regiment: abstracts of pay for periods December 25, 1782, to February 23, 1783, February 24 to April 24, 1783, April 25 to June 24, 1783, abstract of subsistence for period April 25 to June 24, 1783, American Loyalists: Transcript of Various Papers Relating to the Losses Services and Support of the American Loyalists and to His Majesty's Provincial Forces during the War of American Independence, Preserved Amongst the American Manuscripts in the Royal Institution of Great Britain, VIII, 275, 277, 329-32, 389, 391-93.

162. Carl Van Doren, *Secret History of the American Revolution* (New York, 1951), p. 139.

163. *Ibid.*, quoting William Eden to Sir Henry Clinton, November 19, 1778. Franklin and Seabury, well acquainted during the war years, would seem to have been literary collaborators on at least one occasion. Colonel Edmund Fanning requested them to revise the manuscript of his *Declaration and Address of His Majesties Loyal Associated Refugees*, published by Rivington in 1779. Edmund Fanning to Samuel Seabury, April 12, 1779, William Franklin's affidavit, October 29, 1783 (copy), Samuel Seabury Papers.

164. Biographical sketch in Burr, *Anglican Church in New Jersey*, pp. 629-31.

165. Jonathan Odell to John André, December 21, 1779, Van Doren, *Secret History of the American Revolution*, pp. 457-58.

166. New York *Royal Gazette*, December 19, 23, 1778, January 2, 6, February 27, April 21, 1779.

167. *Ibid.*, January 9, 20, February 17, March 6, 24, May 29, June 12, July 3, 17, 1779. "Papinian's" letters, subsequently printed in the *New-York Gazette, and Weekly Mercury*, were also reissued in pamphlet form. Memorial of Charles Inglis, February 10, 1784, American Loyalists: Transcript of the Manuscript Books and Papers of the Commission of Enquiry, XLII, 557-58.

168. Memorial of Samuel Seabury, October 20, 1783, *Ibid.*, XLI, 560.

169. Samuel Seabury to the S.P.G. Secretary, March 29, 1777, S.P.G. Manuscript B 2, p. 665.

170. Thomas Bradbury Chandler to Samuel Seabury, June 2, 1778, Samuel Seabury Papers.

171. Thomas Bradbury Chandler to Samuel Seabury, December 1, 1778, Samuel Seabury Papers.

172. Samuel Seabury to the S.P.G. Secretary, November 22, 1778, S.P.G. Manuscript B 2, p. 666.

173. Charles Inglis to the S.P.G. Secretary, May 6, 1782, *Ibid.*, pp. 284-85.

174. "The Solemn Declaration, and humble Petition of the American Loyalists" to George III, enclosed with Charles Inglis, Samuel Seabury *et al.* to Sir Guy Carleton, December 18, 1782, Lydekker, *Life and Letters of Charles Inglis*, pp. 258-60.

175. Jonathan Odell to the S.P.G. Secretary, August 10, 1782, Dix, *Trinity Church in the City of New York*, I, 439; John Sayre to the S.P.G. Secretary, August 14, 1782, S.P.G. Manuscript B 3, pp. 1000-1002.

176. Sabine, *Biographical Sketches of Loyalists*, I, 290; examination of Colin Campbell's claim for temporary support, [1784], American Loyalists: Transcript of the Manuscript Books and Papers of the Commission of Enquiry, VI, 182-83; memorial of Colin Campbell, March 8, 1784, *Ibid.*, XXXVIII, 195-99; Dix, *Trinity Church in the City of New York*, I, 436, quoting the *New-York Gazette, and Weekly Mercury*, December 31, 1781.

177. Samuel Seabury to William Markham, November 24, 1783, Samuel Seabury Papers.

178. "Agents for the Settlers in Nova Scotia," [1782], American Loyalists: Transcript of Various Papers, VIII, 591; "Articles. Of the Settlement of Nova Scotia, Made With the Loyalists at New York, at the Time of the Peace of 1783," William Odber Raymond, *Glimpses of the Past*: *History of the River St. John A.D. 1604-1784* (St. John, New Brunswick, 1905), pp. 345-46.

179. Instructions for Amos Botsford, Samuel Cummings, and Frederick Hauser, [*c.* September, 1782], American Loyalists: Transcript of Various Papers, VIII, 589-90; Raymond, *Glimpses of the Past*, pp. 346-48; Esther Wright Clark, *The Loyalists of New Brunswick* (Fredericton, New Brunswick, 1955), pp. 31-45.

180. *Ibid.*, pp. 46-51, 72; Raymond, *Glimpses of the Past*, pp. 348-50.

CHAPTER VI

"A FREE VALID AND PURELY ECCLESIASTICAL EPISCOPACY"

1. Charles Inglis to Samuel Johnson, November 10, 1770, Hawks Papers.

2. *Ibid.*; Charles Inglis to Samuel Johnson, December 22, 1770, March 28, April 30, June 17, July 4, 1771, Thomas Bradbury Chandler to Samuel Johnson, December 14, 1770, Hawks Papers; Thomas Bradbury Chandler to Samuel Johnson, March 14, October 26, 1771, Johnson, *Writings*, I, 477, 482. See also Arthur Lyon Cross, *The Anglican Episcopate and the American Colonies* (Cambridge, 1902), pp. 230-40; George MacLaren Brydon, *Virginia's Mother Church and the Political Conditions under Which It Grew* (Richmond, Philadelphia, 1947-52), II, 347-59.

3. Charles Inglis to Samuel Johnson, February 5, November 6, 1771, Hawks Papers; Thomas Bradbury Chandler to Samuel Johnson, October 26, 1771, Johnson, *Writings*, I, 483.

4. Thomas Bradbury Chandler to Samuel Johnson, March 14, 1771, *Ibid.*, I, 476-77; Thomas Bradbury Chandler to Samuel Johnson, December 14, 1770, Hawks Papers; Beardsley, *Samuel Johnson*, pp. 341-42; Samuel Johnson to George Berkeley, November 10, 1771, *Ibid.*, p. 348; Stiles, *Literary Diary*, I, 103-4.

5. See Leonard Elliott Elliott-Binns, *The Early Evangelicals: a Religious and Social Study* (Greenwich, 1953), pp. 38, 139-40, 161, 217, 260-61, 268, 293, 302, 310, 322, 330.

6. George Berkeley to William Samuel Johnson, October 19, 1772, Eben Edwards Beardsley, *Life and Times of William Samuel Johnson, LL.D., First Senator in Congress from Connecticut, and President of Columbia College, New York* (New York, 1876), pp. 96-98; William Samuel Johnson to Myles Cooper, January 18, 1773, Johnson, *Writings*, I, 486-87; Myles Cooper to William Samuel Johnson, February 10, August 9, 1773, *Ibid.*, I, 488-89.

7. Thomas Bradbury Chandler to John Vardill, August 3, December 15, 1774, A.O. 13 (American Loyalists' Claims, Series II)/105, ff. 284-87; John Vardill to William Legge, Earl of Dartmouth, September 1, 1774, November 9, 1784, Dartmouth Manuscripts Nos. 955, 1931, William Salt Library.

8. Thomas Bradbury Chandler to William Samuel Johnson, June 20, 1774, Beardsley, *Samuel Johnson*, p. 368.

9. Chandler, Memorandums, pp. 24, 38.

10. [Samuel Seabury], Proposals for establishing the Church of England in America, [1777], Samuel Seabury Papers.

11. Samuel Auchmuty *et al.* to the S.P.G. Secretary, February 8, 1777, S.P.G. Manuscript B 3, pp. 944-45.

12. Serle, *American Journal*, pp. ix-xxvii; Henry Leigh Bennett, "Ambrose Serle, 1742-1812," *The Dictionary of National Biography*, edited by Leslie Stephens and Sidney Lee (London, 1949-50), XVII, 1192.

13. Serle, *American Journal*, pp. 115-16.

14. *Ibid.*, pp. 116-17.

15. *Ibid.*, pp. 165-246, *passim.*

16. *Ibid.*, pp. 201-2, 204-5.

17. Thomas Bradbury Chandler to Samuel Seabury, May 16, 1777, Samuel Seabury Papers.

18. Chandler, Memorandums, p. 48.

19. *Ibid.*, p. 50. For Lowth and the Church of England in the colonies, see Samuel Johnson to William Samuel Johnson, June 8, 1767, to Robert Lowth, June 25, 1767, October 25, 1768, Johnson, *Writings*, I, 405, 409-10, 448-49; Robert Lowth to Samuel Johnson, May 16, 1771, *Ibid.*, I, 478; William Samuel Johnson to Robert Lowth, January 13, 1772, *Ibid.*, I, 485-86; Robert Lowth to Samuel Johnson, May 3, 1768, May 15, 1770, May 16, 1771, to Thomas Bradbury Chandler, May 29, 1775, Chandler, *Life of Samuel Johnson*, pp. 201-8.

20. Chandler, Memorandums, pp. 53-54; S.P.G. Manuscript Journals, XXI, 200-201.

21. *Ibid.*, XXI, 214.

22. [Samuel Seabury], Proposals for establishing the Church of England in America, [1777], Samuel Seabury Papers.

23. Serle, *American Journal*, pp. 204, 209-10.

24. Charles Inglis, Samuel Seabury, *et al.* to Sir Guy Carleton, March 21, 26, 1783, American Loyalists: Transcript of Various Papers, IV, 173-78.

25. The Ridgefield building was destroyed in 1777, Trinity, Fairfield, and St. Paul's, Norwalk, in 1779, and St. James's, New London, in 1781.

26. Sabine, *Biographical Sketches of Loyalists*, I, 487-88, II, 200, 361; Dexter, *Biographical Sketches of the Graduates of Yale*, I, 240-41, II, 40, 483, 708; Shipton, *Sibley's Harvard Graduates*, IX, 400. Gideon Bostwick is included in the figure of twenty-two clergymen, and his churches at Great Barrington and Lanesboro, Massachusetts, in that of forty-eight churches, for the year 1774. Throughout his ministry (1770-93) Bostwick and his parishes—made up, in part, of emigrants from Connecticut—maintained extraparochial ties with the Churchmen of that state rather than with those of Massachusetts, almost all of whom lived far to the east—within thirty-five miles of Boston. Hooper, *Records of Convocation*, pp. 8, 33, 34, 39, 43, 45, 47, 50; Gideon Bostwick to Henry Caner, July 13, 14, 1773, abstracted in S.P.G. Manuscript Journals, XX, 3. See also *supra*, p. 320 and note.

27. For typical instances of clerical assistance, rendered, in this case, by the missionary at Norwich to the churches of Hebron and New London, see John Tyler to the S.P.G. Secretary, January 9, 1781, October 3, 1782, May 15, 1783, Photostats, S.P.G. Connecticut (Part I) 1635-1782, (Part II) 1783-1852; John Tyler to Samuel Peters, January 9, 1784, Samuel Peters Papers, Church Historical Society.

28. Minutes of the Connecticut Convention, Derby, May 23-25, 1780, Litchfield, June 12-14, 1781, Massachusetts Diocesan Library; Hooper, *Records of Convocation*, p. 9.

29. John Rutgers Marshall to the S.P.G. Secretary, April 24, 1782, S.P.G. Manuscript B 3, p. 965.

30. John Sayre to the S.P.G. Secretary, November 8, 1779, Hawks and Perry, *Documentary History*, II, 204-6; Bela Hubbard to the S.P.G. Secretary, July 19, 1782, abstracted in S.P.G. Manuscript Journals, XXIII, 22-23; Samuel Andrews to the S.P.G. Secretary, May 2, 1783, abstracted in *Ibid.*, XXIII, 139-40; Daniel Fogg to the S.P.G. Secretary, January 24, 1783, Photostats, S.P.G. Connecticut (Part II) 1783-1852.

31. Charles Inglis to the S.P.G. Secretary, May 6, 1782, S.P.G. Manuscript B 2, pp. 284-85.

32. Samuel Seabury to the S.P.G. Secretary, February 27, 1785, Ecclesiastical Letter Book, Samuel Seabury Papers; Jeremiah Leaming to Samuel Peters, January 22, 1787, "Letters of the Reverend Doctor Jeremiah Leaming to the Reverend Doctor Samuel Peters, Loyalist Refugee in London and One Time Bishop Elect of Vermont," *op. cit.*, p. 138.

33. In order to expose the numerical weakness of the Church of England, Connecticut Congregationalists undertook an enumeration with the intention of providing statistics for January 1, 1774. Returns giving a total of 9,966 Episcopalians were received from forty-three of the colony's seventy-six towns by the

census director, Elizur Goodrich of Durham. For twelve of the remaining thirty-three towns, estimates from the 1760's, based on jottings of Ezra Stiles, are available. These give evidence of an additional 3,156 Churchmen, the combined figures totaling 13,122. *Minutes of the Convention of Delegates from the Synod of New York and Philadelphia, and from the Associations of Connecticut; Held Annually from 1766 to 1775, Inclusive* (Hartford, 1843), pp. 62-63; Stiles, *Itineraries and Other Miscellanies*, pp. 58, 71, 110, 112, 113, 172. Since returns from the towns noted by Stiles probably would have exceeded his figures, and since there are no statistics of any sort for twenty-one towns (which in the aggregate are known to have had some, though not many, Episcopalians), the figure of fifteen thousand Connecticut Churchmen on the eve of the Revolution seems reasonable.

34. Samuel Seabury to the S.P.G. Secretary, February 27, 1785 (draft), Samuel Seabury Papers.

35. [William White], *The Case of the Episcopal Churches in the United States Considered*, edited by Richard G. Salomon (n.p., 1954), pp. 8-9, 29-47.

36. See the appendix to the charge which White delivered to the clergy of his diocese in 1807, reprinted in *Ibid.*, pp. 70-72; White's statements in reference to *The Case of the Episcopal Churches* are conveniently brought together in Appendix II of this edition.

37. *Ibid.*, pp. 9-12.

38. Samuel Seabury to the S.P.G. Secretary, February 27, 1785 (draft), Samuel Seabury Papers. Presumably the news which triggered the clergy's measures was the report of the King's formal acknowledgment of independence at the opening of Parliament. This arrived in New Haven, February 20, 1783. Seabury wrote as though the receipt of the preliminary articles had provided the impetus, but it appears that the articles were not generally available in Connecticut until the very day the Convention assembled. Stiles, *Literary Diary*, III, 60, 63.

39. The parsonage still stands and is now preserved as a Seabury shrine. For an illustration, see Beardsley, *Samuel Seabury*, p. 77.

40. Daniel Fogg to Samuel Parker, July 2, 1783, Hawks and Perry, *Documentary History*, II, 212.

41. John Tyler to Samuel Peters, January 9, 1784, October 24, 1785, Samuel Peters Papers; John Tyler to the S.P.G. Secretary, July 1, 1785, Photostats, S.P.G. Connecticut (Part II) 1783-1852. Because of letters he wrote recounting the Woodbury proceedings (cited in other notes), Fogg has generally been considered a participant; but the language of the letters—the use of "they" instead of "we" in describing the actions of the clergy—argues otherwise.

42. Ebenezer Dibble to Samuel Peters, May 3, 1785, "Letters of the Reverend Doctor Ebenezer Dibble, of Stamford, to the Reverend Doctor Samuel Peters, Loyalist Refugee in London, 1784-1793," [edited by E. Clowes Chorley], *HMPEC*, I (June, 1932), p. 63.

43. Isaac Jones, *The Mandate of God, for Israel's Advancement: a Sermon, Delivered in Trinity Church, Milton, and St. Michael's, Litchfield*, Nov. 5, 1845 . . . (Litchfield, 1846), p. 26.

44. Abraham Jarvis, Secretary of the Connecticut Convention, to William White, March 25, 1783, William White, *Memoirs of the Protestant Episcopal*

Church in the United States of America, edited by B. F. DeCosta (New York, 1880), pp. 336-40.

45. White, *Memoirs of the Protestant Episcopal Church*, p. 84; Jacob Duché to William White, December 1, 1784, William White Papers, Church Historical Society.

46. Dexter, *Biographical Sketches of the Graduates of Yale*, II, 39-42.

47. Abraham Jarvis, Secretary of the Connecticut Convention, to Frederick Cornwallis, [William Markham, and Robert Lowth, *c.* March 25, 1783] (draft), [Samuel Farmar Jarvis], "Memoir of Bishop Jarvis," *Historiographer of the Episcopal Diocese of Connecticut*, No. 20, May, 1957, pp. 3-4; Samuel Seabury to the S.P.G. Secretary, February 27, 1785 (draft), Samuel Seabury Papers. The Woodbury gathering was, of course, unaware that Archbishop Cornwallis of Canterbury had died on March 19.

48. Thomas Bradbury Chandler to Samuel Seabury, February 4, 1779, Samuel Seabury Papers; Chandler, Memorandums, p. 68. Seabury, it seems, had been requested to do this service in order to quiet some tender consciences, for most Connecticut churches were conducting services on this plan even before he wrote Chandler. See John Tyler to the S.P.G. Secretary, January 9, 1781, Photostats, S.P.G. Connecticut (Part I) 1635-1782; Stiles, *Literary Diary*, II, 314-15.

49. In 1881-85 Eben Edwards Beardsley and Bishop William Stevens Perry of Iowa, at that time the leading historians of the Protestant Episcopal Church, engaged in a heated dispute as to whether Seabury or Leaming was the second choice of the Woodbury Convention. Beardsley, correctly interpreting the documents and supplementing them with unrivaled personal sources (his boyhood pastor and friend, Ashbel Baldwin, had been present at Woodbury; as a young minister, he frequently had discussed the Convention with Reuben Ives, formerly Seabury's curate at New London), maintained that Leaming was elected first. The dispute appears to have been occasioned by the account of the Woodbury proceedings in Beardsley's biography of Seabury, to which Perry replied with a note appended to Chapter XVI of "Early American Bishops," published in *The Living Church*, August 13, 1881. Beardsley produced a rejoinder, *Choice by the Clergy of the First Bishop of Connecticut* (n.p., 1882?), which the bishop countered with *The Election of the First Bishop of Connecticut, at Woodbury, on the Feast of the Annunciation, 1783, an Historical Review* (Davenport, 1883). Beardsley seems to have had the last word in *The Rev. Jeremiah Leaming, D.D. His Life and Services* (New York, 1885). Undertaking the role of peacemaker, Seabury's great-grandson, William Jones Seabury, came forward in 1883 with an ingenious theory, expounded in *The Election in Order to Consecration of the First Bishop of Connecticut* . . . (New York, 1884). According to the Reverend Dr. Seabury, it was probable that the Woodbury Convention *elected* only Seabury, but intended that Leaming—obviously unfit for the post—should have the courtesy of a refusal. The evidence, however, will not support this view.

50. Samuel Seabury to the S.P.G. Secretary, February 27, 1785 (draft), Samuel Seabury Papers.

51. *Ibid.* See also Abraham Jarvis, *A Discourse . . . Occasioned by the Death of the Right Reverend Samuel Seabury, D.D. Bishop of Connecticut and Rhode-Island* (New Haven, [1796]), pp. 18-19.

52. Such as the following: "During the arduous struggle, the Church in this country was passed over without notice; and we grieve to find that in the conclusion [the preliminary treaty] she was not thought worth regarding. In the severest season of the conflict, none of her faithful members conceived of this as possible; much less did they dream of it as probable." Abraham Jarvis, Secretary of the Connecticut Convention, to Frederick Cornwallis, [William Markham, and Robert Lowth, *c.* March 25, 1783] (draft), [Jarvis], "Memoir of Bishop Jarvis, *op. cit.*, p. 3.

53. Abraham Jarvis to John Moore, William Markham, and Robert Lowth, April 21, 1783 (copy), Samuel Seabury Papers.

54. Samuel Seabury, Sr., to the S.P.G. Secretary, May 5, 1733, S.P.G. Manuscript A 24, p. 320.

55. Samuel Seabury testimonial, April 21, 1783 (copies), Samuel Seabury Papers. Subsequent to this date, S.P.G. missionaries John Beardsley and Samuel Cooke added their signatures.

56. Charles Inglis *et al.* to John Moore, William Markham, and Robert Lowth, May 24, 1783 (copies), Samuel Seabury Papers and the Archives of the Protestant Episcopal Diocese of Connecticut.

57. Samuel Seabury testimonial, June 3, 1783, Samuel Seabury Papers.

58. John Wetherhead to the Loyalist Commissioners, [*c.* November 1, 1784], A.O. 13 (American Loyalists' Claims, Series II)/105, ff. 46-47.

59. Account with James Rivington, 1773-87, Samuel Seabury Papers.

60. Samuel Seabury to the Connecticut clergy, July 15, 1783, "Letters Relating to the Consecration," edited by E. Clowes Chorley, *HMPEC*, III (September, 1934), p. 158.

61. *Ibid.*

62. Charles Inglis *et al.* to John Moore, William Markham, and Robert Lowth, May 24, 1783 (copies), Samuel Seabury Papers and the Archives of the Protestant Episcopal Diocese of Connecticut.

63. Samuel Seabury to the Connecticut clergy, July 15, 1783, "Letters Relating to the Consecration," *op. cit.*, pp. 158-59.

64. Samuel Seabury to Abraham Jarvis, May 3, 1784, *Ibid.*, p. 170.

65. Samuel Seabury to the Connecticut clergy, July 15, 1783, *Ibid.*, p. 159.

66. Samuel Seabury to Myles Cooper, August 31, 1784, Episcopal Chest Papers, Episcopal Theological College, Edinburgh; Vance, "Myles Cooper," *op. cit.*, pp. 281-82.

67. Account Book of Samuel Seabury, Jr., 1783-84, American Antiquarian Society; John Wetherhead to the Loyalist Commissioners, [*c.* November 1, 1784], A.O. 13 (American Loyalists' Claims, Series II)/105, ff. 46-47.

68. Samuel Seabury to the Connecticut clergy, August 10, 1783, to Jeremiah Leaming, September 3, October 20, 1783, "Letters Relating to the Consecration," *op. cit.*, pp. 159-65.

69. *Ibid.*

70. *Ibid.*

71. *Ibid.*

72. Samuel Seabury to the English archibishops and bishops, [*c.* November, 1783] (draft), Samuel Seabury Papers.

73. Samuel Seabury to William Markham, November 24, 1783, Samuel Seabury Papers.

74. Walter Roland Foster, *Bishop and Presbytery: the Church of Scotland, 1661-1688* (London, 1958), *passim.*

75. General accounts of Scotland's Episcopal Church in this period may be found in Grub, *Ecclesiastical History of Scotland*, IV, and in Frederick Goldie, *A Short History of the Episcopal Church in Scotland from the Restoration to the Present Time* (London, 1951). See also the perceptive comments of G. Sutherland, "The Scottish Communion Office Historically Considered," *The Scottish Church Review*, II (February, 1885), pp. 122-23.

76. John Skinner to Jonathan Boucher, May 17, 1786, "Correspondence between the Right Reverend John Skinner, Jr., and the Reverend Jonathan Boucher, 1786," edited by E. Clowes Chorley, *HMPEC*, X (June, 1941), p. 169. Despite the large influx of English families into Scotland, the Scottish Episcopal Church remains a very small body; its membership, 147,000 in 1921, by 1950 had declined to 108,000, about four per cent of Scotland's population. Goldie, *Short History of the Episcopal Church in Scotland*, pp. 124, 147.

77. Henry Broxap, *The Later Non-Jurors* (Cambridge, England, 1924), pp. 260-76.

78. For extended biographical accounts, see the studies of William Walker: *The Life and Times of the Rev. John Skinner, M.A. of Linshart, Longside, Dean of Aberdeen . . .* (London, 1883); *The Life and Times of John Skinner, Bishop of Aberdeen . . .* (Aberdeen, 1887).

79. Broxap, *Later Non-Jurors*, pp. 278-83. See also John Skinner to Robert Kilgour, December 16, 1783, "Consecration of Bishop Seabury: Additional Correspondence of Scottish Bishops," edited by J. Nicholson, *The Scottish Church Review*, I (September, 1884), pp. 589-90; Robert Kilgour to Arthur Petrie, December 20, 1783, *Ibid.*, pp. 590-91; Arthur Petrie to Robert Kilgour, December 27, 1783, *Ibid.*, pp. 591-92.

80. Daniel Fogg to Samuel Parker, July 14, 1783 (copy), Samuel Seabury Papers. See also Samuel Parker to Daniel Fogg, July 17, 1783, *Historiographer of the Episcopal Diocese of Connecticut*, No. 8, June, 1954, p. [6].

81. John Dowden, "Who Was Mr. Elphinston?" *The Scottish Church Review*, II (February, 1885), pp. 103-17; Sabine, *Biographical Sketches of Loyalists*, I, 230-31.

82. James Elphinston to John Allan, November 6, 1783, and enclosed inquiry, also John Allan to Robert Kilgour, November 15, 1783, Episcopal Chest Papers.

83. George Berkeley to John Skinner, October 9, November 18, 1782, January 6, 1783, Episcopal Chest Papers. See also George Berkeley to William Legge, Earl of Dartmouth, October 1, 1782, Dartmouth Manuscripts No. 389.

84. John Skinner to George Berkeley, [*c.* November 15], December 21, 1782, February 22, 1783 (copies), George Berkeley to John Skinner, March 21, [1783], Episcopal Chest Papers. See also John Skinner to Arthur Petrie, October

29, November 23, 1782, January 16, 1783, Charles Rose to Arthur Petrie, December 23, 1782, Robert Kilgour to Arthur Petrie, February 19, 1783, Arthur Petrie Papers, Episcopal Theological College, Edinburgh.

85. John Skinner to George Berkeley, February 22, 1783 (copy), Episcopal Chest Papers.

86. John Allan to Robert Kilgour, December 3, 1783, "Consecration of Bishop Seabury: Additional Correspondence of Scottish Bishops," *op. cit.*, p. 589.

87. Robert Kilgour to Arthur Petrie, November 22, 1783, *Ibid.*, pp. 587-88; Arthur Petrie to Robert Kilgour, November 26, December 27, 1783, *Ibid.*, pp. 588, 591-92; William Falconar to Robert Kilgour, November 29, 1783, *Ibid.*, pp. 588-89; Charles Rose to Robert Kilgour, December 1, 1783, *Ibid.*, p. 589.

88. George Berkeley to John Skinner, November 24, December 10, 12, 1783, John Skinner to George Berkeley, November 29 (copy), December 8, 1783 (copy), Episcopal Chest Papers.

89. Robert Kilgour to John Allan, December 13, 1783, *Forty Years' Correspondence between Geniusses ov Boath Sexes, and James Elphinston,* edited by Elphinston (London, 1791), IV, 293-95.

90. Samuel Seabury to Abraham Jarvis, May 3, 1784, "Letters Relating to the Consecration," *op. cit.*, p. 169.

91. Bela Hubbard to Samuel Peters, January 21, 1784, Samuel Peters Papers; Jeremiah Leaming, Abraham Jarvis, Bela Hubbard to Samuel Seabury, February 5, 1784, Episcopal Chest Papers.

92. "An Act for securing the Rights of Conscience in Matters of Religion to Christians of every Denomination in this State" (attested copy), Samuel Seabury Papers.

93. Jeremiah Leaming, Abraham Jarvis, Bela Hubbard to Samuel Seabury, February 5, 1784, Episcopal Chest Papers. See also Jeremiah Leaming to Samuel Seabury, January 21, 1784, Samuel Seabury Papers; Samuel Andrews to the S.P.G. Secretary, February 10, 1784, Photostats, S.P.G. Connecticut (Part II) 1783-1852; Bela Hubbard to the S.P.G. Secretary, March 17, 1784, abstracted in S.P.G. Manuscript Journals, XXIII, 354-55.

94. Jeremiah Leaming, Abraham Jarvis, Bela Hubbard to Samuel Seabury, February 5, 1784, Episcopal Chest Papers.

95. Samuel Seabury to Jeremiah Leaming, Abraham Jarvis, Bela Hubbard, April 30, 1784, to Abraham Jarvis, May 3, 1784, "Letters Relating to the Consecration," *op. cit.*, pp. 168-70.

96. *Ibid.*

97. Samuel Seabury to Abraham Jarvis, May 3, 1784, "Letters Relating to the Consecration," *op. cit.*, p. 171.

98. Samuel Seabury to Abraham Jarvis, May 24, 1784, *Ibid.*, 171-72.

99. Samuel Seabury to Abraham Jarvis, June 26, 1784, *Ibid.*, p. 173.

100. *Ibid.*; Samuel Seabury to Jeremiah Leaming, Abraham Jarvis, Bela Hubbard, July 26, 1784, to Abraham Jarvis, September 7, 1784, "Letters Relating to the Consecration," *op. cit.*, pp. 174-76; Samuel Seabury to the S.P.G. Secretary, February 27, 1785 (draft), Samuel Seabury Papers.

101. "Objections made to the Connecticut Episcopacy, by the B----- Ministry, as represented to Dr. S----- by his G---- of C---- the beginning of Augt. 1784," Samuel Seabury Papers. See also Thomas Bradbury Chandler to Abraham Beach, September 22, 1784, "Bishop Williams' Scrapbook of Old Letters," *Historiographer of the Episcopal Diocese of Connecticut*, No. 10, December, 1954, p. 6.

102. Samuel Seabury to Abraham Jarvis, September 7, 1784, "Letters Relating to the Consecration," *op. cit.*, pp. 175-79.

103. *Ibid.* See also Bela Hubbard to Samuel Peters, January 29, 1785, Samuel Peters Papers.

104. Clara O. Loveland, *The Critical Years: the Reconstitution of the Anglican Church in the United States of America: 1780-1789* (Greenwich, 1956), pp. 159-60, 173-74, 176-77, 214; White, *Memoirs of the Protestant Episcopal Church*, pp. 21-22, 113-14, also the documents printed as Appendix No. 17, pp. 386-92.

105. Samuel Seabury to Abraham Jarvis, May 24, June 26, September 7, 1784, "Letters Relating to the Consecration," *op. cit.*, pp. 172, 174, 178.

106. Richard Mansfield to Samuel Peters, May 26, 1785, Samuel Seabury Papers.

107. Abraham Jarvis, Secretary of the Connecticut Convention, to the S.P.G. Secretary, May 6, 1783, Photostats, S.P.G. Connecticut (Part II), 1783-1852.

108. See, for example, John Tyler to Samuel Peters, January 9, 1784, Bela Hubbard to Samuel Peters, November 25, 1784, Samuel Peters Papers.

109. George Berkeley to John Skinner, March 21, [1783], Episcopal Chest Papers.

110. Samuel Seabury to Abraham Jarvis, September 7, 1784, "Letters Relating to the Consecration," *op. cit.*, p. 178.

111. Samuel Seabury to Myles Cooper, August 31, 1784, Episcopal Chest Papers.

112. Myles Cooper to Robert Kilgour, September 13, 1784, Episcopal Chest Papers; John Allan to Arthur Petrie, September 14, 1784, Arthur Petrie Papers.

113. Robert Kilgour to Arthur Petrie, September 22, 1784, Arthur Petrie Papers.

114. Robert Kilgour to John Allan, October 2, 1784, Ecclesiastical Letter Book, Samuel Seabury Papers.

115. Samuel Seabury to Robert Kilgour, October 14, 1784, Episcopal Chest Papers.

116. Samuel Seabury to the S.P.G. Secretary, February 27, 1785 (draft), Samuel Seabury Papers.

117. *Ibid.*; examination of Samuel Seabury's claim, September 28, 1784, American Loyalists: Transcript of Various Papers, VII, 84-87.

118. See *supra*, p. 51.

119. Charles Rose to Robert Kilgour, October 5, 1784 (copy), to Arthur Petrie, October 26, 1784, Robert Kilgour to Arthur Petrie, October 13, 1784, John Skinner to Arthur Petrie, October 18, 1784, Arthur Petrie Papers.

120. William Seller to Robert Kilgour, November 6, 1784, Episcopal Chest Papers, quoting [Alexander Murray] to William Seller, October 28, 1784.

121. Samuel Seabury to Jonathan Boucher, December 3, 1784, Ecclesiastical Letter Book, Samuel Seabury Papers; Samuel Seabury to Jeremiah Leaming, Abraham Jarvis, Bela Hubbard, January 5, 1785, "Letters Relating to the Consecration," *op. cit.*, p. 189.

122. Samuel Seabury to George Horne, January 8, 1785 (draft), Samuel Seabury Papers.

123. John Skinner to Robert Kilgour, November 8, 1784, Episcopal Chest Papers.

124. Annotation on the reverse of Samuel Seabury to Myles Cooper, August 31, 1784, believed to be in the handwriting of John Skinner of Linshart, Episcopal Chest Papers; Arthur Petrie to Alexander Jolly, October 23, 1784, "Consecration of Bishop Seabury: Additional Correspondence of Scottish Bishops," *op. cit.*, p. 594.

125. John Allan to Arthur Petrie, November 9, 1784, Arthur Petrie Papers.

126. Samuel Seabury to Abraham Jarvis, September 7, 1784, "Letters Relating to the Consecration," *op. cit.*, p. 178.

127. Samuel Seabury to Jeremiah Leaming, Abraham Jarvis, and Bela Hubbard, January 5, 1785, *Ibid.*, p. 188; Jeremiah Leaming, Abraham Jarvis, and Bela Hubbard to Samuel Seabury, Abraham Jarvis to Samuel Seabury, [both *c.* August, 1784], abstracted in "Minute Book of the College of Bishops in Scotland," quoted in "Intercommunion of the American and Scottish Churches," *The Scottish Ecclesiastical Journal*, I (October 16, 1851), p. 215.

128. John Skinner to Arthur Petrie, November 8, 1784, Arthur Petrie Papers.

129. Robert Kilgour to John Skinner, November 6, 1784, Episcopal Chest Papers.

130. Myles Cooper to Samuel Peters, December 6, 1784, "Letters from the Reverend Dr. Myles Cooper, Formerly President of King's College, New York, Written from Edinburgh to Rev. Dr. Samuel Peters, of London," [edited by E. Clowes Chorley], *HMPEC*, II (March, 1933), p. 45; Samuel Seabury to John Skinner, December 27, 1784, Episcopal Chest Papers.

131. See *supra*, p. 88.

132. Loveland, *The Critical Years*, pp. 29-32.

133. For Seabury's observations on this point, see his letter to the English archbishops and bishops, [*c.* November, 1783] (draft), Samuel Seabury Papers.

134. Samuel Seabury to the S.P.G. Secretary, December 29, 1776, S.P.G. Manuscript B 2, pp. 656-57; Thomas Bradbury Chandler to Samuel Seabury, March 5, 1777, Samuel Seabury Papers.

135. William Seller to Robert Kilgour, November 6, 1784, Episcopal Chest Papers, quoting [Alexander Murray] to William Seller, October 28, 1784.

136. *Ibid.*

137. John Skinner to Robert Kilgour, November 8, 1784, Episcopal Chest Papers.

138. *Ibid.*; Robert Kilgour to Arthur Petrie, October 27, 1784, John Skinner to Arthur Petrie, November 8, 1784, Arthur Petrie Papers; "Minute Book of the College of Bishops in Scotland," *op. cit.*, p. 215.

139. Skinner, *Annals of Scottish Episcopacy*, pp. 16-17; *Seabury Centenary Handbook: a Comprehensive Sketch of the Facts Relating to, and the Results of, the Consecration of Dr. Seabury As the First Bishop of the American Church* (Edinburgh, 1884), *passim.* An old view of Skinner's house is reproduced in *Historiographer of the Episcopal Diocese of Connecticut*, No. 8, June, 1954, p. [5].

140. "Minute Book of the College of Bishops in Scotland," *op. cit.*, p. 215; Alexander Jolly to Robert Kilgour, November 2, 1784, "Consecration of Bishop Seabury: Additional Correspondence of Scottish Bishops," *op. cit.*, p. 595. See also Andrew Macfarlane to Arthur Petrie, September 24, October 2, November 4, December 9, 1784, Arthur Petrie Papers.

141. [John Skinner], *The Nature and Extent of the Apostolical Commission, a Sermon Preached at the Consecration of the Right Reverend Dr Samuel Seabury, Bishop of the Episcopal Church in Connecticut* (Aberdeen, 1785), in *HMPEC*, III (September, 1934), pp. [193]-209. A London reprint appeared in the same year as the original edition.

142. "A Dignified Clergyman of the Church of England" to Robert Kilgour, June 9, 1785, Skinner, *Annals of Scottish Episcopacy*, pp. 60-64.

143. This periodical briefly noticed Seabury's consecration in its February, 1785, issue; a communication correcting several errors in the account, dated March 16 and probably written by Chandler, was printed in April. In the same issue, "L.L.," apparently a Scots Presbyterian clergyman, attacked Seabury and the Scottish Bishops. "An Episcopal Clergyman of the Scotch Church," George Gleig, replied in June, and the controversy thus joined continued for over a year. *The Gentleman's Magazine*, LV (February-November, 1785), pp. 105, 248, 278-80, 437-40, 691-92, 770-71, 776-79, 787-89, 878-79; *Ibid.*, LVI (April-September, 1786), pp. 286-88, 566-67, 633-35, 768; William Walker, *Life of the Right Reverend George Gleig, LL.D., F.S.S.A., Bishop of Brechin, and Primus of the Scottish Episcopal Church* (Edinburgh, 1878), pp. 191-95.

144. John Skinner to Jonathan Boucher, June 25, 1785, "The Seabury Consecration: Additional Letters," edited by E. Clowes Chorley, *HMPEC*, III (December, 1934), p. 254.

145. Goldie, *Short History of the Episcopal Church in Scotland*, pp. 78-79, 85, 99.

146. Alexander Jolly to James Kemp, November 27, 1826, *Fac-Similes of Church Documents: Papers Issued by the Historical Club of the American Church, 1874-1879* (n.p., 1879), pp. [29-31].

147. Beardsley, *Samuel Seabury*, pp. 156-57, based upon a letter from George Grub, November 20, 1879. Grub's father attended the service and often described Seabury's pulpit appearance to him.

148. Concordat between the Episcopal Church of Scotland and the Episcopal Church of Connecticut, November 15, 1784, signed by Robert Kilgour, Arthur Petrie, John Skinner, Samuel Seabury, Samuel Seabury Papers. Conveniently reprinted in Hawks and Perry, *Documentary History*, II, 249-51.

149. Robert Kilgour to Arthur Petrie, February 11, 1784, Arthur Petrie Papers.

150. Robert Kilgour to Arthur Petrie, September 22, October 13, 18, 27, 1784, John Skinner to Arthur Petrie, October 1, 18, November 8, 1784, Alexander Jolly to Arthur Petrie, October 23, 1784, Arthur Petrie Papers; Robert Kilgour to John Skinner, October 2, 1784, Episcopal Chest Papers; Robert Kilgour to John Allan, October 2, 1784, Ecclesiastical Letter Book, Samuel Seabury Papers; Arthur Petrie to Alexander Jolly, October 4, 23, 1784, "Consecration of Bishop Seabury: Additional Correspondence of Scottish Bishops," *op. cit.*, pp. 592-94.

151. "A Proposal for a Concordate betwixt the orthodox and catholick remnant of the British Churches, and the Catholick and Apostolical Oriental Church," dated London, August 18, 1716, in George Williams, *The Orthodox Church of the East in the Eighteenth Century, Being the Correspondence between the Eastern Patriarchs and the Nonjuring Bishops with an Introduction on Various Projects of Reunion between the Eastern Church and the Anglican Communion* (London, 1868), pp. 4-11. The seventh of twelve numbered proposals which form the first part of this document reads: "That in order still to a nearer Union, there be as near a conformity in Worship establish'd, as is consistent with the different circumstances and customs of nations, and with the rights of particular Churches, in that case allow'd of." This proposal found a place in the Connecticut concordat as the opening section of article IV: "With a vew to the salutary purpose mentioned in the preceding Article [intercommunion of the churches of Scotland and Connecticut], they agree in desiring that there may be as near a Conformity in Worship, and Discipline established between the two Churches, as is consistent with the different Circumstances and Customs of Nations. . . ." Similarly, the eighth of twelve numbered points comprising the second section emerged, after considerable paraphrasing, as article II of the Connecticut agreement.

152. John Skinner to Arthur Petrie, October 18, 1784, Arthur Petrie Papers.

153. See *supra*, pp. 362-63.

154. Skinner, *Annals of Scottish Episcopacy*, p. 32, quoting a eulogy of Bishop Skinner delivered July 21, 1816, by an unidentified clergyman. See also the mass of documents in *Ibid.*, pp. 73-232; William Jones, *Memoirs of the Life, Studies, and Writings of the Right Reverend George Horne, D.D., Late Lord Bishop of Norwich* (London, 1799), pp. 148-54; [James Allan Park], *Memoirs of William Stevens, Esq.* (London, 1814), pp. 132-47; *The Theological and Miscellaneous Works of the Late Rev. William Jones, M.A., Minister of Nayland, Suffolk, to Which Is Prefixed, a Short Account of His Life and Writings*, edited by William Stevens (London, 1826), I, xxviii-xxix; Broxap, *Later Non-Jurors*, pp. 282-83; Walker, *Life of the Right Reverend George Gleig*, pp. 200-204; "Correspondence between the Right Reverend John Skinner, Jr., and the Reverend Jonathan Boucher, 1786," *op. cit., passim.*

155. Robert Kilgour, Arthur Petrie, John Skinner "To the Episcopal Clergy in Connecticut in North America," facsimile in *Historiographer of the Episcopal Diocese of Connecticut*, No. 4, May, 1953, p. [4], from the original in the Archives of the Protestant Episcopal Diocese of Connecticut. The archives also has

one of the attested copies of the Scots succession; the other copy, as well as the certificate of consecration and the concordat, are in the Samuel Seabury Papers.

156. John Skinner to George Berkeley, November 18, 1784 (copy), Samuel Seabury to John Skinner, December 3, 1784, Episcopal Chest Papers; Samuel Seabury to Samuel Peters, November 24, 1784, Archives of the Protestant Episcopal Diocese of Connecticut.

157. Myles Cooper to Samuel Peters, December 6, 1784, "Letters from the Reverend Dr. Myles Cooper, Formerly President of King's College, New York, Written from Edinburgh to Rev. Dr. Samuel Peters, of London," *op. cit.*, p. 45; John Skinner to Arthur Petrie, December 13, 1784, Arthur Petrie Papers; John Allan to Samuel Seabury, January 17, 1785, Alexander Allan to Samuel Seabury, January 18, 1785, Samuel Seabury Papers.

158. Arthur Petrie to Thomas Bowdler, July 19, 1785, "Consecration of Bishop Seabury: Additional Correspondence of Scottish Bishops," *op. cit.*, pp. 597-98. Intentionally or no, Seabury followed the policy of Bishop Skinner with regard to the Nonjurors. According to the pastor of the London congregation, upon his return from Aberdeen, he "did not communicate with our small Remnant which might be too insignificant to attract the notice of such a sublime Genius: But makes his court to the Publick Church." John Mansfield to Arthur Petrie, April 7, 1786, Arthur Petrie Papers.

159. William Abernethy Drummond to Samuel Seabury, January 3, 1785, Samuel Seabury Papers; Charles Rose to Arthur Petrie, February 26, 1785, Arthur Petrie Papers.

160. Samuel Seabury to John Skinner, December 27, 1784, Episcopal Chest Papers; Samuel Seabury to Jeremiah Leaming, Abraham Jarvis, Bela Hubbard, January 5, 1785, "Letters Relating to the Consecration," *op. cit.*, pp. 186, 189; George Horne to Samuel Seabury, January 3, 1785, Samuel Seabury Papers.

161. Samuel Seabury to George Berkeley, December 24, 1784 (draft), Samuel Seabury Papers.

162. Samuel Seabury to John Skinner, "February" [March] 11, 1785, Episcopal Chest Papers. See also Samuel Seabury to Sylvester Gardiner, March 15, 1785 (copy), Samuel Seabury Papers.

163. Samuel Seabury to Jonathan Boucher, December 3, 1784, Ecclesiastical Letter Book, Samuel Seabury Papers.

164. Samuel Seabury to George Berkeley, December 24, 1784 (draft), to George Horne, December 24, 1784, January 8, 1785 (drafts), Samuel Seabury Papers.

165. Samuel Seabury to George Berkeley, December 24, 1784 (draft), Samuel Seabury Papers.

166. Samuel Seabury to John Skinner, December 27, 1784, Episcopal Chest Papers.

167. Samuel Seabury's receipt for S.P.G. salary, January 12, 1785, Photostats, S.P.G. Connecticut (Part II) 1783-1852.

168. Samuel Seabury to the S.P.G. Secretary, February 27, 1785, Ecclesiastical Letter Book, Samuel Seabury Papers.

169. John Wetherhead to the Loyalist Commissioners, [*c.* November 1,

1784], A.O. 13 (American Loyalists' Claims, Series II)/105, ff. 46-47; Samuel Seabury to John Skinner, December 27, 1784, "February" [March] 11, December 23, 1785, Episcopal Chest Papers; Reginald V. Harris *et al.*, *Charles Inglis: Missionary, Loyalist, Bishop* (Toronto, 1937), p. 69.

170. Samuel Seabury to Sylvester Gardiner, March 19, 1785 (copy), Samuel Seabury Papers; Samuel Peters to John Tyler, April 4, 1785 (copy), Woodbury Glebe House Papers, Connecticut State Library; Thomas Bradbury Chandler to John Skinner, April 23, 1785, Skinner, *Annals of Scottish Episcopacy*, p. 47.

171. Jacob Bailey to Samuel Peters, April 29, 1785, Bartlet, *Frontier Missionary*, p. 204; Harris *et al.*, *Charles Inglis*, pp. 68-69; *Gospel Messenger, and Church Record of the Diocese of Western New York*, December 21, 1849, quoting John Bours's diary entry, June 20, 1785; New London *Connecticut Gazette*, June 24, July 1, 1785; account with James Rivington, 1773-87, Samuel Seabury Papers.

172. Samuel Seabury to John Rivington, July 25, 1785, Ecclesiastical Letter Book, Samuel Seabury Papers.

173. Samuel Seabury to Abraham Jarvis, June 29, 1785, "Original Documents," *The Churchman's Monthly Magazine*, III (April-August, 1806), p. 278.

174. Samuel Peters to John Tyler, April 4, 1785 (copy), Woodbury Glebe House Papers; John Skinner to Jonathan Boucher, May 17, 1786, "Correspondence between the Right Reverend John Skinner, Jr., and the Reverend Jonathan Boucher, 1786," *op. cit.*, p. 168.

175. Thomas Bradbury Chandler to Samuel Seabury, July 28, 1785, Samuel Seabury Papers.

176. William Morice, S.P.G. Secretary, to Samuel Seabury, April 29, 1785, Samuel Seabury Papers.

177. Samuel Seabury to John Skinner, December 23, 1785, Episcopal Chest Papers.

178. The account of Seabury's reception as Bishop of Connecticut is drawn from the "Minutes of Conventions of the Clergy of Connecticut for the Years 1766, 1784, and 1785," [edited by E. Clowes Chorley], *HMPEC*, III (March, 1934), pp. 59-62. Besides Leaming and Jarvis, the clergy present included Richard Mansfield, Bela Hubbard, Gideon Bostwick, Samuel Andrews, Richard S. Clarke, James Scovil, John Tyler, and John Bowden, formerly an assistant at Trinity Church, New York, who had taken charge of Leaming's old congregation at Norwalk. In view of Tyler's attendance, he can hardly be acquitted of duplicity when, several months later, in requesting Samuel Peters to urge the continuance of his S.P.G. stipend, he stated that he had not received Seabury as his bishop. See John Tyler to Samuel Peters, October 24, 1785, Samuel Peters Papers.

179. "Address proposed" (so annotated) of the Connecticut clergy, August 3, 1785, Samuel Seabury Papers.

180. Address of the Connecticut clergy, August 3, 1785, "Minutes of Conventions of the Clergy of Connecticut for the years 1766, 1784, and 1785," *op. cit.*, pp. 62-64.

181. The phrases within brackets were omitted from the text as delivered:

"The surprize you express at the rejection of your application in England is natural. But where the ecclesiastical & civil constitution are so closely, [& in some respects at least, unhappily] woven together, the first characters in the Church for station & merit may find their good dispositions rendered ineffectual by the [party politics of an unthinking minister, who possibly regards religion no further than as he can make it subservient to his own schemes.] intervention of the civil authority. And whether it is better to submit quietly to this state of affairs in England, or to risk that confusion which, [in such a government as theirs,] would probably ensue, should an amendment be attempted, demands some consideration." Reply to the address of the Connecticut clergy, [August 3, 1785] (draft), Samuel Seabury Papers.

182. Reply to the address of the Connecticut clergy, August 3, 1785, "Minutes of Conventions of the Clergy of Connecticut for the Years 1766, 1784, and 1785," *op. cit.*, p. 64.

CHAPTER VII

"UPON TRUE EPISCOPAL PRINCIPLES"

1. For biographical sketches, see Burr, *Anglican Church in New Jersey*, pp. 583-85; Dexter, *Biographical Sketches of the Graduates of Yale*, II, 446-49.

2. Abraham Beach to William White, January 26, March 22, April 13, 1784, *Journals of General Conventions of the Protestant Episcopal Church in the United States, 1785-1835*, edited by William Stevens Perry (Claremont, 1874), III, 8-11; Abraham Beach to Benjamin Moore, February 27, 1784, Benjamin Moore Papers, General Theological Seminary; Samuel Provoost to Abraham Beach, March 24, April 7, 1784, "Bishop Williams' Scrapbook of Old Letters," *op. cit.*, pp. 4, 5-6; Robert Blackwell to Abraham Beach, April, 1784, *Ibid.*, p. 4.

3. Benjamin Moore to Abraham Beach, March, 1784, *Ibid.*, p. 3.

4. White, *Memoirs of the Protestant Episcopal Church*, pp. 99-102.

5. Abraham Jarvis to Abraham Beach, May, 1784, "Bishop Williams' Scrapbook of Old Letters," *op. cit.*, pp. 4-5.

6. Minutes of the New Brunswick conference, May 11, [12], 1784, Perry, *Journals of General Conventions*, III, 7-8. The minutes imply that all the deliberations took place on May 11; it is clear, however, from White's *Memoirs* that the meeting lasted two days.

7. White, *Memoirs of the Protestant Episcopal Church*, p. 85. White mentions "the more northern clergymen"; in view of the composition of the meeting, this must refer to the four New York Loyalists present: Benjamin Moore, Thomas Moore, Joshua Bloomer, John Bowden.

8. See the minutes of a meeting of the incumbent clergy and lay members delegated by the vestries of the United Churches of Christ Church and St. Peter's and of St. Paul's Church, Philadelphia, March 29, 31, 1784, Perry, *Journals of General Conventions*, III, 35-36; White, *Memoirs of the Protestant Episcopal Church*, pp. 92-94.

9. *Ibid.*, pp. 84-85. White's sentences give the impression that the name of

Connecticut's candidate was revealed to him at New Brunswick. But see Jacob Duché to William White, December 1, 1784, William White Papers.

10. Minutes of the New Brunswick conference, May 11, [12], 1784, Perry, *Journals of General Conventions*, III, 7-8; White, *Memoirs of the Protestant Episcopal Church*, pp. 84-85.

11. Minutes of the Connecticut Convention, New Milford, June 8-10, 1784, Howard Chandler Robbins Collection of Episcopal Bishops' Papers, General Theological Seminary.

12. Abraham Beach to William White, June 19, 1784, William White Papers.

13. Minutes of the Connecticut Convention, New Haven, September 8, 1784, Howard Chandler Robbins Collection of Episcopal Bishops' Papers. See also Daniel Fogg to Samuel Parker, September 28, 1784, Perry, *Journals of General Conventions*, III, 215-16.

14. Abraham Jarvis, Secretary of the Connecticut Convention, to the New York conference, September 9, 1784, Howard Chandler Robbins Collection of Episcopal Bishops' Papers. See also John Tyler to Samuel Peters, December 2, 1784, Samuel Peters Papers.

15. For biographical details, see "Memoir of Rt. Rev. Samuel Parker, D.D., Second Bishop of Massachusetts," *The Evergreen*, II (May, 1845), pp. 131-34; Sprague, *Annals of the American Pulpit*, V, 296-98.

16. Loveland, *The Critical Years*, pp. 9-10, mistakenly depicts Parker as an exponent of "central Anglicanism," holding the mean between Seabury and White. His letters, many of which are cited in this chapter, clearly reveal his High Church position.

17. William White to Samuel Parker, [June ?, 1784], Perry, *Journals of General Conventions*, III, 59-60; Samuel Parker to William White, June 21, 1784, William White Papers; William White to Samuel Parker, August 10, 1784, J. P. Morgan Collection of Episcopal Bishops' Papers, Pierpont Morgan Library.

18. Minutes of the Boston Convention, September 8, 1784, Perry, *Journals of General Conventions*, III, 63-65; Samuel Parker to William White, September 10, 1784, *Ibid.*, III, 62-63. For the guidelines, see the minutes of the Pennsylvania Convention, Philadelphia, May 24, 25, 1784, *Ibid.*, III, 37-39.

19. John Graves, Moderator of the Boston Convention, to the standing committee of the Pennsylvania Convention, September 8, 1784, *Ibid.*, III, 65-66. The same letter, with necessary verbal alterations, was forwarded to the Connecticut Convention and is quoted in Jarvis, "Memoir of Bishop Jarvis," *op. cit.*, p. 6.

20. Minutes of the New York conference, October 6, 7, 1784, Howard Chandler Robbins Collection of Episcopal Bishops' Papers. That the letter from the clergy of Massachusetts referred to in these minutes was their letter of September 8 seems certain; according to the Boston Convention minutes, the letter was to be forwarded to the "Episcopal Clergy in the States of Connecticut, New York & Pennsylvania." White in his *Memoirs* does not mention the Massachusetts letter, thus creating the impression (bolstered by other remarks in that volume) that Connecticut was more isolated in her position than was, indeed, the case. See White, *Memoirs of the Protestant Episcopal Church*, pp. 86-90.

21. Daniel Fogg to Samuel Parker, September 28, 1784, Perry, *Journals of General Conventions*, III, 215-16; Samuel Parker to Daniel Fogg, November 18, 1784, J. P. Morgan Collection of Episcopal Bishops' Papers.

22. William White to [Samuel Parker, June, 1785], J. P. Morgan Collection of Episcopal Bishops' Papers; Samuel Parker to William White, September 14, 1785, William White Papers; *At a Convention of Clergymen and Lay Deputies, of the Protestant Episcopal Church in the United States of America, Held in New-York, October 6th and 7th, 1784* . . . [n.p., 1784] (broadside).

23. Samuel Seabury to John Skinner, December 27, 1784, "February" [March] 11, 1785, Episcopal Chest Papers.

24. John Skinner to Samuel Seabury, January 29, 1785, Ecclesiastical Letter Book, Samuel Seabury Papers; Andrew Macfarlane to Samuel Seabury, February 5, 1785, Samuel Seabury Papers.

25. James Rivington to Samuel Seabury, July 25, 1785, Samuel Seabury Papers.

26. Jeremiah Leaming to William White, July 14, 1785, William White Papers.

27. Jeremiah Leaming to Abraham Beach, July [14?], 1785, "Bishop Williams' Scrapbook of Old Letters," *op. cit.*, p. 7.

28. Samuel Parker's authorization as a proctor of the Boston Convention, July 28, 1785, J. P. Morgan Collection of Episcopal Bishops' Papers.

29. White, *Memoirs of the Protestant Episcopal Church*, pp. 111-12. See also Thomas Bradbury Chandler to Samuel Seabury, July 28, 1785, Samuel Seabury Papers.

30. William White, Samuel Magaw, John Andrews to Samuel Seabury, July 22, 1785, Samuel Seabury Papers.

31. William White to Samuel Parker, [June?, 1784], Perry, *Journals of General Conventions*, III, 60; William White to [Samuel Parker, June, 1785], J. P. Morgan Collection of Episcopal Bishops' Papers.

32. Jacob Duché to William White, December 1, 1784, February 10, 1785, William White Papers. Duché saw a good deal of Seabury while the latter was in England. His son, Thomas S. Duché, painted in the winter of 1784-85 a three-quarter-length likeness of the bishop reproduced in this study. The portrait was immediately engraved, the painter forwarding fifty impressions to Seabury in the summer of 1786. Variously altered, this engraving appeared in many nineteenth-century publications. One of the originals is in the J. P. Morgan Collection of Episcopal Bishops' Papers. See Thomas S. Duché to Samuel Seabury, August 30, 1786, Samuel Seabury Papers.

33. William White to [Samuel Parker, June, 1785], J. P. Morgan Collection of Episcopal Bishops' Papers.

34. Samuel Parker to William White, September 14, 1785, William White Papers.

35. Samuel Seabury to John Skinner, December 23, 1785, Episcopal Chest Papers.

36. Samuel Seabury to William White, Samuel Magaw, John Andrews, Au-

gust 8, 1785, Episcopal Church Papers, William L. Clements Library; Samuel Seabury to William White, August 19, 1785, William White Papers.

37. Samuel Seabury to William Smith, August 15, 1785, William White Papers.

38. Smith's letter is not among the Samuel Seabury Papers, but its contents are recounted in Samuel Seabury to [Jonathan Boucher], December 14, 1785 (copy), Hawks Papers; Samuel Seabury to John Skinner, December 23, 1785, Episcopal Chest Papers; Jonathan Boucher to John Skinner, December 6, 1785, *Annals of Scottish Episcopacy*, pp. 53-54.

39. *An Address to the Members of the Protestant Episcopal Church of Maryland, Containing, an Account of the Proceedings of Some Late Conventions Both of Clergy and Laity, for the Purpose of Organizing the Said Church, and Providing a Succession in Her Ministry Agreeable to the Principles of the American Revolution . . .* (Baltimore, 1784); reprinted, except for the appended sermon by William Smith, in Perry, *Journals of General Conventions*, III, 14-33.

40. Thomas Bradbury Chandler to William White, September 6, 26, 1785, William White Papers. William Samuel Johnson, now a congressman from Connecticut, had supplied Chandler with a copy of the *Journal of the Convention of the Clergy and Laity of the Protestant Episcopal Church, of Virginia, Begun and Holden in the City of Richmond, Wednesday May 18, 1785* (Richmond, 1785). See Thomas Bradbury Chandler to William Samuel Johnson, December 28, 1785, Beardsley, *Samuel Johnson*, pp. 369-70.

41. This expression is used by Loveland in *The Critical Years*, the contrasting proposals of Seabury and Chandler being labeled the "ecclesiastical plan." The present writer considers the latter term unfortunate, since it implies that their views received support only from the clergy.

42. White, *The Case of the Episcopal Churches*, pp. 22-23. For his later comments on the subject, see White, *Memoirs of the Protestant Episcopal Church*, pp. 94-99.

43. *An Address to the Members of the Protestant Episcopal Church of Maryland*, Perry, *Journals of General Conventions*, III, 30; canon No. 11 adopted by the Virginia Convention, May, 1785, quoted in *Ibid.*, III, 50. To these three rights and powers Virginia added that of superintending the conduct of the clergy.

44. Jeremiah Leaming, *A Sermon, Preached before the Convention of the Clergy, of the Episcopal Church in Connecticut; at Middletown, August 3d, 1785 . . .*, in *The Address of the Episcopal Clergy of Connecticut, to the Right Reverend Bishop Seabury, with the Bishop's Answer, and, a Sermon . . . Also, Bishop Seabury's First Charge . . . with a List of the Succession of Scot's Bishops, from the Revolution in 1688, to the Present Time* (New Haven, [1785]), p. 15 of the separately paged *Sermon.*

45. Samuel Seabury to William White, January 8, 1786, William White Papers; William White to Samuel Seabury, February 1, 1786, Samuel Seabury Papers; Samuel Seabury to William White, June "20," [29], 1789, Perry, *Journals of General Conventions*, III, 384-86; White, *Memoirs of the Protestant Episcopal Church*, pp. 91-92.

46. *Ibid.*, pp. 112-13.

47. The General Convention's journal is reprinted in Perry, *Journals of General Conventions*, I, 14-29.

48. The phrase "Protestant Episcopal" was disliked in Connecticut, not for the reasons which influence present-day Anglo-Catholics, but because a "Protestant" church, to an eighteenth-century Connecticut Churchman, meant a body originally organized in opposition to the civil authority. See Jeremiah Leaming to Abraham Beach, September, 1786, "Bishop Williams' Scrapbook of Old Letters," *op. cit.*, p. 9.

49. Among the lay deputies were such Revolutionary figures as James Duane of New York, John Page of Virginia, and Charles Pinckney of South Carolina.

50. Abraham Beach to the S.P.G. Secretary, October 30, 1783, February 8, 1785, "Additional Letters of the Reverend Abraham Beach: 1772-1791," edited by Walter Herbert Stowe, *HMPEC*, V (June, 1936), pp. 134, 138-39; Samuel Parker to William White, June 21, 1784, William White Papers; William White to Samuel Parker, August 10, 1784, J. P. Morgan Collection of Episcopal Bishops' Papers.

51. Samuel Parker to Daniel Fogg, July 17, 1783, *Historiographer of the Episcopal Diocese of Connecticut*, No. 8, June, 1954, p. [6].

52. The Connecticut Convention became the diocesan Convocation once Seabury had been accepted as bishop.

53. Minutes of the Connecticut Convention, Middletown, August 2-5, 1785, "Minutes of the Conventions of the Clergy of Connecticut for the Years 1766, 1784, and 1785," *op. cit.*, p. 61.

54. *SAMUEL, by Divine Permission, Bishop of the Episcopal Church in the State of Connecticut, to the Clergy of the Said Church, GREETING . . . Aug. 12th, 1785* [n.p., 1785] (broadside).

55. January 30 (Martyrdom of Charles I), May 29 (Restoration of Charles II), October 25 (Accession of George III), November 5 (Gunpowder Plot).

56. Thomas Bradbury Chandler to Samuel Seabury, July 28, 1785, Samuel Seabury Papers.

57. Samuel Seabury to Matthew Griswold, September 2, 1785, Gratz Collection, Historical Society of Pennsylvania. See also Samuel Seabury to William Smith, August 15, 1785, William White Papers.

58. William Stevens Perry, *Bishop Seabury and the "Episcopal Recorder;" a Vindication* (n.p., 1863), p. 37.

59. Jeremiah Leaming to Samuel Seabury, December 1, 1785 (copy), Samuel Seabury Papers.

60. Samuel Seabury to Samuel Huntington, October 14, 1786, Ely Collection of Episcopal Bishops' Papers, Yale University; Samuel Huntington to Samuel Seabury, November 4, 1786, Samuel Seabury Papers. The forms are printed in Beardsley, *Samuel Seabury*, p. 265.

61. Samuel Parker to Samuel Seabury, January 28, 1788 (draft), J. P. Morgan Collection of Episcopal Bishops' Papers.

62. *Ibid.*; Samuel Parker to churchwardens of Trinity Church, Newport, August 15, 1785, Mason, *Annals of Trinity Church, Newport*, pp. 173-74; Samuel

Parker to Samuel Seabury, September 12, 1785, Hawks and Perry, *Documentary History*, II, 284-85; Samuel Parker to William White, September 14, 1785, William White Papers. Samuel Farmar Jarvis, who had seen a copy of the Middletown proposals, testified as to their basic character. [Jarvis], "Memoir of Bishop Jarvis," *op. cit.*, p. 6.

63. Samuel Parker to Samuel Seabury, September 12, 1785, Hawks and Perry, *Documentary History*, II, 284-85; alterations in the Prayer Book approved by the Boston Convention, September 7, 8, 1785, Perry, *Journals of General Conventions*, III, 93-98.

64. Samuel Seabury to Samuel Parker, December 29, 1790, William Stevens Perry, *The History of the American Episcopal Church, 1587-1883* (Boston, 1885), II, 131.

65. It is evident from the letters of Parker cited in note 62 that no such significant change as an alteration in the usual manner of reading the creeds was made at Boston: these changes were definitely the work of Seabury and the Convocation committee.

66. Samuel Parker to Samuel Seabury, January 28, 1788 (draft), J. P. Morgan Collection of Episcopal Bishops' Papers.

67. Samuel Seabury to William Smith, August 15, 1785, to William White, August 19, 1785, William White Papers.

68. Samuel Parker to Samuel Seabury, September 12, 1785, Hawks and Perry, *Documentary History*, II, 285; Samuel Parker to William White, September 14, 1785, William White Papers.

69. William Smith to Samuel Seabury, October 2, 1785, Samuel Seabury Papers.

70. For the alterations of the Proposed Book (some of which were made by a second committee after the General Convention's adjournment) and related correspondence, see Perry, *Journals of General Conventions*, III, 110-98.

71. White, *Memoirs of the Protestant Episcopal Church*, pp. 117-19.

72. Samuel Parker to Samuel Seabury, January 9, 1786, Samuel Seabury Papers. Parker, by this date, had received the unbound sheets of the Proposed Book containing Morning and Evening Prayer, the Communion service, and the Collects, Epistles, and Gospels. See also Samuel Parker to William White, January 31, 1786, William White Papers.

73. Samuel Parker to Samuel Seabury, September 12, 1785, Hawks and Perry, *Documentary History*, II, 284-85; Samuel Parker to William White, September 14, 1785, William White Papers.

74. The list of delegates and ministers attending is printed from the manuscript journal in Perry, *Journals of General Conventions*, III, 92. King's Chapel, Boston, the original Episcopal foundation in New England, was among the churches not represented. Under the leadership of lay reader James Freeman (Harvard, 1777) the Chapel, by this date, was fast isolating itself from its sister congregations; on June 19, 1785, the proprietors had voted to adopt a revised Prayer Book adapted to Freeman's Socinian views. This action notwithstanding, the Chapel wardens wrote Seabury shortly after his arrival in Connecticut, requesting that he ordain Freeman. What response they received is not known,

but in March, 1786, when the bishop visited Boston, a committee waited on him and renewed the application. He replied, characteristically, that in a case so unusual he must consult his clergy. As a result, Freeman appeared before the Convocation at Stratford in June, 1786. Interviewed by the clergy (Seabury does not appear to have been present), he was, according to his account, treated with great politeness, but since he made his doctrinal position clear, they could not recommend him for Orders. See, in addition to Henry Wilder Foote, *Annals of King's Chapel from the Puritan Age of New England to the Present Day* (Boston, 1882-96), II, 309-94, *The Diary of William Bentley, D.D., Pastor of the East Church, Salem, Massachusetts* (Salem, 1905-14), II, 418, IV, 141-42; Samuel Parker to William White, January 31, 1786, William White Papers; Samuel Parker to William White, September 15, 1786, Perry, *Journals of General Conventions*, III, 326.

75. Samuel Parker to Samuel Seabury, January 28, 1788 (copy), J. P. Morgan Collection of Episcopal Bishops' Papers.

76. *Ibid.*

77. "Governor and Council" was substituted for Seabury's "Governor and Rulers"; "subordinate Magistrates" replaced "inferior Magistrates"; and in the Massachusetts churches, "Commonwealth" replaced "State." A copy of the broadside, altered for use in Rhode Island or New Hampshire, is in the J. P. Morgan Collection of Episcopal Bishops' Papers. As it appears in the Convention's manuscript journal, the injunction includes several very minor additional verbal alterations, apparently a result of hasty copying. See Perry, *Journals of General Conventions*, III, 93-94.

78. Samuel Parker to Samuel Seabury, September 12, 1785, Hawks and Perry, *Documentary History*, II, 284-85; "Alterations in the Book of Common Prayer proposed & agreed to by the Clergy & Lay Deputies from a Majority of the Episcopal Churches in the States of Massachusetts Rhode Island & New Hampshire met in Convention at Boston Sepr. 7th & 8th 1785," Samuel Seabury Papers; manuscript journal of the aforesaid Convention, Perry, *Journals of General Conventions*, III, 97-99.

79. Samuel Seabury to Samuel Parker, November 28, 1785, J. P. Morgan Collection of Episcopal Bishops' Papers.

80. *Ibid.* Parker afterwards declared that the Connecticut churches had sent memorials to Seabury in Convocation, requesting him not to approve any alterations but those of his August 12, 1785, injunction. It seems certain that these memorials were presented at New Haven, even though Parker ascribed their drafting to the alarm taken at the proceedings of the General Convention, which met two weeks *after* the New Haven session. See Samuel Parker to Samuel Seabury, January 28, 1788 (draft), J. P. Morgan Collection of Episcopal Bishops' Papers.

81. Bela Hubbard to Samuel Parker, September 17, 1785, Hawks and Perry, *Documentary History*, II, 287.

82. William Smith to Samuel Seabury, October 2, 1785, William White to Samuel Seabury, October 18, 1785, February 1, 1786, Samuel Seabury Papers; Samuel Seabury to William White, January 8, 1786, William White Papers.

83. Samuel Seabury to [Jonathan Boucher], December 14, 1785 (copy), Hawks Papers.

84. *Ibid.*; Samuel Seabury to Samuel Parker, November 28, 1785, J. P. Morgan Collection of Episcopal Bishops' Papers; Samuel Seabury to John Skinner, December 23, 1785, Episcopal Chest Papers.

85. Samuel Parker to Samuel Seabury, January 28, 1788 (draft), J. P. Morgan Collection of Episcopal Bishops' Papers.

86. William Smith to Samuel Parker, April 17, 1786, Hawks and Perry, *Documentary History*, II, 291-92.

87. Samuel Parker to William White, September 15, 1786, Perry, *Journals of General Conventions*, III, 324-25.

88. *Ibid.*

89. Samuel Parker to Samuel Seabury, January 28, 1788 (draft), J. P. Morgan Collection of Episcopal Bishops' Papers.

90. Rufus King to Elbridge Gerry, May 8, 1785, *The Life and Correspondence of Rufus King* . . . , edited by Charles R. King (New York, 1894-1900), I, 95; Elbridge Gerry to Rufus King, May 27, 1785, *Ibid.*, I, 101.

91. *The Diaries of George Washington, 1748-1799*, edited by John C. Fitzpatrick (Boston, 1925), II, 421.

92. Richard Henry Lee to unnamed correspondent, October 10, 1785, *The Letters of Richard Henry Lee* . . . , edited by James Curtis Ballagh (New York, 1911-14), II, 388.

93. For biographical details, see John N. Norton, *Life of Bishop Provoost, of New York* (New York, 1859); Sprague, *Annals of the American Pulpit*, V, 240-45; Cadwallader D. Colden and George B. Rapelye, "Memoir of Bishop Provoost," *The Evergreen*, I (July, 1844), pp. 193-200; E. Clowes Chorley, "Samuel Provoost, First Bishop of New York," *HMPEC*, II (June, September, 1933), pp. 1-25, 1-16. Jay and Duane had married nieces of Sarah (Livingston) Alexander, the wife of Provoost's uncle, William Alexander, Revolutionary general and self-styled Earl of Stirling. George Dangerfield, *Chancellor Robert R. Livingston of New York, 1746-1813* (New York, 1960), folding genealogical chart opposite p. 516; Dix, *Trinity Church in the City of New York*, II, 32-33.

94. *Ibid.*, II, 2-30, and accompanying documents, 245-64; Robert R. Livingston to Samuel Provoost, January 14, [1784] (draft), Robert R. Livingston Papers, New-York Historical Society. Some degree of peace was restored to the parish by the subsequent election of Moore as an assistant minister. Abraham Beach to the S.P.G. Secretary, August 4, 1784, "Additional Letters of the Reverend Abraham Beach: 1772-1791," *op. cit.*, pp. 135-36.

95. [Arthur Cleveland Coxe], *Seventy Years Since*; *Or What We Owe to Bishop Seabury, a Sermon Preached in St. John's Church, Hartford, on Sexagesima Sunday, Feb. 27, 1848* (Hartford, 1848), p. 9.

96. White, *Memoirs of the Protestant Episcopal Church*, pp. 163, 187-88. Valuable as is White's volume, it cannot be considered a work of history. In his preface, White explicitly disclaimed any intention of producing such a book, declaring that he chose "to be silent in regard to a few transactions, which, although sufficiently known and discoursed of when they happened, are not of so much importance to the future concerns of the Church, as to induce a wish to perpetuate the remembrance of them; and thereby the personal irritation by which they were accompanied." *Ibid.*, p. 4.

97. His own assertions and his biographer's enthusiastic pages to the contrary, Sharp's efforts were of little importance in securing the consecration of White and Provoost in 1787. See Prince Hoare, *Memoirs of Granville Sharp, Esq. Composed from His Own Manuscripts, and Other Authentic Documents . . .* (London, 1820), pp. 207-35.

98. See, in addition to the letter cited in note 99, Granville Sharp to John Moore, November 19, 1784, September 13, 1785, Hoare, *Memoirs of Granville Sharp*, pp. 212, 219-20; "A Letter to Dr. [Benjamin] Franklin, from Granville Sharp, on the Subject of American Bishops," [October 29, 1785]," *Collections of the Massachusetts Historical Society, First Series* (Boston, 1792-1809), III, 162-64; Granville Sharp to James Manning, December 11, 1785, *Ibid.*, III, 165-66.

99. Granville Sharp to James Manning, February 22, 1785, Samuel Seabury Papers.

100. James Manning to Granville Sharp, July 26, 1785, "A Letter to Dr. Franklin, from Granville Sharp, on the Subject of American Bishops," *op. cit.*, p. 165.

101. Henry Purcell to Samuel Seabury, September 15, 1785, James Rivington to Samuel Seabury, September 19, 1785, Samuel Seabury Papers.

102. *The Address of the Episcopal Clergy of Connecticut, to the Right Reverend Bishop Seabury, with the Bishop's Answer, and, a Sermon . . . Also, Bishop Seabury's First Charge . . . with a List of the Succession of Scot's Bishops, from the Revolution in 1688, to the Present Time.* Advertised as "Just published" in the New London *Connecticut Gazette*, September 23, 1785.

103. Thomas Fitch Oliver, then lay reader at King's Church, Providence, had seen Sharp's letter sometime before April 27, 1785; always a strong supporter of Seabury, he was ordained by the bishop August 7, September 16, 1785. Thomas Fitch Oliver to Samuel Parker, April 27, 1785, Perry, *Journals of General Conventions*, III, 272*n.*; "A Registry of Ordinations by Bishop Seabury and Bishop Jarvis of Connecticut," edited by William A. Beardsley, *HMPEC*, XIII (March, 1944), p. 49.

104. White, *Memoirs of the Protestant Episcopal Church*, pp. 20-21, 139-40.

105. John Jay to John Adams, November 1, 1785, *The Works of John Adams*, edited by Charles Francis Adams (Boston, 1850-56), VIII, 335.

106. Stephen James DeLancey to Samuel Seabury, October 26, 1785, Samuel Seabury Papers.

107. Samuel Provoost to William White, October 25, 1785, William White Papers.

108. "A Registry of Ordinations by Bishop Seabury and Bishop Jarvis of Connecticut," *op. cit.*, pp. 49-52.

109. "Epistle to the Right Reverend Father in God Dr Samuel Seabury Bishop of Connecticut. 1785," Samuel Seabury Papers.

110. Subscription of Colin Ferguson, Henry Van Dyck, Philo Shelton, Ashbel Baldwin, August 3, 1785, Samuel Seabury Papers.

111. Subscription of John Cosens Ogden, March 27, 1788, Samuel Seabury Papers.

112. Samuel Seabury to John Skinner, December 23, 1785, Episcopal Chest

Papers. See also Samuel Seabury to [Jonathan Boucher], December 14, 1785 (copy), Hawks Papers.

113. Walker Maury to Samuel Seabury, October 26, 1785, Samuel Seabury Papers.

114. "A Registry of Ordinations by Bishop Seabury and Bishop Jarvis of Connecticut," *op. cit.*, p. 51.

115. Samuel Spraggs of Mount Holly, New Jersey, and Samuel Roe of Burlington, New Jersey, ordained September 16, 18, 1785; William Duke of Maryland, ordained October 16, 18, 1785; Joseph Pilmore, recently arrived in the United States, ordained November 27, 29, 1785. *Ibid.*, pp. 49-50; Burr, *Anglican Church in New Jersey*, p. 429; Nelson Waite Rightmyer, *Maryland's Established Church* (Baltimore, 1956), p. 180; Diaries of William Duke, 1774-76, *passim*, Archives of the Protestant Episcopal Diocese of Maryland, Peabody Institute; Nelson Waite Rightmyer, "Joseph Pilmore, Anglican Evangelical," *HMPEC*, XVI (June, 1947), pp. 181-98.

116. Charles Wesley to Thomas Bradbury Chandler, April 28, 1785, Samuel Seabury Papers. Seabury spoke without knowing that American Methodists were then being organized into a distinct denomination; the preachers he subsequently ordained had refused any part in this work. To William Smith he wrote, August 15, 1785: "The plea of the Methodists is something like impudence. Mr. [John] Wesley is only a Presbyter, & all his Ordinations Presbyterian, & in direct opposition to the Church of England: And they can have no pretence for calling themselves Churchmen till they return to the unity of the Church, which they have unreasonably, unnecessarily and wickedly broken, by their separation & schism." William White Papers.

117. William Smith to Samuel Seabury, July 12, 1786 (draft), William White Papers. It is doubtful whether this letter was ever sent.

118. *Proceedings of the Convention of the Protestant Episcopal Church in the State of New-York; Held in the City of New-York, on Wednesday June 22d, 1785* (New York, 1787), p. 7; Richard Peters to William White, William Smith, Samuel Provoost, James Duane, Samuel Powell, March 4, 1786, White, *Memoirs of the Protestant Episcopal Church*, p. 394; Samuel Provoost to William White, May 20, June 10, 1786, William White Papers.

119. William Smith to Samuel Seabury, July 12, 1786 (draft), William White Papers.

120. White, *Memoirs of the Protestant Episcopal Church*, pp. 131-32; William Smith of Newport to Samuel Seabury, November 5, 1785, to the "Archiepiscopum Russianum, in Urbi Sancti Petri," May 25, 1792 (copy), Samuel Seabury Papers. To distinguish Smith from his better-known relative, he is designated in all citations in the aforesaid manner; he was rector of Trinity Church, Newport, during the greater part of Seabury's episcopate.

121. William Smith to William White, March, 1786, William White Papers.

122. White, *Memoirs of the Protestant Episcopal Church*, pp. 131-32; Journal of the General Convention, June 20-26, 1786, Perry, *Journals of General Conventions*, I, 35-38.

123. White, *Memoirs of the Protestant Episcopal Church*, pp. 131-32; Journal of the General Convention, June 20-26, 1786, Perry, *Journals of General Conventions*, I, 37-38.

124. Samuel Parker to William White, September 15, 1786, *Ibid.*, III, 325.

125. Certainly there were some persons who did not seek Orders from Seabury, 1785-87, because of his disputed consecration; otherwise, it would be difficult to explain why White and Provoost, who arrived in New York from their consecration voyage, April 7, 1787, should have ordained twenty-one deacons before the end of that year. However, since Seabury had many Southern candidates early in this period, the Smith resolution must account for the fact that the list of them ended abruptly with Henry Moscrop, ordained deacon and priest for Virginia, August 27, 30, 1786. *List of Persons Admitted to the Order of Deacons in the Protestant Episcopal Church, in the United States of America, from A.D. 1785, to A.D. 1857, Both Inclusive*, compiled by George Burgess (Boston, 1874), p. 3; "A Registry of Ordinations by Bishop Seabury and Bishop Jarvis of Connecticut," *op. cit.*, pp. 51-52.

126. Samuel Parker to Samuel Seabury, January 9, 1786, Samuel Seabury Papers; Samuel Parker to William White, January 31, 1786, William White Papers.

127. Samuel Seabury to [Jonathan Boucher], December 14, 1785 (copy), Hawks Papers. See also his equally explicit criticism of what he supposed to be the episcopate envisioned by the General Convention (as well as of the Proposed Book) in *Bishop Seabury's Second Charge, to the Clergy of His Diocess, Delivered at Derby, in the State of Connecticut, on the 22d of September, 1786* (New Haven, [1786]), pp. 11-14, 19-20.

128. Samuel Provoost to William White, December 28, 1785, William White Papers. See also—in the same collection—Samuel Provoost to William White, November 7, 1785.

129. Thomas Bradbury Chandler to Samuel Seabury, December 28, 1785, Samuel Seabury Papers. For Chandler's correspondence with the archbishop, see Thomas Bradbury Chandler to [Jonathan Boucher], June 6, September 5, 1786 (copies), Hawks Papers.

130. Bela Hubbard to Samuel Peters, November 29, 1785, Samuel Peters Papers; "A Registry of Ordinations by Bishop Seabury and Bishop Jarvis of Connecticut," *op. cit.*, p. 50.

131. Wrote Ezra Stiles in 1779: "Provost Smith is a contemptible drunken Character! of tolerable academic general Knowledge. But immoral, haughty, irreligious & profane, *avaricious* and covetous, a consummate Hypocrite in *Religion & Politics*!" Stiles, *Literary Diary*, II, 338.

132. Bela Hubbard to Samuel Peters, November 29, 1785, Samuel Peters Papers; Samuel Seabury to Samuel Peters, December 14, 1785, Archives of the Protestant Episcopal Diocese of Connecticut; Samuel Seabury to [Jonathan Boucher], December 14, 1785 (copy), Hawks Papers; Thomas Bradbury Chandler to Samuel Seabury, February 16, 1786, Samuel Seabury Papers.

133. Thomas Bradbury Chandler to William White, September 26, 1785, William White Papers.

134. Samuel Seabury to John Skinner, December 23, 1785, Episcopal Chest Papers.

135. Charles Inglis to Samuel Seabury, September 14, 1786, Samuel Seabury Papers.

136. Samuel Parker to the churchwardens of Trinity Church, Newport, August 15, 1785, Mason, *Annals of Trinity Church, Newport*, pp. 173-74.

137. Samuel Parker to Samuel Seabury, September 12, 1785, Hawks and Perry, *Documentary History*, II, 285.

138. Bela Hubbard to Samuel Peters, November 29, 1785, Samuel Peters Papers.

139. Samuel Seabury to Samuel Parker, November 28, 1785, J. P. Morgan Collection of Episcopal Bishops' Papers.

140. Samuel Parker to Samuel Seabury, January 9, 1786, Samuel Seabury Papers.

141. Samuel Seabury to Samuel Parker, January 12, 1786, J. P. Morgan Collection of Episcopal Bishops' Papers.

142. Boston *Continental Journal and the Weekly Advertiser*, March 30, 1786; Samuel Seabury to Samuel Parker, April 27, 1786, J. P. Morgan Collection of Episcopal Bishops' Papers.

143. Edward Bass to Samuel Parker, July 7, 1785, March 20, May 6, September 30, 1786, J. P. Morgan Collection of Episcopal Bishops' Papers; Edward Bass to Samuel Parker, January 3, 1786, Hawks and Perry, *Documentary History*, II, 288. Bass and Seabury (and John Adams) were great-great-grandsons of the Pilgrim Father John Alden; however, there is nothing to indicate that either was aware of their relationship. For Bass's ancestry, see Daniel Dulany Addison, *The Life and Times of Edward Bass, First Bishop of Massachusetts* (Boston, 1897), pp. 1-3.

144. Jacob Bailey to Samuel Peters, April 29, 1785, Bartlet, *Frontier Missionary*, p. 207; Samuel Parker to [Jacob Bailey?], November 22, 1788, *Ibid.*, p. 289; Samuel Parker to William White, January 20, 1789, William White Papers; Nathaniel Fisher and William Willard Wheeler to Samuel Provoost, September 18, 1789, Hawks Papers.

145. Richard Peters to William White, William Smith, Samuel Provoost, James Duane, Samuel Powell, March 4, 1786, White, *Memoirs of the Protestant Episcopal Church*, pp. 392-95; Charles Inglis to Samuel Seabury, September 14, 1786, Trinity College; Charles Inglis to William White, June 6, 1786, Perry, *Journals of General Conventions*, III, 301-4.

146. John Moore *et al.* to the General Convention, February 24, 1786, *Ibid.*, I, 36-37.

147. Samuel Provoost to William White, May 13, 1786, *Ibid.*, III, 299; Jonathan Boucher to Samuel Seabury, March 31, 1786, Samuel Seabury Papers; Jonathan Boucher to John Skinner, July 3, 1786, "Correspondence between the Right Reverend John Skinner, Jr., and the Reverend Jonathan Boucher, 1786," *op. cit.*, p. 173.

148. Samuel Seabury to Samuel Parker, May 24, 1786, J. P. Morgan Collection of Episcopal Bishops' Papers.

149. Charles Inglis to Samuel Seabury, September 14, 1786, Trinity College; Charles Inglis to William White, June 6, 1786, Perry, *Journals of General Conventions*, III, 301-4.

150. John Moore and William Markham to William White, William Smith, Samuel Provoost, James Duane, Samuel Powell, Richard Peters, [June, 1786], *Ibid.*, I, 51-55.

151. Charles Inglis, Journal of Occurrences, Beginning Wednesday, October 12, 1785, To Dec. 6, 1786 (copy), pp. 22-24, General Theological Seminary.

152. Charles Inglis to Samuel Seabury, September 14, 1786, Trinity College.

153. Journal of the General Convention, June 20-26, 1786, Perry, *Journals of General Conventions*, I, 31-46; Loveland, *The Critical Years*, pp. 191-92.

154. *Ibid.*, pp. 209-11; Journal of the General Convention, October 10, 11, 1786, Perry, *Journals of General Conventions*, I, 47-62.

155. William White to Samuel Parker, September 1, 1786, J. P. Morgan Collection of Episcopal Bishops' Papers.

156. Benjamin Moore to Samuel Parker, November 4, 1786, Hawks and Perry, *Documentary History*, II, 305.

157. Jonathan Boucher to Samuel Seabury, June 12, 1786, Samuel Seabury Papers; Charles Inglis to Samuel Seabury, September 14, 1786, Trinity College.

158. Charles Inglis to Samuel Seabury, April 3, 1787, Samuel Seabury Papers. Seabury apparently lacked information as to the precise character of the liturgical decisions taken at the Wilmington session.

159. Samuel Seabury to John Skinner, March 2, 1787, Skinner, *Annals of Scottish Episcopacy*, pp. 65-66; Samuel Seabury to John Skinner, November 7, 1788, Episcopal Chest Papers.

160. Samuel Parker to Bela Hubbard, June 1, 1787, J. P. Morgan Collection of Episcopal Bishops' Papers; Perry, *Journals of General Conventions*, III, 343.

161. *Ibid.*, III, 343. Perry's account of the Wallingford Convocation is drawn from a letter of Roger Viets, who was present.

162. Jarvis, "Memoir of Bishop Jarvis," *op. cit.*, p. 6. As published, Jarvis' account states that his father deferred a reply until the annual Convocation of "1788," but this is probably a misprint.

163. Samuel Seabury to John Skinner, March 2, 1787, Skinner, *Annals of Scottish Episcopacy*, pp. 65-66.

164. Samuel Seabury to William Stevens, May 9, 1787, Ecclesiastical Letter Book, Samuel Seabury Papers.

165. Edward Hicks to Samuel Seabury, January 4, 1787, Samuel Seabury Papers.

166. Charles Inglis to Samuel Seabury, April 3, 1787, Samuel Seabury Papers. See also Inglis, Journal of Occurrences, pp. 29-30.

167. Ebenezer Dibble to Abraham Beach, February 25, 1787, "Bishop Williams' Scrapbook of Old Letters," *op. cit.*, p. 9.

168. Samuel Seabury to Samuel Provoost, May 1, 1787, Ecclesiastical Letter Book, Samuel Seabury Papers; Samuel Seabury to William White, May 1, 1787, William White Papers.

169. Samuel Seabury to William Stevens, May 9, 1787, Ecclesiastical Letter Book, Samuel Seabury Papers.

170. Ebenezer Dibble to Samuel Peters, June 13, 1787, Samuel Peters Papers.

171. William White to Samuel Seabury, May 21, 1787, Samuel Seabury Papers. A copy of this letter which Seabury submitted to Samuel Parker for comment is in the J. P. Morgan Collection of Episcopal Bishops' Papers.

CHAPTER VIII

"I HAVE DETERMINED TO GO TO PHILADELPHIA"

1. Jeremiah Leaming to Abraham Beach, August 5, September, 1786, "Bishop Williams' Scrapbook of Old Letters," *op. cit.*, pp. 8-9.

2. Jeremiah Leaming to William White, July 9, 30, 1787, William White Papers.

3. Samuel Parker to William White, July 19, 1787, William White Papers.

4. Biographical sketches: Burr, *Anglican Church in New Jersey*, pp. 605-6; George MacLaren Brydon, "David Griffith, 1742-1789, First Bishop-Elect of Virginia," *HMPEC*, IX (September, 1940), pp. 194-230.

5. David Griffith to William White, May 28, 1787, William White Papers.

6. William White to Samuel Parker, August 6, 1787, J. P. Morgan Collection of Episcopal Bishops' Papers.

7. See Jeremiah Leaming to William White, June 16, 1788, William White Papers.

8. Jeremiah Leaming to William Samuel Johnson, August 13, 1788, Beardsley, *William Samuel Johnson*, pp. 132-33; William Samuel Johnson to Jeremiah Leaming, *c.* August, 1788, *Ibid.*, p. 133.

9. Samuel Parker to Samuel Peters, September 29, 1787, Samuel Peters Papers.

10. John Skinner to Jonathan Boucher, February 21, 1788, "The Seabury Consecration: Additional Letters," *op. cit.*, pp. 258-59.

11. John Skinner to Samuel Seabury, June 20, 1787, Samuel Seabury Papers.

12. Charles Inglis to Samuel Seabury, April 3, 1787, Samuel Seabury Papers.

13. William Stevens to Samuel Seabury, July 4, 1787, Samuel Seabury Papers. See also William Stevens to Samuel Seabury, January 1, 1788, Samuel Seabury Papers.

14. Jonathan Boucher to Samuel Seabury, November 5, 1787, Samuel Seabury Papers.

15. Ashbel Baldwin to Tillotson Bronson, November, 1787, Beardsley, *Samuel Seabury*, p. 318.

16. No copy of this letter is preserved, but its existence is established when the fact that Seabury did receive White's letter of May 21, 1787 (Samuel Seabury Papers) is considered in conjunction with the following letters: Samuel Seabury

to [Jonathan Boucher], November 7, 1788 (copy), Hawks Papers; Samuel Seabury to John Skinner, November 7, 1788, Episcopal Chest Papers; William White to Samuel Seabury, December 9, 1788, Samuel Seabury Papers.

17. Samuel Seabury to Samuel Parker, December 16, 1788, J. P. Morgan Collection of Episcopal Bishops' Papers.

18. William White to Samuel Seabury, December 9, 1788, Samuel Seabury Papers.

19. Samuel Provoost to William White, February 24, 1789, J. P. Morgan Collection of Episcopal Bishops' Papers.

20. Samuel Provoost to William White, August 26, September 24, 1789, William White Papers.

21. Samuel Seabury to [Samuel Parker], May 27, 1789 (draft), Samuel Seabury Papers. For his initial—and rather favorable—reaction to White's letter, see Samuel Seabury to Samuel Parker, April 10, 1789, Hawks and Perry, *Documentary History*, II, 327.

22. Samuel Seabury to Abraham Jarvis, May 11, 1789 (copy), Woodbury Glebe House Papers.

23. Samuel Seabury to William White, June "20," [29], 1789, Perry, *Journals of General Conventions*, III, 384-88.

24. William Smith to Samuel Seabury, July 13, 1789, Samuel Seabury Papers.

25. Samuel Seabury to William Smith, July 23, 1789, Hawks Papers.

26. Journal of the General Convention, July 28-August 8, 1789, Perry, *Journals of General Conventions*, I, 65-66. For Coxe's attitude, see Tench Coxe to William Samuel Johnson, June 20, 1789, William Samuel Johnson Papers, Connecticut Historical Society.

27. Samuel Provoost to William White, July 22, 1789, J. P. Morgan Collection of Episcopal Bishops' Papers.

28. Journal of the General Convention, July 28-August 8, 1789, Perry, *Journals of General Conventions*, I, 71.

29. "An act of the Clergy of Massachusetts and New Hampshire," June 4, 1789, *Ibid.*, I, 70-71.

30. William White to Samuel Parker, July 5, 1787, *Ibid.*, III, 353; William White to Samuel Parker, August 6, 1787, J. P. Morgan Collection of Episcopal Bishops' Papers.

31. William White to Samuel Parker, [December ?], 1788, J. P. Morgan Collection of Episcopal Bishops' Papers.

32. Samuel Parker to William White, January 20, 1789, William White Papers.

33. "A Registry of Ordinations by Bishop Seabury and Bishop Jarvis of Connecticut," *op. cit.*, pp. 49, 52-53; *The Diary of William Pynchon of Salem . . .*, edited by Fitch Edward Oliver (Boston, 1890), p. 149; Bentley, *Diary*, I, 299; Abraham Lynsen Clarke to Samuel Seabury, December 9, 1786, Thomas Fitch Oliver to Samuel Seabury, December 6, 1789, Samuel Seabury Papers; Samuel Seabury to Tillotson Bronson, April 10, 1789, J. P. Morgan Collection

of Episcopal Bishops' Papers; Samuel Seabury to Tillotson Bronson, May 14 (copy), July 2, 1789, Archives of the Protestant Episcopal Diocese of Connecticut.

34. Burgess, *List of Persons Admitted to the Order of Deacons*, p. 3; Samuel Parker to William White, January 20, 1789, William White Papers.

35. Samuel Seabury to [Samuel Parker], May 27, 1789 (draft), Samuel Seabury Papers.

36. "An act of the Clergy of Massachusetts and New Hampshire," June 4, 1789, and appended authorization of Samuel Parker as the clergy's representative, Hawks Papers. These copies appear to be the ones forwarded to Bishop Provoost.

37. Samuel Parker to William White, June 21, 1789, quoted in General Convention to John Moore and William Markham, August 8, 1789, Perry, *Journals of General Conventions*, III, 400.

38. Journal of the General Convention, July 28-August 8, 1789, *Ibid.*, I, 70-74; William Smith to Samuel Seabury, August 16, 1789, Samuel Seabury Papers.

39. White, *Memoirs of the Protestant Episcopal Church*, pp. 162-65; William Smith to Samuel Seabury, August 16, 1789, Samuel Seabury Papers.

40. Tench Coxe to William Samuel Johnson, August 15, 1789, William Samuel Johnson Papers.

41. William Smith to Samuel Seabury, August 16, 1789, Samuel Seabury Papers.

42. Journal of the General Convention, July 28-August 8, 1789, Perry, *Journals of General Conventions*, I, 74-75.

43. The constitution as originally proposed by the first General Convention in 1785, and as amended, by the second General Convention in 1786 and by the first session of the third General Convention in 1789, is printed in *Ibid.*, I, 21-23, 40-42, 83-85.

44. Journal of the General Convention, July 28-August 8, 1789, *Ibid.*, I, 86.

45. Samuel Seabury to Samuel Parker, August 26, 1789, J. P. Morgan Collection of Episcopal Bishops' Papers.

46. William White, William Smith, Samuel Magaw, Francis Hopkinson, Tench Coxe to Samuel Seabury, August 16, 1789, Samuel Seabury Papers.

47. William Smith to Samuel Seabury, August 16, 1789, Samuel Seabury Papers.

48. William White to Samuel Seabury, August 12, 1789, Samuel Seabury Papers.

49. William White to John Moore, [August, 1789], Perry, *Journals of General Conventions*, III, 402-3.

50. Samuel Provoost to William White, August 26, September 17, 24, 1789, William White Papers.

51. William Willard Wheeler and Nathaniel Fisher to Samuel Provoost, September 18, 1789, Hawks Papers.

52. Minutes of a meeting of the churchwardens and vestrymen of St. Paul's, Newburyport, August 30, 1789, Addison, *Life and Times of Edward*

Bass, pp. 270-73; a churchwarden of St. Paul's to the churchwardens and vestrymen of St. Peter's, Salem, August 31, 1789, Hawks Papers.

53. Addison, *Life and Times of Edward Bass*, p. 274; letters, all of them addressed to the churchwardens of St. Paul's, Newburyport: churchwardens of Trinity Church, Boston, September 9, 1789, *Ibid.*, pp. 280-81; churchwardens of Christ Church, Boston, September 9, 1789, *Ibid.*, pp. 277-79; clerk of St. Michael's, Salem, September 6, 1789, *Ibid.*, pp. 276-77; a churchwarden and a vestryman of Queen's Chapel, Portsmouth, September 2, 1789, *Ibid.*, pp. 274-75; churchwardens of Episcopal Church, Holderness, September 12, 1789, *Ibid.*, pp. 282-83.

54. Minutes of a meeting of St. Paul's, Newburyport, September 16, 1789, *Ibid.*, pp. 283-85; committee and churchwardens of St. Paul's to Tristram Dalton and Elbridge Gerry, September 18, 1789, *Ibid.*, pp. 286-89.

55. Samuel Parker to an unnamed brother-in-law, September 27, 1789, Hawks and Perry, *Documentary History*, II, 355.

56. Bentley, *Diary*, I, 139.

57. Minutes of the General Convention's committee of correspondence, August 14, 1789, Hawks and Perry, *Documentary History*, II, 338; William White, William Smith, Samuel Magaw, Francis Hopkinson, Tench Coxe to the Episcopal clergy of Massachusetts and New Hampshire, August 11, 1789, Howard Chandler Robbins Collection of Episcopal Bishops' Papers.

58. Authorization of Samuel Parker as clerical deputy of Massachusetts and New Hampshire, also Parker's instructions, September 8, 1789, Massachusetts Diocesan Library.

59. Edward Bass, Thomas Fitch Oliver, John Cosens Ogden, and Tillotson Bronson to William White, September 8, 1789, Hawks Papers. The Rhode Island pastors were Moses Badger, since 1786 rector of King's Church, Providence, and the younger William Smith, who took charge of St. Paul's, Narragansett, in 1787 and who, at this time, also was serving Trinity, Newport, of which he became rector in 1790. For Seabury's relations with the clergy and churches of Rhode Island, see *supra*, pp. 335-40.

60. Samuel Parker to an unnamed brother-in-law, September 27, 1789, Hawks and Perry, *Documentary History*, II, 355.

61. Samuel Seabury to William White, August 27, 1789, William White Papers.

62. Minutes of the Connecticut Convocation, Stratfield, September 15, 16, 1789, quoted in [Jarvis], "Memoir of Bishop Jarvis," *op. cit.*, p. 7.

63. Minutes of the Connecticut Convocation, Newtown, September 30, October 1, 2, 1790, Hooper, *Records of Convocation*, pp. 34-35.

64. William Smith of Newport to William Smith, September 26, 1789, William Smith Papers.

65. Ebenezer Dibble to Samuel Peters, October 22, 1789, Samuel Peters Papers.

66. Samuel Parker to an unnamed brother-in-law, September 27, 1789, Hawks and Perry, *Documentary History*, II, 355.

67. Tench Coxe to William Samuel Johnson, September 25, 1789, William Samuel Johnson Papers.

68. White, *Memoirs of the Protestant Episcopal Church*, pp. 167-68.

69. *Ibid.*, p. 168; Journal of the General Convention, September 29-October 3, 1789, Perry, *Journals of General Conventions*, I, 93-96.

70. *Ibid.*, I, 75-76; White, *Memoirs of the Protestant Episcopal Church*, p. 169.

71. *Ibid.*

72. "Certificate of the Eastern Delegates Assent to the Constitution," October 2, 1789, William White Papers.

73. Journal of the General Convention, September 29-October 3, 1789, Perry, *Journals of General Conventions*, I, 97.

74. Samuel Provoost to William White, September 24, 1789, William White Papers.

75. Journal of the General Convention, September 29-October 3, 1789, Perry, *Journals of General Conventions*, I, 97.

76. Journal of the House of Bishops, October 5-16, 1789, Perry, *Journals of General Conventions*, I, 115-23; White, *Memoirs of the Protestant Episcopal Church*, pp. 172-73.

77. *Ibid.*, pp. 170-72.

78. See *supra*, pp. 351-354.

79. Abraham Jarvis to Beilby Porteus, undated but written sometime between 1797 and 1808, [Jarvis], "Memoir of Bishop Jarvis," *op. cit.*, p. 7. Jarvis declared that Seabury was supported in this position by the delegations from New Jersey and New York, as well as by himself, Hubbard and Parker. For the General Convention's decisions, as they affected the text of the English Book, see Perry, *Journals of General Conventions*, III, 448-85, where the changes are reprinted from a contemporary pamphlet.

80. White, *Memoirs of the Protestant Episcopal Church*, pp. 176-78.

81. *Ibid.*, pp. 173-76.

82. For the 1787 texts, which differ, for the most part, in but a few details from those adopted in 1789, see Samuel Seabury, Occasional Prayers and Offices (unpaged), Samuel Seabury Papers.

83. Samuel Seabury to [Jonathan Boucher], October 28, 1790 (copy), Hawks Papers. See also Thomas Bradbury Chandler to [Jonathan Boucher], March 3, 1789 (copy), Hawks Papers; Ebenezer Dibble to Samuel Peters, April 15, 1790, Samuel Peters Papers.

84. Thomas Bradbury Chandler to [Jonathan Boucher], December 5, 1785, June 6, September 5, 1786, September 4, 1787, March 3, 1789 (copies), Hawks Papers.

85. William White to Samuel Seabury, October 20, 1789, Samuel Seabury Papers; White, *Memoirs of the Protestant Episcopal Church*, pp. 175-76.

86. Samuel Seabury to William White, November 1, 1789, William White Papers.

87. William White to Samuel Seabury, December, 1789, White, *Memoirs of the Protestant Episcopal Church*, pp. 180-87; William White to Samuel Seabury, January 16, 1790, Samuel Seabury Papers; Samuel Seabury to William White, March 29, 1790, William White Papers.

88. Ebenezer Dibble to Samuel Peters, November 6, 1789, Samuel Peters Papers.

89. Minutes of the Connecticut Convocation, Litchfield, June 2-4, 1790, Hooper, *Records of Convocation*, p. 34.

90. Samuel Seabury to William White, September 1, 1790, William White Papers.

91. Minutes of the Connecticut Convocation, Newtown, September 30, October 1, 2, 1790, Hooper, *Records of Convocation*, pp. 34-35.

92. Bela Hubbard to Samuel Peters, July 5, 1790, Samuel Peters Papers.

93. Minutes of the Connecticut Convocation, Newtown, September 30, October 1, 2, 1790, Watertown, October 5-7, 1791, Hooper, *Records of Convocation*, pp. 37-39.

94. New London *Connecticut Gazette*, April 28, 1791.

95. Minutes of the Connecticut Convocation, Newtown, September 30, October 1, 2, 1790, Hooper, *Records of Convocation*, pp. 35-37.

96. *Ibid.*, p. 37.

97. William White to Samuel Seabury, December 21, 1790, Samuel Seabury Papers; Samuel Seabury to Samuel Parker, December 29, 1790, Perry, *History of the American Episcopal Church*, II, 131.

98. See *supra*, pp. 335-36.

99. John Bowden, *An Address . . . to the Members of the Episcopal Church in Stratford, to Which Is Added, a Letter to the Rev'd Mr. James Sayre* (New Haven, [1792]), p. 28.

100. Possibly Samuel William Johnson (Yale, 1779), the senator's son.

101. Bowden, *An Address . . . to the Members of the Episcopal Church in Stratford, to Which Is Added, a Letter to the Rev'd Mr. James Sayre, passim.*

102. Minutes of the Connecticut Convocation, East Haddam, February 15, 16, 1792, Hooper, *Records of Convocation*, pp. 40-41.

103. Samuel Seabury to [Jonathan Boucher], October 1, 1791 (copy), Hawks Papers.

104. Samuel Seabury to James Sayre, April 23, 1791 (draft), Samuel Seabury Papers.

105. Samuel Seabury "To the Wardens, Vestrymen, & Congregation of Christs Church, Stratford," undated but written after April 23, 1791 (draft), Samuel Seabury Papers.

106. Benjamin Moore to Samuel Peters, August 31, 1792, J. P. Morgan Collection of Episcopal Bishops' Papers; Samuel Seabury to the churchwardens of Christ Church, Stratford, October 12, 1792 (draft), Samuel Seabury Papers.

107. Samuel Seabury to [Jonathan Boucher], October 9, 1793 (copy), Hawks Papers; Samuel Seabury to William White, November 1, 1793, Wil-

liam White Papers; Samuel Seabury to Thomas John Claggett, November 2, 1793, Archives of the Protestant Episcopal Diocese of Maryland.

108. Minutes of the Connecticut Convocation, New Milford, September 25, 1793, Hooper, *Records of Convocation*, p. 45; *SAMUEL, by Divine Permission, Bishop of Connecticut and Rhode-Island, to the Clergy of the Church in Connecticut and Rhode-Island, Greeting. WHEREAS the Rev. Mr. James Sayre* . . . [n.p., 1793] (broadside).

109. William White to Samuel Seabury, December 6, 1793, Samuel Seabury Papers. Hooper, *Records of Convocation*, p. 131, declares that Sayre, after his departure from Stratford, established himself as pastor of Woodbury's Episcopal church and that this parish—in defiance of Seabury—retained him even after his excommunication. Although other writers give similar accounts, there is, in fact, no evidence that Sayre was ever at Woodbury; the reports of his officiating there apparently stem from a mistaken interpretation of the Convocation's minutes for September 25, 1793.

110. Ebenezer Dibble to Samuel Peters, June 13, 1787, June 20, October 22, November 6, 1789, April 15, September 27, 1790, Samuel Peters Papers.

111. Samuel Seabury to Ebenezer Dibble, February 22, 1792, Ecclesiastical Letter Book, Samuel Seabury Papers.

112. The Episcopalians worshipping at Horseneck Chapel were included in the parish of St. John's Church, Stamford.

113. That is, the Church of England; Dibble was born a Congregationalist.

114. Ebenezer Dibble to Samuel Seabury, April 30, 1792, Samuel Seabury Papers.

115. Samuel Provoost to William White, November 9, 1789, William White Papers; Journal of the New York Convention, November 3-5, 1789, *Journal of the Convention of the Protestant Episcopal Church of the State of New-York, Held in the City of New-York . . . 1787 . . . to . . . 1791* (New York, 1792), p. 11.

116. Benjamin Moore to Samuel Parker, April 15, 1790, J. P. Morgan Collection of Episcopal Bishops' Papers.

117. Bentley, *Diary*, I, 168.

118. *Ibid.*, I, 139.

119. James Madison to William White, July 12, 1790, Hawks Papers.

120. William Smith to Abraham Beach, July 2, 1790, "Bishop Williams' Scrapbook of Old Letters," *op. cit.*, p. 12.

121. *Ibid.*

122. Samuel Seabury to [Jonathan Boucher], October 28, 1790 (copy), Hawks Papers.

123. Addison, *Life and Times of Edward Bass*, p. 317; Benjamin Moore to Samuel Parker, April 15, 1790, J. P. Morgan Collection of Episcopal Bishops' Papers.

124. Samuel Parker to the proprietors of Trinity Church, Boston, September 29, 1790 (copy), Howard Chandler Robbins Collection of Episcopal Bishops' Papers. See also Bentley, *Diary*, I, 196-97.

125. Minutes of the Boston Convention, Salem, October 5, 6, 1790, *Ibid.*, I, 206-9. Taking part in the session were representatives of eight Massachusetts congregations and of Queen's Chapel, Portsmouth; the minutes indicate that the other churches of New Hampshire, as well as those of Rhode Island, had also received notifications.

126. Jonathan Boucher to Samuel Seabury, August 1, 1791, Samuel Seabury Papers; Jonathan Boucher, *Reminiscences of an American Loyalist, 1738-1789 . . .*, edited by Jonathan Bouchier (Boston, 1925), p. 48.

127. William White to Samuel Seabury, December 21, 1790, Samuel Seabury Papers.

128. Samuel Seabury to Jonathan Boucher, January 2, 1792, Miscellaneous Manuscripts, William L. Clements Library.

129. White, *Memoirs of the Protestant Episcopal Church*, p. 165.

130. William White to Samuel Seabury, April 26, 1790, Samuel Seabury Papers.

131. James Madison to William White, December 19, 1790, Hawks Papers.

132. White, *Memoirs of the Protestant Episcopal Church*, p. 166.

133. "Bishop Samuel Seabury's Journal 'B'—A Record of Certain Events between May 29, 1791, and November 4, 1795," *Historiographer of the Episcopal Diocese of Connecticut*, No. 12, May, 1955, pp. 5-6.

134. White, *Memoirs of the Protestant Episcopal Church*, pp. 187-89.

135. "Bishop Samuel Seabury's Journal 'B'," *op. cit.*, p. 6. See also Samuel Seabury to [Jonathan Boucher], November 30, 1792 (copy), Hawks Papers.

136. Samuel Seabury, *A Discourse Delivered before the Triennial Convention of the Protestant Episcopal Church in the United States of America, in Trinity-Church, New-York, on the Twelfth Day of September, One Thousand Seven Hundred and Ninety-Two* (New York, 1792), pp. 10, 15. Text: Colossians III.14. "And above all these things put on Charity, which is the bond of perfectness."

137. White, *Memoirs of the Protestant Episcopal Church*, pp. 189-90.

138. The House of Bishops was granted the absolute veto in 1808.

139. "Bishop Samuel Seabury's Journal 'B'," *op. cit.*, p. 6; Samuel Seabury to [Jonathan Boucher], November 30, 1792 (copy), Hawks Papers; White, *Memoirs of the Protestant Episcopal Church*, pp. 191-92.

140. *Ibid.*, pp. 192-94. By 1795 Seabury seems to have reverted to his earlier position; at any rate, he then opposed the adoption of the Thirty-Nine Articles (which were finally adopted by the General Convention in 1801). William White to Samuel Seabury, September 24, 1795, Samuel Seabury Papers.

141. Thomas Coke to the General Conference of the Methodist Church in the United States, January 29, 1808, *The Journals and Letters of Francis Asbury*, edited by Elmer T. Clark, J. Manning Potts, and Jacob S. Payton (London, 1958), III, 382-84; White, *Memoirs of the Protestant Episcopal Church*, pp. 195-96.

142. *Ibid.*, pp. 195-99; Thomas Coke to William White, April 24, 1791, *Ibid.*, pp. 408-12; William White to Thomas Coke, [May, 1791], *Ibid.*, pp. 412-

13; William White to Simon Wilmer, July 30, 1804, *Fac-Similes of Church Documents*, pp. [141-43]; Thomas Coke to Samuel Seabury, May 14, 1791, Samuel Seabury Papers; Asbury, *Journal and Letters*, I, 670-74; Thomas Coke to the General Conference of the Methodist Church in the United States, January 29, 1808, *Ibid.*, III, 382-84.

143. "Bishop Samuel Seabury's Journal 'B'," *op. cit.*, p. 6.

CHAPTER IX

"SAMUEL, BY DIVINE PERMISSION BISHOP"

1. Guy Palmes, Thomas Mumford *et al.* to the S.P.G. Secretary, May 10, 1751, S.P.G. Manuscript B 19, p. 136; Records of St. James's Protestant Episcopal Church, New London, I, 35, 56; Caulkins, *History of New London*, p. 445; Hallam, *Annals of St. James's Church, New London*, pp. 40, 51.

2. "Bishop Samuel Seabury's Journal 'B'," *op. cit.*, p. 9.

3. Inventory of November 28, 1796, Estate of Samuel Seabury, Town of New London, 1796, No. 4722, Connecticut State Library.

4. New London *Connecticut Gazette*, October 14, 1785.

5. *Ibid.*, May 8, 1789, January 8, 1790, August 20, 1795, May 12, 1796; Records of St. James's Protestant Episcopal Church, New London, II, 14; Estate of Samuel Seabury, Jr., Town of New London, 1796, No. 4723, Connecticut State Library.

6. New London *Connecticut Gazette*, April 11, 1792, October 17, 1793; Samuel Seabury to Charles Cooke, September 29, 1791, to Robert Cooke, January 2, 1792, September 10, 1793, to William Stevens, April 28, 1794, to William Ustick, Jr., October 10, 1794, January 5, 1796, Financial Letter Book, Samuel Seabury Papers; Charles Cooke to Samuel Seabury, January 28, 1792, John Moore to Samuel Seabury, July 20, 1795, Samuel Seabury Papers.

7. *Heads of Families at the First Census of the United States Taken in 1790, Connecticut* (Washington, 1908), p. 129; Diary of John Moore, 1788 (unpaged), August 29, September 2 entries, also 1789 (unpaged), September 8 entry, American Antiquarian Society; Seabury, Occasional Prayers and Offices (unpaged), Samuel Seabury Papers; Elizabeth (Powell) Seabury to Samuel Seabury, July 15, 1787, Charles Nicol Taylor to William Crooke, January 4, 1792, Benjamin Moore to Samuel Seabury, October 9, 1792, Violetta (Seabury) Taylor to Mrs. Matthias Nicoll, November 3, 1792, John Moore to Samuel Seabury, May 15, 1795, Samuel Seabury Papers; Samuel Seabury to Charles Cooke, October 28, 1790, Financial Letter Book, Samuel Seabury Papers.

8. Hallam, *Annals of St. James's Church, New London*, pp. 82-84.

9. Stiles, *Itineraries and Other Miscellanies*, pp. 410-11.

10. Beardsley, *Samuel Seabury*, p. 283.

11. Records of St. James's Protestant Episcopal Church, New London, II, 7-14.

12. *Ibid.*, I, 79, 81-94; Historical Sketch of St. James's Church, [*c.* 1807], Samuel Seabury Papers; John Tyler to Samuel Peters, October 24, 1785, Samuel

Peters Papers; Nathaniel Mann to Samuel Peters, June 19, 1787 (copy), Samuel Seabury Papers. New London's Congregationalists settled a new pastor in 1787 at a yearly salary of £140. Stiles, *Literary Diary*, III, 256, 258, 263.

13. Adams, "The Seabury Family," *op. cit.*, pp. 128-29; Records of St. James's Protestant Episcopal Church, New London, I, 77-93.

14. *Ibid.*, I, 77, 79, 83, 85-86, 88; Lawrence Shaw Mayo, *The Winthrop Family in America* (Boston, 1948), pp. 118-37, 154-63, 206.

15. Records of the First Church of Christ, New London, 1670-1888, II, 47, 50, 189, IV, 27, 41, Connecticut State Library; Seabury, Occasional Prayers and Offices (unpaged), Samuel Seabury Papers; Records of St. James's Protestant Episcopal Church, New London, I, 60, 62, 64-65. David Mumford was the son of Seabury's uncle, Thomas Mumford.

16. Caulkins, *History of New London*, pp. 446-47; Hallam, *Annals of St. James's Church, New London*, pp. 56-58; Records of St. James's Protestant Episcopal Church, New London, I, 69-73.

17. Address of St. James's Church to the Episcopalians of Boston, [1785], *Ibid.*, I, 76; Historical Sketch of St. James's Church, [*c.* 1807], Samuel Seabury Papers.

18. Caulkins, *History of New London*, p. 592; Records of St. James's Protestant Episcopal Church, New London, I, 74-76.

19. John Tyler to Samuel Peters, October 24, 1785, Samuel Peters Papers.

20. Samuel Seabury to Samuel Parker, January 12, 1786, J. P. Morgan Collection of Episcopal Bishops' Papers.

21. Records of St. James's Protestant Episcopal Church, New London, I, 76.

22. *Ibid.*, I, 81-82.

23. Hallam, *Annals of St. James's Church, New London*, pp. 69-70.

24. Ashbel Baldwin to Tillotson Bronson, November, 1787, Beardsley, *Samuel Seabury*, p. 318.

25. *Ibid.* See also Ashbel Baldwin to Tillotson Bronson, November 15, 1787, *Ibid.*, p. 315; Diary of Daniel Fogg, 1786-1814 (copy), pp. 29-30, Connecticut State Library.

26. "A Form of Consecrating Churches, Chapels, and Church-Yards, or Places of Burial," Seabury, Occasional Prayers and Offices (unpaged), Samuel Seabury Papers. For Wilson's form, see *The Works of the Right Reverend Father in God, Thomas Wilson, D.D., Lord Bishop of Sodor and Man* (Oxford, 1847-63), VII, 143-49.

27. The procuring of this ornament, now at Trinity College, Hartford, had proved a difficult commission for Inglis. On September 14, 1786, he wrote to Seabury: "Agreeably to your Desire, I called upon Mr. Stone about the Mitre. As no Mitres are worn by our Bishops in England, the Manufacture of them is consequently little known. Neither Stone, nor any other Persons I could hear of, had ever made one. However, I told Stone he must try his Hand. He & I have consulted together at least a Dozen Times; & we also called in a very ingenious Embroiderer to assist us. After consulting a Variety of Books, Cuts, Monuments, &c (for no real Mitre was to be found) we at last fixed on the Size, Materials & Manner of Execution; all of which I hope will meet your Approbation. The

Size I fancy is large enough. The Materials are Paste-Board covered with black Sattin; a Cross, in Gold Embroidery, on the back part. The two Lobes, if I may so call them, lined with white Silk; & each pointed with a gilt Cross, such as is usual on the Mitres of Bishops. The lower Part bound with a handsome black Lace, & the Inside lined with black thin Silk. The Ribbons with which it ties down, are purple & each pointed with a Bit of Gold Lace. My Wish was to have it decent & respectable; without any Thing tawdry, or very expensive about it. What the Expence will be, I know not, & shall order the Bill to be put up with the Mitre, by which You will learn it—it cannot be very great; & therefore if this Mitre does not please or fit You, the next may be made more to Your Mind." Trinity College.

28. The deed of dedication and certificate of consecration are in Records of St. James's Protestant Episcopal Church, New London, I, 80-81.

29. Samuel Seabury, Sermons, IV, 1-38, Samuel Seabury Papers.

30. John Bowden to Isaac Wilkins, August 2, 1786, Perry, *Journals of General Conventions*, III, 320.

31. That the initiative lay with the congregation seems clear. East Plymouth's Churchmen, for example, voted November 10, 1794, "that Mr. Caleb Matthews our Church Clark should attend Convention at Cheshire this present week and Request the Right Revd. Dr. Seabury to attend at our New Church as soon as may be convenient and Consecrate the same according to the rules and Customs of the Episcopal Church." Parish and Vestry Records of St. Matthew's Church at East Plymouth, 1791-1877 (copy, unpaged), Archives of the Protestant Episcopal Diocese of Connecticut.

32. Nelson R. Burr, *Inventory of the Church Archives of Connecticut, Protestant Episcopal* (New Haven, 1940), p. 69, 70, 74, 80, 84, 93, 101, 107, 114, 117, 118, 120, 121, 123, 125, 127, 128, 130, 240; Hooper, *Records of Convocation*, p. 145; "Bishop Samuel Seabury's Journal 'B'," *op. cit.*, pp. 8-10; Seabury, Occasional Prayers and Offices (unpaged), Samuel Seabury Papers.

33. *The Address of the Episcopal Clergy of Connecticut, to the Right Reverend Bishop Seabury, with the Bishop's Answer, and, a Sermon . . . Also, Bishop Seabury's First Charge . . . with a List of the Succession of Scot's Bishops, from the Revolution in 1688, to the Present Time*, pp. 9-15 of the separately paged *Charge*.

34. Samuel Seabury to Daniel Fogg, December 26, 1785 (draft), Samuel Seabury Papers; Diary of Daniel Fogg, 1786-1814, pp. 4, 29-30, 52; "Bishop Samuel Seabury's Journal 'B'," *op. cit.*, pp. 4-5.

35. "Parochiales Notitiae, Being a Private Register Kept by the Rev. Philo Shelton . . . 1785-1825," Edmund Guilbert, *Annals of an Old Parish, Historical Sketches of Trinity Church, Southport, Connecticut, 1725 to 1898* (New York, 1898), pp. 257-58.

36. New London *Connecticut Gazette*, June 30, 1786; John Bowden to Isaac Wilkins, August 2, 1786, Perry, *Journals of General Conventions*, III, 320.

37. For accounts of Seabury's personal appearance during the period of his episcopate, see "Biographical Sketch of Bishop Seabury," *The Evergreen*, I (January, 1844), pp. 4-5; Daniel Burhans to William B. Sprague, January 9, 1850, Sprague, *Annals of the American Pulpit*, V, 157-58; Hallam, *Annals of St. James's Church, New London*, pp. 74-75.

38. Ashbel Baldwin to Tillotson Bronson, November 15, 1787, Beardsley, *Samuel Seabury*, pp. 315-16.

39. Bostwick died in 1793, just after Seabury had ordained Daniel Burhans to assist him; Burhans succeeded Bostwick at Lanesboro, and in 1795 the bishop ordered Caleb Child deacon for Great Barrington. Hooper, *Records of Convocation*, pp. 127-28, 173-75, 177; "A Registry of Ordinations by Bishop Seabury and Bishop Jarvis of Connecticut," *op. cit.*, pp. 56-57; Dexter, *Biographical Sketches of the Graduates of Yale*, II, 731-33; Daniel Burhans to Samuel Seabury, May 29, 1795, Samuel Seabury Papers.

40. Journal of the Connecticut Convention, New Haven, June 6, 7, 1792, *The Journals of the Annual Convention of the Diocese of Connecticut, from 1792-1820* (New Haven, 1842), p. 4.

41. "Bishop Samuel Seabury's Journal 'B'," *op. cit.*, *passim.*

42. *Ibid.*, p. 9.

43. Samuel Seabury to [Jonathan Boucher], July 13, 1792 (copy), Hawks Papers.

44. This group included Gideon Bostwick, John Bowden, Ebenezer Dibble, Daniel Fogg, Bela Hubbard, Abraham Jarvis, Jeremiah Leaming, Richard Mansfield, John Rutgers Marshall, James Sayre (in Rhode Island, 1786-88), and John Tyler. For biographical details, see Hooper, *Records of Convocation*, pp. 124-31, 154-57; Dexter, *Biographical Sketches of the Graduates of Yale*, I, 507-9, 687-88, II, 39-43, 537-39, 684-85, 726-27, 731-33, III, 154-58; Sprague, *Annals of the American Pulpit*, V, 129-34, 234-40, 274-77, 304-8; Eben Edwards Beardsley, *The Lessons of the Past: a Sermon Preached in St. Paul's Church, Woodbury, Conn., September 6, 1871, at the Centennial Celebration of the Settlement of Rev. John Rutgers Marshall, M.A.* (New Haven, 1874), *passim.*

45. Richard Mansfield to Samuel Peters, May 26, 1785, Jonathan Boucher to Samuel Seabury, April 15, 1789, Samuel Seabury Papers; John Tyler to Samuel Peters, April 20, 1786 (copy), Woodbury Glebe House Papers; Samuel Andrews to Samuel Peters, March 6, July 20, 1786, Ebenezer Dibble to Samuel Peters, March 1, August 1, 1788, June 20, 1789, Richard Mansfield to Samuel Peters, June 3, 1788, Bela Hubbard to Samuel Peters, December 27, 1788, June 8, 1789, April 5, 1791, Samuel Peters Papers.

46. Dexter, *Biographical Sketches of the Graduates of Yale*, II, 492-94, 557-59, 568-70, 739-41.

47. Records of St. Peter's Protestant Episcopal Church, Plymouth, 1784-1910, I, 8-10, Connecticut State Library. Similarly, the congregation of St. Matthew's, East Plymouth, voted June 2, 1792, "to Give Mr. David Butler a Call for three quarters of the time to be our Minister," the salary being "Fifty five pounds & his fire wood yearly three Quarters of the time to be paid two thirds in farmers Produce & one third in Cash." Parish and Vestry Records of St. Matthew's Church at East Plymouth (unpaged).

48. Samuel Seabury to Jonathan Boucher, January 2, 1792, Miscellaneous Manuscripts, William L. Clements Library.

49. Biographical data for the twenty-six men whom Seabury ordained, and who worked in his Connecticut diocese (including Berkshire County, Massachusetts) at some time between 1785 and 1796, may be found in Hooper, *Records of*

Convocation, pp. 131-50, 152-53, 157-59, 167-70, 173-79; Dexter, *Biographical Sketches of the Graduates of Yale*, III, 587-89, 602-5, 632-34, 699, IV, 341-43, 386, 391-93, 395-96, 452-55, 485-86, 493-94, 515-16, 720-21; Sprague, *Annals of the American Pulpit*, V, 349-52, 358-63, 389-91, 400-403, 410-25; *The Correspondence of John Henry Hobart*, edited by Arthur Lowndes (New York, 1911-12), III, 76-78, 423-24, IV, 242-43.

50. Of seven men in this category, five were ordained in the years 1790-95; the seven included Seabury's son Charles and Alexander Viets Griswold, subsequently Bishop of the Eastern Diocese.

51. Daniel Burhans to Samuel Seabury, May 29, 1795, Samuel Seabury Papers. Clerical life in the 1790's is interestingly depicted in the "Autobiography of the Rev. Dr. Daniel Burhans (1763-1853)," *Historiographer of the Episcopal Diocese of Connecticut*, No. 13, September, 1955, pp. 1-11.

52. "Biographical Sketch of Bishop Seabury," *op. cit.*, p. 4.

53. Ebenezer Dibble to Samuel Peters, March 1, 1788, Samuel Peters Papers.

54. Bela Hubbard and Samuel Nesbitt, Committee, "To the Episcopal Churches in the State of Connecticut," March 8, 1788, New London *Connecticut Gazette*, April 11, 1788.

55. Stiles, *Literary Diary*, III, 318; *Proposals for Instituting an Episcopal Academy in the State of Connecticut* [n.p., 1789] (broadside).

56. Records of St. James's Protestant Episcopal Church, New London, I, 85; Samuel Seabury to William White, June "20," [29], 1789, Perry, *Journals of General Conventions*, III, 385.

57. Samuel Seabury to John Skinner, November 7, 1788, Episcopal Chest Papers.

58. Samuel Seabury to William Stevens, April 9, 1793, Financial Letter Book, Samuel Seabury Papers.

59. Minutes of the Connecticut Convocation, Watertown, October 5-7, 1791, Hooper, *Records of Convocation*, p. 40.

60. "Bishop Samuel Seabury's Journal 'B'," *op. cit.*, p. 5.

61. Journal of the Connecticut Convention, New Haven, June 6, 7, 1792, *Journals of the Annual Convention of the Diocese of Connecticut*, pp. 3-5. Probably the Convocation had previously worked out a preliminary draft of the constitution; the Convention's journal records that it having been judged "expedient to form an Ecclesiastical Constitution for the Protestant Episcopal Church in Connecticut, a Constitution was laid before them by a member for consideration." It appears that few changes—if any—were made in this document.

62. White, *Memoirs of the Protestant Episcopal Church*, p. 190.

63. Journal of the Connecticut Convention, Middletown, June 5, 6, 1793, *Journals of the Annual Convention of the Diocese of Connecticut*, p. 6; Records of St. Peter's Protestant Episcopal Church, Plymouth, I, 14. It seems likely that the sixth article produced most of the opposition. This provided that when a clergyman excluded anyone from the Communion, he was to transmit a full account to the bishop, whose judgment, taken in Convocation, would be decisive, "unless the person under suspension should think proper to appeal to a council

of bishops." The congregation of St. Michael's, Litchfield, meeting May 27, 1793, amended the article so as to allow the mixed Convention to review the Convocation's decision. Upon finding themselves in the minority, they adopted the constitution in its original form, April 21, 1794. In September, 1793, the Convocation, for reasons not now known, decreed that no clergyman should officiate in St. Paul's, Woodbury, until its people had acceded to the constitution. The operation of this vote was subsequently suspended to allow St. Paul's further time to consider the matter. After some hesitation, the congregation voted approval, November 10, 1794, two days before the expiration of the period of grace. Records of the First Episcopal Society, Litchfield, 1784-1896, pp. 12, 14, Records of St. Paul's Protestant Episcopal Church, Woodbury, 1765-1923, I, 8-9, Connecticut State Library; Minutes of the Connecticut Convocation, New Milford, September 25, 1793, New Haven, June 5, 1794, Hooper, *Records of Convocation*, pp. 45-46; Samuel Seabury to John Clark, May 27, 1794, Ecclesiastical Letter Book, Samuel Seabury Papers.

64. This pattern plainly appears when the entries in Seabury's visitation journal are read in conjunction with the Convocation's and Convention's minutes. See "Bishop Samuel Seabury's Journal 'B'," *op. cit.*, pp. 5, 7, 9, 10; Hooper, *Records of Convocation*, pp. 40-50; *Journals of the Annual Convention of the Diocese of Connecticut*, pp. 3-11.

65. *At a Convention of Lay-Delegates from Several of the Episcopal Societies in the State of Connecticut, Holden at New-Haven, on the Sixth Day of June, 1792* [n.p., 1792] (broadside); Journal of the Connecticut Convention, New Haven, June 6, 7, 1792, Middletown, June 5, 6, 1793, *Journals of the Annual Convention of the Diocese of Connecticut*, pp. 5-7.

66. Memorial of "the several episcopal Societies" of Connecticut, October 14, 1793, Connecticut Archives, Ecclesiastical Affairs, Second Series, V, document 57.

67. Memorial of "the several episcopal Societies" of Connecticut, October 12, 1795, *Ibid.*, V, document 58; Journal of the Connecticut Convention, New Haven, June 4, 5, 1794, Stratford, June 3, 4, 1795, *Journals of the Annual Convention of the Diocese of Connecticut*, pp. 8, 11. Jarvis's often-cited statement that a decade of episcopal labors did not yield Seabury, in the aggregate, a sum equal to the interest of the money he expended in seeking consecration may be somewhat exaggerated. See, in this connection, an account of monies received, June 5, 1793—May, 1794, Samuel Seabury Papers; Beardsley, *Samuel Seabury*, p. 284, quoting the records of Trinity Church, New Haven; Records of Christ Church and the Episcopal Society, Stratford, 1722-1932 (copy), II, 190-91, 193, 230-31, 340-41, 343, and Records of the Protestant Episcopal Church of the Holy Trinity, Middletown, 1750-1937, B, pp. 39, 41, both in Connecticut State Library.

68. Such as General Jedediah Huntington of New London, whose invitation to dinner is in the Samuel Seabury Papers.

69. Stiles, *Literary Diary*, III, 173.

70. New London *Connecticut Gazette*, June 27, 1788.

71. On May 4, 1785, after he had learned of Seabury's consecration, but before the General Association had taken action, Stiles, participating in the ordination of James Noyes as pastor of the First Church, Wallingford, declared him

"a Minister of the blessed Jesus, and a BISHOP of the Church of God under the great BISHOP and Shepherd of Souls." Stiles, *Literary Diary*, III, 160.

72. Abiel Holmes, *The Life of Ezra Stiles, D.D. LL.D.* (Boston, 1798), p. 370. See also Joseph Willard to Ezra Stiles, October 5, 1785, Yale University; "Sidney" in the Hartford *American Mercury*, April 20, 1795; Beardsley, *Samuel Seabury*, p. 237.

73. Stiles, *Literary Diary*, III, 263.

74. *A Sermon, Delivered at the Ordination of the Reverend Henry Channing, A.M. to the Pastoral Charge of the Congregational Church, in the City of New-London, May 17, 1787* (New London, 1787).

75. *A Letter from John Bowden, A.M., Rector of St. Paul's Church, Norwalk, to the Reverend Ezra Stiles, D.D. LL.D., President of Yale-College, Occasioned by Some Passages Concerning Church Government, in an Ordination Sermon . . .* (New Haven, 1788); *A Second Letter from John Bowden . . . to the Reverend Doctor Stiles . . . In This Letter, the Reverend Doctor Chauncy's Compleat View of Episcopacy until the Close of the Second Century, Is Particularly Considered; and Some Remarks Are Made upon a Few Passages of Doctor Stiles's Election Sermon* (New Haven, 1789); *A Letter from a Weaver, to the Rev'd. Mr. Sherman, Occasioned by a Publication of His in the Fairfield Gazette, for the Purpose of "Pinching the Episcopalian Clergy with the Truth"* (New Haven, 1789).

76. Samuel Seabury, *A Discourse, Delivered in St. John's Church, in Portsmouth, New Hampshire, at the Conferring the Order of Priesthood on the Rev. Robert Fowle, A.M. of Holderness, on the Festival of St. Peter, 1791* (Boston, 1791). See also: Samuel MacClintock, *An Epistolary Correspondence between the Rev. John Ogden, Rector of St. John's Church, at Portsmouth, New-Hampshire; and the Rev. Samuel MacClintock, Minister of the Congregational Society in Greenland, on a Variety of Subjects; Principally the High Powers and Prerogatives Claimed by Diocesan Bishops As Successors of the Apostles* (Portsmouth, 1791); John Cosens Ogden, *Letters, Occasioned by the Publication of a Private Epistolary Correspondence . . .* (Boston, 1791); "Bishop Samuel Seabury's Journal 'B'," *op. cit.*, p. 3; John Cosens Ogden to Samuel Seabury, July 13, 1791, Edward Bass to Samuel Seabury, August 15, 1791, Samuel Seabury Papers.

77. Samuel Seabury to Benjamin Gale, March 25, 1789, Ecclesiastical Letter Book, Samuel Seabury Papers. Gale, a physician noted for his interest in science and religious topics, was a son-in-law of Jared Eliot, one of the members of the Cutler-Johnson group who had decided, in 1722, to remain a Congregationalist. For Gale, see Dexter, *Biographical Sketches of the Graduates of Yale*, I, 477-80.

78. [Samuel Seabury], *An Address to the Ministers and Congregations of the Presbyterian and Independent Persuasions in the United States of America, by a Member of the Episcopal Church* ([New Haven], 1790), p. 3. The pamphlet was reprinted at Boston in 1797. Seabury's reasons for issuing it anonymously were probably the same as those which prevented his making any public overtures for a union. "In my situation," he declared in a letter to Gale cited in note 77, "proposals of such a nature would, too probably, be considered as a trap to gain an advantage to myself or my party; or as a matter of triumph over the Church." In the *Address* he insisted that the Presbyterians and Congregationalists make the first move.

79. [Seabury], *An Address to the Ministers and Congregations of the Presbyterian and Independent Persuasions*, pp. 50-51.

80. New London *Connecticut Gazette*, February 12, 1790; Bentley, *Diary*, II, 27, 35.

81. Samuel Seabury, "The Complaint &c," pp. 7-10, 17-20, 25-28, Samuel Seabury Papers. This manuscript seems to have been written in 1795 and was prepared with an eye to publication.

82. New London *Connecticut Gazette*, February 19, 26, March 26, April 16, 23, 30, 1795; Jeremiah Libbey to Samuel Seabury, February 6, March 17, 1795, Samuel Seabury Papers. Libbey, a resident of Portsmouth, New Hampshire, declared that one of his friends had originated the plan for a collection of this sort; he himself proposed it to leading clergymen throughout the United States, but Seabury seems to have been the only one who adopted the plan. In the Hartford *American Mercury*, April 20, 1795, "Sidney" violently attacked Seabury on various grounds, alleging, among other things, that he had personally pocketed the proceeds of charitable collections in the past and would probably do so in the present instance. With its most offensive sentence excised, this letter was reprinted in the New London *Connecticut Gazette*, April 30, 1795. The furious bishop responded with a defense of his character, which—for once—he decided not to publish; the manuscript, dated May 1, 1795, and signed "Crito" is in the Samuel Seabury Papers.

83. "Plain Truth" attacked Seabury for not observing the public thanksgiving in the New London *Connecticut Gazette*, March 12, 1795. The bishop responded with "The Churchman's Apology" (drafts of which are among his papers) in the same newspaper on March 19. Further communications on the subject appeared in the issues of March 26, April 23, 30, 1795. The letter printed April 23, signed "Plain Truth's Sec'ry," is very much in Seabury's style. It criticized the Reverend Henry Channing, whom the writer apparently believed to be "Plain Truth." The *Connecticut Gazette*, September 15, 1791, reprinted from *The Newport Mercury* the letter of "Ignotus Nemo," censuring the Congregationalist Channing for reading the Episcopal burial service at the funeral of a Roman Catholic. "Sidney," in the Hartford *American Mercury*, April 20, 1795, charged that Seabury was the author of this amusing satire.

84. Seabury, "The Complaint &c," pp. 10-17, Samuel Seabury Papers.

85. W. DeLoss Love, *The Fast and Thanksgiving Days of New England* (Boston, 1895), pp. 347-61.

86. Seabury, "The Complaint &c," pp. 28-29, 33-34, Samuel Seabury Papers.

87. For Stiles's explanation of this policy, see Stiles, *Literary Diary*, II, 521.

88. Nathaniel Mann to Samuel Peters, April 20, 1788, Samuel Peters Papers.

89. Samuel Seabury to George Horne, December 24, 1784, to George Berkeley, same date (copies), George Horne to Samuel Seabury, January 3, 1785, Samuel Seabury Papers.

90. Samuel Seabury to [Jonathan Boucher], November 7, 1788 (copy), Hawks Papers. See also Samuel Seabury to William Abernethy Drummond, November 7, 1788, Walter Herbert Stowe, "The Scottish Episcopal Succession and

the Validity of Bishop Seabury's Orders," *HMPEC*, IX (December, 1940), p. 325; Samuel Seabury to John Skinner, November 7, 1788, Episcopal Chest Papers.

91. Samuel Seabury to [Jonathan Boucher], November 7, 1788 (copy), Hawks Papers.

92. New London *Connecticut Gazette*, November 14, 1788.

93. *Proposals for Instituting an Episcopal Academy in the State of Connecticut* [n.p., 1789] (broadside).

94. Bela Hubbard to Samuel Peters, June 8, 1789, Samuel Peters Papers. See also Ebenezer Dibble to Samuel Peters, June 20, 1789, Samuel Peters Papers.

95. Minutes of the Connecticut Convocation, East Haddam, February 15, 16, 1792, Hooper, *Records of Convocation*, p. 41.

96. Journal of the Connecticut Convention, New Haven, June 4, 5, 1794, *Journals of the Annual Convention of the Diocese of Connecticut*, p. 8; "Bishop Samuel Seabury's Journal 'B'," *op. cit.*, p. 9.

97. *Ibid.*, p. 10; Journal of the Connecticut Convention, Stratford, June 3, 4, 1795, *Journals of the Annual Convention of the Diocese of Connecticut*, pp. 10-11.

98. Agreement to erect an academy in Cheshire, October 14, 1794 (copy), Minute Book of the Trustees of the Episcopal Academy of Connecticut (Cheshire), 1810-57, Cheshire Academy Papers, Archives of the Protestant Episcopal Diocese of Connecticut.

99. Various documents relating to the construction of the academy building are among the Cheshire Academy Papers.

100. Eben Edwards Beardsley, *An Address Delivered in St. Peter's Church, Cheshire, October 1, 1844, on Occasion of the Fiftieth Anniversary of the Episcopal Academy of Connecticut* (New Haven, 1844), p. 10.

101. *Ibid.*, p. 7.

102. The academy constitution, adopted by the Convention in June, 1796, is printed in the *Journals of the Annual Convention of the Diocese of Connecticut*, pp. 14-15.

103. Samuel Goodwin to Jacob Bailey, October 5, 1785, Bartlet, *Frontier Missionary*, p. 278.

104. "A Registry of Ordinations by Bishop Seabury and Bishop Jarvis of Connecticut," *op. cit.*, pp. 55-56; Bartlet, *Frontier Missionary*, p. 284.

105. "Bishop Samuel Seabury's Journal 'B'," *op. cit.*, pp. 2-3; "A Registry of Ordinations by Bishop Seabury and Bishop Jarvis of Connecticut," *op. cit.*, pp. 54-55; Samuel Seabury to Samuel Parker, August 26, 1789, J. P. Morgan Collection of Episcopal Bishops' Papers.

106. Ashbel Baldwin to Tillotson Bronson, November 15, 1787, *c.* October, 1788, Beardsley, *Samuel Seabury*, pp. 316, 332-33. The Bolton lands, it appears, were sold and the proceeds used to repay the money which Seabury had borrowed from James Rivington for the expenses of his consecration voyage. James Rivington to Samuel Seabury, October 27, November 9, 1789, February 25, 1792, Samuel Seabury Papers.

107. Samuel Seabury to William White, November 1, 1793, William White Papers.

108. "A Registry of Ordinations by Bishop Seabury and Bishop Jarvis of Connecticut," *op. cit.*, pp. 52, 53, 55; Hooper, *Records of Convocation*, p. 168; Beardsley, *An Address Delivered in St. Peter's Church, Cheshire*, p. 24. The dates given are those for the candidates' ordinations as deacons.

109. Minutes of the Vermont Convention, Sandgate, February 23, 24, 1791, "Notes on the Documentary History of the American Church," *HMPEC*, II (March, 1933), p. 59.

110. Samuel Seabury to Samuel Peters, October 10, 1794, Howard Chandler Robbins Collection of Episcopal Bishops' Papers. See also the Vermont Convention's petition for the consecration of Samuel Peters, June 17, 1795, Hawks Papers.

111. Boston *Continental Journal, and the Weekly Advertiser*, March 30, 1786; *Deacon John Tudor's Diary . . .*, edited by William Tudor (Boston, 1896), p. 101.

112. Boston *Independent Chronicle: and the Universal Advertiser*, April 7, 1786; Boston *Massachusetts Centinel*, April 12, 1786; *New-Haven Gazette, and the Connecticut Magazine*, April 13, 1786.

113. Samuel Seabury, *A Sermon Delivered before the Boston Episcopal Charitable Society, in Trinity Church; at Their Anniversary Meeting of Easter Tuesday March 25, 1788* (Boston, 1788); Diary of John Moore, 1788 (unpaged), March 17-30 entries.

114. Bentley, *Diary*, I, 90.

115. "Bishop Samuel Seabury's Journal 'B'," *op. cit.*, p. 3.

116. Edward Bass to Samuel Seabury, August 15, 1791, Samuel Seabury Papers; Bentley, *Diary*, I, 268.

117. New London *Connecticut Gazette*, April 14, 1786; Updike, *History of the Episcopal Church in Narragansett*, II, 199. There is nothing in the journal of the General Convention to indicate that Seabury sought to use this authorization.

118. Trinity's invitation is not now among Seabury's papers, but these were the terms offered James Sayre, August 27, 1786, after Seabury had declined. Mason, *Annals of Trinity Church, Newport*, pp. 181-82, quoting minutes of a congregational meeting held that date.

119. Samuel Seabury to John Bours, Samuel Freebody, Francis Malbone, Francis Brinley and Charles Handy, July 17, 1786, *Ibid.*, pp. 179-81.

120. Mason, *Annals of Trinity Church, Newport*, pp. 184-86; members of Trinity Church to Samuel Seabury, *c.* 1788, *Ibid.*, pp. 186-87; Samuel Seabury to Samuel Freebody, Thomas Freebody, and Benjamin Gardiner, February 3, 1790, Ecclesiastical Letter Book, Samuel Seabury Papers; also, these pamphlets: James Sayre, *A Candid Narrative of Certain Matters Relating to Trinity Church in Newport . . .* (Fairfield, 1788); John Bours, *An Appeal to the Public, in Which the Misrepresentations and Calumnies, Contained in a Pamphlet, Entitled, a Narrative of Certain Matters Relative to Trinity Church in Newport . . . by . . . the Rev. James Sayer* [*sic*], *A.M., Late Minister of Said Church, Are Pointed Out, and His Very Strange Conduct during the Time of His Ministration at Newport, Faithfully Related* (Newport, 1789); *An Address Presented the Rev. James Sayre, A.M., Minister of Trinity Church, Newport, Previous to His Leaving the Town*;

Together with His Answer after His Arrival at Fairfield, in Connecticut . . . (Newport, 1789).

121. Biographical sketches include: Updike, *History of the Episcopal Church in Narragansett*, II, 111-13; Sprague, *Annals of the American Pulpit*, V, 345-49; William Palmer Ladd, "William Smith, *c.* 1754-1821," Johnson and Malone, *Dictionary of American Biography*, XVII, 358-59.

122. Stiles, *Literary Diary*, III, 330.

123. Samuel Seabury to John Skinner, November 7, 1788, Episcopal Chest Papers.

124. Samuel Seabury to Samuel Freebody, Thomas Freebody, Benjamin Gardiner, February 3, 24, 1790, Ecclesiastical Letter Book, Samuel Seabury Papers; Samuel Seabury to [Benjamin] Gardiner, April 13, 1790 (draft), Samuel Seabury Papers.

125. William Smith of Newport to Samuel Seabury, *c.* 1791, March 18, 1794, Samuel Seabury Papers.

126. See *supra*, p. 308.

127. Bentley, *Diary*, I, 203, 206.

128. Minutes of a vestry meeting, October 10, of a congregational meeting, October 17, 1790, Mason, *Annals of Trinity Church, Newport*, pp. 193-94.

129. In the early records of the Rhode Island Convention, the state and Connecticut are referred to as forming one diocese under Seabury; in fact, however, they were distinct units and are here treated as such.

130. Journal of the Rhode Island Convention, Newport, November 18, 1790, *Journals of the Conventions of the Protestant Episcopal Church in the Diocese of Rhode Island, from the Year A.D. 1790 to the Year A.D. 1832, Inclusive* (Providence, [1859]), pp. 5-7.

131. William Smith of Newport and Moses Badger to Samuel Seabury, November 20, 1790, Mason, *Annals of Trinity Church, Newport*, pp. 196-97.

132. Samuel Seabury to William Smith of Newport and Moses Badger, December 1, 1790, *Ibid.*, pp. 198-99.

133. Samuel Seabury to William White, November 1, 1793, William White Papers; Samuel Seabury to Thomas John Claggett, November 2, 1793, Archives of the Protestant Episcopal Diocese of Maryland; "Bishop Samuel Seabury's Journal 'B'," *op. cit.*, p. 8; Updike, *History of the Episcopal Church in Narragensett,* II, 114, 116, 355-57, 359-67, 419-20; *Correspondence of John Henry Hobart*, II, 414-16; Journal of the Rhode Island Convention, Newport, November 18, 1790, Providence, August 20, 21, 1792, *Journals of the Conventions . . . in the Diocese of Rhode Island*, pp. 6-7, 9-11.

134. Journal of the Rhode Island Convention, Providence, July 31, August 1, 1793, *Ibid.*, pp. 13-16; Perry, *Journals of General Conventions*, I, 210; White, *Memoirs of the Protestant Episcopal Church*, pp. 200-201; William White to Samuel Seabury, September 24, 1795, Samuel Seabury Papers.

135. "Bishop Samuel Seabury's Journal 'B'," *op. cit.*, p. 11.

136. *Ibid.*, pp. 1-2, 7-8, 11.

137. Journal of the Rhode Island Convention, Providence, July 31, August

1, 1793, Bristol, July 8, 1795, *Journals of the Conventions . . . in the Diocese of Rhode Island*, pp. 13-16, 18-21. In 1792 the Rhode Island Convention authorized Connecticut's lay and clerical deputies to represent their church at New York. When the General Convention ruled that a deputy could not act under the appointment of more than one state body, two Connecticut deputies resigned their original appointments in order that Rhode Island might have a delegation. Journal of the Rhode Island Convention, Providence, August 20, 21, 1792, *Ibid.*, p. 12; Journal of the House of Clerical and Lay Deputies, September 12-19, 1792, Perry, *Journals of General Conventions*, I, 150.

138. William Smith of Newport and Moses Badger to Samuel Seabury, April 9, 1792, Samuel Seabury Papers.

139. "A Registry of Ordinations by Bishop Seabury and Bishop Jarvis of Connecticut," *op. cit.*, pp. 56-57.

140. For Usher see Shipton, *Sibley's Harvard Graduates*, XI, 319-21.

CHAPTER X

"THE TRUE & REAL CHRISTIAN SACRIFICE"

1. William Williams, Moderator of the Hampshire Association, to Edmund Gibson, September 10, 1734, Perry, *Historical Collections*, III, 299.

2. See, for example, Richard Mather, *An Apologie of the Churches in New-England for Church-Covenant* (London, 1643), as quoted in Perry Miller, *Orthodoxy in Massachusetts, 1630-1650: a Genetic Study* (Cambridge, 1933), p. 151.

3. Samuel Johnson, *A Short Catechism for Young Children: Proper To Be Taught Them, before They Learn the [Westminster] Assembly's, or after They Have Learned the Church Catechism* (Philadelphia, 1753), in Johnson, *Writings*, III, 594.

4. Samuel Johnson, Sermon from Luke 22: 19, 20, annotated as preached on six occasions between 1740 and 1763, Hawks Papers.

5. *A Short Catechism for Young Children*, Johnson, *Writings*, III, 594.

6. Quoted in Seabury, *Memoir of Bishop Seabury*, pp. 11-12, 14-15.

7. *Ibid.*, p. 16.

8. White, *Memoirs of the Protestant Episcopal Church*, p. 180.

9. Seabury, *Memoir of Bishop Seabury*, pp. 12-13, quoting "Ms. Mem. Dr. Samuel Seabury."

10. See, for purposes of comparison, the extracts from writings of William Laud and Jeremy Taylor and accompanying commentary in W. Jardine Grisbrooke, *Anglican Liturgies of the Seventeenth and Eighteenth Centuries* (London, 1958), pp. 10-36.

11. For a discussion of Johnson's eucharistic theology, illustrated with lengthy quotations from *The Unbloody Sacrifice* and others of his publications, see *Ibid.*, pp. 71-88. The Seabury quotation appears in the sermon "Of the Holy Eucharist" in Samuel Seabury, *Discourses on Several Subjects* (New York, 1793), I, 179.

12. Samuel Seabury, *An Earnest Persuasive to Frequent Communion; Addressed to Those Professors of the Church of England, in Connecticut, Who Neglect That Holy Ordinance* (New Haven, 1789), p. 17.

13. Grisbrooke, *Anglican Liturgies*, p. 73, quoting *The Unbloody Sacrifice.*

14. "Bishop Samuel Seabury's Journal 'B'," *op. cit.*, p. 8.

15. William Smith of Newport, *A Discourse Delivered in St. John's Church, Providence, before the Right Reverend Samuel, Bishop of Connecticut and Rhode-Island, and the Clerical and Lay Delegates of the Protestant Episcopal Church in the State of Rhode-Island . . .* (Providence, 1793), pp. iii-iv.

16. Grisbrooke, *Anglican Liturgies*, pp. 150-59, discusses the formation of the Scots Office; the text is reproduced in *Ibid.*, pp. 332-48. For a more exhaustive treatment, see John Dowden, *The Scottish Communion Office 1764* (Oxford, 1922).

17. William Smith to William White, April 9, 1786, William White Papers; William Smith to Samuel Parker, April 17, 1786, Hawks and Perry, *Documentary History*, II, 291.

18. Samuel Seabury to [Jonathan Boucher], December 3, 1784 (copy), Hawks Papers.

19. Concordat between the Episcopal Church of Scotland and the Episcopal Church of Connecticut, November 15, 1784, Samuel Seabury Papers.

20. Samuel Seabury to [Jonathan Boucher], December 3, 1784 (copy), Hawks Papers. The concordat exaggerated the similarity of the two offices. In that of the First Prayer Book, the Invocation came before the words of Institution, whereas Falconar and Forbes, it will be recalled, followed Johnson's "primitive" sequence: Institution, Oblation, and Invocation.

21. For the assembling of this collection, see Samuel Seabury to John Skinner, December 3, 27, 1784, "February" [March] 11, 1785, Episcopal Chest Papers; John Skinner to Arthur Petrie, January 13, 1785, Arthur Petrie Papers; John Allan to Samuel Seabury, January 17, 1785, Alexander Allan to Samuel Seabury, January 18, 1785, Andrew Macfarlane to Samuel Seabury, January 21, 1785, Samuel Seabury Papers.

22. With about eighteen hundred volumes exclusive of tracts, Thomas Bradbury Chandler had, it appears, the largest library of any of Seabury's Episcopal contemporaries. In it were less than a score of works by Nonjurors and like-minded theologians. See the *Catalogue of Books, for Sale by Mrs. Chandler, in Elizabeth-Town, New-Jersey; Being the Library of the Late Rev. Dr. Chandler, Deceased* (Elizabethtown, 1790).

23. Ebenezer Dibble to Samuel Peters, June 13, 1787, Samuel Peters Papers.

24. Samuel Seabury to John Skinner, December 23, 1785, Episcopal Chest Papers.

25. *Ibid.*

26. William Smith to Samuel Seabury, July 12, 1786 (draft), William White Papers.

27. Reprinted in facsimile in *Bishop Seabury's Communion-Office . . . with*

an Historical Sketch and Notes, edited by Samuel Hart (New York, 1883), pp. 1-23.

28. A collation showing the differences between the two offices is in *Ibid.*, pp. 36-38.

29. *Ibid.*, p. 40.

30. Seabury, *Discourses on Several Subjects*, II, 45-46.

31. Granville Sharp to Benjamin Franklin, October 29, 1785, "A Letter to Dr. Franklin, from Granville Sharp, on the Subject of American Bishops," *op. cit.*, pp. 163-64; Walker, *Life and Times of the Rev. John Skinner*, p. 118.

32. Grisbrooke, *Anglican Liturgies*, pp. 74-75, quoting Johnson's *Unbloody Sacrifice* and his posthumously published *Primitive Communicant* (1738).

33. Seabury, *Discourses on Several Subjects*, I, 169-72.

34. *Bishop Seabury's Second Charge, to the Clergy of His Diocess*, pp. 17-19; Seabury, *An Earnest Persuasive to Frequent Communion, passim*; Seabury, *Discourses on Several Subjects*, I, 163-83.

35. Beardsley, *Samuel Seabury*, p. 263.

36. Hart, *Bishop Seabury's Communion Office*, p. 40.

37. Samuel Seabury to William White, June "20," [29], 1789, Perry, *Journals of General Conventions*, III, 387-88.

38. White, *Memoirs of the Protestant Episcopal Church*, pp. 179-80.

39. *Ibid.*, p. 179.

40. Samuel Seabury to [Benjamin] Gardiner, April 13, 1790 (draft), Samuel Seabury Papers.

41. William Smith of Newport to Samuel Seabury, November 5, 1785, Samuel Seabury Papers.

42. Samuel Seabury to John Skinner, December 23, 1785, Episcopal Chest Papers.

43. William Smith to William White, April 9, 1786, William White Papers; William Smith to Samuel Parker, April 17, 1786, Hawks and Perry, *Documentary History*, II, 291.

44. Benjamin Rush to John Adams, April 5, 1808, *Letters of Benjamin Rush*, edited by Lyman H. Butterfield ([Princeton], 1951), II, 962; *The Autobiography of Benjamin Rush, His "Travels through Life," Together with His Commonplace Book for 1789-1813*, edited by George W. Corner (Princeton, 1948), p. 165.

45. Hart, *Bishop Seabury's Communion Office*, pp. 52-53, reports that some of the Connecticut clergy continued to use the Scots Office long after the liturgical revision of 1789 had taken effect; his evidence, however, seems rather slight. What probably occasioned this belief was the fact that Seabury transposed what is known as the Prayer of Humble Access from its position in the 1789 service (the same position it had held in that of 1662) and read it after the Prayer of Consecration, where it appeared in the Scots Office. This practice was followed by Jarvis and by a Seabury ordinee as late as 1835. Beardsley, *Samuel Seabury*, p. 264; Samuel Farmar Jarvis to William Skinner, August 10, 1822, "Some Letters of Bishop William Skinner of Aberdeen," edited by Edgar Legare Pennington,

HMPEC, XVI (December, 1947), p. 383. Hart's statement is repeated in Francis Procter and Walter Howard Frere, *A New History of the Book of Common Prayer with a Rationale of Its Offices* (London, 1901), p. 240.

46. Seabury, *Discourses on Several Subjects*, I, 183.

47. John Beach to the S.P.G. Secretary, April 12, 1774, Hawks and Perry, *Documentary History*, II, 195; Sprague, *Annals of the American Pulpit*, V, 412; Seabury, Occasional Prayers and Offices (unpaged), Samuel Seabury Papers; Samuel Seabury, Sr.'s, *notitia parochialis*, March 25, 1743, S.P.G. Manuscript B 11, p. 138.

48. Seabury, Occasional Prayers and Offices (unpaged), Samuel Seabury Papers.

49. William Samuel Johnson to Samuel William Johnson, April 20, 1789, William Samuel Johnson Papers.

50. *Bishop Seabury's Second Charge, to the Clergy of His Diocess*, p. 17.

51. The frequency of English celebrations is discussed in Norman Sykes, *Church and State in England in the XVIIIth Century* (Cambridge, England, 1934), pp. 250-51, 254-55. The pattern of New England administrations can be traced in Updike, *History of the Episcopal Church in Narragansett*, III, 90; Records of St. James's Protestant Episcopal Church, New London, I, 58; accounts of Christ Church, Boston, St. Michael's, Marblehead, and Queen Anne's Chapel, Newbury, in 1724, Perry, *Historical Collections*, III, 148, 150, 151; David Mossom to the S.P.G. Secretary, May 5, "1729" [1727], *Ibid.*, III, 255; accounts of Christ Church, Stratford, Trinity, Newport, St. Paul's, Narragansett, King's Church, Providence, and St. Michael's, Bristol, in 1724, Manross, *Fulham Papers*, pp. 11, 122-23; James MacSparran to the S.P.G. Secretary, September 30, 1742, S.P.G Manuscript B 10, p. 36; Ebenezer Punderson to the S.P.G. Secretary, October 12, 1744, S.P.G. Manuscript B 13, p. 296; John Usher to the S.P.G. Secretary, April 2, 1746, S.P.G. Manuscript B 14, p. 55; James MacSparran's *notitia parochialis*, November 25, 1747, S.P.G. Manuscript B 15, p. 135; James Honyman to the S.P.G. Secretary, April 20, 1748, S.P.G. Manuscript B 16, p. 22; Edward Winslow to the S.P.G. Secretary, July 19, 1762, Hawks and Perry, *Documentary History*, II, 31; Rana Cossit to the S.P.G. Secretary, January 6, 1779, S.P.G. Manuscript B 3, p. 967.

52. Address of Samuel Seabury to the congregation of St. James's, New London, [December 25, 1788?], Samuel Seabury Papers.

53. This tract was several times reprinted in the nineteenth century.

54. Seabury, *An Earnest Persuasive to Frequent Communion*, p. [3].

55. *Ibid.*, pp. 8-20.

56. *Ibid.*, pp. 16-17.

57. *Ibid.*, pp. 21-23.

58. E. Clowes Chorley, *Men and Movements in the American Episcopal Church* (New York, 1950), pp. 256-58.

59. George Innes, *A Catechism, or, the Principles of the Christian Religion, Explained in a Familiar and Easy Manner, Adapted to the Lowest Capacities* (New Haven, 1791), p. [2]. For Scottish comment on this point, see Charles Wordsworth, Bishop of St. Andrews, "What Can England Learn from Scotland

in Religious Matters?" *The Scottish Church Review*, I (October, 1884), pp. 676-82.

60. Innes, *Catechism*, pp. 8-9, 21-23, 25, 32, 55-58.

61. *Ibid.*, pp. 25, 45-52.

62. For James Sayre's criticism on this score, see Bowden, *An Address . . . to the Members of the Episcopal Church in Stratford, to Wich Is Added, a Letter to the Rev'd Mr. James Sayre*, pp. 29-33.

63. Abraham Lynsen Clarke, *The Catechism of the Protestant Episcopal Church in the United States of America, with Selected Questions and Answers, on Important Subjects* (Providence, 1798).

64. *The Catechism of the Protestant Episcopal Church in the United States of America, Published at the Expense of a Fund Arising from the Charitable Contributions of the Members of the Protestant Episcopal Church in the State of New-York* (New York, 1802). The section containing the material drawn from Innes has a separate title page. See also Seabury, *Memoir of Bishop Seabury*, pp. 397-98.

65. Whittingham afterwards issued another edition in which the omitted Innes material was printed as footnotes. *A Catechism, Designed As an Explanation and Enlargement of the Church Catechism: Formerly Recommended by the Bishops and Clergy of the Protestant Episcopal Church in the State of New York, to Which Are Added the Omitted Parts of the Original Catechism of Bishop Innes, As Republished by Bishop Seabury* (Baltimore, 1851).

66. James Morss, *The Catechism of the Protestant Episcopal Church in the United States of America, to Which Is Annexed a Catechism Designed As an Explanation and Enlargement of the Church Catechism: Selected from a Catechism, Recommended by the Bishop and Clergy of the Protestant Episcopal Church in the State of New-York, with Some Additions* (Newburyport, 1815); John Henry Hobart, *Catechism Number Three: the Church Catechism Enlarged, Explained and Proved from Scripture, in a Catechism Drawn Up, with Alterations and Additions, from Various Approved Catechisms* (New York, n.d.).

67. Chorley, *Men and Movements in the American Episcopal Church*, p. 122.

68. Innes, *Catechism*, pp. 31, 41, 45-52.

69. Hobart, *Church Catechism Enlarged*, pp. 70-71, 82.

70. James Rivington to Samuel Seabury, January 13, November 9, 1789, May 10, 1790, June 28, 1793, Benjamin Moore to Samuel Seabury, December 7, 1791, January 6, March 29, November 13, 1792, Samuel Seabury Papers.

71. Samuel Seabury, *Discourses on Several Important Subjects* (New York, 1798). Proposals for printing this work by subscription appeared in the New London *Connecticut Gazette*, January 1, 1795.

72. Jonathan Boucher to Samuel Seabury, March 3, 1794, Samuel Seabury Papers.

73. J. M. Danson, "Seabury as a Preacher," *The Scottish Church Review*, I (October, 1884), p. 656. Danson had examined the second edition of *Discourses on Several Subjects* (Hudson, 1815), which included three sermons from the volume issued in 1798.

74. Samuel Seabury to John Skinner, November 7, 1788, Episcopal Chest Papers; Samuel Seabury to [Jonathan Boucher], October 1, 1791, July 13, 1792 (copies), Hawks Papers.

75. Samuel Seabury to William Abernethy Drummond, November 7, 1788, "The Scottish Episcopal Succession and the Validity of Bishop Seabury's Orders," *op. cit.*, pp. 324-25.

76. Eben Edwards Beardsley, *The History of the Episcopal Church in Connecticut* (New York, 1865-68), II, 96-97; also his *Samuel Seabury*, pp. 404-6.

77. See *supra*, pp. 218-19.

78. Chandler, Memorandums, pp. 17-18, 26-27, 30, 45, 48, 51, 53-54, 118; Thomas Bradbury Chandler to Samuel Seabury, July 5, 1777, February 16, 1786, Samuel Seabury Papers; Thomas Bradbury Chandler to [Jonathan Boucher], March 6, 1787 (copy), Hawks Papers.

79. Samuel Seabury to Jonathan Boucher, December 3, 1784, Ecclesiastical Letter Book, Samuel Seabury Papers; Thomas Bradbury Chandler to Samuel Seabury, February 16, 1786, Samuel Seabury Papers; Thomas Bradbury Chandler to John Skinner, April 23, 1785, Skinner, *Annals of Scottish Episcopacy*, pp. 45-46; [Park], *Memoirs of William Stevens*, pp. 140-41.

80. Jonathan Boucher to Samuel Seabury, March 31, 1786, Samuel Seabury Papers; memoranda in Financial Letter Book, Samuel Seabury to William Ustick, Jr., December 28, 1792, October 14, 1794, January 5, 1796, Financial Letter Book, Samuel Seabury Papers.

81. Copies of many of Seabury's letters to Boucher are in the Hawk Papers. For letters to Stevens, see the Ecclesiastical and Financial Letter Books, Samuel Seabury Papers.

82. William Stevens to Samuel Seabury, July 4, 1787, January 1, 1788, March 31, 1789, Samuel Seabury Papers.

83. William Jones of Nayland to John Bowden, 1799, Beardsley, *History of the Episcopal Church in Connecticut*, II, 97.

84. See Broxap, *Later Non-Jurors*, pp. 291-308.

EPILOGUE

"A WILLING HEART TO DO MY DUTY"

1. Samuel Seabury to [Jonathan Boucher], July 13, 1792, October 9, 1793 (copies), Hawks Papers.

2. Samuel Seabury to William White, June 22, 1795 (copy), Samuel Seabury Papers.

3. *An Address to the Members of the Protestant Episcopal Church, in the United States of America* (New York, 1792). White stated (see the first letter cited in note 4) that he had always understood John Bowden to be the author of this publication.

4. William White to Samuel Seabury, September 24, 1795, Samuel Seabury Papers. See also William White to Samuel Seabury, October 27, 1795, Sam-

uel Seabury Papers; White, *Memoirs of the Protestant Episcopal Church*, pp. 205-6.

5. "Bishop Samuel Seabury's Journal 'B'," *op. cit.*, pp. 10-11.

6. Jarvis, *A Discourse Delivered before a Special Convention . . . Occasioned by the Death of the Right Reverend Samuel Seabury*, p. 23.

7. Charles Seabury to John Henry Hobart, October 31, 1802, *Correspondence of John Henry Hobart*, III, 108-9.

8. Stiles, *Literary Diary*, III, 403.

9. Richard Saltonstall to Samuel Peters, March 12, 1796, Samuel Peters Papers; Abraham Jarvis to Samuel Peters, April 4, 1796 (copy), Samuel Seabury Papers.

10. New London *Connecticut Gazette*, March 3, 1796; Daniel Burhans to William B. Sprague, January 9, 1850, Sprague, *Annals of the American Pulpit*, V, 157; Records of St. James's Protestant Episcopal Church, New London, II, 16.

11. Beardsley, *Samuel Seabury*, pp. 455-56, 465-66; Hallam, *Annals of St. James's Church, New London*, pp. 77-79, 101-6.

12. Beardsley, *Samuel Seabury*, p. 467.

13. Abraham Jarvis to Samuel Peters, April 4, 1796 (copy), Samuel Seabury Papers.

BIBLIOGRAPHY

MANUSCRIPT SOURCES

American Antiquarian Society, Worcester.

Account Book of Samuel Seabury, Jr., 1783-84.

Diary of John Moore, 1788, 1789.

Church Historical Society, Austin.

Hawks Papers.

Samuel Peters Papers.

William Smith Papers.

William White Papers.

Columbia University, New York.

John Jay Papers.

Samuel Johnson Correspondence.

Connecticut Historical Society, Hartford.

William Samuel Johnson Papers.

Connecticut State Library, Hartford.

Admissions and Baptisms of the First Congregational Church, Groton, Connecticut, 1727-1811 (copy).

Connecticut Archives, Ecclesiastical Affairs, First Series, III, X, Second Series, V.

Connecticut Archives, Revolutionary War, First Series, I.

Diary of Daniel Fogg, 1786-1814 (copy).

Estate of Thomas Mumford, Town of Groton, 1766, No. 3784; of Caleb Seabury, Town of Groton, 1772, No. 2680; of Samuel Seabury, Town of New London, 1796, No. 4722; of Samuel Seabury, Jr., Town of New London, 1796, No. 4723.

Groton Births, Marriages, Deaths 1704-1853 (copy).

New London Births, Marriages, Deaths 1646-1854 (copy).

New London Land Records (copies), XII-XV, XIX.

Records of Christ Church and the Episcopal Society, Stratford, 1722-1932 (copies), II.

Records of the First Church of Christ, New London, 1670-1888, II, IV.

Records of the First Episcopal Society, Litchfield, 1784-1896.

Records of the Protestant Episcopal Church of the Holy Trinity, Middletown, 1750-1937, B.

Records of St. James's Protestant Episcopal Church, New London, 1725-1874, I, II.
Records of St. Paul's Episcopal Church, Woodbury, 1765-1923, I.
Records of St. Peter's Protestant Episcopal Church, Plymouth, 1784-1910, I.
Records of the Second or North Ecclesiastical Society, Groton, 1725-1826, I.
Woodbury Glebe House Papers (copies).

Episcopal Theological College, Edinburgh.
Arthur Petrie Papers.
Episcopal Chest Papers.

General Theological Seminary, New York.
Benjamin Moore Papers.
Charles Inglis, Journal of Occurrences, Beginning Wednesday, October 12, 1785, To Dec. 6, 1786 (copy).
Howard Chandler Robbins Collection of Episcopal Bishops' Papers.
Samuel Seabury Papers.
Samuel Seabury, Sr., Sermon from Psalm 24:115, annotated as preached at Oyster Bay, May 23, 1762.

Historical Society of Pennsylvania, Philadelphia.
Gratz Collection.

Library of Congress, Washington.
Fulham Palace Manuscripts.
Jacob Bailey Papers.
Photostats, S.P.G. Connecticut (Part I) 1635-1782, (Part II) 1783-1852.
Sir William Johnson Papers.
S.P.G. Manuscript Journals (copies), V, VI, XII-XVIII, XXI-XXIII.
S.P.G. Manuscripts A 23-26, B1-3, 7, 9-11, 13-20.

Massachusetts Diocesan Library, Boston.
Authorization of Samuel Parker as clerical deputy of Massachusetts and New Hampshire, also Parker's instructions, September 8, 1789.
Minutes of the Connecticut Convention, Derby, May 23-25, 1780, Litchfield, June 12-14, 1781.

New-York Historical Society, New York.
Order for the induction of Samuel Seabury as rector of Jamaica, January 12, and certificate of induction, January 13, 1757.
Order for the induction of Samuel Seabury as rector of Westchester, December 3, 1766, and certificate of induction, March 1, 1767.
Robert R. Livingston Papers.

New York Public Library, New York.
Alexander Hamilton Papers.
American Loyalists: Transcript of the Manuscript Books and Papers of the Commission of Enquiry, II, VI, XVII, XXXVIII, XLI, XLII, XLIV.

American Loyalists: Transcript of Various Papers Relating to the Losses Services and Support of the American Loyalists and to His Majesty's Provincial Forces during the War of American Independence, Preserved Amongst the American Manuscripts in the Royal Institution of Great Britain, IV, VII, VIII.

Diary of Edward Winslow, 1754-55 (copy).

Peabody Institute, Baltimore.

Archives of the Protestant Episcopal Diocese of Maryland:

Diaries of William Duke, 1774-76.

Samuel Seabury to Thomas John Claggett, November 2, 1793.

Pierpont Morgan Library, New York.

J. P. Morgan Collection of Episcopal Bishops' Papers.

Public Record Office, London.

A.O. 13 (American Loyalists' Claims, Series II)/105.

Trinity College, Hartford.

Archives of the Protestant Episcopal Diocese of Connecticut:

Charles Inglis *et al.* to John Moore, William Markham, and Robert Lowth, May 24, 1783 (copy).

Cheshire Academy Papers.

Memorandums of Thomas Bradbury Chandler, 1775-86 (copy).

Parish and Vestry Records of St. Matthew's Church at East Plymouth, 1791-1877 (copy).

Philip Bearcroft, S.P.G. Secretary to Thomas Sherlock, October 23, 1753 (copy).

Samuel Seabury to Samuel Peters, November 24, 1784, December 14, 1785.

Samuel Seabury to Tillotson Bronson, May 14 (copy), July 2, 1789.

Transcripts of Early Letters by Samuel Johnson (Stratford), Thomas Bradbury Chandler, John Henry Hobart, 1754-1830.

Charles Inglis to Samuel Seabury, September 14, 1786.

University of Virginia, Charlottesville.

Bruce E. Steiner, Samuel Seabury and the Forging of the High Church Tradition: a Study in the Evolution of New England Churchmanship, 1722-1796 (University of Virginia Doctoral Dissertation, 1962).

William L. Clements Library, Ann Arbor.

Episcopal Church Papers.

Miscellaneous Manuscripts.

William Salt Library, Stafford.

Dartmouth Manuscripts.

Yale University, New Haven.

Ely Collection of Episcopal Bishops' Papers.

Joseph Willard to Ezra Stiles, October 5, 1785.

Bibliography

PRINTED SOURCES

Abstracts of Wills on File in the Surrogate's Office, City of New York, [*1665-1800*] . . . (*Collections of the New-York Historical Society, Third Series,* XXV-XXXVIII). 14 vols. New York, 1893-1905.

Adams, Arthur. "The Seabury Family." *Historical Magazine of the Protestant Episcopal Church,* III (September, 1934), pp. 122-32.

Adams, John. *The Works of John Adams.* Edited by Charles Francis Adams. 10 vols. Boston, 1850-56.

Adams, Samuel. *The Writings of Samuel Adams.* Edited by Harry Alonzo Cushing. 4 vols. New York, 1904-8.

Addison, Daniel Dulany. *The Life and Times of Edward Bass, First Bishop of Massachusetts.* Boston, 1897.

The Address of the Episcopal Clergy of Connecticut, to the Right Reverend Bishop Seabury, with the Bishop's Answer, and, a Sermon . . . Also, Bishop Seabury's First Charge . . . with a List of the Succession of Scot's Bishops, from the Revolution in 1688, to the Present Time. New Haven, [1785].

An Address Presented the Rev. James Sayre, A.M., Minister of Trinity Church, Newport, Previous to His Leaving the Town: Together with His Answer after His Arrival at Fairfield, in Connecticut . . . . Newport, 1789.

An Address to the Members of the Protestant Episcopal Church, in the United States of America. New York, 1792.

American Archives: Consisting of a Collection of Authentick Records, State Papers, Debates, and Letters and Other Notices of Publick Affairs. Fourth Series. Compiled by Peter Force. 6 vols. Washington, 1837-46.

Annals of Trinity Church, Newport, Rhode Island, 1698-1821. Edited by George Champlin Mason. Newport, 1890.

[Anonymous Communications Relating to the Consecration of Samuel Seabury]. *The Gentleman's Magazine,* LV (February-November, 1785), pp. 105, 248, 278-80, 437-40, 691-92, 770-71, 776-79, 787-89, 878-79, LVI (April-September, 1786), pp. 286-88, 566-67, 633-35, 768.

Asbury, Francis. *The Journal and Letters of Francis Asbury.* Edited by Elmer T. Clark, J. Manning Potts, and Jacob S. Payton. 3 vols. London, 1958.

At a Convention of Clergymen and Lay Deputies, of the Protestant Episcopal Church in the United States of America, Held in New-York, October 6th and 7th, 1784 . . . . [N.p., 1784] (broadside).

At a Convention of Lay-Delegates from Several of the Episcopal Societies in the State of Connecticut, Holden at New-Haven, on the Sixth Day of June, 1792. [N.p., 1792] (broadside).

Bartlet, William S. *The Frontier Missionary: a Memoir of the Life of the Rev. Jacob Bailey, A.M.* . . . . New York, 1853.

Beach, Abraham. "Additional Letters of the Reverend Abraham Beach: 1772-1791." Edited by Walter Herbert Stowe. *Historical Magazine of the Protestant Episcopal Church,* V (June, 1936), pp. 122-41.

Beach, John. *A Modest Enquiry into the State of the Dead* . . . . New London, 1755.

Beardsley, Eben Edwards. *An Address Delivered in St. Peter's Church, Cheshire, October 1, 1844, on Occasion of the Fiftieth Anniversary of the Episcopal Academy of Connecticut.* New Haven, 1844.

———. *Choice by the Clergy of the First Bishop of Connecticut.* [N.p., 1882?].

———. *The History of the Episcopal Church in Connecticut.* 2 vols. New York, 1865-68.

———. *The Lessons of the Past: a Sermon Preached in St. Paul's Church, Woodbury, Conn., September 6, 1871, at the Centennial Celebration of the Settlement of Rev. John Rutgers Marshall, M.A.* New Haven, 1874.

———. *Life and Correspondence of the Right Reverend Samuel Seabury, D.D., First Bishop of Connecticut, and of the Episcopal Church in the United States of America.* Boston, 1881.

———. *Life and Correspondence of Samuel Johnson, D.D., Missionary of the Church of England in Connecticut, and First President of King's College, New York.* New York, 1874.

———. *Life and Times of William Samuel Johnson, LL.D., First Senator in Congress from Connecticut, and President of Columbia College, New York.* New York, 1876.

———. *The Rev. Jeremiah Leaming, D.D., His Life and Services.* New York, 1885.

Becker, Carl Lotus. *The History of Political Parties in the Province of New York, 1760-1776.* Madison, 1909.

Bennett, Henry Leigh. "Ambrose Serle, 1742-1812." *The Dictionary of National Biography*, edited by Leslie Stephens and Sidney Lee (London, 1949-50), XVII, 1192.

Bentley, William. *The Diary of William Bentley, D.D., Pastor of the East Church, Salem, Massachusetts.* 4 vols. Salem, 1905-14.

"Biographical Sketch of Bishop Seabury." *The Evergreen*, I (January, 1844), pp. 1-5.

Birket, James. *Some Cursory Remarks Made by James Birket in His Voyage to North America 1750-1751.* New Haven, 1916.

"Bishop Williams' Scrapbook of Old Letters." *Historiographer of the Episcopal Diocese of Connecticut*, No. 10, December, 1954, pp. 1-14.

Bolton, Robert. *History of the Protestant Episcopal Church, in the County of Westchester, from Its Foundation, A.D. 1693, to A.D. 1853.* New York, 1855.

Boston. *Continental Journal, and the Weekly Advertiser.* 1786.

Boston-Gazette, and Country Journal. 1769.

Boston. *Independent Chronicle: and the Universal Advertiser.* 1786.

Boston. *Massachusetts Centinel.* 1786.

Boston. *Massachusetts Gazette.* 1769.

Boston Post-Boy. 1768, 1770-1774.

Boston Weekly News-Letter. 1769.

Bibliography

Boucher, Jonathan. *Reminiscences of an American Loyalist, 1738-1789. . . .* Edited by Jonathan Bouchier. Boston, 1925.

———. *A View of the Causes and Consequences of the American Revolution: in Thirteen Discourses, Preached in North America between the Years 1763 and 1775: with an Historical Preface.* London, 1797.

Bours, John. *An Appeal to the Public, in Which the Misrepresentations and Calumnies, Contained in a Pamphlet, Entitled, a Narrative of Certain Matters Relative to Trinity Church in Newport . . . by . . . the Rev. James Sayer [sic], A.M. Late Minister of Said Church, Are Pointed Out, and His Very Strange Conduct during the Time of His Ministration at Newport, Faithfully Related.* Newport, 1789.

Bowden, John. *An Address . . . to the Members of the Episcopal Church in Stratford, to Which Is Added, a Letter to the Rev'd Mr. James Sayre.* New Haven, [1792].

———. *A Letter from John Bowden, A.M., Rector of St. Paul's Church, Norwalk, to the Reverend Ezra Stiles, D.D. LL.D., President of Yale-College, Occasioned by Some Passages Concerning Church Government in an Ordination Sermon. . . .* New Haven, 1788.

———. *A Letter from a Weaver, to the Rev'd Mr. Sherman, Occasioned by a Publication of His in the Fairfield Gazette, for the Purpose of "Pinching the Episcopalian Clergy with the Truth."* New Haven, 1789.

———. *A Second Letter from John Bowden . . . to the Reverend Doctor Stiles . . . In This Letter, the Reverend Doctor Chauncy's Compleat View of Episcopacy until the Close of the Second Century, Is Particularly Considered; and Some Remarks Are Made upon a Few Passages of Doctor Stiles's Election Sermon.* New Haven, 1789.

Bridenbaugh, Carl. *Mitre and Sceptre: Transatlantic Faiths, Ideas, Personalities, and Politics 1689-1775.* New York, 1962.

Broxap, Henry. *The Later Non-Jurors.* Cambridge, England, 1924.

Brydon, George MacLaren. "David Griffith, 1742-1789, First Bishop-Elect of Virginia." *Historical Magazine of the Protestant Episcopal Church*, IX (September, 1940), pp. 194-230.

———. *Virginia's Mother Church and the Political Conditions under Which It Grew.* 2 vols. Richmond, Philadelphia, 1947-52.

Burhans, Daniel. "Autobiography of the Rev. Dr. Daniel Burhans (1763-1853)." *Historiographer of the Episcopal Diocese of Connecticut*, No. 13, September, 1955, pp. 1-11.

Burr, Nelson R. *The Anglican Church in New Jersey.* Philadelphia, 1954.

———. *Inventory of the Church Archives of Connecticut, Protestant Episcopal.* New Haven, 1940.

Catalogue of Books, for Sale by Mrs. Chandler, in Elizabeth-Town, New Jersey; Being the Library of the Late Rev. Dr. Chandler, Deceased. Elizabethtown, 1790.

A Catechism, Designed As an Explanation and Enlargement of the Church Cate-

chism: Formerly Recommended by the Bishops and Clergy of the Protestant Episcopal Church in the State of New York, to Which Are Added the Omitted Parts of the Original Catechism of Bishop Innes, As Republished by Bishop Seabury. [Edited by William Rollinson Whittingham]. Baltimore, 1851.

The Catechism of the Protestant Episcopal Church in the United States of America, Published at the Expense of a Fund Arising from the Charitable Contributions of the Members of the Protestant Episcopal Church in the State of New-York. New York, 1802.

Caulkins, Frances Manwaring. *History of New London, Connecticut, from the First Survey of the Coast in 1612. . . .* Hartford, 1852.

[Chandler, Thomas Bradbury]. *The American Querist, or Some Questions Proposed Relative to the Present Disputes between Great-Britain and Her American Colonies.* [New York], 1774.

———. *An Appeal to the Public, in Behalf of the Church of England in America.* New York, 1767.

———. *The Appeal Farther Defended; in Answer to the Farther Misrepresentations of Dr. Chauncey.* New York, 1771.

[———]. *A Friendly Address to All Reasonable Americans, on the Subject of Our Political Confusions. . . .* New York, 1774.

———. *The Life of Samuel Johnson, D.D., the First President of King's College, in New York.* London, 1824.

[———]. *What Think Ye of Congress Now? . . . .* New York, 1775.

Chorley, E. Clowes. *Men and Movements in the American Episcopal Church.* New York, 1950.

———. "Samuel Provoost, First Bishop of New York." *Historical Magazine of the Protestant Episcopal Church*, II (June, September, 1933), pp. 1-25, 1-16.

Clark, Esther Wright. *The Loyalists of New Brunswick.* Fredericton, New Brunswick, 1955.

Clarke, Abraham Lynsen. *The Catechism of the Protestant Episcopal Church in the United States of America, with Selected Questions and Answers, on Important Subjects.* Providence, 1798.

Colden, Cadwallader D. and George B. Rapelye. "Memoir of Bishop Provoost." *The Evergreen*, I (July, 1844), pp. 193-200.

A Collection of Tracts from the Late News Papers, &C. Containing Particularly the American Whig, a Whip for the American Whig, with Some Other Pieces. . . . 2 vols. New York, 1768-69.

"Consecration of Bishop Seabury: Additional Correspondence of Scottish Bishops." Edited by J. Nicholson. *The Scottish Church Review*, I (September, 1884), pp. 584-98.

Cooper, Myles. "Letters from the Reverend Dr. Myles Cooper, Formerly President of King's College, New York, Written from Edinburgh to Rev. Dr. Samuel Peters, of London." [Edited by E. Clowes Chorley]. *Historical Magazine of the Protestant Episcopal Church*, II (March, 1933), pp. 44-47.

[Coxe, Arthur Cleveland]. *Seventy Years Since; Or What We Owe to Bishop*

Seabury, a Sermon Preached in St. John's Church, Hartford, on Sexagesima Sunday, Feb. 27, 1848. Hartford, 1848.

Cross, Arthur Lyon. *The Anglican Episcopate and the American Colonies.* Cambridge, 1902.

Dana, James. *An Examination of the Late Reverend President Edwards's 'Enquiry on Freedom of Will.'* . . . Boston, 1770.

Dangerfield, George. *Chancellor Robert R. Livingston of New York, 1746-1813.* New York, 1960.

Danson, J. M. "Seabury as a Preacher." *The Scottish Church Review*, I (October, 1884), pp. 654-66.

Davidson, Philip. *Propaganda and the American Revolution, 1763-1783.* Chapel Hill, 1941.

Dewey, Edward H. "Peter Thacher, 1651-1727." *Dictionary of American Biography*, edited by Allen Johnson and Dumas Malone (New York, 1928-37), XVIII, 389-90.

Dexter, Franklin Bowditch. *Biographical Sketches of the Graduates of Yale College with Annals of the College History.* 6 vols. New York, New Haven, 1885-1912.

Dibble, Ebenezer. "Letters of the Reverend Doctor Ebenezer Dibble, of Stamford, to the Reverend Doctor Samuel Peters, Loyalist Refugee in London, 1784-1793." [Edited by E. Clowes Chorley]. *Historical Magazine of the Protestant Episcopal Church*, I (June, 1932), pp. 51-85.

Dillon, Dorothy Rita. *The New York Triumvirate: a Study of the Legal and Political Careers of William Livingston, John Morin Scott, William Smith, Jr.* New York, 1949.

Diocese of Connecticut: the Records of Convocation A.D. 1790-A.D. 1848. Edited by Joseph Hooper. New Haven, 1904.

Documentary History of the Protestant Episcopal Church, in the United States of America, Containing Numerous Hitherto Unpublished Documents Concerning the Church in Connecticut. Edited by Francis Lister Hawks and William Stevens Perry. 2 vols. New York, 1863-64.

The Documentary History of the State of New York. Edited by Edmund Bailey O'Callaghan. 4 vols. Albany, 1849-51.

Documents Relative to the Colonial History of the State of New-York. . . . Edited by Edmund Bailey O'Callaghan and B. Fernow. 15 vols. Albany, 1853-87.

Dowden, John. *The Scottish Communion Office 1764.* Oxford, 1922.

———. "Who Was Mr. Elphinston?" *The Scottish Church Review*, II (February, 1885), pp. 103-17.

Eliot, John. *A Biographical Dictionary, Containing a Brief Account of the First Settlers and Other Eminent Characters . . . in New-England.* Boston, 1809.

Elliott-Binns, Leonard Elliott. *The Early Evangelicals: a Religious and Social Study.* Greenwich, 1953.

Elphinston, James. *Forty Years' Correspondence between Geniusses ov Boath Sexes, and James Elphinston.* 6 vols. London, 1791.

Fac-Similes of Church Documents: Papers Issued by the Historical Club of the American Church, 1874-1879. [N.p., 1879].

[Fanning, Edmund]. *Declaration and Address of His Majesty's Loyal Associated Refugees, Assembled at Newport, Rhode-Island.* New York, 1779.

Flick, Alexander Clarence. *Loyalism in New York during the American Revolution.* New York, 1901.

Foote, Henry Wilder. *Annals of King's Chapel from the Puritan Age of New England to the Present Day.* 2 vols. Boston, 1882-96.

Foster, Walter Roland. *Bishop and Presbytery: the Church of Scotland, 1661-1688.* London, 1958.

The Fulham Papers in the Lambeth Palace Library, American Colonial Section, Calendar and Indexes. Compiled by William Wilson Manross. Oxford, 1965.

Goldie, Frederick. *A Short History of the Episcopal Church in Scotland from the Restoration to the Present Time.* London, 1951.

Goodwin, Edward Lewis. *The Colonial Church in Virginia. . . .* Milwaukee, 1927.

Grant, Alexander. *The Story of the University of Edinburgh during Its First Three Hundred Years.* 2 vols. London, 1884.

Grisbrooke, W. Jardine. *Anglican Liturgies of the Seventeenth and Eighteenth Centuries.* London, 1958.

Groce, George Cuthbert. *William Samuel Johnson; a Maker of the Constitution.* New York, 1937.

Grub, George. *An Ecclesiastical History of Scotland from the Introduction of Christianity to the Present Time.* 4 vols. Edinburgh, 1861.

Hallam, Robert A. *Annals of St. James's Church, New London, for One Hundred and Fifty Years.* Hartford, 1873.

Hamilton, Alexander. *Gentleman's Progress, the Itinerarium of Dr. Alexander Hamilton.* Edited by Carl Bridenbaugh. Chapel Hill, 1948.

[Hamilton, Alexander]. *The Farmer Refuted; or, a More Comprehensive and Impartial View of the Dispute between Great Britain and the Colonies. . . .* New York, 1775. Reprinted in *The Papers of Alexander Hamilton,* edited by Harold C. Syrett *et al.* (New York, 1961-), I, 81-165.

[———]. *A Full Vindication of the Measures of Congress. . . .* New York, 1774. Reprinted in *The Papers of Alexander Hamilton,* edited by Harold C. Syrett *et al.* (New York, 1961-), I, 45-78.

Hamilton, John C. *The Life of Alexander Hamilton.* New York, 1834.

Hardy, Edward Rochie. "Samuel Seabury, 1801-1872." *Dictionary of American Biography,* edited by Allen Johnson and Dumas Malone (New York, 1928-37), XVI, 530-31.

Harris, Reginald V. *et al. Charles Inglis: Missionary, Loyalist, Bishop.* Toronto, 1937.

Hartford. *American Mercury.* 1795.

Heads of Families at the First Census of the United States Taken in 1790, Connecticut. Washington, 1908.

Hempstead, Joshua. *Diary . . . Covering a Period of Forty-Seven Years, from*

September, 1711, to November, 1758 (*Collections of the New London Historical Society*, I). New London, 1901.

Historical Collections Relating to the American Colonial Church. Edited by William Stevens Perry. 5 vols. [Hartford], 1870-78.

Historical Manuscripts Commission. *Report on American Manuscripts in the Royal Institution of Great Britain.* 4 vols. London, 1904-9.

A History of the Parish of Trinity Church in the City of New York. Edited by Morgan Dix. 4 vols. New York, 1898-1906.

Hoare, Prince. *Memoirs of Granville Sharp, Esq. Composed from His Own Manuscripts, and Other Authentic Documents. . . .* London, 1820.

Hobart, John Henry. *Catechism Number Three: the Church Catechism Enlarged, Explained, and Proved from Scripture, in a Catechism Drawn Up, with Alterations and Additions, from Various Approved Catechisms.* New York, [n.d.].

———. *The Correspondence of John Henry Hobart.* Edited by Arthur Lowndes. 6 vols. New York, 1911-12.

Hoffman, Ross J. S. *Edmund Burke, New York Agent, with His Letters to the New York Assembly and Intimate Correspondence with Charles O'Hara, 1761-1776.* Philadelphia, 1956.

Holmes, Abiel. *The Life of Ezra Stiles, DD. LL.D.* Boston, 1798.

Honyman, Robert. *Colonial Panorama 1775: Dr. Robert Honyman's Journal for March and April.* Edited by Philip Padelford. San Marino, 1939.

Innes, George. *A Catechism, or, the Principles of the Christian Religion, Explained in a Familiar and Easy Manner, Adapted to the Lowest Capacities.* New Haven, 1791.

Jarvis, Abraham. *A Discourse . . . Occasioned by the Death of the Right Reverend Samuel Seabury, D.D., Bishop of Connecticut and Rhode-Island.* New Haven, [1796].

Jarvis, Samuel Farmar. "Memoir of Bishop Jarvis." *Historiographer of the Episcopal Diocese of Connecticut,* No. 20, May, 1957, pp. 3-4.

Johnson, Samuel. *Samuel Johnson, President of King's College, His Career and Writings.* Edited by Herbert and Carol Schneider. 4 vols. New York, 1929.

Jones, Isaac. *The Mandate of God, for Israel's Advancement: a Sermon, Delivered in Trinity Church, Milton, and St. Michael's, Litchfield, Nov. 5, 1845. . . .* Litchfield, 1846.

Jones, Thomas. *History of New York during the Revolutionary War, and of the Leading Events in the Other Colonies at That Period.* Edited by Edward Floyd DeLancey. 2 vols. New York, 1879.

Jones, William. *Memoirs of the Life, Studies, and Writings of the Right Reverend George Horne, D.D., Late Lord Bishop of Norwich.* London, 1799.

———. *The Theological and Miscellaneous Works of the Late Rev. William Jones, M.A., Minister of Nayland, Suffolk, to Which Is Prefixed, a Short Account of His Life and Writings.* Edited by William Stevens. 6 vols. London, 1826.

Journal of the Convention of the Clergy and Laity of the Protestant Episcopal

Church, of Virginia, Begun and Holden in the City of Richmond, Wednesday May 18, 1785. Richmond, 1785.

Journal of the Convention of the Protestant Episcopal Church of the State of New-York, Held in the City of New-York . . . 1787 . . . to . . . 1791. New York, 1792.

The Journals of the Annual Convention of the Diocese of Connecticut, from 1792-1820. New Haven, 1842.

Journals of the Conventions of the Protestant Episcopal Church in the Diocese of Rhode Island, from the Year A.D. 1790 to the Year A.D. 1832, Inclusive. Providence, [1859].

Journals of General Conventions of the Protestant Episcopal Church, in the United States, 1785-1835. Edited by William Stevens Perry. 3 vols. Claremont, 1874.

Journals of the Provincial Congress, Provincial Convention, Committee of Safety and Council of Safety of the State of New York, 1775-1776-1777. 2 vols. Albany, 1842.

Keith, George. *A Journal of Travel from New-Hampshire to Caratuck, on the Continent of North-America.* London, 1706.

Keys, Alice Mapelsden. *Cadwallader Colden: a Representative Eighteenth Century Official.* New York, 1906.

Kilgour, Robert and Arthur Petrie and John Skinner. Facsimile of a letter "To the Episcopal Clergy in Connecticut," November 15, 1784. *Historiographer of the Episcopal Diocese of Connecticut,* No. 4, May, 1953, p. [4].

King, Rufus. *The Life and Correspondence of Rufus King. . . .* Edited by Charles R. King. 6 vols. New York, 1894-1900.

Ladd, William Palmer. "William Smith, *c.* 1754-1821." *Dictionary of American Biography,* edited by Allen Johnson and Dumas Malone (New York, 1928-1937), XVII, 358-59.

Leaming, Jeremiah. "Letters of the Reverend Doctor Jeremiah Leaming to the Reverend Doctor Samuel Peters, Loyalist Refugee in London, and One Time Bishop Elect of Vermont." [Edited by E. Clowes Chorley]. *Historical Magazine of the Protestant Episcopal Church,* I (September, December, 1932), pp. 116-42, 179-203.

Lee, Richard Henry. *The Letters of Richard Henry Lee. . . .* Edited by James Curtis Ballagh. 2 vols. New York, 1911-14.

"Letters Relating to the Consecration." Edited by E. Clowes Chorley. *Historical Magazine of the Protestant Episcopal Church,* III (September, 1934), pp. 158-91.

"List of the American Graduates in Medicine in the University of Edinburgh, from 1705 to 1866, with Their Theses." *New England Historical and Genealogical Register,* XLII (April, 1888), pp. 159-65.

List of Persons Admitted to the Order of Deacons in the Protestant Episcopal Church, in the United States of America, from A.D. 1785, to A.D. 1857, Both Inclusive. Compiled by George Burgess. Boston, 1874.

Love, W. DeLoss. *The Fast and Thanksgiving Days of New England.* Boston, 1895.

Loveland, Clara O. *The Critical Years: the Reconstitution of the Anglican Church in the United States of America: 1780-1789.* Greenwich, 1956.

Lydekker, John Wolfe. *The Life and Letters of Charles Inglis.* London, 1936.

MacClintock, Samuel. *An Epistolary Correspondence between the Rev. John Ogden, Rector of St. John's Church, at Portsmouth, New-Hampshire; and the Rev. Samuel MacClintock, Minister of the Congregational Society in Greenland, on a Variety of Subjects; Principally the High Powers and Prerogatives Claimed by Diocesan Bishops As Successors of the Apostles.* Portsmouth, 1791.

MacSparran, James. *A Letter Book and Abstract of Out Services Written during the Years 1743-1751. . . .* Edited by Daniel Goodwin. Boston, 1899.

Mather, Cotton. *Magnalia Christi Americana; or, the Ecclesiastical History of New England; from Its First Planting, in the Year 1620, unto the Year of Our Lord 1698.* 2 vols. Hartford, 1855.

Mayo, Lawrence Shaw. *The Winthrop Family in America.* Boston, 1948.

"Memoir of Rt. Rev. Samuel Parker, D.D., Second Bishop of Massachusetts." *The Evergreen,* II (May, 1845), pp. 131-34.

Miller, Perry. *Orthodoxy in Massachusetts, 1630-1650: a Genetic Study.* Cambridge, 1933.

[Mines, Flavel S.]. *A Presbyterian Clergyman Looking for the Church.* 2 parts. New York, 1849-53.

"Minute Book of the College of Bishops in Scotland," quoted in "Intercommunion of the American and Scottish Churches." *The Scottish Ecclesiastical Journal,* I (October 16, 1851), pp. 214-18.

Minutes of the Convention of Delegates from the Synod of New York and Philadelphia, and from the Associations of Connecticut; Held Annually from 1766 to 1775, Inclusive. Hartford, 1843.

"Minutes of Conventions of the Clergy of Connecticut for the Years 1766, 1784, and 1785." [Edited by E. Clowes Chorley]. *Historical Magazine of the Protestant Episcopal Church,* III (March, 1934), pp. 56-64.

Moore, William H. *History of St. George's Church, Hempstead, Long Island.* New York, 1881.

Morais, Herbert M. *Deism in Eighteenth Century America.* New York, 1934.

Morgan, Edmund S. *The Gentle Puritan, a Life of Ezra Stiles, 1727-1795.* New Haven, 1962.

Morss, James. *The Catechism of the Protestant Episcopal Church in the United States of America, to Which Is Annexed a Catechism Designed As an Explanation and Enlargement of the Church Catechism: Selected from a Catechism, Recommended by the Bishop and Clergy of the Protestant Episcopal Church in the State of New-York, with Some Additions.* Newburyport, 1815.

Mumford, James Gregory. *Mumford Memoirs, Being the Story of the New England Mumfords from the Year 1655 to the Present Time.* Boston, 1900.

New Haven. *Connecticut Journal.* 1775.

New-Haven Gazette, and the Connecticut Magazine. 1786.
New London. *Connecticut Gazette.* 1785-96.
New-York Gazette. 1754-55.
New-York Gazette; or, the Weekly Post-Boy. 1764.
New-York Gazette, and Weekly Mercury. 1768-69, 1774.
New York. *John Englishman, In Defence of the English Constitution.* 1755.
New-York Journal; or, the General Advertiser. 1774-75.
New-York Mercury. 1754-55, 1762, 1764.
New York. *Rivington's New-York Gazetteer.* 1774-75.
New York. *Royal Gazette.* 1778-79.
Norton, John N. *Life of Bishop Provoost, of New York.* New York, 1859.
"Notes on the Documentary History of the American Church." *Historical Magazine of the Protestant Episcopal Church*, II (March, 1933), pp. 51-61.

Ogden, John Cosens. *Letters, Occasioned by the Publication of a Private Epistolary Correspondence. . . .* Boston, 1791.
Onderdonk, Henry. *The Annals of Hempstead; 1643 to 1832; Also, the Rise and Growth of the Society of Friends on Long Island and in New York, 1657 to 1826.* Hempstead, 1880.
———. *Antiquities of the Parish Church, Jamaica, (Including Newtown and Flushing,). . . .* Jamaica, 1880.
O'Neill, Maud. "Matthew Graves: Anglican Missionary to the Puritans." *British Humanitarianism, Essays Honoring Frank J. Klingberg*, edited by Samuel Clyde McCulloch (Philadelphia, 1950), pp. 124-44.
"Original Documents." *The Churchman's Monthly Magazine*, III (March-August, 1806), pp. 111-15, 154-60, 192-96, 236-39, 276-78, 316-19.
Oviatt, Edwin. *The Beginnings of Yale (1701-1716).* New Haven, 1916.

Papers of the Lloyd Family of the Manor of Queens Village, Lloyd's Neck, Long Island, New York, 1654-1826. [Edited by Dorothy C. Barck]. (*Collections of the New-York Historical Society, Third Series*, LIX-LX). 2 vols. New York, 1927.
[Park, James Allan]. *Memoirs of William Stevens, Esq.* London, 1814.
Parker, Samuel. Letter to Daniel Fogg, July 17, 1783. *Historiographer of the Episcopal Diocese of Connecticut*, No. 8, June, 1954, p. [6].
Peirce's Colonial Lists, Civil, Military and Professional Lists of Plymouth and Rhode Island Colonies . . . 1621-1700. Compiled by Ebenezer W. Peirce. Boston, 1881.
Pennington, Edgar Legare. "Colonial Clergy Conventions." *Historical Magazine of the Protestant Episcopal Church*, VIII (September, 1939), pp. 178-218.
Perry, William Stevens. *Bishop Seabury and the "Episcopal Recorder;" a Vindication.* [N.p., 1863].
———. *The Election of the First Bishop of Connecticut, at Woodbury, on the Feast of the Annunciation, 1783, an Historical Review.* Davenport, 1884.
———. *The History of the American Episcopal Church, 1587-1883.* 2 vols. Boston, 1885.

Proceedings of the Convention of the Protestant Episcopal Church in the State of New-York; Held in the City of New-York, on Wednesday June 22d, 1785. New York, 1787.

Procter, Francis and Walter Howard Frere. *A New History of the Book of Common Prayer with a Rationale of Its Offices.* London, 1901.

Proposals for Instituting an Episcopal Academy in the State of Connecticut. [N.p., 1789] (broadside).

Punderson, Ebenezer. *The Nature and Extent of the Redemption of Mankind by Jesus Christ, Stated and Explained.* New Haven, 1758.

[Purcell, Henry]. *Strictures on the Love of Power in the Prelacy; Particularly in a Late Claim of a Complete Veto, on All the Proceedings of the Clergy and Laity in Legal Convention Assembled, As Set Forth in a Pamphlet, Published Prior to Their Meeting in New-York.* Charleston, 1795.

Pynchon, William. *The Diary of William Pynchon of Salem. . . .* Edited by Fitch Edward Oliver. Boston, 1890.

Quaestiones pro Modulo Discutiendae sub Reverendo D. Thoma Clap, Colegii-Yalensis, Quod Est Divina Providentia, Novo-Portu Connecticutensium, Praeside. In Comitiis Publicis a Laureae Magistralis Candidatis, MDCCXLVIII. [New London, 1748] (broadside).

Quaestiones pro Modulo Discutiendae . . . In Comitiis Publicis a Laureae Magistralis Candidatis, MDCCLI. [New London, 1751] (broadside).

Quincy, Josiah. *History of Harvard University.* 2 vols. Boston, 1860.

Raymond, William Odber. *Glimpses of the Past: History of the River St. John A.D. 1604-1785.* St. John, New Brunswick, 1905.

Records of the Colony of New Plymouth in New England. Edited by Nathaniel B. Shurtleff. 12 vols. Boston, 1855-61.

Rightmyer, Nelson Waite. "Joseph Pilmore, Anglican Evangelical." *Historical Magazine of the Protestant Episcopal Church*, XVI (June, 1947), pp. 181-98.

———. *Maryland's Established Church.* Baltimore, 1956.

Rowe, John. *Letters and Diary of John Rowe, Boston Merchant, 1759-1762, 1764-1779.* Edited by Anne Rowe Cunningham. Boston, 1903.

Rowe, William Hutchinson. *Ancient North Yarmouth and Yarmouth, Maine, 1636-1936, a History.* Yarmouth, 1937.

Rush, Benjamin. *The Autobiography of Benjamin Rush, His "Travels through Life," Together with His Commonplace Book for 1789-1813.* Edited by George W. Corner. Princeton, 1948.

———. *Letters of Benjamin Rush.* Edited by Lyman H. Butterfield. 2 vols. [Princeton], 1951.

Russell, Edward. "History of North Yarmouth." *Old Times: a Magazine Devoted to . . . the Early History of North Yarmouth, Maine*, II (January, April, October, 1898), pp. 169-72, 192-96, 260-66.

Sabine, Lorenzo. *The American Loyalists, or Biographical Sketches of Adherents to the British Crown in the Revolution. . . .* Boston, 1847.

———. *Biographical Sketches of Loyalists of the American Revolution with an Historical Essay.* 2 vols. Boston, 1864.

"St. George Church and Cemetery Records—Hempstead, L.I." *The Daughters of the American Revolution Magazine,* LXXXVII (May, 1953), pp. 670-72.

Sargent, William M. "The Old Church." *Old Times: a Magazine Devoted to . . . the Early History of North Yarmouth, Maine,* IV (January, 1880), pp. 453-65.

Sayre, James. *A Candid Narrative of Certain Matters Relating to Trinity Church in Newport. . . .* Fairfield, 1788.

Seabury, Samuel, Sr. *A Modest Reply to a Letter from a Gentleman to His Friend in Dutchess-County, Lately Published by an Anonymous Writer.* New York, 1759.

[Seabury, Samuel]. *An Address to the Ministers and Congregations of the Presbyterian and Independent Persuasions in the United States of America, by a Member of the Episcopal Church.* [New Haven], 1790.

[———]. *An Alarm to the Legislature of the Province of New-York, Occasioned by the Present Political Disturbances, in North America: Addressed to the Honourable Representatives in General Assembly Convened.* New York, 1775.

———. "Bishop Samuel Seabury's Journal 'B'—A Record of Certain Events between May 29, 1791, and November 4, 1795." *Historiographer of the Episcopal Diocese of Connecticut,* No. 12, May, 1955, pp. 1-11.

———. *Bishop Seabury's Communion Office . . . with an Historical Sketch and Notes.* Edited by Samuel Hart, New York, 1883.

———. *Bishop Seabury's Second Charge, to the Clergy of His Diocess, Delivered at Derby, in the State of Connecticut, on the 22d of September, 1786.* New Haven, [1786].

[———]. *The Congress Canvassed: Or, an Examination into the Conduct of the Delegates, at Their Grand Convention. . . .* [New York], 1774.

———. *A Discourse Delivered before the Triennial Convention of the Protestant Episcopal Church in the United States of America, in Trinity-Church, New-York, on the Twelfth Day of September, One Thousand Seven Hundred and Ninety-Two.* New York, 1792.

———. *A Discourse, Delivered in St. John's Church, in Portsmouth, New Hampshire, at the Conferring the Order of Priesthood on the Rev. Robert Fowle, A.M. of Holderness, on the Festival of St. Peter, 1791.* Boston, 1791.

———. *A Discourse on Brotherly Love, Preached before the Honorable Fraternity of Free and Accepted Masons, of Zion Lodge, at St. Paul's Chapel, in New-York, on the Festival of St. John the Baptist, One Thousand Seven Hundred and Seventy-Seven.* New York, 1777.

———. *A Discourse on II Tim. III. 16. Delivered in St. Paul's and St. George's Chapels, in New-York, on Sunday the 11th of May, 1777.* New York, 1777.

———. *Discourses on Several Important Subjects.* New York, 1798.

———. *Discourses on Several Subjects.* 2 vols. New York, 1793.

———. *An Earnest Persuasive to Frequent Communion; Addressed to Those Pro-*

fessors of the Church of England, in Connecticut, Who Neglect That Holy Ordinance. New Haven, 1789.
[———]. *Free Thoughts on the Proceedings of the Continental Congress. . . .* [New York], 1774.
———. *Letters of a Westchester Farmer.* Edited by Clarence H. Vance. White Plains, 1930.
———. *St. Peter's Exhortation to Fear God and Honor the King, Explained and Inculcated: in a Discourse Addressed to His Majesty's Provincial Troops, in Camp at King's-Bridge, on Sunday the 28th Sept. 1777.* New York, [1777].
———. *SAMUEL, by Divine Permission, Bishop of Connecticut and Rhode-Island, to the Clergy of the Church in Connecticut and Rhode-Island, Greeting. WHEREAS the Rev. Mr. James Sayre. . . .* [N.p., 1793] (broadside).
———. *SAMUEL, by Divine Permission, Bishop of the Episcopal Church in the State of Connecticut, to the Clergy of the Said Church, GREETING . . . Aug. 12th, 1785.* [N.p., 1785] (broadside).
———. *A Sermon Delivered before the Boston Episcopal Charitable Society, in Trinity Church; at Their Anniversary Meeting on Easter Tuesday March 25, 1788.* Boston, 1788.
———. *A Sermon Preached before the Grand Lodge, and the Other Lodges of Ancient Freemasons, in New-York, at St. Paul's Chapel, on the Anniversary of St. John the Evangelist, 1782.* New York, 1783.
[———]. *A View of the Controversy between Great-Britain and Her Colonies. . . .* New York, 1774.
——— and Abraham Jarvis. "A Registry of Ordinations by Bishop Seabury and Bishop Jarvis of Connecticut." Edited by William A. Beardsley. *Historical Magazine of the Protestant Episcopal Church*, XIII (March, 1944), pp. 44-71.
Seabury, Samuel Dorrance. "Seabury Family." *Old Times: a Magazine Devoted to . . . the Early History of North Yarmouth, Maine*, III (July, October, 1879), pp. 373-78, 403-10.
Seabury, William Jones. *The Election in order to Consecration of the First Bishop of Connecticut. . . .* New York, 1883.
———. *Memoir of Bishop Seabury.* New York, 1908.
Seabury Centenary Handbook: a Comprehensive Sketch of the Facts Relating to, and the Results of, the Consecration of Dr. Seabury as the First Bishop of the American Church. Edinburgh, 1884.
"The Seabury Consecration: Additional Letters." Edited by E. Clowes Chorley. *Historical Magazine of the Protestant Episcopal Church*, III (December, 1934), pp. 234-61.
"The Seabury Minutes of the New York Clergy Conventions of 1766 and 1767." Edited by Walter Herbert Stowe. *Historical Magazine of the Protestant Episcopal Church*, X (June, 1941), pp. 124-62.
Serle, Ambrose. *The American Journal of Ambrose Serle, Secretary to Lord Howe, 1776-1778.* Edited by Edward H. Tatum. San Marino, 1940.

Sewall, Samuel. *Letter-Book of Samuel Sewall (Collections of the Massachusetts Historical Society, Sixth Series*, I, II). Boston, 1886-88.

Sharp, Granville. "A Letter to Dr. Franklin, from Granville Sharp, on the Subject of American Bishops." *Collections of the Massachusetts Historical Society, First Series*, (Boston, 1792-1809), III, 162-66.

Shelton, Philo. "Parochiales Notitiae, Being a Private Register Kept by the Rev. Philo Shelton . . . 1785-1825." Edmund Guilbert, *Annals of an Old Parish, Historical Sketches of Trinity Church, Southport, Connecticut, 1725 to 1898* (New York, 1898), pp. 183-273.

Shipton, Clifford Kenyon. *Sibley's Harvard Graduates.* 15 vols. to date. Cambridge, 1933- .

Skinner, John (of Linshart). *An Ecclesiastical History of Scotland, from the First Appearance of Christianity in That Kingdom, to the Present Time. . . .* 2 vols. London, 1788.

[Skinner, John]. *The Nature and Extent of the Apostolical Commission, a Sermon Preached at the Consecration of the Right Reverend Dr Samuel Seabury, Bishop of the Episcopal Church in Connecticut.* Aberdeen, 1785. Reprinted in *Historical Magazine of the Protestant Episcopal Church*, III (September, 1934), pp. 193-209.

Skinner, John and Jonathan Boucher. "Correspondence between the Right Reverend John Skinner, Jr., and the Reverend Jonathan Boucher, 1786." Edited by E. Clowes Chorley. *Historical Magazine of the Protestant Episcopal Church*, X (June, 1941), pp. 163-75.

Skinner, John. *Annals of Scottish Episcopacy, from the Year 1788 to the Year 1816, Inclusive. . . .* Edinburgh, 1818.

Skinner, William. "Some Letters of Bishop William Skinner of Aberdeen." Edited by Edgar Legare Pennington. *Historical Magazine of the Protestant Episcopal Church*, XVI (December, 1947), pp. 373-412.

Smith, Horace Wemyss. *Life and Correspondence of the Rev. William Smith, D.D., . . . with Copious Extracts from His Writings.* 2 vols. Philadelphia, 1879-80.

Smith, William. *Historical Memoirs of William Smith, Historian of the Province of New York, Member of the Governor's Council and Last Chief Justice of That Province under the Crown, Chief Justice of Quebec.* Edited by William H. W. Sabine. 2 vols. New York, 1956-58.

Smith, William (of Newport). *A Discourse Delivered in St. John's Church, Providence, before the Right Reverend Samuel, Bishop of Connecticut and Rhode-Island, and the Clerical and Lay Delegates of the Protestant Episcopal Church in the State of Rhode-Island. . . .* Providence, 1793.

Sprague, William B. *Annals of the American Pulpit.* 9 vols. New York, 1857-69.

Stiles, Ezra. *Extracts from the Itineraries and Other Miscellanies of Ezra Stiles, D.D., LL.D., 1755-1794, with a Selection from His Correspondence.* Edited by Franklin Bowditch Dexter. New Haven, 1916.

———. *The Literary Diary of Ezra Stiles, D.D., LL.D., President of Yale College.* Edited by Franklin Bowditch Dexter. 3 vols. New York, 1901.

———. *A Sermon, Delivered at the Ordination of the Reverend Henry Channing, A.M. to the Pastoral Charge of the Congregational Church, in the City of New-London, May 17, 1787.* New London, 1787.

Stowe, Walter Herbert. "The Scottish Episcopal Succession and the Validity of Bishop Seabury's Orders." *Historical Magazine of the Protestant Episcopal Church*, IX (December, 1940), pp. 322-48.

Sutherland, G. "The Scottish Communion Office, Historically Considered." *The Scottish Church Review*, II (February, 1885), pp. 122-33.

Swiggett, Howard. *The Extraordinary Mr. Morris.* Garden City, 1952.

Sykes, Norman. *Church and State in England in the XVIIIth Century.* Cambridge, England, 1934.

Thacher, Thomas. *A Brief Rule to Guide the Common People of New-England How to Order Themselves and Theirs in the Small Pocks, Or Measles.* Boston, 1677.

Thompson, Benjamin F. *The History of Long Island; from Its Discovery and Settlement, to the Present Time.* 2 vols. New York, 1843.

Thompson, Benjamin F. and Charles J. Werner. *History of Long Island from Its Discovery and Settlement to the Present Time.* 4 vols. New York, 1918.

Troup, Robert and Hercules Mulligan. "Alexander Hamilton Viewed by His Friends: the Narratives of Robert Troup and Hercules Mulligan." Edited by Nathan Schachner. *William and Mary Quarterly, Third Series*, IV (April, 1947), pp. 203-25.

Tucker, Louis Leonard. *Puritan Protagonist: President Thomas Clap of Yale College.* Chapel Hill, 1962.

Tudor, John. *Deacon John Tudor's Diary. . . .* Edited by William Tudor. Boston, 1896.

Tyler, John. *The Rev. John Tyler's Journal, May 4 to November 1, A.D. 1768.* San Francisco, [1894].

Tyler, Moses Coit. *The Literary History of the American Revolution, 1763-1783.* 2 vols. New York, 1898.

Updike, Wilkins. *A History of the Episcopal Church in Narragansett, Rhode Island, Including a History of Other Episcopal Churches in the State.* Edited by Daniel Goodwin. 3 vols. Boston, 1907.

Van Amringe, John Howard *et al. A History of Columbia University, 1754-1904.* New York, 1904.

Vance, Clarence Hayden. "Myles Cooper, M.A., D.C.L., LL.D., Second President of King's College, Now Columbia University, New York City." *Columbia University Quarterly*, XXII (September, 1930), pp. 261-68.

Van Doren, Carl. *Secret History of the American Revolution.* New York, 1951.

Vital Records of Duxbury, Massachusetts, to the Year 1850. Boston, 1911.

Walker, William. *Life of the Right Reverend George Gleig, LL.D., F.S.S.A., Bishop of Brechin, and Primus of the Scottish Episcopal Church.* Edinburgh, 1878.

———. *The Life and Times of John Skinner, Bishop of Aberdeen. . . .* Aberdeen, 1887.

———. *The Life and Times of the Rev. John Skinner, M.A., of Linshart, Longside, Dean of Aberdeen. . . .* London, 1883.

Washington, George. *The Diaries of George Washington, 1748-1799.* Edited by John C. Fitzpatrick. 4 vols. Boston, 1925.

Webster, Richard. *A History of the Presbyterian Church in America, from Its Origin until the Year 1760, with Biographical Sketches of Its Early Ministers.* Philadelphia, 1857.

Wells, William V. *The Life and Public Services of Samuel Adams. . . .* 3 vols. Boston, 1865.

[White, William]. *The Case of the Episcopal Churches in the United States Considered.* Edited by Richard G. Salomon. [N.p., 1954].

———. *Memoirs of the Protestant Episcopal Church in the United States of America.* Edited by B. F. DeCosta. New York, 1880.

[Wilkins, Isaac]. *Short Advice to the Counties of New-York.* New York, 1774.

Williams, George. *The Orthodox Church of the East in the Eighteenth Century, Being the Correspondence between the Eastern Patriarchs and the Nonjuring Bishops with an Introduction on Various Projects of Reunion between the Eastern Church and the Anglican Communion.* London, 1868.

Wilson, Thomas. *The Works of the Right Reverend Father in God, Thomas Wilson, D.D., Lord Bishop of Sodor and Man.* 7 vols. Oxford, 1847-63.

Wordsworth, Charles. "What Can England Learn from Scotland in Religious Matters?" *The Scottish Church Review*, I (October, 1884), pp. 676-82.

INDEX

Index

Index

Index

Index